FAIR
ECONOMICS

NATURE, MONEY AND PEOPLE

BEYOND NEOCLASSICAL THINKING

IRENE H SCHOENE

Published by

Green Books
An imprint of UIT Cambridge Ltd
www.greenbooks.co.uk

PO Box 145, Cambridge CB4 1GQ, England
+44 (0) 1223 302 041

First published in 2015, in England

Irene Schoene has asserted her moral rights under the
Copyright, Designs and Patents Act 1988.

Front cover design by Andrew Corbett
Interior design by Jayne Jones

ISBN: 978 0 85784 309 8 (paperback)
ISBN: 978 0 85784 310 4 (ePub)
ISBN: 978 0 85784 311 1 (pdf)
Also available for Kindle.

Disclaimer: the advice herein is believed to be correct at
the time of printing, but the author and publisher accept
no liability for actions inspired by this book.

10 9 8 7 6 5 4 3 2 1

Contents

1. Prologue

Will Hutton, in his book *Them and Us, Changing Britain – Why We Need A Fair Society* (London, 2011), spoke of the problems with the current economic system:

> "The problem with capitalism is that most of its proponents genuinely believe that it is an immutable force of nature. They think that, like the rest of nature, it works by itself and is best left alone... This is an expression of the best and the worst in human nature – the struggle for improvement and self-betterment and the struggle to defeat the other man or woman. There is only a very limited role for the social or the public in all this. Capitalism is about economic hunter-gatherers being allowed to follow their primeval instincts. Any economic and social construction that gets in the way of those instincts will be counter-productive...
>
> "I argue... that capitalism quickly becomes dysfunctional when it surrenders to primeval hunter-gatherer instincts without fairness. Capitalism is a much more subtle system than most capitalists think. There is a co-dependency between the public and private spheres that creates innovation and business franchise. The public realm is the custodian of fairness, houses the checks and balances that keep capitalism honest and is the architect of the institutions that allow whole societies to take risks and drive forward their economies. There is a genius in capitalism, but the paradox is that it flowers best in an environment that capitalists themselves think is hostile. Paradoxically, fairness is capitalism's indispensable value."

In this book, we examine the origins of the received wisdom, see how it is flawed in the context of the modern world, and how economics can embrace fairness to man and nature.

> "A system of natural philosophy may appear very plausible, and be for a long time very generally received in the world, and yet have no foundation in nature, nor any sort of resemblance to the truth."[1]
>
> Adam Smith

2. Introduction

We live in a curved four-dimensional space-time continuum, in an expanding universe which came into being with a Big Bang, and our understanding of its history continually increases. What was regarded as a true explanation 250 years ago is no longer seen as such, as new questions are asked, new experiments conducted, and new data collected. As more and more facts are gathered and new, different evidence obtained, our understanding of the world evolves. Events that could not be understood before can now be explained. New theories emerge replacing traditional ones in due course. Views formerly treated as facts become, in the light of new evidence, outdated ideas. This is the ongoing process of scientific discovery.

Here is one example: until medieval times, people thought that Earth was the centre of the universe with every heavenly body moving around it. Our planet was seen as a specially created place, which humans were to rule accordingly. Then, in the 16th century, Nicolaus Copernicus (1473–1543), a lawyer and physician,[2] who was also interested in mathematics and astronomy, proved that the Sun rather than the Earth is the centre of the universe. The planet Earth moved around the star we call the Sun. Today we call his insight the Copernican turning point – the change from a geocentric to a heliocentric system. Adam Smith, the so-called 'father of economics', described this turning point as follows[3] (EW p. 76): "As, in the instance before us, in order to connect together some seeming irregularities in the motions of the Planets, the most inconsiderable objects in the heavens, and of which the greater part of mankind have no occasion to take any notice during the whole course of their lives, she (ie philosophy) has, to talk in the hyperbolical language of Tycho Brahe, moved the Earth from its foundations, stopped the revolution of the Firmament, made the Sun stand still, and subverted the whole order of the Universe." When Copernicus "had completed his 'Treatise of Revolutions', and began coolly to consider what a strange doctrine he was about

---

1   In: The Theory of Moral Sentiments (TMS), sixth edition, published 1790 (first published Edinburgh, 1759), this edition published London 2009, foreword by Amartya Sen, p. 368
2   Copernicus was also very interested in economics, eg in money theory, although money theory is not the subject of this work
3   'Essays on Philosophical Subjects', in: *Early Writings* (EW), edited by J. Ralph Lindgren, publisher Auguustus M. Kelley, New York, 1967, p. 76

to offer to the world, he dreaded so much the prejudice of mankind against it, that, by a species of continence, of all others the most difficult to a philosopher, he hid it in his closet for thirty years together. At last, in the extremity of old age, he allowed it to be extorted from him but died as soon as it was printed, and before it was published."

"The conviction that all physical structures could be described in terms of a set of perfect forms – circles, squares, and triangles – limited the development of astronomy until Johannes Kepler broke the bonds of classical thought and discovered that the orbit of Mars was elliptical – a finding that Kepler himself initially considered to be no ore than a pile of dung,"[4] while these insights were major changes in man's understanding of the world – and of himself.

Thomas Kuhn named this revolution in the history of thinking a "paradigm shift",[5] which he explained as a process whereby "former expressions, definitions and experiments get into a new relation with each other."[6]

When, nearly one hundred years after Copernicus, the philosopher, mathematician and astronomer Galileo Galilei (1564–1642) published his support for his system, the Roman Catholic Church placed his work on their list of forbidden books. He had to answer to the Inquisition. It took the Roman Catholic Church until 1992 to rehabilitate Galilei who is seen today as the founder of modern, mathematics-based physics.

Three-hundred and fifty years later we know that the Sun is not situated at the centre of the universe, but in a side spiral of the Milky Way, our galaxy, and we can suppose with reason that there must be millions more planets like Earth within the Milky Way capable of carrying life. Earth was ousted by science from her supposed special place to a more ordinary one. The idea that man and the planet on which he is born have been especially chosen became obsolete. This still seems to cause a kind of humiliation to people who grow up believing that religion gives them the true explanation for their existence, and one cannot help thinking that even today this may be one reason why so many people seem to turn away from science.

In the 18th century, six planets were known to be moving around the Sun: Mercury, Venus, Earth, Mars and Jupiter. In 1781, a seventh planet was discovered by William Herschel (1738–1822) and his sister Caroline, which was later named Uranus.[7] Consequently, humanity's view of the world changed again.

This is the normal progression of science, as normal to us as it obviously was to Adam Smith who, in the 18th century, wrote the first and still highly-respected body of ideas that we today call 'economic theory'. The opening quotation shows that Smith was indeed aware that science is an evolving process and this analysis should be applied to his own theory.

The renowned US thinktank, the Pew Research Center in Washington,

---

4   Elinor Ostrom, *Governing the Commons, The Evolution of Institutions for Collective Action*, New York, 1999, p. 24

5   Thomas Kuhn, *Die Struktur wissenschaftlicher Revolutionen, Frankfurt*, 1976, p. 186–187

6   ibid., p. 160

7   The eighth planet, Neptune, was discovered in 1846, and in 1930 a ninth planet, Pluto, now declassified.

reported in July 2012 that an increasing number of people seem to have lost the belief in a free market society. Only ten per cent of people in Europe and Japan think that their children will be able to enjoy a better life than theirs. It is therefore, as this study shows, high time we developed other models for our life.

That is what this study aims to do: to analyze Adam Smith's work against the background of his time, in order to find out if and how it can still give us a true explanation of events we observe today, and so build a model for life in the 21st century.

At first this might seem to be a strange proposition, as economists and politicians still claim that, "Adam Smith could save the world". Adam Smith's name and his 250-year-old political recipes are so deeply embedded in our society that one might consider analyzing Smith and with him the history of economic thinking a needless and fruitless task.

When we think back to Adam Smith in the 18th century, it seems almost impossible to imagine what life must have been like in his day. When he gives advice, for example, to the colonies in North America, 13 of which declared their independence in 1776, we cannot compare these 13 colonies to the democratic republic of the modern-day United States of America. When he talked about Germany, we should remember that Germany only came into existence in 1871, while before there were various independent German kingdoms such as Hannover, Preussen, Hessen, Bayern, Sachsen and others. Germany as a united kingdom did not become a republic until 1918. The United Kingdom, the kingdoms of England and Scotland were only united in 1706/7, with Ireland joining in 1800, ten years after Smith's death.

When I started studying *The Early Writings of Adam Smith* (EW), consisting of published and unpublished articles,[8] printed five years after Adam Smith's death, *The Theory of Moral Sentiments* (TMS), first published in 1759, when Smith was 36 years old, and *An Inquiry into the Nature and Causes of the Wealth of Nations* (WN), first published in 1776, when Smith was 53 years old, I found that, even though most of Smith's ideas seem still self-evident today, a lot of them are not known at all, while more need to be updated for the 21st century.

The following analysis will explain in detail why Adam Smith's view of the world, the nature of government and economics with the traditional assumptions about 'land', 'labour' and 'money' need to be modernized in order to apply to us today.

This task of modernizing economic thinking is long overdue, and it is essential if we want to understand the environmental as well as the financial crisis[9] we are

---

8   1. Preface to William Hamilton's *Poems On Several Occasions,* printed in Glasgow, 1748;
      2. Articles in the *Edinburgh Review* of 1755;
      3. *Essays on Philosophical Subjects,* not previously published, written perhaps before 1758, compare the editors Black and Hutton's remark on p. 106;
      4. Considerations concerning the *First Formation of Languages,* printed in 1761.

9   Roger Bootle, in: *The Trouble with Markets, Saving Capitalism from Itself,* London/Boston, 2009, wrote: "What has happened to the world economy is not minor and it is not accidental. The Great Implosion, and the possible deflationary, or inflationary, dangers, yet to come, are the direct result of a profound weakness in our economic system – the trouble with markets." p. 64, and resumes: "So the conventional, classically inspired, textbook version of capitalism, free and uncontrolled, has all along been a fairytale." p. 67

in and find solutions to them. No real understanding or solution has been offered by today's mainstream economists. They seem only to be able to repeat Smith's recommendations without considering that our explanations of the world have moved on. I will use a lot of reports from today's media, both print and digital, to compare 18th-century life to that of the 21st and help us formulate an economic theory that is appropriate for our time.

Basing economic theory on real facts, means using a technique which is called "inductive reasoning" "in which individual instances are used to infer a general conclusion. Those individual instances are gained by observation of the world,"[10] remarked Laura J. Snyder, associate professor philosophy at the US St. John's University. She cited the English philosopher Francis Bacon (1561–1626) who overcame the deductive scientific process of Aristotle, that the man or the women "of science must be like the bee, not the spider or ant. The spider 'spins webs out of his own substance', creating theories based only on what he already knows or believes; nothing comes from outside his mind... Bacon also rejected the method of the philosophical ant, which 'only collects, but does not use'. This kind of thinker piles up numerous facts about nature from observation and experiment, but does not create theories that explain those facts... Bacon noted that, contrary to these approaches, the bee both collects and digests the pollen, to make something new: honey. The modern, reformed man of science was to emulate the bee: he must use both observations about the world and reasoning about those observations, to create new scientific theories."[11] So, let's be bees.

I also hope that this study can contribute a little to a better understanding of the so-called 'Adam Smith problem', which refers to an element of contradiction between the multiple ideas in his books. Let's also see what can be done about this.

Giving up assumptions beliefs which were rational in the 18th century and replacing them with rational views based on evidence and facts available rational in the 21st century, can also mean modernizing some political structures, and diverging from Smith's original recommendations. However, this is necessary if society is to develop and attain a truly modern and enlightened structure. It is of course easier said than done. It still seems simpler to invent new products and sell them to customers, who in turn need to learn how to use them, and then, after a certain period of use, find that they have, for example, totally changed their habits of communication. It is easier to change the world through new products than through political analysis and action.

Here is an example of an out-dated expression: we still say 'the Sun is rising' or 'the Sun is setting', although we know that these are expressions derived from a distant past, when people believed that the Earth was the centre of the universe. In fact, we have known for over 500 years that the objective truth is that Earth is moving. The Earth revolves around Sun and spins around its own axis, although we are not conscious of it and we have not found yet words to express that insight. The expression of a moving Sun has a kind of subjective logic, because that is what

---

10   Cf. Laura J. Snyder, The Philosophical Breakfast Club, Four Remarkable Friends Who
     Transformed Science And Changed The World, New York, 2011, p. 39
11   Ibid, p. 41

we, as humans, see every day, we 'see' the Sun rise and set, but this is not from an objective point of view. If we wanted to be objective, we should really name it 'Earthrise' and 'Earthset'.

Given this, one sometimes wonders how long it might take to modernize economic theory and make it reality.

Besides, there will be always people who resist social and political change. They are the ones who profit from traditional views, even when those views have been proved to be out-of-date. And they are mostly the ones who have the power to make themselves heard and be listened to.

Nevertheless, a scientist has to work for a better understanding of the real world. This is what science is all about. Remarkable as Adam Smith's thinking was, his ideas were set down 250 years ago: they cannot be the last word on the subject. No physicist would argue such a case. This means that there cannot be a new economic understanding without an analysis and rethinking of 18th-century ideas. One cannot help but feel that if Adam Smith were alive today, he too would have understood the necessity of modernizing economics. What we need is an economic theory for the 21st century, and political recommendations on how to make people aware of it.

This also means that Adam Smith's theory can no longer be seen as *the* economic theory, but has to be viewed as *an* economic theory, one which is, from today's perspective, no longer capable of offering explanations and solutions to 21st century problems.

But let's modernize very carefully: it does not make sense to throw Adam Smith's economic views immediately on to the scrap-heap of history. There is much to be learned from him and admired, and there is much that can be adopted, adapted and made useful for our century. That is the beauty of historic ideas. And such ideas do not need to come from a political party, they can come from science, by collecting as much reported data as possible from real life, examining it, organizing it into groups, uncovering connections, differentiating coincidental events from essential ones,[12] and comparing data to historic as well as present explanations. This procedure will allow us some kind of hope for change in the future and a glimpse into what that future might be – a future that can and will be totally different from today's reality – not merely a quantitative prolongation.[13] Rather, there can and will be a qualitatively different reality and a different understanding in the same way as the past is different to the present. History is never just a linear development. Therefore, neither history nor work can ever come to an end.

---

12   as Adolf Damaschke in: *Geschichte der Nationaloekonomie*, Jena, 1922, p. 1

13   Michio Kaku argued in an interview with *Der Spiegel*, 39/2012, p. 138 ff, that we will be perfect, referring to his book: *Physics of the Future: How Science Will Shape Human Destiny and Our Daily Lives by the Year 2100*, London, 2011.

3. "Adam Smith could save the world," they claim.

"Adam Smith could save the world," UK politicians claim. From the newest back-bencher to the 'big beasts' – from Conservative and Labour chancellors to a Liberal business secretary, politicians generally concur with this view.

Adam Smith's ideas, laid down in *The Early Writings of Adam Smith* (EW), *The Theory of Moral Sentiments* (TMS) *and An Inquiry into the Nature and Causes of The Wealth of Nations* (WN), seem indeed to rule the world – until today.[1] All of his three publications will be discussed in this study, as Smith is perceived to be the 'classical' economist and the 'father of economics'.

However, despite the seemingly universal claim that Adam Smith could save the world, is it really helpful to refer to the 18th century, when a political economic vision for our own century, the 21st, is needed? Why look back when we could look forward?

Whilst no physicist would dare merely repeat 250-year-old ideas, having instead to consider the latest findings of science, economists are still basing their ideas on Adam Smith's insights and still recommending them to politicians. Indeed, Adam Smith's theories are still treated as facts about how the world works today and always has.

Moreover, the belief that Adam Smith could offer to us, 250 years later, an understanding of how to solve the environmental and financial crisis we suffer from today, suggests a lack of familiarity with his real writings.

Indeed, few will even know what such a reference to Adam Smith means, although most of us come across his picture nearly every day – on a £20 note.[2] This note gives us his lifespan – from 1723 to 1790 – and the following text: "The division of labour in pin manufacturing: (and the great increase in the quantity of work that results)". When we compare the £20 note with the £10 note featuring Charles Darwin (1809–1882), we are, however, reminded that it was Darwin who made the most important discovery of all time, that all life is an evolutionary process. Apparently Darwin's discovery was not seen as being worth the same. Why not? Does this mean that Adam Smith is twice as important as Charles Darwin? Hard to believe. And what about Alfred Russel Wallace?

---

1   This study uses the 1790 version of *The Theory of Moral Sentiments* published in New York 2009, the version of *An Inquiry into the Nature and Causes of the Wealth of Nations*, Petersfield, 2007, and the version of *The Early Writings of Adam Smith*, edited by J Ralph Lindgren, and published by Aguustus M Kelley, New York, 1967.

2   Will Hutton in: *Them and Us, Changing Britain – Why We Need a Fair Society*, London, 2011, p. 148, informed us that a week before Gordon Brown "delivered his last budget statement, the new £20 note was issued with Adam Smith on the reverse – a symbolic statement of his stature in British life with which Brown wanted to associate himself."

3.1. Some data about Adam Smith

Before discussing in detail what Adam Smith wrote, a few details about his life might be interesting.

Smith was born in Kirkcaldy, Scotland, the son of Margaret Douglas, second wife of Adam Smith Senior. His mother came from a wealthy landowning family in Strathendry. Adam Smith was named after his father, Clerk of Court Martial and Customs Commissioner in Kirkcaldy, who unfortunately died a few months before the young Adam was born.

Adam Smith Junior studied at the University of Glasgow and went to Balliol College, Oxford.

In 1752 he was elected professor of Moral Philosophy at the University of Glasgow.

Four years later, Henry Scott, 3rd Duke of Buccleuch, and stepson of Lord Charles Townshend, Chancellor of the Exchequer, offered Smith a job as a tutor, which came with a salary double his income from the University and a pension to the end of his life. Smith accepted.

However, only three years later he returned to London and started work on his second book, *An Inquiry into the Nature and Causes of The Wealth of Nations* (WN).

In 1778, Adam Smith moved to Edinburgh. Smith was appointed Collector of Salt Tax and Commissioner of Customs like his father, jobs he held until the end of his life.

The customs officer and professor Adam Smith was an only son. He is said to have been the very incarnation of an absent-minded professor. He lived with his mother all his life, and in 1784, when she died at the age of 90, his cousin Jean Douglas continued to look after him until her own death in 1788.

Smith never married and had no offspring. He died on 17 July 1790, aged 67, and was buried in Canongate Cemetery in Edinburgh[3].

Although it is almost impossible to imagine what daily life must have been like in the 18th century – without sanitation, electricity, modern transport or ready

---

3   Alan Greenspan noted in *The Age of Turbulence*, London, 2007, p. 265, that "the pendulum of economic thinking began to swing in Smith's favor in the late sixties, ... The comeback has been long and slow, particularly in his native land. A U.S. economist looking for Smith's grave in an Edinburgh churchyard in 2000 reported having to clear away beer cans and debris to read the worn inscription on the stone:
Here are deposited the remains of Adam Smith, Author of *The Theory of Moral Sentiments* and *Wealth of Nations*.
Yet Scotland, too, has come around to according Smith the kind of honour he deserves. The way to the grave is now marked by a newly installed stone that quotes from The Wealth of Nations, and a college near Kirkcaldy has been renamed after Smith. A ten foot-tall bronze statue of him is planned for Edinburgh's Royal Mile. Appropriately, it is being paid for with private funding. And, on a personal note, in late 2004 I was delighted to accept a request from my good friend Gordon Brown, Britain's long-time chancellor of the exchequer and then prime minister, to deliver the first Adam Smith Memorial Lecture in Kirkcaldy. That a leader of Britain's Labour Party, whose roots in Fabian socialism are such a far cry from the tenets espoused by Smith, would sponsor such an occasion is a measure of change. As I will discuss, Britain has endeavoured to join some of the tenets of the Fabians with market capitalism - a pattern that repeats itself to a greater or lesser extent throughout the trading world."

meals, in a country which was almost constantly at war with France,[4] Eric Hobsbawn[5] offered something of a window on that past world, when he commented that life in the 18th century seemed "at once much smaller and much larger than ours. It was smaller geographically, because even the best-educated and best-informed men then living knew only patches of the inhabited globe... Much of the surface of the oceans had already been explored and mapped thanks to the remarkable competence of 18th-century navigators like James Cook, though human knowledge of the sea-bed was to remain negligible until the mid-20th century. The main outlines of the continents and most islands were known, though by modern standards not too accurately. ... Not only the 'known world' was smaller, but the real world, at any rate in human terms. Since for practical purposes no censuses are available, all demographic estimates are sheer guesses, but it is evident that the earth supported only a fraction of today's population... If the population was smaller, so also was the area of effective human settlement... Humanity was smaller in yet a third respect: Europeans were, on the whole, distinctly shorter and lighter than they are today... However, the fact remains that human physique was then, by our standards, very poor, as is indicated by the exceptional value kings and generals attached to the 'tall fellows', who were formed into the elite regiments of guards, cuirassiers and the like... Yet if the world was in many respects smaller, the sheer difficulty or uncertainty of communications made it in practice much vaster than it is today... even before the revolution of the railways, improvements in roads, horse-drawn vehicles and postal services are quite remarkable. Between the 1760s and the end of the century the journey from London to Glasgow was shortened from ten or twelve days to sixty-two hours... but for the great majority of the inhabitants of the world letters were useless, as they could not read and travel... Under the circumstances transport by water was therefore not only easier and cheaper, but often also (except for the uncertainties of wind and weather) faster... The world of 1789 was therefore, for most of its inhabitants, incalculably vast. Most of them, unless snatched away by some awful hazard, such as military recruitment, lived and died in the county, and often in the parish of their birth... There were no newspapers, except for a tiny handful of the middle and upper classes – and few could read in any case... the world of 1789 was overwhelmingly rural, and nobody can understand it who has not absorbed this fundamental fact."

3.2. Adam Smith as an author of classical economics

The attribute 'classical' is normally used with reference to the ancient cultures of Sumer and Egypt, Greece and Rome, to empires and the beginning of democratic structures around the Mediterranean Sea, from which the Enlightenment and the basis for modern Western thinking largely derived. 'Classical' relates to this context,

---

4   during Smith's lifetime, "1743-48, 1756–83", cf. Laura J. Snyder, ibid, p. 33 and 34: "Britons saw France - with its larger population and landmass, its more powerful army, and, no less, its Catholic aristocracy – as a threat to their safety and freedom until the end of the century."

5   Eric Hobsbawn, *The Age of Revolution 1789–1848*, London, 1975, p. 7–11

as in the works of Xenophon (428–354 BC) or Aristotle (384–322 BC), for example.

Adam Smith, by contrast, lived 2,000 years later in the century of powdered wigs, candles and sedan chairs, in the Regency period when the Hanoverian King George III – one of the country's many foreign rulers – reigned over what in the 19th century became the British Empire. Smith's writings can therefore not really be referred to as 'classical'; he can only be identified in the same way as we refer to classical music for example.

Smith analyzsed the people's as well as the government's activities in his time and made recommendations to the Sovereign, how to improve the wealth of a nation, to repeat it: the wealth of a nation, not the wealth of the individual.

3.3. Political economics versus value-free and neutral economic theory

Adam Smith called his theory 'political economics' and characterized it as a 'branch of the science of a statesman or legislator' which 'proposes to enrich both the people and the sovereign' (WN p. 275), the king in the 18th century. Such an understanding has changed. Today the Sovereign is the people.

Smith was eager and proud to give political advice to the King on how to increase wealth – in monetary terms. Therefore, the intention behind his aim to increase wealth was not neutral; it was instead value-driven – driven by making money. Today's frequently uttered claim that (mainstream) economic theory is value-free and neutral therefore cannot be based on Adam Smith, especially when economists regard themselves as advisers to governments in the same way as Adam Smith did. No economic theory can claim to be neutral when it aims at making money. And every economic theory is political. Every economic theory reflects an opinion as to how society should be organized, and which actions are right and which are wrong.

Economic theory always has and always will influence the activities of governments as well as individuals. As Smith stated: "Nothing tends so much to promote public spirit as the study of politics, of the several systems of civil government, their advantages and disadvantages, of the constitution of our own country, its situation, and interest with regard to foreign nations, its commerce, its defence, the disadvantages it labours under, the dangers to which it may be exposed, how to remove the one, and how to guard against the other. Upon this account political disquisitions, if just, and reasonable, and practicable, are of all the works of speculation the most useful. Even the weakest and the worst of them are not altogether without their utility. They serve at least to animate the public passions of men, and rouse them to seek out the means of promoting the happiness of the society."[6] (TMS, p. 217) These remarks reflect Adam Smith's strong belief in the political impact of economic ideas. It is easy to agree with his remarks.

---

6   It would have been a pity to miss Smith's remark by only analyzsing the *Wealth of Nations*.

When today's economists claim that their theories are value-free and neutral, their arguments seemed based in the idea that economic theory is frozen in time.[7] This ignores the historic roots of modern economic theory, the knowledge and understanding that different forms of economics and economies had in the past. However, economics cannot be regarded as static.[8] A theory formulated in the 18th century based on the world view of that time, seems to be accepted uncritically today as if it were somehow 'natural' and valid once-and-for-all-unto-eternity.[9] It is seen as *the* economic theory, not as *an* economic theory. Why has this happened?

As a consequence, the basic parameters of Smith's work have never been thoroughly analyzsed and not really questioned by the public. They seem to be taken for granted even 250 years later, which is actually a very unusual status for a theory which claims to be a science, and not just some technique intended to make money, as Ekkehard Kappler has pointed out.

I would, moreover, take issue with the popular view of economics as a 'dismal'[10] science. Economics is never anything but. Indeed, it should give us the basic understanding how real life works and apply equally to individuals, whether at home or in the work place, whether entrepreneurs or employees, and to governments. It is the basis for how journalists report the daily news and how they interpret it, how lawyers represent legal cases and how teachers in schools and universities educate students entrusted to them. A consistent economic understanding is what unites a culture and keeps a society together. It has today even been extended from Europe to the whole world.

Dismissing economics as 'dismal' suggests a diminished view – accompanied by a sense that we should better stay out of it, as long as the experts understand what they are doing. The question is, do they really? In short, it is up to us to do exactly the opposite: to engage in it. We should no longer be satisfied with entrenched beliefs, we want to have explanations and to participate in something which affects every aspect of our life.

---

7   Roger Bootle, *The Trouble with Markets, Saving Capitalism from itself*, London/Boston, 2009, p. 68: "If you listened to the business school professoriat, you could readily be forgiven for believing that the system we call capitalism, otherwise known as the market economy, was not only the natural state of affairs for humankind but also the eternal one – here since the beginning of time and destined to govern our economic affairs until the crack of doom."

8   ibid., p. 22: "Yet there is another culpable group of people who usually escape scot free from all blame and responsibility. Indeed, I believe they are the ones who are ultimately responsible. I refer to the economists – the long line of professors, thinkers, and teachers who at first propounded and then disseminated the *ideas* that underlay the disaster: the idea that the markets know best; the idea that the markets are 'efficient'; the idea that there was no good reason to be concerned about the level and structure of pay in banking; the idea that bubbles cannot exist; the idea that in economic matters, human beings are always 'rational'; ...; the idea that central banks should be allowed no scope for judgement and should be controlled by tightly described rules; the idea that economic and financial history is another country."

9   compare: Katharina Weinberger, *Kopfzahl-Paranoia, Von der Selbstzerstoerung der Konzerne*, Munich, 2009, p. 167

10 The attributes "dismal" together with "stolid", "dreary" and "without hope" were used by Thomas Carlyle (1795–1881), a Scottish historian, in the 19th century to characterize the work of the cleric and scholar Robert Malthus (1766–1834) as an economist; and therefore they should not be attributed to economic theory in general.

4. From Aristotle to Adam Smith

4.1. Economics or chrematistics

Smith called his theory 'economics', derived from the Greek word 'oikonomia' which comes from 'oikos' meaning the whole house, and 'nomos' meaning convention or social habit.

Thoughts on oikonomia had been written down 2,000 years before Smith, for example *The Oeconomicus*[1] by the genuinely classical author Xenophon, through whom the philosophy of Socrates survived, or by another classical author, Aristotle, in *The Politics (P)*.[2]

As it is highly important for a scientist to define precisely the subject under discussion so that everybody understands exactly what is meant – and what is not – it is interesting to examine Aristotle's definition of economy and compare it with that of Adam Smith.

Aristotle distinguishes between 'oikonomia' meaning household management,[3] and 'chrematistike' meaning making money, the word 'chrematistike' deriving from the Greek word 'chrema' which means money (P p. 80). Therefore, Smith should have called his theory 'chrematistics', because it focuses on money. Smith presents his data in terms of prices. He concentrates more or less on the monetary aspect of reality. In this way, he elevates money from a 'factor of production', from a 'wheel' of the economy as he wrote (WN p. 184), to an aim of economic activity.

To us today, this form of economics seems normal and nearly 'natural', rather than a cultural historical invention from the 18th century. Today, making money is felt to be the only rational of all economic activity. To cite a few examples: Companies are forced by law to use balance sheets to determine how much profit, expressed in money, they have made in the last year; we value a man according to his income (how much do you earn?), taxes are paid in money, governments state their budgets in monetary terms, and believe their political goals to be fulfilled, when money is spent. Monetary considerations define our behaviour and our habits. They seem to rule us.

Economists have invented the term *'homo oeconomicus'* for a man following that logic, and innumerable books have been written about the concept of the totally rational man, whose actions are focussed on money and only on

---

1   Xenophon, *Oeconomicus*, translated by E. C. Marchant, O. J. Todd, Loeb Classical Library, first published 1923, Cambridge/London, 2010, p. 363 and following

2   Aristotle, *The Politics*, translated by T. A. Sinclair, third reprint, 1993

3   The form of household management with its unity of production and consumption was typical far into the 19th century, at least in Germany. Today the household has lost its productive function, as we understand it merely as the place of leisure and consumption. Cf Margarete Freudenthal, *Gestaltwandel der staedtischen, buergerlichen und proletarischen Hauswirtschaft zwischen 1760 und 1910*, Frankfurt/Berlin, 1986

money,[4] while Adam Smith never used the term *'homo oeconomicus'* and therefore cannot be held responsible for it. In summary, it is important to point out and keep in mind that Adam Smith did not focus on the customary household economics of his time, but proposed a break with it. He argued for a qualitative change from what was thought as the norm in the 18th century. However, instead of calling it 'chrematistics' he used the term 'economics'.

4.2. Natural order or cultural invention

A further view Smith shared with Aristotle was the conviction that his ideas reflected the natural order of things. Things are done "by nature..." (TMS p. 259). Nature has given society its laws, distinction of ranks etc. – there are even natural prices for goods. "And Nature, indeed," he mentioned, "seems to have so happily adjusted our sentiments of approbation and disapprobation, to the conveniency both of the individual and of the society, that after the strictest examination it will be found, I believe, that this is universally the case." (TMS p. 219)

"Nature has wisely judged that the distinction of ranks, the peace and order of society, would rest more securely upon the plain and palpable difference of birth and fortune, than upon the invisible and often uncertain difference of wisdom and virtue..." he continues, adding that the "wisdom of nature..." is "benevolent" (TMS p. 267).

The form of economics which was named "chrematistike", ie making money, by Aristotle while referred to by Smith as "economy", was, in his view, more natural than culturally invented. Even prices are ordained by nature: "When the quantity brought to market is just sufficient to supply the effectual demand, and no more, the market price naturally comes to be either exactly, or as nearly as can be judged of, the same with the natural price... The quantity of every commodity brought to market naturally suits itself..." (WN p. 37)

This view of a justification of economics by nature is even shared by a lot of economists these days. How society organizes its economy is mostly viewed as the natural order of things, and therefore unchangeable. These economists seem to view money and markets as autonomous natural entities rather than cultural inventions, as for example reflected in the use of biological terms such as 'growth of the economy' instead of 'increase of turnovers measured in money'.

Therefore let us be very clear: different societies certainly have their base in nature but how they are formed and which norms, laws and customs they follow are

---

4   A few examples are: Reiner Manstetten, *Das Menschenbild der Oekonomie, Der homo oecoomicus und die Anthropologie von Adam Smith*, Freiburg/Munich, 2000;
H. Wolff, *Der homo oeconomicus, Eine nationaloekonomische Fiktion*, Berlin/Leipzig, 1926;
R. B. McKenzie, G. Tullock, *Homo oeconomicus*, Frankfurt/New York, 1984.
Herbert Marcuse called this abstract figure a *One-dimensional man*, Boston, 1964.
Roger Bootle, ibid., p. 80, characterized the *homo oeconomicus* as follows: "Homo oeconomicus is a bloodless, artificial creature who is remarkable in at least one major respect. Although, to the best of my knowledge, he has never set foot on Earth, he has nevertheless left huge footprints all over society."
Cf. too: Frank Schirrmacher, *EGO, Das Spiel des Lebens*, Munich, 2013; Schirrmacher called the *homo oeconomicus* a hypothesis of a person to simulate a human, p. 53

dictated by their specific historic understanding, by culture.[5] As David Korten points out: "Culture is the system of beliefs, values, perceptions, and social relations that encodes the shared learning of a particular human group that is essential to its orderly social function... The processes by which culture shapes our perceptions and behaviour occur mostly at an unconscious level. It rarely occurs to us to ask whether the reality we perceive through the lens of the culture within which we grow up is the 'true' reality. We take for granted it is."[6] Mark Pagel explains the role of culture thus: "Humans had acquired the ability to learn from others, and to copy, imitate and improve upon their actions. This meant that elements of culture themselves – ideas, languages, beliefs, songs, art, technologies – could act like genes, capable of being transmitted to others and reproduced. But unlike genes, these elements of culture could jump directly from one mind to another, shortcutting the normal genetic routes of transmission. And so our cultures came to define a second great system of inheritance, able to transmit knowledge down the generations. For humans, then, a shared culture granted its members access to a vast store of information, technologies, wisdom, and good luck."

Aristotle characterized the technique of exchanging goods by means of money as "not contrary to nature", but that of producing and exchanging them with the sole aim of making money as an "artificial trumpery having no root in nature" (P p. 83). I will therefore, initially, add the attribute 'cult'(ural) when writing about a form of economy using money as an end. This seems preferable to using Aristotle's expression 'chrematistics', a word which is not well known, and I will add the attribute 'nat'(ural) when writing about a form of economy using money as a means.

Smith pointed out that: "Every age and country look upon that degree of each quality... and as this varies, according as their different circumstances render different qualities more or less habitual to theirs, their sentiments concerning the exact propriety of character and behaviour vary accordingly." (TMS p. 239) This clearly shows that Adam Smith had been aware of cultural changes, although he did not go into the details. That he was aware of cultural changes instead of believing in a natural order is an important point, which we will developed further on.

Societies are organized according to the social convention of their time. However, once invented, their norms seem to become quite natural to people. They become what is known as 'second nature'[7] to people, reversing what is natural and what is cultural.

It is important to highlight the difference between nature and culture, as cultural constructions are a human invention and can be changed according to people's insights and needs, when they become aware of some of the consequences of their beliefs and actions. People have the power to change the conventions and

---

5   Mark Pagel, *Wired for Culture, The Natural History of Human Cooperation*, London, 2012, p. 2
6   David Korten, *Agenda for a New Economy – From Phantom Wealth to Real Wealth –*
     A Declaration of Independence from Wall Street, 2nd edition, San Francisco, 2010, p. 248
7   An expression which dates back to the Roman poet Cicero (106–43 BCE)

habits of their era. All that is necessary is to make this clear to people. Who was indeed that French philosopher who said that the confusion of social conventions with natural laws is the most dangerous and unenlightened idea of all?

Robert Green Ingersoll argued that the idea that society mirrored the natural order was typical of the feudal system, which was "supposed to be in accordance with the divine plan. The people were not governed by intelligence," he said, "but by threats and promises, by rewards and punishments. No effort was made to enlighten the common people; no one thought of educating a peasant –of developing the mind of a labourer. The people were created to support thrones and altars. Their destiny was to toil and obey – to work and want... The poor peasant divided his earnings with the state, because he imagined it protected his body; he divided his crust with the church, believing that it protected his soul... He was taught by the king to hate the people of other nations, and by the priest to despise the believers in all other religions."[8]

4.2.1. Nature is a machine created by a supernatural being

When Smith holds society as representative of the natural order of things, he believed that nature was created by a super-natural being external to the living world, similar to the thinking in Aristotle's time.

However, while Aristotle's contemporaries saw natural events as the deeds of different gods, representing different natural forces, Smith believed in one god. In his view, god created the natural world and it had not changed since the time of creation. Smith gave this supernatural being the following names:

"The all-wise Author of Nature ..." (TMS p.93/152/195/351)

"... all-wise Architect and Conductor..." (TMS p. 340)

"... the great Superintendent of the universe..." (TMS p. 341)

"... the great Director of the universe..." (TMS p. 278)

"That great, benevolent, and all-wise Being, who directs all the movements of nature..." (TMS p. 277)

"That Divine Being..." (TMS p. 179)

---

8   Robert Green Ingersoll (1833-1899), *What's God Got to Do with It? God in the Constitution* -1890, Hanover, 2005, p. 26.

How anybody can sum up Smith's theory that his natural order is not only reality, but the existence of this order is based on laws of the dignity of natural science, as well as there is a finalism intrinsic in it because of harmonic thinking, really is beyond one's understanding, especially when we learn in 1922 from Dupont, editor of the works of Robert Jaques Turgot (1727-1781), one of the so-called French physiocrats, that everything which is true in the valuable, but not very readable work which Smith has published can already be found in Turgots 'Considerations', while everything Smith has added is short of exactness and proof. *"Mithin ist Smith's natuerliche Ordnung nicht nur Wirklichkeit, sondern ihre Existenz ist verbuergt durch eine innere Gesetzmaessigkeit von naturwissenschaftlicher Dignitaet, auch wenn dieser infolge des Harmoniegedankens ein Finalismus immanent ist,"* Gerhard Stavenhagen, in: *Geschichte der Wirtschaftstheorie*, Goettingen, 1969, p. 169, and Adolf Damaschke, in: Geschichte der Nationaloekonomie, 1. Band, Jena, 1922, p. 353: *"Alles Wahre in dem wertvollen, aber nur schwer lesbaren Werk, welches Smith seither ueber denselben Gegenstand veroeffentlicht hat, findet sich bereits in Turgots 'Betrachtungen', und alles, was Smith hinzugefuegt hat, ermangelt der Genauigkeit und selbst der Begruendung."*

When Smith stated that this supernatural being has created the world and "governs the universe" with his "benevolent wisdom" (TMS p. 327), he is repeating 18th-century beliefs regarding the origin of the world. According to human understanding at that time, somebody from the outside must have 'generated' the world. The world could not have been understood as self-organized and evolving in time. As Lewis Mumford pointed out the English philosopher Hobbes[9] brushed aside all positive evidence of spontaneous order or self-organization, morality, mutual assistance and autonomy, while glorifying absolute authority as a necessity.[10]

Today, our understanding has moved on due to the advance of physics. We have found scientific explanations for many natural events, although not yet for the question of how the universe came into existence. Was it really a Big Bang or will there be another explanation? Is the Standard Model of Particle Physics a true explanation of the nature of matter? There are still – and perhaps always will be – unsolved and not understood questions.

Smith even believed the super-natural being to be wise, powerful and good, a god who cared for his creation: "... As all events in this world were conducted by the providence of a wise, powerful, and good God, we might be assured that whatever happened tended to the prosperity and perfection of the whole." Today we could mention many examples which have made people doubt that the world is made by a wise and good being for the prosperity and perfection of the world, but we have to admire Smith's belief.

According to Smith this being had not only created the natural world and humankind, but given the world its laws as well. Obeying the laws of their creator is the most important duty for human beings: "That to obey the will of the Deity, is the first rule of duty, all men are agreed." (TMS p. 204)

Provided the divine laws were obeyed, the world would be at peace. Humans had to demonstrate their obedience to god by following his laws and through praying and offering sacrifices to him. If they did this, no harm would come to them. Not even natural disasters?

So when catastrophic natural events did occur, such as volcanic eruptions, destructive storms, floods, droughts or exceptionally bad harvests, then obviously humans had not followed the divine laws. Consequently they needed to be punished. They needed to make sacrifices and hope for divine forgiveness. Humans had to give god or – in classical time: the gods –something back by way of appeasement. Then their obeisance would be rewarded. "It must either be said that we ought to obey the will of the Deity because he is a Being of infinite power, who will reward us eternally if we do so and punish us eternally if we do otherwise ..." (TMS p. 359) "... that Great Superior who is finally to recompense him according to his deeds." (TMS p. 197)

One of the rewards is that obeying the god, humans will be given eternal life, not during their life but after they are dead: "... that the great Author of our nature ... will complete the plan which he himself has thus taught us to begin; and will,

---

9   Thomas Hobbes lived from 1588–1679
10   *Lewis Mumford, Mythos* der Maschine, Kultur, Technik und Macht, Frankfurt, 1978, p. 450

in a life to come, render to every one according to the works which he has performed in this world. And thus we are led to the belief of a future state..." (TMS p. 195). Why after life? Why can't the world be made to function better during people's lives?

This belief of an eternal life certainly cannot be verified by any human. Instead it seems to be more an instrument by which the supernatural being controls humankind. God is, in Smith's words, "... the great Judge of the world..." (TMS p. 156).

However, humans are not only judged by god, they also judge each other. "The all-wise Author of Nature has, in this manner, taught man to respect the sentiments and judgements of his brethren; ... He has made man... the immediate judge of mankind; and has in this respect, as in many others, created him after his own image, and appointed him his vicegerent upon earth, to superintend the behaviour of his brethren." (TMS p. 152)

Smith understood the world, the universe, even human society in a form we now call 'mechanistic'. Obviously, the 2,000 years old Antikythera Mechanism found 1901 is the first man-made device predicting the movements of the Moon and the planets. As far as we can guess, it has been constructed by the Greek Archimedes of Syracuse (287–212 BC). From there it is no wonder that the idea the world is working like a mechanism was taken.[11] However, this mechanism was built on the assumption that Earth is the centre of the universe and every celestial body moves around it. Today such an understanding is considered to be mistaken, although the conviction that the world works like a machine seems to prevail.

In other words, being inventors of machines,[12] people return to the characterizsation of world-as-machine to understand nature, themselves[13] and their social creations, as eg the market.[14] Similarly, they view their own inventions as if they have become subjects, as if they can move on their own. Smith says "... the great machine of the universe is perpetually exhibiting... " (TMS p. 25), and: "The idea of that divine Being, whose benevolence and wisdom have, from all eternity contrived and conducted the immense machine of the universe, so as at all times to produce the greatest possible quantity of happiness..." (TMS p. 279). For him, the world was a machine, and a machine has an external maker – in this case god, whom he likened to a "watch-maker". (TMS p. 105) This idea, which puts humans on a par with a mechanic product, seems now totally inappropriate to us, in the 21st century. It degrades a person and the natural world.

Smith further argues: "Human society, when we contemplate it in a certain abstract and philosophical light, appears like a great, and immense machine,

---

11   Cf.: Jo Marchant, *Decoding the Heavens, A 2,000-Year-Old Computer – And the Century-Long Search to Discover its Secrets*, Cambridge, 2009

12   When at the beginning of February 2013 a robot was constructed from mechanical parts designed to replace failing human organs, it was called a bionic man. Why use the word 'man' for a technical product, as it obviously is no man at all? Why is nobody raising that argument? Why aspire to produce robots for the most intimate personal relationships as sex and care?

13   Rudolf zur Lippe, *Naturbeherrschung am Menschen I + II*, Frankfurt, 1981

14   As did Frank Schirrmacher, in: *EGO, Das Spiel des Lebens*, Munich, 2013, p. 172

whose regular and harmonious movements produce a thousand agreeable effects. As in any other beautiful and noble machine that was the production of human art ..." (TMS p. 371) And the same principle is applied to the economy: "... the machine of economy..." has "turned the rude forests of nature into agreeable and fertile plains, and made the trackless and barren ocean a new fund of subsistence ..." (TMS p. 214). Such a mechanistic view of nature, men and society, especially when different individuals are forced to act as one and on the command of one,[15] are today regarded as totalitarian. Unfortunately, that view is still held by some.

Smith was not alone in his world view. It came into being in the 17th century, as Carolyn Merchant has so admirably shown.[16] Lewis Mumford, however, thought that such ideas had their basis in a much earlier age: "Conceptually the instruments of mechanization 5,000 years ago were already detached from other human activities and purposes than the constant increase of order, power, predictability and, above all, control. With this proto-scientific ideology went a corresponding regimentation and degradation of once autonomous human activities: 'mass culture' and 'mass control' made their first appearance. With mordant symbolism, the ultimate products of the mega-machine in Egypt were colossal tombs, inhabited by mummified corpses..."[17]

It is useful to point out a few differences more between a machine and an organism. Machines cannot act on their own. They are built for a certain purpose. They have to be set into motion and stopped. They repeat only what they are manufactured for. They save human energy, but cannot reflect on what they are doing. Machines have no metabolism.[18] Machines are given by humans the power to move. They cannot repair or heal themselves, while humans and nature have power of creation.[19] Humans can reflect on the possible consequences their actions have, for example expecting a profit from a business deal. People can choose which actions to perform, or not to perform any at all. And they can invent ideas and products which were not there before. People have senses, the use of which make them aware of their environment. They are able to learn from their experiences. People propagate. People make jokes, laugh, make music, write and compute. They can swim, run or ride a bike. They can find new explanations. They are not restricted to a single mode of operation. They can change their culture. In this dynamic view, where humans can initiate and create, lies the most important difference to a mechanistic world view.

---

15   As it is necessary for an army to function as one, that people are at first to be "pushed to their physical and mental limits but also stripped of their individuality in an effort to produce obedient soldiers who accept orders without questions", cited from *The Week* 1 December 2012, p. 56: "Attack ... keep punching": the women being trained for battle", by Sean Rayment

16   Carolyn Merchant, *The Death of Nature. Women, Ecology and the Scientific Revolution*, San Francisco, 1980

17   Lewis Mumford, ibid., p. 24

18   It is indeed very disappointing to read that even Mark Pagel subscribes to the a mechanistic model as an explanation for human life, in: *Wired for Culture, The Natural History of Human Cooperation*, London, 2012, p. 369 for example

19   That most important difference has already been pointed out by Immanuel Kant, remarked W. A. Joehr, 'Organische Wirtschaftsgestaltung?' in: *Die Ganzheit in Philosophie und Wissenschaft*, Wien, published by Walter Heinrich, 1950, p. 111

Today we no longer subscribe to Adam Smith's view of the world. We do not see oceans as "barren", but rather know that organic life began in them, and we do not consider forests as "rude" when they are left on their own. Instead, we know that life depends on natural biodiversity in undisturbed wild lands and seas.

That said, we still find Smith's beliefs repeated in economic ideas, derived from classical theory, such as the assumption that nature is only something outside humans, the 'not-us', a disposable commodity with which man can do as he likes without any consequences to himself. Nature, it seems, only becomes valuable by human 'cultivation' – whatever that means – but is worth nothing when it is left as wild, as uncontrolled by people. I think that this classical point of view is partly responsible for the environmental crisis we are suffering from today.

4.3. Self-interest rules

Adam Smith is also famous for the following remarks, which seem to have underpinned every economic practice and theory to date: "It is not from the benevolence of the butcher, the brewer, or the baker, that we expect our dinner, but from their regard to their own interest. We address ourselves, not to their humanity, but to their self-love." (WN p. 10) These two sentences, written at the beginning of a 656-pages analysis (WN), seem to show that egoistic self-interest rules and, more importantly, *should be* the ruling pattern for society. Self-interest is viewed by him as a kind of natural force, which people follow like a natural law. This claim about self-interest, still prevalent today, is interpreted by Smith in these two short sentences out of 656 pages as an interest focussed on money.

However, reality is not this simple. By talking to these craftsmen, we learn that they are well aware that by offering meat, beer and bread, they produce goods for their fellow citizens who would, without this, perhaps starve. We realize too how proud they are of their task, and that they feel some obligation to deliver good quality products to their customers. Amartya Sen pointed out in the introduction to *The Theory of Moral Sentiments*, these two short sentences provide the whole foundation for the belief, held by most traditional economists today, that Smith is the "Guru of selfishness or self-love".[20]

Sen also discussed the so-called "Adam Smith problem", "the common element of which is the fanciful belief that there is an inconsistency between Smith's arguments presented in the *Moral Sentiments*, which 'attributed conduct to sympathy', and in the *Wealth of Nations*, which allegedly saw behaviour as 'based on selfishness'." (TMS p. ix) Sen regrets that "self-interest dominates the majority of men," and that this only interest has obviously also found its way into politics.

A thorough analysis of Smith's writing shows that there is indeed a difference in the two books (TMS + WN), but it is a difference which Smith himself explains: "That whole account of human nature, however, which deduces all sentiments and affections from self-love, which has made so much noise in the world" – and still

---

20   Peter Bofinger in an article for the *Frankfurter Allgemeine Sonntagzeitung* 24 August 2013, naming egoism a blessing.

does –"but which so far as I know has never yet been fully and distinctly explained, seems to me to have arisen from some confused misapprehension of the system of sympathy." (TMS p. 374) "Sympathy, however, cannot in any sense, be regarded as a selfish principle." (TMS p. 373)

It also seems that the claim for "self-interest" or "self-love" is much older than Smith's writings, and that he obviously was aware of it. Self-interest as a basic category was already mentioned by philosophers like Thomas Hobbes (1588–1679) or John Locke (1632–1704).

Self-interest was understood by Smith as "self-preservation and the propagation of the species": "The preservation and healthful state of the body seem to be objects which Nature first recommends to the care of every individual." (TMS p. 250)

As to the idea of allowing the principle of self-interest to govern society, Smith commented: "The wise and virtuous man is at all times willing that his own private interest should be sacrificed to the public interest of his own particular order or society. He is at all times willing too that the interest of this order or society should be sacrificed to the greater interest of the state or sovereignty," (the King in Smith's time) "of which it is only a subordinate part. He should, therefore, be equally willing that all those inferior interests should be sacrificed to the greater interest of the universe, to the interest of that great society of all sensible and intelligent beings, of which God himself is the immediate administrator and director." (TMS p. 277)

Indeed, the relinquishment of the individual's interest in self-preservation is central to the concept of government, as no individual on their own can defend themselves against the aggression of another country. Indeed, this is an argument used to justify the power governments are granted over the lives and deaths of their citizens. Smith continues: "And hence it is, that to feel much for others and little for ourselves, that to restrain our selfish, and to indulge our benevolent affections, constitutes the perfection of human nature; and can alone produce among mankind that harmony of sentiments and passions in which consists their whole grace and propriety ... so it is the great precept of nature to love ourselves only as we love our neighbour, or what comes to the same thing, as our neighbour is capable of loving us." (TMS p. 30)

This shows that Smith's opinion of the importance of self-interest is not absolute, but always socially related, as "even the greatest ruffian, the most hardened violator of the laws of society is not altogether without an interest in the fortune of others and render their happiness necessary to him, though he derives nothing from it, except the pleasure of seeing it." (TMS p. 13) Therefore his writings can hardly be seen as coming from a guru of pure self-interest. Instead they come from a man who was very much aware of other humans and their rightful interest in their own self-preservation. Smith was obviously not a preacher of pure self-love but his thinking has been fragmented to justify an abstract and unsocial type of egoism.

To clarify: in a money-based culture, people's interest in self-preservation and propagation, is mediated through money. So, the difference between the wider understanding of self-interest expressed in the *Theory of Moral Sentiments*, and the narrower understanding in the *Wealth of Nations* can be explained by the fact that the *Wealth of Nations* is focussed on money. Therefore a wider cultural understanding and a narrower one depending on monetary terms cannot be seen as a contradiction. It is just a different form of understanding, and in no way can that narrower understanding be justified to be the norm for society, as a justification of personal greed.

It would be unfair to refer only to this one side of Smith's writings. We need to consider all his of works. Amartya Sen complained that "unfortunately a big part of modern economics gets both of them wrong in interpreting Smith", and we have to agree with this assessment.

In the *Wealth of Nations*, Smith goes to further extremes with a narrower view of self-interest. His remark about the self-interest of craftsmen leads him on to claim that concentrating on one's own interest is beneficial for the whole of society. Man "generally, indeed, neither intends to promote the public interest, nor knows how much he is promoting it. By preferring the support of domestic to that of foreign industry, (the merchant) intends only his own security; and by directing that industry in such a manner as its produce may be of the greatest value, he intends only his own gain, and he is in this, as in many other cases, led by an invisible hand to promote an end which was no part of his intention. Nor is it always the worse for the society that it was no part of it. By pursuing his own interest he frequently promotes that of the society more effectually than he really intends to promote it." (WN, printed 1776, p. 293) Smith mentioned here an "invisible hand" as a kind of natural mechanism balancing the one-dimensional, egoistic money-based interest of a person as beneficial to society.

Smith also mentioned the "invisible hand" in the *Theory of Moral Sentiment* (printed 1759). Here he writes that the rich "are led by an invisible hand to make nearly the same distribution of the necessaries of life, which would have been made, had the earth been divided into equal portions among all its inhabitants..." (TMS p. 215). The invisible hand,[21] so widely used to justify modern-day economics, is mentioned only once in both books. Smith did not, it seems, give it the emphasis that most economists assume it has even these days.

Smith's idea of the earth being divided into equal portions among all its inhabitants is far more important, whilst astonishingly nobody ever has followed it up yet.

Here it is necessary to point out two things: firstly, Smith's "invisible hand" goes back to Aristotle in *Politics*. Aristotle was – 2,000 years before Smith – already of the opinion that "with every man busy with his own, there will be increased effort all round." (P p.114)

Secondly, the observation that the invisible hand offers a kind of balance between people's egoistic interests can, when analysed precisely, only apply to producers in the economy. If personal greed were the only interest people followed in their life, then no newborn child would survive, no families would stick together, no elderly person would be looked after and no-one would help others in hard times, during wars or famine for example. The narrower definition

---

21   Ulrich Gruber pointed out in: *Die Entdeckung der Nachhaltigkeit, Kulturgeschichte eines Begriffs*, Munich, 2013, p. 50, that church father Augustinus (354–430 CE) was the first to use the metaphor of "God's invisible hand".

of Smith highlights an interest centring on and being reduced to money, whereas in his analysis of the consumer sphere, or the household, the interest of people is not focussed on it. While Smith remarked (WN p. 426), that "consumption is the sole end and purpose of all production", however, he never followed up it up.

The very first time Smith mentions the "invisible hand" is in his *Early Writings* (EW p. 49), published not before 1795, five years after his death. It is assumed that he wrote his *Essays on Philosophical Subjects* before 1758, as he made a remark about the recurrence of a comet, which obviously was Halley's Comet, visible from Earth without astronomical instruments. Halley's seem to have been a kind of omen for people since ancient times, prefiguring the occurrence of important events; its periodic appearance is well documented from 240 BC onward. And the prediction of its re-appearance in 1758 was a successful test of Isaac Newton's physics .

To show the context in which Smith first mentioned the "invisible hand", it is important to cite further sections of the text (EW p. 47-49): "Mankind, in the first ages of society, before the establishment of law, order and security, have little curiosity to find out those hidden chains of events[22] which bind together the seemingly disjointed appearances of nature. A savage, whose subsistence is precarious, whose life is every day exposed to the rudest dangers, has no inclination to amuse himself with searching out, what, when discovered, seems to serve no other purpose than to render the theatre of nature a more connected spectacle to his imaginations... Comets, eclipses, thunder, lightning, and other meteors, by their greatness, naturally overawe him, and he views them with a reverence that approaches to fear. His inexperience and uncertainty with regard to every thing about them, how they came, how they are to go, what went before, what is to come after them, exasperate his sentiment into terror and consternation... As those appearances terrify him, therefore, he is disposed to believe everything about them which can render them still more the objects of his terror. That they proceed from some intelligent, though invisible causes, of whose vengeance and displeasure they are either the signs or the effects, is the notion of all others most capable of enhancing this passion, and is that, therefore, which he is most apt to entertain..."

"Hence the origin of Polytheism, and of that vulgar superstition which ascribes all the irregular events of nature to the favour or displeasure of intelligent, though invisible beings, to gods, daemons, witches, genii, fairies. For it may be observed, that in all Polytheistic religions, among savages, as well as in the early ages of Heavenly antiquity, it is the irregular events of nature only that are ascribed to the agency and power of their gods. Fire burns, and water refreshes; heavy bodies descend, and lighter substances fly upwards, by the necessity of their own nature; nor was the invisible hand of Jupiter ever apprehended to be employed in those matters. But thunder and lightning, storms and sunshine, those more irregular events, were ascribed to his favour, or his anger. Man, the only designing power

---

22 On p. 45 he explains: "Philosophy is the science of connecting principles of nature." "Philosophy, by representing the invisible chains which bind together all these disjointed objects, endeavours to introduce order into this chaos of jarring and discordant appearances, to allay this tumult of the imagination, and to restore it, when it surveys the great revolutions of the universe, to that tone of tranquillity and composure, which is both most agreeable in itself, and most suitable to its nature."

with which they were acquainted, never acts but either to stop or to alter the course which natural events would take, if left to themselves. Those other intelligent beings, whom they imagined, but knew not, were naturally supposed to act in the same manner; not to employ themselves in supporting the ordinary course of things, which went on of its own accord,but to stop, to thwart, and to disturb it. And thus, in the first ages of the world, the lowest and most pusillanimous superstition supplied the place of philosophy."

By the "invisible hand of Jupiter" Adam Smith was obviously referring to the early belief that a natural event was created by a god, in this instance Jupiter, the king of the gods in Roman state religion, which was used as a name for the sky and thunder. In the absence of a scientific and proven explanation for natural events, people invented gods to represent the different natural powers and applied typically human attributes to them. Once invented, these man-made beliefs of whatever kind were treated as real beings with a life and purpose of their own. Despite being human inventions, they are then considered to dictate to people, instructing their subjects on what to do and how to behave, needing to be worshipped and offered sacrifices, as if they were real autonomous beings with needs and desires. It hardly makes sense these days to use Smith's reference to an "invisible hand" to justify selfish behaviour as the ruling pattern for every society.

4.4. Man's nature as social animal

Of man's nature, Smith wrote, that "the word sympathy, in its most proper and primitive signification, denotes our fellow-feeling with the sufferings, not that with the enjoyments, of others." (TMS p. 55) And this fellow-feeling is given to us by nature, by "... natural sympathy..." (TMS p. 86) It means that Smith saw man in relationship with man as well as with nature. Smith refers here to a view which is today necessary to overcome; the split between a person and nature. He thought of humans as animals, instead of following the Descartian split, and about a hundred years before Darwin published *On the Origin of Species by means of Natural Selection* in 1859. In Smith's view, the desire to lead "... is, perhaps, the instinct upon which is founded the faculty of speech, the characteristical faculty of human nature. No other animal possesses this faculty, and we cannot discover in any other animal any desire to lead and direct the judgment and conduct of its fellows." (TMS p. 397) And in his *Early Writings* discussing the inborn faculties of young animals he writes: "It seems difficult to suppose that man is the only animal of which the young are not endowed with some instinctive perception of this kind ..." (EW p. 217). Man is like any other animal forced by nature into "self-preservation and the propagation of the species". These "are the great ends which Nature seems to have proposed in the formation of all animals." (TMS p. 94)

Man is an individual, but at the same time part of nature and a part of his society: "Though every man, may, ... be the whole world to himself, to the rest of mankind he is a most insignificant part of it," (TMS p. 100) he said – an interesting remark which will be considered later. Man "does not look upon himself as a whole, separated and detached from every other part of nature, to be taken care of by itself. He regards himself in the light in which he imagines the great genius of human nature, and of the world, regards him. He enters, if I may say so, into the sentiments of that divine Being, and considers himself as an atom, a particle, of an immense and infinite system, which must and ought to be disposed of, according to the conveniency of the whole." (TMS p. 327) Smith can thus be said to have regarded man as a social animal, as did Aristotle 2,000 years before.[23]

Being part of human society has consequences: "It is thus that man, who can subsist only in society, was fitted by nature to that situation for which he was made. All the members of human society stand in need of each others' assistance, and are likewise exposed to mutual injuries." (TMS p. 103)

Man has to respect the laws of society. "He is not a citizen who is not disposed to respect the laws and to obey the civil magistrate; and he is certainly not a good citizen who does not wish to promote, by every means in his power, the welfare of the whole society of his fellow-citizens." (TMS p. 273) Because "society... cannot subsist among those who are at all times ready to hurt and injure one another." (TMS p. 104) "The very existence of society requires that unmerited and unprovoked malice should be restrained by proper punishment..." (TMS p. 93)

Therefore "justice is the main pillar that upholds the whole edifice. If it is removed, the great, the immense fabric of human society, that fabric which to raise and support seems in this world, if I may say so, to have been the peculiar and darling care of Nature, must in a moment crumble into atoms." (TMS p. 104) And that "the disposition to the affections which tend to unite men in society, to humanity, kindness, natural affection, friendship, esteem, may sometimes be excessive," (TMS p. 286), "but upon the tolerable observance of these duties (justice, truth, chastity, fidelity) depends the very existence of human society..." (TMS p. 188)

Reverence for the above is, said Adam Smith "further enhanced by an opinion which is first impressed by nature, and afterwards confirmed by reasoning and philosophy, that those important rules of morality are the commands and laws of the Deity, who will finally reward the obedient, and punish the transgressors of their duty." (TMS p. 189). Naturally, we would formulate this differently these days.

Nevertheless, we can also state that, according to Adam Smith, there definitely was such a thing as society.

4.5. Male is the norm

While the gods of Aristotle's time were both male and female, the god of the 18th century was considered to be male. Adam Smith called the supernatural being "... this learned and ingenious Father..." (TMS p. 233) and remarked that: "To this universal benevolence... the very suspicion of a fatherless world, must be the most melancholy of all reflections..." (TMS p. 277) When writing about humankind, Smith always used the male gender. Men are the norm. They set the norms. According to him, men create culture, women are at their mercy, often treated as if they are only part of the natural world rather than the civilized state nature.

23   David Brooks, *The Social Animal*, New York, 2011

The other gender, the female, normally constituting the majority of people in a society, was neither in Aristotle's, nor in Smith's time given an equal and fair role. If a woman was mentioned in Smith's work, then only in her function as a wife for a man: "A wife... may sometimes not feel that tender regard for her husband which is suitable to the relation that subsists between them. If she has been virtuously educated,[24] however, she will endeavour to act as if she felt it, to be careful, officious, faithful, and sincere, and to be deficient in one of those attentions which the sentiment of conjugal affection could have prompted her to perform." (TMS p. 187) Women in the 18th century did not have the right to own property, they were not allowed to vote, and their estates would become, when married, the property of their husbands.

Smith's remarks about women illustrate our observation that many of his economic ideas are not neutral and not value-free, but based on 18th-century notions, no longer appropriate for the 21st century. A truly modern economic theory will of course be fairer than that. It can overcome the classical view of the 'other sex' and develop a contemporary model, free of gender bias. (It is truly remarkable that, although many books have been written about Adam Smith's view of men, the persistent bias towards the male has hardly been pointed out.)

Even today, women are still disadvantaged in employment, earning only two thirds of the amount that men earn and therefore collecting lower pensions, being unequally represented in parliaments and in governments,[25] as well as in executive roles and university jobs. According to *The Sunday Times* report of 11 March 2012, "the proportion of women holding senior executive management positions in FTSE 100 companies fell last year despite the government's efforts to address the gender imbalance." Dick Oliver, chairman of BAE Systems is quoted thus: "'Female non-executives on main boards are only part of the story.' 'If we want to tackle discrimination in the workplace, we must have more women in key executive roles. That's the future supply of chief executives and chairmen.'" Naturally, women can never be 'chairmen', but of course they can be called 'chair-women'. The male form in language remains typical in our society.

---

24 Educated in what subject? In following men's interests instead of her own? Why?
    Thomas Tusser (1524?–1580) wrote in: *Five Hundred Points of Good Husbandry*, Oxford 1984,
    p. 157, the following praising women as housewives:
    "I serve for a daie, for a weeke, for a yere,
    For life time, for ever, while man dwelleth here.
    For richer, for poorer, from North to the South,
    For honest, for hardhead, or daintie of mouth,
    For wed and unwedded, in sicknes and health,
    For all that well liveth, in good Commonwealth.
    For citie, for countrie, for Court, and for cart,
    To quiet the head, and to comfort the hart."

25 According to a report of *The Observer* of 24 February 2013, in the UK women make up 17.4% of
    government and 22.3% of Parliament. A recent study by the Centre for Women and Democracy
    of August 2014 found that the UK ranks in place 74 of nations with respect to the percentage of
    women in the lower or single House (*The i* 28 August 2014, p. 6), while Germany was placed at
    22, though in Germany 50.5% of the population are women, and 51% in the UK.

A study by Stefan Bach of the German DIW (Deutsches Institut fuer Wirtschaftsforschung) compared all forms of income, not only wages, but also profits and assets, while before only wages of men and women were regarded. The study came to the conclusion that in Germany the income difference is higher than expected: women have only 49 per cent of the income of men.[26] And: "According to the World Economic Forum, Britain 'has fallen out of the top 20 most gender-equal countries in the world for the first time,' said Oliver Wright in *The Independent*. Average wages for women fell by around £2,700 to £18,000 this year, while earnings for men were unchanged at £24,800."[27]

There is another dichotomy, too: When a women does have a paid job, there is a second unpaid job waiting for her when she returns to her private home. Surely women should have the same right that men claim for themselves to do nothing but rest and recuperate after work?

There is further split: culteconomy (ie the production side) has traditionally been regarded as the active, male realm, while the – hitherto unconsidered – consumption side is seen as passive female one, again no longer justifiable in the 21st century. Nevertheless, the latest study by the Institute for Policy Research, published 11 March 2012, reported that in the UK, even after 40 years of feminism, (unpaid) housework is still primarily a woman's job and the traditional gender roles are still alive. "The IPPR says its research shows that, for real equality, society needs to see men pick up the vacuum cleaner and do their fair share... The revolution in gender roles is unfinished business."

4.6. The two functions of goods

Smith split the functions of goods into two categories, which he describes as follows: "The word VALUE, it is to be observed, has two different meanings, and sometimes expresses the utility of some particular object, and sometimes the power of purchasing other goods which the possession of that object conveys. The one may be called 'value in use'; the other 'value in exchange'." (WN p. 18)

In fact, Aristotle had already argued, 2,000 years before Smith, that all goods have a dual use, two inseparable, but different functions. One is their use value and the other is their exchange value (P p.81), their price.[28] This insight, therefore does not derive, as today's students of economics are still taught, from the writings of Adam Smith, but is much older. We would have wished that Smith that had made its origin clear, as he referred to Aristotle in his *Early Writings*. In this study Aristotle's differentiation between use and exchange value will be considered.[29]

---

26 *Spiegel* online, 27 August 2014

27 *The Week*, 1 November 2014, p. 51

28 One cannot help but be reminded of Oscar Wilde's (1854–1900) famous definition of a cynic as a man who knows the price of everything and the value of nothing.

29 It would not be very meaningful to follow Jeremy Bentham's (1748–1832) utilitarian approach. He assigns utility to both values which conceals their differences.

4.6.1. Slaves as goods

Both Aristotle and Smith, although 2,000 years apart, saw slavery as a given. Slaves are like any other object which can be bought and sold. Women, in particular, were seen as the original commodity and in some places this perception seems to remain.[30]

In classical Greece, most labour was done by slaves. Aristotle stated in *Politics*, that "Humanity is divided into two: the masters and the slaves; or, if one prefers it, the Greek and the Barbarians, those who have the right to command; and those who are born to obey." Some human beings were seen as tools, as objects, with no will of their own, while others were entitled to dispose of them. This was not an unusual opinion, but shared by most at that time.

"Plato," as Hugh Thomas pointed out, "compared the slave to the body, the master to the soul. He took for granted the enslavement of foreigners, though he desired to end that of Greeks."[31] Classical democracy, with its real slave markets, can never be a model for a modern society.

In the Bible, there are, cf. Exodus (or the second book of Moses), chapter 21, verse 21, laws mentioned how to deal with slaves, and it is pointed out that "a slave (he) *is money*".

This division of humanity was still found in the 18th century. Some humans were treated as objects; while others were considered to be the soul or spirit commanding and controlling them. Serfs were the property of landowners, for example, men were sold by the Landgraf von Hessen to fight for the British king against the rebellious colonies in North America.

From the 15th to the 19th century, the slave trade took the form of the so-called Atlantic Triangle, in which about 11–13 million[32] black people were sold by their African leaders for European goods, mostly cloth,[33] and transported to work in the American colonies. "Most of the great enterprises of the first 400 years of colonisation owed much to African slaves," Thomas continues, "sugar in Brazil and later the Caribbean; rice and indigo in South Caroline and Virginia; gold in Brazil and, to a lesser extent, silver in Mexico; cotton in the Guyanas and later in North America; cocoa in what is now Venezuela; and, above all, in clearing of land ready for agriculture. The only great American enterprise which did not use black labour extensively was the silver mining at Potosi in Peru, and that was only because it was at too high an altitude for Africans to be able to work there

---

30 For example the journalist Hans Zippert commented in 'Zippert zappt', *Die Welt*, 4 September 2013, on the idea of Bavarian Prime Minister Horst Seehofer, who suggested the introduction of a toll for foreigners using German motorways, which, if proved effective, could be expanded to include a toll on using Bavarian women as well as Bavarian air. Even a joke mentioning to "use" women as if they are object, should be abstained.

  The internet dating agency Shopaman treats a man as a product, as a commodity, commented by Nora Lysk in *Kieler Nnachricthen* 7 September 2013 p. 14.

31 Aristotle, quoted in Hugh Thomas, *The Slave Trade, The History of the Atlantic Slave Trade: 1440-1870*, New York, 1997, p. 28. It is moving to read the carving on a wall in Delphi by a slave thanking the god Apollo for his freedom.

32 ibid., p. 805–806

33 ibid., p. 797

with their usual energy. The servants of the Americas between Buenos Aires and Maryland were for four centuries usually black slaves."[34] The colonial raw materials were then shipped to Europe to be transformed into final products, and these products shipped back to Africa in exchange for slaves – a most profitable business. Indeed, it has been suggested that the Industrial Revolution which started in the 18th century in Britain, was mostly financed by fortunes made in the Atlantic Triangular Trade.

Slavery was abolished in France in the 1789 revolution, in Britain in 1807, (and in the United States in 1865), 17 years after Adam Smith's death – although it took another 26 years until it was abolished in all British territories, while the slave-owners were compensated with £20 million of taxpayers' money.[35]

Nevertheless, in June 2012, the US Foreign Ministry estimated that up to 27 million people worldwide still live in slave-like circumstances,[36] even though forced labour is today illegal in most countries. UK Prime minister David Cameron said at the opening of an anti-slavery exhibition in the House of Commons in April 2013, "designed to warn MPs of hidden slaves brought into the UK by gangmasters, the trafficked children who vanish and the plight of these domestic serfs... :

'Modern-day slavery crimes in many forms... we have to have a really con-certed approach... to make sure that we look at the rights of those who are affected, and take a criminal approach.'"[37] A recent investigation for a committee of the EU Parliament found out that in the European Union alone about 880,000 people live like slaves, a quarter of whom are sexually exploited.[38] And the Global Slavery Index[39] estimated that in the 21st century there are 35.8 million slaves in the world, people without right, without the liberty to decide where to live, forced to labour without being paid accordingly, especially in Pakistan, India and China, even when the constitution of these countries forbids serfdom. According to Smith slaves "can have no other interest but to eat as much and to labour as little as possible." He was of the opinion that "the work done by slaves, though it appears to cost only their maintenance, is in the end the dearest of any" (p. 252). Such a statement is based on monetary terms, ie how much work the slave owner can

---

34 ibid., p. 794

35 In his book *The Elements of Morality*, Including Polity of 1845, "a decade after the new poor law was enacted," (William) "Whewell sharply noted the irony that at the very time Britain was emancipating the slaves throughout most of its empire, with the Slavery Abolition Act of 1833, it had enslaved its own laborers. A worker was required to sell all of his belongings, including the furniture from his house and the tools of his trade, in order to receive relief in the workhouse. This made it impossible for a man to leave the workhouse and take up his trade again, as he could not earn the money to buy back those tools while in the workhouse, and thus reduced him to permanent 'servitude'", as Laura J. Snyder, in: The Philosophical Breakfast Club, ibid, p. 107, mentioned.

36 And it took the United States of America until the 1960s to extend the civil rights enjoyed by whites to everybody else.
A study in 162 countries by the Walk Free Foundation came in October 2013 to nearly the same result, that 30 million people live still as slaves.

37 Polly Toynbee, in *The Guardian*, 14 May 2013, p. 29

38 *Spiegel* online, 13 October 2013

39 *Der Spiegel* 49/2014, p. 100

get out of his property. Smith reflected the thinking of the time in comparing slaves to cattle – or chattels as they were called: in *America and the West Indies*, he wrote "...blacks indeed, who make the greater part of the inhabitants, both of the southern colonies upon the continent and of the West India islands, as they are in a state of slavery, are, no doubt, in a worse condition than the poorest people either in Scotland or Ireland. We must not, however, upon that account, imagine that they are worse fed, or that their consumption of articles which might be subjected to moderate duties, is less than that even of the lower ranks of people in England. In order that they may work well, it is the interest of their master that they should be fed well, and kept in good heart, in the same manner as it is his interest that his working cattle should be so." (WN p. 614)

Did this view of slaves, as the *"instrumentum vocale"*, the talking tool, who are treated more like cattle than human beings, lead Smith to demand the abolition of slavery? No. It did not.

The difference between a slave and a free man, wrote Smith, is that free men "are capable of acquiring property; and having a certain proportion of the produce of the land," therefore "they have a plain interest that the whole produce should be as great as possible, in order that their own proportion may be so." (p. 253)

As slaves were not able to acquire land, they were not allowed to vote. They had no role to play in society. Smith found that "birth and fortune are evidently the two circumstances which principally set one man above another... His birth and fortune thus naturally procure him some sort of judicial authority." (WN p. 465) This was obviously the natural (and male) order of things. Everybody had his place in society and nobody was allowed to question it.

Smith never demanded universal human rights for every man regardless of property ownership (and certainly not for every woman, as we may demand today), not in *Wealth of Nations* nor in *The Theory of Moral Sentiments* or in his *Early Writing*. So – can he really be called an enlightened scientist?

It is precisely in this thinking, in Smith's view of male and female roles, of free men and slaves, that we found the most important differences between the period from classical times up to the 18th century and our own.

But so far an analysis of the historical situation has not led to a significant change in mainstream thinking or a revision of our political structures so that they are more appropriate for today. This is another reason why the challenge is to formulate a truly modern theory of culteconomics, which, while respecting history, is no longer based on 2,000 year or 250-year-old assumptions.

4.7. Agriculture is the heart of economy

The classical economy in Aristotle's time relied on agriculture, ie big country estates owned by free men where slaves laboured. This is where all the necessities of life were produced. As Xenophon remarked in *Oeconomicus* (p. 409): "We came to the conclusion that for a gentleman the best occupation and the best science is husbandry," although, life, as it was for the Greek would have been quite different if human slaves had not undertaken the labour.

The importance of agriculture was more or less the same in Adam Smith's time. As he stated: "The land constitutes by far the greatest, the most important, and the most durable part of the wealth of every extensive country," (WN p. 156), with slaves or serfs still doing most of the labour. And elsewhere: "In countries therefore, where agriculture is the most profitable of all employments, and farming and improving the most direct roads to a splendid fortune, the capitals of individuals will naturally be employed in the manner most advantageous to the whole society." (WN p. 240)[40] King George III ("farmer George") who made industrious efforts to improve farming, would most certainly have agreed, perhaps Charles Windsor, in his role as farmer, too.

In the UK and in other countries which belonged to the British Empire, all land is still seen as owned by the Crown.[41] The land and the monarch are identical. The laws of tenure still allow people only a freehold or leasehold, but not real ownership. The king often gave land as a kind of present to the aristocrats for their service to him, and he had to give in to the rebellious aristocrats – the big landowners, so despised by Smith, and sign the Magna Carta of 1215. This agreement gave them certain rights which even the king then had to obey.

In Smith's time as well as in Aristotle's, civil rights were based on the proprietorship of land. Ownership of land defined the free man. Everyone's place in society depended on it. If one had money to buy land, one was free. One had the right to vote with the exception of serfs, landless people and women, of course. Status and freedom in society was defined by property and money, not by the same shared basic human rights for everybody, as has already been pointed out.

It is interesting to see that Aristotle even used ownership to characterize democracy: "What really differentiates oligarchy and democracy is wealth or the lack of it. It inevitably follows that where men rule because of the possession of wealth, whether their number be large or small, that is oligarchy, and when the poor rule, that is democracy," (P p. 192), and he made the following criticism of the Greek town of Sparta: "And so a state of affairs has come about which is just the opposite of the happy conditions envisaged by the lawgiver; he has produced a state, which has no money, but is full of individuals eager to make money for themselves." (P p. 149) This statement still seems to hold true today.

Nowadays, we usually divide the annual turnover of sales in a country into three sectors defined by A.G.B. Fisher in 1935: agriculture, forestry, mining, fisheries and market gardening for fruit and vegetables constituting the primary sector; industry the secondary sector and services the tertiary sector.

---

40 How Hans Christoph Binswanger could state in: *Geld und Magie, Eine oekonomische Deutung von Goethe's Faust*, Stuttgart, 2010, p. 140, that Smith promoted industry, is totally incomprehensible, as industry certainly had started, but was not totally developed yet in Smith's time. Such a judgement could only be arrived at by noticing Smith's insights about the importance of the "division of labour" in manufacturing, but ignoring those about the importance of agriculture.

Laura J. Snyder, ibid, came to the same conclusion, p. 120, ascertaining that it was Charles Babbage (1791–1871) in his book *Economy of Machinery and Manufacturers*, published 1832, i.e. 56 years later than *The Wealth of the Nations*, who placed the factory at centre stage.

41 Kevin Cahill, *Who Owns the World*, Edinburgh, 2006

These three sectors follow totally different patterns, as will be discussed later, here it is only important to register that the primary sector, agriculture, no longer plays the major role as it did 250 years ago. From being the most important sector of the economy, agriculture has declined to a marginal one. Here are the latest figures showing the contribution of agriculture to the Gross Domestic Product (GDP) in the United Kingdom, the United States of America and Germany:[42]

Share of agriculture in the Gross Domestic Product (GDP) in 2008

in the United Kingdom	0.67 %
in Germany	0.87 %
in the United States of America	1.31 %

Smith's recommendations were certainly useful in his time –when agriculture was the major sector – but they can neither be valid nor appropriate in the 21st century, when about three quarters of GDP derives from the third sector of services.

A hundred years after Smith developed his theories, industry – that is, the production of goods on a far larger scale than the cottage industry and craftsmanship of the 18th century – became the most important part of the economy. The invention of technologies, for example the steam engine (by James Watt), and the fabric system (by Richard Arkwright[43]) changed what people regarded as normal life. That change is known as the 'Industrial Revolution'. Smith did not live long enough to experience it.[44] The United Kingdom was the first nation to undergo this process, industrializing agriculture as well.[45] Eric Hobsbawm called it "the greatest transformation in human history since the remote times when men invented agriculture and metallurgy, writing, the city and the state". This revolution he said "has transformed, and continues to transform the entire world..."

However, the "great revolution of 1789–1848 was not the triumph not of 'industry' as such, but of *capitalist* industry; not of liberty and equality in general but of *middle class* or *'bourgeois'* liberal society; not of 'the modern economy' or 'the modern state', but of the economies and states in a particular geographical region of the world (part of Europe and a few patches of North America), whose centre was the neighbouring and rival states of Great Britain and France."[46]

Hobsbawm differentiated between two revolutions, "the French revolution of 1789 and the contemporaneous (British) Industrial Revolution", but also spoke of a "dual revolution",[47] seeing the America Revolution of 1776 – the declaration of independence of 13 North American former colonies – as the "stimulator" of the French revolution. In an industrial society, labour is forced to leave home.

---

42 According to the German Statistisches Bundesamt, Wiesbaden, for 2008
43 Lewis Mumford, however, was convinced that the fabric system was not invented by Arkwright but by Venetian Arsenal officers in the 13th century, ibid. p. 504
44 For example in 1847 Parliament passed the 10 Hours Act restricting the working hours for young people in the textile mills to 10 hours a day.
45 Peter Mathias, *The First Industrial Nation, The Economic History of Britain*, 1700–1914, London, first published 1969
46 Eric Hobsbawm, *The Age of Revolution*, p. I
47 Ibid,. p. ix

Labour is dissected into smaller and smaller parts and can then be replaced by machines. Labouring people need to live by means of money, they need to be employed, selling their labouring abilities for money to others.

4.8. The two functions of money

According to Aristotle, money has two inseparable sides, serving both as a means of exchange and as an end in itself, so it has exchange value and use value. Aristotle discussed these differences characterizing the former, which he saw as natural, and the latter as unnatural.

When Adam Smith called money the "wheel of circulation" (WN p. 184), he was referring to money as means, and neglected to point out its second function as an end. Elsewhere in his writings, however, he treated money as if it were the end purpose of all economic activity, though he still called it "economics", when should have used the term 'chrematistics', as pointed out previously.

Today we see Smith's focus on only one function of money is repeated. For example consider Glyn Davies's definition of money[48] as "anything that is widely used for making payments and accounting for debts and credits", or Niall Ferguson's definition: "Money... is a medium of exchange, which has the advantage of eliminating inefficiencies of barter; a unit of account, which facilitates valuation and calculation; and a store of value, which allows economic transactions to be conducted over long periods as well as geographical distances. To perform all these functions optimally, money has to be available, affordable, durable, fungible, portable and reliable."[49] The function of money as a means is mentioned, but the function of money as an end is not considered – and this in the economic climate of 2012! Truly remarkable.

And whilst in Adam Smith's time the use value was more or less identical with the exchange value of money, as in silver and gold coins, these days the two values are at odds. This divergence was caused by the use of paper money. Paper money, ie banknotes, was introduced in England in the 17th century, although it was known and used in China long before. By the beginning of the 18th century, Davies noted, paper forms of money already "exceeded metallic money in total in England and Wales, and by the middle of the century, paper money considerably exceeded specie money in Scotland also."[50]

This separation of the use value from the exchange value comes with a consequence: it means that any amount of (exchange) value can be printed on a paper note. The exchange value can rise almost limitlessly, whilst the use value declines as the material on which the exchange value is printed consists of a mere slip of paper worth next to nothing. And this process of diminution of the use value has been continued with the invention of electronic cash.

---

48   Glyn Davies, *History of Money – From Ancient Times to the Present Day*, Cardiff, 2005, p. 29, Davies identified ten functions of money, differentiating between micro- and macro-economic (p. 27-28), but these are not relevant here.
49   Niall Ferguson, *The Ascent of Money, A Financial History of the World*, London, 2009, p. 24
50   ibid. p. 279

It is remarkable to see that another development has taken place. People have invented fake paper money with zero exchange value, as introduced into India and other Asian countries. These zero-rupee notes were created in 2007 by the organization Fifth Pillar, founded by Vijay Anand. The fake notes of which 2.5 million are said to be in circulation, are used to pay corrupt civil servants who are asking for bribes. As Ana Lehmann from *Deutsche Welle* reported on 18 March 2010, the anti-corruption organization Transparency International estimated that 95 per cent of Indian people had experiences with bribes, making especially poor people even poorer. So, paying bribes with notes of zero exchange value should increase the awareness of corruption and help to abolish it.

5. Adam Smith's extraordinary new ideas

5.1. Exchange is the basic principle

Adam Smith was right to state: "In civilized society he" (man, of course) "stands at all times in need of the co-operation and assistance of great multitudes, while his whole life is scarce sufficient to gain the friendship of a few persons. In almost every other race of animals, each individual, when it is grown up to maturity, is entirely independent, and in its natural state has occasion for the assistance of no other living creature. But man has almost constant occasion for the help of his brethren, and it is in vain for him to expect it from their benevolence only." (WN p. 9)

From this, he concluded, comes the human propensity to "truck, barter, and exchange one thing for another", (WN p. 9) one of the inherent principles given to men by nature.

These remarks are not only true for a civilized society – whatever 'civilized' means. Humans are indeed in constant need of communication and exchange. However, Smith mentioned only the exchange between man and man: he considered only the social side of the whole picture. What Smith forgot to point out is the basic fact that human beings as natural animals have an innate need for constant interaction with nature; that is with the natural environment in which they live. Their life depends on this. Take breathing for example: breathing is a natural process which man constantly experiences and cannot give up at will if he wants to stay alive. We are scarcely aware of this process because it is an unconscious process involving interaction with nature. We take surrounding air into our body and give back to our environment the gas we no longer need. If man wants to venture into an environment where there is no breathable air, he

---

1   quoted from: Sylvia Nasar, *Grand Pursuit, The Story of Economic Genius*, London, 2011, p. 84

has to take this most important ingredient for life with him, e g when climbing mountains 8,000 metres high or deep-sea diving. The natural environment will always vary according to local conditions.

Everything that we live on, that we eat, has been alive and has been part of nature. We take from nature these elements that are fundamental to our lives, and give back to nature the residues we no longer need. Every material thing we produce ultimately has its origin in nature and its end in nature. Minerals, metals, water and energy resources are all extracted from nature, although, as we have learned to produce more and more synthetics, we seem to no longer be aware of that basic connection. Viewing man as a natural being, as Smith did, therefore makes it necessary to refer to our basic interactions with nature as the foundation and source of all life.

The other point which has to be made is that when speaking of truck, barter and exchange, Smith compares activities with totally different meanings. His remarks are, again, not exact enough. Truck and barter means to substitute one set of goods or one item for another without the use of the culturally invented means of exchange, money. Then he uses the word 'exchange' which has a commercial connotation. Goods are exchanged using money with the aim of making money. This exchange is known as trade. Commercial trade, however, answers to totally different rules, which will be discussed later.

There is also, however a naturally occurring type of 'exchange' – or rather: interaction between people – without the involvement of money. This is so self-evident that Adam Smith did not bother to mention it. It happens within a group of people who live in the same household. These people share living conditions, physical and verbal 'exchanges', rooms, meals, times of ill-health, maintenance tasks and so on. This kind of interaction is based on the principle of caring for each other, and such caring and sharing is not exchanged by means of or with the aim of making money.

This type of 'exchange' relates to one side of the economic principle, which aims at making the most out of given means. The other side of the economic principle is to reach a given aim with the least means. The former is, in my view, the aspect which is underrepresented or even left out when discussing economics. It is the household economy, the natural economy Aristotle was referring to, and the basis of all economic theory. Adam Smith was at least aware of this when he stated that the aim of all production is consumption, although consumption is not taken on in his theory. Although this forgotten side of the economy is today considered more or less passive and dependent on a means of financial income (ie paid employment), there is something basic "produced" in households which economics seems to forget: life.[2] It is therefore important to remind ourselves that today's pattern of life has not been created by nature but by social construction during history. For example, it is now seen as normal to leave home to go to work, yet 250 years ago manufacturing was mostly home-based, known as the cottage industry. The home was not seen primarily as a place for free time, recreation and

---

2   compare: Claudia von Werlhof, ‚Comments on *Shadow-work* by Ivan Illich', a paper read at the ECOROPA Conference 'Towards an Ecological Economy', in Kassel, September 1980

leisure, as it is today, and there was no need for a lengthy daily commute, which has today created the need for fast and reliable mass transport to and from work.

Today production and consumption are diverged. In the vast majority of cases, production normally takes place outside the house while – even when a few people seem to be able to work from home – consumption takes place in the home.

The natural basis for life is mutual 'exchange', but without a medium and without the aim of making money. This is true both for people and for nature itself. Humans are constantly 'exchanging' with nature and with other natural beings, and the form this takes varies between societies, being influenced by social rules and customs as well as the natural environments in which different societies exist. I propose that the word 'exchange' should be replaced with the word 'interaction'. The term 'interaction' does not have monetary connotations and it encompasses not just the exchange of products for money, but the whole interactive process of taking and giving between man and man as well as between man and nature.

5.2. The history of money

In chapter IV of the *Wealth of Nations*, entitled 'Of the Origin and Use of Money', Smith explains how money was invented. One would assume that this invention which is so central to Smith's work – and to society, would be worth a long and thorough exploration but he dedicated only four-and-a-half pages of his 656-page volume to its history.

He described the progression from money-as-a-means to money-as-the-end-of-all-economic-activity as follows: "Every man thus lives by exchanging, or becomes, in some measure, a merchant, and the society itself grows to be what is properly a commercial society." (WN p. 15) Here again he showed a confused understanding, regarding people's interaction with each other as well as with nature as being based on money. He makes no distinction between natural interaction and commercial exchange, which uses money as a means and as an end, when in fact they are quite different. Again, his definition is not exact enough.

Following his logic, Smith must have viewed the introduction of a medium of exchange as having no impact on the interaction process. This is also a misrepresentation, as every 'medium' comes with its own intrinsic rules and therefore has both influences and consequences.

By mentioning that money has an origin, Smith implicitly hinted at the fact that money has not existed throughout human history, but came into being at a certain historic date. Time is an important factor to be considered.

Taking the dimension of *time* into account, we have to remind ourselves, again, that Smith's theory of economics is not *the* economic theory, but an economic theory formulated 250 years ago at a time when candles, powdered wigs and sedan chairs were normal. It is therefore worthwhile trying to formulate an economic theory based on people's natural habits of interaction, direct and indirect, and then develop from that basis a new theory which explains today's model of interaction, mediated by money and markets.

Aristotle said, as pointed out earlier, that it is natural to use money as a means of exchange. He called this form of exchange "economy", but regarded it as rather unnatural to exchange goods with the aim of making money. This he named *"chrematistike"*. To him, money as a means is natural while money as an end is not. (P p. 81)

Today we find Aristotle's differentiation helpful, because we have realized thanks to Adam Smith's remarks about *"The Origin and Use of Money"* that money is not a natural, but a cultural concept. Nature never invented a means for her interactions. Humans did, about 7,000 years ago. Hence we have named an economy using money, which can take different forms, a *'cult*economy'. The expression *'cult*economy', however, does not do justice to the difference between a society that uses money as a means and one where money is viewed as the end of all economic activity. This distinction should be made very clear, and it should be reflected in the words we use. I am therefore suggesting a reversal of the terms 'cult' and 'economy' to form the word 'economi*cult'* when describing a culture which has money as its aim. Usually the word 'capitalism' is used to characterise such a form of economy, but this term neither conveys its development nor makes transparent the substitution of the means for the end. The word 'economi*cult'* makes it much clearer.

This substitution of money as a means with money as end of the economic activities went hand in hand with a change in religious thinking. In the 17th century the idea was invented that striving to make money was tantamount to pleasing God and devoutly following his laws.[3] Up to now this view seems to have defined economics.

Thinking this through, a few consequences come to mind: if money-as-means is substituted with money-as-the-end, so that everything is defined in monetary terms, there no longer seem to be any limits, even to human needs. And when today's economicult theorists look back at history, for example to Tudor times, they use to express their findings exclusively in money terms. However, this does not really make sense, as in Tudor times most people did not depend solely on a monetary income, nor was their only aim to make money. Even Adam Smith has pointed out this fact. In those days, people had the use of a patch of land to work on and live from. Smith was fully aware of this as he wrote: "(Cottagers)... are a sort of out-servant of the landlords and farmers. The usual reward which they receive from their master is a house, a small garden for pot-herbs, as much grass as will feed a cow, and, perhaps, an acre or two of bad arable land... The daily or weekly recompense which such labourers occasionally received from their

---

3   Bertrand Russell, in: *History of Western Philosophy*, first published 1946, Abingdon, 1996, pp. 181–182, explained this as follows: "With the Reformation, the situation [ie the attitude to money] changed. Many of the most earnest Protestants were businessmen, to whom lending money at interest was essential. Consequently first Calvin, and then other Protestant divines, sanctioned interest. At last the Catholic Church was compelled to follow suit, because the old prohibitions did not suit the modern world. Philosophers, whose incomes are derived from the investments of universities, have favoured interest ever since they ceased to be ecclesiastics and therefore connected with landowning. At every stage, there has been a wealth of theoretical argument to support the economically convenient opinion."

masters, was evidently not the whole price of their labour. Their small tenement made a considerable part of it." (WN p. 77) Smith even criticised other writers who focused purely on monetary aspects and therefore took a much restricted view with the following remark: "This daily or weekly recompense, however, seems to have been considered as the whole of it by many writers who have collected the prices of labour and provisions in ancient times, and who have taken pleasure in representing both as wonderful low." (WN p. 77) But then he forgot his own insight and did likewise, referring only to money.

Smith lived at the time of the Enclosures, when people began to be denied the use of common land, which had been their ancient custom. "... before enclosure the cottager was a labourer with land, after enclosure he was a labourer without land. The economic basis of his independence was destroyed. In the first place he lost a great many rights for which he received no compensation."[4] The majority of people became subjected to employment, ie working for somebody in exchange for money. From then on they had to rely on their financial income alone. People lost their self-producing power and had to depend on the purchasing power of money. Karl Polanyi named this process "The Great Transformation".[5]

This concentration on monetary terms considers only a quantitative category, as this can be expressed in money. And when everything is measured in quantitative terms, the work people do without involving money is no longer seen as valuable – not by economicult theorists. Today, all economic activity is considered to have one aim: making money. A balance sheet shows the result of the business expressed in money. The annual figures of the General Domestic Product of a country, showing the market value of all officially recognised goods and services, is stated in money. This transformation has become so natural to us that no one questions it. We just take it for granted that everything is expressed in monetary terms – how else can it be? But why should the annual result of production be expressed exclusively in money terms, when money is only one factor of production and there are two more known factors of production, ie land and labour? Why, for example, is there not one politician calling for annual reports on the number of labouring hours and its changes in time, or the use of natural resources in physical measurements? Such questions are considered so 'off-the-wall' that they are not asked. Money is the only goal we are aiming at. Money has become the only rational aim, the end of every human activity, even in our private lives. We are living in an economicult society.

5.3. The relativity of prices in time or the continually changing buying power of money

Another of Smith's insights was that money has an infinite capacity for change with regard to its buying power. Money, he wrote "the great wheel of circulation is altogether different from the goods which are circulated by means of it."

---

4   J. L. Hammond and B. Hammond, *The Village Labourer 1760–1832, A Study of the Government of England before the Reform Bill*, first published 1911, London, 1967, p. 100

5   Karl Polanyi, *The Great Transformation*, Boston, 1944

However, "the revenue of the society consists altogether in those goods, and not in the wheel which circulates them."[6] And: "In computing either the gross or the net revenue of any society, we must always, from whole annual circulation of money and goods, deduct the whole value of the money, of which not a single farthing can ever make any part of either. It is only the ambiguity of language which can make this proposition appear either doubtful or paradoxical. When properly explained and understood, it is almost self-evident." (WN p. 184) It seems we are still not paying enough attention to Smith's remarks when the possession of money makes us feel richer than the possession of goods which can be bought with money.

"Though the weekly or yearly revenue of all the different inhabitants of any country, in the same manner, may be, and in reality frequently is, paid to them in money, their real riches, however, the real weekly or yearly revenue of all of them taken together, must always be, great or small, in proportion to the quantity of consumable goods which they can all of them purchase with this money. The whole revenue of all of them taken together is evidently not equal to both the money and the consumable goods, but only to one or other of those two values, and to the latter [consumable goods] more properly than to the former [money]. (WN p. 185)

It was Smith who first pointed out that the price people pay at a certain time in history does not say anything about their real buying power. This needs to be taken carefully into consideration when comparing prices. "At the same time and place, therefore, money is the exact measure of the real exchangeable value of all commodities. It is so, however, at the same time and place only." (WN p. 24) "As it is the nominal or money price of goods, therefore, which finally determines the prudence or imprudence of all purchases and sales, and thereby regulates almost the whole business of common life in which price is concerned, we cannot wonder that it should have been so much more attended to than the real price." (WN p. 25) The ever-changing buying power of money over time was obviously not given enough attention by scientists before Smith. Today the phrase 'money illusion' is used when only the nominal and not the real value of money at a certain time is considered.

Smith's recommendations have been generally adopted. If one looks into the figures published today by the national statistical offices, they are always given in nominal prices as well as in real prices, ie price minus inflation in time. And only real prices can be compared with each other.

Smith's insight into the infinitely changing buying power of money, into the necessity of considering the time factor leads to additional questions: Why should economic data only be given in always changing (money) terms? Would it not make more sense, for example, to compare the physical quantities according to the standards of the International System of Units (SI) for comparing different categories in time? Or at least, add these to the monetary figures?

---

6   It should be pointed out that the words 'wheel' and 'circulate' follow an idea so often heard, that everything moves in a circle. A wheel rolls on, arriving at the same point from which it started. This, however, forgets to consider that the whole purpose of the wheel's move is to go on in time. The expression 'circle' omits the category time, and it therefore should no longer be used.

5.4. Production is only one side of the economy

Smith made another important point when he said that, "consumption is the sole end and purpose of all production..." and regretted that "the interest of the consumer is almost constantly sacrificed to that of the producer; and it seems to consider production, and not consumption, as the ultimate end and object of all industry and commerce." (WN p. 426) In Smith's view, "the interest of the producer ought to be attended to, only so far as it may be necessary for promoting that of the consumer." After such statements, we would have expected him to include a theory of consumption in the *Wealth of Nations*, as he sees consumption as the "end and object of all industry and commerce". But the *Wealth of Nations* did not stretch to this subject. Smith neglected the consumption side as well, and this is how we follow it today. Consumption is not important to economists. Economicult theory concentrates on the production side of all human activities.

It is easy to understand why economicult theorists even these days concentrate on production, as   after all only the manufacturing and sale of products secures the goal of making money. Consumption does not. Economicult theory is controlled by, and viewed from money terms. Consumption is based on a totally different set of values to those typical for production.

However, Smith made one of his now famous remarks about this consequence: "To found a great empire for the sole purpose of raising up a people of customers, may at first appear a project fit only for a nation of shopkeepers.[7] It is, however, a project altogether unfit for a nation of shopkeepers, but extremely fit for a nation whose government is influenced by shopkeepers. Such statesmen, and such statesmen only, are capable of fancying that they will find some advantage in employing the blood and treasure of their fellow-citizens, to found and maintain such an empire." (WN p. 397)

A genuinely modern version of economic theory therefore cannot go on neglecting consumption, instead it has to discuss both sides of the economic process, production and consumption. And herein lies another challenge.

5.5. Land and labour produce the real wealth of a nation

Smith's insight was that the real wealth of a country derives from the annual produce of land and labour, as already pointed out in chapter 4.7: "The land constitutes by far the greatest, the most important, and the most durable part of the wealth of every extensive country."[8] (WN p. 156) But he added: "It would be too ridiculous to go about seriously to prove that wealth does not consist in money, or in gold and silver; but in what money purchases, and is valuable only

---

7   This description of the UK being a nation of shopkeepers became famous when Napoleon is said to have used it, too.

8   It is therefore wrong to claim, as Hans Christoph Binswanger does in: *Geld und Magie, Eine oekonomische Deutung von Goethes Faust*, Stuttgart, 2010, p. 23–24/46, that Adam Smith did not mention the works of nature and that he thought only human labour constitutes wealth.

for purchasing. Money, no doubt, makes always a part of the national capital; but it has already been shown that it generally makes but a small part, and always the most unprofitable part of it..." (WN p. 282). Smith's remark that the real wealth of a country derives from the annual produce of land and labour might indeed surprise. One wonders what an economic theory would look like if his insights were to be taken seriously – for theory as well for practice?

We should not be astonished by this, however, as Smith here follows a tradition of British philosophers such as Thomas Hobbes[9] (1588–1679) or William Petty[10] (1623–1687). Let us remind ourselves that it was Petty who said that labour is the father and active principle of wealth, as land is the mother.

This "... whole annual produce of the land and labour of every country" Smith wrote, "... naturally divides itself, it has already been observed, into three parts; the rent of land, the wages of labour, and the profits of stock; and constitutes a revenue to three different orders of people; to those who live by rent, to those who live by wages, and to those who live by profit. These are the three great, original, and constituent, orders of every civilized society..." (WN p. 161). Here we find for the first time what is now seen as the three factors of production: land, labour[11] and capital. Viewing land, labour and capital as the factors of production derives, naturally, from the view of someone who employs them.

It becomes interesting to analyze what Smith meant by the 'land' and 'labour' from which he saw the real wealth of a country deriving. This is not as obvious as one might perhaps think.

5.5.1. Land

Adam Smith understood 'land' as it was seen at his time – and from the perspective of an entrepreneur – as a commodity which can be bought, owned and sold.

This point of view is interesting if it is contrasted with a remark of one of his contemporaries, Gilbert White of Selborne (1720–1793), a keen observer of the land and the people. His book *The Natural History of Selborne*, printed in 1788 by T. Bensley of London, 18 years after the first mention of such a project, is the fourth most published book in English.

Richard Mabey remarked in 1977 in his introduction to White's work:[12] "More than any other single book it has shaped our everyday view of the relations between man and nature... He was perhaps the first writer to talk of animals – and particularly birds – as if they conceivably inhabited the same universe as human beings... This is a new note in nature writing – and not just because of the accuracy and percipience of the observations..." The birds Maybe observed "... are

---

9   Thomas Hobbes, *Leviathan*, 1651

10   William Petty, *A Treatise of Taxes and Contribution*, 1662

11   This assumption seems to be centuries older, as Israel Finkelstein and Neil Asher Silberman, in: *The Bible Unearthed, Archeology's New Vision Of Ancient Israel And The Origin Of Its Sacred Texts*, New York, 2002, p. 215, pointed out: "The Assyrians viewed all the lands, animals, resources, and peoples of the areas the had conquered as objects - as chattel - that could and should be moved or exploited to serve the best interests of the Assyrian state."

12   p. ix–x

real, not puppets – 'bundles of responses' – or links in some taxonomic chain. They are living birds in a living and closely observed situation. With no more than a hint of anthropomorphism, White suggests that their lives have a richness and rhythm of their own. And by describing them on a summer evening in a particular English village, he is able to awake in us the possibility of a human response to them... White was more interested in the relationships between living animals than in the relationships between their taxonomically significant parts," asking: "How was this unexceptional country parson able to go against the whole tenor of science in his time, and rise to such a position of eminence in both natural history and literature?"

As Mabey pointed out: "A hundred years before Darwin, he realized the crucial role of worms in the formation of soil."[13]

So let's hear White in his own words even when it is a long citation:[14] "Dear Sir, I was much gratified by your communicative letter on your return from Scotland, where you spent, I find, some considerable time, and gave yourself good room to examine the natural curiosities of that extensive kingdom, both those of the islands, as well as those of the highlands. The usual bane of such expedition is hurry; because men seldom allot themselves half the time they should do: but, fixing on a day for their return, post from place to place rather as if they were on a journey that required dispatch, than as philosophers investigating the works of nature. You must have made, no doubt, many discoveries and laid up a good fund of materials for a future edition of the British Zoology; and will have no reason to repent that you have bestowed so much pains on a part of Great Britain that perhaps was never so well examined before.

It has always been matter of wonder to me that field-fares, which are so congenerous to thrushes and blackbirds, should never choose to breed in England: but that they should not think even the highlands cold and northerly, and sequestered enough, is a circumstance still more strange and wonderful. The ring-ousel, you find, stays in Scotland the whole year round; so that we have reason to conclude that those migrators that visit us from a short space every autumn do not come from thence.

And here, I think, will be the proper place to mention that those birds were most punctual again in their migration this autumn, appearing, as before, about the 30th of September: but their flocks were larger than common, and their stay protracted somewhat beyond the usual time. If they came to spend the whole winter with us, as some of their congeners do, and then left us, as they do, in spring, I should not be so much struck with the occurrence, since it would be similar to that of the other winter birds of passage; but when I see them for a fortnight at Michaelmas, and again for about a week in the middle of April, I am seized with wonder, and long to be informed whence these travellers come, and whither they go, since they seem to use our hills merely as an inn or baiting place.

Your account of the greater brambling, or snow-fleck is very amusing; and strange it is that such a short-winged bird should delight in such perilous voyage

---

13   p. xviii
14   I have chosen his letter no xxvi of December 8, 1769, to Daines Barrington as an example.

over the northern ocean! Some country people in the winter time have every now and then told me that they have seen two or three white lark on our downs; but on considering the matter, I begin to suspect that these are some stragglers of the birds we are talking of, which sometimes perhaps may rove so far to the southward.

It pleases me to find that white hares are so frequent on the Scottish mountains, and especially as you inform me that it is a distinct species; for the quadruped of Britain are so few, that every new species is a great acquisition.

The eagle-owl, could it be proved to belong to us, is so majestic a bird that it would grace our fauna much. I never was informed before where wild-geese are known to breed.

You admit, I find, that I have proved your fen *salicaria* to be the lesser reed-sparrow of Ray; and I think that you may be secure that I am right; for I took very particular pains to clear up that matter, and had some fair specimens; but, as they were not well preserved, they are decayed already. You still, no doubt, insert it in its proper place in your next edition. Your additional plates will much improve your work.

De Buffon, I know, has described the water shrew-mouse: but still I am pleased to find you have discovered it in Lincolnshire, for the reason I have given in the article on the white hare.

As a neighbour was ploughing in a dry chalky field, far removed from any water, he turned out a water rat, that was curiously laid up in a *hybernaculum* artificially formed of grass and leaves. At one end of the burrow lay above a gallon of potatoes regularly stowed, on which it was to have supported itself for the winter. But the difficulty with me is how this *amphibius mus* came to fix its winter station at such a distance from the water. Was it determined in its choice of that place by the mere accident of finding the potatoes which were planted there; or is it the constant practice of the aquatic rat to forsake the neighbourhood of the water in the colder months?

Though I delight very little in analogous reasoning, knowing how fallacious it is with respect to natural history; yet, in the following instance, I cannot help being inclined to think it may conduce towards the explanation of a difficulty that I have mentioned before, with respect to the invariable early retreat of the *hirundo apus*, or swift, so many weeks before its congeneres; and that not only with us, but also in Andalusia, where they also begin to retire about the beginning of August.

The great large bat (which by the by is at present a nondescript in England, and what I have never been able yet to procure) retires and migrates very early in summer: it also ranges very high for its food, feeding in a different region of the air; and that is the reason I never could procure one. Now this is exactly the case with the swifts; for they take their food in a more exalted region than the other species, and are very seldom seen hawking for flies near the ground, or over the surface of the water. From hence I would conclude that these *hirundines*, and the larger bats, are supported by some sorts of high-flying gnats, scarabs, or *phalaenae*, that are of short continuance; and that the short stay of these strangers is regulated by the defect of their food.

By my journal it appears that curlews clamoured on to October the thirty-first; since which I have not seen or heard any. Swallows were observed on to November the third. * The little bat appears almost every month in the year; but I have never seen the large ones till the end of April, nor after July. They are most common in June, but never in any plenty; are a rare species with us."

This is a description of the land, indeed. What a pity that White's understanding of it did not find more admittance into Smith's writings.

Kevin Cahill, for example, defines 'land' as "the earth upon which we stand, from whence we obtain our food and water and upon which we live. That earth has many shapes, components and dimensions, and it extends under water, in lakes and rivers and under the sea and beyond the coastline. In general... land is the physical surface of the state in all its many shapes and dimensions."[15] It seems a far more appropriate description than the narrower view expressed by Smith about the 'land'.

Karl Polanyi saw the definition of 'land' by Smith as another word for nature. He was of the opinion that nature is not produced by man, and therefore cannot be seen as a production factor or as a ware or commodity.[16]

Therefore we can assert that an economicult theory based on Smith's assumptions has an understanding of nature. It is not nature-forgotten as a lot of economists claim.

Now the question has to be asked: how can 'land', meaning nature, be rewarded for its use by Smith, if bearing in mind the fact that money is not a concept of nature, and therefore has no meaning for nature? Smith used an intellectual trick to find a solution to this problem: instead of offering 'land' (alias nature) something in return for its service to man, he recommended paying the landowner. As a landowner is a natural being, there is a kind of a justification for such a jump from rewarding land/nature to paying the landowner money. With regard to land/nature Smith explained: "The interest of the first of those three great orders" land/nature, labour and money "... is strictly and inseparably connected with the general interest of the society." Landowners, he commented "... are the only one of the three orders whose revenue costs them neither labour nor care, but comes to them, is it were, of its own accord, and independent of any plan or project of their own." (WN p. 162) It comes to them by itself, that is, by nature. Nature produces resources, and the landowner seizes the natural produce as his or her own.

Smith pointed out some consequences to this view: "That indolence which is the natural effect of the ease and security of their situation, renders landowners too often, not only ignorant, but incapable of that application of mind, which is necessary in order to foresee and understand the consequence of any public regulation." (WN p. 162)

What Smith suppressed therefore, when concentrating on money, is the fact that land/nature is much more than a production factor. Land/nature cannot make any sense of money, only the landowner can. Land (meaning nature) is the

15   Kevin Cahill, *Who owns the World–the hidden facts behind landownership*, Edinburgh, 2006
     p. 166
16   Karl Polanyi, *The Great Transformation*, Boston, 1944

basis for life – as we know it. We depend on our natural environment – with every breath. This side of nature gets overshadowed by monetary considerations, when in reality it is the all-important basis. Today this fact can no longer be ignored.

Furthermore, it must be added that Smith's view of nature would have been totally different from our own in the 21st century. In Smith's time, Earth was thought to be only a few thousand years old, and the Sun, around which Earth orbits, was assumed to be the centre of the universe. According to our knowledge today, however, Earth is about 4.5 billion years old, and is situated in a distant spiral arm of the local galaxy, the Milky Way. This has at its centre, as seems to be the case with every other galaxy, a black hole. The solar system of which the Earth is a part moves around this centre. And as there are billions of stars, only in the Milky Way, we can assume that there are billions of other stars and billions of other planets like Earth. Furthermore, we have evidence that the universe is dynamic and expanding, had a beginning and will, therefore, possibly have an end.

5.5.2. Labour

Smith obviously did not see the need to define his concept of 'labour', whereas for today's theorists it is essential to have an exact definition of one of economics' most basic categories. This will be explored later. Smith wrote: "The property which every man has in his own labour, as it is the original foundation of all other property, so it is the most sacred and inviolable." 'Labour' here is seen by Smith as a commodity like any other, which man can dispose of as he wants, without regard for example to its natural conditions.

Indirectly Smith pointed out that 'labour' can also mean a group of dependently working people: "The interest of the second order, that of those who live by wages, is as strictly connected with the interest of the society as that of the first," ie landowners. When labour, "this real wealth of the society, becomes stationary, his wages are soon reduced to what is barely enough to enable him" (or her) "to bring up a family, or to continue the race of labourers... The order of proprietors may perhaps gain more by the prosperity of the society than that of labourers; but there is no order that suffers so cruelly from its decline. But though the interest of the labourer is strictly connected with that of the society, he is incapable either of comprehending that interest, or of understanding its connection with his own. His condition leaves him no time to receive the necessary information, and his education and habits are commonly such as to render him unfit to judge, even though he was fully informed. In the public deliberations, therefore, his voice is little heard, and less regarded..." (WN p. 162)[17]

Smith's use of the term 'labour' obviously referred to Thomas Hobbes (1588–1679). It was Hobbes who remarked, a hundred years before Smith, that a man's "labour is a commodity as well as any other thing".[18] Hobbes made this

---

17   One really wonders how Smith's view relates to the neoclassical perspective of fully informed citizen making rational choices.

18   Thomas Hobbes, *Leviathan*, published first in 1651, ninth edition, Cambridge, 2006, p. 171.
     In modern times Guenter Woehe, *Einfuehrung in die Allgemeine Betriebswirtschaftslehre*, Munich, 1973, p. 211, noted that in economics a human being is a means, not an end.
     Cf. too: Ralf Reichwald, *Arbeit als Produktionsfaktor*, Munich/Basel, 1977

remark in the context of his time, when 'labour' or men as serfs could be bought and sold. And it is not very far-fetched to assume that Hobbes derived his view of 'labour' from the slave market. The only difference was that a free labourer was able to sell his own labour, being the "owner" of it.

Smith recommended that 'labour' be rewarded liberally, meaning generously. "The liberal reward of labour... as it is the necessary effect, so it is the natural symptom of increasing national wealth. The scanty maintenance of the labouring poor, on the other hand, is the natural symptom that things are at a stand, and their starving condition, that they are going fast backwards." (WN p. 48)

There is no argument in the *Wealth of Nations* to justify the claim so often heard today, that the costs of labour are too high and should be reduced.[19] Smith had indeed a totally different opinion regarding labour to today's economicult theorists. He explained: "The liberal reward of labour... as it is the effect of increasing wealth, so it is the cause of increasing population. To complain of it, is to lament over the necessary cause and effect of the greatest public prosperity." And: "The wages of labour are the encouragement of industry, which, like every other human quality, improves in proportion to the encouragement it receives. A plentiful subsistence increases the bodily strength of the labourer, and the comfortable hope of bettering his condition...Where wages are high, accordingly, we shall always find the workmen more active, diligent, and expeditious than where they are low..." (WN p. 53) Let us remember that these days the law requires that everyone should be paid a minimum wage, while only a 'living wage' would allow people surviving on relatively low pay to live in London for example.[20]

Smith followed Hobbes in defining 'labour' as a commodity, ie working for someone in exchange for money. This view of labour is based on abstract thinking, as in reality 'labour' cannot be bought and sold like any other good without the labouring person applying his labouring ability. And therefore it is questionable whether the 'labour' executed by men and nature really is the same as what "produces value and is the real measure of value". (WN p. 20, 22, 24/ WN p. 233) What does the labour of an entrepreneur or an artist or even the labour of a professor of philosophy and customs officer mean? When his 'labour' is not bought? How is this labour valued? Should perhaps an economy be built on relying on labour – of nature and of man – as its natural basic principle, rather than on money, the cultural invention? But what is labour, then?

In today's economy the meaning of 'labour' is split – at least – twice, and its understanding depends on money. Money defines whether it is seen merely as cost for the employer, or if it is the result of an entrepreneur's work, as the latter is not seen as cost, but as profit.

This also comes with the consequence that 'labour' which is not offered on the market and not defined in terms of money, does not seem to have any value. By

---

19 And it seems that one business strategy to achieve this is to introduce 'Zero-hour contracts', meaning that people have a contract to labour, but have to wait until the company needs them, and are only paid when working. It is estimated that nearly one million employees in the UK are nowadays labouring under such conditions, according to *The Independent* 6 August 2013, p. 14.

20 compare for example the article 'The man cleaned Nick Clegg's office. He also fought for a living wage: Then he was punished' in *The Observer*, 11 November, 2012, p. 14

concentrating on paid 'labour' we have lost, it seems, the importance and value of our own work. We seem to value only a part of our whole activity, the 'labour' which is mediated by market and money. We have made money, the means of economic activity, to determine even our understanding of ourselves. A historic human invention is used to define a human being. In recent years, we have even grown accustomed to expressing our own ability to labour as 'human capital'. How could people have let this happen?

Besides, what should we think of a theory which claims to be a 'science', when even its basis, 'labour', has not one exactly defined but at least two different meanings, depending on money? Such an approach would be unthinkable in physics, so why is nobody questioning it in a social science, in economicult theory?

By viewing 'labour' as a commodity and by creating a market for 'labour', Hobbes – and in the same tradition, Smith – separated 'labour' from the labouring person. This can only be done in the abstract. It is an intellectual trick, because it is self-evident that in reality 'labour' is an expression for the working ability incorporated in a person, from whom it cannot be detached. In real life we find working *people* in factories, and not labour. Therefore the conclusion has to be that the separation of 'labour' and a labouring person is the real division of labour.

Separating the ability to labour from the person who labours is an abstract concept, and a very convenient one in an age where a market for people (ie a slave market) is no longer acceptable. We can now name this market a 'labour market' – a change of terminology but nothing more. In an enlightened and modern society this historic construct should no longer be used, because it contains an outdated assumption about the nature of 'labour', even though today a labouring person is permitted to sell his own labouring ability which he was not able to do before. Today we are fully aware that nobody can sell 'labour' without selling himself or herself. No longer can humans be seen (through their labour) as instruments, as means[21] of production, and they can no longer view their own ability as a means. "Always recognise that human individuals are ends, and do not use them as means to your end,"[22] demanded Immanuel Kant (1724–1804), the German enlightened philosopher who defined 'enlightenment' as "man's leaving his self-caused immaturity. Immaturity is the incapacity to use one's intelligence without guidance of another... *Sapere aude!* have the courage to use your own intelligence! is therefore the motto of the Enlightenment."[23]

Today we understand that man cannot buy a person, so nobody can have property in another as Thomas Paine (1737–1809) famously expressed it in the

---

21 Although we might doubt it on reading in the *Computerwoche* 4 February 2013 that the computer company Hewlett-Packard informed their 1,100 IT-specialists via email of the closure of the production plant in Ruesselsheim, Germany. Hewlett-Packard had taken on these specialists in 2008 after buying the IT company EDS, an outsourcing partner of General Motors and Opel. Employees are evidently still treated no differently from any other wares which can be bought and sold.

22 Immanuel Kant, *Was ist Aufklaerung?* Berlinische Monatsschrift, December 1784

23 Immanuel Kant, *Kritik der reinen Vernunft*, 1781

Rights of Man[24], an idea which seems to go back to the Greek philosopher Zeno.[25] The Declaration of Human Rights was issued by the United Nations on 10 December 1948. The Street of Human Rights was built in Nuremberg, Germany in 1988[26] as a response to the history of the city during the Nazi atrocities, and also in remembrance of the Nuernberg trials of 1945–1946 when the major war criminals were sentenced.

The historic view of 'labour' has to change for its 'producers' as well as for its 'buyers'. The 18th century concept is no longer appropriate for a modern society today, as Paine for example pointed out: "That which may be thought right and convenient in an age, may be thought wrong and found inconvenient in another. In such cases, who is to decide, the living or the dead?"[27]

Land and labour, nature and humans produce the real wealth of a country, Adam Smith argued. However, this one of his many insights has had no consequences until today.

Smith began his inquiry into the nature of the *Wealth of Nations* with an explanation of the importance of the division of labour. He characterizes the division of labour, as "...the necessary, though very slow and gradual, consequence of a certain propensity in human nature... " (WN p. 9) and explained: "When the division of labour has been once thoroughly established... every man thus lives by exchanging, or becomes, in some measure, a merchant, and the society itself grows to be what is properly a commercial society." (WN p. 15) Smith is referring here to the independent individual craftsman, the norm at his time, who controls the products he makes, owns them and offers them for sale on the real market, where he competes with other producers for a buyer. There he can exchange his products for money, which enables him to buy the goods he needs which he does not produce himself.

This, however, is not what is going on in today's companies. In a factory, dependent employees have to perform set tasks, in which they rarely have a say. In doing so they give up their own free will and follow the command of their employer for an agreed time in exchange for money. And their tasks are easily executable and exchangeable by other employed labourers.

In a factory, the overall manufacturing process is subdivided into small units, with labour even separated into 'head and hand'[28], the sub-products of which are then combined according to the business plan of the company. By concentrating on one small task, the labourer can produce more. Smith explained this process by using the example of pin-making. He wrote: "A workman... could scarce, perhaps, with his utmost industry, make one pin in a day, and certainly could not make twenty." (WN p. 3) Concentrating on small repetitive tasks, the labourer gets more done. He is more profitable. If the manufacturing process "is divided into a number of branches, of which the greater part are likewise peculiar trades", for

---

24 Thomas Paine, *Rights of Man*, Part One, first published in Britain in 1791, London, 1985, p. 42.
     Paine is said to have first formulated his thoughts in 'the Legacy White Hart Hotel' in Lewes.
25 as pointed out by Robert Green Ingersoll, *What's God Got to Do with It?* Hanover, 2005, p. 84
26 www.menschenrechte.nuernberg.de – in English
27 Thomas Paine, ibid., p. 45
28 compare: Richard Sennett, *The Craftsman*, London, 2008, p. 52

example into "about eighteen direct operations", "... ten persons... could make among them upwards to forty-eight thousand pins in a day... But if they had all wrought separately and independently... certainly could not each of them have made twenty, perhaps not one pin a day..."

Smith used the words "branches", "peculiar trades", "operations" and "subdividing" to explain this fragmentation of tasks into small parts. "In every other art and manufacture, the effects of the division of labour are similar to what they are in this very trifling one, though, in many of them, labour can neither be so much subdivided, nor reduced to so great a simplicity of operation. The division of labour, however, so far as it can be introduced, occasions, in every art, a proportionable increase of the productive powers of labour." (WN p. 4) By this he meant being productive for the employer producing more products in the same time. However, is it also fair to the labourer?

In a factory the fragmented parts of the whole product are now put together according to the entrepreneur's plan; they are never internally exchanged on a kind of market. And the labourer does not own the part he has produced, and consequently he cannot sell that single part to an internal market (even if this possibility existed), competing for a price in money. What is needed inside a corporation is co-operation – co-operation to fulfil a given task with the aim of manufacturing a special product. But this necessary co-operation does not seem to have become a principle of economicult theory.

Competition, on the other hand, has.[29] Yet competition happens only when the product is ready for sale outside the company on the market. Therefore the manufacturing process within a company cannot be called 'division of labour', and 'division of labour' cannot be seen as a natural category. As so often, Smith has not been exact in his expression. He compares the subsequent process on the market to the production process within a company, when in fact the latter has nothing to do with the division of labour, but should instead be referred to as a fragmentation of tasks.[30]

Such a fragmentation comes with consequences for the labourer. The smaller the individual task, the more repetitive and boring the job. Less and less of a person's labouring ability is needed, and less and less training is necessary. The German unions therefore introduced, years ago, a publicly financed programme of enriching tasks in productions, known as 'Humanising Labour'.

Through the fragmentation of tasks, 'labour' costs per unit can be reduced. In the end these dissected tasks can be replaced and performed by machines,[31] owned

---

29 It is often heard these days, we have to point out, that companies try to introduce the market principle of competition in a company by aiming to make departments compete with others, although such a procedure was never found to be successful, as the example of Sears showed, according to *Money Week* 26 July 2013, p. 31

30 Lewis Mumford, *Mythos der Maschine, Kultur, Technik und Macht*, Frankfurt, 1978, p. 23, argued that this thinking does not have its source in the so-called industrial revolution which began in the 18th century, but in ancient Egypt, in the organisation of an archetypical machine composed of humans as parts.

31 Compare this with the keynote speech of Matt Atkinson, digital marketing head at Tesco. "Asked if the store might employ 'robots on the shop floor', he commented: 'Some people would say we already do," reported by Hugh Muir, *The Guardian*, 23 May 2013, p. 47

by the company. Then the entrepreneur is no longer dependent on the co-operation of his fellow men, but is in full control of the machines. Ultimately, production can be carried out autonomously by machines without the need for cooperation with other human beings. And where a labourer works on given tasks in his own way and at his own speed according to his own nature, his experience and interest, as well as his health, machines operate entirely according to the purpose of their owner.

This process of rationalisation of labour sets labouring people free, meaning it makes them redundant of their tasks. In other words, 'labour' is not only defined by money, but can also be replaced by money. Perhaps, therefore, the decision to portray Adam Smith and his recommendations on the "division of labour" on the £20 banknote was one of pure irony?

Is this really the freedom we are looking for? Would it not be preferable to "free" people *in* their 'labour' rather than *from* their 'labour' as both Lewis Mumford and Andre Gorz demanded?

The process of standardization and mechanization of 'labour' reduces the person who is looking for a job to an even more passive status than that of a dependent worker, as he then becomes merely a consumer, unless he finds another employer, of course. By rights, there is no reason why people should be treated this way in any economy.[32] Why do we think it justifiable to routinely replace human beings with machines?

If the wealth of the country lies in the annual produce of land and labour, meaning nature and man, to quote Adam Smith, does this wealth really increase if less and less labour is needed for which fewer and fewer people are working? Where does it lead?

Smith himself had already thought about the consequences of such fragmentation of tasks: "The man whose whole life is spent in performing a few simple operations, of which the effects too are, perhaps, always the same, or very nearly the same, has no occasion to exert his understanding, or to exercise his invention in finding out expedients for removing difficulties which never occur. He naturally loses, therefore, the habit of such exertion, and generally becomes as stupid and ignorant as it is possible for a human creature to become... His dexterity at his own particular trade seems, in this manner, to be acquired at the expense of his intellectual, social, and martial virtues. But in every improved and civilized society this is the state into which the labouring poor, that is, the great body of the people, must necessarily fall, unless government takes some pains to prevent it." (WN p. 506) Can it therefore be concluded that Adam Smith was the first to demand (at least an elementary) general education for people?[33] Another consequence of his recommendations for making 'labour' monetarily more productive might be

---

32   Chris Mullin assessed this phenomenon as follows: "The growth of 'oursourcing' is producing a class of employee who can be picked up and dropped at will without qualifying for holidays, sickness or redundancy pay or any of the other hard-won benefits we used quaintly to associate with civilisation. Slowly, but surely, we are heading backwards towards the nineteenth century." in: *Decline and Fall*, London, 2011, p. 398

33   Mentioned by Helmut Reichelt, in: *Adam Smith, Pipers Handbuch der politischen Ideen*, published by Iring Fetscher und Herfried Muenkler, Muenchen, 1985, p. 603

perhaps that it has been made too far-reaching so that costs are not being reduced but increased.[34]

Allowing money to define education and letting the gap between private and public education to become bigger and bigger, cannot, then, be an option for any government. In Smith's words: "The education of the common people requires, perhaps, in a civilized and commercial society, the attention of the public, more than that of people of some rank and fortune." (WN p. 507) Compare this to the statement by US Education Secretary Arne Duncan, that the worst of the colleges which have been set-up simply to make a profit are "saddling students with debt they cannot afford in exchange for degrees and certificates they cannot use". This brought Dylan Ratigan[35] to the following conclusion: "The misdirection of education money parallels the perverse misalignment of interests that we saw in the health care industry, where we pay for bureaucracy and disease treatments, when what we actually want is improved health. In education, we pay crippling amounts of money for expensive buildings, over-the-top athletic programs, high administrative salaries, frequent testing, and teacher job security rather than what we need: improved learning."

And finally, to name a few more consequences, the assumptions of 'land' and 'labour' as commodities include the split between nature and man. This split was taken for granted by Rene Descartes (1596–1650), when he characterised nature as *res extensa* and man as *res cogitans*, meaning that nature only exists outside of man, and that humans are something other than nature, as they are endowed with a spirit, with the ability to think. It seems that we still live in the tradition of such an assumption. In a genuinely modern theory of economics, neither human beings nor the natural world can be viewed as or treated as commodities, as neither are entities produced for and traded on the market. These are historic assumptions, no longer appropriate for the 21st century.

5.6. The state and people's elected representation

In Smith's time, 'the state' meant the absolute monarch as sovereign,[36] and the interests of 'the state' could be contrary to those of ordinary people to the extreme – especially when the people were forced to pay taxes to their ruler and become his soldiers, sacrificing their own life for the king's interest. This sovereign has changed. Two-hundred and fifty years later the state can no longer be considered as contrary to the people; rather a state includes all its inhabitants, both the legislative representatives of people and the executive government as well as the

---

34 At a UK NHS surgery when the doctor wants a blood test, the patient is advised to make an appointment with a nurse who will then take a blood sample. This appointment takes a few days to happen. Then the patient has to wait for a week until the results are in. At least 10 days have passed, costing more time and travel expenses for the patient, during which he is not yet treated and therefore does not get better. Why can't the procedure be the same as in other countries?: when a doctor wants a blood test, he takes the sample immediately and calls back with the results in 24 hours.

35 Dylan Ratigan together with G. Lichtenberg and Dr. Jeffrey Spees, *Greedy Bastards*, New York, 2012, p. 125/128

36 Louis XIV is supposed to have said: "*L'etat c'est moi*", ie I am the state.

citizens who elect them. Today most people in the West live in a democratic state. Government is 'by the people for the people', and not by an unelected monarch who came into his job by inheritance, claimed his power from god, set the law, was defined by with the land he governed and could not be prosecuted.[37] Today everybody, man or woman, freeholder or tenant, is free to choose his or her representation in Parliament. The elected Parliament has supremacy. With birth into society comes the basic human right to participate in society, a right which is bound to every living person and can neither be denied nor taken away from him.

According to Charles de Secondat, Baron de Montesquieu (1689–1755), the power of the people as sovereign should be divided into three: The elected Members of Parliament have the law-giving powers, they decide on the budget and taxes and they control the government. The government is the executive power. And the third power, the judiciary, makes sure that laws are followed by everyone. It is elected by Parliament.

It is understandable that Smith makes a distinction between the people and the state/king, because that was the condition of public life in his time, but the continuation of this separation of state and people today is totally anachronistic as it fails to acknowledge that, in a democracy, the state is the people. Yet still, this notion persists. The state is seen to mean the government – a government which derives its power from the people and acts on their behalf, as well as assuming the role of trustee of taxpayers' money.

It is interesting to see what Adam Smith had to say about the task of government: "The civil magistrate is entrusted with the power not only of preserving the public peace by restraining injustice, but of promoting the prosperity of the commonwealth, by establishing good discipline, and by discouraging every sort of vice and impropriety; he may prescribe rules, therefore, which not only prohibit mutual injuries among fellow-citizens, but command mutual good offices to a certain degree... Of all the duties of a law-giver, however, this, perhaps, is that which it requires the greatest delicacy and reserve to execute with propriety and judgement. To neglect it altogether exposes the commonwealth to many gross disorders and shocking enormities, and to push it too far is destructive of all liberty, security and justice." (TMS p. 99) Further on, he states that, "every independent state is divided into many different orders and societies," all of which "are dependent upon the state to which they owe their security and protection. That they all subordinate to that state and established only in subservience to its prosperity and preservation, is a truth acknowledged by the most partial member of every one of them. It may often, however, be hard to convince him that the prosperity and preservation of the state require any diminution of the powers, privileges and immunities of his own particular order or society." (TMS p. 272)

---

37 One wonders sometimes why there are still relics of the king's law in the UK, eg the vast majority of members of the second House of Parliament, the House of Lords, is not elected, and the Crown has a say in bills before they become law, as Lord Berkely wrote in *The Guardian* 1 September 2012, p. 14: "We are in the 21st century, not in the 18th century and it is crazy to think they are even trying to do this. The royal family should give up this special privilege and we should all obey the law of the land. Just because they have private estates, private incomes and land from several centuries ago doesn't mean they should have the right to interfere."

The first duty of a government, as Smith saw it, is "defending the society from the violence and injustice of other independent societies," which "grows gradually more and more expensive, as the society advances in civilisation." (WN p. 461)

The second duty is "that of protecting, as far as possible, every member of the society from the injustice or oppression of every other member of it, or the duty of establishing an exact administration of justice." (WN p. 462)

And on the government's obligation to defend the country, Smith had the following to say: "Men of inferior wealth combine to defend those of superior wealth in the possession of their property, in order that men of superior wealth may combine to defend them in the possession of theirs."

"Civil government, so far as it is instituted for the security of property, is, in reality, instituted for the defence of the rich against the poor, or of those who have some property against those who have none at all."

This shows that Adam Smith had a real sense of fairness – and expressed it in a rather ironic way. One wonders how such thoughts would be formulated today?

"The third and last duty of the sovereign or commonwealth, is that of erecting and maintaining those public institutions and those public works, which though they may be in the highest degree advantageous to a great society, are, however, of such a nature, that the profit could never repay the expense to any individual, or a small number of individuals; and which, therefore, cannot be expected that any individual, or small number of individuals, should erect or maintain." (WN p. 470) These tasks include those for "facilitating the commerce of the society and those for promoting the instruction of the people", "good roads, bridges, navigable canals, harbours etc., education of the youth" (WN p. 472). This was applicable even during the classical period, as Pericles (443–429 BCE) demonstrated in Athens. These are obligations of the government, not of private interest. These tasks should not be made the business of private interest, otherwise Parliament would have no control over them. As it shows, Smith never demanded government to be reduced, and never called for privatisation of its duties. Specifically, he did not demand that private companies should be given powers of border control, policing, law courts, prisons, defence, inland revenue, and above all, education. The governments' obligations need to be especially transparent, controlled and answerable to a legitimate Parliament, which cannot be expected of private interests.

And why should control over spending taxpayers' money be given up by Parliament by privatisation of public works? Why is it thought to be rational that taxpayers' money should be used to make private profits? Everyone understands that this means an easy profit and a loss of the constitutional controlling rights of Parliament. Why do the members of Parliament go along with this? Why do they allow their legitimated power to be undermined?

It is noteworthy and unfathomable, that a lot of people justify the policy of privatisation with reference to Adam Smith. This attitude is not justifiable.

5.6.1. Business interests and their influence on politics

The first and most important difference between the 18th century and today is that Smith lived at a time when the majority of businesses consisted of individual craftsmen and artisans such as bakers, butchers and bankers whereas we live in a century of large global corporations – sometimes even larger and therefore more important than national states – which through their economic power, are far more effective at persuading the public and governments that they can do a better job of looking after public services. Power, it seems, still comes with money, but it should not take away the legitimate rights of a Parliament.

Bearing in mind that, according to the democratic constitution of the modern state, the people are sovereign, it is interesting what Smith had to say about businesses and their influence on politics: "The rise of profit operates like compound interest. Our merchants and master manufacturers complain much of the bad effects of high wages in raising the price..." (but) "they say nothing concerning the bad effects of high profits; they are silent with regard to the pernicious effects of their own gains; they complain only of those of other people." (WN p. 64)

"... the clamour and sophistry of merchants and manufacturers easily persuade (landlords, farmers and labourers) that the private interest of a part, and of a subordinate part, of the society, is the general interest of the whole." (WN p. 84)

"People of the same trade seldom meet together, even for merriment and diversion, but the conversation ends in a conspiracy against the public, or in some contrivance to raise prices ..." (WN p. 84)

"The pretence that corporations are necessary for better government of the trade is without any foundation." (WN p. 85)

"The plans and projects of the employers of stock regulate and direct all the most important operation of labour, and profit is the end proposed by all those plans and projects... Merchants and master manufacturers are, in this order, the two classes of people who commonly employ the largest capitals, and who by their wealth draw to themselves the greatest share of the public consideration... As their thoughts, however, are commonly exercised rather about the interest of their own particular branch of business, than about that of society, their judgment, even when given with the greatest candour – which it has not been upon every occasion – is much more to be depended upon with regard to the former of those two objects, than with regard to the latter.

Their superiority over the country gentleman is, not so much in their knowledge of the public interest, as in their having a better knowledge of their own interest than he has of his... To widen the market, and to narrow the competition, is always the interest of the dealers...

The proposal of any new law or regulation of commerce which comes from this order, ought always to be listened to with great precaution, and ought never to be adopted till after having been long and carefully examined, not only with the most scrupulous, but with the most suspicious attention. It comes from an order of men, whose interest is never exactly the same with that of the public." (WN p. 163)

"The government of an exclusive company of merchants is, perhaps, the worst of all governments for any country whatever." (WN p. 368)

Reading these remarks about private business interests raises the following question: was Adam Smith well ahead of his time regarding the influence of businesses on politics, or are governments these days, with their virtually hidden aim to oblige vested interests, behind their time?

The decision concerning the way in which a society is constituted and they way in which humans live in it is primarily the obligation and the responsibility of the people. This should be written in the constitution of every country. Their rights can never be denied, never be separated from them and transferred to non-natural entities such as business corporations. It seems that Adam Smith's remarks are still valuable. They could have been made today.

5.6.2. Liberate markets, free enterprise

Let's listen to what Adam Smith had said about the claims to liberate markets and free enterprise. When discussing this category, however, we always have to bear in mind that in Smith's time the whole political system, with the King at the top, was totally different from today's democratic society. Therefore a lot of Smith's remarks only make sense with respect to his historic background.

Nevertheless, they are very interesting: "That security which the laws in Great Britain give to every man, that he shall enjoy the fruits of his own labour, is alone sufficient to make any country flourish, notwithstanding these and twenty other absurd regulations of commerce; and this security was perfected by the Revolution", (of 1688), "much about the same time that the bounty was established. The natural effort of every individual to better his own condition, when suffered to exert itself with freedom and security, is so powerful a principle, that it is alone, and without any assistance, not only capable of carrying on the society to wealth and prosperity, but of surmounting a hundred impertinent obstructions, with which the folly of human laws too often encumbers its operations: though the effect of those obstructions is always, more or less, either to encroach upon its freedom or to diminish its security. In Great Britain industry is perfectly secure; and though it is far from being perfectly free, it is as free or freer than in any other part of Europe." (WN p. 349). If this remark was true 250 years ago, then why it is necessary these days, in a democratic state in which everyone participates and people are the sovereign, to demand more freedom for businesses, for the market? And: freedom from what? Freedom from the influence of others, from rules equal for all, from people with the same rights as those who are demanding more?

Smith talked about the freedom of the individual, but at the same time made it subject to the laws of justice. So for him freedom did not mean absolute freedom outside human society, so to speak, but freedom within society. He wrote: "All systems, either of preference or of restraint, therefore, being thus completely taken away, the obvious and simple system of natural liberty establishes itself of its own accord. Every man, as long as he does not violate the laws of justice, is left perfectly free to pursue his own interest his own way, and to bring both his industry and capital into competition with those of any other man, or order of men. The sovereign" (ie King) "is completely discharged from a duty, in the attempting to perform which he must always be exposed to innumerable delusions, and for the proper performance of which, no human wisdom or knowledge could ever be sufficient; the duty of superintending the industry of private people, and of directing it towards the employment most suitable to the interests of the society." (WN p. 444) *Employment in the interest of society*, it should be emphasized.

Nowhere in Adam Smith's work can we find this demand, so commonly claimed these days, that markets should be liberated and enterprises freed from the laws of society. Rather Smith prescribes that individuals be free from a sovereign's oppression to make their own decisions, but with due regard for the society they live in and its laws. Why are his ideas today reported in such a fragmented and distorted way?

To understand the difference between freedom for people and freedom for a market, it is necessary to discuss briefly the concept of a 'market'. It is a place where people encounter manufactured products and services, where real producers set up their stalls offering to real consumers their produced goods which might be fruit and vegetables, plants and salads, fish, animals, eggs, meat, bread, flowers or services. The offered products might vary according to season and location, depending on the natural environment where they are produced, but every market has always needed and still needs real market regulations to make sure the market day is executed peacefully, as Horst Kurnitzky[38] reminds us.

The material products offered on the market, such as food, need to be sold quickly, as they will decay in time. Most food products are not pre-wrapped, ready to be taken away, but offered in their freshly-harvested state, awaiting inspection by consumers using all their senses to make a good choice about the freshness of the goods. Producers compete there for real customers in order to sell their real goods in exchange for money. Consumers can choose what they need and want to buy by using money. Producers look for the best price they can get for their perishable goods, therefore sales ideally need to be made on the same day. The real market[39] brings producers and products into a direct relationship with consumers. Producers and consumers may even form long term relationships as overheard by the following remark: "My eggler woman just told me that her husband is in hospital suffering from the same health problem as uncle Tom (or Dick or Harry), would you believe it?" Kurnitzky saw this real market as the birthplace of public life.[40]

From this real market the retail market has developed. Here are real producers replaced by retailers, who do not themselves produce anything, but buy-in and then offer ready-made products to customers. The direct relationship between the real producer and the real consumer becomes indirect.

A retail market normally offers a wider range of additional products, such as clothes, household wares, furniture, pet food and so on.[41] The retail products can be longer-lasting, which is in the interest of the retailers, as the goods lose their quality less rapidly. But eventually they must be sold, as money can only be made

---

38   Horst Kurnitzky, *Der heilige Markt*, Frankfurt, 1994, p. 36

39   like the award-winning Saturday market in Stroud, South Gloucestershire, for example

40   ibid, p. 72

41   These stages in market development are only for abstract description. Such a clear separation is obviously not possible in reality.

by selling them on. This development is still continuing. The market – meaning real producers in contact with real consumers – is made more and indirect, a deviation from its true origin. For example, today it is possible to buy a country's total coffee harvest for the following year and sell it on all over the world without once having to connect with the real product, its real producer or its real end consumers. This kind of market exchange is still referred to as a 'market', though in reality it bears no resemblance to the real market as we visualize it from experience.

The financial market is an example of the kind of market derived from the real, and still called 'market', though it no longer has anything to do with the sale of real end consumer goods or involves a real relationship between producers and consumers. On the financial market, for example, the commodity being sold is a share of a company's ownership, not real goods or services. The new owner of shares of a company might only be interested in their produced commodities to the extent that they generate for him a share of that company's profits once the goods are sold. The relationship between both sides of the market has become totally indirect. A special form of the financial market is the derivatives market, where the products sold and bought have become even more immaterial, more virtual, for example credit default swaps. These are commodities representing a kind of insurance against possible risks arising from deals on the market. Here it is possible to buy and sell so-called structured financial vehicles representing deals for various financial products derived from real goods and services. These markets came into being in recent years. They are based on three or four assumptions. First of all, there is no need for material goods to be traded but only a financial representation of these. Secondly, the seller does not need to own the goods he is trading. Third, it is not necessary to use your own money for trading, as banks and investment companies for example use their customers' money for their own interest, the money these have deposited in the banks for safe-keeping and growth as the banks pays interests on the deposited money. Finally, the traded financial products do not even have to offer a real value, as long as a privately owned agency gives them a good rating.

Therefore, if we use the word 'market' and wish to persist in using this expression, we should always try to make it clear which form of market we mean, the real market or the abstract and derived market. The trading on the derived market is still undertaken with the aim of making a profit from buying and selling. However, it is only an abstract representation of the real market. And no market can act on its own. It cannot be made responsible for an individual's activities when trading. However, this is an often-heard excuse. A market is not an individual, not a person, but only a description of sellers and buyers and their relationships as we have experienced them at a real market. It is an abstract idea. Unfortunately, when the same word 'market' is used in the context of a derived market it obscures rather than illuminates its real nature. And the concept should never be used to set its own rules to be obeyed by real people.

It is, in particular, totally inappropriate to use the market idea as a rulebook instructing society on how it should understand and run its 'real life' markets. This has to be decided by real living people. The idea that real people should respect or even obey 'the market' has obviously been derived from the same line of thinking, which assumes that money can move itself. How, then, can anybody claim that markets should be liberated? A justification of such a claim cannot be found in Adam Smith's work. The only demand that can be justified by him is that individuals should be free to choose their own fate within their historic culture (ie in his time, free from the absolute power of the king as the sovereign). If anyone today demands that markets should be liberated, I would suggest that the response should be: we are to liberate people and democratise the economy.

The other point, which is frequently forgotten amid such calls for the unfettered freedom of markets, is that every market answers to its own intrinsic rules. It seems rather strange that people are often not aware of these market rules or concerned about making them absolutely clear. This will, necessarily, be discussed later in this book.

Incidentally, one might ask why are the people who call for the liberation of markets from public regulation, the same ones who demand public subsidies[42] to bail out bankrupt banks or to hand out sums like £9 million to build a new Nissan car factory in Sunderland? Why are they happy to subsidise the nuclear industry, which called for long-term guaranteed profits, when EU law forbids such subsidies, and the government in 2010 promised to obey this law? One wonders what will become of the other governments' promises that the nuclear industry has to finance the decommissioning of nuclear power plants as well as disposing safely of its long-term radioactive waste itself.[43] Is this not a contradiction? Adam Smith, the so-called 'father' of economicult theory certainly did not support such claims to be free from regulation and taxes. He wanted to free individuals within their society, not to liberate markets.

Any observer of reality social commentator will observe that it is remarkable how people respond to objections to their demands. It seems a lot easier to manufacture a new product, say for the communication market, rather than face any objections concerning the ways in which society is governed. Nowadays it may be

---

42 Philip Collins wrote of "Irresponsible companies and the welfare bill" in *The Times* published in *The Week* 10 November 2012, p. 50: "Whenever businessmen gather it doesn't take long before they are demanding gifts from the Government... whether it is lower taxation and lighter regulation, or the sort of business-friendly proposals contained in Lord Heseltine's plan for growth, *No Stone Unturned*". We may compare this to Adam Smith's remarks in chapter 5.6.1. "British companies should be asking what they can do for the country. And the most important step is to start paying their staff properly." And here again, Adam Smith's remarks in chapter 5.5.2 springs to mind when we read: "Companies haven't been playing fair: they've been taking a greater share of GDP as profit, at the expense of the share going to employees. This 'private failure' of the labour market has fallen on the public purse. Between 2003 and 2008, the income of a typical British family grew by only £160 a year, but that increase – such as it was – came via the state through tax credit and benefits. The managers of joint-stock companies need to go back to their public obligations: 'They should all publish the percentage of their employees who get tax credit, and wear a large number like a badge of shame.'"

43 *Der Spigel* reported in December 2012 No.49, p. 18, that decommissioning a nuclear power station is a lengthy task costing at least €500 m for each unit. For the nuclear power station in Brunsbuettel in Germany, for example, more than 300,000 t of contaminated rubble and scrap metal have to be removed, 10,000 t of which are supposed to be disposed of safely at a permanent disposal site, yet no such site is currently in operation worldwide.

true to say that those who design products can control and command global change, and that change is more easily achieved this way rather than through the assessment and implementation of new laws for a given society.

5.6.3. The necessity of regulating banks

Adam Smith never pleaded for some kind of absolute freedom from the influences of society, but always considered freedom in relation to society.

In this way, Smith recommended the regulation of the banks: "To restrain private people... or, to restrain a banker... is a manifest violation of that natural liberty, which it is the proper business of law not to infringe, but to support. Such regulations may, no doubt, be considered as in some respect a violation of natural liberty. But those exertions of the natural liberty of a few individuals, which might endanger the security of the whole society, are, and ought to be, restrained by the laws of all governments; of the most free, as well as of the most despotical. The obligation of building party walls, in order to prevent the communication of fire,[44] is a violation of natural liberty, exactly of the same kind with the regulations of the banking trade which are here proposed." (WN p. 208) One has to remind oneself that the word 'bankruptcy' originated from banks.

Smith then goes on to make a few remarkable comments about directors of joint-stock companies: "The divided capital of the Bank of England amounts, at present, to ten million seven hundred and eighty thousand pounds. The directors of such companies, however, being the managers rather of other people's money than of their own, it cannot well be expected that they should watch over it with the same anxious vigilance with which the partners in a private copartnery frequently watch over their own. Like the stewards of a rich man, they are apt to consider attention to small matters as not for their master's honour, and very easily give themselves a dispensation from having it. Negligence and profusion, therefore, must always prevail, more or less, in the management of the affairs of such a company." (WN p. 483)

And, in contrast to what we are given to believe these days, Adam Smith never said at any point that the financial sector produces the wealth of a nation.

5.6.4. The necessity of paying taxes

In former times, taxes were seen as the income of the sovereign/king – and of the church. Taxes were paid in natural goods, produced by common people, who were under obligation to the landlord to defend them. "The revenues of the ancient Saxon kings of England are said to have been paid, not in money, but in kind, that is, in victuals and provisions of all sort. William the Conqueror introduced the custom of paying them in money." (WN p. 17) Tythe barns where these goods were stored are a relic of this early form of paying taxes. For us today, it is the norm to pay taxes in money. This shift from payments in kind to payments in money has an advantage for those who receive them. Money can be spent on anything, while the usefulness of most food is limited in time, as has already been

---

44   we still call it a 'firewall' today

pointed out. Paying taxes to the sovereign became, more or less, the duty of the poorer people, and one which they often revolted against. Rich people and corporations have always seemed to find ways to pay minimal tax or no tax at all. Today they put money in off-shore accounts in so called 'tax havens' for example.[45] Why these have not yet been abolished is a key question for the 21st century.[46] Smith explains that the sovereign was "obliged to content himself with taxing those who were too weak to refuse to pay taxes. The great lords, though willing to assist him upon particular emergencies (for example in warfare[47]), refused to subject themselves to any constant tax, and he was not strong enough to force them." (WN 555)[48]

---

45 It should be noted that most of the so-called tax-havens and offshore-banking centres are in the ownership of the British Crown, 13 out of 24, according to Kevin Cahill, *Who Owns the World*, p. 56.

   And when Prime Minister David Cameron announced that he would take bold step at the next G8 meeting to shut down tax havens, only the most naive would expect results to follow as no tax haven sees itself as such. So it is not the Prime Minister's fault if nothing changes: a typical example of politics as a symbolic gesture.

   Newspapers reported in April 2013 that millions of figures on tax avoidance were sent to the International Group of Investigating Journalists (ICIJ) in Washington. The German banking regulator BaFin announced in due course that it would take a good look into the banks which manage assets for rich clients. It turned out that German banks had 25 representations with banking licences in 22 tax havens.

   On 25 April 2013 *Der Spiegel* reported that 47,000 tax avoiders have already come clean and paid an additional €2,05 Mrd € to German tax offices.

46 *The Observer* 11 November, 2012, reported, on "… the water giants that pay no tax on profit: Three of Britain's biggest water companies paid little or no tax on their profits last year when rewarding their executives and investors, *The Observer* can reveal. Thames Water and Anglian Water paid no corporation tax on the profits made from their utility business while Yorkshire Water kept its payment to the Inland Revenue in the low millions.

   All the companies made hundreds of millions of pounds in operating profits and some have rewarded their senior executives with performance-related bonuses, and investors with huge dividends. Martin Baggs, the chief executive of Thames Water, which enjoyed a £76 m tax rebate in 2012, was given a bonus of £420,000 on top of his £425,000 salary and is in line for a further windfall of £1 m based on company performance through to 2015." p. 1
   "Britain's privatised water firms are run by a byzantine structure of private equity financing: They have no trouble making profits and paying dividends but seem to have little cash for projects such as sewerage modernisation. Instead the customer foots the bill." p. 6

47 Smith calls "the art of war… certainly the noblest of all arts", (WN p. 454) an opinion which we today in the age of the atomic, hydrogen and neutron bomb, destroying everything alive while keeping dead material intact, find impossible to share.

48 Smith's remark seems reminiscent of today's situation, the only difference being that the current elected government is more strongly legitimised, albeit totally in favour of the rich. What kind of democracy is it where a government favours 1,000 individuals but burdens 62,217,761 million others?
   Michael Meacher MP (Labour) wrote the following letter to *The Guardian*, 29 April 2012:
   "The annual *Sunday Times* Rich List yields four very important conclusions for the governance in Britain. It shows that the richest 1,000 persons, just 0.003% of the adult population, increased their wealth over the last three years by £155 bn. That is enough for themselves alone to pay off the entire current UK budget deficit and still leave them with £30 bn to spare.
   Second, this mega-rich elite, containing many of the bankers and hedge fund and private equity operators who caused the financial crash in the first place, have not been made subject to any tax payback whatever commensurate to their gains. Some 77% of the budget deficit is being

What happened in the 18th century, however, should not be the same in the 21st century where everyone is equal and is bound to obey legislation. Citing the example of FC Bayern chairman Uli Hoeness, Roland Nelles asked, why people who have apparently everything, need to bunker away in Switzerland? "What's so bad about an annoying 25 per cent capital gains taxes if you're still left with comfortable life at Lake Tegernsee?, he asked. "Why this greed or avarice? These are the egomaniacs of our time." Instead of them helping to foot the bill for public services, taxes for schools, kindergardens, hospitals, police forces and roads are the obligation of the citizens who remains loyal to the society whose benefits they enjoy. Paying taxes is for 'other people' whose money is taken by the state automatically every month, that is the tax swindler's understanding of the state. They only call for the community when it benefits them, e.g. in times of need. It is as if they accept the saying: 'Weak shoulders should bear more than strong ones.'[49] The idea that politics should favour the rich was never supported by Adam Smith: "The subjects of every state ought to contribute towards the support of the government, as nearly as possible, in proportion to their respective abilities... In the observation or neglect of this maxim, consists what is called the equality or inequality of taxation." (WN p. 536) Each according to their abilities... this well-known phrase was coined by Adam Smith. Who would have thought so?

Smith's remarks are indeed enlightening. We should also remember that nowadays we no longer pay taxes for the maintenance of a sovereign king. We pay taxes as civilians to finance the public infrastructure everybody depends on, even rich people. When this relationship between the people and the government is neglected, then the state indeed can be seen as a kind of anonymous power, unrelated to the citizens, and therefore people might oppose it.

Nor did Smith plead for no taxation or less taxation, when he argued that everybody should shoulder a fair share of the burden, according to their ability.

The better-off people are often the ones who feel that they have the power to change things. With the command of money obviously comes the idea of commanding others, who can be bought to work for them, a perception which seems to be shared by the poorer members of society. Smith drew our attention to this fact: "This disposition to admire, and almost to worship, the rich and the powerful, and to despise or, at least, to neglect persons of poor and mean condition, though necessary both to establish and to maintain the distinction of ranks and the order of society, is, at the same time, the great and most universal

---

recouped by public-expenditure cuts and benefit cuts, and only 23% is being repaid by tax increases. More than half of the tax increases is accounted for by the VAT rise, which hits the poorest hardest. None of the tax increases is specifically aimed at the super-rich.

Third, despite the biggest slump for nearly a century, these 1,000 richest are now sitting on wealth greater even than at the height of the boom just before the crash. Their wealth now amounts to £414 bn, equivalent to more than a third of Britain's entire GDP. They include 77 billionaires and 23 others, each possessing more than £750 m.

The increase in wealth of this richest 1,000 has been £315 bn over the last 15 years. If they were charged capital gains tax on this at the current 28% rate, it would yield £88 bn, enough to pay off 70 % of the entire deficit. It seems, however, that Osborne takes the notorious view of the New York heiress, Leona Helmsley: 'Only the little people pay taxes.'" (author's emphasis)

49 *Der Spiegel* online 22 April 2013

cause of the corruption of our moral sentiments." (TMS p. 73) According to Adam Smith, the better-off should in fact pay relatively higher taxes and shoulder a greater burden than poor people. And the government should make sure that there are no special deals for the wealthier classes.[50]

The British chancellor George Osborne[51] argued in his 2012 budget speech that politicians (in particular conservative politicians) all over the world are calling for taxes to be cut. However there is no proof that tax cuts make the economy grow.[52] "Explaining away that reality is 'one of the most serious challenges to modern conservatism," concludes David Leonhardt.

Nick Cohen in *The Observer* 19 May 2013,[53] made the interesting comment: "If you want to understand any society, look at its tax system. If one man or a clique can tax at will, you can conclude the society is a dictatorship or oligarchy. If you have reasonably progressive and universal taxes, you can assume it is a

---

50   The Public Accounts Committee (PAC) heard that the CEOs of Amazon, Google and Starbucks, 3 American multinational companies, which do not pay tax in the UK because they claim that they make losses, they pay profits into other countries as a way to avoid tax.

    The Independent noticed on 3 December 2012, p. 6, that: Amazon reported in 2011 a turnover of £ 207 m, on which it paid tax of £ 1.8 m, while providing the PAC with information showing that for 2011 £3.35 bn of its sales were from the UK, 25% of all sales outside the United States. Google recorded revenues of £396 m in the UK in 2011 and paid corporation tax of only £6 m, yet it is estimated that it actually earn £2.75 bn of revenue from its operations in the UK with an estimated pre-tax profit of £836 m. And "Starbucks told the PAC it had made a loss for 14 of the 15 years it has been operating in the UK. But it also briefed shareholders that its UK business was successful and it was making 15% of its global profits in the UK. Its estimated pre-tax profit for the year was £59.6 m, on which it paid £ 0 in tax."

    The i reported 16 May 2013, p. 9: "Amazon revealed that it last year paid just £3.1 m in total taxes on sales of £4.2 bn. Its corporation tax bill was just £2.44 m – less than the £2.5 m it received from the Scottish Government in inducements to build a new distribution warehouse in Dunfermline."

    Kieler Nachrichten published 1 October 2014 that Apple has profited in Ireland for years from illegal tax reductions and that the EU commission will now look into it.

    The Week of 17 November 2012, p. 51, reported about the discussion citing Jonathan Guthrie in *The Financial Times*: "Politicians 'talk up multilateral crackdowns on avoidance while trying to lure footloose company registrations with loopholes and low rates.' Then they turn on the executives. The hypocrisy is breathtaking."

    The Week of 8 December 2012, p. 4, reported that: "Consumers angry about the amount of UK tax paid by some big multinational companies have claimed their first victory. On Sunday, following months of public outcry over its tiny corporation tax contributions, Starbucks admitted that it had opened talks with HMRC over its tax affairs, saying it 'needed to do more'. The announcement was made the day before MPs branded Starbucks, Amazon and Google 'immoral' for avoiding tax." Really, paying tax should not depend on "talks", but on the law, and if the law has holes, then they should be fixed by Parliament – if there is a will to do so.

    Owen Jones in: 'Do the right thing, Mr Schmidt,' *The i*, 20 May 2013, p. 13, reported the following calculation: "And while the 0.7% of social security spending lost to fraud costs the tax-payer £1.2 bn, tax justice pioneer and chartered accountant Richard Murphy estimates avoidance is worth £25 bn a year. Guess which one the state cracks down on without mercy or hesitation?"

51   George Osborne also wrote a foreword to the *Wealth of Nations*

52   David Leonhardt wrote in *The New York Times*, reported in *The Week* 29 September 2012 p. 17 that a "new, nonpartisan analysis by the Congressional Research Service has concluded that since 1945, changes to the top tax rate 'do not appear correlated with economic growth'..."

53   p. 37

modern democracy. Britain has elements of democratic taxation. The same rules on occasion apply to everyone. But other parts of the system resemble the *ancien regime* of pre-revolutionary France. Only in our case the privileged estates the government exempts from taxation are the corporations rather than the aristocracy and the church... The result for vested interests can be summarised in one statistic. Between 1999 and 2011, British companies' profits increased by 58 per cent but revenues from corporation tax increased by just 5 per cent... The old complaint that there is one law for the rich and another for the rest does not do justice to the debasement of public authority in Britain. When it comes to tax, too often there is no law for the rich whatsoever."

So why is the country not at least doing everything in its power to reduce tax avoidance as it would bring in money to balance the deficit, especially when it is so overloaded with debts? Why have all attempts to fix loopholes in tax regulations been abandoned? And why, as Polly Toynbee asked,[54] is HMRC's staff being reduced "by 10,000 when the EU puts UK tax evasion at £70 bn?"
It remains to be seen whether the latest spring 2013 EU-initiative to tackle tax avoidance by extending the obligation to report on capital gains will actually lead to any improvements.

However, what Mr Osborne, an admirer of Adam Smith, forgot to put into practice, was Smith's aspiration that one tax should be abolished – the tax on wages. Smith called a tax on wages "absurd and destructive", (WN p. 563). He explained how taxes on wages lead to higher wages, and higher wages to higher prices for the same amount of food. Employed people will suffer, because taxation reduces their buying power. The only party to gain from a tax on wages is the sovereign, the king. One wonders why not one politician today following Adam Smith's advice in demanding the abolition of a tax on wages, when so many believe that Smith's ideas could save the world?

And it is not another real irony that Members of Parliament, along with well-paid civil servants (especially those who work in HM[55] Revenue and Customs, which is responsible for tax payments) have used personal service companies with the aim of allowing them "to avoid PAYE tax and national insurance contributions"?[56]

5.6.5. Governing the American colonies

When the cover of the *Wealth of Nations* states that its contents gave comfort to the colonial revolutionaries, as "attested by the number of America's founding fathers who bought it for their libraries", one cannot but wonder if the founding fathers ever read what they put on their bookshelves. For example Adam Smith never mentioned that the North American colonies were not void of people when the new settlers from Europe arrived and claimed their land. Gordon S. Wood regretted that "... the European invasion of the New World had drastically reduced the numbers of the native peoples," and indicated how many indigenous people

---

54 in *The Guardian* 18 June 2013, p. 32
55 Besides: Why is the British tax office in a democratic state called "Her Majesty's"?
56 *Private Eye*, No 1307, 10 February 2012, p. 5

in the different regions of this huge country had died mainly through the spread of diseases unfamiliar to them. "At the beginning of the Seven Years' War, the problems of restless and angry Native Americans in the West compelled the British government for the first time to take over from the colonies the direct control of Indian affairs. Two British officials, one each for the northern and southern regions, now had the task of pacifying tribes of Indians, whom one of the superintendents described as 'the most formidable of any uncivilized body of people in the world'."[57]

Smith must have had been aware of the injustice done by the new settlers to the natives. What happened to their own freedom? And how did he justify the European settlers' claiming of their land? Was this a fair treatment – especially considering perhaps what the consequences would have been had Native Americans tried to do the same, to colonize Britain?

Adam Smith expressed the view that the debt of the British king, accumulated in the North American War of Independence, should be shared by the colonies: "It is not contrary to justice, that both Ireland and America should contribute towards the discharge of the public debt of Great Britain. That debt has been contracted in support of the government established by the Revolution; a government to which the Protestants of Ireland owe, not only the whole authority which they at present enjoy in their country, but every security which they possess for their liberty, their property, and their religion; a government to which several of the colonies of America owe their present charters, and consequently their present constitution; and to which all the colonies of America owe the liberty, security, and property, which they have ever since enjoyed. That public debt has been contracted in the defence, not of Great Britain alone, but of all the different provinces of the empire. The immense debt contracted in the late war in particular, and a great part of that contracted in the war before, were both properly contracted in defence of America." (WN p. 617) One wonders how the "colonies" would have responded to that if they had been aware of Smith's writings.

Only a few months after the publication of the *Wealth of Nations*, 13 American colonies declared their independence from Britain and created the now enlarged United States of America. They gave themselves a constitution which is based on equal human rights.[58] Robert Ingersoll (1833–1899) commented on this as follows: "In 1776 our fathers endeavoured to retire the gods from politics. They declared that 'all governments derive their just powers from the consent of the governed. This was a contradiction of the then political ideas of the world; it was, as many believed, an act of pure blasphemy – a renunciation of the Deity. It was in fact a declaration of the independence of the earth. It was a notice to all churches and priests that thereafter mankind would govern and protect themselves. Politically it tore down every altar and denied the authority of every 'sacred book', and appealed from the Providence of God to the Providence of Man. Those who prom-

---

57   Gordon S. Wood, *The American Revolution, A History*, London, 2005, p. 8

58   Noah Webster (1758–1843), compiler of dictionaries, was of the opinion that an independent nation should also have its own language, as discussed by Mark Pagel in: *Wired for Culture*, London, p. 305

ulgated the Declaration adopted a Constitution for the great Republic."[59]

Laws were now made by emancipated men and legitimized by their fellow men. They were no longer perceived as being given by God.

In summary, Smith can in no way be called an apostle of *'laissez-faire'* economics.

5.7. The impartial spectator

Another of Adam Smith's extraordinary ideas was that a person should not act merely on a whim of his egoistic fancy, but that: "We should view ourselves, not in the light in which our own selfish passions are apt to place us, but in the light in which any other citizen of the world would view us." (TMS p. 162) This view should take the form of a kind of "impartial spectator" within each of us. "The man within the breast, the abstract and ideal spectator of our sentiments and conduct... " (TMS p. 177)

Analysing this, Smith explained: "It is reason, principle, conscience, the inhabitant of the breast, the man within, the great judge and arbiter of our conduct. It is he who, whenever we are about to act so as to affect the happiness of others, calls to us, with a voice capable of astonishing the most presumptuous of our passions, that we are but one of the multitude, in no respect better than any other in it; and that when we prefer ourselves so shamefully and so blindly to others, we become the proper objects of resentment, abhorrence, and execration. It is from him only that we learn the real littleness of ourselves, and of whatever relates to ourselves, and the natural misrepresentations of self-love can be corrected only by the eye of this impartial spectator." (TMS p. 159)

Man is presented with a kind of inner censor or mirror of his own behaviour: "Bring him into society, and he is immediately provided with the mirror which he wanted before." (TMS p. 134).[60]

The impartial spectator advises a person on what is right and wrong, he is seen a kind of objective judge of man's behaviour. This means that a person's behaviour is always connected to the norms and rules of his culture at a certain time. These different social norms and rules, when internalised, serve us all as a guide: "Every faculty in one man is the measure by which he judges of the like faculty in another. I judge of your sight by my sight, of your ear by my ear, of your reason by my reason, of your resentment by my resentment, of your love by my love. I neither have nor can have, any other way of judging about them." (TMS p. 25).

This faculty of social judgement was seen by Smith as part of our nature. It should, however, be treated with caution because "... we approve of another man's judgment, not as something useful, but as right, as accurate, as agreeable to truth

---

59 Robert Green Ingersoll, *What's God Got to Do with It? God in the Constitution – 1890*, Hanover, 2005, p. 28

60 Roy Porter in: *Enlightenment, Britain and the Creation of the Modern World*, London, 2000, p. 201, pointed out that this idea goes back to David Hume (1711–1776), a friend of Adam Smith: "Hume held that beliefs and actions should be tempered by self-criticism, detachment and a desire to cultivate domestic affection and friendship: only thus could social approval be secured. Here, finally, lies the contribution of Adam Smith."

and reality: and it is evident we attribute those qualities to it for no other reason but because we find that it agrees with our own." (TMS p. 26)

The impartial spectator inside a man is used as a – necessary – corrector of his self-interest, and lead him to consider and respect his fellow-men's interest: "If he would act so as that the impartial spectator may enter into the principles of his conduct, which is what of all things he has the greatest desire to do, he must, upon this, as upon all other occasions, humble the arrogance of his self-love,
and bring it down to something which other men can go along with." (TMS p. 101)

The impartial spectator leads men towards social responsibility: "The most vulgar education teaches us to act, upon all important occasions, with some sort of impartiality between ourselves and others, and even the ordinary commerce of the world is capable of adjusting ourselves and others, our active principles to some degree of propriety," (TMS p. 160). These remarks by Smith, which seem to be totally neglected, are still useful today. "We must view them" Smith argued, "neither from our own place nor yet from his, neither with our own eyes nor yet with his, but from the place and with the eyes of a third person, who has no particular connexion with either, and who judges with impartiality between us." (TMS p. 157)

Roy Porter differentiated the many roles of Smith's impartial spectator. "It could be the identity of a real person ('the attentive spectator') in concrete situations, whose approval was valued. On a higher plane, the 'impartial spectator' lay more within the imagination than in the world – he was the 'supposed spectator of our conduct'. At the most sophisticated level, the figure was thoroughly internalized as 'the abstract and ideal spectator', or, in other words, conscience. This internal tribunal – the 'demi-god within the breast' – was thus a monitor, an 'alter ego', conjured up to negotiate social intricacies."[61]

Smith, in short, was always aware that every person is in a relationship with other people. He never sees a man as a total individual, but always as part of his society, in a very similar way to Aristotle's 'zoon politicon', and therefore as someone who takes into considerations his interdependence with others. As Smith said elsewhere: "Without this sacred regard to general rules, there is no man whose conduct can be much depended upon. It is this which constitutes the most essential difference between a man of principle and honour and a worthless fellow." (TMS p. 188)

He also noticed how hard this is to follow, however: "So partial are the views of mankind with regard to the propriety of their own conduct, both at the time of action and after it; and so difficult is it for them to view it in the light in which any indifferent spectator would consider it..." (TMS p. 182)

"There are some situations which bear so hard upon human nature, that the greatest degree of self-government, which can belong to so imperfect a creature as man, is not able to stifle, altogether, the voice of human weakness or reduce the violence of the passions to that pitch of moderation, in which the impartial spectator can entirely enter into them." (TMS p. 33)

---

61 Ibid., p. 202

"This self-deceit, this fatal weakness of mankind is the source of half the disorders of human life. If we saw ourselves in the light in which others see us,[62] or in which they would see us if they knew all, a reformation would generally be unavoidable." (TMS p. 182)

With the impartial spectator, Smith has not only introduced the idea of an objective voice inside an individual[63] reminding them of their social dependency and responsibility. He also requires that we consider not only a subjective, but also an objective view of things, as any statement always depends on personal and cultural awareness and time. Furthermore he has introduced the option that everyone shares the same rights, and that the views of the others need to be respected. Smith always considers carefully the relationship between an individual and society, and we would not be going too far as to interpret this as fairness. Today, we are of course keen to extend this kind of regard for our fellow natural beings as well as extending it to nature, the outside to men as well as the inside to mankind.

5.8. What to take into the 21st century

So, what should we take from Adam Smith's theory when it comes to formulating an economic theory for the 21st century? What has stood the test of time?

The first point, obviously, is to continue the use of the word 'economy' for the subject in question, while at the same time ensuring that the historic forms of economy – and economics as the theory for them – are clearly described and distinguished (thereby making it clear how each form derives from the basis of what Aristotle named the "natural" form of exchange, the household economy where no means of exchange is used). This is necessary not only to put today's form of economy into its historical context, but also to show that those forms of interaction previously considered to be natural exchanges, and therefore eternal, are in fact a cultural construction of people in their time.

The next point is to make sure that the basic principle of economy is exchange, but not necessarily an exchange which is defined exclusively by monetary terms, as money is a relatively recent historical invention. Therefore, we have to explore the meaning of exchange in greater depth.

Additionally there is no reason, why the concept of land/nature and labour/person economic theory has, should be merely defined by money terms, viewing them as commodities.

---

62   How easy to compare Smith's statement with the poem to a louse by Robert Burns (1759-1796), also referred to in Roy Porter's *Enlightenment*, p. 203:

O wad some Pw'r the giftie gie us
To see oursels as ithers see us!
It wad frae mony a blunder free us,
An foolish notion:
What airs in dress an'gait wad lea'e us,
An' ev'n devotion!

63   Is this reminiscent of Sigmund Freud's idea of a super ego?

Adam Smith wrote that land and labour produce the real wealth of a nation. He discussed social relations in the economicult at length, ie the role of the sovereign king, the role of government and the role of businesses and of banks. His economic theory placed people in the context of their society, something sometimes economicult theorists seem to have forgotten.

However, what Smith omitted to discuss was the relationship of people with nature. On one side, he saw nature as 'land' and referred to it in monetary terms, while on the other side referring to man as a natural animal. One of the most important insights the environmental debate had produced is that the Descartesian split between nature and natural human beings, between *res extensa* and *res cogitans*, so common to us today, is a historic invention. It began to become the norm in the Renaissance and was totally accepted from the 19th century on, however, even then it was only typical for occidental thinking, as Philippe Descola pointed out.[64] This differentiation can no longer be seen as a fact. And with it, the view is to be abandoned that nature is infinite passive dead matter, over which man has total control, while man himself is an active, rational, spiritual being. Such an assumption about a split between nature and man was sometimes even used to characterize the differences between the genders with women likened to nature. Instead a modern understanding of nature as a dynamic, alive, self-organized and continuously evolving process has to be introduced into economic theory.

Smith, a kind of "product" of his time, had not yet totally followed the Descartesian split. He saw humans as social animals living according to the natural order of things. Today we need to agree to Descola's word that to be modern means to become naturalistic.[65]

There are further differentiations to be overcome too, the one between man and his labour, whereby it has been made possible to view labour as a commodity like any other which can be traded on a (labour) market, as well as the split between (paid) labour in a company and (unpaid) labour in the household. These assumptions, along with the split of people into (active) producers and (passive) consumers, are no longer necessary. It is no longer necessary for them to be defined by monetary terms. *One* consistent understanding of labour is essential, as in every scientific theory there can only be one exact definition of its most basic category.

Furthermore, Adam Smith's works also cannot be said to focus exclusively on the rule of money, although his ideas apply equally to a society using the cultural invention of money-as-a-means and to a society using the cultural invention of money-as-an-end-of-economic activity. Amartya Sen has commented that "the spirited attempt to see Smith as an advocate of pure capitalism, with complete reliance on the market mechanism guided by pure profit motive, is altogether misconceived. Smith never used the term 'capitalism'."

We can also add that he never used the term "*homo oeconomicus*".

---

64 Philippe Descola, *Die Oekologie der Anderen,* Berlin, 2014, mentions that neither Japan or China seem to have the same idea about nature being external to man on p. 88.

65 ibid, p. 112

Smith "was not aiming to be the great champion of the profit-based market mechanism, nor was he arguing against the importance of economic institutions other than the markets..." said Sen (TMS p. xiii). His observations are right indeed.

It looks therefore as if certain writers have interpreted Adam Smith's work in such a way that it serves their own interests. They seemed to have needed a 'father' to justify their own ideas, and someone who lived 250 years ago, can be easily used for this purpose. However, they have referred only to a selection of his ideas. They have not considered all of them. They neglected the ones which did not suit them. Therefore they did not do justice to him. But they had the power to influence economics, politics and society according to their fragmented interest, even today.

This, obviously, should not have happened, as these ideas have much more to do with historical assumptions than with knowledge, and they are no longer appropriate for the 21st century. However, analyzing Adam Smith's works has allowed us to take on board some of the points he made and learn from them. Therefore let us summarize what we should take forward, when a modern economic theory has to break away from classical and neoclassical assumptions:

- If exchange is seen as the basic principle on which every economy and ever economic theory is based, then we propose that interaction is a better word for it, as it does not come with the connotation of money.
- It is people who move money; money cannot move on its own as if it were a living person.
- Real life supersedes money terms.

- A deeper understanding of the history of money is necessary.
- Past societies have invented different forms of economic activities, and their differences need to be considered.
- Today's economy is not *the* natural form of economy, but a cultural invention in a specific historic time.
- No society can allow itself to be defined exclusively in money terms. Money is a useful culturally invented means, but it should never be viewed as if it sets the rules for society.
- Money can never define people, nor can it replace people's right to equally participate in their particular society.
- In a democratic society, emancipated people are the sovereign. They set the framework of laws for everyone.
- People need to be free *in* their labour, not free from their labour.
- People need to be free *in* their society, not from their society.
- A democratic society needs to work in the interest of all people. A public service is for the many and not for money.
- The elected parliament has supremacy as it represents the legitimized power. The government is executing parliaments' decisions. It has to be at the service of and accountable to its electors. It has to build and run the infrastructure.
- Everything has two sides. Production is only half of economic activity. Con-

sumption, the other side, has to be considered too.
- Everybody in society participates and contributes. Everybody pays taxes according to their means.
- Wage income is to be exempt from taxes.
- The economic pattern can no longer be based on agriculture.
- Land/nature and labour/people produce the real wealth of a nation.
- Nature has to be respected as the base of all life. Only rewarding land owners with money is not sufficient.
- Humans are natural beings and – at the same time – part of their society in the historical culture.
- Nature, of which humans are part, cannot be treated as if it were peripheral to human lives, or a commodity at man's disposal. Nature has its own end and comes with its own intrinsic value.
- Regarding various divisions between paid and unpaid labour, the split of labour has to be overcome, as well as the separation of labour from the labouring person. *One* consistent understanding of labour should be at the base of any scientific theory.
- Neither human beings nor society, the economy or the universe can be regarded as machines.
- The 18th century's age of Enlightenment claimed that no human being should be seen as a production factor, a tool, a commodity, as mere goods or as a pure means for the purpose of somebody else, even if a person sells his ability to work to someone in exchange for money.
- Self-interest is not free from the rules of nature and culture, society and environment.
- People act mostly from a subjective point of view, but there is an objective point to be considered.
- If Earth were to be 'divided into equal portions among all its inhabitants', every person born there should have the same basic right to make use of it in the same way.

To conclude this analysis of Adam Smith's works, no real modern *cult*economic theory can be formulated without analyzing and then overcoming classical and neoclassical assumptions. It is not enough to propose 'new economics' or 'eco-economics' or ' evolutionary economics' or 'sustainable economics' "or green economics" while retaining such outdated views about men and nature.
Instead, every theory has to be based on the empirical reality, and every theory should allow us a better understanding of reality. What is the core of traditional classical and neoclassical economics, is not exchange among people with the help of the means "money", but a different quality of exchange, i. e. the substitution of the means for the end of all exchange – without making this clear. However, every theory, even economics, is expected to explain *why* the world is constructed in this way and why it should be like this. Therefore we can conclude that the way Western societies today are constructed is not the work of nature, but the work of human culture. Mainstream economic theory cannot be legitimized justified and

referred to as reference to the natural order of things.

There always is and always will be a need for change (naturally, not only with respect to the role of money). Society can develop, for example from a halfway modern one to a fairer and properly modern one – this is not a 'utopia' but possible. Neither work, nor history has come, or will ever come to an end. Life is a continuously evolving process. However, by destroying living nature and transforming it into dead matter, in the way that we are damaging our environment currently, we are reversing the process of evolution. The question is: Why do we still think that is rational?

6. A few spotlights on today's crises

To get a feel for how we reached our current state of economics it is useful to shine a spotlight on a few of today's crises. This chapter features extracts from various publications.

6.1. Economics is in crisis. But why aren't political scientists and sociologists offering an alternative view?

by permission of Aditya Chakrabortty, *The Guardian*, 17 April 2012, p. 5

"When the history of how a good crisis went to waste gets written up, it will surely contain a big chapter on the failure of our academic elites. Because just like the politicians, the taxpayer-funded intellectuals at our universities have missed the historic opportunities gifted to them by the financial collapse. And it will be the rest of us who pay the price.

At the start of the banking crisis, the air was thick with the sound of lachrymose economists. How did they miss the biggest crash since 1929? Professors at the LSE were asked that very question by the Queen – and were too tongue-tied to reply. A better answer came from Alan Greenspan, until recently the most powerful economist on the planet, who went to Capitol Hill and confessed to a "flaw" in his model of the world. Clearly, the economic crisis was also a crisis of economics.

With the all-powerful dismalists temporarily discredited, an opportunity opened up for the sociologists, the political scientists and the rest to charge in, have their say – and change the way public policy is shaped.

If all that sounds like a battle of the -ologies to you, then consider: no discipline has so profoundly shaped Britain or America over the past 30 years as mainstream economics, with its almost unshakeable faith in markets. Displace that narrow, straitened form of economics from its position as the orthodoxy on modern capitalism, and you have a shot at changing capitalism itself.

So have the non-economists grasped their moment? Have they hell. Look at the academic conferences held over the past few weeks and it's as if Lehman Brothers never fell over.

Britain's top political scientists met in Belfast, and you'd have thought there would be plenty in the crisis for them to discuss, from the technocrat governments installed in southern Europe to the paralysis of British politicians in the face of the banks. But no: over the course of three days, they held exactly one discussion of Britain's political economy.

Perhaps you have more faith in the sociologists. Take a peek at the website for the British Sociological Association. Scroll through the press-released research, and you will not come across anything that deals with the banking crash. Instead in April 2010, amid the biggest sociological event in decades, the BSA put out a notice titled: "Older bodybuilders can change young people's view of the over-60s, research says."

Or why not do the experiment I tried this weekend: go to three of the main academic journals in sociology, where the most noteworthy research is collected, and search the abstracts for the terms 'finance' or 'economy' or 'markets' since the start of the last decade.

Comb through the results for articles dealing with the financial crisis in even the most tangential sense. I found nine in the *American Sociological Review*, three in *Sociology* ("the UK's premier sociology journal"), and one in the *British Journal of Sociology*. The BSA has 2,500 members – yet this is the best they could do.

Sociologists are reliably good at analysing the fallout from crises: the recessions, the cuts, the dispossessed, the repossessed. I'd expect them to be in for a busy few years. But on the upstream stuff, the causes of this crisis, they are practically silent. Indeed, leave aside three remarkable books from Karen Ho, David Graeber and Alexandra Ouroussoff, all of whom are anthropologists (and all discussed here previously), and the bigger picture is still in the hands of those formerly shamefaced, but now rather assertive, economists. One promising initiative has just begun on the Open Democracy website called Uneconomics, where non-economists do chip in on the upstream causes of the crisis. But that's it: a cheap and cheerful internet forum. The Second International it ain't.

It wasn't always like this. One way of characterising what has happened in America and Britain over the past three decades is that people at the top have skimmed off increasing amounts of the money made by their corporations and societies. That's a phenomenon well covered by earlier generations of sociologists, whether it's Marx with his study of primitive accumulation, or the American C Wright Mills and his classic *The Power Elite*, or France's Pierre Bourdieu.

But those sociologists were unafraid to stray outside their disciplines. Compare that with the picture of today's teacher, forever churning out publications for their discipline's top-rated journals. Not much scope there to try out a speculative research project that might not fly, or to collaborate with specialists in other subjects.

Nor is there much encouragement to engage with public life. Because that's what's really missing from the other social sciences. When an entire discipline does what the sociologists did at their conference last week and devotes as much time to discussing the holistic massage industry ("using a Foucauldian lens") as to analysing financiers, they're never going to challenge the dominance of mainstream economics. And it's hard to believe they really want to."

6.2. Pitiless Samaritans

How Margaret Thatcher and her German disciples changed democracy to conform with the market

by Barbara Supp, Journalist, published in: *Der Spiegel No 6*, 6 February 2012, with permission of *Der Spiegel*, translated by the author

"She is still alive, but probably no longer aware of how much she has changed Europe, and Germany too. She said: "There is no such thing as society. There are only individual men and women." She talked a lot about individuals taking responsibility for themselves and about chains which needed to be cast off, and she meant it.

Now she is praised in the cinema as the old, now senile, former iron lady, and at the same time talks are taking place in Great Britain about her funeral. Should it be a state event? Does she deserve it?

Margaret Thatcher, former British Prime Minister, has a big share of responsibility for the crisis in which Europe, capitalism and democracy find themselves at present, but this is scarcely discussed, perhaps because of piety. Or because her contribution is underestimated, even today.

Now, as many cower under the force of the markets, submissive as to a force of nature, it helps to remember: It was people who gave authority to the markets.

Margaret Thatcher has played a key role in this process and the results are still being felt.

Think back to October 25 years ago, for example. A law was passed, which seemed to bring modern times to the City of London: an end to the division between trading at the stock exchange for one's own account and trading for a third party. An end to stable fees for financial transactions. Unlimited admission of foreign companies. London became the financial centre of the world.

The 'Big Bang'. At that time astonished people watched the absurd speed with which computer trading was facilitated. A new class of young greedy bankers emerged, with a morality portrayed a year later in the US movie *Wall Street*. Nobody understood at the time that this 'Big Bang' was political, a decisive attempt to disempower the state.

There are people who salute a weakened state.

Margaret Thatcher had done it. Imperturbable in her belief, harsh in her tone: "People must look to themselves first," was how she saw it. Radical liberty for the markets, that was her mission. She did not just want to deregulate, reduce taxes, privatise. "Economics are the method; the object it to change the heart and soul," she said. How successful she became.

It sounds Anglo-American, that thinking of Thatcher and Ronald Reagan back then, and of the Tea Party today, however it has oozed into Germany too. It has become standard government procedure, in a complicated way.

Thatcher sometimes lectured obstinate party politicians, taking her cue from free market prophet Friedrich von Hayek: "That is it what we believe." Thus she spoke.

This disempowerment of the state has happened much more quietly, discreetly and pervasively in Germany, and this has subsequently influenced the whole of Europe. It has not been publicly proclaimed as the state's objective, but has come into politics through advisors, companies, universities, associations: through experts.

Experts. That sounds intelligent and independent.

Some of these experts are well known, but others are sometimes more important than those one hears lecturing constantly in talk shows. In the 90s, a well-known expert in economic circles wrote that, the power of the state should be reduced as a mater of great urgency. Resistance to this was to be expected. To counter this, a solution might be to reduce taxes. The dictate of empty public coffers would be helpful. A shocking deficit would be needed.

In this way it would be possible to reduce the state. Totally undisguised, the idea was that the state should be diminished, becoming less powerful and poorer, as a matter of principle, not because of necessity. The writer of this was no off-the-wall maverick. It was Herbert Giersch, a scientist who died one-and-a-half years ago at a great age. Giersch was for decades the 'doyen' of German political economics. He was advisor to the government, founding member of the Council of Economic Experts – or the 'Five Wise Men', director of the Kiel Institute for the World Economy, an impressive compendium writer and instructor of several generations of economists, who today to be found in banks, associations and companies. One of the leading neoliberal economic scientists, and, like Thatcher, an apostle of Hayek, he influenced all classical market and entrepreneur-friendly politics.

In the past, there were those with a different point of view, the Keynesians in terms of employment and purchasing power, who argued for sensible wages and, if necessary, the intervention of the state. Today they are rarely seen. There was a quiet rebellion in the lecture halls, originating in the USA in the 80s, but with more consequences for Germany than over there. Hans-Werner Sinn, who belongs to the opposite camp, has estimated the share of this minority at 5 %. Now there is no longer any diversity, according to Peter Bofinger, one of the 'Five Wise Men' and, as a Keynesian, one of the last of his kind: "Analysis and therapy are dominated by one school. Reduce taxes, reduce wages, save, privatise, deregulate. The markets will sort it." These are "the common recommendations", given to people who seek the support of science. As if there is no other choice.

The belief in these experts is fed by the hope that they are not driven like politicians by power lust and party bias. There is an illusion that an 'expert' is a totally unbiased independent party with no attitude, no interests, no point of view, no biography. As if something like pure knowledge on two legs existed, without human interpretation, without the human dimension.

The expert Mario Monti, an economist who became Prime Minister, and is now tasked with saving Italy and eventually also the Euro and Europe, has been greeted by the directors of business associations with great praise: "He has known the markets for a long time, and is familiar with liberalisation, privatisation and reduction of public spending." In his cabinet of technocrats sits a minister of the business association and two former bankers. He himself was a long-time advisor to Goldman Sachs. As he does not belong to any party, he is celebrated in portraits as an 'independent', as one, who is "remote from trench-warfare". But he is not. An expert never is.

On a winter evening in the brilliance of Essen's Philharmonic Hall, the Alfred-Krupp-Halle, with its light wood and perfect acoustics, a gentleman with a charming Swiss accent is addressing an audience of about 2,000 guests, entrepreneurs, politicians, SME representatives and managers.

"Why," Josef Ackermann asks, "are bankers talking about the future of Europe? Would it not be better if they held back with their political advice? And sorted out their own future?" Ackermann, the departing chief of Deutsche Bank, a private bank, Ackermann, who represents to the people outside, the Occupy-protestors, the face of greed and crisis. He is quick in his response. Because, as an economic leader, his interference is "not only allowed", but "indeed required". What does he want? More privatisation, deregulation and flexibility. The failure of the market should be fought with even more market freedom.

The crisis is also his crisis, the crisis of the banks, of the bankers, who contributed considerably to the financial- and debt predicament. But that is not a problem. It is as if his central role makes him stand out even more from the others. He talks, and the auditorium listens in silence. He talks as a global traveller, hearing critical questions and touching facts from "his partners in the Asiatic-Pacific region", he talks as one who is powerful, authoritative, in the know.

That there have been "excesses" he occasionally admits. But his words are sustained at all times by his belief in the market.

The market will sort it, if left to itself: Joseph Vogl, cultural scientist and author of *Das Gespenst des Kapitals*,[1] calls it "oikodicy" – a doctrine of justification by faith in the market, similar to the theological doctrine of justification by faith in god. Now, as the foul by-products of unfettered markets are so openly visible, as doubts are expressed even by people who have previously accepted the market economy, they are treated by believers as if they do not exist or are not important.

Embarrassed Vogl describes this "indestructible conviction of liberal economics, that the market is an exemplary scene of order, integrated mechanisms, equalisation and therefore of social rationality".

It is indeed a weird rationality, this reasoning of the market – if bankrupt states were hungry people waiting for Samaritans, then the logic of these markets would be thus: You are nearly dead, said the Samaritan to the first starveling. If I give you bread now, you must return it to me – and if you survive, you must return it tenfold. You are weak, but you will recover, he said to the second. I will give you a load of bread, later you must give me back three. You have forgotten your lunch, he said to the third. I will give you bread. Tomorrow you must give me back more.

When it comes to the market, the helpers from the IWF, EU and European Central Bank are no more compassionate. They hand out bread, but they demand from the starvelings a strict regime.

---

1   translated into English: The spectre of capital

Why it is necessary to subscribe to that logic – that is for the common experts to explain. They interpret the market as priests do the will of the Lord. They praise the brakes on debt, born out of the dictate of empty coffers, and recommend them Europe wide, based on the German example. They praise Germany's Agenda 2010, the economic reforms of the Social Democrat chancellor Gerhard Schroeder, likewise, as a model for Europe. An agenda of reforms, relying on privatisation, deregulation of labour and financial markets and tax reduction, which was staggeringly close to the recommendations off the market liberal Giersch in the 80s – this is now an "Agenda for German economic policy".

There is no longer praise for the concepts of the heretics, who plead: Let us raise taxes on wealth, inheritance and capital, on private fortunes that have been growing in equal measure to the money which has been disappearing from the public coffer. No praise either for the 'heretical' idea that Greece could be helped to its feet again, economically speaking, with a kind of Marshall Plan.

"There is no alternative" was the favourite saying of Margaret Thatcher. "No alternative" is an expression Angela Merkel too likes to use, when she has come to a decision. She is in favour of democracy controlled by the market.

Outside on the streets, among the Occupy camps and demonstrations, people hoped that the economic crisis of 2008 would encourage the state to fight back, to find its role again. However, that did not happen. They were told that Germany has come through the crisis pretty well. If one looks to the export numbers as measure, then this is true. If we judge by the gap between poor and rich, then it is less true than ever.

"There is no such thing as society", Margaret Thatcher said.

Perhaps it is time, to listen to the heretics. And to the people outside, who do not want to give up their belief in democracy. **"**

6.3. Banking Wasn't Meant to Be Like This

What will their future be – and what is the government's proper financial role?

by (permission of) Michael Hudson, President of The Institute for the Study of Long-Term Economic Trends (ISLET), Wall Street Financial Analyst, Distinguished Research Professor of Economics at the University of Missouri, Kansas City, from his blog, published in German in *Frankfurter Allgemeine Sonntagszeitung*, 5 February, 2012

"The inherently symbiotic relationship between banks and governments recently has been reversed. In medieval times, wealthy bankers lent to kings and princes as their major customers. But now it is the banks that are needy, relying on governments for funding – capped by the post-2008 bailouts to save them from going bankrupt from their bad private-sector loans and gambles. Yet the banks now browbeat governments – not by having ready cash but by threatening to go bust and drag the economy down with them if they are not given control of public tax policy, spending and planning. The process has gone furthest in the United

States. Joseph Stiglitz characterizes the Obama administration's vast transfer of money and pubic debt to the banks as a "privatizing of gains and the socializing of losses. It is a 'partnership' in which one partner robs the other." Prof. Bill Black describes banks as becoming criminogenic and innovating "control fraud." High finance has corrupted regulatory agencies, falsified account-keeping by "mark to model" trickery, and financed the campaigns of its supporters to disable public oversight. The effect is to leave banks in control of how the economy's allocates its credit and resources.

If there is any silver lining to today's debt crisis, it is that the present situation and trends cannot continue. So this is not only an opportunity to restructure banking; we have little choice. The urgent issue is who will control the economy: governments, or the financial sector and monopolies with which it has made an alliance. Fortunately, it is not necessary to re-invent the wheel. Already a century ago the outlines of a productive industrial banking system were well understood. But recent bank lobbying has been remarkably successful in distracting attention away from classical analyses of how to shape the financial and tax system to best promote economic growth – by public checks on bank privileges.

How banks broke the social compact, promoting their own special interests
People used to know what banks did. Bankers took deposits and lent them out, paying short-term depositors less than they charged for risky or less liquid loans. The risk was borne by bankers, not depositors or the government. But today, bank loans are made increasingly to speculators in recklessly large amounts for quick in-and-out trading. Financial crashes have become deeper and affect a wider swathe of the population as debt pyramiding has soared and credit quality plunged into the toxic category of "liars' loans."

The first step toward today's mutual interdependence between high finance and government was for central banks to act as lenders of last resort to mitigate the liquidity crises that periodically resulted from the banks' privilege of credit creation. In due course governments also provided public deposit insurance, recognizing the need to mobilize and recycle savings into capital investment as the Industrial Revolution gained momentum. In exchange for this support, they regulated banks as public utilities.

Over time, banks have sought to disable this regulatory oversight, even to the point of decriminalizing fraud. Sponsoring an ideological attack on government, they accuse public bureaucracies of "distorting" free markets (by which they mean markets free for predatory behaviour). The financial sector is now making its move to concentrate planning in its own hands.

The problem is that the financial time frame is notoriously short-term and often self-destructive. And inasmuch as the banking system's product is debt, its business plan tends to be extractive and predatory, leaving economies high-cost. This is why checks and balances are needed, along with regulatory oversight to ensure fair dealing. Dismantling public attempts to steer banking to promote economic growth (rather than merely to make bankers rich) has permitted banks to turn into something nobody anticipated. Their major customers are other financial institutions, insurance and real estate – the FIRE sector, not industrial firms. Debt leveraging by real estate and monopolies, arbitrage speculators, hedge funds and corporate raiders inflates asset prices on credit. The effect of creating "balance sheet wealth" in this way is to load down the "real" production-and-consumption economy with debt and related rentier charges, adding more to the cost of living and doing business than rising productivity reduces production costs.

Since 2008, public bailouts have taken bad loans off the banks' balance sheet at enormous taxpayer expense – some $13 trillion in the United States, and proportionally higher in Ireland and other economies now being subjected to austerity to pay for "free market" deregulation. Bankers are holding economies hostage, threatening a monetary crash if they do not get more bailouts and nearly free central bank credit, and more mortgage and other loan guarantees for their casino-like game. The resulting "too big to fail" policy means making governments too weak to fight back.

The process that began with central bank support thus has turned into broad government guarantees against bank insolvency. The largest banks have made so many reckless loans that they have become wards of the state. Yet they have become powerful enough to capture lawmakers to act as their facilitators. The popular media and even academic economic theorists have been mobilized to pose as experts in an attempt to convince the public that financial policy is best left to technocrats – of the banks' own choosing, as if there is no alternative policy but for governments to subsidize a financial free lunch and crown bankers as society's rulers.

The Bubble Economy and its austerity aftermath could not have occurred without the banking sector's success in weakening public regulation, capturing national treasuries and even disabling law enforcement. Must governments surrender to this power grab? If not, who should bear the losses run up by a financial system that has become dysfunctional? If taxpayers have to pay, their economy will become high-cost and uncompetitive – and a financial oligarchy will rule.

The present debt quandary

The endgame in times past was to write down bad debts. That meant losses for banks and investors. But today's debt overhead is being kept in place – shifting bad loans off bank balance sheets to become public debts owed by taxpayers to save banks and their creditors from loss. Governments have given banks newly minted bonds or central bank credit in exchange for junk mortgages and bad gambles – without re-structuring the financial system to create a more stable, less debt-ridden economy. The pretence is that these bailouts will enable banks to lend enough to revive the economy by enough to pay its debts.

Seeing the handwriting on the wall, bankers are taking as much bailout money as they can get, and running, using the money to buy as much tangible property and ownership rights as they can while their lobbyists keep the public subsidy faucet running.

The pretence is that debt-strapped economies can resume business-as-usual growth by borrowing their way out of debt. But a quarter of U.S. real estate already is in negative equity – worth less than the mortgages attached to it – and the property market is still shrinking, so banks are not lending except with public Federal Housing Administration guarantees to cover whatever losses they may suffer. In any event, it already is mathematically impossible to carry today's debt overhead without imposing austerity, debt deflation and depression.

This is not how banking was supposed to evolve. If governments are to underwrite bank loans, they may as well be doing the lending in the first place – and receiving the gains. Indeed, since 2008 the over-indebted economy's crash led governments to become the major shareholders of the largest and most troubled banks – Citibank in the United States, Anglo-Irish Bank in Ireland, and Britain's Royal Bank of Scotland. Yet rather than taking this opportunity to run these banks as public utilities and lower their charges for credit-card services – or most important of all, to stop their lending to speculators and gamblers – governments left these banks operating as part of the "casino capitalism" that has become their business plan.

There is no natural reason for matters to be like this. Relations between banks and government used to be the reverse. In 1307, France's Philip IV ("The Fair") set the tone by seizing the Knights Templars' wealth, arresting them and putting many to death – not on financial charges, but on the accusation of devil-worshipping and satanic sexual practices. In 1344 the Peruzzi bank went broke, followed by the Bardi by making unsecured loans to Edward III of England and other monarchs who died or defaulted. Many subsequent banks had to suffer losses on loans gone bad to real estate or financial speculators.

By contrast, now the U.S., British, Irish and Latvian governments have taken bad bank loans onto their national balance sheets, imposing a heavy burden on taxpayers – while letting bankers cash out with immense wealth. These "cash for trash" swaps have turned the mortgage crisis and general debt collapse into a fiscal problem. Shifting the new public bailout debts onto the non-financial economy threatens to increase the cost of living and doing business. This is the result of the economy's failure to distinguish productive from unproductive loans and debts. It helps explain why nations now are facing financial austerity and debt peonage instead of the leisure economy promised so eagerly by technological optimists a century ago.

So we are brought back to the question of what the proper role of banks should be. This issue was discussed exhaustively prior to World War I. It is even more urgent today.

How classical economists hoped to modernize banks as agents of industrial capitalism

Britain was the home of the Industrial Revolution, but there was little long-term lending to finance investment in factories or other means of production. British and Dutch merchant banking was to extend short-term credit on the basis of collateral such as real property or sales contracts for merchandise shipped ("receivables"). Buoyed by this trade financing, merchant bankers were successful enough to maintain long-established short-term funding practices. This meant that James Watt and other innovators were obliged to raise investment money from their families and friends rather than from banks.

It was the French and Germans who moved banking into the industrial stage to help their nations catch up. In France, the Saint-Simonians described the need to create an industrial credit system aimed at funding means of production. In effect, the Saint-Simonians proposed to restructure banks along lines akin to a mutual fund. A start was made with the Crédit Mobilier, founded by the Péreire Brothers in 1852. Their aim was to shift the banking and financial system away from debt financing at interest toward equity lending, taking returns in the form of dividends that would rise or decline in keeping with the debtor's business fortunes. By giving businesses leeway to cut back dividends when sales and profits decline, profit-sharing agreements avoid the problem that interest must be paid willy-nilly. If an interest payment is missed, the debtor may be forced into bankruptcy and creditors can foreclose. It was to avoid this favouritism for creditors regardless of the debtor's ability to pay that prompted Mohammed to ban interest under Islamic law.

Attracting reformers ranging from socialists to investment bankers, the Saint-Simonians won government backing for their policies under France's Second Empire. Their approach inspired Marx as well as industrialists in Germany and protectionists in the United States and England. The common denominator of this broad spectrum was recognition that an efficient banking system was needed to finance the industry on which a strong national state and military power depended.

Germany develops an industrial banking system

It was above all in Germany that long-term financing found its expression in the Reichsbank and other large industrial banks as part of the "holy trinity" of banking, industry and government planning under Bismarck's "state socialism." German banks made a virtue of necessity. British banks "derived the greater part of their funds from the depositors," and steered these savings and business deposits into mercantile trade financing. This forced domestic firms to finance most new investment out of their own earnings. By contrast, Germany's "lack of capital… forced industry to turn to the banks for assistance," noted the financial historian George Edwards. "A considerable proportion of the funds of the German banks came not from the deposits of customers but from the capital subscribed by the proprietors themselves. As a result, German banks "stressed investment operations and were formed not so much for receiving deposits and granting loans but rather for supplying the investment requirements of industry."

When the Great War broke out in 1914, Germany's rapid victories were widely viewed as reflecting the superior efficiency of its financial system. To some observers the war appeared as a struggle between rival forms of financial organization. At issue was not only who would rule Europe, but whether the continent would have laissez faire or a more state-socialist economy.

In 1915, shortly after fighting broke out, the Christian Socialist priest-politician Friedrich Naumann published Mitteleuropa, describing how Germany recognized more than any other nation that industrial technology needed long-term financing and government support. His book inspired Prof. H. S. Foxwell in England to draw on his arguments in two remarkable essays published in the Economic Journal in September and December 1917: 'The Nature of the Industrial Struggle', and 'The Financing of Industry and Trade.' He endorsed Naumann's contention that "the old individualistic capitalism, of what he calls the English type, is giving way to the new, more impersonal, group form; to the disciplined scientific capitalism he claims as German."

This was necessarily a group undertaking, with the emerging tripartite integration of industry, banking and government, with finance being "undoubtedly the main cause of the success of modern German enterprise," Foxwell concluded (p. 514). German bank staffs included industrial experts who were forging industrial policy into a science. And in America, Thorstein Veblen's *The Engineers and the Price System* (1921) voiced the new industrial philosophy calling for bankers and government planners to become engineers in shaping credit markets.

Foxwell warned that British steel, automotive, capital equipment and other heavy industry was becoming obsolete largely because its bankers failed to perceive the need to promote equity investment and extend long-term credit. They based their loan decisions not on the new production and revenue their lending might create, but simply on what collateral they could liquidate in the event of default: inventories of unsold goods, real estate, and money due on bills for goods sold and awaiting payment from customers. And rather than investing in the shares of the companies that their loans supposedly were building up, they paid out most of their earnings as dividends – and urged companies to do the same. This short time horizon forced business to remain liquid rather than having leeway to pursue long-term strategy.

German banks, by contrast, paid out dividends (and expected such dividends from their clients) at only half the rate of British banks, choosing to retain earnings as capital reserves and invest them largely in the stocks of their industrial clients. Viewing these companies as allies rather than merely as customers from whom to make as large a profit as quickly as possible, German bank officials sat on their boards, and helped expand their business by extending loans to foreign governments on condition that their clients be named the chief suppliers in major public investments. Germany viewed the laws of history as favouring national planning to organize the financing of heavy industry, and gave its bankers a voice in formulating international diplomacy, making them "the principal instrument in the extension of her foreign trade and political power."

A similar contrast existed in the stock market. British brokers were no more up to the task of financing manufacturing in its early stages than were its banks. The nation had taken an early lead by forming Crown corporations such as the East India Company, the Bank of England and even the South Sea Company. Despite the collapse of the South Sea Bubble in 1720, the run-up of share prices from 1715 to 1720 in these joint-stock monopolies established London's stock market as a popular investment vehicle, for Dutch and other foreigners as well as for British investors. But the market was dominated by railroads, canals and large public utilities. Industrial firms were not major issuers of stock.

In any case, after earning their commissions on one issue, British stockbrokers were notorious for moving on to the next without much concern for what happened to the investors who had bought the earlier securities. "As soon as he has contrived to get his issue quoted at a premium and his underwriters have unloaded at a profit," complained Foxwell, "his enterprise ceases. 'To him,' as *The Times* says, 'a successful flotation is of more importance than a sound venture.'"

Much the same was true in the United States. Its merchant heroes were individualistic traders and political insiders often operating on the edge of the law to gain their fortunes by stock-market manipulation, railroad politicking for land giveaways, and insurance companies, mining and natural resource extraction. America's wealth-seeking spirit found its epitome in Thomas Edison's hit-or-miss method of invention, coupled with a high degree of litigiousness to obtain patent and monopoly rights.

In sum, neither British nor American banking or stock markets planned for the future. Their time frame was short, and they preferred rent-extracting projects to industrial innovation. Most banks favoured large real estate borrowers, railroads and public utilities whose income streams easily could be forecast. Only after manufacturing companies grew fairly large did they obtain significant bank and stock market credit.

What is remarkable is that this is the tradition of banking and high finance that has emerged victorious throughout the world. The explanation is primarily the military victory of the United States, Britain and their Allies in the Great War and a generation later, in World War II.

The regression toward burdensome unproductive debts after World War I

The development of industrial credit led economists to distinguish between productive and unproductive lending. A productive loan provides borrowers with resources to trade or invest at a profit sufficient to pay back the loan and its interest charge. An unproductive loan must be paid out of income earned elsewhere. Governments must pay war loans out of tax revenues. Consumers must pay loans out of income they earn at a job – or by selling assets. These debt payments divert revenue away from being spent on consumption and investment, so the economy shrinks. This traditionally has led to crises that wipe out debts, above all those that are unproductive.

In the aftermath of World War I the economies of Europe's victorious and defeated nations alike were dominated by postwar arms and reparations debts. These inter-governmental debts were to pay for weapons (by the Allies when the United States unexpectedly demanded that they pay for the arms they had bought before America's entry into the war), and for the destruction of property (by the Central Powers), not new means of production. Yet to the extent that they were inter-governmental, these debts were more intractable than debts to private bankers and bondholders.

Despite the fact that governments in principle are sovereign and hence can annul debts owed to private creditors, the defeated Central Power governments were in no position to do this.

And among the Allies, Britain led the capitulation to U.S. arms billing, captive to the creditor ideology that "a debt is a debt" and must be paid regardless of what this entails in practice or even whether the debt in fact can be paid. Confronted with America's demand for payment, the Allies turned to Germany to make them whole. After taking its liquid assets and major natural resources, they insisted that it squeeze out payments by taxing its economy. No attempt was made to calculate just how Germany was to do this – or most important, how it was to convert this domestic revenue (the "budgetary problem") into hard currency or gold. Despite the fact that banking had focused on international credit and currency transfers since the 12th century, there was a broad denial of what John Maynard Keynes identified as a foreign exchange transfer problem.

Never before had there been an obligation of such enormous magnitude. Nevertheless, all of Germany's political parties and government agencies sought to devise ways to tax the economy to raise the sums being demanded. Taxes are levied in a nation's own currency. The only way to pay the Allies was for the Reichsbank to take this fiscal revenue and throw it onto the foreign exchange markets to obtain the sterling and other hard currency to pay. Britain, France and the other recipients then paid this money on their Inter-Ally debts to the United States.

Adam Smith pointed out that no government ever had paid down its public debt. But creditors always have been reluctant to acknowledge that debtors are unable to pay. Ever since David Ricardo's lobbying for their perspective in Britain's Bullion debates, creditors have found it their self-interest to promote a doctrinaire blind spot, insisting that debts of any magnitude could be paid. They resist acknowledging a distinction between raising funds domestically (by running a budget surplus) and obtaining the foreign exchange to pay foreign-currency debt. Furthermore, despite the evident fact that austerity cutbacks on consumption and investment can only be extractive, creditor-oriented economists refused to recognize that debts cannot be paid by shrinking the economy. Or that foreign debts and other international payments cannot be paid in domestic currency without lowering the exchange rate.

The more domestic currency Germany sought to convert, the further its exchange rate was driven down against the dollar and other gold-based currencies. This obliged Germans to pay much more for imports. The collapse of the exchange rate was the source of hyperinflation, not an increase in domestic money creation as today's creditor-sponsored monetarist economists insist. In vain Keynes pointed to the specific structure of Germany's balance of payments and asked creditors to specify just how many German exports they were willing to take, and to explain how domestic currency could be converted into foreign exchange without collapsing the exchange rate and causing price inflation.

Tragically, Ricardian tunnel vision won Allied government backing. Bertil Ohlin and Jacques Rueff claimed that economies receiving German payments would recycle their inflows to Germany and other debt-paying countries by buying their imports. If income adjustments did not keep exchange rates and prices stable, then Germany's falling exchange rate would make its exports sufficiently more attractive to enable it to earn the revenue to pay.

This is the logic that the International Monetary Fund followed half a century later in insisting that Third World countries remit foreign earnings and even permit flight capital as well as pay their foreign debts. It is the neoliberal stance now demanding austerity for Greece, Ireland, Italy and other Eurozone economies. Bank lobbyists claim that the European Central Bank will risk spurring domestic wage and price inflation if it does what central banks were founded to do: finance budget deficits. Europe's financial institutions are given a monopoly right to perform this electronic task – and to receive interest for what a real central bank could create on its own computer keyboard.

But why is it less inflationary for commercial banks to finance budget deficits than for central banks to do this? The bank lending that has inflated a global financial bubble since the 1980s has left as its legacy a debt overhead that can no more be supported today than Germany was able to carry its reparations debt in the 1920s. Would government credit have so recklessly inflated asset prices?

How debt creation has fuelled asset-price inflation since the 1980s

Banking in recent decades has not followed the productive lines that early economic futurists expected. As noted above, instead of financing tangible investment to expand production and innovation, most loans are made against collateral, with interest to be paid out of what borrowers can make elsewhere. Despite being unproductive in the classical sense, it was remunerative for debtors from 1980 until 2008 – not by investing the loan proceeds to expand economic activity, but by riding the wave of asset-price inflation. Mortgage credit enabled borrowers to bid up property prices, drawing speculators and new customers into the market in the expectation that prices would continue to rise. But hothouse credit infusions meant additional debt service, which ended up shrinking the market for goods and services.

Under normal conditions the effect would have been for rents to decline, with property prices following suit, leading to mortgage defaults. But banks postponed the collapse into negative equity by lowering their lending standards, providing enough new credit to keep on inflating prices. This averted a collapse of their speculative mortgage and stock market lending. It was inflationary – but it was inflating asset prices, not commodity prices or wages. Two decades of asset price inflation enabled speculators, homeowners and commercial investors to borrow the interest falling due and still make a capital gain.

This hope for a price gain made winning bidders willing to pay lenders all the current income – making banks the ultimate and major rentier income recipients. The process of inflating asset prices by easing credit terms and lowering the interest rate was self-feeding. But it also was self-terminating, because raising the multiple by which a given real estate rent or business income can be "capitalized" into bank loans increased the economy's debt overhead.

Securities markets became part of this problem. Rising stock and bond prices made pension funds pay more to purchase a retirement income – so "pension fund capitalism" was coming undone. So was the industrial economy itself. Instead of raising new equity financing for companies, the stock market became a vehicle for corporate buyouts. Raiders borrowed to buy out stockholders, loading down companies with debt. The most successful looters left them bankrupt shells. And when creditors turned their economic gains from this process into political power to shift the tax burden onto wage earners and industry, this raised the cost of living and doing business – by more than technology was able to lower prices.

The EU rejects central bank money creation, leaving deficit financing to the banks

Article 123 of the Lisbon Treaty forbids the ECB or other central banks to lend to government. But central banks were created specifically to finance government deficits. The EU has rolled back history to the way things were three-hundred years ago, before the Bank of England was created. Reserving the task of credit creation for commercial banks, it leaves governments without a central bank to finance the public spending needed to avert depression and widespread financial collapse.

So the plan has backfired. When 'hard money' policy makers limited central bank power, they assumed that public debts would be risk-free. Obliging budget deficits to be financed by private creditors seemed to offer a bonanza: being able to collect interest for creating electronic credit that governments can create themselves. But now, European governments need credit to balance their budget or face default. So banks now want a central bank to create the money to bail them out for the bad loans they have made.

For starters, the ECB's €489 billion in three-year loans at 1% interest gives banks a free lunch arbitrage opportunity (the 'carry trade') to buy Greek and Spanish bonds yielding a higher rate. The policy of buying government bonds in the open market – after banks first have bought them at a lower issue price – gives the banks a quick and easy trading gain.

How are these giveaways less inflationary than for central banks to directly finance budget deficits and roll over government debts? Is the aim of giving banks easy gains simply to provide them with resources to resume the Bubble Economy lending that led to today's debt overhead in the first place?

Conclusion

Governments can create new credit electronically on their own computer keyboards as easily as commercial banks can. And unlike banks, their spending is expected to serve a broad social purpose, to be determined democratically. When commercial banks gain policy control over governments and central banks, they tend to support their own remunerative policy of creating asset-inflationary credit – leaving the clean-up costs to be solved by a post-bubble austerity. This makes the debt overhead even harder to pay – indeed, impossible.

So we are brought back to the policy issue of how public money creation to finance budget deficits differs from issuing government bonds for banks to buy. Is not the latter option a convoluted way to finance such deficits – at a needless interest charge? When governments monetize their budget deficits, they do not have to pay bondholders.

I have heard bankers argue that governments need an honest broker to decide whether a loan or public spending policy is responsible. To date their advice has not promoted productive credit. Yet they now are attempting to compensate for the financial crisis by telling debtor governments to sell off property in their public domain. This 'solution' relies on the myth that privatization is more efficient and will lower the cost of basic infrastructure services. Yet it involves paying interest to the buyers of rent-extraction rights, higher executive salaries, stock options and other financial fees.

Most cost savings are achieved by shifting to non-unionized labour, and typically end up being paid to the privatizers, their bankers and bondholders, not passed on to the public. And bankers back price deregulation, enabling privatizers to raise access charges. This raises the economy's cost base and thus lowers its competitive advantage – just the opposite of what is promised.

Banking has moved so far away from funding industrial growth and economic development that it now benefits primarily at the economy's expense in a predator-like extractive manner, not by making productive loans. This is now the great problem confronting our time. Banks now lend mainly to other financial institutions, hedge funds, corporate raiders, insurance companies and real estate, and engage in their own speculation in foreign currency, interest-rate arbitrage, and computer-driven trading programs. Industrial firms bypass the banking system by financing new capital investment out of their own retained earnings, and meet their liquidity needs by issuing their own commercial paper directly. Yet to keep the bank casino winning, global bankers now want governments not only to bail them out but to enable them to renew their failed business plan – and to keep the present debts in place so that creditors will not have to take a loss.

This wish means that society should lose, and even suffer depression. We are dealing here not only with greed, but with outright antisocial behaviour and hostility.

Europe thus has reached a critical point in having to decide whose interest to put first: that of banks, or the 'real' economy. History provides a wealth of examples illustrating the dangers of capitulating to bankers, and also for how to restructure banking along more productive lines. The underlying questions are clear enough:

- Have banks outlived their historical role, or can they be restructured to finance productive capital investment rather than simply inflate asset prices?
- Would a public option provide less costly and better directed credit?
- Why not promote economic recovery by writing down debts to reflect the ability to pay, rather than relinquishing more wealth to an increasingly aggressive creditor class?

Solving the Eurozone's financial problem can be made much easier by the tax reforms that classical economists advocated to complement their financial reforms. To free consumers and employers from taxation, they proposed to levy the burden on the 'unearned increment' of land and natural resource rent, monopoly rent and financial privilege. The guiding principle was that property rights in the earth, monopolies and other ownership privileges have no direct cost of production, and hence can be taxed without reducing their supply or raising their price, which is set in the market. Removing the tax deductibility for interest is the other key reform that is needed.

A rent tax holds down housing prices and those of basic infrastructure services, whose untaxed revenue tends to be capitalized into bank loans and paid out in the form of interest charges. Additionally, land and natural resource rents – along with interest – are the easiest to tax, because they are highly visible and their value is easy to assess.

Pressure to narrow existing budget deficits offers a timely opportunity to rationalize the tax systems of Greece and other PIIGS countries in which the wealthy avoid paying their fair share of taxes. The political problem blocking this classical fiscal policy is that it 'interferes' with the rent-extracting free lunches that banks seek to lend against. So they act as lobbyists for untaxing real estate and monopolies (and themselves as well). Despite the financial sector's desire to see governments remain sufficiently solvent to pay bondholders, it has subsidized an enormous public relations apparatus and academic junk economics to oppose the tax policies that can close the fiscal gap in the fairest way.

It is too early to forecast whether banks or governments will emerge victorious from today's crisis. As economies polarize between debtors and creditors, planning is shifting out of public hands into those of bankers. The easiest way for them to keep this power is to block a true central bank or strong public sector from interfering with their monopoly of credit creation. The counter is for central banks and governments to act as they were intended to, by providing a public option for credit creation.**"**

6.4. Battle is joined on bonuses – and high time too

John Plender, *The Financial Times*, **April 21/April 22 2012, p.8**

"When more than half the shareholders in Citigroup vote against or abstain on a multimillion-dollar pay plan for Vikram Pandit, chief executive, and his fellow directors, something is clearly afoot. So, too, in the UK, where shareholder pressure this week caused Bob Diamond, chief executive of Barclays, to forgo half his bonus for 2011, just days before the bank's annual meeting. Do these unexpected events presage the start of a capitalist revolution – a shareholder assault on further pillaging of banks by executives whose mediocre performance has customarily been rewarded with huge bonuses and equity-related incentives?

Some institutional investors are certainly determined to alter the distribution of rewards between bank executives and shareholders. In the case of Barclays they have extracted a promise of increased dividends. Whether this will suffice to pre-empt a significant protest vote remains to be seen. While the insurer Standard Life has declared itself satisfied, others feel that after months of engagement with Barclays on the issue this was a case of too little, too late.

The amazing thing is that it has taken so long for the worms of the institutional investment world to turn, though in fairness to institutional investors in the UK where 'say on pay' votes were introduced earlier than in the US, significant protest votes have been registered against bank bonuses since 2009. Yet the fact remains that bankers' pay is one of history's great heists – a gigantic reward for failure.

It is worth recalling just how devastatingly costly the bankers have been for the world. Soon after the collapse of Lehman Brothers in 2008, Andrew Haldane of the Bank of England calculated that the net present value of the cumulative loss of global output resulting from the crisis could be – hold on to your seat – anywhere in money terms between $60 tn and $200 tn. In addition, the high level of public sector debt in the US and Europe partly reflects the huge cost of bailing out financial institutions.

Of course, it was not just bankers who were responsible for the crisis. Yet it is important to note that Mr Haldane also demonstrated that the profits on which bonuses had been paid were largely illusory. For most of the 20th century the long-run return on equity in UK banking moved in line with the underlying growth rate of the UK economy.

Then from 1986 to 2006 the return on equity jumped from 2 per cent to an annual average of 16 per cent. Yet the return on assets was largely stagnant over the period. In effect, the managers of banks took to the roulette wheel. They juiced up rotten returns by shrinking their equity capital and taking on more risk. This pattern was repeated across much of the developed world.

Here, then, is a mature industry that nonetheless attracts the cream of university graduates and pays entrepreneurial rewards for erratic and mediocre performance. And financial institutions that are too big to fail continue to enjoy an implicit subsidy from the taxpayer while complaining, in many cases, that they are not able to cover their cost of capital. So the rebellious institutions undeniably have a point and their protest will undoubtedly affect future behaviour among the banks. But can they bring about a wider return to sanity in setting bankers' pay?

The prospects on either side of the Atlantic are different. In the US it is much harder to vote directors off the board if they have performed badly in their compensation committee role. The 'say on pay' vote is only advisory. In a legalistic culture where many business people routinely take things to the legal limit, some bankers may decide to tough it out even if a majority votes against the pay package.

They would do that in the knowledge that the likelihood of a backlash from Capitol Hill is not great given that the banks are one of the biggest providers of campaign finance to politicians. Indeed, the recipients of Wall Street's largesse are busy doing all they can to dilute the Dodd-Frank Act's provisions to tighten financial regulation in response to the crisis.

More complex circumstances prevail in the UK. After the onset of the crisis, a culture of deference prevailed because politicians were acutely conscious of how much the banks had delivered in terms of employment and tax revenues. They were reluctant to believe that the golden goose was mere base metal. Now reality has set in. Vince Cable, the business secretary, is consulting on whether to make the 'say on pay' vote binding and on a host of other options, including increasing diversity on remuneration committees.

Because UK institutions have more power to fire directors than their US counterparts, they could also strengthen their hand by voting more aggressively against those remuneration committee chairs who do a poor job. While they increasingly do this at the companies where an egregious pay package has been proposed, they rarely vote against remuneration committee chairs at other companies where they are nonexecutive directors.

Perhaps the most beneficial thing they cold do would be to spearhead a move back towards old-fashioned cash rewards. Equity incentives were, after all, counterproductive at Lehman Brothers, Bear Sterns, Merrill Lynch and elsewhere. And the complexity of pay and incentive packages nowadays is almost as unfathomable as the nature of the risks in the structured products and derivatives the banks have been so busily peddling.

As for the bankers, in this credit-constrained, more risk-averse time, they should remember the adage of Leon Fraser, second president of the Bank for International Settlements, who said "it is better to have loaned and lost than never to have loaned at all". When he was around, they didn't need the prospect of a bonus to make a loan. **"**

6.5. High-frequency trading drives cable contest

Philip Stafford in London, in: *The Financial Times,* **21/22 April 2012, p. 15**

"Two telecoms companies have claimed they will create the fastest trading connection between London and New York, a development that highlights growing demand from investors for high-speed trading between the world's financial centres.

The link, which will cut about six milliseconds – or thousandths of a second – of time from existing speeds, is the work of Reliance Globalcom, part of the Indian telecoms group, and Perseus Telecom, a small Irish company.

The project reflects a race to meet the growing demand to provide hedge funds and banks with the fastest possible trading times around the globe. Investors are pushing the barriers of physical geography to eke out tiny advantages and exploit tiny discrepancies in prices of the same assets on different exchanges and trading venues, a practice known as high-frequency trading.

Fibre-optic cables had not been laid under the Atlantic for a decade but new cables between London and New York are due to come into operation next year, costing about $300m.

The cable from Reliance and Perseus will use an existing cable owned by Flag Atlantic, which floats 3,000 m below sea level between Long Island, New York, and Land's End in the UK. Those depths are below the normal operations of commercial trawlers and even submarines.

Currently it takes about 65 milliseconds to trade between London and New York. New equipment on the ends of the line, say the companies, will shave milliseconds off that time. The second phase of the project, in which cabling will be replaced and completed later this year, will take times below 60 milliseconds.

Some high-frequency trading groups have complained that the high cost of new cables has been passed on to customers. Manoj Narang, chief executive of Tradeworkx, has labelled that "a gigantic tax on the industry".

A link between London and Hong Kong opened last year cut a round trip between the two financial hubs to 176 milliseconds.

Internet and trading services to Egypt and the Middle East were hit in 2008 when a cable outside Alexandria was damaged and took nearly two years to fully repair."

6.6. Where Did the Good Jobs Go?

from: *Greedy Bastards! How We Can Stop Corporate Communists, Banksters, and Other Vampires from Sucking America Dry*, p. 59–63

Dylan Ratigan, Host of MSNBC's *The Dylan Ratigan Show* and former global managing editor for corporate finance at Bloomberg News has developed and launched more than half a dozen broadcast and new media properties including CNBC's *Fast Money* and *The Dylan Ratigan Show*, and a non-profit foundation, Get Money Out, together with G. F. Lichtenberg and Dr. Jeffrey Spees, 2012.

"Our economy used to be based on making things ourselves, which provided jobs for Americans as well as consumer goods. But more and more, we consume products that are made, packaged, and assembled abroad, which means that the jobs have gone abroad, too – most notably to China. According to the *Wall Street Journal*, most people who lost jobs in the recent recession found new ones, but at lower pay. In fact, over one-third of those lucky enough to find new employment had to accept pay cuts of at least 20 per cent.

Pay cuts? We haven't experienced real, sustained pay cuts since the 1930s. We all know that the 2008-09 recession was terrible, but what is unusual is that the recovery has been terrible too. Only certain segments of the economy improved. Seemingly, productivity increased. Profits increased. The stock market recovered. Corporate profits rose, giving corporations extra money for investing. Interest rates remained at historic lows, so it was cheaper than ever to borrow money to invest. But the job market and domestic investment market didn't recover. All that corporate cash had to go somewhere. Why wasn't it going into new ventures, and research and development, and expanding existing businesses, creating a surge in new jobs?

We know that a lot of money is being sucked into the banking casinos, but certainly not all of it. Where was all that free trade money?

The simple answer is that the money had already been divided up. Part of it is going to finance manufacturing in China and part of it is staying here with our bankers and the super rich. Big industry – minus Engine, and automakers among others – was investing far more in China than here. American banks (which we subsidize!) were increasing their lending to China rather than lending capital here. Andrew Liveris, CEO of the Dow Chemical Company, put it bluntly: "US companies – run by patriotic people – are moving off-shore at the fastest rate in history."

The fact is, if you and I had a spare $100 million to invest, we'd be tempted to send it to China too. It's so much easier to make money investing in that country's short-term growth at our long-term expense, whether you're a major corporation, a private investor, or a bank. But why should it be? Why?

The reason why is because of government policy. Our current, highly regulated trading arrangements benefit international investors who want to profit from sending capital to low-wage countries such as China. You can read the evidence yourself. In December 2005, a little-known but extremely powerful group of American economic policy makers met in what's called the Federal

Open Market Committee (FOMC) meeting. The FOMC is the policy-making body of the Federal Reserve; the people around that table decide whether to lower or raise interest rates, monitor instability in the financial system (or bury their heads in the sand; whatever the case may be), and discuss various regions of American and their economic performances. You might have glimpsed the power of this group if you've ever watched the stock market go crazy after the Fed has moved to bail out the world economy (or not).

One of the men in the room at the time, Dallas Fed president Richard Fisher, had a complaint about China. As revealed in the minutes of the December 2005 meeting, Fisher was bitter about the enormous quantity of Chinese goods flowing into America. He pointed out that this was creating "disinflation", or lowering prices and wages for Americans, and that the CEOs he was talking to were frustrated about the tide of goods and services coming in to the country. Except that Fisher wasn't griping that there were too many Chinese imports; he was angry that there *weren't enough* imports. Even though China had built special export-only ports for shipping goods out of China, the American ports can't absorb what China wants to sell us because of what he called "work rules" – in other words, unions, being "slow to adjust". This presented a huge problem, Fisher continued, because it was blocking his CEO contacts from outsourcing as much work abroad as quickly as possible. In his words, they were not "exploiting globalization" fast enough.

Disturbingly, in that same meeting, Fisher *bragged* about the weakness, at that time, of Ford: "My most delicious irony is the fact that similarly dated Vietnamese debt now trades on a price basis richer, and on a yield basis lower, than that of Ford Motor Company." A developing Asian country was financially stronger, as measured by the value of its debt, than one of the most significant employers in the United States. The response from his fellow bankers? Laughter.

Why would the Dallas Federal Reserve Bank president celebrate the strength of Chinese exports and Vietnamese debt? Simple: moving work to China weakens American workers. When you can't find a job, or your only choice is to accept a pay cut or face layoffs, you're much less likely to strike. That means multinational corporations benefit twice when they move manufacturing to China. Not only do they get to pay Chinese workers extremely low wages but they also build the leverage to lower wages and limit the rights of their US employees.

Now, you might consider this an outrage. And you might wonder why it wasn't reported widely in 2005 that a powerful economic player like Richard

Fisher was openly arguing for shipping the US manufacturing base to China faster than it was already happening, at the urging of corporate CEOs in Texas. Are you sitting down? The reason it wasn't reported at the time is that transcripts of FOMC meetings were kept secret for five years. (And that five-year lag is an *improvement* – it used to be that the meetings were secret and the transcripts shredded.) This transcript was released only in 2010, while the world financial system was melting down. So very few read it, let alone reported on it. Besides, five years later, it's old news, right? So why would any journalist report it as significant?

But it is significant. The US national strategy is and has been for many years now, to move as much production to China as quickly as possible. It is stated outright by powerful policy makers, not when and where the public is paying attention. This is the strategy of CEOs and political decision makers like Richard Fisher: promote disastrous policies that are misaligned with the interests of hard-working Americans. Just make sure to do it from behind closed doors.

Before I go on to describe the basics of our trading relationship, and why it is a destructive, short-term greedy model, you should recognize that just by knowing what the people who set these policies believe, you have weakened their power. What I am about to describe is upsetting, but remember, you can solve only what you have the courage to see. By learning, you are helping America to begin to conduct itself differently.**"**

6.7. High street shops offer fresh produce and personal service,

Response letters to the Editor of *The Sunday Telegraph*, 19 February, 2012

"SIR – Justin King, the chief executive of Sainsbury's, thinks that people do not have time to shop in the high street (report February 12). He is wrong. My local shopping street at Hoole, in Chester, has a butcher, a baker, a greengrocer, a delicatessen and a fishmonger. We find it more convenient to visit several shops there than to drive to an out-of-town supermarket.

At a supermarket, one walks up and down crowded aisles looking for goods that have been relocated or are no longer stocked. On completing that lonely task, there are queues at the tills and the long drive home.

In my high street, I am served personally by shopkeepers who care. I buy the quantity I need because it is not ready-bagged.

The produce is fresh and, despite what supermarkets tell us, often cheaper or comparably priced. Visiting several shops is still quicker, more friendly and better for the environment than making that journey out of town.

Mr King's views have little to do with what people want and rather a lot to do with what Sainsbury's shareholders want.

Ian Fantom, Guilden Sutton, Cheshire

SIR – I'm slightly baffled by the lure of supermarkets, and I wonder at the packed car parks that lie on the fringes of every settlement in Britain.

I admit that it is convenient for Ocado to deliver the boring, bulky stuff, but independent shops offer better shopping. They are also easier on the pocket: though their prices may not compete with supermarkets', one doesn't over-buy; you simply get what you went for.

Since abandoning the retail behemoths for my local shops, end-of-week, out-of-date food has all but disappeared from my kitchen and there's substantially less packaging to recycle.

It is enjoyable to shop from people whose names I know and who know mine, who ask how I am and can chat about what's going on in the neighbourhood.

Local shopping beats the supermarket experience any day and keeps the flame of independent business burning.
Giovanna Forte, London E2

SIR – By offering every kind of product – newspapers, clothes, pharmaceuticals, tourism, banking and coffee – the supermarkets are sucking the life out of local economies. But the death of high streets reduces the buying power of the very communities on which the supermarkets rely. They are also being hit by rising transport and distribution costs, which will eventually favour local produce.

Bristol is introducing its own currency in an attempt to revive the high street, following similar initiatives in Totnes, Lewes, Stroud and Brixton. I hope the Bristol pound will prevail against the enemies of the high street.
John Busby, Lawshall, Suffolk

SIR – We should bulk up our high streets and downsize the supermarkets – they can then be converted into prisons or whatever. That way we will continue to meet friends every day, and will not be lonely and depressed by having to spend £5 in petrol to wander aimlessly around an emporium for hours on end not speaking to anyone.
Don Stuart, Stokesley, North Yorkshire**"**

6.8. Our digital masters must themselves be watched

Jonathan Freedland, *The Guardian*, 2 March, 2012, p. 47

"As far as I know there is no secretive government agency that keeps a trio of strange, other-wordly teenagers in a waterpool, wires attached to their brains, exploiting their eerie ability to see into the future. But, that detail aside, the 2002 film *Minority Report* can claim – like the 'precogs' in the pool – to have predicted the future with uncanny accuracy.

The film depicted a mid-21-century world of robotics and assorted gadgetry, with a few striking specifics. The first was the way Tom Cruise and friends used computers. No laborious typing on keyboards, just swishing and swiping with their fingers. Well, that future didn't take long to arrive. Thanks to Steve Jobs and his touchscreen gizmos, *Minority Report*-style hand movements are already here ... this week we took another step towards it, thanks to that all-pervasive presence in our lives: Google.

On Thursday, Google took down the barrier that had, until now, prevented it joining the dots of your electronic life. It had already been logging all your Google searches, remembering what you looked for and when, as well as watching what you watched on YouTube, photographing your house for Street View and, if you use a Google smartphone, knowing where you've been and maybe where you are right now. It had been using that information to generate, to take one example, the ads that appear on your Google search page based on your past these separate silos of information.

Now it will. Thanks to a change in its privacy policy, Google can make deductions based on one aspect of your online activity and use that to sell you things in another. If you watched football clips on YouTube, an ad for upcoming matches might appear beside your inbox. Perhaps that will strike you as efficient rather than sinister, but consider this: if you use a Google email service, then Google will be reading your emails too. It's true there is no human pair of eyeballs gazing at your daily correspondence: the 'reading' is of the electronic, algorithmic variety. But it will be just enough, as my colleague James Ball put it in *The Guardian* yesterday, that if you sent an email to a friend announcing 'I am pregnant!', your next browsing experience could well be interrupted by ads for maternity wear. Just like *Minority Report* imagined it.

Perhaps Hollywood thrillers are not the best guide to what's scary and what's safe. Maybe we shouldn't shudder at the warning that when an online service is free, you're not the customer – you're the product, a valuable source of data ripe for commercial exploitation. It's possible that this sounds creepier than it is. Perhaps all this knowledge held in Google's vaults of humming, blinking servers will only ever be used to help us go shopping or find a decent restaurant.

But there are other possibilities. What if some of that information leaked or got lost? What if Google chucked out a few old servers containing millions of our emails, in just the same way that the last government managed to lose the personal details of 25 million British citizens? Google now holds so much data that industry watchers assume it is a target for state espionage; assume indeed that every self-respecting intelligence agency in the world is trying 'to get an engineer into the Google server room'. The company has accused China of attempting to hack its Gmail service, trying to read the emails of US officials and Chinese dissidents.

It should give us pause, too, that if the US government wanted to subpoena emails between, say, a journalist and a confidential source, Google could, if it chose, simply hand over those emails without even telling those involved. The power lies with Google, not the people who sent or received the messages. And power is the right word. If knowledge is power, then Google is a global super-power, the match of any government. It doesn't raise armies or levy taxes, but its reach and influence are enormous – and getting bigger. The trouble is, our political vocabulary does not quite know how to speak about this kind of power.... "

6.9. UK's £1.5 bn for climate change aid

**Richard Gray, Science Correspondent, *The Sunday Telegraph*,
19 February 2012**

"Nearly £1.5 billion has been spent tackling man-made climate change by the Government department responsible for fighting poverty abroad, it can be revealed.

The Department for International Development (DfiD) has funded projects which it says will either reduce carbon emissions abroad or attempt to deal with the effects of predicted changes in the earth's climate.

In the past four years DfiD has spent £900 million on climate change projects, with nearly two thirds of that being spent in the past financial year under the Coalition. A further £533 million has already been committed up to 2013.

The biggest recipients of the climate change aid are India and Indonesia, two countries considered to be rapidly emerging economies.

The disclosures – made under the Freedom of Information Act – will raise fresh questions over how foreign aid is spent, and comes after an Indian minister described British aid to the country as "peanuts", which ministers in London had begged Delhi to continue accepting.

DfiD is one of only two departments not affected by the Government's austerity drive, with a budget last year of £8.4 billion.

The figures released by the Government reveal that total spending on tackling climate change overseas rose from £ 61 million in 2007–08 to more than £883 million in 2010–11.

During that time, DfiD saw the biggest increase in spending on climate change with funding for projects now 45 times higher than four years ago. The department now also employs 66 specialist climate and environmental advisers.

Among the aid provided was a £4.7 million project in Indonesia aimed at helping the government there provide "more effective leadership and management of climate change programming".

Another project encouraged Indian farmers to use foot pumps to draw water from underground rather than diesel powered pumps.

A project in western Kenya to help indigenous Nganyi rainmakers being undermined by extreme weather conditions caused by changes in the climate was launched in 2008 as part of a £25 million climate change adaptation programme funded by DfiD.

It aimed to bring the rainmakers together with government meteorologists to produce a "consensus forecast" combining satellite data and computer models with traditional techniques, such as observing wildlife and pot blowing, where herbs are placed into a pot buried in the ground into which the rainmaker blows through a pipe, listening for coming winds.

In total £3.5 billion of public money has been paid out or allocated to projects addressing climate change abroad since 2007–08.

Although DfiD accounts for the bulk of the spending, other departments also spent significant amounts abroad. The Foreign and Commonwealth Office spent more than £71 million on climate change and energy programmes overseas in the past two years.

This included a "Low Carbon High Growth Strategic Fund" operating in developed and developing countries including Poland, China, India, Brazil, Saudi Arabia, Japan, Indonesia and Mexico.

The Department for Environment, Farming and Rural Affairs has spent more than £233,000 attending climate change talks and has also allocated £10 million for a project to tackle deforestation in the Brazilian Cerrado.

As revealed by *The Sunday Telegraph* last year, the Department for Energy and Climate Change also spent £537 million on "developing an international agreement on climate change" and promoting low carbon technologies in developing countries since 2007-2008. It plans to spend a further £1 billion by 2015.

Last night Conservative MPs said the expenditure had to be closely examined.

Douglas Carswell, MP for Clacton, said: "It is not a priority for us to be spending these large amounts of public money on climate change when there is hardship at home".

But Andrew Mitchell, Secretary of State for International Development, said it was in Britain's best interest to help other countries tackle climate change because it is a global problem.

He said: "Climate change will hit the poorest hardest and leave many more people susceptible to flooding, failing crops and food shortages. We can only help these people if all countries – rich and poor – work together." **”**

6.10. We can't afford cut in pollution – Spelman

John Vidal, Environment editor, *The Guardian*, 28 February, 2012

"The environment secretary, Caroline Spelman, has rejected key sections of a critical report on air pollution by a committee of MPs, arguing the government cannot comply with EU laws and deadlines because it would cost too much.

In a formal response to the environmental audit committee, the Department for Environment, Food and Rural Affairs (Defra) said it did not dispute evidence presented in November that air pollution was the second biggest public health risk in Britain after smoking, and was linked to nearly one in five deaths a year in London.

But for the first time, the government admitted that the costs of meeting EU pollution targets may not match the benefits.

"The government... supports further EU ambitions to reduce health and environmental impacts of air pollution ... However, there was never an intention for any of the [EU] deadlines to force measures that would impose disproportionate costs on society. Deadlines... must reflect both the availability of measures and the affordability of implementation relative to the benefits," Defra told MPs.

Britain has some of the worst air pollution in Europe, mostly from traffic, but has consistently failed to meet targets and timetables to reduce both the quantity of soot in the London air (known as PM10s) and of nitrogen dioxide (NO_2), a gas emitted mainly from burning diesel fuel.

Faced with draconian European fines, it has argued successfully in Europe that it needs more time to meet deadlines. In yesterday's response to the MPs, the government claimed it would meet targets for PM10s this year, but it would not be able to meet NO_2 targets, even by an extended deadline of 2015.

It accepted that the London 2012 Olympics could be hit by air pollution, but said that would be largely beyond its control. "The most likely health risk arising from air pollution during the Olympic Games is from an ozone event... where the combination of air masses from continental Europe and warm weather with prolonged sunshine lead to elevated levels... Scope for local action in these circumstances is extremely limited, as such events are meteorologically driven and need long-term international commitments to reduce emissions of precursor pollutants," it said.

It disagreed strongly with the committee which argued that air pollution costs Britain £10 bn a year with 925,000 people exposed to NO2 exceeding the legal limit.

Friends of the Earth's London campaigner, Jenny Bates, said: "The government is shunning EU deadlines for cleaning up our air. Ministers are putting thousands of lives at risk and hitting the poorest and most vulnerable people the hardest." **"**

6.11. Market forces are the spanners in Whitehall's works

Alasdair Palmer, *The Sunday Telegraph,* **19 February, 2012**

""We are creating a much leaner, more effective Whitehall machine," insisted Francis Maude, the Minister for the Cabinet Office, last week. The Coalition, he says, is going to ensure that the Civil Service "manages its finances like the best-run businesses".

I am all in favour of a leaner Whitehall machine. But who ever wanted the fat monster we have now? No minister set out to create it. If Mr Maude's promises have a familiar ring, it's because just about every politician over the past two decades has promised a "leaner, more effective Whitehall". Not one has achieved it. Instead, the amount paid to civil servants has gone up, and the amount they achieve has gone down.

Mr Maude says he is going to tackle the "shocking £21 million a year the public sector loses to fraud". How about the many billions it loses each year because of incompetent decisions by civil servants?

The roll call of colossally costly bungles is as depressing as it is perversely impressive: the GP's contract that increased average pay by 40 per cent while decreasing the amount of work GPs are required to do; the billions spent on the NHS computer system that doesn't work; the procurement of helicopters that turn out not to be airworthy and cost hundreds of millions to make safe; the £800 million spent on trying to reduce the rate at which students drop out of university, to no effect whatever; the £500 million spent on building eight new call centres for the fire service that will never be used, but will cost several million pounds a month to maintain, empty, for the next 25 years; the £2.2 billion that was paid to the wrong people in the first year tax credits were introduced... and so on and on.

Tony Blair was going to make Whitehall more efficient when he arrived at No 10 in 1997. He was impressed by *Reinventing Government*, an American book that suggested reforming the state by establishing market-type incentives for civil servants: performance-related pay, bonuses, short-term contracts. Civil servants got bonuses all right, but their effectiveness did not increase. They made as many bad decisions as they always had, if not more: the fire service call-centre debacle was arranged by civil servants on performance-related pay.

One of the reasons why nothing has changed is that 'market incentives' for civil servants are a con: market mechanisms do not operate on the state. If someone who runs a company does not provide goods or services at a price that people are willing to pay, or pays himself too much or does not invest enough in increasing productivity, then that firm, if the market works, will go bust and he will be out of a job. The market imposes its punishment mercilessly.

But the state does not operate in the market. Its money comes from taxes, not from consumers exercising choices. There is no punishment for incompetent decision-making, other than the judgment of your peers – and in the Civil Service, they tend to sympathise with how difficult it is to do the job. So what happens when 'performance-related pay'" is introduced? Civil servants just pay themselves more for less effective performance. Officials in the Ministry of Defence, for instance, have given themselves £40 million in bonuses so far in this financial year.

In fact, the only check on the inefficiency and incompetence of civil servants is their own integrity. And here is the central problem with encouraging them to think like businessmen. We expect businessmen to maximise their profits: it is the essence of the market's 'invisible hand' that we're all better off if they do, while the ones who don't provide what the rest of us want go to the wall. But if civil servants think like businessmen, they may simply enrich themselves, with no risk of finding themselves out of a job – which is what has happened since 'market incentives' were introduced into government. If Mr Maude is to have a chance of reducing Whitehall's wasted billions, he will have first to stop officials pretending to be businessmen.**"**

6.12. A better way to hit the rich

Aidan Harrison, Rothbury, Northumberland, in *The Week*, 15 September 2012 p. 29

"To: *The Independent*
Can Vince Cable and Ed Balls possibly explain their obsession with introducing new taxes on the rich before they look at the much simpler option of removing the huge, blatant loopholes in the current system of capital and property taxation which only benefit the enormously wealthy?

Why, for example, do we persist with the bizarre system of bands for council tax under which a £50 m mansion pays only twice as much as the smallest flat? Many developed countries such as Sweden have a straightforward flat-rate annual tax of around 0.7 % on all properties. Inheritance tax is riddled with escape clauses available only to the wealthiest. Why, for example is any middle-class family home worth more than £375,000 liable to inheritance tax at an eye-watering 40 %, while farmland worth up to tens, or even hundreds of millions of pounds, is completely exempt?

Most middle-class old people tend to hang on to their wealth until they die in case they need to pay for care, leaving their family's inheritance liable to the 40% tax. In contrast, the ultra-rich can hand over unlimited millions completely tax-free if it is done seven years before death.

By turning a blind eye to these grossly discriminatory and utterly unjustifiable loopholes for an idle minority, surely all politicians of Left, Centre or Right are making a mockery of their supposed wish to encourage a 21st-century society based on hard work, fairness, social mobility and meritocracy?**"**

6.13. Alcohol: should we put the price up?

The Week, 31 March 2012, p. 20

"It was the sight of ambulances on standby outside nightclubs that made me realise the scale of the problem, said Libby Purves in *The Times*. If "grown-ups can't go out dancing without expecting casualties'" then something is badly amiss. The problem isn't new: for years, this country has failed to get to grips with its culture of heavy drinking. But now alcohol-related hospital admissions "stand at record levels" of more than a million a year, and there are more than 4,000 deaths a year from alcoholic liver disease – the only major cause of death which is still on the rise. And that's before you add in the social mayhem caused by bingeing. So I'm glad the government has at last decided to introduce a minimum price of 40p per unit of alcohol in England. It "shouldn't affect pubs or decent quality drink", but it will make it harder for young people to "pre-load" on cheap supermarket booze so that they're "off their face" before even hitting town.

When we talk about drink in Britain, we're often really talking about class, said Paul Vallely in *The Independent on Sunday*. The minimum price is aimed at the "staggering, vomiting lager-oiks and their teetering, white stilettoed girlfriends": the Chablis-quaffing professionals won't be affected. Yet according to the Office of National Statistics, it's the upper and middle classes who are the heaviest drinkers. So this policy is "as snobbish as it is unfair on the vast majority of poor people who drink sensibly and whose pockets will be hit unnecessarily". Strange how the "moral panic" about drinking has grown more hysterical in recent times, said Dominic Lawson in *The Sunday Times*. In reality, there has been a steady decline (about 20 % in the past five years) in per-capita consumption of alcohol. Even the NHS is guilty of exaggerating the damage: the "doubling" of "alcohol related admissions" reported last year came after it had broadened its definitions to include anything that could conceivably be linked to alcohol.

Even so, drunkenness is now a part of English life, said Philip Hensher in *The*

Independent. Walk out of your door anytime after 11am and within ten minutes – if you live in a town – you'll meet someone who's plastered. Yet the cost of such drunkenness, in terms of lost lives, broken health and billions spent by the NHS, is never factored into the price (under £3) of a three-litre bottle of strong white cider, or the branded lagers sold below cost price as loss leaders. A minimum alcohol price is a useful first step in alerting people to those costs. People should be "free to drink themselves stupid" every night. But they should have to pay real money to exercise that particular choice."

6.14. Who is making the money as private firms move in on the public sector?

Daniel Boffey, Policy Editor, *The Observer*, 26 February, 2012, p. 8–9

"The sudden resignation of Emma Harrison as David Cameron's handpicked "family tsar" has cast a spotlight on the number of lucrative contracts awarded to private firms, by both coalition and Labour governments, to carry out work previously undertaken by the public sector

Fresh to his job as prime minister, with boundless energy and hope, David Cameron told assembled locals at a Relate centre in Leeds that he had made a fantastic new signing to his team trying to improve the lot of families.

"She refuses to believe some people are lost causes and has a proven track record," the prime minister boasted, "which is why I have asked her to come on board to help us." Less stuffy state bureaucracy; more focused, personalised support. "Emma Harrison understands that," Cameron chirped.

Fourteen months on, and things don't look so sunny. Harrison has not only quit as the Cameron's "family tsar", but also as the boss of A4E, the company she formed 25 years ago, following the arrests of four members of its staff on suspicion of fraud.

Harrison says she doesn't want the "media attention" around her to damage her firm's prospects. There is a £15 m contract for the rehabilitation of prisoners to be awarded, for which A4E is still the preferred bidder. The company still has £438 m of contracts under the Work Programme. And along with a money advice service and some apprenticeship work, A4E is still earning about £180m a year by carrying out services on behalf of the state. There is a lot to lose.

But how has A4E, a company with an "abysmal" record, according to parliament's public accounts committee, got so rich?

The clue may lie in its company accounts. "At present, A4E's sectors benefit from a broad cross-party consensus," it says. In other words, ministers, be they Labour or Conservative, have come to believe that private profit-hunting firms do it best – and cheaper.

It was the agenda that Oliver Letwin, the coalitions' policy minister, was getting at last July when he told a thinktank that the public sector had failed to improve its productivity in the past 20 years and that the public sector needed "fear and discipline" instilled into it.

Critics say the same agenda is driving the reforms being pursued by the health secretary, Andrew Lansley which would encourage GPs to look beyond NHS hospitals when they seek a surgeon. From schools to universities, hospitals to prisons, it is the agenda that is increasingly seeking private or independent entities to take over from the state.

Circle Healthcare, run by a former Goldman Sachs executive, is already managing one NHS hospital that had amassed unwieldy debts. The *Observer* has learnt that Circle is seeking control of another three hospitals by 2014, according to a trading update delivered to the stock market last week.

In higher education, Montague Private Equity is in talks to take over the formerly charitable College of Law in London, as the latest figures from the Department for Business, Innovation and Skills reveal that the amount of money given to private institutions by the state in the years from £15m to £33m. The Ministry of Justice last week announced the tender of contracts worth up to £3bn for electronic tagging of prisoners.

These sums seem huge, but the political consensus that Harrison cites in her company accounts says it would cost more if the state carried out these services. The consensus has treated big private outfits such as A4E well. Smaller independent firms and charities argue that it has treated them too well, and at their expense. At a recent meeting with the employment minister, Chris Grayling, the third-sector outfits, particularly those which had worked with the long term unemployed, complained that big private firms were taking all the business and muscling them out of any pay days. Those who attended the meeting did not leave with the impression that the government was going to act.

John Pugh, a Liberal Democrat MP, said he feared for the public sector and wants Harrison's so- called consensus to be debated in the open. "A clear consistent ideology, not pragmatism, is driving this. Under vague slogans like 'diversity and choice' or 'opening up public services', you can engineer a situation where direct public sector provision in effect disappears as public bodies and private firms become utterly indistinguishable."

Welfare
Current value to the private sector: Around £5 bn over the next seven years
Big earner: Therese Rei, managing director of Ingeus, whose company paid £3.8 m in dividends last year – Rein holds around 97% of its shares

Schools
Current value to the private sector: Around £7.2 bn
Big earner: Majorie Scardino, chief executive of Pearson, had a base salary of £60,000 in 2010 and took home a bonus of £1.6 m

Health
Current value to the private sector: Around £24.2 bn
Big earner: John Griffith-Jones, co-chairman of KPMG, paid £2.62 m

Prisons
Current value to the private sector: Around £4 bn
Big earner: Nick Buckles, chief executive of G4S, earned £1.42 m, comprising his base salary, benefits and a performance-related bonus

Higher Education
Current value to the private sector: Around £33 m
Big earner: Carl Lygo, chief executive BPP, was paid £435,000 in 2010"

Figures are for 2010

6.15. Sheila Dillon interviewed Fuchsia Dunlop from Shanghai, author of *Shark's Fin and Sichuan Pepper, a sweet-sour memoir of eating in China,* published 2011

Transcript from BBC Radio 4's *Food Programme*, broadcast Sunday, 4 March 2012

"Q: The way we eat at least in the West has changed more in the last 60 years than in the couple of thousand that went before. And most of us have taken to our mass produced and globalized eating habits with relish, despite the evidence that it is not good for us or the rest of nature. But at a different stage of this fast moving drama is the most populous nation on Earth, China...

A: I first went to live in China in 1994 in the capital of the Sichuan province Chegdu. At that time there really weren't supermarkets in this big city. People did not have big fridges in their houses. Every neighbourhood would have a little fresh produce market where farmer came to sell two or three kinds of vegetables. So most people did their shopping on a daily basis, coming back with fresh live fish, fresh meat and vegetables, and cooking at home. And there were lots of small restaurants, serving freshly made food. Everything used just a few basic seasonings like soya sauce, sugar and sesame oil and chillies and pepper and everything else was really fresh.

So one of the things that struck me at that time was, how very very well people ate. When I first lived in Chengdu that was just before any Western fast food joints were in town and over a few years I was spending a lot of time there, having seen a lot of McDonald schemes and a lot of supermarket branches across the city. There wasn't at that time I think one Chinese chain which offered similar sorts of food, and they have grown and grown. The sad thing is that the Chinese children, middle class children, who can afford to eat in these places are becoming a kind of hooked on them. There was this kind of attitude that it was right and convenient and also a bit kind of chic, I suppose.

Q: When you first arrived in China in the mid-90s, it was a healthy country. It was being studied for its health programmes. Low level of heart disease cancer etc. Now we are told that that is changing. Is it a change that you were aware of when you were there?

A: Well, very much aware of the rising of obesity, although you know, Chinese people in general are much slenderer than people in Europe or America. And that is one thing you immediately notice. There are more and more children who are quite clearly overweight and adults. And people I have known for years they used to be very healthy eating and there are now a bit overweight, eating too many pastries and eating out in too many restaurants.

And you only use to look at many statistics, like breast cancer and diabetes and obesity, you know, and fatty liver disease, to see it is not just an impression, it is a serious change and it is getting worse very year.

Q: So when did you first notice this change? If people started mentioning that word healthy, talking about nutrients?

A: Talking about healthy eating is a very ancient art of Chinese culture, but talking about scientific nutrients, I think has come in when China started opening up in the 90s, why people become more aware of the foreign discussions about food. Because I remember having a conversation with a lot of chefs and food editors of magazines and people in the late 90s. And they would be saying to me Sichuan food is a bit too oily or Chinese food is a bit too oily.

But talking about Western nutrients was very scientific. It was something they should be learning from. So perhaps we can learn from the Japanese on the presentation and the aesthetics of food and from the West on nutrients.

I used to say to them: Are you crazy? You get all the problems of the West, you know, and we may be told more scientifically about nutrients, but we have these problems with obesity and people not to know what to cook and what to eat.

And I would say to them: You have this amazing food culture and everyone really seems to understand how to use food and to nurture the mind and body, and how to live really well. So I found it very strange that people do not take more pride in their own food culture which has so much to offer, not just in terms of flavour and the pleasure of foods but also in living well and in good health and balanced.

Q: And if you do want to cook now, if you go out buying ingredients have those ingredients changed? Is it harder to get the traditional things in the cities?

A: Well, a lot of processed products have, a sort of shortcut food, have been available, that weren't before, international brands, Hong Kong brands, bottled sauces are used by every restaurant kitchen, and more affluent people shop in supermarkets, where there is more ready prepared food, and the street markets that used to be, have disappeared. So it is becoming a bit more difficult to find those really fresh and raw ingredients.

Q: What do you really think, watching China go through that process?

A: It is really painful to see so much potential being lost so quickly. And with so many aspects of Chinese society one wishes that people here would actually look what happened in the West and learn some lessons from it, not wanting to go along the same path. But sadly it seems the same as we have with the problem of traffic and cars and pollution, it seems as an inevitable stage they are going through. So one hopes they are looking for more healthy solutions. **"**

6.16. A tax on your conservatory will be just the beginning

- **Curbing our reckless guzzling of natural resources may not win votes, but politicians can't be coy about it -**

Gaby Hinsliff, *The Guardian*, 11 April 2012, p. 29

"There are few more risky places to stand in modern politics, so legend has it, than between a suburban voter and a longed-for-conservatory. The dream of an extra room that's too hot in summer and too cold in winter supposedly runs so deep in middle England's psyche that the shadow cabinet minister Douglas Alexander once said Labour should only be led by someone who understands it. What, then, to make of the fact that the coalition proposes making them more expensive?

Short of a windfall tax on golf clubs, there seems no quicker way to inflame suburban wrath than making people fit compulsory energy-saving measures as the price of being allowed a conservatory – unless it's enforcing a hosepipe ban that makes it harder to wash the car at weekends. (Not for nothing did Tony Blair say he knew the 1992 election was lost when he "met a man polishing his Sierra" in the suburbs, who no longer voted Labour: the emotional tie between man and shiny paintwork defies rational analysis.)

But unfortunately for the coalition and its successors, this is only the start of a very awkward conversation.

Politicians of all parties fall over themselves now to swear there's no money left in the kitty, yet remain oddly coy about suggesting that within a generation there may not be enough water left either – or enough affordable oil, or cheap food – to maintain the cheerily wasteful lives that many of us take for granted.

Our dank and soggy nation is slowly drying out, with half of England and Wales deemed 'water-stressed'. Oil isn't running out as fast as once feared, as new fields beneath the melting Arctic ice or buried in Texan shale are exploited – but they're harder and riskier to drill, pushing up the price per barrel. Demand for meat is soaring as emerging nations get a taste for protein-heavy westernised diets.

Yet it may take the environmental equivalent of a run on the banks – some short, sharp, urgent shock – before British politicians start discussing that other kind of austerity, one involving cuts not to spending but to the reckless guzzling of natural resources.

The reason the coalitions' husky-hugging tendency has been in retreat is that the hair-shirt-stuff – drive and fly less, eat fewer burgers, shower faster – is traditionally a vote-loser. But so, until recently, was the case for spending less. What would it take for the stigma now attached to rampant consumerism and cheap credit to spread to conspicuous overconsumption of petrol or water?

The mysterious affair of Richard Benyon's hosepipe suggests one answer. When photographs surfaced in *The People* of a gushing tap in the grounds of the environment minister's country pile, he furiously insisted the hose must have been turned on deliberately by reporters: the paper, meanwhile, insists its team merely popped round for a chat and spotted it. (Ironically, it turns out the Benyons aren't even subject to the hosepipe ban, having their own private borehole. As one does.)

But whatever the truth, it's now clearly risky for anyone in public life to possess a suspiciously green lawn while their constituents – or customers in the case of the Southern Water chairman Colin Hodd, attacked by another tabloid for having a river running conveniently through his own garden – face scorched earth. In times of plenty, we're relatively relaxed about what others have or do: but lean times change everything, as any beleaguered banker could confirm.

Water envy hasn't quite taken up where bonus envy left off, of course. But the prospect of drought across much of southern England, together with lingering threats of a fuel strike (or of a painful oil price spike driven by tensions in the Middle East), does expose our resource-hungry lifestyle for the precarious thing it is. And that may just change the terms of debate.

When panic buyers recently sucked garages dry, much was made of the flaws exposed in a 'just in time' delivery system for petrol: but the deeper message was what it said about our dependence on the car. Warning signs should flash when people would rather fill jam jars with lethally flammable petrol than be without wheels even for a day – or indeed would risk a £1,000 fine, as some undoubtedly will, just to stick the sprinklers on.

Nothing will change overnight, despite the 'Proud to be Dirty' car bumper stickers optimistically issued by Thames Water, encouraging customers to leave their Sierras unpolished for the nation. But painstakingly purifying water, via more than half a dozen complex and expensive processes, just to slosh it over your hatchback or pour it into the lawn from whence it came? For the first time last weekend, I wondered.

There's always a reason to do nothing in politics. It's always possible that rain will suddenly fall in biblical proportions, kicking all this into the long (and suddenly lush) grass. Or perhaps the climate-change deniers will, against all the odds, somehow be proved right. More plausibly, maybe human ingenuity will triumph, and we'll learn to make synthetic oil from algae or distil seawater cheaply – or grow meat in test tubes, sidestepping the planet's inability to support enough grazing animals to satisfy future demand. Nature tends to exact revenge for such wheezes, of course, but perhaps we're clever enough to override all that.

But if not, then a hard conversation looms about the viability of everyday habits to which we feel blithely entitled. Just as we have with public spending, we'll have to debate where scarcer natural resources should be targeted and why: who deserves extra protection, which lifestyle choices it is reasonable to support.

We'll have to examine things politicians prefer to shove under the carpet from compulsory water metering and road pricing to the idea floated at different times by both Miliband brothers (but never adopted) of carbon rationing, under which everyone gets a basic annual allowance for everything from driving to heating to long-haul flights, and those wishing to exceed their carbon ration would pay through the nose to do so.

So while there is indeed nothing wrong with wanting a conservatory, there is something not quite right about assuming life can go on just as it always has. Stand by your wicker furniture: this is only the beginning.**"**

6.17. Outsource to easyCouncil? Not in our name

John Harris, Barnet, in: *The Guardian,* **12 November 2012, p. 34**

"I once sat in a radio studio and watched, with some horror, as a well-known current affairs presenter fielded a call about the last government's reckless use of the private finance initiative. The person at the other end of the line sounded very well-informed, but he was cut off within five seconds. "Sorry, you're sending me to sleep," says the host, and that was that. The implication was clear: this stuff was the preserve of anoraks, and best left that way.

The same applied to privatisation writ large, and an agenda so mired in acronyms and general tedium that, circa 2006–7, it almost disappeared from debate. But now, with G4S having so bungled their Olympics contract and the cutting edge of outsourcing reaching the police, this most crucial of issues is back. Moreover, in one corner of London, there is a full-scale citizens' revolt against a huge switch from public to private that defies rational belief.

In 2009, the local Tory council expressed its enthusiasm for a notion known as "easyCouncil", which referred to a simple if hair-raising principle: that in straitened times, local authorities should be like budget airlines, offering a basic set of services, and charging for optional extras. Now, the big deal is officially called "One Barnet". This denotes 70% of the council's functions – first supposed 'back office' services, and the such core functions as environmental health, planning, transport, even crematoriums – being handed to the private sector, on the basis of two 10-year contracts, together worth over £1 bn.

Similar plans have been floated in Suffolk, only to be halted by Tory dissent.

In Cornwall, last month saw the ousting of the county council's Conservative leadership, and the suspension of a £800 m privatisation programme. But in Barnet, the first contract will be signed on 6 December, with a second to follow in the New Year (the frontrunners are BT, Capita and EC Harris, a self-styled "global built asset consultancy").

Those in charge claim that in the face of swingeing cuts from Whitehall, the scheme will eventually lead to savings of £111 m over the contracts' duration; the project's opponents reckon such figures have been pulled from the sky.

Piloting such a radical plan takes a certain kind of pioneering zeal, and the ability to keep your head while all about are losing theirs.

The council's chief executive quit in early October and a high-profile local Tory named Brian Coleman turned on the plans two weeks ago, claiming that "the concept of One Barnet is fundamentally un-Conservative and ignores localism. It is totally New Labour, in fact." Recently, there was an unexpected decision to keep waste services in-house. But on the really big stuff, the ruling Tory-group – led by Richard Cornelius, who survived a vote of confidence last week – are holding their nerve. Last Thursday, I spent the evening at a community centre in North Finchley, watching a 150-strong crowd make impassioned arguments against all this, to a panel that included Cornelius. The event had been organised by an umbrella group called the Barnet Alliance for Public Services, and the questions came thick and fast.

Why 10-year contracts? To make it worth the companies' while, said Cornelius. What would happen if either of the successful bidders hit the buffers? No need to worry: they had been "checked" for all such eventualities. Shouldn't the public have been consulted before such a drastic change? 2010's election was effectively a consultation, he said, rather passing over the fact that the Tories never mentioned anything remotely resembling One Barnet in the course of the campaign. Why had no financial case for keeping services in-house been worked out, at least as a comparator? There was no answer.

The Barnet rebellion's tribunes are five forensic, workaholic bloggers who go by the name of Citizen Barnet, Barnet Eye, Mr Mustard, Mrs Angry (aka Broken Barnet) and Mr. Reasonable.

The de facto HQ of the revolt is Friern Barnet public library, squatted since September and turned into a 'people's library', in opposition to the council's plan to close it, and sell the land to a property developer. And the local upsurge includes many people beyond the usual suspects – not least, irate ex-Tory voters, who cannot quite believe their council is doing something so mind-boggling.

Barnet already has a questionable record on outsourced contracts, and the downgrading of services. The great British headache that is parking is a good example: in such areas as North Finchley, where coin-in-the-slot machines have all been removed, the service has been handed to a company called NSL, and signs advise you to pay using your mobile phone (I tried this, and having encountered inexplicable difficulties, was put on hold for 40 minutes, before giving up; local traders say business has dropped by 40%).

There is also plenty of noise about even more vital services that have been fragmented and refashioned out of all recognition: day care for adults with disabilities, for instance, is now handled by a 'local authority trading company', and has been taken out of purpose-built centres into local church halls.

What's happening in Barnet goes back to the absolute fundamentals. This is a local story with terrifying national significance. People here are fighting for their most basic of rights. Once One Barnet is rolled out, so called commercial confidentiality will smother service delivery, and contracts will have to remain in place for a decade, irrespective of which party wins elections. Put simply, democracy is close to being snuffed out.**"**

6.18. Tackling the energy 'trilemma'

Damian Carrington, *The Guardian*, 24 November 2012, p. 9

"There is a simple way to think about the complex energy policy decisions made this week: it is a £200 bn bet on the UK's energy future. What's more, the money on the table belongs to you. Win or lose, every electricity and gas customer will pick up the tab for this wager for decades to come.

In such a high-rolling game, you would have hoped for cool heads. Instead, 'unholy war' was waged behind the scenes at Westminster, a senior participant told me. Worse, the boiling row within the coalition was driven as much by ideology and party politics as cold, hard facts. In fact, the opposing sides had 'different facts', the source said.

All sides agreed on one thing. The problem the much-delayed energy bill seeks to solve is a fiendish one. It requires predicting the future and is not so much a dilemma as a trilemma. The solution must keep the lights on while preventing energy bill payers from being fleeced and tackling climate change. Furthermore, we are not starting from a strong position. Two decades of under-investment in our energy infrastructure has left a dirty and decaying system.

Action was unavoidable, meaning the question was not will energy bills go up, but by how much? The more adventurous punters may be happy that George Osborne refused to curb his new dash for gas, spiced as that prospect is by the possibility of a shale gas revolution in the UK. Gas prices will plummet, say fracking supporters, so why waste so much money on renewable energy? Never mind that relying on gas puts the nation on the rollercoaster ride of fossil fuel geopolitics. The fact, for example, that half of the UK's gas imports come through the strait of Hormuz, which Iran has threatened to close, just adds to the excitement.

With risky bets, of course, the odds are long. No one outside the fracking industry thinks shale gas is a silver bullet for the UK's trilemma. Nor is anyone placing serious money on European gas prices declining, not least because demand is rising so fast elsewhere.

The alternative wager, backed by the Liberal Democrats, was a more diverse flutter – a bit of gas, renewable energy and nuclear. But energy secretary Ed Davey was out-muscled by Osborne and only a bit of the nation's stake money is backing this bet. This means that, despite the green sector being one of the few growing parts of the UK's torpid economy, those jobs are now more likely to go abroad.

Where does this leave us? Given that keeping the lights on is non-negotiable and that cutting carbon emissions is a legal requirement, the critical factor is cost. At this point, the complexity of the energy bill starts to make the financial engineering that crashed the economy look like primary school arithmetic. In the arcane algebra of contracts-for-difference, capacity mechanisms and carbon floor prices, there are plenty of hiding places for jackpot wins for energy companies at their customers' expense.

Ministers are in effect negotiating with one company for the nuclear power it believes will soon be needed. This is hardly likely to deliver a bargain for bill-payers. Those building new gas plants are demanding payments too, in case carbon targets mean the plants can only run part-time. Of course, renewable providers are also arguing hard for their subsidies. But they have a trump card: while the cost of gas and nuclear power is rising, the cost of green energy and its subsidies is already falling.

The greatest failing of the new energy policy is the woeful underplaying of the cheapest option of all: energy efficiency. Almost all the incentives are aimed at producing more power, none at reducing demand. Why is the UK planning for an increase in electricity demand of up to two-thirds in 2050, when Europe's manufacturing powerhouse, Germany, is planning for a 25% cut?

As a nation we have now pretty much paid our money and taken our choice. The coalition has staked a good bit of our money on Osborne's bet that international gas prices won't spike and that the UK's shale gas hype bubble won't burst, meaning relatively cheap, clean wind power can be passed up without consequence. We still have a bit of the plan that emphasises exploiting the renewable resources on our doorstep, creating a secure and sustainable energy system.

But overall, in the great energy gamble, we've chosen a long odds bet rather than to back the favourite and we will pay the price."

6.19. How to escape the zombies

Tim Bennett, *Money Week*, 23 November 2012, p. 12

"Anyone who thinks tax is irrelevant to the way you invest should watch out for a huge loophole – companies' ability to claim tax relief on the interest they pay on their borrowings. This bizarre anomaly (dividends paid to shareholders are not tax deductible in the same way) has created what *The Evening Standard*'s Anthony Hilton, among many others, calls "zombie firms". These are bloated with borrowing, "permanently weakening the business and making it more vulnerable to shocks". How do firms get into such a dire position and how can you avoid them?

The joy of tax relief
Companies like debt for a very good reason: because of the tax relief available, taking on debt turbocharges returns for shareholders. Take two firms, which each make £40 m in sales, incur £20 m in costs and so have profits before interest and tax of £20 m. Let's say company A is 100% funded by its shareholders, to the tune of £100 m. Company B is 50% funded by shareholder equity, and 50% with debt of £50 m. The debt carries an interest rate of 10%. As a result, the profit after interest costs for company A is £20 m, while profit after interest for company B is £15 m (£20 m profit minus £5 m interest).

Now comes the tax dodge, Say both firms pay corporation tax at a rate of 25%. Company A suffers a tax charge on its profits of £5 m (£20 m x 0.25). So its profits after interest and tax are £15 m (£20 m – £5 m). Company B gets to offset £5 m of interest before being hit for tax. This means its corporation tax charge is based on profits of £15 m, so its tax charge is £3.75 m (£15 m x 0.25) and its profits after interest and tax £11.25 m (£15 m – £3.75 m). Here's the point – what is the return on equity for each? ... For the 100% equity funded firm it's a respectable 15% (£15 m/£100 m). But for the debt funded firm it's 22.5% (£11.25 m/£50 m). Yet both firms made the same profit and started out the same size and even do the same thing!

As Allister Heath notes in *The Daily Telegraph*, "firms with lots of debt pay less corporation tax than those with none, even if the companies are identical in every other way". This is madness: it encourages the likes of private-equity firms to load up companies with lots of debt in a rising market, squeeze out dividends while they can, and leave a debt-laden husk at the end of it.

Hilton would like to see one immediate change to the system: abolish corporation tax relief on debt. As he says, "equity investment would get a boost, which would make British business more soundly based and better focused."

How to avoid buying a zombie

Sadly, this kind of reform isn't about to happen overnight – there are too many vested interests benefiting from the status quo. So in the meantime, the fastest way to spot a debt-bloated zombie is by looking at the gearing ratio and interest cover.

Gearing is the relationship between debt and equity funding as a percentage. So using my two firms, company A had gearing of 0%, while company B had gearing of 50%. You might like a bit of gearing during a rising market, as it boosts returns, but in today's volatile markets, low gearing is generally a good sign.

Also check interest cover – a company's ability to pay interest out of profits. In my example, company A has no problems as there was no interest bill to cover. Company B had profits before interest of £20 m and a £5 m interest bill. So cover is £20 m/£5 m, or four times. The absolute minimum I would accept in today's climate is two to three times. Anything less and you could end up with a zombie."

6.20. Starbucks: time for a consumer boycott

'Talking points' in: *The Week* **24 November 2012**

"Poor Starbucks. It has tried so hard, said Christina Patterson in *The Independent*: it has opened more than 700 cafes in the UK, mostly in places where there already were cafes; it has persuaded millions of us that coffee is best drunk in bucket-sized cups, with lashings of milk or even shots of syrup, to disguise the coffee taste; and it has kept costs down by paying its staff the minimum wage. Yet last year it failed to make a profit, even on a turnover of £398 m. In fact, in 14 of the 15 years it has been trading in the UK, Starbucks has made a loss on an accumulated turnover of £3 bn. Summoned by the Public Accounts Committee last week to explain why the firm makes no money, and has paid no corporation tax last year, Starbucks' chief financial officer could only shrug his shoulders and tell incredulous MPs: "It's a failing."

But of course, it's not a failing at all, said Alice Thomson in *The Times* – it's a desired outcome. Starbucks, like many multinationals, uses complex (legal) structures to channel revenue to countries with low taxes. For instance, it pays a royalty for the use of its logo in the UK to another Starbucks firm in the

Netherlands. For similar reasons, Google's advertising space is run by a team in low-tax Ireland. Amazon, which has 15,000 staff in the UK, generated sales of more than £3 bn here last year, but the money went to a firm in Luxembourg, which has 500 employees. (The UK firm is just a service company.) The result is that, like Apple and Facebook, these behemoths pay little or no tax on revenues generated in the UK, while taking advantage of tax-funded benefits such as good roads and a healthy workforce. So much, you might say, for their 'Don't Be Evil' mission statements and cosy talk of community responsibility. But you can't blame the money men: their duty is to their shareholders. So the pressure must come from us. The 'little people' who pay their taxes must boycott the giants who do not. Only then will they have a compelling reason to mend their ways, and pay their share.

Yet this time, it's not only grass-roots protesters who are up in arms, said Will Hutton in *The Observer*. Finally, businesses are breaking ranks to warn that 'bad' capitalism poses a very real threat to our economy. As John Lewis's managing director Andy Street warned last week, tax-dodging multinationals can out-invest rivals paying full UK tax, threatening their ability to grow and survive. The UK corporate tax base is being further undermined by the rise of private equity – Boots, for instance, is now based in Switzerland. It's time for the state to take a real interest in who owns our companies, and how they organise their operations.**"**

6.21. America's dirtiest war

The film *Breaking the Taboo* and the campaign to legalise drugs

by permission of Lars Jensen, published in: *Frankfurter Allgemeine Sonntagszeitung*, 9 December 2012, p. 26, translated by the author

"There is bad news for the bosses of Latin American drug cartels, for the Taliban in their poppy fields and for the African dictators, who finance their power with drug money. The news comes from Colorado and Washington (the state, not the town), where this week law makers legalised the possession of marijuana. It comes from Portugal and the Czech republic, where the decriminalization of hard drugs is showing amazing results. From Baltimore where new police tactics revolutionising the control of drug dealers and from Cartagena, where American states governers first declared that war on drugs was lost and demanded the end of prohibition.

Now Kate Winslet is also intervening. On Friday the film *Breaking the Taboo* opens in the United States, as part of a campaign of the same name, in which Hollywood stars, rappers, athletes, scientists and the ex-presidents Clinton and Carter are taking part. The aim: to enlighten the Americans about the role of their nation in a war raging in more countries than were involved in the Second World War. The United States are the biggest serious importer of hard drugs, and it was President Nixon, who declared "total war against public enemy number one' in 1971. Against whom the war was declared was never clear, because drugs cannot be shot. Yet the American army is fighting in at least thirty sovereign states; in the forests of Belize or Honduras American drones are flying and American missiles are exploding.

At home, the front-line is situated in the quarters of the urban poor, the police arrest 1.5 million people per year, and the courts sentence draconically for the smallest offences. This enables prison corporations such as the "Corrections Corporation of America' to pay extravagant dividends because they not only get 50,000 $ per prisoner per year from the state, but can also exploit prisoners as if they were serfs. The human rights activist Michelle Alexander calls this situation "nothing but a modern slave trade'. At present 7.2 million people – more than 3% of the adult population – under "correcting observation' as it is called, are in prison or outside under probation. These people happen to be overwhelmingly black and poor, and are not allowed to vote or to rent public accommodation. Without accommodation they cannot get a job. What is the solution? Right, they sell drugs on the next street corner. The government pays 40 billion $ a year for this. While the price for a gramme of cocaine adjusting for inflation sank from 669 $ to 177 $ since 1981.

The ignorance of people concerning the drug war is unlimited. Because other American wars seem to be more important. And because most victims of that war belong to the lower social groups, whose fate rarely interest the media.

But a few months ago the discussion spread from the professional magazines of criminologists and sociologists into the mass media. In October Eugene Jareckis' excellent film documentation *The House I Live In* described how the war on drugs was a concept against the poor from the beginning. A judge reported in tears how he had to send hundreds of young black men to prison for 15 years and more for possessing only a few grammes of crack. A prison warden explains the business model of his sector: corporations such as CCA offer a structurally weak community hundreds of new jobs in a new prison: "If you build the prison we certainly will fill it.' In the meantime most of the federal states invest more money in prisons than in universities.

The House I Live In inspired a debate which even spread to entertainment magazines such as the *New Yorker Magazine* whose front page two weeks ago read: "The end of prohibition – the orderly retreat from the worldwide war on drugs". The article proclaimed what science has demanded for years: the ordered decriminalization and taxation of drugs, combined with an area wide offer of therapy instead of punishment. This would cancel the business model of the cartels, offer addicts a more dignified life and thirdly minimize supply criminality.

Hallucinogenic drugs will never disappear, they have existed from the beginning of civilisation. But America could lessen the by-products for society and help neighbouring countries to end the orgies of violence – if it only had the will.

Guatemala's president Otto Perez Molinz had started the discussion at the American congress in Cartagena: "We have to give up all the ideological positions such as prohibition. We need a more realistic policy, we need a regulation of the drug industry." When someone like Perez says this, American politicians should sit up and take notice. In the 80s Perez had led the war on drugs in his country as a general under the command of the Americans. His scorched earth tactics financed by the United States and supported by American soldiers, culminated in military offences in the Ixil-triangle at the end of 1982. 2,744 people died who were suspected of being involved in drug dealings.

Thirty bloody years later Guatemala is nearly collapsing: drug money controls all institutions of society, cartels dominate two thirds of the country, and the murder rate in Guatemala City is only higher in Tegucigalpa, capital of Honduras. There has been much reporting of the 60,000 dead people who are mourned in Mexico in the drug war since 2000. Less is known about the fact that Mexican cartels are pushing to the south and that the murder rate in countries such as Guatemala has been driven to tenfold that of Mexico. When in spring eighty women and children were cut to pieces by machetes Perez had evidently had enough. The hard liner gave up his pro-American position. "It cannot go on like this any more", he said on Fox News – of all places: "We cannot fight violence with more violence. We have to throttle the demand for drugs from America". Referring to a study by the 'Global Commission on Drug Policy' he said: "Whenever police and the military destroy a cartel it is replaced by another; if they destroy a coca plantation the price for coca rises for a short time so that even more farmers start planting coca."

President Obama reacted with a wonderful speech that brought tears to people's eyes. A few days later he expanded the war on drugs. He not only sent 200 elite soldiers to Guatemala, but troops and drones to Ghana, Nigeria, Kenya. At home he continued the policy of his predecessors: his government pushed much harder against the producers of medical marihuana than the Bush regime.

Those who have been following the war on drugs for a little bit longer will wonder why Bill Clinton supports *Breaking the Taboo*. In his time 'Plan Columbia' constituted a crime against international law. In the name of the war on drugs, thousands of American soldiers helped to spray large parts of the country with Agent Orange with devastating consequences for men and nature. Later on it was discovered that the Americans had sprayed mostly regions into which left wing guerillas had retreated. Drug plantations of America friendly paramilitaries were spared.

'Plan Columbia' was a business programme favourable to multinational corporations: Monsanto delivered the spray, Sikorsky the helicopters, Blackwater the soldiers. Protected by troops of the Pastrana-government Occidental Petroleum increased its oil exports from Columbia tenfold – in return America increased military help for Pastrana tenfold. He then sent death squads to the insubordinate inhabitants of the country. 'Plan Columbia' was registered with the Drug Enforcement Administration (DEA) as an anti-drug campaign.

More than ten thousand employees work in 64 countries for the DEA, and rarely are their motives and actions transparent. The end result after 39 years: drugs are as cheap as they have ever been, producers are powerful enough to control governments; and banks feed half a billion narco dollars into the international banking system each year. If there is no change Ronald Reagan's forecast will come true: 'This war will go on for hundred years. Or even longer.'

One region which gives some grounds for hope is Baltimore whose desperate drug scene inspired the serial *The Wire* and where the police in 2005 arrested 108,000 out of 660,000 inhabitants. A commander named Frederick Bealefeld observed the prisons overflowing but the situation in the streets worsened with more than 300 murders occurring annually. Bealefeld changed tactics: He no longer arrested small criminals but concentrated on violent criminals known to the police. Street dealers he left undisturbed. He also convinced the town in 2007 to offer therapy at focal points. In 2011 there were 106 murders, and the police arrested only 65,000 civilians.

According to Professor Peter Reuter from the University of Maryland the number of addicted went down continually with the start of Bealefeld's revolution. "Old drugs addicts are dying", Reuter says, "'and fewer young people are becoming addicts because they are no longer trapped in the vicious circle of criminality." For those who make their money through drugs and the war on drugs this is not good news.**"**

6.22. Expensive helplines

Letter from John Healey, Labour MP, London, to *The Independent,* **cited in** *The Week,* **29 December 2012, p. 18**

"Your front-page report 'The great HMRC telephone rip-off' was right to point out the high cost to HMRC customers of premium rate 0845 numbers. But this practice goes on throughout government. My research has shown that 148 of the Department for Work and Pensions' helplines – or 87% – are 0845.

The most vulnerable, poor and distressed people have to call these numbers to claim change or enquire about sickness and disability benefits, carers' support, jobs, pensions, child support and even crisis loans. Well over 30 million people call just seven of the DWP's most-used helplines each year, but many give up on getting through after being kept on hold and charged. In one example, more than one in three calls to the employment and support allowance helpline are abandoned before they are answered, but on average over five minutes after they have been connected.

Callers to the incapacity benefit reassessment line wait nearly 13 minutes without being answered before they hang up. That means some people who can ill afford it are being charged more than £5 without even getting through.

The DWP and HMRC tell us they don't profit from having 0845 numbers, but someone is making money from these calls. If it's the Government, it's immoral. If it's only the telephone company, it's a very bad deal for taxpayers. Calls to such public service lines should be free.**"**

6.23. The Republicans need a dose of Lincoln's human factor

The party's swing even further to the right has prevented compromise in American politics

> Rupert Cornwell, 'Out of America', in: *The Independent on Sunday*, 30 December 2012, p. 28

"Yes, it's fiscal cliff countdown time. Will the Republican-controlled House of Representatives and the White House strike a deal to avert the looming tax increases and budget cuts before tomorrow's deadline? Or is tomorrow really the deadline? And, despite the doom-mongering, does it really matter? Some eminent economists now argue it would be better if we do go over the cliff.

But the cliff-talk obscures the real story: how this impasse has been reached because the Republican Party, prisoner of its extreme conservative wing, for whom tax cutting is all, has simply gone off the rails. If you don't believe me, then consider Norman Ornstein and Thomas Mann, of the conservative American Enterprise Institute and the liberal-centrist Brookings Institution respectively, both of them dispassionate, experienced observers of the US political scene, about as unpartisan as you can get.

Yet, in their book earlier this year on the dysfunctional system that has spawned the fiscal cliff debacle, entitled *It's Even Worse than It Looks*, Mann and Ornstein let slip any pretence of even-handedness. "One of our two major parties, the Republicans," they write in exasperation, "has become an insurgent outlier – ideologically extreme, contemptuous of the inherited social and economic policy regime, scornful of compromise, unpersuaded by conventional understanding of facts, evidence and science, and dismissive of the legitimacy of its political opposition."

The Republicans, in short, have lurched so far to the right that politics in the normal sense of give and take, of taking other points of view into consideration, has become virtually impossible. Yes, Democrats must bear some of the blame for the stalemate, but only a small part. Their move to the left is far less than the Republican shift rightward.

Ronald Reagan is the saint to whom modern conservatives mouth ritual devotion. But Reagan, always, ready to make a deal when he had to, would be lost amid today's Republican zealotry, where moderates have been systematically expelled and ideology is now all. But it was not always thus – as a couple of things reminded me last week.

The first was the turn for the worse in the health of George H W Bush, Reagan's Republican successor in the White House. Bush is now 88 and in intensive care, being treated for bronchitis. Happily, the last news was more encouraging: "Put the harps back in the closet," was his mood, according to a spokesman.

Bush is America's oldest living former president. More to the point, he's the sort of Republican you don't find any more, a patrician moderate and East Coast establishment gentleman who might have been a bit out of touch on occasion, but whose heart was in the right place. Yet the elder Bush is anathema to great swathes of his party.

His sin was to have abandoned his celebrated 1988 campaign pledge of "Read my lips, no new taxes", when economic facts of life obliged him to strike a deficit reduction deal, two years later, with the Democrats who then controlled Congress. The deal helped to pave the way for the boom later in the decade, but it is an article of faith for modern Republicans that the broken pledge was responsible for his 1992 election defeat. Never again, they said – and so it has been.

The other reminder came from a Republican of the 19th century, whose occupancy of the White House prevented the country from sliding off an existential cliff, in comparison with which the 2012 fiscal variety is the gentlest incline.

Steven Spielberg's *Lincoln* is being released in the UK on 25 January, and don't miss it. Not only does Daniel Day-Lewis deliver an unforgettable portrayal of America's greatest president, as he seeks passage of the 13th amendment, banning slavery, through the House of Representatives in the final months of the civil war (and his own life). It is also perhaps the most realistic cinematic depiction ever of how the US political system, with its separation of powers, works.

Lincoln knows his opponents' foibles. He wheedles, flatters and cajoles; he appeals to their best instincts and, when necessary, their worst. On occasion, he stretches the truth almost to breaking point. And, in the end, he rounds up the votes required, without betraying his principles.

The message of the movie is not so much that compromise is essential in politics (although it is). Rather, it is that politics is ultimately about people and how humans interact with one another. Obviously, there is a lesson for President Obama as he seeks a way down from the cliff-edge. Wheedling and flattering is not his style; all too often, he seems contemptuous of the human spadework at which Lyndon Johnson excelled.

But the greater lesson, laying bare the terrible flaw of US politics as currently practised, is that this human factor has vanished from the Republican Party. When only ideological purity matters, everything else is pointless. Even LBJ wouldn't have had a prayer with the Tea Party.

Worst of all, the mess is of the Republicans' own making. They hold a 233-200 majority in the House, even though they lost the popular vote in congressional elections by over half a million. Americans, in other words, didn't vote for a Republican House in 2012. They got one however, thanks to the gerrymandering of Republican-controlled state legislatures.

But gerrymandering also makes seats vulnerable in primaries to intra-party challengers claiming greater ideological purity. Thus moderates are driven out and extremists take over. Now, however, the revolution is devouring its own. Before Christmas, the House Speaker, John Boehner, was humiliatingly forced to withdraw fiscal cliff legislation, as dozens of Republican members, arch-purists all, rebelled. A party that loses control of itself is surely doomed. America teeters on the fiscal cliff – but, for Republicans, the political cliff that looms is steeper still.**"**

6.24. Market and Family

by permission of Christiane Hoffmann, in: *Frankfurter Allgemeine Sonntagszeitung*, **23 December 2012, p. 8**

"It is a pity that I do not have any influence on the *Arbeitgeberverband* (in English: employers' association). Otherwise I would like to give its president, Mr Hundt, a hot tip for Christmas: Dear Mr Hundt, I would say, have you ever thought of demanding shorter pregnancies? Nine months no longer need be the rule. Besides every women wants to give birth by Caesarean. Therefore 38 weeks would do. By the time the baby is ready; after that it only makes itself more comfortable inside. Women could give birth two weeks earlier and start working two weeks earlier. What a rise in productivity that would be! In Germany it would amount to 1.3 working weeks in the last year alone. Such a fast-track-pregnancy-law would have been a real advantage in terms of European competition: German mothers breed faster.

No, really. We live faster, more condensed, more effectively orientated lives. Although a little bit more can always be done. We have the G8 reform with shorter studying times, and now Mr Hundt promised to shorten parental leave – as soon as there are enough crib places for babies. Parents, industry demands should work as soon as possible after the birth of a child. Because: everything takes too long – always. Family leave, parental leave, sabbatical, sick leave. Everywhere time is wasted. We simply have too much time in which people are not working. And while we're at it, we are dying too slowly too.

But back to women. Or better to the labour market. These are related because for the labour market women always seem to be the best regulator. When men go to war, women go to work. When men are done with war, women go home again. When unemployment is high, unemployment for women is still higher. When the labour market is empty, women leave the broom in the corner and go to the office. But then the families minister said that families are "not an object of economic disposal". It is good that she said it, but it isn't. And how long will she be able to hold when global competition and Chinese rivalry come into the equation? Parental leave – employers say – makes it hard for women to come back to the labour market. But is that an argument against it? We have to ask ourselves: is it not for our benefit for women, mothers, fathers, families? Was the extension of childcare and parental allowances not intended to give women, men and families freedom of choice? Was the whole discussion about compatibility of family and workplace only concerned with the ability of women to work?

No, it is about us and it should be about us. The needs of the labour market and the needs of women, economisation and equality are two different things. Women who work are not powerless victims of capitalism – just as women who prefer to stay at home looking after their children are not powerless victims of patriarchy. And talking of victims: why is nobody complaining that men – for hundreds of years, from the beginning of time – have had to bow to the dictates of economics?

Mothers and fathers who want to work do not have the same interests as businesses – they do not want to be constantly disposable, they need more free time, the possibility of sabbaticals, more flexibility in terms of hours and location. But if they want to work they do have a similar interest to businesses, and they would be stupid not to use it: that of making conditions, for example.

What parents do not need is to argue about the economic value of their children, to sell them as future employees and contributors to pension schemes. If we go along with the idea that only potentially productive, high-performing people are worthy of our attention, time and affection – how should a colleague justify the fact that she needs free time to look after her mother with dementia? How should a family with a Down's syndrome child justify their decision not to abort it, given that it makes no sense in terms of social cost-benefit-calculation?

In short: we should not answer the economic demand with economic arguments. Otherwise we accept that there is no other measure. Good is what is right from a moral point of view and not what is useful for the market. There have to be places where the economic imperative does not prevail.

That would be wonderful: the family as space where time and attention can be available in abundance – and without calculation."

6.25. Hello 999, this prostitute is so ugly it's criminal

The Daily Telegraph, 14 June 2013, p. 9

"A man dialled 999 to complain that a prostitute he had arranged to meet was too ugly.

He told police that he wanted to report the woman under the Sale of Goods Acts. She had advertised herself "in the private section of the newspaper" but was not as attractive as he had expected, he said.

West Midlands Police said: "The caller said he had arranged to meet a prostitute outside a hotel and he did not like the look of her.

"He said she made herself out to be better than she was. When he took issue with this she took his car keys, ran out of the car and then threw them back at him."

The call was terminated by the 999 handler a short time later, and Sergeant Jerome Monran, based at Solihull police station, called the man back to give him some advice.

Sgt Moran said: "He genuinely believed he had done nothing wrong and that the woman should have been investigated for misrepresentation. I told him that she had not committed any offences and that it was his actions, in soliciting for sex, that were in fact illegal.

"Unhappy with the response, he then insisted on coming down to the police station to debate the matter."

Despite the man refusing to give his details, police have been able to identify him and have sent him a letter warning him about his actions.

The Sale of Goods Act 1979 gives consumers legal rights, stipulating goods which are sold must be of satisfactory quality, be fit for purpose and match the sellers' description."

6.26. Selling off our Utilities to Foreign Governments

Jeffrey Henderson, professor of international development, University of Bristol, to *The Guardian*, published in *The Week*, 26 October 2013, p. 29

"So, we're to have Chinese companies providing our nuclear-generated electricity. Can the Chancellor explain why it is OK to have companies owned by foreign governments – including by communist ones – controlling major chunks of the British economy (all Chinese nuclear-generating companies are 100% state owned, while EDF, the principal partner in the new Hinkley Point power station, is 85% owned by the French government), while it is not OK to have companies owned by the British Government participating in the economy (eg Royal Mail), except in emergency situations (eg RBS). What sort of ideologically distorted hypocrisy are we being subjected to here, and what are its implications for the longer-term future of the British economy?

And if UKIP is so concerned with the leaking of British sovereignty to foreign powers, which this development underlines spectacularly, how about parking your obsessions with the EU for once and paying attention to who owns the British economy?"

6.27. Orthodox economists have failed their own market test

- Students are demanding alternatives to a free-market dogma with a disastrous record.

Seumas Milne, *The Guardian*, 21 November 2013

"That's something we all need. –

From any rational point of view, orthodox economics is in serious trouble. Its champions not only failed to foresee the greatest crash for 80 years, but insisted such crises were a thing of the past. More than that, some of its leading lights played a key role in designing the disastrous financial derivatives that helped trigger the meltdown in the first place.

Plenty were paid propagandists for the banks and hedge funds that tipped us off their speculative cliff. Acclaimed figures in a discipline that claims to be scientific hailed a '"great moderation" of market volatility in the run-up to an explosion of unprecedented volatility. Others, such as the Nobel prize-winner Robert Lucas, insisted that economics had solved the "central problem of depression prevention."

Any other profession that had proved so spectacularly wrong and caused such devastation would surely be in disgrace. You might even imagine the free-market economists who dominate our universities and advise governments and banks would be rethinking their theories and considering alternatives.

After all, the large majority of economists who predicted the crisis rejected the dominant neoclassical thinking: from Dean Baker and Steve Keen to Ann Pettifor, Paul Krugman and David Harvey. Whether Keynesians, post-Keynesians or

Marxists, none accepted the neoliberal ideology that had held sway for 30 years; and all understood that, contrary to orthodoxy, deregulated markets don't tend towards equilibrium but deepen the economy's tendency to systemic crisis.

Alan Greenspan, the former chairman of the US Federal Reserve and high priest of deregulation, at least had the honesty to admit his view of the world had been proved "not right". The same cannot be said for others. Eugene Fama, architect of the "efficient markets hypothesis" underpinning financial deregulation, concedes he doesn't know what "causes recessions" – but insists his theory has been vindicated anyway. Most mainstream economists have carried on as if nothing had happened.

Many of their students, though, have had enough. A revolt against the orthodoxy has been smouldering for years and now seems to have gone critical. Fed up with parallel universe theories that have little to say about the world they're interested in, students at Manchester University have set up a post-crash economics society with 800 members, demanding an end to the introduction of a pluralist curriculum.

They want other schools of economic thought taught in parallel, from Keynesian to more radical theories – with a better record on predicting and connecting with the real world economy – along with green and feminist economics. The campaign is spreading fast: to Cambridge, Essex, the London School of Economics and a dozen other campuses, and linking up with university groups in France, Germany, Slovenia and Chile.

As one of the Manchester society's founders, Zach Ward-Perkins, explains, he and a fellow student agreed after a year of orthodoxy: "There must be more to it than this." Neoclassical economics is after all built on a conception of the economy as the sum of the atomised actions of millions of utility-maximising individuals, where markets are stable, information is perfect, capital and labour are equals – and the trade cycle is bolted on as an afterthought.

But even if it struggles to say anything meaningful about crises, inequality or ownership the mathematical modelling erected on its half-baked intellectual foundations give it a veneer of scientific rigour, valued by students aiming for well-paid City jobs. Neoclassical economics has also provided the underpinning for the diet of deregulated markets, privatisation, low taxes on the wealthy and free trade we were told for 30 years was now the only route to prosperity.

Its supporters have an "almost religious mentality", as Ha-Joon Chang – one of the last surviving independent economists at Keyne's Cambridge – puts it. Although claiming to favour competition, the neoclassicals won't tolerate any themselves. Forty years ago, most economics departments were Keynesian and neoclassical economics was derided. That all changed with the Thatcher and Reagan ascendancy.

In institutions supposed to foster debate, non-neoclassical economists have been systematically purged from economics faculties. Some have found refuge in business schools, development studies and geography departments. In the US, corporate funding has been key. In Britain, peer review through the 'research excellence framework' – which allocates public research funding – has been the main mechanism for the ideological cleansing of economics.

Paradoxically, the sharp increase in student fees and the marketisation of higher education is creating a pressure point for students out to overturn this intellectual monoculture. The free marketeers are now being market-tested, and the customers don't want their product. Some mainstream academics realise that they may have to compromise, and have been colonising a Soros-funded project to overhaul the curriculum, hoping to limit the scale of change.

But change it must. The free-market orthodoxy of the past three decades not only helped create the crisis we're living through, but gave credibility to policies that have led to slower growth, deeper inequality, greater insecurity and environmental degradation all over the world. Its continued dominance after the crash, like the neoliberal model it underpins, is about power not credibility. If we are to escape this crisis, both will have to go.**"**

6.28. The left is too silent on the clunking fist of state power

- Government's role is vital, but an arrogant and centralised state is as big a problem as the out-of-control market -

by John Harris, *The Guardian*, 6 January 2014, p. 24

"This will be the year of the intrusive, oppressive state. Obviously, this will not much distinguish it from 2013, 2012 or 2011. But still: fundamental issues for government and its reach into our lives are now bubbling away as never before, and may well reach boiling point over the next 12 months.

The fallout from Edward Snowden's revelations goes on: in the US, the latest stories concern a National Security Agency programme aimed at breaking all forms of digital encryption, while the debate about legislating to curtail surveillance powers rages. Here, by contrast, there is something jaw-dropping about how little the three main UK parties have to say. Britain has blazed a trail for the collection of enormous amounts of personal data, with a blasé attitude proving that the prospect of any oversight has been far from the thoughts of those in charge. But aside from such Lib Dems as Julien Huppert and Vince Cable, and the Conservatives' David Davis and Dominic Raab, who speaks out?

Meanwhile, the modern Conservative party evidently wants to accelerate Britain's progress towards being a country of spot checks and roving billboards instructing illicit migrants to hand themselves in, and the rest of us to grass them up. Large parts of the welfare state increasingly look not like a safety net, but a mess of traps, intended to enforce complete obedience under pain of destitution. Doctors, nurses and teachers work to central diktat as never before.

The political right has big problems here: it uses the rhetoric of small government but enforces its opposite. But so too does the left. Far too many on my side of politics still have their heads in the sand, holding on to a ragbag of notions that now bears no serious examination: that so-called civil liberties should always come a distant second to schools, hospitals and such like; that the centralised, snooping, target-driven state can be our friend, so long as it can be once again captured by Labour and put to the correct uses; and that from the NHS to the BBC, so long as giant and unwieldy institutions can be kept away from the private market, all will be well.

At the heart of all this is an attachment to the achievements of the Labour government of 1945–51, and a stifling myth it is time we buried. 1945 was the high point of a kind of statecraft that has little to teach us today. Yet its legacy is still here, across the left spectrum, in the politics that reduces socialism to higher taxation and bigger government; that screams 'nationalise it' when corporate interest messes up and 'ban it' when it encounters something it doesn't like.

If you doubt this, consider what the essential functions of the modern state look like to any politicised person under 30. The state comes to the rescue of banks while snatching away benefits. It strides into sovereign countries, and commits serial human rights abuses. It subjects doctors, nurses and teachers to ludicrous targets. It watches us constantly via CCTV, and hacks your email and phone data. It farms out some of its dirtiest business to private firms. This is not a vision of modern government invented by the current lot: in Britain, it decisively came to life thanks to Tony Blair and Gordon Brown. Whether knowingly or not, they demonstrated an essential truth: that contrary to the vanities of the 'free market', neoliberal capitalism needs the big centralised state to clear its way and enforce its insanities.

In December last year, I closely followed an upsurge of protest on university campuses across the UK, and spoke to some if the young people involved. They were socialists, to all intents and purposes: they want a more equal society, and an education system oriented around something higher than the idea of maximising their earning potential. But they had no illusions about how much of their focus was on the clunking fist of state power: their recurrent cry was "Cops off campus", and they testified to such ingrained parts of modern university life as spot checks on foreign students by police and Border Agency personnel, and the bonds that tied the cops to private security contractors. They were all experts on the surveillance state. Moreover, they are part of a generation whose meetings have no platform speakers, who insist the world should take on the horizontal characteristics of social media. The big state, whatever purposes it is put to, is anathema to them.

In orthodox politics there are occasional flashes of recognition of how much we need to tame, and then radically remodel, government. Localism, when it actually amounts to something coherent, is part of the noise. So is (was?) the big society, and the radical ideas about the devolution of power that Jon Cruddas is trying to bring to the Labour party. If you want a flavour of the journeys that need to be taken, have look at Compass: once broadly aligned with the Brownite wing of Labour but now a breeding ground for a new kind of creative, non-hierarchical, left politics. You know the signs of something different when you see them: if you're in the right company, people talk passionately about housing co-operatives, local poverty projects and sustainability initiatives, and credit unions. They want the revival of local councils. Crucially, they also argue for what's missing from the left's agenda: a cutting down of the surveillance state, exacting oversight of the security services, and strict limits on data collection.

None of this is an argument for anarchism or the stupid form of Tory politics which believes that so long as public spending can be pushed below a certain share of GDP, liberty will be assured. It is not intended to overlook what only the state can do: redistribute income; confront corporate power; forge the international agreements we need to fight everything from climate change to corporate tax avoidance. But there is no argument for extending those truths into the kind of boundless leviathan that Britain has ended up with. The truth is that the arrogant, centralised state is as much of a problem as the out-of-control market, and the dominion of one is symbiotically related to the tyranny of the other. From that, all else follows. The future politics of the left will either be pluralist, localist and libertarian or it will shrivel.**"**

6.29 Editorial

by Jeremy O'Grady, *The Week*, 15 March 2014

"I know we should marvel at the transformative power of capitalism ("We're all capitalists now", as Labour's Chuka Umunna says) but there's something vile about it, too. It leaves no corner of existence unfingered; it takes anything good, true and beautiful and bastardises it. The glories of classical music become soundtracks for airlines; Bob Dylan a T-shirt; the counterculture a fashion poster. Nike has muscled in on the loneliness of the long-distance runner; tour operators and Tri-Advisor have tamed the world's wild places. No one can now stare at the Pacific "silent, upon a peak in Darien" – not without sharing it on Facebook. The corporations have colonised[2] the wide open spaces of the internet and burrowed their way into honest journalism (*see p. 15*):

Beware the ads that look like journalism
by Andrew Sullivan, *The Sunday Times*:
Do you remember 'advertorials'? Once a common feature of newspapers, these were ads that took the form of pseudo-articles – "The economic potential of Bahrain!" – often paid for by government agencies. You probably never read them, says Andrew Sullivan, because editors took care to ensure that this stuff couldn't be mistaken for real journalism. But all that's changing. Today's 'media mavens' are setting out to produce ads that are indistinguishable from editorial, for one simple reason: advertisers will pay for it. Online banner ads don't work: no one clicks on them. But disguise ads as editorial, and people will read them and, crucially, share them,providing advertisers with clear evidence that their message is hitting home. This money-spinning approach was pioneered by the website BuzzFeed; but serious news site are getting in on the action. Last month, for instance, *The Guardian* unveiled something called *Guardian* Labs, which will produce content in association with Unilever. Newspapers are "becoming ad agencies, creating ads that look like Journalism". But it's not journalism, and it's certainly not "honest journalism".

---

2   an expression coined by the German philosopher Juergen Habermas

Apple – check out its nauseating iPad Air ad, *What Will Your Verse Be?* – has even staked out poetry and what it means to be human.

And now they're hijacking our sense of smell – the sense, as Proust reminds us, most closely linked to memory and the emotions. Last week *The Times* reported on a firm called ScentAir UK which sells lab-manufactured smells to thousands of retailers. Travel agents can seduce you with the scent of Mediterranean pine, bookshops with a whiff of coffee and chocolate fudge cookies. It's not just that the authentic shrivels and dies: all experience becomes an arch wherethrough gleams a company logo. Capitalism corrupts, and corporate capitalism corrupts absolutely.**"**

6.30 Why we fear Google

by Matthias Doepfner, CEO of Axel Springer SE, Germany, *Frankfurter Allgemeine Zeitung,* **17 April 2014, english version online**

"Dear Eric Schmidt,

In your text 'A Chance for Growth' in the *Frankfurter Allgemeine Zeitung* you reply to an article which this newspaper had published a few days earlier under the title 'Fear of Google'. You repeatedly mention the Axel Springer publishing house. In the spirit of transparency I would like to reply with an open letter to highlight a couple of things from our point of view.

We have known each other for many years, and have, as you state, had lengthy and frequent discussions on the relationship between European publishers and Google. As you know, I am a great admirer of Google's entrepreneurial success. In just a few short years, starting in 1998, this company has grown to employ almost 50,000 people worldwide, generated 60 billion dollars in revenue last year, and has a current market capitalization of more than 350 billion dollars. Google is not only the biggest search engine in the world, but along with YouTube (the second biggest search engine in the world) it also has the largest video platform, with Chrome the biggest browser, with Gmail the most widely used e-mail provider, and with Android the biggest operating system for mobile devices. Your article rightly points out what fabulous impetus Google has given to growth of the digital economy. In 2013, Google made a profit of 14 billion dollars. I take my hat off to this outstanding entrepreneurial performance.

Google doesn't need us. But we need Google

In your text you refer to the marketing cooperation between Google and Axel Springer. We were also happy with it. But some of our readers have now interpreted this to mean that Axel Springer is evidently schizophrenic. On the one hand, Axel Springer is part of a European antitrust action against Google, and is in dispute with them regarding the issue of enforcement of German ancillary copyright prohibiting the stealing of content; on the other hand, Axel Springer not only benefits from the traffic it receives via Google but from Google's algorithm for marketing the remaining space in its online advertising. You can call it schizophrenic – or liberal. Or, to use one of our Federal Chancellor's favourite phrases: there is no alternative.

We know of no alternative which could offer even partially comparable technological prerequisites for the automated marketing of advertising. And we cannot afford to give up this source of revenue because we desperately need the money for technological investments in the future. Which is why other publishers are increasingly doing the same. We also know of no alternative search engine which could maintain or increase our online reach. A large proportion of high quality journalistic media receives its traffic primarily via Google. In other areas, especially of a non-journalistic nature, customers find their way to suppliers almost exclusively through Google. This means, in plain language, that we – and many others – are dependent on Google. At the moment Google has a 91.2 per cent search-engine market share in Germany. In this case, the statement "if you don't like Google, you can remove yourself from their listings and go elsewhere" is about as realistic as recommending to an opponent of nuclear power that he just stop using electricity. He simply cannot do this in real life – unless he wants to join the Amish.

Google's employees are always extremely friendly to us and to other publishing houses, but we are not communicating with each other on equal terms. How could we? Google doesn't need us. But we need Google. And we are also worlds apart economically. At 14 billion dollars, Google's annual profit is about twenty times that of Axel Springer. The one generates more profit per quarter than the revenues of the other in a whole year. Our business relationship is that of the Goliath of Google to the David of Axel Springer. When Google changed an algorithm, one of our subsidiaries lost 70 per cent of its traffic within a few days. The fact that this subsidiary is a competitor of Google's is certainly a coincidence.

Not only economic, but also political

We are afraid of Google. I must state this very clearly and frankly, because few of my colleagues dare do so publicly. And as the biggest among the small, perhaps it is also up to us to be the first to speak out in this debate. You wrote it yourself in your book: "We believe that modern technology platforms, such as Google, Facebook, Amazon and Apple, are even more powerful than most people realize (...), and what gives them power is their ability to grow – specifically, their speed to scale. Almost nothing, short of a biological virus, can scale as quickly, efficiently or aggressively as these technology platforms and this makes the people who build, control, and use them powerful too."

The discussion about Google's power is therefore not a conspiracy theory propagated by old-school diehards. You yourself speak of the new power of the creators, owners, and users. In the long term I'm not sure about the users. Power is soon followed by powerlessness. And this is precisely the reason why we now need to have this discussion in the interests of the long-term integrity of the digital economy's ecosystem. This applies to competition, not only economic, but also political. It concerns our values, our understanding of the nature of humanity, our worldwide social order and, from our own perspective, the future of Europe.

The greatest opportunity in the last few decades

As the situation stands, your company will play a leading role in the various areas of our professional and private lives – in the house, in the car, in healthcare, in robotronics. This is a huge opportunity and a no less serious threat. I am afraid that it is simply not enough to state, as you do, that you want to make the world a "better place". The Internet critic Evgeny Morozov has clearly described the position that modern societies need to take here: This is not a debate about technology, and the fascinating opportunities it presents. This is a political debate. Android devices and Google algorithms are not a government program. Or at least they shouldn't be. It is we the people who have to decide whether or not we want what you are asking of us – and what price we are willing to pay for it.

Publishers gained their experience here early – as the vanguard for other sectors and industries. But as long as it was simply a question of the expropriation of content (which search engines and aggregators use but don't want to pay for), only a few were interested. But that changes when the same thing applies to people's personal data. The question of who this data belongs to will be one of the key policy issues of the future.

You say in your article that those who criticize Google are "ultimately criticizing the Internet as such and the opportunity for everyone to be able to access information from wherever they happen to be." The opposite is true. Those who criticize Google are not criticizing the Internet. Those who are interested in having an intact Internet – these are the ones who need to criticize Google. From the perspective of a publishing house, the Internet is not a threat, but rather the greatest opportunity in the last few decades. 62 per cent of our corporate profit today comes from our digital business. This means that we are not talking about the Internet here, but only about the role that Google plays within it.

The "fair criteria" are not in place

It is in this context that of the utmost importance are competition complaints submitted four years ago by various European publishers' associations and Internet companies against Google at the European Commission in Brussels. Google is a prime example of a market-dominating company. With a 70 per cent global market share, Google defines the infrastructure on the Internet. The next largest search engine is Baidu in China with 16.4 per cent – and that's because China is a dictatorship which prohibits free access to Google. Then there are search engines with market shares of up to 6 per cent. These are pseudo-competitors. The market belongs to a single company. Google's share of the online-advertising market in Germany is increasing from year to year and is currently around 60 per cent. For comparison: *The Bild* newspaper, which has been considered as market-dominating by the German Federal Cartel Office for decades (which is why Axel Springer was not allowed to buy the TV company Pro SiebenSat.1 or regional newspapers), has a 9 per cent market share of printed advertisements in Germany. By comparison Google is not only market-dominating but super market-dominating.

Google is to the Internet what the Deutsche Post was to mail delivery or Deutsche Telekom to telephone calls. In those days there were national state monopolies. Today there is a global network monopoly. This is why it is of paramount importance that there be transparent and fair criteria for Google's search results.

However, these fair criteria are not in place. Google lists its own products, from e-commerce to pages from its own Google+ network, higher than those of its competitors, even if these are sometimes of less value for consumers and should not be displayed in accordance with the Google algorithm. It is not even clearly pointed out to the user that these search results are the result of self-advertising. Even when a Google service has fewer visitors than that of a competitor, it appears higher up the page until it eventually also receives more visitors. This is called the abuse of a market-dominating position. And everyone expected the European antitrust authorities to prohibit this practice. It does not look like it will. The Commissioner has instead proposed a "settlement" that has left anyone with any understanding of the issue speechless. Eric, in your arcitle you talk about a compromise which you had attempted to reach with the EU Commission. What you have found, if the Commission does decide on the present proposal, is an additional model for Google of advertising revenue procurement. There will not be any "painful concessions" but rather additional earnings.

A betrayal of the basic idea behind Google

The Commission is seriously proposing that the infrastructure-dominating search engine Google be allowed to continue to discriminate against its competitors in the placement of search results critical to success. As "compensation", however, a new advertising window will be set up at the beginning of the search list, in which those companies who are discriminated against will be able to buy a place on the list. This is not a compromise. This is an officially EU-sanctioned introduction of the business model that in less honourable circles is referred to as protection money – i.e. if you don't want me to kill you, you have to pay me.

You know very well that this would result in long-term discrimination against and weakening of any competition.

Meaning that Google would be able to develop its superior market position still further. And that this would further weaken the European digital economy in particular. I honestly cannot imagine that this is what you meant by compromise. But I do not want to reproach you and Google for this. You, as the representative of the company, can and must look after its interests. My criticism is directed at the European Competition Commission. Comissioner Almunia ought to reflect once again on whether it is wise, as a kind of final official act, to create a situation that will go down in history as a nail in the coffin of the already sclerotic European Internet economy. But it would above all be a betrayal of the consumer, who will no longer be able to find what is most important and best for him but what is most profitable for Google – at the end a betrayal of the basic idea behind Google.

A remarkably honest sentence

This also applies to the large and even more problematic set of issues concerning data security and data utilization. Ever since Snowden triggered the NSA affair, ever since the close relations between major American online companies and the American secret services became public, the social climate – at least in Europe – has fundamentally changed. People have become more sensitive about what happens to their user data. Nobody knows as much about its customers as Google. Even private or business emails are read by Gmail and, if necessary, can be evaluated. You yourself said in 2010: "We know here you are. We know where you've been. We can more or less know what you're thinking about." This is a remarkably honest sentence. The question is: Are users happy with the fact that this information is used not only for commercial purposes – which may have many advantages, yet a number of spooky negative aspects as well – but could end up in the hands of the intelligence services and to a certain extent already has?

In Patrick Tucker's book *The Naked Future: What Happens in a World that Anticipates Your Every Move?*, whose vision of the future was considered to be "inescapable" by Google's master thinker Vint Cerf, there is a scene which sounds like science fiction, but isn't. Just imagine, the author writes, you wake up one morning and read the following on your phone: "Good morning! Today, as you leave work, you will run into your old girlfriend Vanessa (you dated her eleven years ago), and she is going to tell you that she is getting married. Do try to act surprised!" Because Vanessa has not told anyone yet. You of course are wondering just how your phone knew that or whether it's a joke, and so you ignore the message. Then in the evening you actually pass Vanessa on the sidewalk.

Can competition generally still function in the digital age?

Vaguely remembering the text from the phone, you congratulate her on her engagement. Vanessa is alarmed: "How did you know I was engaged?" she askes. You're about to say, "My phone sent me the text," but you stop yourself just in time. "Didn't you post something to your Facebook profile?" you ask. "Not yet," she answers and walks hurriedly away. You should have paid attention to your phone and just acted surprised.

Google searches more than half a billion web addresses. Google knows more about every digitally active citizen than George Orwell dared to imagine in his wildest dreams in 1948. Google is sitting on the entire current data trove of humanity like the giant Fafner in *The Ring of the Nibelung*: "Here I lie and here I hold." I hope you are aware of your company's special responsibility. If fossil fuels were the fuels of the 20th century, then those of the 21st century are surely data and user profiles. We need to ask ourselves whether competition can generally still function in the digital age if data are so extensively concentrated in the hands of one party.

There will be a winner

There is a quote from you in this context that concerns me. In 2009 you said: "If you have something that you don't want anyone to know, maybe you shouldn't be doing it in the first place." The only sentence that is even more worrying comes from Mark Zuckerberg when he was on the podium of a conference with you and I in the audience. Someone asked what Facebook thinks of the storage of data and the protection of privacy. And Zuckerberg said: "I don't understand your question. If you have nothing to hide you have nothing to fear."

Ever since then I have thought about this sentence again and again. I find it terrible. I know that it was certainly not meant that way. Behind this statement there is a state of mind and an image of humanity that is typically cultivated in totalitarian regimes – not in liberal societies. Such a statement could also have come from the head of East Germany's Stasi or other secret police in service of a dictatorship. The essence of freedom is precisely the fact that I am not obliged to disclose everything that I am doing, that I have a right to confidentiality and, yes, even to secrets; that I am able to determine for myself what I wish to disclose about myself. The individual right to this is what makes a democracy. Only dictatorships want transparent citizens instead of a free press.

Officials in Brussels are now thinking about how the total transparency of users can be avoided by restricting the setting and storage of cookies on the Internet (with which it is still possible today to find out which website you clicked on at 10.10 a.m. on 16 April 2006), in order to strengthen consumer rights. We do not yet know exactly how this regulation will turn out, any more than we know whether it will do more good than bad. But one thing is already certain – if it comes to pass, there will be a winner: Google. Because Google is considered by experts to be the absolute leader in the development of technologies which document the movements and habits of users without setting cookies.

Something the EU has so sorely missed in the past

Google has also made provisions as far as the antitrust proceedings in Brussels on fair search are concerned. It is expected that the whole procedure will be decided in Google's favour. But if not, it would also be safeguarded. Concessions and restrictions that have been wrung out in lengthy proceedings, limited to Google's European domains, would be ineffective in an agreement because Google is able, using Android or Chrome, to arbitrarily determine that the search will no longer be carried out from a web address but by using an app. This means that Google will be able to withdraw from all the commitments it has given, which to this day are still bound to the Google domains such as google.de.

Will European politics cave in or wake up? The institutions in Brussels have never been so important. An archaic question of power is to be decided. Is there a chance for an autonomous European digital infrastructure or not? It is a question of competitiveness and viability for the future. Voluntary self-subjugation cannot be the last word from the Old World. On the contrary, the desire of the European digital economy to succeed could finally become something for European policy, which the EU has so sorely missed in the past few decades: an emotional narrative.

You don't have to be a conspiracy theorist

16 years of data storage and 16 years experience by tens of thousands of IT developers has established a competitive edge which can no longer be offset with economic resources alone. Since Google bought 'Nest' it knows in even more detail what people do within their own four walls. And now Google is also planning driverless cars, in order to compete in the long term with the car industry from Toyota to VW. Google will then not only know where we drive our cars but how we are occupying ourselves when we are in the car. Forget Big Brother – Google is better!

Against this background it greatly concerns me that Google – which has just announced the acquisition of drone manufacturer 'Titan Aerospace' – has been seen for some time as being behind a number of planned enormous ships and floating working environments that can cruise and operate in the open ocean What is the reason for this development? You don't have to be a conspiracy theorist to find this alarming, especially if you listen to the words of Google founder and major shareholder Larry Page.

What impact does it have on our society?

He dreams of a place without data-protection laws and without democratic accountability. "There's many, many exciting and important things you could do that you just can't to because they're illegal", Page said back in 2013, continuing "... we should have some safe places where we can try out some new things and figure out what is the effect on society, what's the effect on people, without having to deploy kind of into the normal world."

Does this mean that Google is planning to operate in a legal vacuum, without troublesome antitrust authorities and data protection? A kind of superstate that can navigate its floating kingdom undisturbed by any and all nation-states and their laws?

Until now the concerns were the following: What will happen if Google continues to expand its absolutely dominant market power? Will there be even less competition? Will the European digital economy be thrown back even further compared to the few American super corporations? Will consumers become even more transparent, more heteronomous and further manipulated by third parties – be it for economic or political interests? And what impact do these factors have on our society?

It is not the fear of old analog dinosaurs

After this disturbing news you need to ask yourself: Is Google in all seriousness planning for the digital supra-state in which one corporation is naturally only good to its citizens and of course "is not evil"? Please, dear Eric explain to us why our interpretation of what Larry Page says and does is a misunderstanding.

I am aware that the problems which are caused by new digital super-authorities such as Amazon and Facebook cannot be solved by Google alone. But Google could – for its own long-term benefit – set a good example. The company could create transparency, not only by providing search results according to clear quantitative criteria, but also by disclosing all the changes to algorithms. By not saving IP addresses, automatically deleting cookies after each session, and only saving customer behaviour when specifically requested to do so by customers. And by explaining and demonstrating what it intends to do with its floating group headquarters and development labs.

Because the fear of growing heteronomy by the all-determining spider in the web is not being driven by an old analog dinosaurs, who have not understood the Internet and are therefore afraid of everything new. It is rather the digital natives, and among them the most recent and best-informed, who have a growing problem with the increasingly comprehensive control by Google.

Impressive and dangerous

This also includes the fiction of the culture of free services. On the Internet, in the beautiful colourful Google world, so much seems to be free of charge: from search services up to journalistic offerings. In truth we are paying with our behaviour – with the predictability and commercial exploitation of our behaviour. Anyone who has a car accident today, and mentions it in an e-mail, can receive an offer for a new car from a manufacturer on his mobile phone tomorrow. Terribly convenient. Today, someone surfing high-blood-pressure web sites, who automatically betrays his notorious sedentary lifestyle through his Jawbone fitness wristband, can expect a higher health insurance premium the day after tomorrow. Not at all convenient. Simply terrible. It is possible that it will not take much longer before more and ore people realize that the currency of his or her own behaviour exacts a high price: the freedom of self-determination. And that is why it is better and cheaper to pay with something very old fashioned – namely money.

Google is the world's most powerful bank – but dealing only in behavioural currency. Nobody capitalizes on their knowledge about us as effectively as Google. This is impressive and dangerous.

Is it really smart to wait?

Dear Erich Schmidt, you do not need my advice, and of course I am writing here from the perspective of those concerned. As a profiteer from Google's traffic. As a profiteer from Google's automated marketing of advertising. And as a potential victim of Google's data and market power. Nevertheless – less is sometimes more. And you can also win yourself to death.

Historically, monopolies have never survived in the long term. Either they have failed as a result of their complacency, which breeds its own success, or they have been weakened by competition – both unlikely scenarios in Google's case. Or they have been restricted by political initiatives. IBM and Microsoft are the most recent examples.

Another way would be voluntary self-restraint on the part of the winner. Is it really smart to wait until the first serious politician demands the breakup of Google? Or even worse – until the people refuse to follow? While they still can?

Mathias Doepfner**"**

6.31 HSBC files

- Tax dodging was systematic. The response from the bank and the politicians is anything but -

Editorial, *The Guardian*, p. 30, 10 February 2015

""'Values', wrote the Rev Prebendary Stephen Green go beyond 'what you can get away with.' Reassuring words from the part-time priest who for years ran one of the world's biggest banks, before being brought into government by David Cameron. Courtesy of the HSBC files, however, we now know that this bank, when under his stewardship - first as chief exec, later as chair - was involved in concealing 'black accounts' from the taxman, servicing the secretly stowed funds of corrupt businessmen and allowing the withdrawal of 'bricks' of untraceable cash.

In the face of these ugly facts about his old bank's Swiss operation, Lord Green has said only that it is for HSBC, and not for him, to comment on that institution's past and current behaviour. No wonder. His obvious refuge would be to claim that, as the boss of a global business in London, he had other worries and could not be expected to know every detail of what distant colleagues in Geneva were up to. Sadly for him, this potential shelter took a battering from something else he wrote: 'For companies, where does this (ethical) responsibility begin? With their boards, of course. There is no other task they have which is more important. It is their job ... to promote and nurture a culture of ethical and purposeful business throughout the organisation.

The chief defence offered by HSBC corporately is that the Swiss skullduggery reflected the federated structure of the bank's past, as if this structure had been merely an inheritance of historical accident, which had latterly been put right. Suspicious minds will wonder whether these structures were instead a reflection of moral evasion. They will be encouraged by yet another thing that Lord Green wrote, this time very much in dog-collar mode: 'Compartmentalisation ... is a besetting sin of human beings.'

Even if Lord Green simply failed to notice what a rogue Swiss operation was up to, rather than looking away, his failure to grip it was serious. A clergyman's feet of clay are an eye-catching detail, particularly because - as an acknowledged expert on ethical finance - he is advising the archbishop of Canterbury on how to shake up the Church of England, advocating more vicars in an MBA mould. The real issues, however, go both deeper and wider. At root, this is a story about the culture of a crooked form of capitalism.

The Treasury minister, David Gauke, yesterday faced, and failed to deal with, the obvious questions about whether any of Lord Green's coalition colleagues had thought to ask him about the Swiss dodges after Revenue & Customs got hold of the files in 2010, but the truly dispiriting thing about the Commons session was the questions that 3,000-plus cases that HMRC investigated on the strength of the Swiss cache have contributed to just a single prosecution, and even then of someone who was already being pursued? Desperate families on benefits, who can be hounded all the way to prison for failing to declare cash-in-hand work, will discover that in angry disbelief. Rather than regarding itself as a law enforcer, HMRC would appear to approach the wealthy in a softly-softly spirit of 'negotiate, and see what you can get'. And why when illegal evasion as well as lawful avoidance appears to have been indulged, is the only discussion about prosecutions about individual clients, and not the pursuit of the bank as a whole?

Then there is the most fundamental question of the lot, at least for those unexotic citizens who are happy to work for a salary on the understanding that it will be taxed at source then paid into a British bank. Namely, what valid reason could there be for squirrelling funds in Switzerland? Even as it concedes past problems with tax, HSBC insists that there are 'numerous legitimate reasons to have a Swiss bank account', but neglected to expand on what these might be. Save for the odd individual with Swiss family links or plans to invest in a real Swiss business, are these reasons really so self-evident that they don't need require spelling out? If private banking overseas is to be tolerated at all, then, in the light of the systematic malpractice laid bare this week, the onus should surely shift on to the individual to explain why it is needed.

That, however, is not the approach that the UK has taken to date. From George Osborne's patchy stich-up of tax deal with Switzerland, which failed to bring in the promised revenue, to the extraordinarily forgiving 'amnesty with interest' that Mr Gauke offered to evaders who had dabbled in Liechtenstein, tax dodging is approached first as a matter for haggling and only secondly as a crime. The smooth movement of the former tax chief Dave Hartnett from HMRC to an advisory post with HSBC last year confirms the cosiness

Citizens who work hard to pay their own taxes are nonetheless looking at cuts to cherished services for years to come. They are entitled to rage against the rich who dodge their own obligations, the bankers who assist them, and the politicians who still refuse to get tough."

> "Philosophers have, of late years, considered chiefly the tendency of affections, and have given little attention to the *relation* which they stand in to the cause which excites them."
> Adam Smith, *The Theory of Moral Sentiments*[1]

7. On course to a modern culteconomic theory

7. 1. The modern understanding of *land* and *labour* =[2] nature and people and the interaction between them

Adam Smith claimed that exchange is the basic principle of economics and that 'land' and 'labour' create the wealth of nations. In the following, the words 'land' and 'labour' will be replaced by words which give them their real meaning, ie nature and people.

Although Smith stated that "nature labours beside man" – one of his extraordinary insights – he concentrated his thinking on exchanges between humans only.

He did, however, share our modern view of humans as natural beings. Seeing man as part of nature, rather than as the opposite to nature, necessitates that the interaction of man and nature is included into an economic theory. Therefore, broadening the point of view about the human condition lies at the very basis of modern culteconomic theory.

The first step, naturally, is to analyze our understanding of nature, followed by our understanding of man. Respecting Aristotle's insights, although not following him blindly, it is then necessary to describe the natural form of interaction between nature and humans, keeping in mind that it is from this natural form that the cultural form of exchange derived; 'cultural' meaning using a means of exchange which was invented about 7,000 years ago, in the Neolithic age.

---

1 TMS, p. 24, accentuation by the author
2 "... to avoid the tedious repetition of these words: 'is equal to': I will set as I do often in work use, a pair of parallels, or Gemowe lines of one length, thus: =, because no 2 things, can be more equal." Robert Recorde (ca. 1512-1558), introduced the equals sign in 1557, in: "The Whetestone of Witte whiche is the seconde parte of Arithmeteke; containing the extraction of rootes; the cossike practise, with the rule of equation; and the workes of Surde Nombers," as noted by Mark Forsyth, in: *The Etymologicon, A Circular Stroll Through the Hidden Connections of the English Language*, London, 2011, p. 177

Generally speaking, even today nature seems to be seen by a lot of people as the *res extensa*, the external matter, whereas they think of themselves as spiritual beings with consciousness. This understanding of nature derives from the religious belief that humans were created by God to rule over nature, as expressed in the Bible: "Men are made to subdue Earth and have dominion over everything" (Genesis I, 26+28), an understanding mirrored in Roman as well as in Napoleonic law. It led to the assumption – upheld for centuries – that humans could deal with nature however they liked. There would be no consequences either for nature or for them by this kind of domination. Nature is the dead matter, outside of humans, which does not have awareness or soul, nor will or purpose of its own. Nature is seen as limitless and stable, remaining as it was created, unchangeable, forever the same.

In classical Greece, mathematics became the tool to understand nature, to measure, weigh and define it, a method abstract from people's real experiences, from natural location, from daily life, from nature's seasons. It was seen as objective comprehension. Bertrand Russell referred to it as follows: "I should agree with Plato that arithmetic, and pure mathematics generally, is not derived from perception. Pure mathematics consists of tautologies, analogous to 'men are men', but usually more complicated. To know that a mathematical proposition is correct, we do not have to study the world, but only the meanings of the symbols... Mathematical truth, therefore, is, as Plato contends, independent of perception; but it is truth of a very peculiar sort, and is concerned only with symbols."[3] We have to remind ourselves that in reality we do not find straight lines, right angles or full circles, these are abstract symbols created by humans with the aim of building models in search of rational explanations as well as predictions of natural events.

Sheldrake pointed out that such an understanding causes a "major problem,"[4] as "most of our experience is not mathematical. We taste food, feel angry, enjoy the beauty of flowers, laugh at jokes. In order to assert the primacy of mathematics, Galileo and his successors had to distinguish between what they called 'primary qualities', which could be described mathematically, such as motion, size and weight, and 'secondary qualities', like colour and smell[5] which were subjective. They took the real world to be objective, quantitative and mathematical. Personal experience in the lived world was subjective, the realm of opinion and illusion, outside the realm of science."

In the 17th century, however, people began to realise that nature was not that constant but must have changed over time, as people found fossils which they tried to categorize.[6] Nature, they had to conclude, had undergone radical changes,

---

3   Bertrand Russell, *History of Western Philosophy*, London and New York, first published 1946, 1996, p. 153, and very similar Y. S. Brenner in: *Theories of Economic Development and Growth*, Bury St. Edmunds, 1966, p. 148–149: "In fact the whole substitution of rationalized mathematical functions for the human relations of real life seems highly doubtful."

4   Rupert Sheldrake, *The Science Delusion*, London, 2012, p. 30

5   Why the floral industry ever thought it a good idea to bring flowers which no longer have any scent to the market isn't really understandable.

6   eg by John Woodward, *Essay Towards a Natural History of the Earth*, published in 1695, cited in:

it has a history,[7] one which must date back millions of years, far longer than any-body's individual lifetime. Once upon the time, everything had been different. Earth's continents had a different shape, and there were very different species of plants and animals millions of years ago.[8] People in the 17th century came to the conclusion that nature is not static, but is a dynamic, ongoing and self-organised process, that continues in the present day, meaning that as nature has history, it also will have a future, different from the present and unknowable to us.

Our understanding of nature can now be driven forward from two opposite approaches, one that looks deeper into the world, into the very consistency of matter, or one that looks into the world away from planet Earth, into the nature of the Milky Way and the universe.

When Edwin Hubble (1889–1953) discovered in 1922 that the observable universe with its billions and billions of galaxies was expanding, formulating the so-called Redshift Law in 1929, it was assumed that there must have been a time, billions of years ago, when the universe would have been concentrated in one single point from which this expansion started. The Big-Bang-Theory was born. It was conjectured – and still is today because we do not yet seem to have a better explanation – that the Big Bang caused the universe to come into being and that this must have happened 13.82 billion years ago. Therefore, the questions we are still curious about, are: What caused the Big Bang? What was 'there' before the universe existed? And even: What does 'there' mean, when space and time only came into existence with the universe? Could something have derived from noth-ing? And what does 'nothing' mean? Or is the universe perhaps an eternally contracting and expanding process? In 'warped space-time'?[9] And can there be other universes? Is Earth the only planet which (or do we need to say: who) has produced life, when there are billions and billions of other galaxies with billions and billions of stars and billions and billions of planets? How can we ever find out if consciousness has been developed – even in different forms – somewhere else? Will we ever be able to make contact with other life forms? Such questions, however, could not have been asked in the 18th century. And they are not only of interest to scientists.

The other way to approach an understanding of nature is to penetrate deeper and further into matter, until we find the smallest possible parts from which natu-ral material is constructed.

This idea that there are tiny unchangeable parts of the same quality, so tiny that they couldn't be split further, goes back to Leucippos of Miletus (about 465 BCE), teacher of Democritus, who coined the name for them: atoms. In the classical world, this was a totally new concept of seeing nature, as people at that time were familiar with only four elements: air, water, fire and soil.

However, when in the 20th century it was found out that atoms themselves consist of smaller particles, and in 1911 Ernest Rutherford (1871–1937) build the

---

Enlightenment, Discovering the World in the 18th Century, by Kim Sloan and Andrew Burnett (d.), London, 2003, p.94

7   compare: Carl Friedrich von Weizsaecker, Die Geschichte der Natur, Goettingen, 1979
8   Geophysicist Alfred Wegner (1880-1930) discovered the shift of the continental drifts in 1915.
9   compare: Stephen Hawking, The Universe in a Nutshell, London, 2001

atom model, physicists tried to split the atom into such sub-atomic particles. The reason for doing so obviously was not only to allow a better understanding of matter, but also because they wanted to join these particles together to build a new material with atoms of a heavier weight than those found in nature – a task which only seemed possible by human synthesis.

When elementary physicists split particles further, they came to unexpected results. They found that the quality of matter changes. On a subatomic level, matter appears not only as a material object but also as a wave of energy, meaning that the nature of matter is double-sided. The source of these insights involved various experiments with light.[10]

Max Planck (1858–1947) named these double-sided sub-atomic particles 'quantum', and developed a theory of quantum mechanics, which led to a further scientific revolution in the process to understand nature. This not only affected natural science but philosophy too. Matter, it seems, can no longer be understood as an *object* existing in exact locations in a quantitative and static way, but needs to be seen as a dynamic, self-organized and open process, which has an inherent tendency to exist, as well as its counterpart, anti-matter, a probability.[11] Werner Heisenberg (1901–1976) stated that 'quantum mechanics forbids, at any given moment, the precise determination of both the position and the momentum of a particle'.[12] (p. 232)

With Albert Einstein (1879–1955) came a further step forward in the endeavour to define and understand nature when he published his theory of special and general relativity, showing that space-time is bending light. "By curving space and time, general relativity changes them from being a passive background against which events take place to being active, dynamic participants in what happens... In general relativity ... time and space do not exist independently of the universe or of each other."[13] Einstein also found that matter and energy can be transformed into each other, as all matter is condensed energy, while gravity, one of the four basic forces, is caused by bending space-time.

Manjit Kumar has shown how Einstein struggled to come to terms with this new understanding, especially with Niels Bohr's (1885–1962) apprehension, that "it was no longer possible to make the separation that existed in classical physics between the observer and the observed". (p. 244)

---

10   Incidentally, light travels at a constant speed of nearly 300,000 km per second, the same everywhere in the universe. That means besides other things, that when looking into the sky we are not able to view the universe as it is at the moment, but as it was. With more and more powerful telescopes we are able to look back in time, and, therefore, perhaps, might one day be able to understand how the universe came into existence. One cannot help but think that nature 'wants' us to know that.

11   Ernst Bloch, a German philosopher (1885–1977) described in his book *Die Lehren von der Materie*, published Frankfurt, 1978, the historic process of a steadily evolving and therefore changing understanding of matter over the centuries of scientific research

12   According to Manjit Kumar, *Quantum, Einstein, Bohr and the Great Debate about the Nature of Reality*, London, 2009

13   Stephen Hawking, ibid, p. 35

Whilst Einstein's view was that there is "an observer-independent reality", the Copenhagen interpretation of quantum theory says that "particles do not have an independent reality, they do not possess properties when they are not being observed", summarized by the American physicist John Archibald Wheeler "no elementary phenomenon is a real phenomenon until it is an observed phenomenon."[14]

This 20th century revolution of the classical view of nature is described by Bertrand Russell as follows: "One result of the work we have been considering is to dethrone mathematics from the lofty place that it has occupied since Pythagoras and Plato, and to destroy the presumption against empiricism which has been derived from it... *Common sense thinks of the physical world as composed of 'things'*[15] which persist through a certain period of time and move in space. Philosophy and physics developed the notion of 'thing' into that of 'material substance', and thought of material substance as consisting of particles, each very small, and each persisting throughout all time. Einstein substituted events for particles... From all this it seems to follow that events,[16] not particles, must be the 'stuff' of physics. What has been thought of as a particle will have to be thought of as a series of events. The series of events that replaces a particle has certain important physical properties, and therefore demands our attention; but it has no more substantiality than any other series of events that we might arbitrarily single out. Thus 'matter' is not the part of the ultimate material of the world, but merely a convenient way of collecting events into bundles."[17]

Events happen in time. And Adam Smith seems to have been aware of this well ahead of his time when he stated: "Mankind, in the first ages of society, before the establishment of law, order, and security, has little curiosity to find out those hidden chains of events which bind together the seemingly disjointed appearances of nature." (EW p. 47)

The findings of physics, about 100 years old, however, have not yet been made useful for economics. Therefore I propose to implement the modern, contemporary view of the world into economic theory at last. We should not wait any longer, unless we want to be stuck in the past.

Life evolved from inorganic matter about 3.5 billion years ago, as algae acquired photosynthesis, a metabolism, growth, propagation and the production of oxygen, thereby transforming Earth from a dead into a living planet.[18] According to Norbert Elias, we call events-in-time processes.[19]

As life develops it affects its environment and the environment affects life. Out

---

14 Manjit Kumar, ibid, p. 312
15 And our use of language needs to reflect this too, preferring the verb to the noun.
16 It is hardly possible to resist the temptation to mention the words of Harold Macmillan (1894–1986), British Conservative Prime Minister from 1957 - 1963: "Events, dear boy, events." Macmillan, it seems, must indeed have understood a lot of physics.
17 Bertrand Russell, *History...*, p. 741
18 In the 1970s, James Lovelock and Lynn Margulis coined the word '*Gaia*' for the living self-organised planet Earth, an idea which goes back to James Hutton (1726–1797), the 'father of geology'.
19 *The Civilizing Process*, Norbert Elias, London, first published 1939, this edition 1969

of the basic organic life of plants grew animals, able to roam, and then human animals, able to understand causes and effects of their own activities.

Therefore, the traditional view of the world has to be abandoned. Nature can no longer be viewed and treated as infinite, static and dead, but has to be seen as an ongoing process of development. Nature can no longer be understood merely as external to humans over which they are supposed to have total control. In the 21st century, humans have to be considered as part of nature, as creatures who have evolved through the dynamic process of natural evolution.

Now everything seems to be related: not only are humans at one with Earth's nature, humans also need to be understood in connection with the whole universe, as the heavy elements in the human body were originally baked in exploding stars, in supernovae.

The historical religious belief that men has been created as he is today by a (male) god cannot be upheld. Nature, we know today, is able to produce not only life, but consciousness, or, to express it the other way around, consciousness is a function of matter.[20] Nature is not 'the other', but a product of human involvement. Therefore today's challenge should be called:

Forward to nature.[21] And definitely not: back to nature.[22]

It is not only land=nature that is still viewed by economicult theorists as a sole object that can be bought and sold on a market, but 'labour' too. Labour is seen as a good with which its owner can do as he pleases.[23] As already mentioned, this was the first split between labour and a labouring person – the real division of labour. Labour is regarded, even by the labourer himself, as if it is a thing. In an economicult the 'owner' of his labour is free to sell it to anyone, because he is forced to sell his labour in exchange for a cash income, as he needs money to buy the commodities on which his life depends. As we learned, in a society where everything is commodified, referred to and defined in terms of money , labour is too. Oskar Negt mentioned that labour is only understood in terms of gainful employment, which is not due to man's nature, but is the product of historical development.[24] It led to man's alienation from his own ability. Andre Gorz has

---

20 Gregory Bateson, *Geist und Natur, Eine notwendige Einheit*, Frankfurt, 1984

21 Gernot Boehme, *Die Natur vor uns*, Kusterdingen, 2002.
   It is hard to understand how anyone can claim as Verena Postel does in: *Arbeit im Mittelalter*, Berlin, 2006, p. 7, that the modern 'ecological' demand to work in harmony with the natural cosmos instead of transforming it autonomously and autocratically according to human ideas is essentially a revival of ancient and early medieval views of nature. "*Die moderne 'oekologische' Forderung, sich mit der Arbeit in den natuerlichen Kosmos einzufuegen, statt ihn autonom und eigenmaechtig nach menschlichen Vorstellungen umzugestalten, ist im Grunde eine Wiederbelebung antiker und (frueh-) mittelalterlicher Naturauffassung.*"
   Author's translation: The modern 'ecological' call to work in harmony with the natural cosmos instead of transforming it autonomously and autocratically according to human ideas, is essentially a revival of ancient and early medieval views of nature.

22 Robert N. Watson, *Back to Nature, The Green and the Real in the Late Renaissance*, Philadelphia, 2006

23 George Bataille writes that capitalistic society generally reduces humanity into a mere thing, a commodity, in: *Die Aufhebung der Oekonomie*, Munich, 1985, p. 164

24 Oskar Negt, *Lebendige Arbeit, enteignete Zeit, Politische und kulturelle Dimensionen des Kampfes um die Arbeitszeit*, Frankfurt/New York, 1984, p. 184: "*Dass die Arbeit ausschliesslich unter dem*

characterized this view when he wrote that there are only two kinds of activities left for society, those that are aimed at earning money and those (games, spectacles, tourism, therapy, sport with expensive equipment) which depend on money as the necessary means.[25] And the whole production in a household, the 'poetic' sphere of self-work[26] was transferred into the public economic sphere of industry and goods exchange.[27]

This concept of labour was then split up once more, into working in one's own interest as a self-employed person or an artist perhaps and labouring for somebody for whom it is merely a cost factor, with this type of work performed overwhelmingly by men in a company working for an employer; while women's work was and is sometimes considered to be working without the exchange of money in a household.

Within paid labour, there are further divisions. Today, one can be employed by a labour-leasing company which buys and sells labour but does not employ the purchased labour itself, instead hiring it out to the actual providers of products or services. In Germany the number of people in such employment has trebled from 300,000 in 2003 to more than 900,000 today, as reported in the magazine *Der Spiegel*, April 2012.[28]

Within companies themselves, there are yet more divisions of labour: into the labour of highly paid senior directors, and well-educated, skilled and reasonably paid labourers in offices and factories, and low paid workers with only minimal training. And this threefold split of paid labour is to be completed by a fourth division: female labourers, even when well-educated and skilled and working in the same jobs and positions as their male counterparts, are – on average – only paid two thirds of their salaries, leading to the consequence that these women will have a smaller monthly pension than men when they retire.

Why we still allow these divisions to be regarded as acceptable, even logical, is hardly discussed. People seem to take such divisions for granted, as justifiable and even natural, that for example self-selected economic (male) leaders should have

Gesichtspunkt der Erwerbsarbeit gesehen wird, gruendet sich nicht auf die Natur des Menschen, sondern ist Produkt einer geschichtlichen Entwicklung."

25   Andre Gorz, Kritik *der oekonomischen Vernunft*, Berlin, 1989, p. 221:
     "Der Gesellschaft bleiben nur noch zwei Taetigkeiten ueber, einerseits Taetigkeiten, die das Geld-verdienen zum Zweck haben, und andererseit die Taetigkeiten (Spiele, Spektakel, Tourismus, Therapien, Sportarten mit teuren Ausruestungen usw.), die das Geld als notwendiges Mittel voraussetzen."

26   The word '*Eigenarbeit*' which I translate as 'self-work', was coined by Ernst Ulrich and Christine von Weizsaecker, in: *Anders Arbeiten – anders Wirtschaften*, published by Joseph Huber, Frankfurt, 1979; Paul Ekins, however, referred to it in: *The Living Economy*, London, 1986, as "own work". However 'own' has the connotation with a kind of property.
     From such a point of view, also the dispute about John Locke's expression that "every man has a *property* in his own person", in: *Second Treatise of Government*, first published 1690, Indianapolis, 1980, p. 19, can be better understood. Self-ownership of man and woman is characteristic for every human, not an external possession.

27   Ibid: *"Die gesamte haeusliche Produktion hingegen, die 'poietische' Eigenarbeit wurde aus der Privatsphaere in die oeffentliche oekonomische Sphaere der Industrie und des Warenverkehrs hinausverlagert."*

28   *Der Spiegel* No 17/2012, p. 77

some kind of natural right to be paid disproportionately large salaries. And we have to state that even the unions, which are supposed to fight for equal rights for male and female labourers, do not seem to be overeager in campaigning for fairer pay for women. Even they tend to accept these divisions as immutable.

It is interesting to look more closely at the salaries of senior executives.

This category shows the highest pay rises compared with all other categories of dependent labour.[29] Executives of German DAX-30-companies were paid 94 per cent more in 2011 compared to the year 2001, whereas the salaries of average employed labourer fell by 3 per cent over the same period. This shows that the division of labour between those who are getting richer and those who are losing out, is widening rapidly – and not only in Germany.

However, one of the effects of this widening gap is that there is now talk of a law making the owners of stock companies responsible for deciding how much employees should be paid, including salaries, share options, pension pots and bonuses and other incentives. It is really hard to understand why this was not solved already in the past. Obviously, it will be very interesting to see if such an initiative becomes law, as the bonus culture and additional payments to executives have grown so exorbitantly – a pattern which the civil service seems to have copied – even when profits were low or losses made. This group of labourers seems to have taken the power into their own hands, advancing from the position of dependent employees to a status very similar to that of an independent entrepreneur. And they have been allowed to get away with it.[30] This is totally unfair, not only to the shareholders of the companies concerned, but to other labourers as well, as no other group of dependent labourers has been able to do the same.

The word 'labour' itself has many more meanings than it's usual use referring to paid labour, and a few of these at least should be mentioned: 'Labour' can mean a task given to a person, the process of labouring, the result of labouring, or a group of people who are employed for money.[31] However, all these meanings of labour are assumptions, an abstraction of reality. In reality, naturally 'labour' is not an object which can be sold, even by its supposed 'owner'. Labour is not an exchangeable object independent from a human being, because the person has always to apply his own ability. Therefore any view claiming 'labour' is a good or ware like any other is wrong. No employer can dispose of 'labour' as he can do with other commercial merchandise. No employee can dispose of his labour, as labour is a built–in ability of himself. 'Labour' – be it of nature or of man – is not a good produced for the market, and it comes with its own purpose.

In a company we find real labouring people, not abstract 'labour'.[32] Indeed the

29 As reported in *Der Spiegel* No 18/2012, p. 76
30 One could observe a very similar development in government where civil servants, responsible for executing politics and answering to parliament, have copied the bonus culture.
31 Ernst Michael Lange, *Das Prinzip Arbeit*, Frankfurt, Berlin, Wien, 1980
32 Perhaps it should be mentioned that there is another division concerning how humans describe themselves, eg Mark Pagel writes in: *Wired for Culture*, London 2012, p. 325: "... people's brains seem to know what they are going to do before the owners of those brains are made aware of the decision." The question is who is the 'I' who 'owns' a brain? Is it not the fact that a person and his brain are one? We have, disappointingly enough, not yet found words to describe what we really are.

economicult idea of labour is a deceptive and annoying constructions. We have shown how the meaning of 'labour' has derived from the classical time of the slave trade, but it is hard to understand why this meaning has not yet been relinquished, when slave markets were abolished hundreds of years ago.

Consequently, in the 21st century the idea of a 'labour market' can finally be replaced by a culteconomic theory based on real facts, not on outdated assumptions of what 'labour' should be. In the 21st century it should be possible to treat 'labour' as what it is, an ability incorporated in and inalienable from a natural being.

And if there are people who believe that today's economicult society is already modern, enlightened and liberal, then they need to be reminded that as long as 'labour' is seen as a kind of commodity, an object dividable from a labouring person, than we find, it is not. Instead, today's society can only be characterized as 'semi-modern'. Let us never forget: when we talk about 'labour', we are talking about a living person, an organism.[33]

This is the hope: that there will be a culteconomy in which real people with their real natural ability interact with their outside nature as well with their own kind.

When Adam Smith stated that 'nature labours besides man', he referred to this connotation of 'labour' to describe nature and men. So, the real modern definition of 'labour' needs to be consistent with nature as well as well as with a person, overcoming the various social divisions that exist today.

These requirements are met when culteconomy follows the definition of labour which is used in physics: *'Labour is the product of force-times-distance divided by time.'* Here, labour is defined as an ability or an energy or a power incorporated in all living matter. By using such an understanding of the labouring *ability* we can finally implement a modern, consistent and exact definition of labour. Also, we can overcome any understanding of it that is expressed purely in terms of money.

Furthermore, labour, it seems, has another rarely discussed connotation, which should be pointed out: that it is an outwardly applied power. If I work for example on a product or a service, I use my labouring ability on it. This is the common understanding. But such a view only concentrates on the one side of labour, because before I am able to apply my labouring power to something, for example flour, yeast and water, I have to identify the materials which I am to apply my labour to. Observing them, they give me the necessary information about themselves, which I perceive.

We have to conclude that labour has two sides, an outward ability of application and at the same time an inward ability to absorb information, a unity of perception and action, as Viktor von Weizsaecker[34] called it. Richard Sennet saw

---

33   which consists of colonies of interacting micro-organisms, according to Robert N. Watson, in: *Back to Nature*, Philadelphia, 2006, p. 12

34   Viktor von Weizsaecker, *Der Gestaltkreis, Theorie der Einheit von Wahrnehmen und Bewegen*, Frankfurt, 1973, first published 1940; cf also: Rupert Sheldrake, *The Science Delusion, Freeing the Spirit of Enquiry*, London, 2012, p. 220, and Carl Friedrich von Weizsaecker, *Der Garten des Menschlichen*, Munich/Wien, 1978, p. 206

it as the "intimate connection between hand and head."[35]

And it is interesting to note that Adam Smith had a very similar insight: "What we feel while we stand in the sunshine during a hot, or in the shade during a frosty, day, is evidently felt, not as pressing upon the body, but as in the body. It does not necessarily suggest the presence of any external object, nor could we from thence alone infer the existence of any such object. It is a sensation which neither does nor can exist anywhere but either in the organ which feels it, or in the unknown principle of perception, whatever that may be, which feels in that organ, or by means of that organ. When we lay our hand upon a table, which is either heated or cooled a good deal beyond the actual temperature of our hand, we have two distinct perceptions: first, that of the solid or resisting table, which is necessarily felt as something external to, and independent of, the hand which feels it: and secondly, that of the heat or cold, which by the contact of the table is excited in our hand, and which is naturally felt as nowhere but in our hand, or in the principle of perception which feels in our hand." (EW p. 191) "... the Internal Sensation, and the External Cause of that Sensation, come in our conception to be so strictly connected, that in our ordinary and careless way of *thinging*[36] we are apt to consider them as almost one and the same thing, and therefore denote them by one and the same word. The confusion, however, is in this case more in the word than in the thought; for in reality we still retain some notion of distinction, though we do not always evolve it with that accuracy which a very slight degree of attention might enable us to do." (EW p. 192) Perception and action are one. Labour has dual quality.

It follows, that labour is a reciprocal process, one side of which is taking in information, the other applying it. Both sides of labour are inseparably connected, one can not exist without the other. Common sense views the outgoing side of labour as active, and the 'in-taking' side as passive. Herein lies another one of the reasons why the analysis of economicult theory cannot be satisfied with discussing merely the outgoing side of labour, ie the production of goods, but has to consider the 'in-taking' side too. In economics, this corresponds to production, being active, and consumption, which is seen as passive.

The understanding of labour as a reciprocal process can also be extended to the scientific approach. Scientific analysis can, in a way, be considered as the in-taking side, gaining necessary information, before labour can be outwardly applied.

But then we encounter a problem. When a scientist wishes to analyze a stone for example, splitting it into its elementary parts to gain knowledge of how it is composed, then we have to state that such a procedure is only an appropriate way for analyzing non-living matter and cannot be used for analyzing life, because trying to split a living organism into its elementary parts would have the unavoidable result of killing it. Moreover, this traditional method of gaining knowledge will not teach the scientist how the plant lived, of the nature of its interactions with its surroundings, or the local conditions that enables it to live, grow and propagate. We have to come to the conclusion that the traditional procedure of analyzing an object is not really appropriate for living matter as plants, animals or humans.

---

35   Richard Sennett, *The Craftsman*, London, 2008, p. 9
36   Obviously it is meant to read 'thinking', but makes a lot of sense in relation to this analysis.

Consequently, the traditional scientific procedure has to be widened. It has to be extended to include the relationship between the analyzing scientist as the subject of the process, and the object of his interest. It depends also on the scientist's personal view of his object; whether he sees it as a material object or an energy wave. The former idea that matter can be viewed independently and objectively and without somebody, a scientist, making it his object of interest, has to be put to rest. The modern way of gaining knowledge about life is to analyze the reciprocal interaction between the scientific subject and the object of his interest.

7.2. Widening the perspective – from object to process

Now it can be shown how the scientific analysis of an object can be extended into an interactive process taking place between the subject and the object of analysis. Let's do that step by step:

The choice to make something into an 'object of interest' is not objective, but subjective. The selection process showing the interest of the scientist is hitherto not included into the discussion. But the object is viewed as if it presents it on its own.

The traditional way of gathering knowledge about an object is to single it out from its natural environment:

O

object of interest

and then divide it into its components:

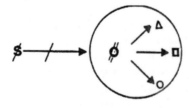

object of interest

To compose or produce something, the different parts are then combined according to interest:

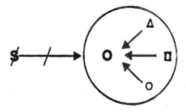

object of interest

This is the procedure typical for today's procedure. It is, however, an incomplete procedure, as mentioned, and can give only incomplete knowledge, as not all the information is collectable, but only part of it. What is missing for example is the information indicating how the object lived and under which conditions, what it needed to preserve its life.

Such information could not be gathered by this procedure. It was neglected.[37]

To demonstrate this graphically, the following page contains a picture. It was drawn by Harmon and published by Stuttgart, 1978, in: *Unsere Welt – ein vernetztes System*[38] by Frederic Vester (1925 - 2003), a German biologist.

The picture serves to show the traditional method of gaining knowledge, this is to measure the number of small squares that can be recognized, their height, width and colour. When all this information is written down, we traditionally believe that the necessary data about the object has been collected, and our knowledge about the object is exact. We now know everything about the object which we need to know, so the assumption goes.

On the contrary, it can be shown that if we allow the data to become less and less exact, eg when the graphic is viewed from a distance from, perhaps 10 metres, then it can be discovered that the drawing shows much more information than just different squares in a range of shades from white to black. Now the relations between the different squares can become clear. It gives us the face of Abraham Lincoln. Salvador Dali, as an artist, obviously was aware of these largely neglected relations, and he has used this insight to create his oil painting '*Gala mirando el Mar Mariterraneo*', painted in 1974/5 and exhibited in the Teatro Museo Dali in Figueres.

We are now convinced that the hitherto unnecessarily reduced understanding of compiling information about an object does not give us all the information, because it neglected the relations between the details.

The first step in broadening our scientific approach therefore has to be: to include the observing subject – the scientist – in the process, as knowledge can only be gathered by a subject. That subject is traditionally excluded in the traditional scientific approach.[39]

---

37   Henri Poincrae's famous remark cited by Mircea Eliade, in: *Die Religionen und das Heilige*, Frankfurt, 1986, p. 13: "*Darf ein Naturforscher, der den Elefanten immer nur unter dem Mikroskop studiert hat, glauben, dieses Lebewesen hinreichend zu kennen?*"
Translated: "Is a natural scientist who has only ever studied the elephant under a microscope entitled to believe that he knows all there is to know about this beast?"

38   p. 166

39   Cf. the introduction of a subject as an objective factor, in: Rudolf zur Lippe, *Am eigenen Leibe, Zur Oekonomie des Lebens*, Frankfurt, 1979, p. 25

Drawing by Harmon

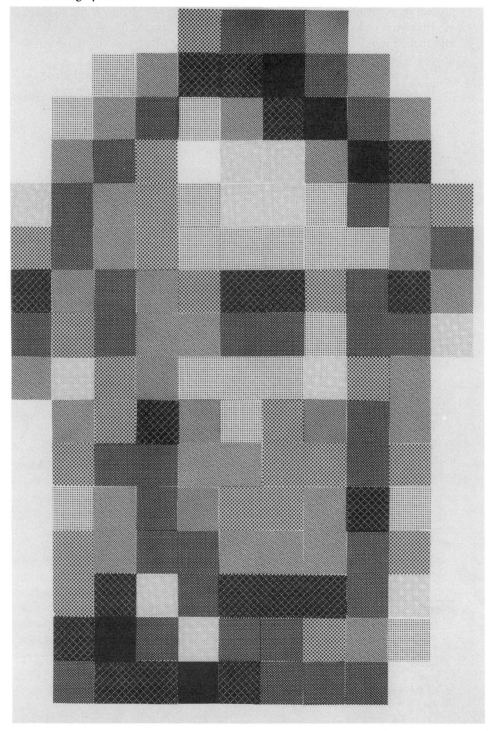

subject with interest   object of interest

This subject's role as receiver is excluded in the diagram above. When the subject wants information about a chosen object, then he becomes the receiver of the information as the object is releasing information to him:

subject with an interest   object of interest

receiver of information   giver of information

The procedure develops from a one-dimensional to a reciprocal process. Object and subject are now viewed as interacting with each other; meaning that what was formerly considered a 'mere object' now becomes the subject of the process when giving information to what was formerly considered a 'mere subject' the human being, the scientist. Their roles have become interchangeable. When the former subject chooses an object according to his own interest, the former 'mere object' becomes now an active part releasing information. The object's *raison d'être* and its own interest in keeping its metabolism going and in propagation can no longer be seen as exempt, as without this consideration the scientific knowledge of an object would be incomplete. As life is a dynamic and open process, taking place in four-dimensional space-time, the openness of this reciprocal interaction is shown by a broken line, as seem in the diagram overleaf:

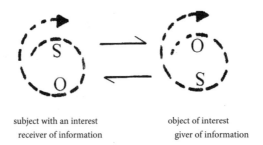

subject with an interest
receiver of information

object of interest
giver of information

Now a final step is necessary relating to the whole logic of the process:

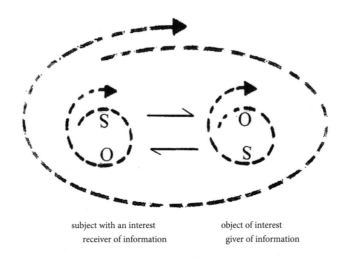

subject with an interest
receiver of information

object of interest
giver of information

Further comment is necessary regarding the process of reciprocal interaction to gain knowledge: When economists discuss events, they often use the image of a 'cycle' or 'circle'. A circular metaphor, however, is not appropriate, as a circle is an abstract idea not found in nature. Furthermore, a circle can easily be drawn on paper, the end joining the starting point, but it can only be drawn without realizing that time has irretrievably moved on. In comparison, if we write down a word by hand, we are very well aware that this is an activity in time, a movement from the left to the right, connecting one letter with the next. Therefore, the circular metaphor should be replaced with the helical or spiral one, of which we know different kinds, eg the Archimedean spiral where distances between the lines stay the same, or the Duerer spiral where the distances extend. In reality, flowers grow in a helical form, DNA is organised as a double helix and galaxies show it. 5,000 years ago, stonemasons cut spiral patterns into the stones of the Neolithic temples in Malta while even 7,000 years ago people of the Naqada culture in Egypt decorated vases with a spring showing that ancient cultures must have had already an idea about its importance. The Milky Way, our local galaxy where Sun and Earth are located, also has the form of a spiral – with four huge arms.

You can try to experiment on your own to transform a circle into a helix or spring: take a coil of wire or an extending cable and place it on the floor before you in a circle, then stand up and slowly draw one end up to you, counting the time. You will notice, how in time you can change a circle into a helix. And if you pick up the coiled wire, taking one end in your left hand and the other end in your right, and then pull both ends slightly, again counting the time, you will notice that the circle is transformed into another shape, a sine wave, typical for sound oscillations or more prosaically, the ups and downs of everyday life.

7.3. The process of direct natural reciprocal interaction

Let's summarize what we have found so far: our understanding of 'land' as the factor of traditional economicult theory could be developed into the self-organized, dynamic and open process of natural evolution, leading from inorganic to organic matter, and from life to consciousness. Perhaps we shall ask the question: "... what if all self-organizing systems are subjects?"[40] and answer it as follows: "The *organism*, not the machine, provides the appropriate metaphor"[41] for our understanding of how natural phenomena – plants, animals, men, even planets – interact with each other.[42] And our understanding of the former factor 'labour' could be developed into an inalienable ability of nature and humans to interact. Manjit Kumar – rather poetically – called these new views "a quantum dance of give-and-take,"[43] while the process of "give-and-take" is double-sided, an entity of human perception and action, of head and hand. It is respecting nature's laws – but in the different forms of the ever-changing human culture, a dynamic process,[44] in which humans are actively participating. Now, neither 'land' nor 'labour' need to be defined according to monetary terms which is limiting. Interaction is a reciprocal process in which every participant plays a role. And furthermore, interaction is no longer concentrated on exchanges between men, but is extended to exchanges between men and nature, it comprises the natural reciprocal[45] process of interaction between humans as well as with nature, and such an understanding of the basic economic principle goes far beyond classical and neoclassical ideas.

---

40 Rupert Sheldrake, *The Science Delusion*, London, 2012, p. 334
41 David C. Korten, *Agenda for a New Economy, From Phantom Wealth to Real Wealth*, San Francisco, 2010, p. 259
42 eg when trees emit certain scents to attract insects thus helping them to get rid of pests or when microbes and bacteria help men to digest, likewise planets' orbits can change in accordance with their reciprocal pull, especially in the case of the largest planet in the solar system, Jupiter.
43 Manjit Kumar, *Quantum ...*, p. 232
44 compare: Norbert Elias (1897-1990), *The Civilizing Process*, London, 1969
45 As explained in chapter 5, it seems more appropriate to use the word 'interaction' than the word 'exchange' to describe the basic principle as the last concentrates on the object exchanged while the first focuses on the process.

It is now possible to draw a diagram of the natural reciprocal interaction between nature and human beings respecting its different historic forms, and this can be described as follows:

Reciprocal interaction between nature and man
- A human being is an entity to itself while at the same time a part of nature.[46] A person perceives nature with his natural senses, feeds from the outside nature and returns unusable waste to it.[47]
- Through his direct interaction with nature the person evolves from an animal into a human being, developing consciousness.

Reciprocal interaction between man and man[48]
- Every person lived or lives together with others. Specific habits and norms how to live are created by the member of the group into which everybody is born. People learn from each other.
- Different cultural habits and norms are imposed on the members of the group forming their particular culture, thus becoming second nature to them.

Reciprocal interaction between human culture and nature
- The human community deals with the local nature in its specific historic way.
- Nature affects the specific culture according to its conditions in which a culture is established, such as geography, climate, seasons etc.

A few remarks need to be added regarding the process of reciprocal interaction:
- The natural process of reciprocal interaction is not mediated by a means.
- The direction of the interaction depends on the participants. It can lead to value cooperation or competition.
- The process of interaction is naturally influenced by the various personalities, habits, experiences, knowledge, beliefs and also gender and age of the participants.
- Ideally, reciprocal[49] interaction should be equally fair[50] to all the participants as every partner has the same right to be active and needs to have his point of

---

46 Gregory Bateson, *Oekologie des Geistes*, Frankfurt, 1981, p. 410 ff
47 An example of why it is important to see man and nature existing within a continual process of interaction is offered by the study of the Centre for Advanced European Studies and Research, Bonn/Germany, when the scientists found that chemicals from "common household products such as toothpastes, soaps and plastic toys have a direct impact on human sperm which could help to explain rising levels of male infertility", which makes us understand the consequences of our own activities, published in The *i* 12 May 2014, p. 6.
48 Here 'culture' is used as in: Mark Pagel, *Wired for Culture, The Natural History of Human Cooperation*, London, 2012
49 Will Hutton wrote in: *Them and Us, Changing Britain – Why we need a fair society*, London, 2011, p. 47, "Reciprocity... at the core of social relationships... indicates that human beings expect to be treated as they treat others."
50 Will Hutton, ibid, p. 21: "Fairness is the indispensable value that underpins good economy and society, and it will be the foundation stone of any sustainable new order."

view respected. The question we need to ask is: what does this mean with regard to nature? Do we treat nature as well as nature nurtures us?

- In this process, we often observe the attempt of one person to convince or dominate the other, or the total resistance of one person to the other, or even the intention of one person to deceive the other. "Natural selection will have equipped us not only with the emotions to take advantage of others, but with a bag of tricks to enhance those deceptions – charm, flattery, lack of empathy, self-deprecation, and an ability to hide or fake emotions. It will also... have favoured an ability to hide our emotions from ourselves, the better to deceive others... On the other hand, if deception can return the rewards we think it does, then natural selection will also have favoured keen abilities for detecting it... to help us spot who is a social cheater and who is following the rules."[51]

- In the process of reciprocal interaction spoken language as well as body language is used, in various forms. Whatever form of interaction takes place, and however fortunate or unfortunate the outcome for one of the participants, it is still an interaction.

- The process of reciprocal interaction is open, ie it continues for as long as the participants engage in it.

- Normally we are not fully aware of the process of reciprocal interaction. It seems that when a process is repeated again and again, the information about it is stored in our unconscious memory, which we rely on in order to re-using it. Once we have learned to drive a car, for example, it is as if our hands and feet instinctively know what to do. We do not have to remind ourselves of every necessary movement which needs to come next. By repeating the same procedure, the process is ritualized. This helps us by saving time, which is a necessity if you consider the consequences of having to think every situation through afresh. As Oliver Sacks described it: "When we walk, our steps emerge in a rhythmical stream, a flow that is automatic and self-organising".[52] Repeated interactions can even lead to a kind of rhythmic pattern creating melodies. This calls to mind the chants invented by people working together. "Rhythm in this sense, the integration of sound and movement, can play a great role in coordinating and invigorating basic locomotor movement,"[53] Sacks noticed. "The embedding of words, skills, or sequences in melody and meter is uniquely human. The usefulness of such an ability to recall large amounts of information, especially in a preliterate culture, is surely one reason why musical abilities have flourished in our species."[54] He then considers what enables us to bind together sight, sound, smell and emotions: " Such binding in the nervous system is accomplished by rapid, synchronized firing of nerve cells in different parts of the brain. Just as rapid neuronal oscillations bind together different functional parts within the brain and nervous system, so rhythm binds together the individual nervous systems of a human community."[55]

---

51 ibid p. 312
52 Oliver Sacks, *Musicophilia,* New York, 2008, p. 270
53 ibid, p. 262
54 ibid, p. 260
55 ibid, p. 269

It seems that such binding does not only take place within the human brain itself, but also takes place between one human and another. We can comprehend what others are going through because of having developed so-called mirror neurons. Christian Keysers,[56] a scientist at the University of Groningen, in the Netherlands, emphasized in an interview with *Der Spiegel* that perception and action are not, as long accepted, separate worlds. The gap is bridged by mirror neurons. Mirroring is a process by which we experience others' sensations, emotions and actions vicariously. The whole body is involved, resonating so to speak with that of the other person. This results in an effortless bond which underpins so much human cooperation. Fundamentally speaking we are not really separate individuals but elements of a social fabric. Is what I am saying here my idea or yours? He answered himself that it is neither, it is the result of our interaction.

The following diagram illustrates the direct natural reciprocal process of interaction:[57]

---

56 29/2013 p. 124, "*Es ist eben nicht so, wie man lange dachte, dass Handeln und Wahrnehmen getrennte Welten seien. Die Spiegelneuronen ueberbruecken die Grenze... Das Spiegeln ist ein Mitspueren, Miterleben, Mittun, das die eigenen Koerpererlebnisse und Erfahrungen benutzt. Der ganze Koerper ist daran beteiligt. Er schwingt mit dem Koerper des anderen Menschen gewissermassen mit. So entsteht eine muehelose Verbindung, die so vielem menschlichen Zusammenwirken zugrunde liegt... wir sind im Grunde gar keine einzelnen Individuen, sondern Bestandteile eines eng vernetzten sozialen Gewebes. Ist das, was ich jetzt sage, meine Idee oder Ihre? Ich wuerde sagen: Weder - noch, es ist das Ergebnis unserer Interaktion.*"

57 Irene Schoene, *Oekologisches Arbeiten*, Wiesbaden, 1988, p. 281.
    This diagram describing the direct natural reciprocal process of interaction and the one that follows when the direct process is mediated, I first published in 1983 in: '*Ansaetze fuer oekologisch orientiertes Arbeiten*', in: *Loccumer Protokolle 25, Oekologisch orientierte Forschung in Naturwissenschaft, Technik und Oekonomie, Dokumentation einer Tagung der Evangelischen Akademie Loccum vom 28,–30, Oktober 1983*, Rehburg-Loccum, published 1984, p. 144 and 146.
    Both diagrams describe *the direct natural reciprocal process of interaction as a continuous activity, a movement*.
    When from this basis the idea of a 'triangle of sustainability' was suggested, however, the new understanding was switched back to a static object or to things, but let us not give up trying to convince our fellow-beings that life is an active process and not an object.

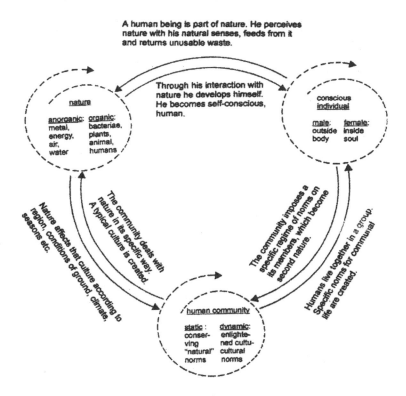

In natural and direct reciprocal interaction there is no means of exchange, and nature has never developed a means/medium for its processes of interaction. The invention of a medium of exchange is an entirely human invention, which John Locke had already pointed out in the 17th century.[58]

Before describing the form reciprocal interaction can take when mediated by money and the market, it is quite useful to point to Ernst Haeckel (1834–1919), German biologist and friend of Charles Darwin, who coined the word 'ecology', and discuss what 'ecology' has to do with it.

Haeckel wrote in his book *Generelle Morphologie der Organismen*[59] that by "ecology" we mean the whole sphere of the organism's relationship with its external environment which, in a wider sense, can be deemed to include all conditions of existence. He explains that the term should refer to the process which began about 3 billion years ago, when bacteria developed and started propagation. Blue algae invented photosynthesis building up the atmosphere essential for life.

We now understand that ecology describes direct relationships between humans and their natural and cultural environment. The term 'ecology' can therefore never be a substitute for 'nature', for 'environment' or even simply for 'green'.

---

58 John Locke, *Second Treatise of Government*, ibid., paragraphs 49 & 50, p. 29.

59 published Berlin, 1866, p. 286.: "*Unter Oecology verstehen wir die gesamte Wissenschaft von den Beziehungen des Organismus zur umgebenden Aussenwelt, wohin wir im weiteren Sinne alle 'Existenz-Bedingungen' rechnen koennen.*"

Haeckel coined a word for 'relationships between' living organisms, but not an additional kind of definition for an object, although today people indeed use the term 'ecology' more or less in an objectified way. (This is – as has already been pointed out – an outdated view, seeing the world in the form of things, when we should view it rather as events. However, it may be that this approach is changing at the moment, as nowadays we seem to talk so much about relationships.)

Having defined the natural basic pattern as reciprocal interaction, it is now possible to discuss where we can experience it in daily life.

7.3.1. The process of reciprocal interaction in the private household

It was Aristotle who gave men's activity the name '*oeconomia*' describing the rules and habits of life in the '*oikos*' (Greek), which included land, house, tools, cattle, materials, slaves/chattels, wife, children and relatives, the male free Greek, the '*oikodespotes*', owned. What was produced on the land and in the house was consumed by the members of this household. The use of a means of exchange in the household did not make sense for this kind of economy, in the same way that a means of exchange is not used within for example a car factory to put the separate parts of a product together.

This classical historic form of interaction – self-contained and not mediated by market and money – is the basis for what we understand by the term 'economy'. We call it natural economy or '*nateconomy*', as it resembles the natural direct interaction without a means[60] as explained in chapter 5. Carl Linnaeus, later Carl von Linne (1707–1778), a Swedish natural scientist and a contemporary of Adam Smith, who was the first to classify organisms, understanding humans as primates, named it '*oeconomia naturae*'.[61] However, the Greeks knew and used a means = money, invented about 7,000 BCE as a medium of exchange[62] to gain the few goods that were too specialized to be produced in their own individual *oikos*. We have called the kind of economy where an invented means (ie money) is used a cultural economy or '*culteconomy*'. We should emphasize again the fact that in classical times, money never had the role we appoint to it today.

We have seen that Aristotle already differentiated between interactions where money is used as a means (culteconomy) and those where money is used as the end of exchange. For the latter, Aristotle invented the term '*chrematistike*'. We

---

60   This differentiation had been made by the German Enlightenment philosopher Georg Wilhelm Friedrich Hegel (1770–1831), *System der Sittlichkeit*, first published 1802/03, in: *Fruehe politische Systeme*, by Gerhard Goehler (ed.), Frankfurt, Berlin, Wien, 1974, p. 43, when he pointed out that in the family the man is the master and administrator, but not the owner. As administrator he only appears to have free power of disposal. Every member of the family contributes to the mutual use of products, but they do not acquire individual ownership. Use is direct and immediate. Hegel must have known Adam Smith's work as he referred to it here and there.

61   According to Ulrich Grober, *Die Entdeckung der Nachhaltigkeit, Kulturgeschichte eines Begriffs*, Munich, 2013, p. 128, who pointed out that Linne took over this expression from the English physio-theologist Thomas Burnet, who understood it in 1690 as the well ordering of the great Family of living Creators.

62   "... by a tacit and voluntary consent..." mentioned Locke, ibid, p. 29

have called this form of economic activity, where the culturally invented means is made the purpose and the end of all interaction, economicult to show very clearly that the end is substituted for the means.[63] The economicult form of economy has been made the norm about 2,000 years after Aristotle, from the 18th century on. However, we today seem to view this form as the natural economy, clearly a misunderstanding.

Before showing a diagram of economicult interactions mediated by and geared towards money, it is useful, in order to show the importance of the changes, to begin by describing the direct, unmediated interactions in a household economy in more detail.

The basis for all economic activities is contained in the so-called economic principle, which has – like so many other things – two sides. One side aims at making the most out of a given means, while the other aims at using the least means possible to gain a set end. It is clear to see that the first side refers to the household economy. This side of the economic principle can therefore also be called the household principle.

When trying to describe interactions in the household economy, it is necessary to go back a few years, to compare how these have changed over time. Looking back only a few decades, household economics, as one of the three economic theories (management theory/microeconomics and national economics/macro-economics) was thought to constitute valuable knowledge. It was taught in universities. Nowadays, it rarely is any more.

Today life is divided into two parts, into production in the economicult sphere on one hand and the consumption side at home on the other, into formal and informal activities, private and public. This split occurred in the 18th century, when labour was no longer performed at home, but started to be outsourced to factories. At the same time, the home began to be divided into different rooms for different purposes, eg cleaning, sleeping, cooking and eating,[64] and for different ages.

Today working in the household is seen as the private, passive side of life, as *re*-production, while labouring in a company represents the active and productive side, as it is paid and aimed at making a profit. In reality, however, it is precisely the other way around: a company produces the means for life. Economic activity is for reproduction, while people and nature produce life itself in their own home. It shows that even the words 'production' and 'reproduction' are characterized by using monetary terms.

Companies are seen as a 'thing'[65] that one works for, although a company

---

63 Karl Polanyi, characterized this in *The Great Transformation*, p. 186: "*Die Wirtschaft ist nicht mehr in die sozialen Beziehungen eingebettet, sondern die sozialen Beziehungen sind in das Wirtschaftssystem eingebettet.*" Author's translation: The economic system is no longer embedded in society, but rather society is embedded in the economy.

64 Richard Sennett reminds us in: *The Craftsman*, ibid, p. 53, that "in the Middle Ages craftsmen slept, ate and raised their children in the places where they worked."

65 It seems that viewing the world in terms of *things* (hypostatisation) is more common for men than for women. Scientists from the Universitee Libre in Brussels have discovered that men seem to have a deep-rooted habit of perceiving the opposite sex as an object, reported in: *Psychological Science*, April 2012.

might be nothing else but the place where an entrepreneur labours, a kind of objectification of his own work.

In such companies, employees who are totally unfamiliar with each other have to cooperate. The 'factory system' has been made the norm. It was initiated by Richard Arkwright in Cromford, Derbyshire, in 1771. The system dictated that everyone had to start working at the same time, rest at the same time and finish at the same time, day in and day out, in return for money; an idea which seems so 'normal' to us today.[66]

We can now say that economicult theory is obviously formulated from the point of view of and in the interest of the entrepreneur. It is a theory of managing the labouring ability of other people. Few entrepreneurs can get rich by applying their labour alone, but become wealthier only by employing other people. And it is, in a way, no wonder that economicult theory cares little about the private side of consumption, where interaction is not mediated by money and the means is not made into the end.

Let's go into the changes that people have made in their household economy in recent years. Reciprocal interaction in a private household consists of keeping people alive by looking after them, feeding them and keeping them healthy. This means trying to understand their needs and fulfilling them, be they babies, or the ill or elderly; washing, drying, ironing and mending clothes, shoes and other belongings of household members; sewing, knitting, doing handicraft; bringing children into the world and educating them, teaching them reading, writing, counting, cooking, how to keep themselves and their home clean, dispose of waste safely, etc., so that they grow into a healthy person capable of standing on their own feet and earning a living. It is also important to teach children to respect other people and help them to understand the behaviour and motives of those people, who may have different ideas and aims in life. Parents or carers must teach them to control their aggression, attempting to interest them in the way a society is run; support them in taking up sports or playing instruments, reciting poetry, using libraries, viewing paintings; giving them a chance to discuss and communicate their feelings and experiences; all of this so that one day they may be able to participate actively in their community. And also maintaining the home; keeping it running smoothly, clean and aired, free from insects and vermin, using utilities such as water and energy efficiently, learning how to decorate the home usefully and pleasingly, whatever the taste; managing the money income, so that a person is never in too much debt and always able to meet obligations; making time for social interactions, such as seeing family and friends; reading; communicating with each other during shared meals, airing ideas about the world, politics, religion; singing, dancing or playing a spot of football, golf or tennis; doing a bit of woodwork or maintaining a garden, where we can enjoy the result of our own interaction with nature in the form of herbs, flowers, fruit and vegetables; and last but not least going for walks, or just relaxing and enjoying the sunshine; going on holidays to see new places and experience other cultures in order to broaden our

---

66 Cf. H. Treiber, H. Steinert, *Die Fabrikation des zuverlaessigen Menschen, Ueber die 'Wahlverwandschaft' von Kloster und Fabrikdisziplin*, Munich, 1980

interest in life. This is also the time, when charity work and volunteering in the community shop can be done. All these various and totally different interactions have to be learned through experience, and when knowledge of these interactions is incorporated in a person, they turn into a kind of 'technique', which can be applied almost without thinking. The interactions become abilities stored on some subconscious level, a kind of natural rationalization of a person's efforts, like the acquired ability to swim or to ride a bicycle. All these interactions have a non-monetary value, as Richard Sennett has pointed out,[67] in his definition of crafts-manship: "Craftsmanship names an enduring, basic human impulse, the desire to do a job well for its own sake."

These diverse interactions have to be repeated all the time. They are a never-ending lifelong process, in which every activity which is 'produced' is consumed at the same time.[68] And all these activities are direct interactions which do not involve the exchange of money or the aim of making money, but of ensuring that people apply their abilities, learn more, live with others, stay alive and remain in good health.[69]

It is still the norm that these unpaid interactions in a household are consid-ered (by men) to be the natural realm of the wife. When a man proposes marriage, this often means he can dispose of the woman's labour for his personal well-being[70] as well as the household tasks, even when she has a professional paid job. A study by the think tank UK Institute for Public Policy Research published 11 March 2012 concluded that "after decades of feminism, housework is still the job of a woman, with just one in 10 men doing more than their partner" and concludes that "for real equality, society needs to see men pick up the vacuum cleaner and do their fair share."[71]

The labour in a household is not paid and not aimed at making money, and therefore, in an economicult society, it is unvalued and treated as not existent. It is for example also excluded from the Gross Domestic Product (GDP). We live in a culture which does not value what we do ourselves, but only values what is done in exchange for money. As a consequence: we even define our own abilities in monetary terms.

Innumerable books had been written about household management. Let's take just one as an example: the News Chronicle *"Everything within – a Library of Information for the Home"*.[72] It offers information about "every vital interest of the Home" which it claims "has been dealt with authoritatively", starting with the

---

67   Richard Sennet, ibid., p. 9
68   Hannah Arendt, *Vita activa oder vom taetigen Leben*, Muenchen, 1981, p. 81
69   An understanding of labour, that already John Locke shared, ibid, in paragraph 27.
70   The American writer Rebecca Solnit pointed out that it is still common for men to deny women their own decisions. In her view, the attitude: "I have the right to control you," is the first authoritarian step towards violence, and she concludes: "We have an abundance of rape and violence against women in this country and on this Earth, though its almost never treated as a civil rights or human rights issue, or a crisis, or even a pattern. Violence doesn't have a race, a class, a religion, or a nationality, but it does have a gender," in: *A Rape a Minute, a Thousand Corpses a Year, Hate Crimes in America (and Elsewhere)*, on TomDispatch.com 24 January 2013.
71   www.dailymail.co.uk
72   Printed in London and Edinburgh, presumably in the 1930s, emphasis from the book

"Business of the Home", proceeding to "Cookery and Catering and then to the "Medical Dictionary" and to the "subject of Beauty Culture". It claims that "'Everyday Facts' provide an invaluable source of much indispensable knowledge, whilst 'Home Management' and the 'Home Handyman' are essentially for home-lovers of both sexes. 'Games and Amusements' occupy a large section, and 'Questions and Answers' throw light on nearly five hundred problems of the utmost interest in every imaginable direction, from classical days to our own times." It's tone suggests that in the household one is free to do whatever one likes – especially in the case of men – and describes how and when these things should be done.

However, even when it seems that 'nothing' much is happening when viewed from the outside, people are interacting with each other as well as with their natural and social environment; they breathe in and out, as mentioned, showing that we cannot live without reciprocal interaction with nature.

In the household we seem to enjoy free time, free from the pressures of the formal economicult. This free time is not only the basis for life, it was seen by enlightened philosophers as the yardstick for people's freedom and autonomy. The free time in the life-world[73], was once seen as inspiring the cultural development and to improve the formal part of life for more individual freedom. However, in today's economicult the life-world seems to be dependent on and defined by formal production, whose norms influence our free, independent time more than the norms of free time have influenced the formal sphere. It is not too far-fetched to conclude that this is caused by making monetary terms rule.

Household management obviously varied and varies according to its cultural and historical context. Before World War II it was more or less the norm to employ people to help with the household chores, people who did not live in the household, eg the 'white' woman. She would come in every four weeks to repair the linen. The butcher would pop in to help slaughter the swine and to help preserve its meat for the winter. The gardener would come to turn up the vegetable patch and tell us about his experiences with a new variety of Italian spinach.[74] He would also help to cut and stack wood for the winter. If necessary, a nurse would offer herself to look after a sick household member. All these people did these jobs because they were paid for doing them. The cash income, brought in by the head of the household, defined what help the household could afford. In bigger houses, more helpers were necessary who lived 'in service'. With 'hired help' the regular and necessary contribution of every household member to execute the essential tasks changed from a daily obligation for all to a paid occupation for a few; however, it is still direct human reciprocal interaction.

Today the hiring of human helpers has been replaced by products in which the working capacity is stored: hoovers, washing and drying machines, dishwashers, fridges and freezers, microwaves, sewing machines and so on. Instead of paying for helping hands we buy machines to help us, again depending on the disposable

---

73   In German '*Lebenswelt*', in English 'lifeworld', is a concept, coined by Edmund Husserl (1859–1938) and pursued by Juergen Habermas, in: *Theorie kommunikativen Handelns*, Frankfurt, 1981

74   Remember, there are still autumn produce shows in this country where people proudly present the results of their efforts.

income of the household or the credit it can afford.

In a sense, a process similar to the one implemented in manufacturing companies has taken place in the household economy. Human labour has been dissected into small, special tasks, and then these have been incorporated into machines, replacing human helpers. With it, the labouring process in the households has transformed from direct human reciprocal interaction into the use of standardized material objects.

In a company we call this process the 'rationalization of labour'. It is intended to make labour more productive as it allows to produce more goods in a given time, as machines never grow tired, ill or unwilling to repeat the same thing over and over again. In this way, the labour costs for an item can be reduced, a factory can offer its products at a lower price, and it is thus in a better position to compete for customers, because the economic assumption is that customers always go for the cheapest. This process is seen by economicult theorists as a kind of natural law. Economic production has to take place with less and less human labour – hence the slogan about the 'end of work'.[75] And as there are more and more people in the world needing paid jobs, we can only sustain levels of employment by producing new commodities.

There is, however, another reason for replacing human labour with machines, which should not be forgotten: machines are totally owned by and at the disposal of the buyer (we think). Machines will execute the process for which they are built – and nothing else. With machines there is no argument, no feedback, and no new ideas. So the company becomes less dependent upon employed labour. And machines do not need health insurances or pensions. They are sorted out when written off. Less human labour is necessary for production. Only a few, less-trained labourers are needed to control machines. The production process is changed from one of human interaction to one of interaction with a machine, in the factory as well as in the household, although male labourers seem to complain less about the loss of human contact than do machine-using housewives, who object more to their resulting social isolation as 'green widows'.

We see this transformation happening not only in corporations and households, but also in the interaction of consumers with producers of a service. Here too the personal service is now replaced by a machine, whether the consumer likes it or not. When buying bus tickets, for example, there is no longer a conductor to make the sale, but an automaton, or when using a subway train there may be no driver. Of course, many would prefer to retain park-keepers, drivers and conductors, as people seem to behave in a far more civilized manner when a human being is around, probably because their relationship with other people is different to their relationship with machines.

However, while the preference for using machines instead of human services can be easily understood in the case of a company (total control, reduction of costs, higher turnout) such monetary gain is not the aim in the private household. The household is the owner of the machines, but the household does not employ machines to make money. Machines can make household labour easier to carry

---

75   Jeremy Rifkin, *The End of Work*, New York, 1996

out and a lot faster – it would be silly to suppress this point – but this change comes with a few 'buts' to be considered:

The household members first have to raise the household budget to be able to buy a machine. Investments in machines normally cost more than employed helpers. Furthermore machines need electricity to run, as well as insurance, maintenance and repairs, for which money has to be provided. Therefore the family members have to earn more, bringing in more income, sometimes even from two employments, labour more or borrow[76] and pay back the debt. They are forced to making themselves more dependent on labour than they would need to be, if buying would not have been their aim.

The replacement of direct human interaction by interaction with machines in the household does not only affect the housewife; it also affects the labour of the (male) head of the household. Given the split between male and female labour in the household, it is usually men who do repairing jobs, for which they also can employ more and more machines in the interest of speed and convenience. These days there are extremely sophisticated machines for the household on the market, enabling men to do more and more work themselves. However this do-it-yourself (DIY) labour, is replacing reciprocal interaction with craftsmen as decorators, builders, carpenters, plumbers or mechanics.

Besides, there are machines on the market which offer to replace one's activity and learned technique, thus transforming a self-determined and open individual human effort into an external controlled object manufactured by any producer, sellable and useable by anyone who pays for it. Let me give an example: when we labour for long hours in an office in front of a computer screen, we often feel the need to get up and move about. So the obvious thing would be to use our commuting time in the morning to walk to the office and back home in the evening, or if this is not possible, get off the bus or the tube a bit earlier and walk a few hundred yards every day or use a bicycle. This is, however, not the norm these days. Cycling is rarely included in the normal working day, whereas using a cycling machine at the gym is, even though it goes nowhere! Today we have internalized this as a norm to the extent that we no longer find it extraordinary.

Naturally, we can buy a real bike and use it for commuting, even to do a bit of shopping on the way home from the office, eg for an evening meal with friends.

If we make the decision to buy a bike and use it daily, we have to decide on which type and where to buy it and at what price. These days retail centres have replaced family owned shops on the high streets of our towns and villages. So we may decide to investigate one of the retail giants to see what bikes they have on

---

76 It would have been interesting to compare data on private household debts, eg that of the UK, USA and Germany. The public household debts are stated in chapter 7.3.2. – but in Germany households are not legally obliged to inform the Statistische Bundesamt, Wiesbaden, about their debts. Therefore it is only possible to refer to the Bank for International Settlement's 82nd Annual Report, published 24 June 2012, p. 1–2, which states: "Household debt remains close to 100 per cent of GDP" (Gross Domestic Product) "in some countries, including Ireland, Spain and the United Kingdom."

Will Hutton, on the other hand, noted in: *Them and Us*, London, 2012, p. 361 that the private debt of the British people amounted to 328 per cent of GDP.

offer. Retail centres offer more choice and need more space than normal shops, and are therefore built out of towns, where land is relatively cheap. Consequently, it is in our own time and at our own cost that we visit the retail centre and choose and pick up the preferred bike. Often there is very little human interaction involved in this process. These retail giants can normally offer more goods, and at cheaper prices because they have cut their distribution costs as well as employed labour, as instead of being served by a shop assistant or even the owner of the shop, the customer does these jobs himself and then pays at the check-out himself using machines. We contribute our own time and our own effort for free, so that the retailer makes more money than he could by employing people and delivering the bike.

Alternatively, we can have a look into the internet and research what kind of bikes are on offer where and at what prices. If you choose this form of buying you will have a similar experience. Shopping via the internet is certainly easier: you do not need travelling to a retailer, as you do the shopping in your own home using your own machine. You are still spending your time, but less of it, as the bike will normally be delivered to you. However, you will not venture outside going to the shopping centre, will not see where it is, how it is built or which other shops are nearby. And internet shopping leads to a reduction of real retailers on the high street. As you sit at home, safe in your chair, you might be able to connect electronically with the whole world, being at the same time deprived of direct impressions and first–hand experiences. You cannot touch the bike you have chosen and you cannot smell it. Your contact is restricted to seeing it. Such an reduction of all our senses is now the norm – at least in the Western world.

There is another change which we seem to have happily accommodated in recent years, no longer finding it extraordinarily. Let's assume that you also have already bought a television set, the biggest one available, which will transform your home into a kind of cinema, to the envy of your neighbours. Let's find out what changes this machine brings into your life. Watching television, for whatever purpose, means that you sit motionless in front of a screen, gazing at a programme, the script for which someone has written months ago, which was then financed, produced and recorded. For you, however, it is actually happening. You might even feel some kind of contact between you and the electronic image on the screen, eg when the same journalist reads the news every night, so that you imagine that you know him as a person, and that he means you directly when he says 'good evening'. Watching a television programme is not a direct and open reciprocal human interaction, where you can actively participate and influence the rules yourself; watching a television programme is being involved with a standardized product delivered by a machine. As you watch a film, your own activities, even your mobility, are reduced, as you have to sit down and keep your eyes on the screen. Moving around is impossible, because you might miss some information if you look away. You need to remain passive.[77] And as other people's

---

77   The change which has taken place is obviously described from an adult point of view. According to *The Week*, 2 June 2012, psychologist Dr. Aric Sigman warned in a speech at the Royal College of Paediatrics and Child Health, that parents "who use the technology as a 'babysitter' could be

remarks will distract your attention, so they obviously are unwelcome.

Watching a television play is not like reading a book, where your mind is activated as you create your own pictures about what you are reading, and where you can change your position, or listening to a radio, where you can walk from one room to the other. Watching television or playing computer games might be restful after a long day's work, but by limiting our whole interactions with the world to viewing, we are deliberately diminishing them. This should be seen as an extraordinary act, but for us today it is normal. And it might have the most astonishing consequences: if, coming into the office in the morning, your colleague might begin telling you about a TV programme he watched the evening before as if it had been a real event rather than he or she being part of passive, canned, entertainment largely created for money. Perhaps in future any such programme should come with a warning: 'Attention: this is not real life but imaginary, second hand life!' so that people would not mix up the world of television consumption with real unmediated participation. And I feel that it is no wonder that TV news about real events are being increasingly replaced by so-called 'news' about the latest film. Produced reality is taking over reality. Television is scarcely 'a window on the world' any more, but has been changed into 'scripted reality' with the aim of making money.[78] Neil Postman (1931–2003) has written about this remarkable transformation.[79].

This contrived reality, especially when consisting of entertainment based on action, horror, murder, violence, catastrophes, fights and battles reinforces the economicult rationale that goods need to be replaced with new ones. The economicult truth is: the faster the depreciation, the more products need to be bought, and only by selling new products can more money be made.[80]

Using machines feels safe and reliable. We own the machine. We take for granted the fact that the response of a machine will always be the same. Machines are predictable, we know exactly what to expect. We seem to be totally in command. We have even the power to destroy the machine. Direct and open

---

bequeathing their children lifelong health problems, including heart disease and type 2-diabetes, and stunting their intellectual development, too."

A similar remark was made by Renate Zimmer, educational scientist at Germany's Osnabrueck University in *Frankfurter Allgemeine Sonntagszeitung* on 3 February, p. 63, reporting about the Spielwarenmesse International Toy Fair in Nuernberg: "*Virtuelle Spiele liefern vorgefertigte Erfahrungen aus zweiter Hand, ihnen fehlt fast immer das ganzheitliche sinnliche Wahrnehmen und die soziale Herausforderung...*". Author's translation: Virtual games deliver second-hand experiences which almost invariably lack the element of holistic sensual perception and social challenge...

78 As reported by *Der Spiegel* 50/2011, p. 161
79 Neil Postman, *Amusing Ourselves to Death*, New York, 1985
80 Cf. Frank Schirrmacher, EGO, *Das Spiel des Lebens*, Muenchen, 2013, p. 240, pointed out that the real estate agent Bernard London published in 1932 the crucial recommendation: "*Die Ueberwindung der Depression durch geplante Veraltung*". Author's translation: Overcoming the depression using planned obsolescence.

BBC 2 TV reported in a documentary 'The Men Who Made Us Spend' about it.

"In the 1920s, the Phoebus cartel of the world's biggest electrical companies – including Osram, Philips and General Electric – hammered out a deal to increase profits. This involved reducing a light bulb's lifespan from 2,500 hours to 1,000." *RadioTimes* 12–18 July 2014, p. 46.

reciprocal human interaction is replaced by interaction with a standardized object, manufactured by a company without any personal involvement of the purchasing consumer. One wonders why these days people do not have a say in what is produced, and how it is produced (which is what is missing in comparison to the 18th century when you would ask a craftsman to produce what you want), and in the end, how it can be safely returned to the natural environment or re-cycled at the end of its life.

These days labour may come back into the home; the employer might allow us to work at home, if the job can be done using a computer, because he is now able to control his employees by machine. For the employee, working from home feels more independent as he will have more time for himself since he does not need commuting time. However, home working has the consequence of excluding people from the process of direct and ongoing human interaction in the office, and in the long run we will be less involved with what is going on there, which is not desirable for anyone.

To repeat it: the process of interaction with a machine is different from human reciprocal interactions. First, we need to learn how a machine works. We need to receive information from it, learn how it operates. Machines are normally specialized tools made for one purpose, while human interaction is open and can be creative. Naturally, we have more control over a machine than a person, who comes with all his own rights, aims, behaviours, feelings, thoughts and preferences which have to be taken account of and respected. But the control over a machine has the effect of distracting us from our direct environment, as we observe every day when people in towns and villages become distracted by electronic, intangible information on their mobile phones and forget to keep aware of their environment.[81] A desire for control might be one of the reasons that many people prefer to use machines rather than interact with people directly.

However, while people believe they are in control, they hardly notice how the machines they are using might influence them.[82] For example, when digitalized information is exchanged via computer and a server, this allows the internet service provider to store this information, without any of these companies having asked their customers for permission to do so and without the user being aware of this. So, when you think you are communicating with a friend, there is always | a third party involved with a particular impersonal interest, as information about you can be sold on to whoever will pay for it. Such data is removed from an individual and treated as if it is a commodity, when it is often only meant to validate your identity or similar. Privacy and anonymity, though constitutional

---

81   The actor Frank Langella came to the following conclusion, in *The Week* 19 January 2013, p. 10: "'I work with a lot of younger actors, and so many fall crazy for each other, go to bed – and then within a couple of days they're lying in bed and each is texting... God, when I was a young man, when you got into bed you were there for years. You lusted for each other, loved each other, were interested in each other. In the morning you made breakfast for each other, all the natural courtship things.' But today's young people seem to view sex the same way they would a new app. 'Let's get the business done, then do something else.'"

82   All these consequences were discussed a few decades ago in the Intermediate Technology Development Group by E. F. Schumacher in: *Small is Beautiful, A Study of Economics as if People Mattered*, London, 1973, and George McRobie in: *Small is Possible, London,* 1981.

rights, have lost their value in the age of digital communication.[83] In fact, a study by the University of California in 2007 found that the boom in digital technology not only changes the way we interact with each other, but also causes fundamental changes in our brains.[84]

The process of replacing direct and open human interaction with interactions mediated by machines (at a cost and with the aim to make money) has been described as 'colonization of the lifeworld'[85], a shift from an open participative process into a standardized thing, a materialized commodity. I call it the *industrialisation of life*.[86] And one of its consequences is that money is given a far bigger role, as money dictates which and how many machines we can buy. Free and independent time is made more and more dependent on monetary terms. And with it, the household principle of making the most out of a given means is reversed into trying to achieve an end with the least means, in other words, buying a consumer product at the cheapest price and least money spent.

There is another point to make about how the open process of direct human reciprocal interaction has been transformed into a 'finished thing'. While it was the norm about 50 years ago to buy the basic raw ingredients for a meal and cook them, today it has become customary to buy ready-made meals from supermarkets or takeaways.

The labour required to prepare and cook our own meals is thereby drastically reduced. The food industry offers convenience meals which only need to be heated. When we are hungry, we do want to eat now! Immediately! Why spend the time preparing and cooking? Getting our hands dirty? Why wait? It is noticeable that, especially in big US cities, today flats are built without kitchens, as people apparently only need microwaves to heat their 'ready-meals', thus saving the building company the expense for fitting a kitchen. The whole range of possible self-activity in the kitchen is thus reduced to one activity – that of buying. While Hegel has recognized that man has evolved from animal status through his own activities, it is less clear whether the activities of people today, often only concentrated on shopping, can support such statement.

Again, we have to mention the cost: ready-meals are more expensive than buying raw food and cooking it. Naturally these offers from the food industry

---

83 It has been made the law in various countries for companies to be able to sell people's data without their knowledge and without those people profiting from it themselves. Also it seems that governments are cooperating with internet companies to get their hands on peoples' data, e.g. the PRISM and XKEYSCORE actions of the American NSA or the TEMPORA actions of the British GCHQ. Such governments' interest is always justified by arguing that it can prevent terrorist activities and criminality to increase security. But what about peoples' basic rights to privacy and the inviolability of their communication and their homes? What if non-democratic governments use the data to spy on people?

84 Reported by *Frankfurter Allgemeine Sonntagszeitung* 28 July 2013, p. 6

85 Cf. again: Juergen Habermas, *Theorie kommunikativen Handelns*, Frankfurt, 1981

86 So, driving can be called 'industrialized self-movement': one sits more or less motionless but attentive, only moving eyes, hands and feet now and then, to control the technical object which moves with us inside it, while the car industry believes that its future lies in developing cars which even operate without the control of a driver. However, what we really need is to achieve more 'self-moving' than moving things.

to do it all for you do not come free, but have to be paid for by the customers. Again, money becomes the term which defines what and how much you can consume. Although if one wants the household budget to last longer, following the household principle, it is cheaper to choose the quantity and quality of food personally, to buy it raw, wash, peel, cut and cook it yourself, than to pay for the food industry's products.

Also, raw fruit and vegetables keep fresh much longer. Today we are well aware that we should favour locally grown food, as it does not have to be transported over long distances and for long periods, and it is certainly fresher than food flown in from other continents and climates.

Ready-made meals are also full of preservatives, as the producers are anxious not to lose money due to short shelf-life. Preservatives in your food can lead to allergic reactions. Additionally, convenience food normally comes with a lot of chemical additives, eg flavourings, added sugar, salt and fat.[87] Moreover, the taste of the ready-made food is determined by the food industry. They do not offer the opportunity to develop our own taste, but subject us to someone else's decision concerning the taste of a meal. This may be totally different from our own preferences. We can only choose to eat what is offered on the shelves of the supermarket.

This is what is left of the freedom one was supposed to enjoy in one's free time, a choice between produced goods which someone else has designed and prepared to sell to us, whilst we are not involved in the decision-making process of creation at all. Is this the model for direct fair and democratic participation? Hardly.

When you prepare your own raw vegetables for your choice of meal, you are presented with far more sensory information. The vegetables will activate your own faculties much more intensely. You notice their natural form, perhaps the different tastes of their different parts. When you wash, peel and cut the vegetables, you experience how rough, smooth or slippery their skin feels; for example how many layers an onion has, how it affects your eyes, when you peel and cut it, how you can see and smell the juices running out. You learn how to handle the vegetables and fruit carefully, so as not to damage them unintentionally; you notice how a fresh onion changes colour and then caramelizes with cooking, and you smell the aroma it produces. You respect your food much more.

You can taste it when it is raw and notice how the taste has changed when cooked; you can experiment with herbs and spices and develop your own preferences, trying out some new recipe; perhaps develop new skills in making a sauce. Every perception and action enhances your interaction with the natural world.

---

87 *The Week* 2 June 2012 cites as follows: "A north London council is about to become the first to take a stand against the proliferation of fast-food restaurants, to limit their potentially adverse effects on the health of the local population, says *The Times*. Officials in Haringey have discovered that there are many more fast-food joints in the parts of the borough with the highest obesity rates and lowest life expectancy among men. In Tottenham Green, for instance, in the east, there are 14 takeaways, and a life expectancy for men of 72.5 years; in Fortis Green to the west, there are three and a life expectancy of 81.5. Similarly, in some wards in the east, up to 50% of ten-year-olds are obese, while in parts of the west, the proportion is as low as 15 %. In considering planning applications from fast-food outlets, officials will in future take into account their impact on health and their proximity to schools."

Perhaps you suddenly start to enjoy cooking for others, as you notice that it gives you a lot of pleasure to prepare a meal and test your own abilities. You gain a lot of satisfaction when other people enjoy what you have carefully prepared – even if, as usually happens, your efforts do not turn out the way you want it.

You feel it with your hands, smell it, taste it, you get to know what you like to eat what agrees with you or what is better for you to avoid. In time you even develop a habit or a technique of cooking a meal or carrying out other tasks in the household. You may find there are some household tasks you are especially good at, or some that you love to do. It was really moving for me to watch the BBC 1 programme *Countryfile* on 7 March 2013 which showed how pupils from Carshalton Boys School in Surrey grew herbs, fruits and vegetable and cooked them. It was great to watch the knowledge these boys gathered, the confidence they acquired as they learned about their health benefits, the skills they adopted and their pride in their achievements. Directly grown and freshly prepared healthy food even helped them to do better in exams.

Everything you do increases your interaction with the world, your understanding of it, your experience and your knowledge. You might even want to learn how to prepare vegetables from other countries, and find out if you like them. The direct interaction with the world sharpens all your senses and also your aesthetic sense of how to present the food and how to lay the table. The whole process might give you, in the end, more pleasure if you share it with others than spooning up ready-made meals resting on your lap as you watch television.

Through the process of direct reciprocal interaction with nature, humans have learned which environments plants will grow and survive in, which plants taste good and are useful for consumption, which are helpful for everyday ailments, and which are best avoided. Widening our interaction with the natural world is the open process by which man has profited and developed from animal to human. Let's not forget this. By using ready-made meals we deliberately limit our experience,[88] restrict our opportunities of experience and invent fewer techniques of our own, but have to pay more! The question therefore is, if the development of consciousness is brought about by reciprocal interaction, as Michael Gazzaniga[89]

---

88 Kristin Wartman reported an example of the consequences in the HuffingtonPost.com as quoted in *The Week*, 3 December 2011, under the headline "The pizzas that turned into vegetables": "If any doubts remained as to who America's elected representatives really work for... they were settled last month 'when Congress announced that frozen pizza was a vegetable'. The proclamation was a response to new nutrition guidelines that would have increased the amount of fruit and vegetables in school lunches. But after large food companies such as ConAgra and Schwan had spent $5.6 m lobbying against the rules, lawmakers decided that the tomato sauce on a frozen pizza qualified it as a vegetable. How disgraceful! If you read what goes into a 'traditional 4x6in school pizza', made by ConAgra, it's clear that 'it's not even a pizza, much less a vegetable'. What makes Congress's surrender all the more abject is that this processed rubbish is not just making children fat but forming their palates. Research shows that a constant diet of 'sugary, salty and fatty products' adjusts taste preferences to the point where 'simple, real foods taste bland and unappealing', ensuring that people keep eating junk. Even a group of retired generals criticised Congress, declaring its decision a national security issue given that obesity has become the leading medical disqualifier for military service. What will it take for US lawmakers to stand up to Big Food?"

89 Michael Gazzaniga, *Who's in Charge?* New York, 2011

argues, why should we deliberately restrict that process – instead of enlightening and enlarging it? Because we think we do not have time to do it? Because all our friends are eating a take-away? Or because someone wants to sell us something we think is quick and cheap?

We live today in a culture where money seems to be needed for every human activity. To go to a cinema, theatre or concert you first need money to buy a ticket; to play a sport you naturally need the appropriate clothes and equipment; and to pay to join a sports club; and even your household chores call for the purchase of machines, the biggest Aga, the most expensive espresso maker, the largest fridge.

Today, when we want to contact each other, we use internet services and emails, connecting through computers and mobile phones. These mediated services seem to have nearly replaced direct human reciprocal interaction, e.g. who hasn't seen, at some point, a couple having a meal in a restaurant, not talking to each other, but paying attention to their mobile phones as not to miss any messages? Has answering a phone become more important than communicating with our closest partner? These days, even our direct contact is mediated through things, bought with money on the market. Repeating the simple pattern of buying has replaced man's infinite opportunities for self-activity.

So we see a form of social fragmentation, as the wide range of self-activities is reduced to just one, buying. As such it is rather interesting to compare Smith's insights about the fragmentation of labourers' tasks: 'The man whose whole life is spent in performing a few simple operations, of which the effects too are, perhaps, always the same, or very nearly the same, has no occasion to exert his understanding, or to exercise his invention in finding out expedients for removing difficulties which never occur. He naturally loses, therefore, the habit of such exertion, and generally becomes as stupid and ignorant as it is possible for a human creature to become... His dexterity at his own particular trade seems, in this manner, to be acquired at the expense of his intellectual, social, and martial virtues.' And if in the concluding sentence I replace the 'labouring poor' with 'consumers' the modern parallel becomes clear: "But in every improved and civilized society this is the state into which the *consumers*, that is, the great body of the people, must necessarily fall, unless government takes some pains to prevent it."[90] Are we discussing Smith's insight? And does any government take precautions, regarding dependent work as well as independent activities? Or do governments think that if people only have a greater choice of ready-made anonymous products, this is enough to secure them liberty, freedom, welfare and real participation?

Given this development, how can such a society be called free and modern, promising to offer everyone the same opportunities for active and democratic participation? When instead reciprocal interactions are reduced and replaced by a choice of marketed products, which other people have decided to produce aiming to sell them for a monetary profit to people, when the prerequisite is that they first have to sell themselves to others in exchange for money so that they are able to buy such (so called time-and-labour-saving) products? Thinking about it, perhaps you will find this kind of socio-cultural model as remarkable as I do.

---

90 Cf. chapter 5, p. 22

This is the change that happened quietly and mostly unnoticed over the last decades. But no society has ever made a democratic decision that this should be the way forward.

Therefore, the economicult model for society can only be called semi-free and semi-modern, while a really free and modern society is still to be achieved.

7.3.2. The process of reciprocal interaction in the public household[91]

There is still another form of household to which the same household principle applies. It is the public one, the one we refer to as government.

Let's first remind ourselves that in a democratic society the power lies in the hands of the people. People elect the Members of Parliament as their representatives. Parliament has supremacy as it is the only elected and therefore legitimate body. Its members elect the executive government as well as the independent judiciary. The three public powers – legislative, executive and judiciary – must be kept strictly separate in accordance with rules about the division of powers.

No Member of Parliament could therefore be at the same time a member of government, otherwise he would not be able to fulfil his obligation of holding the executive to account. As soon as an MP is appointed a member of government he needs to resign and his vacant seat needs to be filled in by somebody else, perhaps the next candidate on the party's list.

The power of people to elect a government by voting for Members of Parliament and their parties is one of the innate civil rights in a democratic society. Every person is born with it. It can never be taken away from a person[92] – and only suspended if someone is found guilty of a criminal offence against society.

However, we find that there is still an electoral system in place which allows businesses to vote as if they were real people. While a business vote was abolished in all other UK local authority elections as recently as 40 years ago, the City of London corporation, "the nation's last rotten borough[93]," is still left with this right. "The principal justification for the non-resident vote is that about 330,000 non-residents constitute the city's day-time population and use most of its services, far outnumbering the City's residents, who number around 7,000. Nevertheless, the system has long been the cause of controversy." Do the non-resident people working for the corporations pay their taxes in the City of London? Obviously not. They pay them where they live. So why should they be allowed to vote in London

---

91 This might be an unfamiliar expression in the English-speaking world, it means the annual budget, but I prefer to use the German expression 'public household'.

92 It was suggested by a member of the Conservative Party that government should not allow people to vote who do not pay taxes and live off government support, ie tax payer's money, so every student, every housewife and every pensioner would lose his right to vote? This would really mean going back to the old days when voting was made dependent on assets.

93 According to George Monbiot: "Our country is being rebuilt in aid of corporate power", *The Guardian* 28 February 2012, p. 30. He adds: "The government, supported by the corporate press, is engaged in a naked attempt to rebuild the life of this country around the demands of business... Cameron is creating an economy in which much of the private sector depends on state contracts, and in which the government's core responsibility is to provide them."

as representatives of corporations *and* then in their home town? Why is London still one of the most unequal places in the world? Is this fair? And why has it still its own police force?

The votes still granted to the (mostly financial) businesses are based on the following rules: "Bodies employing fewer than ten people may appoint one voter; those employing ten to 50 people may appoint one voter for every five employees; those employing more than 50 people may appoint ten voters and one additional voter for each 50 employees beyond the first 50." This means that instead of 7,000 voters the city has 23,000. Where is the political demand to change such a system, one wonders? Where are the prosecutors to take the government to court for such an unconstitutional stratagem? And on what basis does a corporation decide how their representatives should vote?

Companies are corporate bodies under public law, they have not come into existence through natural law in the way that people have. Corporations are a cultural invention from a certain time in history. They cannot claim to have the same rights as a person[94]. A company is a social construction with limited responsibility, while a person has full responsibility. And their employees vote in the constituency where they live and not where they work, otherwise they could vote twice, doubling their influence, which would be totally unfair to other citizens. So when an elected Prime Minister claims that people should believe corporations and trust them,[95] then he has to be reminded that belief and trust are not democratic categories. Instead transparency, control and regulation are. Belief and trust are categories from history, and it would be rather foolish to bring them back. Democracy is not based on randomness, but on accountability.

People have the power to elect their government, and governments must be held to account by the people for whom it works. MPs need to answer questions from their constituents as to what they are doing, and how they will vote when a new law is considered or a political question needs to be answered.

As a Member of Parliament's term of office is generally four years, the people in the constituency can choose another person to represent them if they find out, that their MP has acted against their wishes.

People do not only have the right to vote for the Members of Parliament, they also have the right to stand for Parliament themselves. The right to choose one's government is reciprocal, it is both, an active and a passive right. People and their representation in Parliament, as well as in government, are connected in a process of reciprocal interaction. The more people use their rights and get involved, the more their opinions will have to be heard and considered.

It is the right of Parliament to vote on every item of expenditure a government plans to make. Voting for the annual budget is, in a way, the most important legal

---

94   Jeremy O'Grady pointed out in *The Week* 28 March 2015, that 'it was in 1819 that the US Supreme Court first recognised corporations as having the same legal rights as individuals.'

95   And it is really dangerous when a party leader, in this case Nigel Farage from UKIP, "cheerfully admits" that their manifesto, their aims, have been bought ready-made from the Institute of Economic Affairs. 'Why wouldn't you just buy their stuff off the shelf?'" as reported in *The Week* 10 August 2013, p. 10. Why is a party leader not questioned by his followers when their rights are taken away?

matter that Parliament decides, its "Koenigsrecht", the king's right, as it is called in Germany[96]. Via the budget, proposed by government each year, the Members of Parliament can actually see and control what a government wants to do, the culminating point of the political year.

The budget is where the costs are set out in detail: for the expenditure of the different departments in a government, for political projects and for the employment of civil servants, for supporting citizens who might not be able to afford to pay a lawyer (as without such support only rich people can achieve justice),[97] the cost for all three powers, including the cost of the allowances for MPs, the costs for a Head of State, the costs for executing laws, and for courts. Every detail in a government's spending plan is listed in the budget. It is up to the MPs to make changes, eg to the number of civil servants employed in a ministry, or to the amount spent on office refurbishment or to costs of telephone calls, and then decide on the whole budget which will become law in due course. The budget consists of taxpayers' money, while the government is only its trustee.

When the decisions of Parliament are published in detail for the whole country to view, the MPs have to inform their constituents how much money will be spent in their regions and on what public infrastructure. This is what most constituents want to know. Will a new railway line finally be built? Will a canal finally be deepened to allow more transport on water? Will a new hospital get the go-ahead? Will a new police service be moved into the region, a new school being built, and the hospital be allowed to employ more nurses? Will there be a new training centre established to support jobless people in finding paid employment?[98] Will the waste disposal policy be altered? Will agriculture be supported by a new scientific institution controlling the quality of food? Will a new high-speed train line be realized allowing people to travel faster, at a lower cost and with lower emissions between the cities compared to flying, as it is already the case in France, Switzerland, Germany

96   as the king as sovereign has been replaced by elected representatives of the people. It is interesting to refer here to Owen Jones, *The Establishment*, London, 2014, p. 292 f: "In modern Britain, sovereignty does not really rest with people. Neither the European Union nor any other single institution has, above all others, deprived the people of its sovereignty. It is the Establishment that really reigns supreme. It is this Establishment that has curtailed and trimmed British democracy, ensuring Britain is a country rigged in favour of a tiny, self-aggrandizing elite. And until that changes, democracy in Britain will be imperilled."

97   And when the present UK Conservative-Liberal government decided to cut deep into legal aid, the consequences for citizens are that even the judiciary is made dependent on monetary terms, when it should be approachable by everyone on equal terms, independent of gender, belief, age, nationality or assets.

98   It was reported in *The Guardian* 29 August 2012 p. 8, that "funded from the European social fund, 6,000 Londoners aged 18 - 24 in 16 boroughs will be made to do 13 weeks unpaid work as a condition of claiming their £56-a-week-benefit, if they have contributed less than six months of national insurance payments. As well as charities, some will be made to work for businesses that provide a clear 'community benefit'." Liz Wyatt from Boycott Workfare said: "Chris Grayling, the employment minister" and lord-mayor Boris "Johnson are clutching at straws. After seeing their last youth workfare scheme fall apart after public anger at young people being forced to work in Tescos and Holland & Barrett, they are trying to rebrand their latest efforts as being for so-called community benefit. But this will not fool the public who know that workfare in any guise is unacceptable."

and Japan – or perhaps an integrated traffic policy[99] might even be implemented?

Whilst Adam Smith saw defence, justice and the building and maintaining of public works such as mobility and education as the obligations of government, ie as public services on which everyone relies, even companies, we have to take into consideration the fact that there is much more to do for any government these days. It must run diplomatic services necessary to support relations with other countries, support social services and secure pensions, secure an equal and free approach to justice, support the health service, science and universities, cultural facilities such as museums, the performing and the visual arts, health prevention and sports, supply fresh water and treat sewage, make sure the natural environment is protected from further damage, support gender equality and, last but not least, support the all-important creation of new jobs, jobs, jobs.

Today government even contributes to the wages paid in the private sector instead of forcing corporations to reward their employees fairly. Owen Jones remarked: "To ensure that ... underpaid workers have an adequate standard of living, they receive tax credits 'topping up' their take-home pay - subsidized, of course, by the taxpayer. In 2009-10, for example, the government spent £27.3 bn on such tax credits. Between 2003-4 and 2010-11, a whopping £176.64 bn was spent on them. Now, tax credits are a lifeline for millions of working people who would otherwise be languishing in abject poverty. But that does not detract from the fact that tax credits are, in effect, a subsidy to bosses for lower pay. Employers hire workers without paying them a sum of money that allows them to live adequately, leaving the state to provide for their underpaid workforce."[100] It is remarkable, he wrote, that those who want to roll back the state, milk it mostly.[101]

If a government wants to change any aspect of a budget law during the year, for example if it wishes to borrow more than the members of Parliament have approved, it has to approach Parliament again for agreement on a change of the decided annual budget.

In recent years a change has taken place in politics. It seems that the power of Parliament is undermined by the government when it comes up with a proposal for a new laws. It seems to have become a law in itself that the government now formulates the first draft of a law, and not Parliament. Additionally, these days such a new law is not formulated by an elected minister, but by the unelected civil servants in a ministry. We have noticed that the administration, on occasion, has discussed a new law secretly with business associations and other organisations in order to get their consent without the knowledge of MPs. This is an offence against the rights of Parliament – although it happens. And if Parliament does not do anything to stop this, or a constitutional court does not step in, the misuse will go on.

---

99   as in Switzerland, Germany, Austria or Italy, called: 'One ticket, one time-table and one policy'?
100 Owen Jones, *The Establishment, And How They Get Away With It*, London, 2014, p. 178
101 Cf. p. 49

In particular, no government should ever be allowed to sign contracts, eg with international investors, which are not changeable by Parliament,[102] otherwise its sovereignty would be nil. Yet, exactly this is happening. When a country wants its natural resources developed, it often needs international investment and knowledge. And the consequence seems to be that global corporations can take away people's rights to their own autonomy in their country. However, for corporations, and for financial organizations, it is not legitimate to deprive people of their civil rights by letting money dominate. We must find ways to stop this. "When you allow corporations to roam global markets, you make them more powerful than nation states; when you 'roll back the state', you reduce the power of the people in each nation; when you 'cut back regulation', you allow the biggest corporations to dominate and exploit their territories; when you break trade unions and tear up employment laws, you allow those corporations to ride rough-shod over those who work for them. The simple, beautiful idea that people should run their own societies disintegrates, allowing the few to rule and the many to follow," Nick Davies wrote.[103]

It is necessary for Parliament to put the law-making responsibility back into its own House. Parliament, not government, should draft laws. Parliament should decide if a country goes to war, not government. A government is only the executive power, executing Parliament's decision. The members of a government are appointed for as long as the period between elections lasts. The only continuity one finds in a ministry is its civil service.

Sometimes it happens that a new minister is not sufficiently informed about the tasks of his new appointment, and therefore has to be put in the picture, by the civil servants working in his ministry. These people may have received vocational training for their jobs and have worked there for years and years, while the new minister can come from any profession. If he or she has not been a politician working in their specific field, he or she is dependent on the experience and knowledge of their employees. It is then certainly possible that some civil servants may try to exercise their influence over such a person. Many plays have been written about this discrepancy between politicians and the administration – to the amusement of the public. Besides, it is understandable that some civil servants might not want to involve a new minister too much – who may perhaps only be in post for a few months. He or she might want to change things at a fundamental level or the way politics in their particular ministry is run. He or she might aim at replacing some employees with their own trusted people from their own constituency. It is under-

---

102 Greg Muttitt, described in: *Fuel on the Fire, Oil and Politics in Occupied Iraq*, London, 2011, p. 196 f. how international investor companies in the oil industry "effectively became immune from new laws. Using a measure known as a stabilization clause, contracts froze or 'stabilized', the body of law with which investors had to comply. If a government wanted to pass a new law affecting investors at any point during the length of a contract – which could be up to 40 years – it had to either exempt investors from the law or pay the cost of their complying. Foreign investors thereby gained greater rights than not only domestic companies but also citizens. Every person in a country has to comply with whatever law is in force at any time, even if there is a cost to doing so, but not foreign companies with a stabilization clause."

103 Nick Davies, *Hack Attack, How The Truth Caught Up With Rupert Murdoch*, London 2014, p. 406

standable then, that such a minister will be blocked, or perhaps given a prepared speech, already written for a former minister from another party, to the amusement of everyone, apart from the new minister. All understandable from a human point of view, but totally contrary to the fact that civil servants, while embodying the real and continuous power of an administration, do not have any right to behave as if they were elected representatives of the people. Unelected civil servants, I have often found, having been a Member of Parliament myself, like to act in pursuit of their own aims in a self-legitimized manner.

One of these aims, most certainly, is opposing any reform of the public service.

These days government has established many regulatory organizations outside of the governing ministries,[104] and therefore outside of the political realm, such as Ofsted for schools, Ofqual for qualifications and examinations, Ofcom for the communications industry, Ofwat for water and sewage, Ofgem for electricity and gas, the Gambling Commission or the Office of Rail Regulation (ORR). Such organizations are seen as if they are politically 'neutral', and therefore it seems acceptable that they, rather than government regulate private industries.

Another government idea is setting-up so-called 'quangos'. According to *The Guardian*, 29 August 2013, p. 8, a new NHS (National Health Service) commissioning board, situated in Leeds, will take over £30 bn of health spending for patients from the next year, which "will dwarf government departments such as the Home Office and will in effect regulate the 200 GP clinical commissioning groups and fund complex hospital specialities such as cancer. Even its incoming chief executive, Sir David Nicholson, warned that it could become the 'greatest quango in the sky'." So why are new quangos set up, when the Prime Minister promised before the last election that a Conservative government would cut their number and shift power from bureaucracy to democracy? Why is policy still outsourced and why are these quangos still taking away the rights of Parliament? To what extent can the legitimate Members of Parliament be said to be in control?

On 19 January 2012 Amol Rajan commented in the newspaper The *i* on the 'Big Society' which Prime Minister David Cameron wants to install: "First, the Big Society represents an audacious raid into Labour territory. Former Labour minister James Purnell admits ... that he was struck by the adoption of Labourite principles, such as on co-operatives; Maurice Glasman, now of Blue Labour fame, says he was seeing his life's work with London Citizens stolen from him by the Tory enemy. Second, even within conservatism, the Big Society has a distinguished and long pedigree... Third, and most crucially, the Big Society is yet to be reconciled with austerity. It may be a boom-time fantasy. Voluntary organisations might be cheaper and more efficient than state bodies. But they still need money. When their funding from individuals, corporations, and trusts disappears in a recession, they need more state help, not less."

---

104 *Der Spiegel*, 39/2013, p. 20, reported that the Bundesrechnungshof, the German federal auditing office, criticized in a report dated 13 June 2013 that the federal administration regularly employed external people from companies and institutions, for up to as long as two years. The Bundesrechnungshof saw this as a collusion of interest and complained that the neutrality of the administration is compromised by such practice.

As there is nothing 'neutral' in politics, as everything is based on pre-requisitions and consequences, it is impossible to understand why governmental obligations should not be carried out directly as this is exactly the task of a ministry. Why outsource them?[105] Other countries have not gone down this path, so why has the UK? And how is government legitimizing outsourcing its own obligations, if a quango cannot be held to account by Parliament? Why has Parliament agreed to reduce its legitimate power? What else are civil servants in a ministry supposed to do if they are not executing policies and the laws and regulations decided by Parliament?

These days it has become the norm for public services to be privatized. Even the core obligations of any government, where public power is applied, as in border controls and customs, police and the legal system, prisons and defence and tax collection have been made the job of private companies, for a fee of course, including a profit. Taxpayers' money is used to allow private corporations to profit from them. Lower expenditures for public services could be returned to people in the form of reduced prices or lower taxes, while profits from private companies go to the owners of the companies – financed with taxpayers' money.

The argument for outsourcing public services mostly heard is, that private companies can offer these services cheaper[106] and more efficiently. So, if the public service and the public servants seem to be incapable of executing their already limited obligations, sometimes even being corrupt, why does the government not introduce reforms to become more efficient? Instead we learn that the Prime Minister's long-term adviser Steve Hilton expressed the following view about the public service: the authority of politics should be reduced to commissioning. Then outsiders should step in formulating political strategies, and the private sector should implement the policies. At what point did this become a legitimate strategy? And where is the public outcry against such distorted ideas, which are undermining the only legitimized public body, Parliament?

One reason for privatization is, of course, that a highly indebted government[107] can gain money by selling public services to private companies as they sometimes pay for the take-over. With this fresh money a government can then, perhaps, reduce existing debts or use the money for new expenditure. But this money can only be spent once – once an organisation is sold it no longer brings in revenue.[108]

---

105 When 'Bob' a "star programmer earning a six-figure salary at an American infrastructure company" outsourced his own job to a Chinese software company he was sacked. "...exploitation is for employers, not staff", wrote Steven Poole in: *The Guardian,* 18 January 2013, p. 34

106 One wonders that this myth is still repeated, when we know that for example "the actual worth of the completed project was £54.7 bn, but the taxpayer is projected to pay them £310 bn when it finally pays the contractors off," Owen Jones noted in The *i* 14 November 2013, p. 15, referring to G4S for security services for the Olympics and PFI for building schools and hospitals which were leased back to the state. "Free-market triumphalism is endemic among the British elite, but rarely challenged. It's time to start exposing it as the sham it is," he concluded.

107 "Reclassification of Network Rail will add £30 bn to public debt", reported *The Guardian* 18 December 2013, p. 30

108 It was reported on 22 April 2013 that the British government – according to Mark Russell, manager of the Shareholder Executive – is obviously planning another big privatization programme, selling for example its share of Urenco, the Royal Mail, the Met Office and the Land Registry.

That civil servants also argue the case for privatization is understandable. It ise in their interest to reduce their workload and diminish their responsibility, so, if something goes wrong, it is always possible to blame a politician, but never a civil servant. Zoe Williams[109] commented that privatization is the "attempt to privatize... anger" about results, a natural enough human aim, but not a constitutionally legitimate one.

Let's give a few examples of what the newspapers have recently reported about privatization:

The first mentioned report is by Steve Richards in The *i* 19 July 2012, p. 13. Richards wrote about the failure of the company G4S to fulfil its contract for delivering 10,000 security personnel to guard the Olympic Games in London. G4S is the world's biggest security firm, running security services worldwide, and police operations and prisons in the UK. It is also the world's third biggest employer with 660,000 jobs globally. Its contract was worth £280 million. Two weeks before the opening ceremony on Friday 2 July 2012, it was reported that G4S could not deliver. Instead of 10,000 people they had so far recruited only 4,000. Also, there was no accommodation for 10,000 security personnel in London, no training and no uniforms. The government needed to call in British soldiers for the job, soldiers whose job it is to ensure a country is well defended from outside threat, not operate inside a country. Parliament questioned the CEO of G4S, Nick Buckles, for an explanation in the Home Affairs Committee, and it turned out that the contract between the Home Office and G4S did not allow for Parliamentary scrutiny. This raises the question of whether this was done deliberately or was simply an error in administration. Consequently, Parliament could not hold G4S responsible, and – surprisingly – the contract did not come with a penalty clause. One cannot help but wonder that Parliament endured this. So the CEO told the Committee that "the company still expected to collect £57 m for its contribution to the Olympic Games, an expectation, as Richards comments[110] that brings to mind once more that damning phrase from the old Britain: 'rewards for failure'."

The second example is from Randeep Ramesh, social affairs editor of *The Guardian*.[111] The company in question is Atos, a French company, which had a contract worth more than £3 bn. The value of its contracts was "now more than a third higher than the amount outsourced by the last government," Ramesh stated. Atos "conducts medical assessments for benefit claims on behalf of the government". According to the report "... disabled protesters will deliver a coffin filled with 85 pages of complaints from people and their families who have been told they

---

109 *The Week*, 15 September 2012, p. 15

110 A few weeks later G4S shareholder Neil Woolford of Invesco Perpetual "described Buckle's forced appearance before MPs as like watching ' a medieval persecution'. 'If this is the way Parliament wants to treat business,' he added, 'don't be surprised when businesses decide this isn't the country for them." *The Week*, 1 September 2012, p. 41. Buckle left G4S in 2013. What clearer illustration can there be of how the only legitimate power, Parliament, judges the issue solely in monetary terms – typical for an economicult?

111 *The Guardian*, 29 August 2012, p. 6

have to get a job despite suffering from serious impairments. They point out that 1,100 people died last year after failing the test for the new benefit..." "However, the assessments have been widely criticised and it has emerged that 40 per cent of people appeal against the decisions – with 38 per cent of those successful." "While 10 government departments have contracts with the firm, its most high-profile deal sprung from a Labour pilot project in 2008 to decide whether people were fit to work or eligible for Employment and Support Allowance (ESA)..." "Greatrex, whose investigation into Atos led to the National Audit Office this month calling for an overhaul of the government's medical testing contract with the company, said the firm 'would not fix its reputation by sponsoring the Paralympics'." Besides: why is Parliament not demanding a report from the government on its entire spending and subsidies.[112] It does not seem right that only occasional data here and there is published by newspapers, and the only legitimate body, Parliament, is left in the dark. One can only wish that government would put as much effort into making tax dodgers pay their dues as they put into privatization.[113]

---

112 Owen Jones, *The Establishment*, ibid, p. 174-175: "... fossil-fuel companies enjoy generous state subsidies. They benefit from the slashing of VAT on the consumption of petrol, gas and coal from 20 per cent to 5 per cent, potentially saving them billions. On top of that, fossil-fuel companies enjoy tax breaks, including tax allowances on the production of oil and gas, which save them up to £300 million a year. In the 2012 budget, Osborne increased allowances for North Sea small oil and gas fields, and granted a new £3 billion allowance for drilling around the Shetland Islands.

Fossil fuels also inflict costly damage on the environment, which is why the International Monetary Fund suggests that, unless the cost is taken into account by the price of fossil fuel, then this represents a subsidy too. These government subsidies are huge. According to the OECD, well over £3 billion worth of subsidies go to natural gas alone.

The British nuclear industry is another beneficiary to state subsidies. Although the government rejects the 'subsidy' label, in April 2013 the environmental audit committee of MPs estimated that the nuclear industry benefits from an annual subsidy of £2.3 billion a year. Nuclear-power operators are protected with a limited liability. If there was a nuclear disaster, they would only have to contribute £140 million to deal with the resulting costs; the government has floated hiking this amount to £1 billion, although that has yet to happen. The rest would have to be paid for from the public purse, drastically reducing nuclear operators' insurance costs. What's more, the state shoulders most of the financial burden for the cost of future decommissioing and cleaning up of nuclear waste, which has spiralled from estimates of £56 billion in 2005 to over £100 billion today."

"Perhaps nothing encapsulates state-subsidized capitalism like the UK arms industry. The Campaign Against the Arms Trade (CAAT) has examined the subsidies showered on the sector on an annual basis ... The CAAT found that, in total, arms exports received a government subsidy worth £890 million each year..."

And what about the finance industry? There is no VAT to be paid on financial deals. Is this not another subsidy?

113 *Private Eye* No. 1362, p. 29, published in an article called 'Government wealth cheque': "Despite George Osborne's platitudes to last month's G 20 meeting in Australia – 'It is not fair if big companies avoid their taxes by shifting their profits around artificially' – the *Eye* has discovered that the government has signed its most significant PFI deal to date (a new £190 m children's hospital at Alder Hey in Liverpool) with tax haven-based companies, thus conniving in precisely the sort of tax avoidance the chancellor was talking about."

The Guardian, 9 July 2014, printed a list of "Top Tory's links to offshore banker", donators to the Conservative Party with (perfectly legal) tax avoidance accounts on Jersey. Is it too far fetched if one wonders why the UK government does not close tax havens?

The latest public service to be privatized (October 2013) is the Royal Mail. The government "... sale will increase government revenue and thus reduce budget deficits, it is said." However, as mentioned, public assets can only be sold once. "In the same vein, the government has patted itself on the back for selling (and planning to sell) the shares of the bailed-out banks at a profit, further reducing deficits," wrote Ha-Joon Chang[114] pointing out: "Don't be fooled by all the boring language of bookkeeping, however, behind it lies an ambitious project to restructure British society fundamentally by expanding the domains of our life that are subject to market forces," with the consequence, that: "Thanks to cuts in social spending, the disabled and the elderly have had to buy more expensive supports from the market – or, more typically, put up with greater discomfort and indignity. With cuts in unemployment benefit, an increasing number of workers have been forced to accept zero-hour contracts and other employment conditions that are more fitting for developing countries, if not exactly for the Victorian era." Use of services which were in the past a responsibility of the government and free for all, as paid for by taxpayers, is now dependent on money. "When Royal Mail joins the list, we can be assured that deliveries to remote areas will become less frequent and/or more expensive while postal workers will have greater workload and less time for human contact."

The other objectionable element of privatization is that the government chose, "Lazards, Goldman Sachs and five other banks to advise on the sale," *The Guardian,* 1 April 2014 reported. "Privatization fees alone totalled £12.7 m, according to the National Audit Office report."

"The banks recommended an asking price as low as 330p a share... It is now 562p." So the government could have sold the Royal Mail for a much higher price. "Panmure Gordon estimated a £1 bn undervaluation (which proved conservative)," a loss of this amount was the consequence for the public household, ie the taxpayer. Furthermore, it turned out that the same banks giving advice were "also placing shares with clients," therefore "Chinese walls are put in place to separate 'sellers from buyers' within offices. But is this really possible in the City of London, where Chinese walls are most likely made of rice paper?" asked the newspaper.

And two days later it was reported by *The Guardian* that there were "16 investors who reneged on a deal to remain long-term shareholders in the Royal Mail... in return for being granted priority status and extra allocations of shares." Perhaps only the government was wondering, however, that "... within weeks of the float these investors had sold more than half of their stock at a profit estimated at more than £300 m." And when the Labour opposition in the House of Commons asked who these 16 investors were, Business Secretary Vince Cable refused to name them.

However, on 1 May 2014, *The Daily Telegraph,* p. B 1, made public a few hedge funds, amongst them "Third Point, the aggressive US hedge fund, Landdowne Partners and Och Ziff... Abu Dhabi Investment Authorities, the Kuwait Investment Office, and GIC, an arm of the Singapore government" as well as George Soros "the investor who famously made £1 bn shorting the pound in 1992", leaving you wondering how anyone imagined such foreign companies

114 *The Guardian* 11 October 2013, p. 38

would secure the future of a public service for the British people.

Newspapers took these examples to question the rationality of outsourcing public services.

They reported on the government of Margaret Thatcher (Conservative) where, e.g. water utilities were privatised.[115] The former publicly run companies were criticised because too much drinking water was lost in the ground from leaking pipes. Did privatisation then stop that loss of valuable drinking water? Indeed not. But the directors now earn a lot more than before they went private[116]. And what happened to the railways? They had to be taken back partially into public ownership, because privatisation, introduced by Prime Minister John Major, was not working either. "Commuters now routinely spend 15 per cent of their income travelling to work on what is now the most expensive rail network in Europe... this is the reality of Britain's railway: a byword for bewildering fragmentation, unreliability and exorbitant cost – and a gigantic scam for siphoning off public money into the pockets of monopoly contractors," commented Seamus Milne.[117]

So – will there be a change in the government policy of privatisation? Will there be a turn-round in government thinking? Or are there more projects in the pipeline – without Parliamentary control?

What about the Health Minister's idea of letting private corporations profit from the National Health Service, or the Education Minister's idea of turning schools and universities[118] into profit-making enterprises, probably even with

---

115 It also seems that the EU plans to privatize public water utilities, which has unleashed a storm of protest in Germany. Water is a human right and not a business model. Water utilities are best kept in public hands and not in the hands of multinationals, said SPD, GRUENE and the SSW according to the *Kieler Nachrichten*, 30 January 2013. They appealed to people to take part in a petition to the EU-citizen initiative www.right2water.eu/de And the protest was successful. EU commissioner Michel Barnier promised on 21 June 2013 in Brussels that he would exempt water supply from privatization.

116 Cf. chapter 5.6.4.

    The Week, 17 November 2012, p. 48 quoted Rebecca Burn-Callander in: *Management Today*: "'Something is rotten in the state of utility companies,' says Rebecca Burn-Callander. Even as several water firms are embroiled in a tax-avoidance scandal, the Financial Services Authority and the energy regulator Ofgen are investigating 'unusual' movements in the wholesale gas market. Allegations of market-rigging were tabled by a former employee of ICIS Heren - an energy price-reporting agency, whose figures are used as the basis for large supply contracts between energy firms and gas suppliers. The whistleblower alleges that traders regularly fed his company fictitious numbers to inflate profits. 'Sound familiar? That's because we've been here before with Libor.' Much like the interbank lending rate, wholesale gas deals 'aren't brokered through a robust and transparent electronic system, but thrashed out between companies' – making prices easier to manipulate. The Big Six energy firms deny any knowledge of market–rigging. But other whistleblowers are now coming forward. This looks like 'a further unravelling' of the 1980s utilities privatizations. 'First trains, then water, and now gas are slowly showing their cracks.'"

117 *The Guardian* 29 August 2012, p. 30

118 According to *The Guardian*, 12 November 2012, p. 33, Prof. Howard Hotson, co-founder of the Council for the Defence of British Universities, claimed that "public spending on higher education was lower in the UK than almost any other developed country, while business spending on research and development was equally low and falling" before the idea was introduced that universities should be managed like private corporations. "These management models impoverish teaching, undermine creativity, trivialize research and alienate teachers. Worse still,

teachers without appropriate qualifications?

And what about the welfare-to-work contract? The private company Serco[119] "is in line to win a multimillion-pound contract to run the National Citizen Service".[120] *The Observer* stated that "Pilot NCS programmes, aimed at bringing together 16- and 17-year-olds from different backgrounds to undertake character-forming community work, have been run by around 60 charities over the last year." Where is the Parliamentary control? Where is democracy going?

Another privatization strategy is called Public Private Partnership, for example for the London Underground, which had ailed, leaving the tax payer to pick up the bill for the disaster.

Instead of cutting back debts, new schemes seem to come into practice: *Private Eye* reported in No. 1319 about a brand new PFI scheme, which will allow the PI corporations borrowing money to finance the contracted work, not from the financial market but instead from the government or rather: the taxpayer, and then rent the built infrastructure back to the government for 30 years. This means, of course, that the government has to borrow more from the financial markets, and that the public household's debt is rising while private companies save money.

Let's have a look into the development of government debts in relation to the Gross Domestic Product (GDP) based on data as released in September 2011 by the International Monetary Funds:

---

this market system transforms students from active apprentices in the craft of higher learning to passive consumers attempting to leverage their purchasing power into high lifetime earnings."

119 "Serco on the fiddle: in July, Serco – one of the most prominent of the Government's outsourcers – was found to have overcharged the Ministry of Justice for electronic tagging," reported *The Week* 7 September 2013, p. 41, ... "The total loss to the taxpayer was around £50m. Was that Serco's only dirty little secret? Not a bit of it, said Robert Lea in *The Times*. The ministry now accuses the contractor of 'fiddling the figures' on a £285m contract to run prison vans. That's two alleged frauds in six week. Nice going. With ministers now threatening to strip Serco of all Government contracts unless it cleans up its act, shares have plummeted so far that the group is 'headed for expulsion from the FTSE 100'. If Serco, which also runs air traffic control towers, border control services and hospitals, is banned from 'the Whitehall austerity bazaar', it's certainly in trouble, said Alison Smith in the *Financial Times*. Government contracts (here and abroad) account for most of its revenues. It's the same old story, said Mark Leftly in *The Independent on Sunday*: Serco's bosses have lost control of the sprawling 'empire'. They hadn't a clue what those 'at the bottom' were up to 'Keep track of criminals? Serco can't keep track of itself."

The Week, 14 December 2013, p. 13, published in "The end of the road for Serco?" that "after 25 years of extraordinary growth, the company that has become ubiquitous in British public life, delivering services for the Government in hospitals, Army bases and job centres, is threatening to come unstuck." When outsourcing started under Thatcher's government in the 1980s, "last year Whitehall outsources £40 bn to the private sector (a 4,000-fold increase in 20 years); local councils another £90 bn." About 90 % of its staff are ex-civil servants, and they've taken their expertise overseas..." Serco had more than 120,000 staff running 700 contracts around the world. "The National Audit Office warned last month that the Big Four" G4S, the French-owned Atos, Serco and Capita "were now so entwined with some departments – the MOD plans to outsource 40 % of its entire budget in 2015... that the country couldn't survive without them. In short, if Serco were to fail – like the banks – it would have to be bailed out, as its rival, G4S, was by the Army when it failed to deliver security guards on time for the Olympics."

120 As reported by *The Observer*, 5 August 2012, p. 21, "Serco set to take charge of 'big society' initiative"

Future gross governments' debts
as a percentage of national GDP

	2013	2014	2015	2016
United States of America	128.930 %	141.363 %	153.195 %	165.394 %
United Kingdom	97.700 %	97.101 %	103.060 %	115.386 %
Germany	82.957 %	84.058 %	86.123 %	88.036 %

This new financing scheme whereby private corporations borrow from the government/taxpayer instead of the financial markets is not yet included here.[121]

The PFI "companies will become very expensive middlemen". This raises the question of why the government is not running the projects itself? "The truth is that those building infrastructure and their many consultants have, after mainlining PFI for around 15 years, become hooked on it... As the *Eye* has regularly pointed out, the Whitehall unit responsible, Infrastructure UK, is staffed entirely by PFI industry stalwarts." Does one need to wonder any more how the public household is exploited by private corporate interests?

We can always hope that there will be a real change in the privatization policy of government, but it seems realistic to suppose that such a change will not happen in the next few years, and not without public pressure. Larry Elliott and Dan Atkinson named the "three gods"[122] government believes in these days: liberalization, privatization and competition. Nothing will change as long as the market' ideology is followed and the idea of public service is wilfully forgotten.

Another point to mention is, that not only government, but also Parliament, as well as the wider public, have all come to accept the view that a policy is executed once money has been spent. However, money is only a means, a medium. It might well be that nothing has changed in people's real lives, even if all the money has been spent according to the decided budget. In the end, there must be alternative measures by which the public can judge whether a political strategy was successful.

One may even fear that MPs' understanding of their job – to formulate and control the tasks of the government's – has also changed from one of public service to one of pure representation, a mere formality, and their personal interest is geared largely towards the making of money– supported more and more by

---

121 When the public debt is discussed, a remarkable argument takes place. When it is stated that the United Kingdom "borrowed £ 120.6 bn in the last year" eg then this is judged as "a reduction of just £300 m on what it borrowed the previous year," (The *i* 24 April 2013, p. 41).

This additional borrowing of £120.6 bn in 2012 closes the gap between government spending and tax income. Describing it in this way might lead citizens to think that the public debt has gone down. Far from the truth. The new borrowing is added to the existing old public debt meaning that the latter grew by £120.6 bn in 2012, and in 2011 by £120.9 bn. It was not a reduction of the total public debt but an increase.

One also wonders how much the amount of money necessary for serving the public debt will have to rise if interests rates go up? Are interest rates perhaps kept artificially low to enable the government to serve the public debt? And: Are Parliaments really aware of the extent of the problem that will need to be dealt with one day?

122 Larry Elliott and Dan Atkinson, *The Gods that Failed*, London, 2008, p. 16

lobbyists.[123] The 2011 scandal about parliamentarian allowances, which MPs claimed from taxpayers for accommodation, washbasin plugs, adult films or duck-houses, and how they let their London properties to other MP's, and lived in other houses in order to claim the rent, and also their interest in – highly paid – second jobs besides their official duties is not really convincing the public that their representatives are trustworthy and work for the common good. This is a development from service to self-service, we notice. So when constituents do not hold their MPs to account, nothing will change for the better.

"Governments are not giant corporations,"[124] said Peter Preston, quoted by Chris Mullin, a former MP and a minister himself. A democratic country is no GB plc or Germany AG. Governing is not a commercial job. And if a government is reporting once a year about the state of the country, this is not a usual business report. *A public service is for the many and not for money*, as an anonymous demonstrator in Madrid shouted into the microphones of the British broadcasters on Saturday 21 May 2011: "We are demonstrating for democracy. The government is here for the people, not for the market."

By the way – and not *buy* the way: Where has the idea that MPs and civil servants in government should be a role model for the citizens vanished to? We used to expect them live their lives in a way that showed the majority how they should live eg if a government calls itself "the greenest government ever", where are the public buildings, such as hospitals, schools, care homes, police stations, prisons, museums and so on, that offer guidance and inspiration in terms of energy saving through insulation, using renewables to generate electricity on their roofs? It seems that setting an example is no longer the way government interprets its role, but it understands itself more in terms of governing the life of others Those in government do not appear to practise what they preach. Governing is no longer understood as reciprocal interaction.

So, what do people think about politics nowadays? Does it try to engage more people or turn people off? One fears the latter, thus Parliament, government and the public sector are left uncontrolled instead of bringing them to account? When US economist Jeffrey Sachs told *Der Spiegel*[125] that in the USA the political system has adjusted to the interests of rich people, as these people finance the political parties, the election campaigns and employ public relations experts to help their preferred candidates get elected in foreign countries. In the last few years, politics is being commodified not democratized. It is not the way forward. It is not progress. Of course, it is understandable that a government doesn't want to give the public too much information about what it does and aims for. But will people still be prepared to pay their taxes for the type of public sector we have been discussing? Or will a strong demand for reforms finally arise from a public sovereign to this type of government? And what does it say about the future of a democratic society, where more, not less participation of the people is needed? One wonders and one fears.

---

123 The Austrian MEP, Hans-Peter Martin, reported that he received offers from lobbyists amounting to €65,000 from 2011 to 2013. The number of EU-lobbyists in Brussels is estimated at 15,000. It is no wonder that MEPs take over opinions from vested interests.

124 *A view from the Foothills: The Diaries of Chris Mullin,* London, 2010, p. 156

125 5/2014, p. 67

7.4. The process of reciprocal interaction mediated by money and market

We have seen that the process of free and direct reciprocal interaction is the basic pattern for every kind of human activity, in every cultural form of economy and in relation to the (culturally developed) natural environment.

Direct immediate reciprocal interactions are still found in the private and in the public household, where they depend on the rationality, compassion, ideas and customs of their participants, although there is change. We have observed a trend in recent decades whereby these free, direct and open reciprocal interactions are being substituted with ready-made ones mediated by money and market.[126] Although in the last few years there have been protests against the power of banks and the economy, there has scarcely been protest against the role the market should play in a society. In the words of Will Hutton.[127]: "The doctrine 'there is no alternative to the market' lives on, a first-order strategic error."

The claim is that a derived market should be free. We should no longer assume that our current (real) market operates according to rules that we have set, instead the now abstract derived market is expected to be self-determining, replacing direct human reciprocal interactions with indirect ones. This gives rise to the question, of whether direct reciprocal interactions are preferable to indirect monetarized ones? And: should the political aim to liberate derived markets be sustained or abandoned?

To be able to make a well-informed, rational decision, it is necessary to analyze the consequences which follow the change from a free and direct to an indirect and mediated process of interaction. To analyze these, the meaning of 'market' needs to be discussed. The first necessary statement therefore obviously needs to be a definition. What is called a market in economicult theory needs to be made clear.

A market[128] is a place in time where real producers of real goods and real consumers meet, eg a food market. Here producers exhibit all their wares, so that consumers can make a choice about what they want to purchase, depending on the quality of the offerings, their presentation, their health and state of freshness, but also depending on the prices the real producer wants to achieve and the real consumer wants to pay. A real market is based on the open process of reciprocal interactions between consumers and producers. The producer makes a decision on what to produce based on what has sold in the past and therefore hopefully

---

126 Cf. Michael J. Sandel, *Was man fuer Geld nicht kaufen kann, Die moralischen Grenzen des Marktes*, New York, 2012, p. 13, said that the most fateful change of the last three decades was not the increase of greed. It was the expansion of the markets and their values into areas of life, where they do not belong.

127 *Them and Us, Changing* Britain – *Why we need a fair society*, London, 2011, p. 399

128 "The great pre-20th-century county markets and livestock fairs were supremely social events that contextualized the process of buying and selling so that outcomes were fair. You could see, touch and feel what you were buying – and you would always look into the eyes of the seller to establish if you were being hoodwinked... The market was an interpersonal and fair means of creating and sustaining trust. In that way, fair outcomes could be achieved. For the foundation of human interaction is reciprocity." Will Hutton, ibid, p. 92

will sell in future. His decision, based on experience, is made long before his productive interaction with nature started.

However, the real consumer has some influence on the producer. The real consumer does not have to buy any offered product, if for example it does not seem to be fresh. He can choose what to buy, although he can only buy what is offered. He might even have a slight influence on price, for instance as prices are often lowered near to closing times of the real market to save the producer taking unsold goods home. It is therefore to the advantage of the consumer to visit the market late if he wants to spend less money. Even when the goods are nearly sold out and his choice is perhaps limited compared to start of the real market, he might find acceptable fruit and vegetables and spend less. This is one of the reasons why consumers love real markets.

Today, it is a joy to observe that real food markets are again being set up in towns. They are bringing a lot of life back into the high streets which are cluttered mostly with charity shops and chain stores.

We see that in a real market, consumers have a degree of influence when inter-acting with producers, even when money is used for the exchange process, perhaps enough to feel that they are the subjects and not the objects of the market.

The English word 'market' goes back to the Latin '*mercatus*'[129] for trade or fair, referring to Mercury, the Roman god of trade and the messenger of the gods. The Latin '*mercator*' means a merchant; '*mercennarius*' was the word for the wage of hired soldiers. The English word 'merriment' means a feast, and we find the same root in 'meritorious', which has two meanings in Latin, the second being 'owing', while in the case of the English word 'merit' the first meaning is used, the other meaning of 'fair gain' having been forgotten. The Latin verb '*merere*' also shows more than one meaning: 'deserve', 'earn', 'win', 'acquire' and 'do a good service'. It goes back to the ancient Greek '*meiromai*', which meant to get a share of, and/or to be inflicted on one by fate.

From this real market the abstract idea of a market, henceforth referred to as the market' is derived. The claim of economicult theorists is that this abstract idea of a market' should be free[130] to rule itself. Furthermore: the derived market' should be made the model for all people's interactions in society, an idea which in

---

129 When comparing the Latin word '*mercatus*' with the modern word 'market', we find a vowel shift from 'e' and the 'a'. Would it be too far fetched to assume that the internet site comparethemarket.com played with these changes, by using meerkats?

130 Roger Bootle, in: *The Trouble with Markets, Saving Capitalism from Itself*, London/Boston 2009, p. 24, responded to that claim as follows: "Belief in this theory led to an unquestioning faith in 'the market'. Markets are driven by selfish behaviour. This is not a criticism, it is a description. But the result is supposed to be maximum efficiency, and hence prosperity for all. Never mind the selfishness: greed is good. Never mind the huge gaps in income and wealth this system causes: huge wealth at the top cascades down to those at the bottom. Never mind the sense of injustice: people get an income commensurate with their contribution, as measured by the forces of supply and demand. Never mind the apparent chaos and instability: the world is bound to be uncertain, and the market system absorbs and transforms uncertainty to deliver the best of possible outcomes in the circumstances. In short: nevermind."

But we should mind! It is our lives which are affected and we should be free to decide for ourselves how we would like to live and actively participate in our society.

recent years has had the biggest influence on economic theory – and on politics. From the economy of real markets, market' economics was derived which means that more and more human interactions are to be mediated by money and market, and every direct human interaction, such as raising children, looking after old people, housekeeping, hobbies or lovemaking should become activities for the aim of making money.[131] Genuine human feelings towards other humans would be replaced by the desire for financial profit. Naturally, all direct reciprocal interactions can occasionally do with a bit of professionalism, but by making money the ruling factor, we transform our interactions with each other – as with nature – to the extent that they become indirect, abstract and alienated.

The next point to make is that the transformation from direct reciprocal inter-actions to market' activities does not leave these exchanges neutral or impartial as economicult theorists believe. True, the market' does not follow ethics or morals, but money; and it also influences the process of interaction according to its own rules, as will now be discussed.

The ability to labour, for example, is changed into a commodity, for the labourer as well as for the employer. Sandel describes it as as when we try to turn living experiences into a commodity, we run the risk of spoiling the experience itself.[132]

The market' exchange corrupts direct experiences and replaces them with its own intrinsic rules. These consequences seem to have been forgotten, therefore they have to be pointed out. Everything which is introduced into the process of direct interaction influences it by mediation.[133] As Detlev S. Schlichter has remarked for example: "Money is never neutral, has never been neutral, and can never be made to be neutral. From the moment that human society made the transition from direct trade (barter) to indirect trade via media of exchange, a new element entered economic relationships. Money allowed great advances in human cooperation on markets, but money has its own dynamics and inevitably also constitutes a source of occasional disturbance and of economic volatility."[134] He calls the expansion of the market' and its rules into every area of peoples' lives including those where they should never play a role, the most fateful change of the last three decades.[135] Sandel concludes that, what is missing from recent politics, is the question of the function and range of a market'.[136]

Since their invention and implementation, however, the market' dynamics

---

131 From which governments profit as it is obligatory to pay taxes on the deals.
  The distinction from a so-called "black" market' is that illegal commodities like drugs are exchanged and taxes withheld.
132 Michael J. Sandel, *Was man fuer Geld nicht kaufen kann, Die moralischen Grenzen des Marktes*, New York, 2012, p. 51
133 Marshall McLuhan, who would have been 100 years old in July 2012, characterized this in 1967 with the words "the medium is the message".
  When referring to facts reported by media, magazines, newspapers, broadcasting houses or television stations, we must always be aware that these facts are mediated and interpreted, deliberately or otherwise, according to the media's own interests.
134 Detlev S. Schlichter, *Paper Money Collapse, The Folly of Elastic Money and the Coming Monetary Breakdown*, Hoboken, 2011, p. 146
135 Michael J. Sandel, ibid, p. 13, giving numerous examples of this change.
136 Ibid, p. 18

have become the norm and are today so internalized that people are virtually unaware of them. But the question is, why should the market' with its senseless rules be preferred to a system of rules which has been publicly discussed and chosen, legitimized by an elected Parliament?

Behind that abstract idea of free markets' – and the view that the rules of the free market' should govern society instead of the people – there naturally lies a hidden interest, which means that business interests up for monetary profit should not be inconvenienced by public influence. The few can command the many, but the many are not allowed to set rules for the few. When the only legitimized power, Parliament, proposes new rules, corporations often respond with the threat of leaving the country and moving somewhere else, somewhere where, for example, protection laws for the environment, and human rights perhaps scarcely exist. So public regulation, they argue, would cause the country to lose jobs and tax revenue. Obviously, no politician can want to be responsible for that. In the end, the argument for free markets' is very similar to that for an absolute king like George III, who makes the law, lords it over the people and chooses the government, rather than having a Parliament elected by people. It still seems that a core aim of many corporations is to undermine public legitimation, trying to roll back everybody's right for participation in society.[137] 'We are outside the law,' they seem to claim.

The only remarkable thing is that when a public subsidy[138] is transferred from the taxpayers' purse to a private company or when the public household bails out a private bank or 'quantitative easing' is applied – so far amounting to £ 375 billion in the UK – we never hear any calls to leave the market' alone and let the market' be free from public interference.[139] Of course it is in the interest of governments to

---

137 George Monbiot in *The Guardian* 18 October 2011, p.31, described this issue as follows: "Freedom is what all these groups claim to stand for. But the freedom they promote is of a particular kind. They are not campaigning for freedom from hunger or poverty. They are not demanding free access to health and education. They are not lobbying for freedom from industrial injuries, exploitation, pollution or unscrupulous banking. When these libertarians say freedom, they mean freedom from the rules that prevent their sponsors behaving as they wish: mistreating their workers, threatening public health and using the planet as their dustbin."

138 *The Week*, 15 June 2013, p. 14, printed an article by Aditya Chakrabortty from *The Guardian*: "I once accused Richard Branson of relying on public subsidy for much of his profits... I was wrong... A forensic analysis of the numbers behind privatized rail, it reveals that 'the only way Branson and the vast majority of train barons make their profits is through handouts from the taxpayer.' Take Virgin Rail's west coast mainline service. If you tot up the direct subsidies it received between 1997 and 2012, it comes to £2.79 bn in today's money. Then there are the upgrades to the service worth around £9 bn – again largely funded by taxpayers. Along with other franchises, Virgin has also benefited from a vast hidden subsidy from Network Rail which, by investing in rail infrastructure even as it was lowering track access charges, has accumulated £30 bn in taxpayer-guaranteed debt. Truly, this is 'a looking-glass version of capitalism'. We hand billions to private firms; they take a fat clip and pay us back the rest; and if it doesn't work out, they just walk away..."

Why does a government not stop handing out subsidies and gives companies instead supporting MEANS which, in the long-term, need to be paid back into the public purse? Why make it one paid amount and not a payment that comes back into the budget because it is revolving?

139 We never hear that claim that the market' should be free in the case of the agricultural policy of the European Common Market. The CAP involves giving public subsidies to private farmers, independently of the quantity of food they produce. In 2011 it represented 44 % of the EU's €126,5 bn budget, according to *Der Spiegel* 6/2013 p. 66. Small farms (4,916,590 = 62.5 %)

keep the private sector up and running, not only for people to be employed, but also for the government itself, as it borrows from the private sector to balance the budget, a process of reciprocal interaction par excellence. However, private business interests have no public legitimation, nor can they ever give a country its rules, or replace a government's legitimacy on matters such as running a prison or going to war. On the contrary, no business can function without a public framework of agreed rules, without public infrastructure and without the consent of people. Claiming it could and should is only an attempt trying to roll back legitimate public power and replace it again with personal interest, a step back in history.

If we were to ask economicult theorists, who believe in free markets' and who, as individuals, want to participate in society, why they like to give up reciprocal interaction what would their answer be? Do they, personally, want to give up their public rights and obey the market's rules? It's hard to imagine.

One of the reasons for the claim that the market' should be free to regulate itself instead of being regulated by the people derives from the argument, that a market' is more efficient[140] than a public service. Let's try to find out if this argument holds true.

---

received €1.9 bn in 2009, while large farms (30,870 = 0.4 %) got €6.2 bn.

Nowadays subsidies are even handed out when farmers leave the land to nature and stop working it. The Common Market was set up by the Treaty of Rome 1957, although it is not a 'market' at all. One wonders sometimes whether it was established in the interests of big land-owners.

George Monbiot seems to have come to a very similar conclusion, when he commented in *The Guardian* 27 November 2012, p. 29: "It is a source of perpetual wonder that the people of Europe tolerate this robbery. Farm subsidies are the 21st century equivalent of feudal aid: the taxes medieval vassals were forced to pay their lords for the privilege of being sat upon. The single payment scheme, which accounts for most of the money, is an award for owning land. The more you own, the more you receive. By astonishing coincidence, the biggest landowners happen to be among the richest people in Europe. Every taxpayer in the EU, including the poorest, subsidizes the lords of the land: not once, as we did during the bank bailouts, but in perpetuity... Flooding of the kind blighting the UK is exacerbated by grazing in the hills, which prevents trees and scrub from growing. The sparser the vegetation, the faster the water runs off. Woodland and scrub preserve more carbon – both above and below ground – than pasture does. There has been a catastrophic decline in farm wildlife in the past few decades, as a result of grazing, drainage, sheep dip residues poisoning the streams and farmers' clearance of habitats. Last week's shocking report on the state of the UK's birds shows that while 20% of all birds have been lost since 1966 on farmland the rate is over 50%. The subsidy system doesn't just encourage this destruction: it demands it..."

140 The "efficient market" theory was first published by Eugene Fama (born 1939), University of Chicago, in: 'Efficient Capital Markets: A Review of Theory and Empirical Work', in: *The Journal of Finance*, May 1970, where Fama "emphasizes that the hypothesis of market efficiency must be tested in the context of expected returns". This idea was picked up and used to justify privatization of public tasks with taxpayers' money, irrespective of the fact that government is a public service for the many and not for money.

Roger Bootle, ibid, remarked too that the idea that "we would all be better off if the market were left completely alone has no support from evidence, simply because no modern society has ever tried this – and with very good reason." p. 76

It is also interesting to note that the argument for self-regulation is always used for the market' and for money, but never for nature, although we know that nature is the only force which is able to create, the only force able to create consciousness, the only force able to create order and intelligence, and which therefore stands against the law of entropy?

However, before doing so it seems necessary to remind ourselves that no market' can act by itself as if it were be an autonomous being. It cannot move or make decisions on its own, as it is always people who make these decisions. A market' is only an abstract idea, not a living organism who can act on his or her interest. It needs people who believe in the abstract idea of a market' and act accordingly, while these are – it should not be forgotten – the same people who profit from it. They are the same people who have the power to convince others that the market' has a will of its own, and the market' rules have to be followed, thereby shaping reality accordingly; and they call this liberalism. How can this be considered any kind of freedom, though, when the decisions of people are obstructed and the intrinsic rules of the market' have to be followed? In the words of Christina von Braun money governs, not the other way around. Either a trader follows the rules of money or he fails. It is the process of abstraction, which makes it possible for money to become the subject of history. Money is the subject because it has its own dynamic, which no subject can penetrate, let alone control. And the same is true of the people who make money by this process. This process of the personalization of money, as if it were a self-moving entity with an identity of its own, started early in the 19th century.[141]

Rudolf Wolfgang Mueller commented on it that to become the 'subject of history', money has to incite subjects to place themselves at its service, and to experience this service as freedom, autonomy and fulfilment of the ego. This is the contradiction: capitalists, who strive eagerly and feverishly for individual profit, place themselves in the service of the 'autonomy' of money. But they still feel themselves to be free, equal and autonomous subjects, they do not feel that they have subjected themselves to a general subject, the self-moving value. This is an insight which money does not allow them.[142]

Money is not a living being, it cannot make its own decisions, it cannot move on its own. It is people who exchange the means for the end, this is the objective truth behind our subjective everyday experience. To make the role of money

---

141 Christina von Braun, *Der Preis des Geldes, Eine Kulturgeschichte*, Berlin, 2012, p. 259, "*Entweder der Traeder verhaelt sich nach den Bestimmungen des Geldes, oder er versagt... Es ist der Abstraktionsprozess, der es dem Geld ermoeglicht, zum Subjekt der Geschichte zu werden... Das Geld ist Subjekt, weil es eine Eigendynamik hat, die kein Subjekt durchschaut, geschweige denn beherrscht. Das gilt auch fuer die, die bei diesem Prozess Geld machen.*"

142 Rudolf Wolfgang Mueller, *Geld und Geist, Zur Entstehungsgeschichte von Identitaetsbewusstsein und Rationalitaet seit der Antike*, Frankfurt, 1977, p. 89. "*Um zum 'Subjekt der Geschichte' zu werden, muss das Geld Subjekte dazu anregen, sich in seinen Dienst zu stellen und diesen Dienst als Freiheit, Autonoie und Erfuellung des 'ich' zu erleben. Das ist der Widerspruch: 'Kapitalisten', die mit Eifer und 'fieberhaft' nach individuellem Gewinn streben, stellen sich in den Dienst einer Eigengesetzlichkeit des Geldes. Dennoch empfinden sie sich als 'freie, gleiche und autonome Subjekte', sie empfinden nicht, dass sie einem 'allgemeinen Subjekt, dem sich selbst bewegenden Wert, unterworfen sind.' Dieses Wissen darf das Geld nicht zulassen. 'Das Bewusstsein von Autonomie, Freiheit und Gleichheit muss also selbst als unvermeidliches Produkt der Bewegung des Wertes als Kapital' begriffen werden.*"
(Remark: Let's not fall into the same trap of thinking, it is not money which does not allow that – as it is done by people, it is people who do so.)

clearer, I propose that we substitute the word 'money' with its non-inverted mean-ing: MEANS.[143]

In the future, it is necessary to abstain completely from assigning any kind of autonomy to money. It is neither money nor the market' that act as living subjects, behind them are people with an interest in gaining more MEANS. They have rather successfully made others believe that money and the market' are subjects, that they have a human-like consciousness, a capacity to perceive and act, ideas which only express their assumptions.

Besides, paper money itself is only a near-worthless piece of paper with a few numbers printed on it.[144] It has no use value, but it is exchange value. It is only when people believe that it can always be exchanged for real goods[145] and real services, and when people treat it as an aim instead of a means, when they trust that the value printed on that piece of paper has real use value, then it becomes so, provided that every person in the world shares this belief. The near worthlessness of the paper's MEANS becomes even more clear when electronic money is consid-ered. Von Braun cites the famous remark by Marc Shell: "The matter of electric money does not matter."[146]

When reciprocal interactions are transformed by mediating them through money and the market' and this becomes the model for a society and the habit for everyone, people get the impression that there is no alternative, there is no other choice than to follow this pattern.

The task of science therefore is to show how such an idea has been made the norm and come to dominate our daily life. And when the rules as well as the consequences of it become transparent and the veil which covers money and the

---

143 It is interesting to learn that the German Jesuits in the 17th century coined the phrase 'der Zweck heiligt die Mittel', translated: 'the end justifies the means', while the English say just the opposite: The end doesn't justify the means.

144 Banknotes are money with no intrinsic value, Birger Priddat pointed out, in:, Geist der Orna-mentik, Ideogrammatik des Geldes, in: Kapitalismus als Religion, by Dirk Baecker (ed.), Berlin, 2003, p. 31

145 One wonders what it really means these days when £ paper notes say: I promise to pay the bearer on demand the sum of...? Is the Bank of England still promising to replace £5, £10 or £20 notes with the equivalent amount of gold? And has anybody tested this promise?

146 Ibid, p. 251, Marc Shell, The Economy of Literature, Baltimore and London, 1978.
In their efforts to replace cash with virtual money the banks are trying to convince consumers never again use notes and coins, but only debit and credit cards. This would mean for consum-ers the end of anonymity which the use of coins and notes guarantees, as the banks would know exactly who is spending what and where, while the banks profit from every transaction people make. Besides, we can run out of cash, but we can never run out of plastic money, so people can be nudged into spending more and perhaps consequently borrowing more from the banks. A really creative way to increase the banking business.

market'[147] is lifted, then the opportunity for change – although not in the financial sense, but in the sense of a different rationality – seems to be possible.

The money and market' model is in no way suitable for a sustainable future, as it based on a number of abstract assumptions: for instance that 'land is a factor of production'; that 'nature is the (green) matter external to a human being'; that 'economy is nature-forgotten'; that 'labour is a commodity', and not a human ability; that infinite 'growth' is possible on a finite planet, that things can, once owned, be disposed of as one fancies without any effects, that a machine is the model for the world; instead of us recognizing that we are in a process of reciprocal interaction with our fellowmen and with nature.

Therefore, we can no longer allow human beings, who are born free and equal with inalienable rights as well as obligations, to let themselves to be defined by money and the market'. When the intrinsic rules of the market' are listed on the following pages, however, today's common concept of the market' as an autonomous being is adhered to, as this is easier for reference purposes. We must remain aware, however, that it is neither money nor the market' which 'rules' us, instead there are people behind the veil of money who try to lord it over others, encouraging us to believe that these are the norms to follow. This is the hidden secret behind the free market' philosophy, its deception.

This is why it has been preferable to call the basic pattern for the activity of nature and human beings the process of direct reciprocal interaction, before now showing how the intrinsic rules of the market' work, and how they transform reciprocal interaction when this is mediated via the market'. The below diagram[148] shows the change that occurs when the direct reciprocal process of interaction is mediated by money and the market', this is then followed by a fully expanded list describing the intrinsic rules:

---

147 Uwe Steiner, *'Die Grenzen des Kapitalismus'*, in: *Kapitalismus als Religion*, ibid, p. 41, remarks that the banknote creates a ghostly life on its own, as the token is taken for the thing itself. Instead of viewing it as a means to create wealth, the emperor believes himself wealthy by its very possession. Thus the money only serves to increase his debts, for which it originally stood. "*Gespenstisches Eigenleben entfaltet der Geldschein, weil in ihm der Schein fuer das Wesen selbst genommen wird. Anstatt in ihm das Mittel zu sehen, Reichtum ueberhaupt erst zu schaffen, meint der Kaiser, mit dem Geld bereits in dessen Besitz zu sein. So vermehrt er mit dem Geld nur die Schulden, fuer die es urspruenglich stand.*"

148 Irene Schoene, *Oekologisches Arbeiten*, Wiesbaden, 1988, p. 289

Reciprocal interaction mediated by money and market'

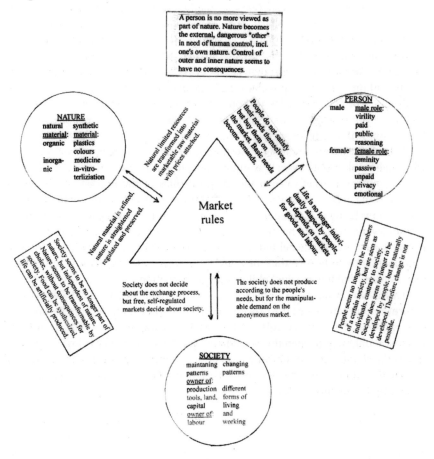

These are the sixty abstract and objective market' rules, none of which is per se 'good' or 'bad', but neither are they neutral, as all effect our lives:

1. Sellers and buyers on a market' always want to achieve something they do not have, as exchanging the same thing would not make sense. The two sides of the market' therefore are always unbalanced and asymmetrical.

2. The market' is supposed to equalize the two sides of supply and demand.

3. The market' divides producers and consumers. Producers appear active as they are manufacturing a product; consumers appear to be passive, only responding to offers, which have to be pushed into the market with enormous, expensive marketing campaigns. Consumers have no influence over the decision as to where manufacturers produce their products.

4. The market' synchronizes different qualities by relating them to the same measure, to prices.

5. The market' prefers the quantitative aspect = price, all qualitative dimensions are neglected.
6. The market' abstracts from the real needs of a consumer. His interests can never be completely answered, because his real needs differ from time to time and person to person.
7. The market' always needs offers. What is not offered cannot be bought.
8. The market' decides the price level through competition, as only the cheapest priced goods are likely to be bought.
9. The market' isolates seller from buyer, both of whom are taking part in the same process, but who follow different interests.
10. The market' allows anonymity and a lack of involvement or responsibility, as the buyer only has to hand over cash without giving information about himself.
11. The market' limits the open process of reciprocal interaction by relating it to and mediating it via money.
12. The market' substitutes the open reciprocal interaction process with a finished object.
13. People behave differently towards a market' product than they might in reciprocal interaction with others. Social behaviour is never respectful to machines; only to other people. Replacing patrolling policemen with observation cameras makes little sense.
14. Replacing one's power of reciprocal interaction with a market' product creates emotional distance. In warfare, for example, it seems easier to kill an enemy remotely from the distance by pressing a button firing a drone than to use a knife in direct man-to-man combat.
15. The market' makes everything achievable. Rather than allowing us to do something ourselves, it offers us the chance to buy. Instead of singing ourselves we can listen to the world's best singers on youtube.com; instead of playing football, we buy tickets and watch a football games; instead of practising sport, we purchase the right sports clothes to look sporty; instead of getting around under our own steam, we sit quietly in an armchair steering a car.[149] Even nature, even human sympathy becomes packaged for purchase.
16. The market' replaces various human abilities with one standardized one, buying.
17. The market' preserves. Only products which do not ripen or age keep their value. Even employees.
18. The market' means that the products have to be presented fresh and young, ready for consumption and appealing to the eye. A person offering his or her ability to labour for somebody also needs to conform to that demand. And of course a whole industry has developed to help people achieve this goal. Personal trainers can be employed, or cosmetic operations can be bought from a young age, to make us look fitter. Personal coaches and shoppers can be employed to enhance the individual's look.
19. The market' solidifies the assumption of money as a self-moving end-in-itself, rather than being socially invented MEANS.

---

149   I have called this 'industrialized self-movement'.

20. It becomes acceptable for the market's deception to replace reality. It seems sufficient for politicians to talk about changing a problematic situation for the better, rather than actually doing so. The current president of the German Social Democratic Party, Siegmar Gabriel, has characterized this as "simulated government". Politicians replace actions with words. It becomes important that they sell themselves to the public as movers and shakers, whilst not really acting at all. In the old days, people who substituted word for actions were called in German 'Maulhelden' (in English: 'loudmouths'). These days, when everybody substitutes words for deeds, people are hardly able to differentiate between a show-off and a genuinely effective leader.[150]

21. The markets' separate people and their data. Today, information about people is stored by electronic communication technology and processed mostly without peoples' knowledge, and sold to others for money, information which is mainly disclosed through electronic social networks. When asked whether they see this as a problem, many people reply that they have nothing to hide. That might be true individually. But it is also true that in this way personal data is turned into a commodity, raw material for commercial interest.[151] Who was it, incidentally, who made the now famous remark that in using an electronic social network you are not using a free product, but become the product yourself? Who wants to be treated as 'material' for other people's business?

22. The market' replaces the real economy, i.e production and consumption, by concentrating on finance. It seems that real material production (and consumption) involves a detour which is no longer necessary, as money, an end in itself, is the only thing which one strives for. David C. Korten reported a conversation he "had some years earlier with Malaysia's then minister of forestry. He told me in all seriousness that Malaysia would be better off once all its trees were cut down and the proceeds were deposited in interest-bearing accounts, because interest grows faster than trees."[152]

23. The market' initiates production, it regulates, calculates, plans and controls itself.

---

150 And especially the show-offs often do not seem to like real change.

151 'Informational self-determination', the German constitutional ruling whereby a person's consent has to be obtained before buying or selling personal data has not yet been enshrined in law. In the last few weeks (autumn 2012) it has transpired that even German city councils have sold data of their registered residents in order to make money.

152 David C. Korten, *Agenda for a New Economy, From Phantom Wealth to Real Wealth*, San Francisco, 2010, p. 30. Korten traced this opinion back to John Edmunds, finance professor at Babson College and the Arthur D. Little School of Management, Babson Park, Mass/USA.

"Professor Edmunds is telling government policymakers that they should no longer concern themselves with producing real wealth by increasing the national output of goods and services that have real utility. They should put all that aside. They can grow their national economies faster with less exertion by securitizing real assets so that investors can put them into play in financial markets... a policy, the Anglo-Saxon countries have followed since."

This totally overturns Adam Smith's insight that real wealth is created by nature and human labour. John Edmunds's comments in 1996 merely echo Colin W. Clark's in his *Blue Whale Economic Analysis* of 1973. When the latter asked: "What practice would yield the whalers and humanity the most money, ... the disconcerting answer was "kill them all and invest the money," as Edward O. Wilson records, in: *The Future of Life*, London, 2002, p. 113

24. The market' demands regularity.
25. The market' rationalizes. Only the cheapest offer will find a buyer.[153] If products are offered cheaply enough, anything can be sold, assumes economicult theory.
26. The market' separates perception from action. The consumer is interested in the offered product, while at the same time handing over money.[154]
27. Viewing market' exchange from the point of exchange of money rather than the exchange of a good, we observe that the seller wants to sell his product for more than it has cost him to produce it, while the buyer wants to pay the least money for it. From the monetary point of view, therefore, buyers and sellers reverse their roles. The seller becomes the demander of money and the buyer the supplier of money. From the point of exchanging goods the seller supplies and the buyer demands.
28. Markets' tend to ignore the quality of the exchanged products. Everything can sell, if offered cheaply enough, even if the buyer has no particular use for a product.
29. The seller on the market' does not make money by producing a good, but only by selling it. Selling, selling, selling is his sole aim and this is what all his efforts are directed towards.
30. The market' ignores the difference between kin and stranger, everyone has to cooperate with everyone else, abstracting from people's real feeling of likes and dislikes.
31. The market' separates purchase from use, temporally and spatially.
32. The market' exchanges the basics of life, eg fresh water which historically could be drunk directly from a brook or river, and is today made into an industrially-produced bottled product.
33. The market' splits man from his own nature, and society from its natural base.
34. The market' ignores the real experience of producing something and the pride and satisfaction of having been able to do so.
35. The market' changes products into money and money into products.
36. The market' reverses the MEANS with the end.
37. The market' transforms self-work into time for consumption and leisure and mediates it with money.
38. The market' reverses the roles of producer and consumer, for example in the so called 'labour' market' as people who produce labour are the suppliers, but are viewed as depending employees, while these who consume the labour are seen as independent employers.
39. The market' appears to rule people, instead of people setting the rules for the market.[155]

---

153 We have just seen this in practice, when thousands of East German pupils suffered from diarrhoea and sickness, having eaten in their school meals frozen strawberries produced in China. *Der Spiegel* 42/2012, p. 30
154 Alfred Sohn-Rethel, *Geistige und koerperliche Arbeit*, Frankfurt, 1973, p. 51
155 Horst Kurnitzky made the following remark in: *Der Heilige Markt,* Frankfurt, 1994, p. 194, that the belief in the market as something we can safely leave to regulate itself, turns the market into a transcendental supersubject.

40. The market' makes people passive, as they no longer learn to involve themselves through effort, but only need to know one activity, buying.

41. The market' gives people easy confidence; once you learn once you learn how to purchase something, that is all that needs to be repeated. The market' replaces the variety of doing with the simple activity of buying.

42. The market' replaces one's own habits of active behaviour with external demand.

43. The market' replaces self-organised processes with organizations from the outside.

44. The market' lures people into the illusion that they have autonomous disposal power over the purchased product, while in reality they are in a process of reciprocal interaction with the bought object. Before they can use the product, they have to learn how by following its instructions.

45. The market' alienates people from their own abilities to act. Their working ability is changed into a factor which they can sell – deliberately and without selling themselves, it is assumed.

46. The market' alienates people from their sociability and their social abilities.[156]

47. The market' sales are higher if a product can be sold to every individual. Shared use reduces sales figures.

48. The market' even turns life into a commodity, as the geneticist James Watson told Congress in the 1970s (reported by Ross Douthat in NYTimes.com, and cited in The Week 7 July 2012). A new kidney costs €70,000.[157] Markets' for fertilization, propagation and cloning are set up, and this will be the future of economicult, enabling life to be patented by companies.[158] People will only start to notice the unwanted consequences when they learn that plant seeds can no longer be used for sowing, but have to be bought year after year as the seeds have been modified in such a way that they no longer germinate, thus securing a constant income for big companies.

49. The market' seems to replace verbs with nouns, eg acting with action, moving with movement, labouring with labour, dealing with deal, increasing with 'growth'.

50. The market' seems to give people the power of disposal because of their ownership of an object.

---

156 As pointed out by Richard Sennett, in: Together: The Rituals, Pleasures and Politics of Cooperation, London, 2012

157 According to the Frankfurter Allgemeine Sonntagszeitung, 19 August 2012, p. 39

158 The Sueddeutsche Zeitung , 27/28 October 2012, p. 22, listed the patents on animals already granted by the European Patent Agency EPA as follows: 194 "cancer" mouse (EP 298807), 2001 Dolly the sheep (EP 0849990) and chimpanzee (EP 1572862, EP 1409646) which the organization No Patents On Life objected together with the Gen-ethisches Netzwerk and the Gesellschaft fuer oeklogische Forschung und Testbiotech.

51. The market' even seems to decide which party wins an election and therefore who runs for office of president of a country,[159] as no election campaign can be successfully run without funds.[160]

52. The market' takes people's responsibility for their actions away. Events are never a person's own fault but always that of the market'.

53. Obeying the market' comes with an easy explanation and no effort at all. We do not need to get involved, we do not need to come to an opinion, we only have to follow its rules.

54. The market' dissects and reconnects – but on its own terms, the well known principle of *divide et impera*, named these days 'division of labour'.

55. The market' not only exchanges everything for money, but does it in a dual sense, as the money changes from being the MEANS to the end at the same time. Market' is only another word for this exchange *and* interchange.

56. Through the market' everything is mediated and is made indirect. In the past the ingredients for a meal such as a pasta bake could be bought locally as the local butcher bought pigs and cattle from farmers he knew and slaughtered and matured the meat himself, so people could rely on his personal service and his interest in offering his customers good quality. These days, however, ready-made meals can involve up to "450 different parties – from farmers to renderers, meat traders to processors, packers to retailers –" which are making money out of it at every stage, as the financial services firm KPMG found.[161]

57. It is not only people who in their role as consumers replace their dominant activities with the purchase of products on the market', even businesses do. Take pharmacists for example. Their business has been transformed from self-making medicines for individual patients according to their own knowledge and experience to selling anonymous ready-made 'specialities'.

58. The market' even brings a 'third' party into direct reciprocal relationships, when for example companies insure their employees against death without their knowledge and permission, and bag the insurance money when the over-worked employee dies.[162]

59. Market' postpones the possibility of a free, self-controlled and self-reliant life to later, eventually even into 'life' after death. Making money today, giving up a carefree life in the hope of being carefree in the future perhaps, is what keeps up the momentum of the Western world, remarked Volker Weidemann in 'Geld? Was fuer ein Widersinn', in *Frankfurter Allgemeine Sonntagszeitung* [163].

60. The market' transforms direct immediate and reciprocal interaction into indirect exchanges, also in a spatial sense. It replaces the locality principle with the monetary principle. Whereas, for example, when it was only important to

---

159 US President Barack Obama is said to have spent about $1 bn on his re-election campaign, money which did not come only out of his own or his party's pocket, but was collected from rich individuals and institutions. One wonders what their payback consists of.

160 We should be very careful to restrict that rule in future, as otherwise even in a democracy choosing representatives of the people will depend on money and market'.

161 As reported in *The Week* 9 March 2013, p. 11

162 Michael J. Sandel, ibid, p. 166

163 29 September 2013, p. 42

recruit local players to a football club, and people were proud when they won against another location, these days this principle is no longer followed, as players can be bought from anywhere, if a club can raise the transfer money for them. So the locality in the clubs' names has in a way lost its meaning. The football clubs Bayern Muenchen or Manchester United no longer consists of players coming from Muenchen or Manchester, instead they are bought in from all over the world. Nor are football clubs local organizations anymore, these days they are bought by any club who can afford it.

The same is of course true of local water, gas or oil suppliers. They are no longer owned and controlled locally, but by global organizations, even by state controlled companies like the French Electricite de France EDF. And last but least, the same phenomenon is observed when a country like Malta[164] starts to grant citizenship to outsiders for money – citizenship which comes with the free choice to live anywhere in Europe.

Another effect is that companies owned by global businesses no longer act in the local interest, when for example "UK Power Networks (UKPN) owned by the Hong Kong tycoon Li Ka-shing's offshore-controlled family business left thousands of customers without electricity on Christmas Day"[165] when we read that £630 m profit "may also have funnelled... back to its Hong Kong and offshore parent companies in dividends and interest repayment on money they lent UKPN since taking it over in 2010" instead of being invested into better electricity supply for local customers.

61. And last but not least, extending the abstract idea of a free market' by MEANS of global trade agreements restricts countries' full sovereignty to decide their own policies.[166]

Therefore, we have to conclude that a market' is not neutral. It is the opposite, it has influences on people, but without discussing these intrinsic rules, people will not be aware of them. The market' disrupts direct involvement and interactions and reconnects them again according to its own rules, thus interchanging everything from direct to indirect and from individual to standardized: 'with the help of money'[167] is turned into 'for money'[168]. This transformation by the MEANS of money is typical for a culturally invented economicult, not for a nateconomy.

---

164 *The Spiegel* 47/2013 reported that besides Malta also Cyprus, Greece, Hungary, Latvia, Portugal and Spain offer citizenship for sale.

165 *The Independent on Sunday*, 5 January 2013, p. 9

166 cf. Naomi Klein, *This Changes Everything, Capitalism vs. the Climate*, London, 2014, p. 70ff

167 As in a cultecomonic society which has invented money and uses it as a MEANS.

168 As in an economi*cult* society where money has been made the end of every activity. This important difference is disavowed in the pamphlet *Spread This Wealth* by C. Jesse Duke which claims according to Thomas Frank *We don't need no regulation* in: *The Guardian Weekend* 7 January 2012 p. 31, that "A tree exchanges oxygen for carbon dioxide. A fire exchanges heat for oxygen. Atoms exchange electrons to become other atoms. Plants collect light to make chlorophyll, which nourishes animals, which become food for other animals and man, and so on. Everything in nature is constantly exchanging." This is true. We called it the nateconomy. For it, nature has not invented a MEANS. The natural exchange, however, had been mediated, and then the medium had been made into the end.

Furthermore, when the economicult theory claims that markets' satisfy every need, even needs people did not know they had before a product is offered, we have to remind them that statement is also wrong, *as the market' can never fulfil the most important of all humans' needs, the need to be self-active.* This need cannot be satisfied by buying, but only by doing. It also requires that people are active in satisfying the following: the need to stay healthy, the need for strong reliable affection, the need to be loved or feel compassionate, the need for companionship or the need to find out about things, and to view them from a fresh point of view.

This begs the question, why basic human needs in a democracy, according to which everyone has to have his say, should be allowed to be replaced by intrinsic market' rules? Why should money be treated as an end in itself, when it is only a MEANS or a "wheel" (Adam Smith) of economic activity? And why should the freedom of people in their free time be transformed through the mediation of money and market'? Can this deep cultural change which has happened, really be justified because only a minority of people profit from it?

The philosopher Dieter Thomae seemed to be of a similar opinion when he compared economicult and family life in the household. He argued[169] that economicult is concentrated on egoism, profit, volatile capital, risk, high flexibility and an ongoing ability to change, while family life, the nateconomy, is dealing with the responsibility for others as a continuous process, as neither of the future parents know at the beginning where it will lead to, therefore a kind of risk assessment is impossible. As a rule, a child will incur a six-digit sum over a lifetime, without any chance of predicting the outcome. Alternatively, you can invest € 500,000 relatively securely on the capital market. It is altogether more secure to buy shares than to raise a child. And when he was asked if he sees a chance for reconciliation between family and capitalism, he answered that he does not from the point of the system. But obviously from the point of a human. No human is totally taken over by economic logic. Experiences of happiness which comes with family life, have a major attraction.[170]

Is it not much more worthwhile and much more democratic to openly discuss which rules people would like to follow, instead of asking them to obey abstract, quasi-autonomous self-serving laws which nobody has consciously decided about? And is the claim that people should follow the intrinsic market' rules not more or less contrary to the process of Enlightenment which aims at freeing people from the dictates of self-appointed minority? The question is: can a country really call itself a democracy when people are excluded from making the rules about how they want to live? Why not dare to implement a democracy with everybody participating, by virtue of their basic human rights? And why not build a strategy for achieving that – directly? In a democracy people rule, neither the market' nor money, as the latter are not subjects like living human beings.

---

169 "*Der Kapitalismus zersetzt die Familie – ganz subtil*", in *Frankfurter Allgemeine Sonntagszeitung* 16 December 2012, p. 39.

170 "*Vom System her eigentlich nicht. Aber vom Menschen her schon. Der ist naemlich nicht ausschliesslich von oekonomischer Logik besessen. Die Gluckserfahrungen, die Familie eben auch mit sich bringt, haben noch immer eine ziemlich hohe Anziehungskraft.*"

Therefore, the political strategy cannot be to liberate markets', but obviously has to focus on the liberation of people from abstract rules they have had to say in, as such rules make them dependent and not free.

Besides: the call to liberate markets' – or in other words: to liberate people with money from public laws – is only a political demand. It is not justifiable by scientific evidence.

And this is perhaps the moment to point out that there are, here and there, certain organisations and movements arising which do try to make truly democratic decisions and act on a wider agenda than concentrating on money. One of them is the campaign for fair trade, which means – among other criteria – that no child labour is used and the real producers receives a good price for their products. In Germany, the town of Eckernfoerde in Schleswig-Holstein, the most northern of the 16 Bundeslaender, has just declared[171] itself the 100th Fairtrade Town in Germany. The Fair Trade campaign started in 2000. Garstang in Lancashire named itself the first global Fairtrade Town, offering fairly produced and traded products. Today there are more than 1,000 of Fairtrade towns in 23 countries. These are small, but essential steps towards developing peoples' awareness. According to Der Spiegel 41/2014, p. 69, German people spent in 2013 about €784 million on fair trade products.

However, a recent study by the University of London, financed by the British government, came to the conclusion that there is a very unfair side to it as farm labourers did not really profit from it. And there is still a lot of criticism about how "fair" the products really are, but generally, Fairtrade has brought more transparency for customers about the way how their food is produced and traded.

So in answer to the call to liberate the market' we must respond: Let us abandon this political claim. Let us concentrate on freeing the people. There is a lot still to be done. Let us abandon the idea that it is money which should be the ruler and the end of all human activity.

Instead – let us treat money as MEANS. A means has its uses, but it has to follow the laws set by free people in a democracy – this is the modern culteconomy which we are aiming for, a worthy goal indeed. ."We can't change the physical reality, so we must change the political reality," Naomi Klein pointed out in a Spiegel interview[172] on 25 February 2015.

---

171 Kieler Nachrichten, 20 October, 2012

172 Spiegelonline 25 February 2015, presenting the German version of her latest book This Changes Everything, Capitalism vs. The Climate, New York, 2014

8. Reciprocal interaction and what money has to do with it

In the last chapters we have found that the process of direct open reciprocal interaction is the basic principle for the relationship between humans and nature, which take different forms according to the particular culture in history, for example in the 21st century the natural direct interaction is transformed into mediated interaction with the aim to gain money. In this way the formerly cultural invented MEANS of exchange is transformed into its end.

We have discussed the different divisions which are the consequence of this transformation, so typical for our culture today: between humans and nature, between humans and their inalienable ability to labour, humans and the society they are living in, as well as the fragmentation of human tasks. We have explained how these divisions were due because the medium of interactions – money – was changed from a MEANS to the end of every human activity, and how every human activity has now become defined by it, with the consequence of more unequal than fair distribution.

These divisions and fragmentations have begun very slowly and without conscious decision making in historic times. They are accepted as typical of today's so-called Westernised nations, in which the Christian religion played and still plays an important role. Although in countries with other religious backgrounds they have barely happened at all, at least not to the same degree, today they are found throughout the whole world in Western Christian nations as the norm in terms of how to live, how to work and how to organise society.[1]

The relationship between Christian religious beliefs and the rise of an economicult had attracted already the attention of many scientists, eg the sociologist Max Weber[2] (1864 - 1920), Professor of National Economics at the University of Munich, Germany. This relationship between religious thinking and economicult will now be discussed in more detail, making it necessary to go into the history of money a little bit deeper.

---

1 Ian Morris based his theory: *Why the West rules – for now*, London, 2010, on a so-called "geographic advantage" of the West, on "maps, not chaps". That the Western model of life has become the worldwide norm is according to Morris due to the geographic position of the West, and not due to people, a logic which is not followed here.

2 Max Weber, *Die protestantische Ethik und der Geist des Kapitalismus'*, in: *Gesammelte Aufsaetze zur Religionssoziologie*, Tuebingen, 1920

It would be interesting to find if there is a relationship between the invention of money and the natural process of reciprocal interaction, as reciprocal interaction is the basic principle of man's as well as nature's activity, which both are, to extend the famous notion of Paul Watzlawick, *unable not to interact*.

Of course, it is hardly possible to reconstruct the history of money. We think that money was invented about 7,000 years ago, but where, by whom, how and how it became universal use, will never be found out.

What we can state, however, is, that it must have been created by people who were already able to use a certain level of abstract thinking. Creating a MEANS for interactions, to which both partners of the process refer in order to exchange different quantities and qualities of products, also requires much persuasiveness. These people had to convince their fellow men to adopt and believe in that idea and practise it in their daily activities. It seems our ancestors could hardly have been primitive men on whom we should look down with a feeling of superiority. Instead we have to give them full respect for their invention. They must have had already agonised over the problem of how to make exchanges fair. If, for example, a lamb was to be exchanged for a portion of rice, there was the problem of deciding how much rice should be handed over for the animal. Using a MEANS of exchange makes the process easier, but at the same time mediated. Using MEANS is very useful as it can be divided into smaller and smaller units, which cannot be done with an animal, as it would die, but the problem of negotiating a price for a good has to be solved. If a lamb is to be exchanged for rice, the value of each good should be equivalent – at least in the opinion of their owners, while the reason of exchange is that the participating people each give what they have and receive what they do not have but want. Besides, the invention of a MEANS for their exchange makes additional sense, as money does not need to be watered and fed, nor does it smell, or make a noise, and it can be stored. It can be easily hidden. And even small amounts of it can represent a high value.

In ancient times different materials were used as MEANS, for example shells, stones, snails. It was about 2,700 years ago in Greek Asia Minor that metal coins started to be used; the same kind of coins we know today. Niall Ferguson described that invention as follows:[3] "Money, it is conventional to argue, is a medium of exchange, which has the advantage of eliminating inefficiencies of barter; a unit of account, which facilitates valuation and calculation; and a store of value, which allows economic transactions to be conducted over long periods as well as geographical distances. To perform all these functions optimally, money has to be available, affordable, durable, fungible, portable and reliable. Because they fulfil most of these criteria, metals such as gold, silver and bronze were for millennia regarded as the ideal monetary raw material. The earliest known coins date back as long ago as 600 BC and were found by archaeologists in the Temple of Artemis at Ephesus (near Izmir in modern-day Turkey). These ovular Lydian coins, which were made of the gold-silver alloy known as electrum and bore the image of a lion's head, were the forerunners of the Athenian *tetradrachm*, a standard silver

---

3   Niall Ferguson, *The Ascent of Money, A Financial History of the World*, London, 2009, p. 25

coin with the head of the goddess Athena on one side and an owl (associated with her for its supposed wisdom) on the obverse."

However, it has to be recognized that, at this time in history, coins were of the same use value as the metal they were made from. Use value and exchange value were identical. A silver coin weighing an ounce of silver would be worth US$/oz 31.43 today.[4] Today a piece of almost worthless paper[5] can have total different exchange values, according to the numbers that are printed on it, ie $1, $10, $20 or $100. And our coins are no longer worth the metal they are made of, but only represent the value embossed on them. Today we have to rely on the promise of the banks issuing the money that it will pay the inscribed value to anybody who presents it. Today money is "trust inscribed", as Niall Ferguson stated. Everybody has to believe "in the person issuing the money he uses or the institution that honours his cheques or transfers."[6]

The point, however, that Ferguson and other economicult theorists neglect is the religious background from which money descended, as Glyn Davies pointed out: "Economists, and especially monetarists, tend to overestimate the purely economic, narrow and technical functions of money and have placed insufficient emphasis on its wider social, institutional and psychological aspects. However... money originated very largely from non-economic causes: from tribute as well as from trade, from blood-money and bride-money as well as from barter, from ceremonial and religious rites as well as from commerce, from ostentatious ornamentation as well as from acting as the common drudge between economic men."[7]

8.1. Reciprocal interaction and religious ritual

Literature about the religious roots of money goes back to the 19th century, for example to Bernhard Laum (1884 - 1974),[8] Professor of National Economics at the University of Marburg, Germany. In 1924 Laum published *Heiliges Geld, Eine historische Untersuchung ueber den sakralen Ursprung des Geldes,*[9] and his expertise was used by Horst Kurnitzky, in: *Triebstruktur des Geldes, Ein Beitrag zur Theorie der Weiblichkeit,*[10] as well as by Christina von Braun in her recent publication *Der Preis des Geldes.*[11]

In Laum's investigation about the religious roots of money he came to express doubts as to whether in the Homeric age, it is appropriate to talk of a general

---

4   According to silver.de
5   Although if you are saving a note and wait a few years, let's say 200, then a paper note can
      perhaps be worth €225,000, the amount of money for which the last existing official Australian
      10-shilling-note from 1817 was bought at auction in Sydney, reported *Spiegel* online, 27 March
      2014.
6   Ibid, p. 31
7   Glyn Davies, in cooperation with Julian Hodge Bank Ltd., *A History of Money, From Ancient-
      Times to the Present Day,* Cardiff, 2002, p. XVIII
8   Or: Ernst Curtius, *Der religioese Charakter der griechischen Muenzen,* Berlin, 1870
9   Barlin, 2006; cf. also: Ernest Bornemann, *Psycholoanalyse des Geldes,* Frankfurt, 1977
10   Berlin, 1974
11   Berlin, 2012

MEANS of exchange from which the measure of value could have derived.[12] Naturally there was an exchange of goods outside the self-sustained Greek household, but a general MEANS against which everything was exchanged and to which everyone aspired, had not yet been invented. According to Laum, money could therefore not have been derived from trade. He came to the conclusion that money derived from ritualised belief[13] – and in a way, even today money still works on the basis of a belief system.

To follow up this argument, it is necessary to explore a bit deeper the religious thinking of that time, even look at the way people in ancient times made sense of natural events. As they did not have trustworthy explanations for natural events, catastrophes, epidemics or the origin of the world, they based their explanations on human experience. And human experience shows that if an event happened, someone must have caused it. It seems logical that therefore there must have been superior beings who created the world. They gave the different natural forces the status of gods,[14] eg sun, light and truth were represented by the god Phoebus Apollon (Greek and Roman), fire by the god Hephaestus (Greek)/Vulcan (Roman), husbandry, harvest and the helix of life and death by the goddess Demeter (Greek)/Ceres (Roman), water and the sea, floods, droughts and earthquakes by the god Poseidon (Greek)/Neptune (Roman), wisdom, courage, inspiration and the arts by the goddess Athena (Greek)/Minerva (Roman), the wilderness and wild animals by the goddess Artemis (Greek)/Diana (Roman), and the sky, weather, thunder and lightning by the highest ranking and therefore king of all gods, Zeus (Greek)/Jupiter (Roman).[15] He was married to the goddess of birth and marriage, Hera (Greek)/Juno (Roman), the highest-ranking goddess in each religion, with the by-name Moneta,[16] meaning: 'remind' and 'remember'.

These goddesses and gods[17] were seen as responsible for everything that happened. The Greek concept of invisible beings manifest in the natural forces of the world is quite different from the one the Christian's envisage of an invisible, supernatural entity existing outside of the world. When disastrous storms devastated the country or flooding occurred, according to the Greeks these catastrophes were caused by the gods Zeus or Poseidon. The people interpreted such events as a sign that the god in question was angry with humans. Perhaps people did not praise

---

12   p. 18: "... wir in homerischer Zeit ueberhaupt von einem allgemeinen Tauschmittel, aus dem der Wertmesser haette entstehen koennen, sprechen duerfen."

13   Ibid, p. 26 and further on

14   James George Frazer, in: *The Golden Bough, A Study in Magic and Religion*, first published 1890, A New Abridgement from the Second and Third Editions, Oxford, 1994, p. 390, called this "the mythical personification of nature".

15   As the highest ranking god was male, we would call this religious thinking patriarchal. Worshipping the great mother goddess in a matriarchal society had already come to an end.

16   Horst Kurnitzky, *Triebstruktur des Geldes*, ibid, p. 24

17   The Greek deities are supposed to have lived on Mount Olympus in the north of Greece.
        Only a few well known Greek and Roman deities are here listed; there were many others all over the world. In the region of Northern Europe for example, the Vikings, or the Celts, living in what is now Austria, France, Germany, Ireland, Switzerland and the UK had similar gods and goddesses representing natural forces, eg Taranis, the Celtic equivalent to Zeus/Jupiter. The Celts sacrificed both humans and animals to the gods.

him enough or had not followed his rules.[18] It was necessary then to pacify that god, and this was done by following a special ritual or by offering him a gift. Charles Freeman wrote: "Ancient Greece vibrated with spiritual presences. Mediation with the gods took place through prayer and sacrifice. The sacrifice was the central point of almost every ritual."[19] For example, we can still see carvings of the goddess Artemis near the amphitheatre of Philippi in northern Greece, with an inscription to the goddess that an offering was made to her in gratitude.

This would be the normal procedure for humans as well. If someone, had damaged your house, then he had to give you compensation that you have suffered from his wrongdoing – fairness at its most basic. Human beings expect to be treated as they treat others, therefore Will Hutton's description of fairness as an "indispensable value that underpins good economy and society..."[20] is understandable.

Human experiences were referred to the behaviour of the gods. The gods were seen as quarrelling with each other, becoming envious, defrauding and stealing, they married each other and had children.

Let's remind ourselves[21] that Adam Smith argued in a very similar way:[22] "Mankind, in the first ages of society, before the establishment of law, order and security, have little curiosity to find out *those hidden chains of events* which bind together the seemingly disjointed appearances of nature. A savage, whose subsistence is precarious, whose life is every day exposed to the rudest dangers, has no inclination to amuse himself with searching out what, when discovered, seems to serve no other purpose than to render the theatre of nature a more connected spectacle to his imaginations... Comets, eclipses, thunder, lightning, and other meteors, by their greatness, naturally overawe him, and he views them with a reverence that approaches to fear. His inexperience and uncertainty with regard to every thing about them, how they came, how they are to go, what went before, what is to come after them, exasperate his sentiment into terror and consternation... As those appearances terrify him, therefore he is disposed to believe everything about them which can render them still more the objects of his terror. That they proceed from some intelligent, though invisible causes, of whose vengeance and displeasure they are either the signs or the effects, is the notion of all others most capable of enhancing this passion, and is that, therefore, which he is most apt to entertain."

These "*hidden chains of events*" Smith explained as follows: "Philosophy is the science of connecting principles of nature." "Philosophy, by representing the

---

18 Charles Freeman, in: *The Closing of the Western Mind, The Rise of Faith and the Fall of Reason*, New York, 2009, p. 250, cited William James: "One of the great consolations of the monastic life is the assurance that we have that in obeying we can commit no fault. The Superior may commit a fault in commanding you to do this or that, but you are certain that you commit no fault so long as you obey, because God will only ask you if you have duly performed what orders you received... Here the abdication of the power to think for oneself is complete." Enlightenment, by contrast, means thinking for yourself.

19 Ibid, p. 9

20 Will Hutton, *Them and Us, Changing Britain – Why We Need a Fair Society*, London, 2011, p. 21

21 As already mentioned in chapter 4.3

22 *The Early Writings of Adam Smith*, edited by J. Ralph Lindgren, New York, 1967, p. 47, author's italics

invisible chains which bind together all these disjointed objects, endeavours to introduce order into this chaos of jarring and discordant appearances, to allay this tumult of the imagination, and to restore it, when it surveys the great revolutions of the universe, to that tone of tranquillity and composure, which is both most ·agreeable in itself, and most suitable to its nature."

And Smith continues two pages later: "Hence the origin of Polytheism, and of that vulgar superstition which ascribes all the irregular events of nature to the favour or displeasure of intelligent, though invisible beings, to gods, daemons, witches, genii, fairies. For it may be observed, that in all Polytheistic religions, among savages, as well as in the early ages of Heavenly antiquity, it is the irregular events of nature only that are ascribed to the agency and power of their gods. Fire burns, and water refreshes; heavy bodies descend, and lighter substances fly upwards, by the necessity of their own nature; nor was the *invisible hand of Jupiter* ever apprehended to be employed in those matters. But thunder and lightning, storms and sunshine, those more irregular events, were ascribed to his favour, or his anger. Man, the only designing power with which they were acquainted, never acts but either to stop or to alter the course which natural events would take, if left to themselves. Those other intelligent beings, whom they imagined, but knew not, were naturally supposed to act in the same manner; not to employ themselves in supporting the ordinary course of things, which went on of its own accord, but to stop, to thwart, and to disturb it. And thus, in the first ages of the world, the lowest and most pusillanimous superstition supplied the place of philosophy."[23]

Such thinking must have long been seen as normal, as already the antique historian Diodorus Siculus stated around 50 years before the Common Era: "Now the Ethiopians (Meroites), as historians relate, were the first of all men...[24] And they say that they were the first to be taught to honour the gods and to hold sacrifices and processions and festivals and the other rites by which men honour the deity... And they state that, by reason of their piety towards the deity, they manifestly enjoy the favour of the gods, inasmuch as they have never experienced the rule of an invader from abroad; for from all time they have enjoyed a state of freedom and of peace one with another, and although many powerful rulers have made war upon them, not one of these has succeeded in his undertaking."[25] Laum found that in the epics of Homer this state of the gods already exists.[26]

It was essential to honour the gods if people wished to live in peace. As the gods were thought to protect the people, the people had to make sure that the gods were favourably disposed towards them. Therefore praying to the gods and sacrificing to them was unavoidable. A ritual of mutuality.[27] That is the process of reciprocal interaction as defined.

---

23 As already mentioned, it seems outdated nowadays to use the term 'invisible hand' to legitima-
    tize egoistic behaviour (relying on 'the invisible hand' to turn it into a benefit for all).
24 It has been proved 2,000 years later, that homo sapiens is of Recent African Origin.
25 Diodorus Siculus, in: *Historical Library*, written ca. 60 - 30 BCE, cited from: Selina O'Grady, *And
    Man created God, Kings, Cults, and Conquests at the Time of Jesus*, London, 2012, p. 79
26 P. 30: "...in den homerischen Epen steht dieser Goetterstaat bereits fertig vor us."
27 Bernhard Laum, ibid., p. 37

It is perhaps of interest to add what the *Oxford Concise Dictionary of World Religions* says about sacrifice:[28] "The offering of something, animate or inanimate, in a ritual procedure which establishes or mobilises a relationship of mutuality between the one who sacrifices (whether individual or group) and the recipient – who may be human but more often is of another order, e.g. god or spirit. Sacrifice pervades virtually all religions, but it is extremely difficult to say precisely what the meanings of sacrifice are – perhaps because there are so many different meanings. Sacrifice is clearly much more than technique: it involves drama, ritual, and action, transforming whatever it is that is sacrificed beyond its mundane role: in general, nothing that is sacrificed has intrinsic worth or holiness before it is set apart; it is the sacrifice that gives it added value. Sacrifice has been understood as expiation of fault or sin; as propitiation of an angry deity; as apotropaic (turning away punishment, disaster, etc.); as purgation; as an expression of gratitude; as substitutionary (offering to God a substitute for what is rightly his, eg the first-born; as commensal, establishing union with God or with others in a community; as *do ut des* ('I give in order that you may give', an offering in order to evoke a gift in return); as maintaining cosmic order (especially in Hindu sacrifices); as celebration; as a means of coping with violence in a community; as catharsis; as a surrogate offering at the level of power and its distribution ..."[29]

The most important sacrifice a god could command from the people was naturally their highest ranking person, the (male) leader, the king. The king/ leader/hero lived on Earth, but his power – and the legitimation of his family's rule – was given to him by the gods. Freeman is of the opinion that: "The concept of the monarch as either a god himself or was specially favoured by the gods, became one of the most important aspects of Hellenistic and Roman imperial rule... the assimilation of Christianity into the Roman state cannot be understood without it."[30] At the same time, the god-king was and head of church.[31]

In matriarchal ritual as described by James George Frazer in: *The Golden Bough* the male hero, representing the Earth, was seen as the companion of the mother goddess, and it was always he who "comes to a sad end, and whose death is annually mourned,"[32] thus representing the death of vegetation in winter and new green shoots in spring, a kind of ritually regenerating sacrifice. According to Mircea Eliade, heaven and earth are the archetypical couple, the "leitmotif" of general mythology.[33] Sigmund Freud came to the same conclusion when he wrote: "At one period – it is hard to say when – great mother deities appeared, probably before the male gods, and they were worshipped beside the latter for a long time

---

28   Published by John Bowker, New York, 2000, p. 498
29   Cf. Marcel Mauss, *The Gift*, London, 1966, where Maus describes different historic forms of the necessity to return something in exchange for a gift.
30   Charles Freeman, *The Closing of the Western Mind*, ibid, p. 41
31   A role that the British monarch still holds. Let's not forget that the leader/king needed some kind of legitimation for his rule, so a supernatural power who gave him his power is useful.
32   James George Frazer, *The Golden Bough*, p. 390
33   Mircea Eliade, *Die Religionen und das Heilige, Elemente der Religionsgeschichte*, Frankfurt, 1986, p. 276: "

to come. During that time a great social revolution had taken place. Matriarchy[34] was followed by a restitution of the patriarchal order[35] ...The male gods appear at first as sons by the side of the great mother; only later do they clearly assume the features of the father. These male gods... are numerous, they have to share their authority, and occasionally they obey a higher god."[36]

Offering[37] the son of heaven to the gods meant that he had to lose his life, on Earth, but being dead was not the end of life for him as he went back to heaven, 'living' there in all eternity. Nigel Davies[38] pointed out that human sacrifice can indeed find its utmost expression in a voluntary act if performed by a person who pledges his life for the common good, as a soldier does for example when he risks his own life to save his country from being conquered by the enemy.

Today, while killing a person and sacrificing them to the gods is seen as a most cruel and horrible act based on superstition, we can perhaps find a kind of rationality even in such a horrendous act, if we consider just how many people might be left suffering from a natural catastrophe[39], leaving them without the essentials for life, and less people would have a better chance of survival..

Let's speculate a little further: when the god-king should not have been offered to the gods because his personality, knowledge and experience was needed, then it might become rational to sacrifice the next in line, ie the king's firstborn son.[40] And when the king, in his role as high priest, was not able to sacrifice his own son as he did not have the heart to kill him, then it became necessary to install childless men, priests, who made a professional job out of the offering and the service to the gods. The consequence was that the functions of a priest and a monarch[41] were split, a division of worldly and spiritual power which today is typical in most countries.

The repeated ritual of offering strengthened daily consciousness concerning

---

34 Johann Jakob Bachofen, *Das Mutterrecht*, first published 1861 in Stuttgart, this edition Frankfurt 1975,
    or: Ernest Bornemann, *Das Patriarchat, Ursprung und Zukunft unseres Gesellschaftssystems*, Frankfurt, 1975;
    Elizabeth Gould Davis, *Am Anfang war die Frau, Die neue Zivilisationsgeschichte aus weiblicher Sicht*, Munich, 1977;
    Heide Goettner-Abendroth, *Die Gottin und ihr Heros, Muenchen, 1983*;
    Erich Neumann, *Die grosse Mutter, Eine Phaenomenologie der Weiblichen Gestaltungen des Unbewussten, Zuerich*, 1985;
    Robert von Ranke-Graves, *Die Weisse Goettin, Sprache des Mythos*, Reinbek, 1988
35 Gunnar Heinsohn, in: *Privateigentum, Patriarchat, Geldwirtschaft, Eine soziatheoretische Rekonstruktion zur Antike*, Frankfurt, 1984, p. 42, noted that M. Vaerting had already formulated in 1921 the theory of the pendulum swing of monosexual dominance.
36 Sigmund Freud, *Moses and Monotheism* New York, first published 1939, 1967, p. 105
37 The English word 'offer' as well as the German '*opfern*' derive from the ancient Greek '*opheilo*', which meant to be obliged, as in 'I owe you'.
38 Nigel Davies, *Opfertod und Menschenopfer*, Frankfurt, Berlin, Wien, 1981, p. 11: "Menschliches Opfer kann in der Tat seinen hoechsten Ausdruck in einer freiwilligen Tat erreichen, wenn sie ein Mensch ausfuehrt, der sein Leben als Unterpfand fuer das Gemeinwohl hingibt."
39 for example the eruption of Thera volcano Thera in the 15th century BCE, now known as Santorini, Greece
40 Compare Christina von Braun, ibid, p. 41
41 A single hereditary head of state, derived from the Greek word *monos* = single, alone

the importance of the process of reciprocal interaction. Everyone was made aware of it each time, with every repetition.

Here are two things to note: people were keen to find an explanation for events which at that time they could not make sense of, that is a very human trait. And further, if a catastrophe occurs, we look for a particular cause for this event. We think, it must have been caused by someone, as a child is fathered by a man. It does not come into existence on its own. The effort to find an explanation led to another consequence, another split, the division between material nature on one side and the spirit, the gods, on the other, as Horst Kurnitzky pointed out.[42]. The French philosopher Rene Descartes (1596–1650 CE) formulated it as the difference between *res extensa*, the extended matter, and *res cogitans*, the conscious matter, as already mentioned.

However, it is not necessary to base our understanding of nature on Descartes's expression. With equal legitimacy we can follow the Dutch philosopher Baruch Spinoza (1632–1677 CE) in his view that nature and spirit are an identity, because in the process of evolution consciousness was created by nature in animals – to different degrees. Stuart Hampshire, one of the most eminent British philosophers of the 20th century, wrote about Spinoza: "It is Spinoza's fundamental argument... that there can be only one substance which is *causa sui*, and that this single substance must be identified with the universe conceived as a whole; this unique all-inclusive totality he therefore calls 'God or Nature' *Deus sive Natura*."[43] "If the Universe were conceived to consist of two (or more) such substances – and Descartes, in his all-embracing distinction between Thought and Extension, the mental and the physical worlds, had in effect made this supposition – then an explanation would be required of why just two (or more) such substances exist; for, according to Spinoza (...) everything can be explained as the effect of some cause, and to suppose anything else is immediately to abandon the hope of rational understanding; for rational understanding simply consists in knowledge of

---

42   Horst Kurnitzky, *Der heilige Markt*, Frankfurt, 1994, p. 106

It is interesting to show how Mircea Eliade in: *A History of Religious Ideas, From the Stone Age to the Eleusinian Mysteries*, Chicago, 1978, p. 354, explained the differences of religious belief between Israel and Canaanites, the country the children of Israel lived in after their exodus from Egypt: "The prophets do not disappear in the last years of the Exile and the postexilic period... But their message develops what could be called the 'theology of salvation' outlined by Jeremiah. So it is legitimate at this point to estimate the role of prophecy in the religious history of Israel. What strikes us first about the prophets is their criticism of the cult and the ferocity with which they attack syncretism, that is, Canaanite influences, what they call 'prostitution'. But this 'prostitution', against which they never cease to fulminate, represents one of the most widespread forms of cosmic religiosity. Specifically characteristic of agriculturalists, cosmic religiosity continued the most elementary dialectic of the sacred, especially the belief that the divine is incarnated, or manifests itself, in cosmic objects and rhythms. Now such a belief was denounced by the adherents of Yahweh as the worst possible idolatry, and this ever since the Israelites' entrance into Palestine. But never was cosmic religiosity so savagely attacked. The prophets finally succeeded in emptying nature of any divine presence. Whole sectors of the natural world, the 'high places,' stones, springs, trees, certain crops, certain flowers – will be denounced as unclean because they were polluted by the cult of the Canaanite divinities of fertility. The pre-eminently clean and holy region is the desert alone, for it is there that Israel remained faithful to its God."

43   Stuart Hampshire, *Spinoza and Spinozism*, Oxford, 2005, p. 40

causes."[44] "The vulgar distinction," Hampshire found, "based on imagination and not on reason, between God and Nature has always been tied to the distinction between the Creator and his Creation; God is imagined as an artificer and Nature, including man, as his artefact..." and "The common Jewish and Christian idea of creation necessarily involves this dualism...". As he noted "... it was convenient in scientific practice to regard the Universe as a giant clockwork mechanism, which, once wound up and set in motion by the Supreme Clock-maker in accordance with his design and laws of motion, revolved on its own (except perhaps for occasional interferences in the mechanism by the maker, called miracles). The advantage of this conception, as developed in the great Deist compromise of the 18th century, was that it allowed men of science and men of religion to declare their doctrines and discoveries without the danger of mutual trespass or conflict. The scientist could investigate the laws of nature, while acknowledging that the laws which he discovered were evidence of God's design; the theologian, while accepting the existence of natural laws as evidence of God's purposeful design, could speak of the act of creation as a mystery and as the test of faith." Therefore – with our modern insight – let us abandon this dualism, follow Spinoza's insights and perceive nature as a living and creative substance, as *natura naturans*.

Coming back to the split between nature and spirit, it can only have been a small step from believing in various invisible gods representing the natural forces to one god, who has created the world with all.

However, this one god is no longer inside the world, but supposed to live outside, in heaven, a supernatural being. Aristotle called him the "supreme 'unmoved mover'".[45] He is thought to have created the world as we experience it today[46] with everything and everyone in it, giving the world his laws to obey. Forever, the world is the same as it was created.

Here again, we note the different characteristics which are given to the female and the male gender: the male is the active agent. It is through a male, by fathering, that creation happened.

In a religious context this is called 'monergism', the doctrine that creating is entirely the work of the Holy Spirit, as nature is incapable of it. This must have been the understanding of the time.

The first people to come up with the idea of one god of creation ruling the world, were the ancient Egyptians and their pharoah Amenophis IV, reigning

---

44 Ibid, p. 43
45 Charles Freeman, *The Closing of the Western Mind*, ibid, p. 24
      Stuart Hampshire described this as follows: "To say that God is the immanent cause of all things is another way of saying that everything must be explained as belonging to the single and all-inclusive system which is Nature, and no cause (not even a First Cause) can be conceived as somehow outside or independent of the order of Nature. Any doctrine of a transcendent God, since 'transcendent simply means 'outside the order of Nature', or any doctrine of God as Creator distinguished as transient cause from his creation, involves this impossibility; it introduces the mystery of an inexplicable act of creation, an act which is somehow outside the order of events in Nature." ibid, p. 45
46 Meaning that neither men nor planet Earth has undergone any changes, that they have no history. No continental shift, no early oxygen producing plants, no dinosaurs, no fossil fuel building, no change between sea and land, no ice ages, no Neanderthal man has ever existed.

from 1351–1334 BCE or 1340–1324 BCE – historians are not sure of the exact dates. He later called himself Akhenaten as he worshipped the one god, the sun[47], Aten. Pharao Akhenaten made his belief state religion, against the resistance of the people and priests of Egypt who were used to their gods. We could call him the first sun king. His successor, Tut-ank-Amun, his son-in-law, turned back to the old gods, when Akhenaten died.

Were we to look for a rationale behind the worshipping of the sun, we could perhaps suppose that the most terrible disaster must have happened to the people at that time; perhaps a comet impact or the eruption of a super volcano, which might have made the sun disappear for a long time, so that vegetation, animals and men were suffering. By praying and sacrificing to the sun god eventually it came shining through again, so people might have believed their efforts had been effective. Consequently, the sun god must have been thought to be the most important god as without sunshine there is no life.[48] Indeed, pictures cut in stone show Akhenaten and his queen with the sun's rays behind them, and the golden crowns of kings or queens still seem to carry the same symbolism.

Jews (about 3,500 years ago) and later on Christians (about 2,000 years ago) and Muslims (whose belief goes back to Mohammed, writer of the Koran, who lived about 1,400 years ago)[49] took on the belief of one male invisible external god who created the world as it is today. All three religions were created in roughly the same area of the Middle East, today Iraq, Israel and Saudi-Arabia.

In Leviticus, part of the Old Testament of the Bible (and this third Book of Moses is equivalent to the third book of the Jewish Torah)[50], there are many rules

---

47   and wrote a famous hymn to Aten.
St. Francis of Assissi also wrote a poem to Brother Sun in the 13th century CE.
48   Cf perhaps T. Lucretius Carus, who lived from 95 BCE to 54 CE, in: *Von der Natur der Dinge*, Leipzig, 1831, chapter V, where he wrote that once upon the time the sun had left its course, but was brought back again on course by Phoebus, a by-name for Apollon, the Greek god of sun and light.
49   Greg Muttitt pointed out in: *Fuel on the Fire, Oil and Politics in Occupied Iraq*, London, 2011, p. 20, that Islam has a different understanding of 'labour' than the West, for example when he wrote that "Sadr's" (Muhammad Baqir al-Sadr, Iqtisaduna) "economics places the human being at its centre. When it comes to production, this means the worker; indeed for Sadr, the only justification for private ownership is physical work, as it is work that improves the situation of society." This is similar to Adam Smith's notion. "But here is the difference: since the worker is the owner, he should make the decisions. This is the opposite of the Western model, where the providers of capital are the owners and decision-makers. A capitalist is not permitted to own the products of workers he hires – the criterion is *direct* labour. A result of the prohibition on earning income without work is that concentration of wealth based on accumulation is not possible. One can only become as rich as one's personal capacity to work allows."
It is of course very interesting to see a different understanding of 'labour' working for a different country, although the difficulty of its implementation in a Western country would be that Islamic economics is based on the belief that this understanding derives from god, whereas we know that economics can not have been derived from nature/god, but consists of ideas and decisions made by people living in different historic cultures.
50   Cf. the latest archeological finds, in: *The Bible Unearthed*, Archeology's New Vision of Ancient Israel and the Origin of its Sacred Texts, by Israel Finkelstein and Neil Asher Silberman, New York, 2001

laid down about the relationship between god and his people based on reciprocal interaction, as for example:[51]

"Ye shall make you no idols nor graven image, neither rear you up a standing image, neither shall ye set up *any* image of stone in your land, to bow down unto it: for I *am* the Lord your God.

2. Ye shall keep my sabbaths, and reverence my sanctuary: I *am* the LORD.

3. If ye walk in my statues, and keep my commandments, and do them;

4. Then I will give you rain in due season, and the land shall yield her increase, and the trees of the field shall yield their fruit.

5. And your threshing shall reach unto the vintage, and the vintage shall reach unto the sowing time: and ye shall eat your bread to the full, and dwell in your land safely.

6. And I will give peace in the land, and ye shall lie down, and none shall make *you* afraid: and I will rid evil beasts out of the land, neither shall the sword go through your land.

7. And ye shall chase your enemies, and they shall fall before you by the sword.

8. And five of you shall chase an hundred, and an hundred of you shall put ten thousand to flight: and your enemies shall fall before you by the sword.

9. For I will have respect unto you, and make you fruitful, and multiply you, and establish my covenant with you...." and "42. Then I will remember my covenant with Jacob[52], and also my covenant with Isaac, and also my covenant with Abraham[53] will I remember; and I will remember the land," to "46" as the last of chapter 26. "These *are* the statutes and judgments and laws, which the LORD made between him and the children of Israel in mount Sinai by the hand of Moses."

The last citation refers to the exodus of the children of Israel led by Moses.

Freud drew our attention to his name by pointing out that 'Moses' is not a proper name, but the Egyptian word for 'son'. During their exodus the son Moses was thought to have been given by god the laws which the children of Israel would be to obey in the future. Numerous rules are set out for offerings, for example in chapter 17:

"And the LORD spake unto Moses, saying,

2. Speak unto Aaron, and unto his sons, and unto all the children of Israel, and say unto them; This *is* the thing which the LORD hath commanded, saying,

3. What man soever *there be* of the house of Israel, that killeth an ox, or lamb, or goat, in the camp, or that killeth *it* out of the camp,

---

51   Cited from: Leviticus 26, in: *The Holy Bible*, Containing the Old and New Testaments, Trans-
      lated out of the Original Tongues and with the former Translations diligently compared and
      revised by His Majesty's special command, A.D. 1611, Appointed to be read in Churches,
      printed in London and published by The British and Foreign Bible Society, 146 Queen Victoria
      Street, p. 149 - 151, emphasis according to the Bible. In German one can say: *Ich lese dir die
      Leviten*, which means to lay down the law to them.

52   Who was given the name Israel

53   Who is said to have been the progenitor of the people of Israel as well as of the Arabs, being
      born in the town of Ur, a farmer of animals. He supposedly emigrated to Egypt with his family
      for a better life.

4. And bringeth it not unto the door of the tabernacle of the congregation to offer an offering unto the LORD before the tabernacle of the LORD; blood shall be imputed unto that man; he hath shed blood; and that man shall be cut off from among his people:

5. To the end that the children of Israel may bring their sacrifices, which they offer in the open field, even that may bring them unto the LORD, unto the door of the tabernacle of the congregation, unto the priest, and offer them for peace offerings unto the LORD..." Indeed the altar, the sacrificing table, only came only into the church when these blood offerings stopped.

   Or in chapter 22 of Leviticus:

"17. And the LORD spoke unto Moses saying,

18. Speak unto Aaron, and to his sons, and unto all the children of Israel, and say to them, Whatsover *he be* of the house of Israel, or of the strangers in Israel, that will offer his oblation for all his vows, and for all his freewill offerings, which they will offer unto the LORD for a burnt offering,

19. *Ye shall offer* at your own will a male without blemish[54], of the beeves, of the sheep, or of the goats.

20. *But* whatsoever hath a blemish, that shall ye not offer: for it shall not be acceptable for you.

21. And whosoever offereth a sacrifice of peace offerings unto the LORD to accomplish *his* vow, or a freewill offering in beeves or sheep, it shall be perfect to be accepted; there shall be no blemish therein.

22. Blind, or broken, or maimed, or having a wen or scurvy, or scabbed, ye shall not offer these unto the LORD, nor make an offering by fire of them upon the altar unto the LORD..."

   When considering these rules for offering it should be noted that a development has taken place in god's demand, compared with the Old Testament that the first-born son had to be sacrificed. In chapter 17, 19 god first announced to Abraham, who was said to be have been 99 years old and his wife ninety: "And God said, Sarah thy wife shall bear thee a son indeed; and thou shalt call his name Isaac: and I will establish my covenant with him for an everlasting covenant, and with his seed after him." When Isaac was born and circumcised as god commanded, god tempted Abraham.

   Chapter 22, 2: "And he said, Take now thy son, thine only son Isaac, whom thou lovest, and get thee into the land of Moriah; and offer him there for a burnt offering upon one of the mountains which I will tell thee of."

   When they got there, this is what happened:

"6. And Abraham took the wood of the burnt offering and laid it upon Isaac his son; and he took the fire in his hand, and a knife; and they went both of them together...

10. And Abraham stretched forth his hand, and took the knife to slay his son.

11. And the angel of the LORD called unto him out of heaven, and said, Abraham: and he said, Here *am* I.

---

54 "... For sacrifices cattle 'without spot or blemish' was important..." wrote Glyn Davies, *History of Money*, p. 44

12. And he said, Lay not thine hand upon the lad, neither do thou any thing unto him: for now I know that thou fearest God, seeing thou hast not withheld thy son, thine only *son* from me.

13. And Abraham lifted up his eyes, and looked, and behold behind *him* a ram caught in a thicket by his horns: and Abraham went and took the ram, and offered him up for a burnt offering in the stead of his son."

This well-publicised story shows the change in the history of offerings: no longer is it necessary for a human to be sacrificed. A human can be replaced with an animal.

The substitution of an animal as a scapegoat for a human is discussed in the writings already mentioned by Christina von Braun Glyn Davies, Nigel Davies, James George Frazer, Horst Kurnitzky and Bernhard Laum.

Especially, Kurnitzky told us about the transition from human to animal sacrifice. Specifically, he discussed pig[55] offerings in ancient Egypt and mentioned religious taboos with respect to pigs and their keepers, arguing that the pig was one of the first cultural products, together with women the first form of property and, as a sacrificial animal, also an early form of money.[56]

Kurnitzky also draws attention to the relationship between pigs and money, as for example, money is still saved in a box we call 'piggy bank', and people in Germany still say 'Schwein gehabt' when they had a lucky escape – from being sacrificed, perhaps?

Selina O'Grady allows us some kind of insight into the historic situation with reference to people of monotheistic belief and the (pagan) Roman cult of gods:[57] "Monotheist Jews forcibly converted the Palestinian regions of Galilee and Idumaea in the second century BC. Monotheist Christians would later knock the heads off pagan statues, spit as they passed temples, ruthlessly suppress other cults and heavily penalize the Jews. Augustus,[58] on the other hand, was happy to acknowledge the Jews' God and 'ordered that for all time continuous sacrifices of whole burnt offerings should be carried out every day at his own expense as a tribute to the most high God', according to the Jewish Alexandrian philosopher, Philo. Pagan Rome was, by virtue of its polytheism, much more tolerant of other gods, though the Roman religion – its gods and festivals – predominated. But failure to participate in or contribute to the Roman cults was considered suspicious, a sign of potential disloyalty, since it was through the cults, and above all through the countless festivals associated with them, that Rome tried to make its subjects Romans, to give them a pride in Rome and a sense of solidarity... As a good client king, Herod the Great ordered that the priests of the Temple should make daily sacrifices (two lambs and a bull) 'on behalf of' Augustus and 'the people of Rome'. These sacrifices would become a running sore for a growing number of Jews, until in AD 66 the Temple priests final refused to perform them.

---

55   Horst Kurnitzky, *Triebstruktur des Geldes, Ein Beitrag zur Theorie der Weiblichkeit*, Berlin, 1974, p. 97

56   Ibid, p. 129: "... eines der ersten Kulturprodukte, zusammen mit den Frauen die erste Form des Eigentums und als Opfertier zugleich eine Vorfrom des Geldes."

57   Selina O'Grady, ibid, p. 116

58   Augustus, the first Roman emperor, lived from 63 BCE to 14 CE.

Their refusal marked for Josephus[59] the true beginning of our war with the Romans.'"

8.2. Replacing reciprocal interaction with a symbol

Whilst the first step in the history of sacrificial rites was replacing a human with an animal, the next step giving something back to god was the replacement of the animal. Over a lengthy process, the real sacrifice (animal) is replaced by a symbol in form of a coin depicting the sacrifice or tools of sacrifice, von Braun pointed out.[60] The offering of a living being was replaced by a symbol, an inanimate object, ie round yellow coins of gold, a material which is never changing, one of the noble elements, resembling and therefore symbolising the disc of the sun[61] - or even the full moon. In the synagogue the firstborn, i.e. the eldest child, *–belongs to God in the same way, as the believer offers the first tithe of all herds and fruits of the field to God. The offering of the firstborn can be replaced by money, however.*[62] This replacement of a living being with a symbol is, in a way, still found today when e.g a soldier is decorated with a medal of coin-like appearance, for offering his life for his country, or, if an athlete is similarly rewarded with a medal for offering his ability to win in the Olympic Games for his country.

It would be appropriate to refer to Horst Kurnitzky in this context, as he is of the opinion that offering money in replacement for something living derives from cult, and not from religion.[63] It is therefore useful make the definition of cult clear by citing O'Grady.[64] "In modern usage 'cult' has become a pejorative term for groups with strange or distasteful ideas under the control of a strong leader. Religious historians, however, tend to use 'cult' in its traditional sense of *cultus*, literally 'care', referring to the ritual practice involved in worshipping a god. The difference between a cult in this sense, and a religion is a difficult one, but hinges on the relative importance of beliefs. I try to use the word 'cult' in its

---

59   Titus Flavius Josephus was a Jewish historian who lived from 37–100 CE.
60   Christina von Braun, *Der Preis des Geldes*, p. 19: "Im Laufe eines laengeren Prozesses trat an die Stelle des realen Opfers (Opertieres) ein Symbol – in Form einer Muenze, auf der das Opfer oder Opferwerkzeuge dargestellt wurden."
61   "The cult of *Sol Invictus* had been imported from Syria in the third century... So when Constantine began using the sun as a mark of imperial power, often portraying himself on coins or statues with rays coming from his head, he was exploring a well-recognized symbol of both spirituality and power." Charles Freeman, *The Closing of the Western Mind*, ibid, p. 157
     Detlev S. Schlichter remarked in *Paper Money Collapse*, Hoboken, 2011, p. 236, that gold "is the oldest and most consistently used form of money throughout human civilization." "Gold is the least corrosive of all metals. It does not decay. It is indestructible. It is perfectly divisible. Its value is easily ascertainable. It is sufficiently scarce without being too rare. .. It is global. It is cosmopolitan. It is apolitical," p. 238
     It is noteworthy that, when cigarettes were used as money in West Berlin after World War II, there was a brand with the name 'Gold Dollar'.
62   Ibid, p. 156: "In der Synagoge... gehoert der Erstgeborene – also auch das aelteste Kind – Gott, so wie der Glaeubige von allen Herden und Fruechten der Felder den ersten Zehnt Gott darbringt. Das erstgeborene Kind kann jedoch durch ein Geldgeschenk ausgeloest werden."
63   Horst Kurnitzky, *Triebstruktur des Geldes*, p. 23
64   Selina O'Grady, *And Man created God*, ibid, p. 5, highlighted by the author

academic, neutral sense, concentrating on ritual practice. I use the word 'religion' for a set of beliefs which would include all or some of the following: an explanation for the origin of the universe and mankind, some sort of deity, a goal for humans to reach involving some kind of afterlife, and a moral code for living."

Again, if we want to find a rational explanation for this – although nobody knows the reasons and it can only be another guess – we could go back to the same natural disaster which caused the sun to be blocked out for a long time, so that there was scarcely something growing. When there is a shortage of food, animals may have become too valuable to be sacrificed. It could have been more important for people to eat them to keep themselves alive as we live of living matter. Gold – as sacrificed to the ancient temple in Delphi and stored there in the treasure houses of the ancient Greek city states, for example, might have some value for humans as a symbol, as jewellery or on icons or for decorative purposes in churches,[65] but metal, a non-living thing, does not have a lot of use in a community of starved people, as nobody can eat it.

Another factor important for the history of money was the Christian religion, whose message of salvation is strikingly similar to that of money. Both involve a symbol that takes material form: a word 'becomes flesh'. The history of Western money is unthinkable without the Christian religion; however it is remarkable how little significance this role is accorded in economic theories, concluded Christina von Braun,[66] and we can add, because we do not have to be economical with the truth: because Christians are used to live with the illusion of Passover, they also accept the money illusion,[67] the illusion that paper money has real use value, and everyone needs to aim at it.

When in today's Holy Communion the believer receives a piece of bread and a sip of red wine, the priest declares that these will turn into the flesh and blood of Jesus Christ. The belief of the transformation of bread and wine into the body of the son and lamb of god is called the transubstantiation doctrine. It was introduced by the IV Lateran Council in 1215 CE, and goes back to the New Testament Markus 14, to the last Passover of Jesus and his disciples which reads:
"22: And as they did eat, Jesus took bread, and blessed, and brake *it*, and gave to them, and said, Take, eat: this is my body.
23. And he took the cup, and when he had given thanks, he gave it to them: and they all drank of it.
24. And he said unto them, This is my blood of the new testament, which is shed for many."

---

65 It is necessary to mention that gold is less useful than silver, which is needed in industry.

66 Christina von Braun, *der Preis des Geldes*, ibid. p. 11: "Ein anderer Faktor, der fuer die Geschichte des Geldes eine wichtige Rolle spielte, war die christliche Religion, deren Heilbotschaft eine frappierende Aehnlichkeit mit der des Geldes aufweist. Hier wie dort ein Zeichen, das sich materialisiert: ein Wort, das 'Fleisch wird'... Die Geschichte des westlichen Geldes ist ohne die christliche Religion nicht zu denken, aber es ist bemerkenswert, wie gering diese Rolle in den Wirtschaftstheorien veranschlagt wird."

67 Ibid, p. 115: "Weil Christen es gewohnt sind, mit der 'Illusion' des Abendmahls zu leben, akzeptieren sie auch die 'Geldillusion'."

Von Braun is therefore of the opinion that it is not gold that is the cover for money, but human life.

In German language the so-called 'money illusion' is more transparent, as a banknote is called a '*Geldschein*'. The word '...schein' has a lot more meanings than 'note', eg shine and appearance, deception and pretence. It gives a clearer idea that it there is no use value in itself, but that it only represents an exchange value as a symbol – provided everyone believes in it. Adam Smith indicated this when he claimed that real wealth derives from nature and from labour. "All value is mediated through the veil of human symbolism," remarked the Skidelskys.[68]

Von Braun also points out that the relationship between sacrifice and money becomes obvious, when we consider that the German word for money '*Geld*' is related to the Germanic word '*gelt*' which means an offering or a sacrifice to the gods.[69] In English, another Germanic language, the word 'geld' means to castrate, eg a horse.

We can also refer to the Greek word for money *chrema*, which Aristotle used. In many languages it is remembered in the word 'crematorium' deriving from the Latin '*cremare*' which means 'to burn a dead body' or 'burnt offering to the god Jupiter'.[70] Uwe Steiner pointed out that according to the Deutsche Woerterbuch the word '*kelt*' is the name for heathenish worshipping.[71]

Even today in church service, for example after the harvest is brought in, grains and vegetables are exhibited in god's house, and a collection-bag is handed round to put offerings in form of money into it. These rituals are reminders of the reciprocal interaction between people and their creator, to whom they will return for eternal life after they die.

The New Testament differs from the Old Testament in terms of its rules of sacrifices in that the latter tells the story of the last offering. Reading the New Testament in this sense, we learn that god's own son, his lamb and a king in his own right, sacrificed himself to abolish once and for all the sins of the people. Thus with his death all human obligation to give something back in return to god have ended, once and for all. While other religious believers still make offerings it is no longer necessary for Christians. The process of reciprocal interaction with god/ nature has come to an end. The Jesus story makes us aware how this process of offerings ended, and refers on the other hand to the ancient custom of offering a human being: at the beginning the king, then the first-born son, then an animal.

It was the temples, which first coined money – and convinced the believers to exchange their real products for an abstract MEANS, installing money dealers in the temple. And it is quite easy to imagine that this situation then developed into a general presentation of goods for exchange against money, into a fair,[72] a word with the substantive meaning of 'exhibition'. The noun '*Messe*' in German can be

68   Robert and Edward Skidelsky, *How Much is Enough, The Love of Money and the Case for the Good Life*, London, 2012, p. 143
69   Charles Freeman, *The Closing of the Western Mind*, ibid, p. 70
70   And when the bloody offering of a living being comes to an end, the offering stone, the altar, can be brought inside the temple.
71   Uwe Steiner, '*Die Grenzen des Kapitalismus*', in: *Kapitalismus als Religion*, ibid, p. 41
72   Deriving from old English '*faeger*' and Old High German '*fagar*'

used for both a religious service and an exhibition of products. The word 'fair' has also a meaning as an adjective: any exchange should take place in a fair and honest way, so that both sides, give and take, offering and buying, are treated equally and no side would suffer an overreach.[73] Therefore let me propose that in the future we no longer use the word 'market' but the word 'fair'– as it comes with this double meaning, and both of it are useful.

Today it is the government, whether democratic or autocratic, that has the exclusive right to supply us with the MEANS of exchange, coin metal coins and print paper money notes, and threatens to punish anybody who would try to copy them.

Jesus had the money dealers thrown out of the temple:[74]

15. "And they come to Jerusalem; and Jesus went into the temple, and began to cast out them that sold and bought in the temple, and overthrew the tables of the money-changers, and the seats of them that sold doves;

16. And would not suffer that any man should carry *any* vessel through the temple.

17. And he taught, saying unto them, Is it not written, My house shall be called of all nations the house of prayer? But ye have made it a den of thieves.

18. And the scribes and chief priests heard *it*, and sought how they might destroy him: for they feared him, because all the people was astonished at his doctrine."

The action is understandable if we view the story from the perspective pointed out, that the obligation to give something back to nature/god has come to an end, with reference to the ancient tradition of human sacrifice.[75]

However, it seems that with the end of this tradition, which had been strengthened by daily ritual, as for example thanking god for the food before eating, it has gone from our consciousness that we are natural beings in an inalienable process of reciprocal interaction, of giving and taking, with the natural co-world around us.

It is interesting to refer in this connection to some passage from Paul, first from his letter to the Romans (chapter 14), and then from his first letter to the Corinthians (chapter 10) about how to worship and obey the one invisible god:

"17. For the Kingdom of God is not meat and drink; but righteousness, and peace and joy in the Holy Ghost.

18. For he that in these things serveth Christ *is* acceptable to God, and approved of men."

And:

"25. Whatsoever is sold in the shambles, *that* eat, asking no questions for conscience sake:

26. For the earth *is* the Lord's and the fulness thereof.

27. If any of them that believe not bid you *to a feast*, and ye be disposed to go; whatsoever is set before you eat, asking no question for conscience sake.

---

73 This double meaning of 'fair' was exactly my reason for calling these thoughts 'Fair Economics'.

74 The New Testament, as above, Mark 10, chapters 15–18

75 Which was still understood up to the 20th century demanding that men are to sacrifice their lives for their country and women for their family.

28. But if any man say unto you, This is offered in a sacrifice unto idols, eat not for his sake that shewed it, and for conscience sake: for the earth *is* the Lord's, and the fulness of it..."

For Paul, Earth has been created by the one god, therefore there is no reason to give something back as god owns everything.

Additionally, with the end of the practice of sacrifice the tradition of eating the sacrificed animal together also ended. Previously, when an animal or other food was offered, after the religious service ended, it would have been divided among the worshippers. Everybody would get their share of the roast and nobody would go hungry. But with the end of the sacrificial ritual, the roast no longer needed to be shared with others.[76] Self-interest could take over.

We can draw a further conclusion: When a sacrifice was executed, this can be seen as a kind of interaction with nature. The body would go back to Earth. When an animal or other food such as plants were offered, this became more of a social interaction, as the sacrificed food[77] was afterwards consumed together. And when real food was replaced by a symbol as gold, the interaction process with nature must have come to an end, as giving back gold has only a social meaning, as it was given to priests specialising in processing the ritual as in ancient Egypt.

It is also now understandable why Walter Benjamin concluded in 1921, nearly 100 years ago, in *Kapitalismus als Religon*[78] that three characteristics of the religious structure of capitalism are, however, recognisable at present. First, capitalism is a pure religious cult, perhaps the most extreme that ever was. This consecration of the cult connects with a second characteristic of capitalism, the permanent duration of the cult. Third this is a cult that engenders blame. Capitalism is presumably the first case of a blaming cult, rather than a repenting cult. An enormous feeling of guilt not itself knowing how to repent grasps the cult.

In the old days, the noble metals silver and gold[79] were used as legal tender. Today only small coins are made of metal, although not of noble metal, where the use value of the metal is not identical with the exchange value, and the higher exchange values are printed on paper notes, while the government backs up these forms of money with the promise that they can be exchanged any time into the real thing, as mentioned. To keep this promise to people governments built up reserves of gold. Today the ten states with the biggest gold reserve are according to an article in *The Telegraph*:[80]

---

76 And one wonders indeed, if this could be the reason why religious organisations feel the need to carry out so much charity and relief work for those in need.

77 It reminds us of the still practised ceremony of Thanksgiving.

78 Published by Dirk Baecker, Berlin, 2003, p. 15: "Drei Zuege jedoch sind schon in der Gegenwart an dieser religioesen Strktur des Kapitalismus erkennbar. Erstens ist der Kapitalismus eine reine Kultreligion, vielleicht die extremste, die es je gegeben hat... Mit dieser Konkretion des Kultus haengt ein zweiter Zug des Kapitalismus zusammen: die permanente Dauer des Kultus... Dieser Kultus ist zum dritten verschuldend. Der Kapitalismus ist vermutlich der erste Fall eines nicht-entsuehnenden, sondern verschuldenden Kultus. Er ruft staendig wachsendes Schuldbewusstsein hervor, etwas wieder gut machen zu muessen."

79 Or an alloy of them is called electron

80 3 July 2011

- USA with 8,133 t
- Germany with 3,401 t[81],
- IMF (the International Monetary Fund) with 2,814 t
- Italy with 2,451.8 t
- France with 2,435.4 t
- China with 1,054.1 t
- Switzerland with 1,040.1 t
- Russia with 824.8 t
- Japan with 765.2 t
- Netherlands with 612.5 t
- The United Kingdom holds 310.3 t gold, putting it in 17th place, valued at $13.8 bn in 2011.[82]

However, it has to be added that the above amounts of gold are only those held by the public household. It was reported on 12 December 2012[83] that German private households own nearly 8,000 t gold with a value of €393 bn, as a study by the Steinbeis-Hochschule of Berlin revealed. According to the study, German people have invested more money in gold than in company shares. Every German adult owns an average amount of 55 g gold jewellery.

The remarkable thing is that if a coin is made of a noble medal, but not even legal tender, it holds its value over time much better or even rises, compared to coins or paper money which has only exchange value. This is another reason why people not only buy jewellery or bullions from the governments and also special commemoration medals made of gold or silver.

About 40 years ago the gold standard, the practice of backing up money with gold as use value, was abandoned in many countries. However, this is not the place to discuss the advantages and disadvantages of a country promising to the people that their money will be turned into gold on demand.[84]

Today's economists think that backing up a currency with gold or use value is no longer necessary. Therefore, when we talk about money these days, we only

---

81   *Frankfurter Allgemeine Sonntagszeitung* 28 October 2012, p. 45, reported that 1,536 t of Germany's gold is stored in New York, 450 t in London, 374 t in Paris, as it would have been too dangerous to hold it in then West Germany in case the USSR invaded, and 1,036 t in Frankfurt at the Bundesbank. In the next three years the Bundesbank will bring back 150 t. *Spiegel* online reported 24 December 2013 that the Bundesbank has brought back from New York and Paris 37 t gold valued at about €1.1 bn, and will bring back a total of nearly 700 t by 2020, so that half of the total amount of gold will be stored in the now united Germany. *Spiegel* online 22 December 2014 reported that the schedule to bring back 674 tons of Germany's gold from USA, France and UK, is on schedule.

82   The Swiss Gold Initiative demanded that the Swiss National Bank should hold 20 per cent of assets in gold. The World Gold Council has published data about the worldwide gold assets, showing that 78.6 per cent of Portugal's currency reserves are in gold, the figure in Switzerland is only 7.7 per cent, EU has 26 per cent, China only one per cent and Canada as a big gold mining country only 0.2 per cent of its reserves in gold.

83   By *Kieler Nachrichten* , p. 5

84   Although it does not need to be gold, and the reference to the sun god is no longer necessary, any other natural resource of a country with a real use value would do as well, for example coal, gas or oil.

refer to so called 'fiat money', money which is purely based on people's belief that they will get back its value, when they exchange real it for real goods. Incidentally, many people will never see a gold coin, although a lot of them buy gold as a kind of hedge against the danger of inflation, ie as protection against the possibility that their money might lose value.

The replacement of the 'do ut des' process with a symbol or a thing – a metal coin or a paper note – for reciprocal interaction had the following effects:

- a split between nature and gods representing the natural forces in the world,
- a change from many gods in the world to one external supernatural god, who is believed to have created the world,
- a split between the material side of nature as the outside of humans and a kind of spiritual inside,
- and therefore division between nature and humans, who are no longer viewed as natural, but only as spiritual beings, created by the external supernatural god,
- with humans being given the natural world as their outside objects to command and control,
- with humans being able to command and control their fellow-beings as if they would be the objects of his wants, but not the subjects of their own life,
- the replacement of the process of reciprocal interaction, of give and take, in which man is connected to nature, with a symbol, a dead object.

And we can now conclude that Detlev Schlichter's[85]remark: "Money has evolved organically and spontaneously from the voluntary actions of trading individuals," is not the whole truth. Firstly, money has not *organically evolved* but people have created it, however no person ever has consciously decided about it and its consequences, which already John Locke mentioned. And secondly, money was not created by trading individuals, but by humans as a substitute for the process of giving and taking, of sacrificing to the gods.

8.3. Reciprocal interaction alive

Today we no longer need to believe the ancient assumption that there are gods in nature, as our understanding of nature has grown and is still doing so. Once upon a time, the idea that natural events are caused by gods and goddesses may have been an acceptable explanation, but today this can only be called a myth. Events in the natural world can today be explained by physicists who understand the workings of the world as an ongoing process.

The same should be valid for economists. Idolatry of nature and the split between nature and an individual today is no longer needed. According to our modern understanding, nature is the basis of all life, and humans can be seen as natural beings in need of a constantly ongoing process of reciprocal interaction

---

85 In: *Paper Money Collapse, The Folly of Elastic Money and the Coming Monetary Breakdown*, ibid, p. 35

with each other as with nature, whatever the form this process may take in the different historic cultures. Let us remind ourselves: Nature does not need people, but people cannot live without being connected to nature, and nature is an evolving process, not a dead object subject to the whims of humankind.

Whereas our ancestors may have had daily rituals that kept them continuously aware of the process of give and take, of perception and action, today this awareness is lost.

Even when people today are expected to give something, they prefer to give money instead of themselves and their time, as was observed by James Boxell, Home Affairs Correspondent of the *Financial Times*. He viewed evidence from a FT/Harris poll as "dealing a fresh blow to David Cameron's vision of a 'Big Society'... But it also shows they are much less happy about being asked to volunteer to support community projects and reject the idea that they have a personal responsibility to do so to 'make the world a better place'... Some 77 per cent of British people said they had given to charity in the past 12 months. This was far higher than the other European countries and above the 71 per cent in the US. However, only a quarter of British people agreed they should be 'encouraged to give up some of their time to help support public services'. This was far lower than in the other countries and well below the 42 per cent of US people who considered it their duty to participate. Only 15 per cent of UK respondents thought they had a responsibility to improve the world by getting involved with worthy causes."

This raises the question of how to revive the awareness about the importance of the give-and-take principle and of practising it every day, even when we know that the daily process of reciprocal interaction cannot be revived by a religious ritual.

That this awareness has been lost is no minor problem. The environmental crisis, the extinction of plants and animals as well as the reality of global warming can only be understood and dealt with when we see our real selves as natural beings in reciprocal interaction with nature. A basic understanding of the process of reciprocal interaction tells us that these problems do not arise naturally, ie by nature, although a lot of people would like to make us believe this, but that they are the consequences of our cultural form of interaction with nature and other people.

And from this insight we are able to make a judgement regarding how rational it is for businesses to claim that protecting the natural environment is too costly for them. Only by understanding the process of reciprocal interaction can we view ourselves as the authors of the environmental crisis and at the same time as well as the victims. Horst Kurnitzky reminded us that to break down the world of things and objects into the relationships and conflicts from which they derive, is the task of science – their truth.[86] And according to the Skidelskys: "Economics is not just any academic discipline. It is the theology of our age, the language that all interests, high and low, must speak if they are to win a respectful hearing in the courts of power."[87]

---

86   Horst Kurnitzky, *Der Heilige Markt*, ibid, p. 72: "h–... die Welt der Dinge und Sachen wieder in die Verhaeltnisse und Konflikte aufzuloesen, denen sie entstammen."

87   Robert and Edward Skidelsky, *How Much is Enough?*, ibid., p. 92

What is necessary, therefore, is to make sure this new found principle of direct reciprocal interaction forms our basic understanding of human activities, to avoid future illusions about ourselves and nature.

We could of course try to raise our awareness through the process of breathing or eating, by remembering that we take air and food into our bodies and release the waste into our natural environments. These are examples of the basic process of perception and action, of taking in and giving out. But there might perhaps be other ways to raise our awareness and live it consciously every day. How this can be achieved is a question to be discussed in the next chapters. But before, we can draw a few final conclusions.

Mainstream economic theory to date is only semi-modern. It is based on outdated beliefs and assumptions about nature and the condition of man, on the substitution of direct natural reciprocal processes with a culturally invented object, and on substituting this MEANS with the end of people's activities. These are the characteristics of an economicult, not of nature.

What is necessary is a truly modern *cult*economic theory for the 21st century where nature and every person are viewed as subjects with their own rational faculties, where they cannot be viewed any more as mere objects. And the culturally invented MEANS can no longer be seen as the self-moving subject, which intrinsic laws people have to obey, as this was an illusion, a deception.[88]

We can now agree with Roger Bootle's comments:[89] "What has emerged is a set of beliefs – and an accompanying set of kneejerk reactions to almost any issue – which hardly bears at all on practical matters, yet which unthinkingly favours free markets as the solution to almost any problem. Ironically, in seeking so assiduously to become a science, modern economics has turned itself into a religion. The god to whose worship this religion is dedicated is 'The Market'", and money which is the end purpose of 'the market' although the paper or electronic money we use today is only based on the belief and on the trust that it can be exchanged into real valuables. Besides "nothing sedates rationality like large doses of effortless money..." one of the most successful US money maker, Warren Buffet,[90] reminds us and he clearly has a lot of experience of this.

This chapter will conclude with two quotations from *The Gods that Failed*[91] as the authors' description of bankers as the new Olympians could not be more apt: "... mere mortals and their governments need the Olympians a lot more than the Olympians need them. It is extraordinary to see how successful has been this piece of propaganda, across the decades, across the continents and across

---

88 This was expressed by G. Katona, cited by P. Meyer-Dohm, '*Wirtschaftswissenschaft als Wissenschaft vom Menschen*', in: *Themen*, Universitaet Witten/Herdecke, April 1984, p. 12: Economy "... *studiert 'das Verhalten des Geldes' oder 'das Verhalten der Preise', als seien Geld und Preise die selbst handelnden Subjekte, die den Wirtschaftsablauf beeinflussen, und nicht die Menschen, die ueber Geld verfuegen oder Preise setzen*," translated: "Economics studies the behaviour of money or the behaviour of prices as if money and prices were the self-acting subjects influencing the course of economic events, and not the people who dispose about money or fix the prices."

89 Roger Bootle, *The Trouble with Markets, Saving Capitalism from Itself*, ibid., p. 234

90 Cited from: Larry Elliott and Dan Atkinson, *The Gods that Failed*, ibid., p. 231

91 Ibid, p. 286 and 289

political party lines. Even after the current crisis saw Big Finance whining like druggies facing cold turkey for public bail-outs and state-supplied cheap credit, the illusion, amazingly, persists of a feat of mass hallucination worthy of the classical gods of antiquity."

However, what Elliott and Atkinson think is necessary is "... to bring their activities back under democratic control. But by 'under democratic control' we do not mean, as at present, under the oversight of the new Olympians' technocratic opposite numbers in unelected national and trans-national bodies, whether Britain's Financial Services Authority or the International Monetary Fund. These Olympian officials exist precisely to promote the financial Olympians' agendas; their answer to every systemic problem is more competition, free trade, a smoother functioning of the very machine that has caused the trouble in the first place. On the contrary, we would argue that the New Olympians have hollowed out the democratic process precisely by removing more and more powers from political control and handing them over to the cadre of technocrats... Action to redress the democratic deficit..." is therefore the thing to do.

But before discussing the steps forward with the aim to create a genuinely modern democratic culteconomy, let us consider where and how the awareness of reciprocal interaction is still found even in today's economy.

"It is time to abandon dream-world economics and embrace real-world, scientific economics."

Prof. Richard Werner, University of Southhampton[1]

9. Reciprocal interaction in the three economic sectors

The last chapter concluded with the observation that the principle of reciprocal interaction is in its most basic form practised in the economy, but mostly we are not aware of it. In chapter 7, we found it hidden in both the private and the public range of nateconomy. Now we will try to show where it is practised, even if a MEANS of exchange is introduced.

To do this we will follow a method which was invented by Allan George Barnard Fisher (1895–1976), already cited: Fisher used to separate economic activities into three sectors according to their typical pattern. His idea to divide and categorize the economic sectors is today followed by the offices for statistics all over the world. We will now discuss the different patterns typical for each economic sector:

9.1. The primary sector: Agricultural goods

Fisher defined the primary sector by including everything which is harvested from nature, such as food or wood, for example. This sector contains the products of agriculture, forestry and fishery. So we can state that the primary sector represents our direct human interaction with nature.

The goods of this sector can only be produced where the natural conditions allow it. Production is location-dependent, depends on the geography as well as the consistency and fertility of the soil, the climate and its location on Earth. Whether it is in the North or in the South will affect it, and whether it takes place near the sea or up in the mountains, for not every seed will germinate under the same conditions as certain plants will not grow, flower and fruit in certain locations.

Humans have to rely on nature's goods on which they live. They are dependent on nature's production of fresh air and clean water, the first and most basic provisions, not only for themselves, but for every living being on the land or in the air or in the water. Humans cannot manufacture these basic provisions for life, while

---

1   in a letter to *The Guardian*, Tuesday, 20 March 2012, p. 35 'Reply'

they are obviously able to spoil or even poison them, if they are not aware of or do not care about the consequences of their activities. Therefore, production in the primary sector cannot be decided about autonomously by humans.

Such natural goods are usually identified with the colour green.

Humans can observe, and they have done so for thousands of years, the particular natural conditions of their special location. They have learned to respect it, adapt to it and profit from it, eg by cultivating plants with bigger fruits or finding remedies for their illnesses, such as salicylic acid from willow trees, or spiraea to fight fever and pain. Other things humans have learnt include building ships for transport on water and navigating them by observing the stars, building banks against flooding, or draining swamps by digging canals.

Humans are in competition for food with other living beings, and they have tried over thousands of years to eliminate or at least to control a lot of other living species. For a long time, humans have observed animals and learned how to domesticate and breed them.

Obviously, humans cannot avoid influencing nature when they plant seeds and water and fertilize them to produce crops. However, the growth of these crops is essential nature's work. Only nature – not humans – can 'produce' animals, vegetables and fruit.

Incidentally, no two plants of the same species look or taste exactly the same, owing to the conditions under which nature produces them. Only their appearance looks the same, so that we can categorize them as a banana plant, for example.

Dependency on nature is the most important characteristic of the primary sector. Ulrich Grober commented[2] on how, for example, until the 18th century, human activities were limited by the quantity of trees available for building and by the amount of charcoal available for energy supplies. Men understood that they should not use more of each than could be regenerated by nature, and coped with it. They managed forests sustainably.

Grober then described how men's attention was diverted from respecting the living, growing regenerating woods on Earth to concentrating to the use of subterranean woods of hard fossil coal. With this change the respect for the limitation of natural growth was forgotten. He wrote that our civilization was from its beginnings up to the Industrial Revolution based solely on sustainable raw materials and the renewable energies of biomass, wind and water. All what was needed to be added was human and animal power. All these resources were constantly regenerated through the movement of air, the water cycle and the photosynthesis of plants. The constant supply of sunlight kept the *oeconomia naturae* in motion. There was virtually no waste. Everything was absorbed into the great cycle of nature.[3]

---

2   in: *Die Entdeckung der Nachhaltigkeit, Kulturgeschichte eines Begriffs,* Muenchen, 2013, p. 182

3   Ibid, "... beruhte von den Anfaengen bis zur industriellen Revolution allein auf nachwachsenden Rohstoffen und den erneuerbaren Energien von Biomasse, Wind und Wasser. Dazu kam nur noch: die Muskelkraft von Mensch und Tier. All diese Ressourcen entstehen staendig neu: durch die Bewegung der Luft, den Kreislauf des Wasser, die pflanzliche Fotosynthese. Allein der bestaendige Zufluss an Sonnenlicht haelt die oeconomia naturae in Gang ... Es gab so gut wie keinen Muell. Alles verschwand wieder im grossen Kreislauf der Natur."

Why people changed their focus from using wood – which could be annually renewed, and is therefore a potentially unlimited natural resources – to the use of fossil fuels, which are most definitely finite and which we still focus on today, is a question which has not yet been sufficiently answered. From the point of view of today's understanding, it seems really hard to follow. Although there is one obvious reason: renewable resources are free to use for everybody, while coal and oil have to be mined and then bought from the owner of the land.

We would like to propose that the word 'production' for mining these limited resources should no longer be used, as it can lead to the erroneous idea that humans have the power to decide what is 'produced', and in what quality and quantity. On the contrary, the primary sector shows the process of direct, immediate and unmediated reciprocal interaction between nature and humans, in which nature is transformed by human activity, while humans depend on nature.

The most important characteristic for the activities in the primary sector is to grow food to support life, and not primarily to make money by selling it on the market, as we do not have a choice of abandoning this kind of activity and doing something else instead. We need to eat and drink, although the form in which meals and beverages appear differs from society to society and from present to past. As the Prince of Wales pointed out in a speech at the Terra Madre conference in Turin, Italy, on 23 October 2004, "agriculture is not only the oldest, but also the most important of humanity's productive activities. It is the engine of rural employment and the foundation stone of culture, even of civilization itself."

This interaction does not only occur on what was formerly called the 'production side', the expropriation of resources from nature, but is also found in the human consumer side. Nature's food cannot be preserved eternally, as it will decompose in time and then lose its value, both for the grower as well as for the consumer who wants to consume it. Every kind of food has to be eaten relatively quickly. Transport and storage time has to be as short as possible so that food is as fresh as possible when it reaches the consumer.

Preservation technologies such as drying, pickling, boiling, freezing or mixing food with preservatives were invented, however, today it is known that the chemicals used in such preservation techniques cause allergic reactions in more and more people and therefore need to be controlled very carefully in future.

Once we are aware of the necessity for humans to co-operate with nature in the process of reciprocal interaction, we also realize that, if humans want to increase their use and consumption of nature, natural resources will recede. So care must be taken not to over-exploit air, soil and water as otherwise nature's ability to grow will be affected, and this will result in negative consequences for humans themselves.

Advertising to increase food sales is permissible, as food is a material good but humans daily need for food is not unlimited. A concerted attempt to increase sales on the part of the seller – for example of meat – resulting in a higher amount of meat purchases obviously does lead to more profit for the seller, but does not lead to better health for the consumer; quite the opposite.[4]

---

4   A study by Professor Sabine Rohrmann of University Zurich/Switzerland found that "diets laden

Lewis Mumford mentioned that "... all natural wealth, represented in the concrete form of food, clothing, furniture, houses, gardens, fields, has definite limits of production and consumption, fixed by the nature of the commodity and the organic needs and capacities of the user. The idea that there should be no limits on any human function is absurd: all life exists within narrow limits of temperature, air, water, food; and the notion that money alone, or power to command the services of other men, should be free of such definite limits is an aberration of the mind."[5]

9.2. The secondary sector: Industrial commodities

Contrary to the dependency on nature we have outlined for goods in the primary sector, industrial material goods can be produced at anytime, in any quantity and in any place. From the viewing point of this sector, human dependency on nature – so typical of the primary sector – is indirect. The secondary sector of the economy includes all production of such commercialized merchandize. The matter of what, where and in what quantity this type of merchandize is produced seems to have become the quasi-autonomous decision of the producer. The entrepreneur has positioned himself in total control of the production process. He creates the vision for new technologies and new products. And therefore he is the one who decides how the future of society will be shaped – according to the commodities he brings to the market'. The 'raw' materials for his products can be bought from anywhere and shipped to any location for final production. Any industrially-manufactured article looks identical to the other. Industrial products as well as industrialized production can be standardized. On a highly technical level, the goods can be produced by machines, almost without human involvement. The manufactured merchandize is often called ' 'white' and 'brown', and labourers who still produce them are 'blue collar' workers.

Goods from the secondary sector can be produced and stored independently of season and well ahead of their sale with virtually no loss of quality and profit, which was a problem with primary sector goods. They can be transported to any location where the conditions of sale seem favourable. Transportation time is no longer so important. The only limiting factor is the cost.

Advertising can now show an article, which, when paid for, will change from being owned by its producer to being owned – and hence totally controlled – by the consumer. Advertising is used to arouse consumers' interest in buying an article. Their involvement in the economic process is limited to a choice of ready-made products.

The more that is produced and sold, the more profit can be made. Profit can always increase, and this is the aim of the producer. How much money is made seems to be up to human industriousness alone. The more one works, the more

---

with pies, sausages, and ready meals can lead to an early death, according to research involving half a million people that highlights links between processed meat and heart disease and cancer", as reported by *The i* 7 March 2013, p. 18

5   Lewis Mumford, *The Myth of the Machine*, New York, 1967, p. 315;
     Kenneth Boulding made the same point.

money one can make. The lifetime of products is even perhaps artificially short-ened, as only through the sale of new wares can new profits be realized. While food consumption is limited to peoples' natural needs, money does not succumb to that law. It has no limits. It can become infinite, as Thomas Aquinas (1225–1274) was already aware in the 13th century. The more profit a producer gains, the richer and more important he is seen to be in a monetary defined society.

The consequence of these changes is that humans tend to forget or at least neglect the awareness of their dependency on nature. Instead they appear to be in total control of nature. And they are not aware that the impact their activities has on nature will ultimately have an effect on themselves. Fossil fuels are produced by nature in a process of anaerobic decomposition of dead plants over millions of years, but humans seem to forget that through their consumption these supplies will come to an end after a consumption time of only 150 years. They forget that their use of fossil fuels comes with the emission of carbon dioxide into Earth's atmosphere, with dramatic effects for the global climate and therefore for all life. This is the reason why it is now seen as advisable to restrict the use of finite fossil fuels, and focus on renewable fuels which do not produce this problem.

The typical pattern of the secondary sector not only fails to consider the fact that humans are in a process of reciprocal interaction with nature, but has also helped to close our minds to its consequences. We can only be thankful that these forgotten consequences have begun to be discussed in recent decades, at first by the biologist Rachel Carson (1907–1964) in *The Silent Spring*, published in 1962.

9.3. The tertiary sector: Intangible services

All products which do not fall into the first two categories were placed by Fisher into the so-called 'tertiary sector' of the economy and called 'services'. Therefore the third sector is more or less viewed as a kind of residual category, perhaps due to its heterogeneous nature.

The French economist Jean-Baptiste Say (1767–1832) named its products "immaterial" produced by so-called 'white collar' labourers. So let us now find out if we could perhaps also find a typical pattern for the production of these intangible or immaterial services, so that there would be a more appropriate description for them than the basic category 'residual'.

Immaterial services encompass[6] the following: retail and wholesale trade, transport and communications, finance and insurance, accommodation such as: hotels and B&Bs, restaurants and bars, dry-cleaners and laundries, personal hygiene services as massage, sports, cinemas, theatres, opera and other entertain-ments, pawn and betting shops, publishing of books, newspapers and magazines, surgeries and veterinary clinics, lawyers and accountants, advertising, real estate and travel agencies, leading even to organizations without any commercial aim at all, such as: religious organizations, care institutions, unions, communal associa-tions, specific associations of professionals, the police, defence, job centres, the diplomatic service and foreign embassies, private and public households (which

---

6   According to the Statistische Bundesamt in Wiesbaden, Germany

are included in the tertiary sector, as neither follows a commercial aim, although they do use money).

The term 'voluntary or charitable sector', so often used as a description of the tertiary sector, is wrong, as we find in this sector not only households and other non-profit organizations but professional, paid services as well.[7] We have to remind ourselves that a lot of industrial goods require services, such as marketing, distribution and legal services, or the building of a house requires the services of architects, structural engineers, accountants, lawyers.

The same applies when we no longer include the cost of 'labour' within the overall cost of a product, but list labouring hours and costs it separately. Labouring is a typical immaterial service which a worker applies to a given task in exchange for a paid salary. However, we are so used to seeing labour melt into the cost of a product, that we rarely give it the necessary attention as a tertiary service. It is another example of the fact that economicult theory is only viewed from the side of a producer. Otherwise 'labour' would be detailed in the service sector.

Besides, the tertiary sector includes different levels of the role of money: some services are offered in exchange for money, other organizations exist without any commercial aim, such as charities, and households which are not only there for non-profit making aims, but also do not exchange their 'products' by the use of MEANS.

Furthermore there are other services normally hidden in the shadow of economicult thinking, eg neighbourly help, illicit work, criminal activities, gambling, prostitution, fencing or tax avoidance. These cannot be categorized in terms of money as their monetary value is hard to specify.

However, if all these services, which often aren't reported, were to be included into the tertiary sector, we would find that this sector is even bigger than it appears today. This raises the question of whether its importance is really sufficiently acknowledged. And it reminds us that the tertiary sector does not really fit into the normal characterization of an economy, where only a quantitative measure, money, is used as criteria for classification. Given all of these difficulties, it is not really surprising that only a few economicult theorists are interested in this sector.

Discussing this sector further, we find that some of the services are direct, eg therapeutic massages, while others are indirect, eg travel agent services; some services, such as advertising, relate to material products, and others, such as legal advice, relate to people.

When the tertiary sector is described, this is done from the point of view of the secondary sector where standardized products of a material commodity are dealt with. This does not do justice to the service sector, because:

- A service is an immaterial process. Once produced it is immediately consumed.
- Services can never be produced in advance.
- Services cannot be stored in the same way as material goods.
- Services cannot be initiated or decided about independently by the producer.
- The consumer is the initiator of a service, eg when an employee recruits the

---

7   The definition of a 'service economy' is a much better description than its definition as a 'voluntary sector'.

work of a labourer. He is then the consumer of this service/labour. A service is produced to satisfy consumer demand. Therefore services are called 'consumer-oriented'.

- The consumer does not initiate production to make money, but to get a service.
- Therefore, in the tertiary sector the consumer is not the passive receiver. In a service-based society[8] the consumer has an active role. This different under-standing has to be accepted and respected by the producer, and it could cause confusion if the producer of the service is not aware of this. The more detailed the consumer gives to describe the service he wants, the better service he gets, eg when visiting a MP's surgery to complain about a problem with the passport office.
- When the consumer requires a service, he wishes it to be personalized and customized. A standardized service would not do. One service does not fit all. Handcrafted products typify this expectation. Therefore, services cannot become standardized in the same way as the secondary production processes and secondary products. Consequently, producers often have their staff dressed in uniforms to give the consumer the impression that he can expect the same quality, for example, judges in court are uniformed.
- Advertising for a service is difficult, as an intangible service cannot be presented visually.
- When a service is required by a consumer and delivered by a producer, it is consumed immediately. Producer and consumer have to meet at the same time and at the same location - the pattern of reciprocal interaction as described.
- As long as the process is ongoing, both consumption and production occur. The process is open[9] as it is ongoing, while in the other two sectors products can be finished and offered ready-made.
  Philip Herder-Dorneich has accordingly characterized the different relationship between consumers and producers in the tertiary sector as an "uno-actu" principle.[10]
- And Alvin Toffler has proposed that consequently the participants in this reciprocal process should no longer be differentiated into consumers and producers, but called pro*sumers*,[11] as this would be a better description for the reciprocal interaction of perception and action.
  Dirk Helbing of the Eidgenoessische Technische Hochschule in Zuerich, Switzerland, called them prod-*users*, a description that unfortunately can be too easily mistaken when spoken, for 'producer', and therefore can not be recommended.
- When a service is requested and paid for by the consumer, the exchange of money and the consumption/production of the service take place at different

8   There are a number of authors who have pointed this out, to mention just one: Alan Gartner, Frank Riessmann, *The Service Society and the Consumer Vanguard*, New York, 1974
9   CF. Andre Gorz, *Kritik der oekonomischen Vernunft*, Berlin, 1989, p. 218ff
10 Philip Herder-Dorneich, *Wirtschaftssysteme*, Opladen 1972, as well as: *Honorarreform und Krankenhaussanierung*, Berlin, 1970.
11 Alvin Toffler, *The Third Wave*, New York, Toronto, London, Sydney, Auckland, 1980.

moments in time. Before – for example – we can watch a film in a cinema, we need to buy a ticket. The activity of viewing is distanced from the service we want. When we take clothes to the dry cleaner, we receive a receipt for the money paid in advance for the cleaning service, which will be exchanged against the clothes when they are ready to be picked up. When we book a hotel through a travel agent we receive a voucher for our payment which will be exchanged for accommodation when we check into the hotel. It shows, in the service sector the exchange of money against the desired service is indirect. Money can be paid long before the actual service is delivered or at a different place. The paying process is decoupled from the process of uno-actu production and consumption.[12]

- It is further evident that services, once bought, cannot be sold on, as is possible with a material product.
- Intangible services are generally regarded as sustainable as no material is used for their production.
- In conclusion, in the tertiary sector we find the pattern of reciprocal interaction working, while in the second sector this pattern is transformed into the quasi-autonomous decision of the (so-called) producer.[13]

---

12 This decoupling is further extended when a person is paid to queue for the client in order to buy tickets for a special opera or theatre performance.

13 It is remarkable that economicult theory argues that it is the unlimited wants of consumers which drive an economy, and that therefore consumers are responsible for the fact that more and more products are offered for sale. This seems to be a very poor argument following the producers' own interest for making money by selling, as J. K. Galbraith has already pointed out, cited in Robert and Edward Skidelsky, *How Much is Enough*, ibid, p. 210.

If Adam Smith is right that all production is for consumption, then consumers should indeed play the initiating role for production. We should build a culteconomy where the roles of producer and consumer are better interrelated as they are both equal citizens while split in economicult theory.

The following table shows the differences between the secondary and the tertiary sector at a glance:

Secondary Sector Commodity	Tertiary Sector Service
tangible object or standardized service product	intangible activity
finished product	ongoing process
storable product	transient process
preservable object	dynamic process
transportable	not transportable, bound to location
resaleable	not resaleable
standardized commodity	individual service
anonymous ware	personal service
can be advertised by showing product	can be advertised by promising a service
use of natural material and energy	human energy rather than natural material
Secondary Sector production	**Tertiary Sector production**
production in total control of producer	production on demand of consumer
supply-oriented	demand-oriented
highly technical standardized production	production depending on human performance
production by division of labour	
production is accountable in money, quantitative	production by holistic working
formal sector	production is monetariseable, but qualitative
ready planned product	formal and informal sector
economic principle: producing with least means	product uncertain, not plannable
aim: production for exchange on market for profit	economic principle: make most out of given means
	aim: production for exchange on market for profit **and** production for reciprocal interaction without monetary target
Secondary Sector Relationship between producer and consumer	**Tertiary Sector Relationship between producer and consumer**
producer in total control of production process/	producer and consumer share uno-actu activity
consumer in total control of consumption	consumer is active in production process
active producer/consumer passive, only chooses products	producer and consumer are "prosumer"
exchange on market: ware against money	exchange on market: service production and consumption on demand/money decoupled from production
consumption is decoupled in time and location from production	+ consumption
exchange exclusively money-oriented	exchange against proof of legitimised claims, tickets
anonymous producer/anonymous consumer	producer and consumer are in relationship with each other
producer/consumer relationship mediated by market' and money, indirect	producer/consumer relationship direct
producer is responsible for product after sale	prosumers are responsible for service production with money
production for money	

From the above analysis it is now possible to formulate an exact definition of the tertiary sector – according to its own logic: services are direct open and unmediated immaterial processes of reciprocal interactions initiated by the receiver, work-intensive and sustainable, initiated and delivered in an uno-actu process between the prosumers who are totally free – inside the norms of their society – to decide about their quality and quantity, while the exchange of a MEANS is indirect and uncoupled from this direct process, being offered at a different time or place. In wikipedia.org we find the following facts about the tertiary sector:[14]

Output of tertiary sector in 2011

	in billions of US$[15]	composition of GDP
United States of America	11,554.714	76.7 %
Germany	2,576.322	71.0 %
United Kingdom	1,927.720	77.7 %[16]

We see that the service sector represents the most important part of these economies.

However, the pattern of direct reciprocal interaction is reverted into the secondary industrial one when a direct, open and personal service is turned into a standardized anonymous disposable commodity, offered and sold ready-made to passive customers, regardless of whether it fulfills their needs or not, as it is the interest of the supply side, for example the banking sector being a case in point.

9.4. The shift in relative shares

So far the three economic sectors have been described from the point of their own intrinsic logic, i.e. from a qualitative point of view. This is now followed by a quantitative analysis. Then we will compare the qualitative with the quantitative results to find out if they are in accord with each other or if they differ. And if they differ – as they might – we know that a quantitative analysis can never be enough on its own. Whilst the qualitative analysis goes deeper into details, the quantitative only allows us to count the same. Therefore it is always advisable to analyse objects from both sides. I call this procedure cross analysis as it allows a deeper vertical

---

14 Please also note: Jonathan Gernshuny, *Die Oekonomie der nachindustriellen Gesellschaft*, Frankfurt, 1981;
Daniel Bell, *Die nachindustrielle Gesellschaft*, Reinbek, 1979

15 It is perhaps necessary to point out here that data given in billions do not have the same meaning everywhere. While a US billion is equal to 1,000 million, in Germany such a figure with 9 '0's is called a 'Milliarde'. A German billion consists of 1,000 Milliarden and has 12 '0's. One can only hope that these differences are always respected.

16 Ian Jack pointed out in *The Guardian* 7 January 2012 that there is also an historic reason for the prevalence of the service sector in the UK: "… England's public schools and ancient universities held it" manufacturing "at arm's length. Finance became the acceptable business profession for gentlemen. In the words of another historian, Martin Wiener, finance 'involved the extraction of wealth by associating with people of one's own class in fashionable surroundings, not by dealing with… the working and lower-middle classes.' In this way the City became part of the elite and 'could call upon government much more effectively than could industry to favour and support its interests.'"

and a wider horizontal insight into a structure at the same time[17]. It can be viewed as a co-ordinate system.

When the three economic sectors are discussed from the quantitative side, we will notice that the importance of each sector for the whole economy has changed over time. As mentioned, agriculture, the primary sector, was in Adam Smith's time the most important sector. Today, this is no longer the case, as already been pointed out.

To show this shift in relative importance between the three economic sectors over time, I will use data from Germany, as it is the same for the whole word. And it is necessary to point out that the shift can only be identified when the whole economy is divided into sectors.

9.4.1. The shift in employment

First, let's see how the number of working people in the three economic sectors has changed. For the purpose of comparison, this data needs to be presented in relative, i. e. percentages, rather than in absolute figures.

Working people in the three sectors in the Federal Republic of Germany[18] in per cent				
sector	1950	1970	1991[19]	2011[20]
primary	23.3	8.5	4.2	1.6
secondary	43.3	48.8	40.9	28.2
tertiary	33.4	42.7	54.9	70.2
total	100.0	100.0	100.0	100.0

It is immediately noticeable that the primary, secondary and tertiary sectors of the German economy have undergone a change in importance – as everywhere in the last decades in highly developed countries. The amount of people working in the primary sector is continually reduced from 1950 compared to 2011. The secondary sector had increased its number from 1950 to 1970, but shows then a continuous decline, while the tertiary sector has continuously increased the number of employed people over the years, now spanning to two-third of all working people.[21]

---

17 The British jazz pianist Rod Kelly pointed out that in music, harmony seems to be vertical while melody is horizontal.

18 The term 'working persons' includes independently working people and employed people. Data from 1950 to 1980 cited from: Irene Schoene, *Schleswig-Holstein – eine Dienstleistungsgesellschaft, in: Schleswig-Holstein Eine politische Landeskunde*, published by Landeszentrale fuer Politische Bildung, Schleswig-Holstein, 1992, p. 178

19 According to Statistisches Jahrbuch fuer die Bundesrepublik Deutschland 1993, p. 116, 1 April

20 Data from: *Mikrozensus, Fachserie 1, Reihe 4.1.1 Bevoelkerung und Erwerbstaetigkeit 2011*, published by the Bundesamt fuer Statistik, Wiesbaden, p. 159, including from 1999 onwards the five former East German regions.

21 It should be added that these increases/decreases were the same for the time before 1950, but to make the point it is sufficient to show just the last 50 years.

9.4.2. The shift in the Gross Domestic Product

As the data on employment alone is not sufficient to prove the shift from primary to tertiary sector, we also need to consider the figures of the Gross Domestic Product (GDP) – again for Germany – to find out if this trend is showing there as well. The GDP (Brutto-Inlands-Produkt (BIP) in German) is, according to the Statistisches Bundesamt,[22] a measure of a nation's annual production – and nothing more. It sums up the (exchange) value of all products and services in prices. That way it can be compared to previous years to find out if an economy has increased in size.[23] And if the GDP has risen, this signifies, in the words of Detlev Schlichter, that "more mutually beneficial exchanges among members of society have occurred. Consequently more material needs have been fulfilled and more people have marginally improved their material well-being."[24]

There is also a point to be made about the quality of the data. Because it is summed up in monetary terms, only activities which have been exchanged on the market can be considered. That means that all human activities which are not mediated by money and market' are left out, as if they do not play a role in determining a nation's wealth.[25] Robert Kennedy made this clear in a speech at the University of Kansas on 18 March 1968: "Too much and for too long, we seemed to have surrendered personal excellence and community values in the mere accumulation of material things. Our Gross National Product, now, is over $800 billion dollars a year, but that Gross National Product – if we judge the United States of America by that – that Gross National Product counts air pollution and cigarette advertising, and ambulances to clear our highways of carnage. It counts special locks for our doors and the jails for the people who break them. It counts the destruction of the redwood and the loss of our natural wonder in chaotic sprawl. It counts napalm and counts nuclear warheads and armored cars for the police to fight the riots in our cities... And the television programs which glorify violence in order to sell toys to our children. Yet the gross national product does not allow for the health of our children, the quality of their education or the joy of their play. It does not include the beauty of our poetry or the strength of our marriages, the intelligence of our public debate or the integrity of our public officials. It measures neither our wit nor our courage, neither our wisdom nor our learning, neither our compassion nor our devotion to our country, it measures everything in short, except that which makes life worthwhile..." The data gives information, but this information is not enough to see the GDP as a measure of well-being.

---

22 Statistischs Bundesamt, Wiesbaden, Germany, *Wichtige Zusammenhaenge im Ueberblick 2011*, p. 8

23 The word "growth", although commonly used for this increase, should not be used, as "growth" is a word from the biological world, in which life is self-organized, while money is a cultural MEANS, not able to act on its own.

24 Detlev S. Schlichter, *Paper Money Collapse, The Folly of Elastic Money and the Coming Monetary Breakdown*, Hoboken, 2011

25 This will be discussed in Chapter 11

Gross Domestic Product (BIP) in the three sectors
in the Federal Republic of Germany
in per cent

sector	1950[26]	1970[27]	1989[28]	2011[29]
primary sector	12.1	5.7	1.7	0.9
secondary sector	54.6	54.5	41.4	30.8
tertiary sector	33.3	39.8	56.9	68.3
total	100.0	100.0	100.0	100.0

While it is relatively easy to add up the number of working people, it is much more complicated to measure a country's annual Gross Domestic Product (GDP) (in German: Brutto-Inlands-Produkt (BIP)). The German Statistische Bundesamt[30] gives us information on how the data is collected, as it is necessary for the comparison of the GDP of one country with the data of another country for a particular year. The regulation was legislated for by the European Union (EU) No. 2223/96 and 1392/2007. From 1999 onwards the European national product system has been made the basis for that accounting. It regulates definitions, concepts, meanings, classifications, time and the regularity of the data, whilst making sure that the European system of national accounting is also in accord with the worldwide System of National Accounts (SNA) of the United Nations.

That said, it is interesting to look into the change of the relative importance of each of the three economic sectors. In the GDP data we find the clearer trend confirmed: both the primary and the secondary sector have continually decreased over time, and the winner is the tertiary sector which has continually increased.

9.4.3. The shift in the use of natural resources

Information on the relative change of use of natural resources is hard to cite at present, as the data has not yet been systematically collected and therefore cannot yet be compared over time. Collection and comparison of the use of natural resources is, however, necessary, as this will allow us to find out if a real shift in the use of natural resources has taken place, given that the tertiary sector does not focus on material products, but on immaterial ones. If such a shift is found, then we could indeed conclude that society is moving away from being a material industrial society into a post-industrial society, based on immaterial services, a model which is expected to be more sustainable.

Such data on the change of use of natural materials should, however, not be expressed in money terms, as money is not a currency of nature, but in physical

---

26 Statistisches Jahrbuch 1952, p. 452
27 Statistisches Jahrbuch 1973, p. 519
28 Irene Schoene, *Schleswig-Holstein – eine Dienstleistungsgesellschaft*, ibid, p. 176
29 Including from 1999 onwards the former five East German regions.
       For 2011 the data refers to the Gross Domestic Product in terms of Gross Value Added and not as BIP, as the BIP is reduced by taxes on goods and by subventions, but this is not important for the argument.
30 Statistisches Bundesamt, *Wichtige Zusammenhaenge im Ueberblick*, ibid., p. 4

terms, as length, contents, weight, electricity consumption and so on.

After decades of discussion, the German Statistische Bundesamt has started to collect and publish some of such information about the use of material resources. This is a welcome start, but it needs to continue over more successive years, in order to compare the annual data and draw conclusions from it.

The Statistische Jahrbuch 2012 published the following data on the turnover with nature[31] in terms of physical quantities:

Use of natural resources in physical quantities in Germany for the year 2010

water extraction from groundwater, spring water, rivers, lakes and barrages in total	33,047 m cubicmetres[32]
waste balance of which 69 % was recycled	372,930,000 tons[33]
emissions of **greenhouse gases** into the atmosphere <u>for 2009</u>	937,262,000 tons CO_2 equivalent[34]
use of **primary energy resources** in the economy as a whole of which: in private households	10,358 peta joules 3,900 peta joules[35]
electricity generation = secondary energy from primary energy resources of which: from renewable resources	554,304 giga watt hours[36] 1,703 peta joules[37]
net **generation of heat**	142,118,914 mega watt hours[38]

While metres and tons are abstract terms of the International System of Units (SI), 'watt' and 'joule' are named after British scientists: 'joule' is a unit of energy, work or heat named after the English physicist James Prescott Joule (1818–1889) and 'watt' is named after the Scottish engineer James Watt (1736–1819) used to measure the rate of energy conversion or transfer.

---

31 The Statistische Bundesamt published on page 463 a few more highly aggregated indicators of the German sustainability strategy with respect to ecology and economy starting in 2002.
32 Statistisches Jahrbuch 2012, p. 447
33 Ibid, p. 453
34 Ibid, p. 460
35 Ibid, p. 458
36 Ibid, p. 552
37 Ibid, p. 459
38 Ibid, p. 553

9.5. Quantitative and qualitative explanations

The shift in the relative importance of the three sectors is called structural change. The reasons for this structural change will now be discussed to find out how this shift has been understood by economists.

9.5.1. Quantitative explanations

Ernst Engel[39] reasoned that the structural shift in the importance of the three economic sectors is a kind of natural process based on changing consumer habits in highly developed countries. Consumers seem to have more immaterial needs with rising income. An example is that people with more income can afford to travel more and visit other countries.

Then there was Ludwig Berekoven[40], explaining that people in highly developed countries seem to have a higher demand for professional paid services instead of satisfying their needs within their own households. An example is that there are now professionals offering their services as organizers of family get-togethers such as memorial days, birthdays or weddings. These professionals suggest ideas as to how the day could be spent, which would otherwise perhaps not have been considered by the family concerned.

Martin Jaenecke, on the other hand, argues that in highly developed countries the demand for immaterial services rises because the damage caused by the industrial society generates the need for more repairs, a kind of iatrogenic understanding. Problems, he found, are technocratically economized. It does not result in a political and administrative preventive strategy to tackle the causes of stress, but a continuously ongoing battle against their symptoms which, though expensive, initiate short-term growth. [41] An example is a person who feels stressed due to the demands of his or her job because of the necessity to commute, as reasonably priced accommodation near his or her workplace has become less. Consequently, the demand for doctor's services or alternative health treatment rises. Then, as more and more people complain of stress and claim they are 'burnt-out', the health system will conclude that there are new kinds of illnesses,[42] and will accordingly offer new treatments. Thus, when a person consults the health service, whether national or private, the doctor can offer more medication which results in turn to the production of new drugs and more drugs which generate even a rising income for the health professionals.

---

39 Ernst Engel, in: *Handwoerterbuch der Sozialwissenschaften*, Band 3, Stuttgart, Tuebingen, Goettingen, 1961

40 Ludwig Berekoven, *Der Dienstleistungsmarkt in der Bundesrepublik Deutschland*, Goettingen, 1983

41 Martin Jaenicke, *Wie das Industriesystem von seinen Missstaenden profitiert*, Opladen, 1979, p. 9: "Nicht die politisch-administrative, vorsorgliche und einmalige Unterbindung von Missstandsursachen, sondern die teure, aber kurzfristig wachstmstraechtige kontinuierliche Symptombekaempfung ist das Resultat."

42 According to *Der Spiegel* 4/2013, p. 113 in: 'Wahnsinn wird normal', 46 % of US Americans fulfil the criteria for psychological illness.

One of the explanation-seeking scientists was the French economist Jean Fourastie (1907–1990). The English title of his book was *The Great Hope of the Twentieth Century*[43], and his explanation is especially interesting as he predicted that employment in the primary and secondary sector would decrease because of rising productivity by technical rationalization. It would then be left to the tertiary sector to offer new jobs as productivity in the tertiary sector could not be increased in the same way as in the primary and secondary sector.

However, Fourastie could not have foreseen that, with the coming of the 'third wave' of new information and communication technologies, new possibilities for rationalizing services would be available.

Another interesting explanation was delivered by Ha-Joon Chang.[44] He argued that today's rich countries have "*not* become post-industrial in the economic sense. Manufacturing still plays the leading role in their economies. In order to see this point, we first need to understand why de-industrialization has happened in the rich countries. A small, but not negligible, part of de-industrialization is due to optical illusions, in the sense that it reflects changes in statistical classification rather than changes in real activities... A UK government report estimates that up to 10 per cent of the fall in manufacturing employment between 1998 and 2006 in the UK may be accounted for by some manufacturing firms, seeing their service activities becoming predominant, applying to the government statistical agency to be reclassified as service firms, even when they are still engaged in some manufacturing activities." "It looks as if we are spending ever higher shares of our income on services not because we are consuming ever more services in absolute terms but mainly because services are becoming ever more expensive in relative terms."

In this way, Chang points out the important argument that GDP statistics – quoted in terms of turnover on market´s – might lead to illusionary views, as rising prices do not necessarily mean rising sales due to rising consumer demands.

9.5.2. Qualitative explanations

Detlev Schlichter is of the following opinion: "Theories that center on the large entities of GDP, the price index, the unemployment rate, and so forth are fundamentally unable to capture the crucial processes of resource allocation and of the alignment of the economic activity with consumer preferences. These processes, by definition, operate beneath such aggregates. The statistical aggregates can, if anything, give only a faint and often misleading image of them."[45]

His argument is also worth considering, and therefore the quantitative explanation needs to be complemented by a qualitative one, based on the qualitative differences between the secondary and tertiary sector as we have identified.

Services within households are not provided in exchange for money. This is due to the market' expectations, where only professional services have a

---

43   Jean Fourastie, *The Great Hope of the Twentieth Century*, 1950
44   In: *23 Things They Don't Tell You About Capitalism*, New York, 2011, p. 92 onwards,
        Chang is also the author of: *Bad Samaritans*, London, 2007.
45   Detlev S. Schlichter, ibid, p. 186

value. People's habits have changed in this respect over the years, for example, many of us now prefer to have breakfast in a coffee shop rather than at home.

The next step is that the market' changes its offer from a service to the sale of an individually owned machine. Now we can consume the same quality of coffee as offered by the professional coffee shop in our own home. We buy a very expensive coffee machine which comes with its own branded and portioned coffee capsules with which it exclusively works. Drinking that coffee at home on your own may perhaps be less fun than going into a coffee shop where you can socialize, but owning the latest coffee machine may give you a better indication of your level of affluence. This change from coffee shop to individual coffee automat reflects the fact that individuals are more numerous than coffee shops and therefore provide a bigger market' for the producers of coffee machines. And this is not only true for coffee makers, but for transport too, as the market' for individually owned cars is bigger than the market' for public transport vehicles.[46]

Thirty years ago, Jonathan Gershuny[47] predicted such a change from tertiary sector to self-service by the use of a private machine. Gershuny's theory has something to offer, as we have seen when discussing the qualitative change in services in recent decades from reciprocal interaction to the one-sided power of disposal by producers.

There is something that Gershuny did not foresee, however: that the direct process of direct reciprocal interaction, from which the exchange of money is decoupled, has been replaced by the direct exchange of material things for money, not only in the production sphere of the economy, but also on the consumption side. And we have noticed that, with this change, the open and direct process of reciprocal interaction between living people is transformed again into the (imaginary) control of a finished material object. We might say that 'thinging' has been employed. Instead of people giving a service, a material thing is giving the service.

Whereas people used to pay a decorator to renovate a house, for example, this professional activity is now superseded by 'doing-it-yourself', as you can now buy the tool necessary for the job enabling everyone to execute such a tasks (not least because the price of a decorator's service seems to have become too expensive).

In the so-called market sphere we have noticed a similar change: employers view it as too costly to employ people, as they cannot be controlled in the same way as machines. Therefore employers have divided tasks into smaller ones and then substituted them with machines.

Let us note a few more examples: we are no longer able to buy a train ticket directly from the conductor on the train, but are forced to buy it from a ticket machine, if not well in advance of a journey via the internet, using our own home computer. The convenience of a direct personal service and paying on board and the possibility of spontaneously jumping on the next train, is gone. It might be that train operators can now predict how many travellers are likely to use a train at a certain time and then provide perhaps a few more seats, but the direct

---

46 One really wonders how this will again shift when it becomes normal for everyone to use 3-D-printers for the production of goods.

47 Jonathan Gershuny, *After Industrial Society? Emerging Self-Service Economy*, London, 1981

interaction with a person is replaced with using a machine. Instead of being served in a shop and paying the shop assistant, we gather the goods ourselves and use a self-service checkout to pay for them. Instead of being checked in with our suitcases at the airport by a helpful airline employee, we are now forced to obtain our boarding passes from a machine which has already decided where you should sit, although it is sometimes possible to amend the seat. The latest development is the requirement to use a mobile phone to pay for a parking ticket, as this method is easier for companies offering parking spaces, and banks profit from it. Cash is no longer wanted.

This also raises the question of why people should be interested in travelling to other cities or visiting other countries when the services offered there are already known to us, as the same shops are found in the same shopping centres. Starbucks or Costa, McDonald's or KFC, GAP, H+M or ZARA are everywhere. The shop windows in other countries show the same standardized products, produced in those not yet highly industrialized countries where people earn only a fraction of the labour cost in this country and where no human rights or environmental regulation might have yet become the law. When the world is becoming everywhere the same, where would development come from? If every product is available globally what happens to cultural diversity? If everything is decided according to monetary terms, where will new and different ideas be generated to help societies evolve into truly modern, enlightened ones?

The process of direct and open reciprocal interaction which was the pattern typical for the service sector has been transformed and deformed into one-sided control. The open, reciprocal and non-material process has been reified in accordance with the capacity and purpose of a manufacturer's design. A personal service has been changed into standardized objectification.

Consumers give their invisible helping hand to this development. They prefer machines which seem to give them (one-sided) control. When talking directly to a person, you get an answer, when emailing someone, we do not expect to get an immediate response,[48] therefore we do not have to respond to it. If we tweet a rude remark we do not want our identities to be known at all. It seems that a kind of illusionary feeling of power over a machine makes us prefer to use this medium instead of a real person.[49] Today, we entertain ourselves with pre-manufactured

---

48   *The Guardian*, 2 March 2012, reported on a young man who "began taking out loans on his iPhone, as he walked into town to meet friends; the money would be in his account before he reached the cash machine... He liked the way there was no need to talk to anyone, no paper bills that his parents might see. 'Because it's done online, there's no human interaction, it is a lot less difficult ... it means that I can hide it. The online is a huge aspect of it. I wouldn't want to talk to somebody about it. The web doesn't ask questions. The website wouldn't judge me."

49   And there is another kind of change. This comes with buying something from the internet – as I experienced myself. When I purchased an antique side table, I made my decision because of five pictures which were provided on the internet. I printed the pictures as a hard copy to show to my partner. Then the sale was agreed. However, when the furniture arrived it turned out that it had huge water rings on its top. Such damage can never be repaired. These affected its quality. I would never have bought the table for this amount of money if I had seen the damage before. But the damage did not show on the pictures I printed. So I looked on internet again, and this time there were seven pictures, of which two clearly showed the water rings. I therefore could

films or computer games instead of inventing our own games with our friends. No wonder a lot of people get easily bored as they no longer know what to do with themselves when they are prevented from using a machine. If this procedure is the norm in today's societies then they are failing to use the more modern and more democratic pattern of the tertiary services, with all the attendant opportunities for fulfilling direct personal needs and individual participation. Instead, we are forced to go back to the pattern typical of the secondary sector. Another example is experienced in Nuremberg, Germany, where trains are operated by computers instead of drivers, however overseen by employees, and it is no exaggeration to say that personal driving will soon be replaced by computers. The claim is this will make car driving safer as *Der Spiegel* reported 5/2013, p. 98, because no other invention in the history of civil engineering, neither aircraft nor electricity nor nuclear power has caused so much harm as the car. Every 30 seconds someone dies in traffic somewhere in the world - that's well above a million deaths a year. According to estimates by the World Health Organisation, this number is set to go on rising with the increasing motorization of emerging countries.[50]

This is another argument of pure quantitative reasoning: when the use of industrial products harms people, more complex industrial products are necessary rather than a totally different and qualitative approach. If we become ill from eating some highly manufactured ready-made meal enriched with additives, preservatives and chemical residues, the solution is to swallow more highly industrialized products in the form of medicines rather than giving up on ready-made meals and deciding to cook a meal personally.

More and more, living processes are replaced with dead objects.[51] It seems almost a pity, one might say, that people – alias consumers – are still needed to buy products. Would it not be preferable to achieve a market' where consumers would not be necessary at all or at least can be forced into purchases? We can only congratulate ourselves that we as consumers cannot be replaced and that we have the freedom to decide if we want a product and which one.

It is easy to see why, in highly developed countries, a kind of consumer revolution has started, based on the search for better quality services, for example preferring bread from artisan bakeries as an alternative to industrially-produced bread.

---

not hand back the table, as the dealer argued that I had seen the damage before and yet agreed to buy it. How could I have proven that he had cheated? Such a deceit could not have happened if I had seen the item in reality, but – by the use of the medium – the dealer was able to trick me into buying the furniture and at a higher price than it was worth. It was obviously a case for the Office for Fair Trading, to which I reported the dealer.

50 *"Keine andere Erfindung der zivilen Technikgeschichte, weder das Flugzeug, noch die Elektrizitaet oder die Atomkraft hat so viel Unheil angerichtet, wie das Auto. Alle 30 Sekunden stirbt auf der Welt ein Mensch im Strassenverkehr - weit ueber eine Million Tote im Jahr. Die Zahl duerfte nach Schaetzung der Weltgesundheitsorganisation mit der zunehmenden Motorisierung in den Schwellenlaendern weiter steigen."*

51 It seems that in future warfare – or formerly: self-defence – will be executed with "killer robots". The *Observer*, 24 February 2013, quotes Dr. Noel Sharkey, a leading robotics and artificial intelligence expert, professor at Sheffield University: "Robot warfare and autonomous weapons, the next step from unmanned drones, are already being worked on by scientists and will be available within the decade."

This revolution, sometimes called the slow food movement, also encourages the purchase of locally grown fruit and vegetables from local producers as opposed to those produced by multinational companies with no respect for different seasons and the different local cultures.

The process of industrialization – first introduced in Great Britain – began in the primary sector of agriculture, fishery and forestry. Fields were enlarged and monocultures laid out so that bigger and bigger machines could be employed. Fields were no longer left to regenerate in a seven-year-rotational growing system. Instead, their productivity was enhanced by introducing industrial fertilizers, insecticides and fungicides. Crops were selected and animals bred that were more productive, using antibiotics to cure illnesses occurring in industrial chicken sheds where thousands of the same birds were crammed, with the possible consequence that sick people, having already ingested high doses of antibiotics through their food, might become immune to their beneficiary effects, when the antibiotics are really needed. On 16 February 2012 14,500 ducks were killed in Germany after the bird flu virus H5N1 was found on a breeding farm.

Animals became 'things' produced by man, with no rights of their own. Chicken, pigs and other livestock were housed in huge stalls, totally against their natural habits. Poultry was fattened so quickly that sometimes their legs could no longer carry them. The sea was exploited with ever-larger fishing equipment, leading indeed to barren oceans. Monocultures of trees, creating easy opportunities for pests and fire, were planted.

Genetically modified crops were pushed into the market' with the argument that the world has to feed a growing number of inhabitants, although the consequences of GMO food for people's health were unknown.

Did we know that: "GMO farmers must now go back each year to the five multinationals that control the" seed "industry – Monsanto, Dow, Bayer, Syngenta, DuPont and BASF; a new sort of vassalage."[52]

Species-appropriate husbandry was transformed into industrialized production – along with the message that the public's objections to such a change were sentimental, and emotions should not govern economic aims.

The Prince of Wales remarked on this change from agri-culture to agri-industry[53] pointing out a few consequences as follows: "Imposing industrial farming systems on traditional agricultural economies is actively destroying both biological and social capital and eliminating the cultural identity which has its roots in working on the land. It is also fuelling the frightening acceleration of urbanization throughout the world and removing large parts of humanity from meaningful contact with Nature and the food they eat."[54] And we go along with it.

What is this fascination that humans seems to have with the disposability of things, with automation, robots, artificial intelligence, and now even with microchips and sensors in our clothes?[55] Is this, sometimes called 'the Californian

---

52 *The Week*, 6 October 2012, p. 15
53 The Prince of Wales speech at the BBC Radio 4 Food and Farming Awards, London, 25 November 2009
54 The Prince of Wales speech at the Terra Madre conference, ibid.
55 *Frankfurter Allgemeine Sonntagszeitung*, 6 July 2014, p. 15

dream', really the only course we can take into the future? And who decides about it? Or do these new ideas merely follow the rationale of money? In neglecting the diversity of natural life are we not restricting nature's ability to evolve rather than supporting it on its course forward? Why do economists, producers and politicians still assure us that this how what the future will look? Without our involvement, without our participation? Are there no other alternative ideas around? More democratic options available? No other logic?

I think that the way towards a fairer future will be through implementing the direct and open process of reciprocal interaction (as it is found in the tertiary sector) as the pattern for development, as this seemed to have worked for nature for more than four billion years.

It is especially depressing to listen to politicians these days claiming that we need more industrialization, more jobs in industry, the secondary sector. This only shows how badly informed most politicians are as they do not seem to be aware of the importance of the relative shift of the three economic sectors. Therefore, what is definitely needed is a change in the structure of statistical data. They should be qualified according to the different patterns typical for the three sectors, and 'labour' should no longer be included in sectors where it does not belong when summing up market' turnover figures.

How this correlates with banking as part of the tertiary sector will now be discussed.

Let us remind ourselves that the secondary sector of the economy follows as well as represents the classical and neoclassical assumptions about nature and humans which are seen as if they are factors of production. Until such out of date assumptions are consigned to the scrapheap of history no society of the 21st century can claim to be modern. Today, we live in societies which are only semi-modern.

The change to the pattern of reciprocal interaction, however, is possible. Such a society would be based on a modern understanding of nature and people with money as MEANS, and decoupled from direct reciprocal interaction. This means simply that the typical tertiary pattern for services that we have identified needs to become the basis for a transformation of all aspects of life, similar to the way the typical pattern of the secondary sector has affected our lives and still is doing today.

Such a conscious and well-founded decision about making the tertiary pattern the basis of our activities has not yet been tried. Perhaps, now in the 21st century we can try it. I think it's high time to do so, for the sake of nature around us and for us as natural human beings.

9.5.3. Banking – a typical service

Banking is a service, a process between a banking company and a customer who initiates it. All details about the typical pattern for services also apply to banking.

2007 saw the beginning of what we call now the 'banking crisis'. This crisis first became apparent for everyone when in the United States of America in September 2008 the investment bank Lehman Brothers, the fourth largest investment bank in USA, shut down because of bankruptcy. It turned out that it was not the only one.

9.5.3.1. The importance of financial services

The extent of the contribution of banking services to the total national gross domestic product (GDP) is shown here in £ for the United Kingdom, in € for Germany as one of the EURO-countries, and in $ for the United States of America over the decade 2000–2010:

Share of banking (and insurance[56]) services in the National Gross Domestic product (GDP)
in per cent

	2000	2005	2009	2010
Germany[57]	8.3 %	9.9 %	5.0 %	5.3 %
USA[58]	7.7 %	8.1 %	8.3 %	8.4 %
United Kingdom[59]	5.2 %	7.8 %	10.4 %	9.4 %

The data gives a basic idea about the extent of the banking (and insurance) services for the three different countries and their development in recent years.

It is interesting to note that the United Kingdom has doubled its banking services from 2000 to 2009. As Will Hutton comments:[60] "One of the most

---

56 Banking and insurance services are not separated for Germany or the USA.

57 According to: *Bruttowertschoepfung in jeweiligen Preisen nach Wirtschaftsbereichen*, Statistisches Bundesamt, Statistisches Jahrbuch 2012, p. 324, and Statistisches Jahrbuch 2008, p. 633.

58 According to the US Census Bureau, *Statistical Abstract of the United States*: 2012, p. 730, at current prices.

59 I have found data about the UK banking and insurance services in the paper: '*Financial Services: contribution to the UK economy*', standard note SN/EP/06193 by Lucinda Maer and Nida Broughton for the Library of the House of Commons, which provides data to the Members of Parliament, although the figures are quoted in GVA (gross value added) instead of GDP (gross domestic product) with the remark: "GVA data for financial services should be used with some caution, as there is some debate as to how it should be measured, for example, what should be included and how to adjust the figures for risk." Furthermore, the data relates only to 2011 prices.

60 in: *Them and Us, Changing Britain – Why we need a fair society*, London, 2011, p. 139

It is perhaps interesting to add that Prime Minister David Cameron wants London to become a centre of Islamic finance as he told the 9th World Islamic Economic Forum WIEF (1,800 delegates from 115 countries, *The Daily Mail* pointed out) in London on 29 October 2013 by issuing a sukuk, the first Islamic bond. This bond is different, however, as Islam has a more ancient understanding of borrowing money than Western countries, and the payment of interest is still not allowed. So a sukuk needs to be constructed differently: it gives an investor a share in the ownership of a project, and his profit derives from the project's profit. Therefore, it is not only a matter of semantics.

remarkable phenomena of modern times is the growth of British big finance. No other leading industrialized country has allowed its financial sector to grow so large and so influential, or to crowd out so much other productive activity in the rest of the economy... the new business model was (and is) 'to make money from money'."

When it comes to Germany, however, it is claimed that the country is "over-banked". This seems to be a critical remark about banking, neglecting criticism of the fact that the share of financial services in the UK had doubled in nine years. Perhaps the view that Germany is overbanked reflects the fact that there are (too) many local banks in Germany, so banking is not as centralized as in other countries. However, this could be seen as positive as it serves people in the locality where they live. On the other hand is the reason behind this criticism perhaps, that the banking structure in Germany is different to that in the UK and USA. In Germany 50 per cent of banking is municipally controlled, 25 per cent are cooperatives, as the Volksbanken und Raiffeisenkassen, and only 25 per cent are private banks.

If one branch of the economy doubles its relative importance in such a short term, it certainly demands special attention from any government. People owning banks and people working in this branch become especially significant. Any government will listen to them in one way or another. At the same time, governments would be thinking to introduce regulations to limit the risks which could possibly derive from such dominance over the whole economy, as the bigger one branch of the whole economy grows, the more damaging it will be if it fails. Consequently it would be much less risky for every economy if no branch would be allowed to grow to such importance, especially one which trades the MEANS for all economic actions.

So when the banking crises swept from the US to Europe, the government of the United Kingdom had to step in and find a solution to stop bankrupt banks from bringing the whole economy down. With Northern Rock, the UK government was the first public body using taxpayers' money to bail out failing banks.

9.5.3.2. Reasons for the banking crisis

The banking crisis was triggered by the fact that American banks were equipped with insufficient proprietary capital, while being overloaded with losses from mortgages (as the banks' customers were not able to pay them back) and the results of highly risky investments – or rather: gambles – and so called structured financial derivatives. Note: the higher interests/profits offered the more risky the investment. The banks had loaned money – at low interest rates – to people they convinced could and should own a house, but who in reality weren't able to meet their obligations when the interest rate started rising. It turned out that the banks had been not careful enough to check the financial solidity of their customers. Previously, it had been normal practice for banks to examine the creditworthiness of those looking for mortgages very thoroughly. Now it was all about selling. The banks satisfied themselves that prospective borrowers had enough annual incomes or assets, that they could shoulder the monthly pay back rates as the relationship between borrowers and banks would typically last up to 25 years. Then the borrower would finally own the house, the deeds of which were clear of obligation. During this lengthy period the bank could look forward to a steady income from the borrower's monthly pay-back. Obviously, the banks were convinced that house prices would keep rising, so even if a few debtors were not able to pay back their mortgages, the bank would always stay in the black as the security for the mortgage was in the houses which could be sold on.

The traditional form of banking service before it changed and the crisis arrived, was described in *The Guardian* as follows, "Martin Wheatle, the FSA managing director said banks used to be a place 'where you would go in, stand in a queue and have a pleasant chat with the clerk', but some time ago financial institutions had changed their view of consumers from someone to serve to someone to sell to."[61]

The traditional kind of banking service or relationship between bank and customer which even today most citizens in any country still take for granted,[62] changed as the banks discovered that they did not need to enter into such a long relationship with their customers, as they could make a quicker and supposedly higher profit by selling on their customers' debts and mortgages,[63] for which additional fees could even be charged.[64] This process has been described in detail by Gilian Tett in: *Fool's Gold, How Unrestrained Greed Corrupted a Dream, Shattered Global Markets and Unleashed a Catastrophe*. And it goes without saying that, by selling their customers' mortgages, the banks would no longer bear the risks of financing customers in their own books. So the new business model for banks became: selling customers a mortgage, collecting a fee, and selling it on, reducing the relationship with their customers. Selling valid securitized debtor obligations to buyers implies that banks need to put a price on them. Let us see, how Ian Stewart, emeritus professor of mathematics at the University of Warwick[65] explained what was done: "It was the holy grail of investors. The Black-Scholes

---

61 6 September 2012, p. 4

62 It is also true that in recent decades people with a tiny income have had difficulty finding a banking service at all, for example a giro account. Here banks are behaving very carefully, as opposed to selling banking products to customers who can hardly afford them, clearly because giro accounts cannot be sold on.

63 Handing-out credits or mortgages is always documented in a contract between bank and customer. When banks believe that they can sell-on such agreements single-sided, they are breaking the contracts. The customer should be able to go to court against it and terminate the contract immediately, as he would never be able to act in the same way.

64 I would like to point out that the banks' practice of charging fees for their services is a relatively new idea. Decades ago banks profited from investing their customers' money deposited in giro or saving accounts; today's banks put additional fees on every service, from opening a giro account to printing statements of accounts. And it seems that governments have also learned from the fee innovation. In former times they financed their budgets through taxes and every service was free. These days they claim an additional fee from citizens, eg for issuing a passport.

It is interesting to note that the EU Parliament fears apparent plans by EU countries to limit transparency on banking products – the very opposite of what is necessary, as the *Sueddeutsch Zeitung* reported on 18 June 2013. While the new regulation "*Mifid*" is said to protect bank customers more efficiently, the European Council's draft has deleted the paragraph on cost transparency.

65 In: "*Is this the equation that caused the crash?*", *The Observer*, 12 February 2012, p. 18 and 19

equation, brainchild of economists Fischer Black and Myron Scholes, provided a rational way to price a financial contract when it still had time to run... It opened up a new world of ever more complex investments, blossoming into a gigantic global industry. But when the subprime mortgage market turned sour, the darling of the financial markets became the Black Hole equation, sucking money out of the universe in an unending stream. Anyone who has followed the crisis will understand that the real economy of businesses and commodities is being upstaged by complicated financial instruments known as derivatives.[66] These are not money or goods. They are investments in investments, bets on bets. Derivatives created a booming global economy, but they also led to turbulent markets, the credit crunch, the near collapse of the banking system and the economic slump. And it was the Black-Scholes equation that opened up the world of derivatives... So derivatives could be traded before they matured. The formula was fine if you used it sensibly and abandoned it when market conditions weren't appropriate. The trouble was its potential for abuse. It allowed derivatives to become commodities that could be traded in their own right. The financial sector[67] called it the Midas Formula and saw it as a recipe for making everything turn to gold. But the markets forgot how the story of King Midas ended. Black-Scholes underpinned massive economic growth.[68] By 2007, the international financial system was trading derivatives valued at one quadrillion dollars per year. This is 10 times the total worth adjusted for inflation of all products made by the world's manufacturing industries over the last century. The downside was the invention of ever-more complex financial instruments whose value and risk were increasingly opaque. So companies hired mathematically talented analysts to develop similar formulas, telling them how much those new instruments were worth and how risky they were. Then, disastrously, they forgot to ask how reliable the answers would be if market conditions changed. Black and Scholes invented their equation in 1973; Robert Merton supplied extra justification soon after. It applies to the simplest and oldest derivatives: options... The equation was so effective that it won Merton and Scholes the 1997 Nobel prize in economics. (Black had died by then, so he was ineligible.)... But the main way to make money on derivatives is to win your bet – to buy a derivative that can later be sold at a higher price, or matures with a higher value than predicted... The early success of Black Scholes encouraged the financial sector to develop a host of related equations aimed at different financial instruments. Conventional banks could use these equations to justify loans and trades and assess the likely profits, always keeping an eye open for potential trouble. But less conventional businesses weren't so cautious. Soon, the banks followed them into increasingly speculative ventures."

And it was not only the banks, but governments too – for example Schleswig-Holstein, one of the 16 German Bundeslaender, which started dealing in deriva-

---

66 ... which are, according to Alex Brummer, *Bad Banks, Greed, Incompetence and the Next Global Crisis*, London, 2014, p. 270, amounting "to $600 trillion or 12 times the total output of the world economy, a figure that is 20 per cent higher than it was during the pit of the recession in 2009".

67 Banking services are not a 'sector' of the economy, but a branch of the tertiary sector.

68 Instead of 'growth', the word 'increase' should be used.

tives to manage its public household debt, for which a special law was made and the administration extended.

"Any mathematical model of reality relies on simplifications and assumptions. The Black-Scholes equation was based on arbitrage pricing theory, in which both drift and volatility are constant. This assumption is common in financial theory, but it is often false for real markets. The equation also assumes that there are no transaction costs, no limits on short-selling and that money can always be lent and borrowed at a known, fixed, risk-free interest rate. Again, reality is often very different... Large fluctuations in the stock market are far more common than Brownian motion predicts. The reason is unrealistic assumptions... many bankers and traders forgot the model had limitations.

They used the equation as a kind of talisman – a bit of mathematical magic to protect them against criticism if anything went wrong. Banks, hedge funds, and other speculators were soon trading complicated derivatives such as credit default swaps – likened to insuring your neighbour's house against fire – in eye-watering quantities. They were priced and considered to be assets in their own right. That meant they could be used as security for other purchases... As everything got more complicated, the models used to assess value and risk deviated ever further from reality. Somewhere underneath it all was real property values would keep rising for ever, making these investments risk-free... At the forefront of these efforts is complexity science, a new branch of mathematics that models the market as a collection of individuals interacting according to specified rules. These models reveal the damaging effects of the herd instinct: market traders copy other market traders. Virtually every financial crisis in the last century has been pushed over the edge by the herd instinct... The facility to transfer billions at the click of a mouse may allow ever-quicker profits, but it also makes shocks propagate faster..."

Stewart concludes his findings with the following remarks – and I apologize for citing him at such length, but his explanation is so worth doing it: "Despite its supposed expertise, the financial sector performs no better than random guess-work... The system is too complex to be run on error-strewn hunches and gut feelings, but current mathematical models don't represent reality adequately. The entire system is poorly understood and dangerously unstable..."

Not everyone believed his explanation. "Some people like to blame the economic crisis on the complicated mathematics used in obscure financial models, says Chris Arnade. The real cause is much simpler and less sexy – and the maths involved is basic. It is leverage: something every new Wall Street employee learns. In plain English: instead of having enough own capital, borrowed money is used to boost returns. In the boom years, investors took advantage of low interest rates and easy credit to do just that. The pursuit of profit led them to exploit it to the limit, which meant loading up with more and more debt. This didn't matter as long as the good times lasted – the borrowed money simply inflated returns. But when the good times ended – when subprime mortgage borrowers defaulted on their loans because they couldn't afford them, and hence rates rose and credit terms were squeezed – suddenly everyone found themselves with more debt than they could afford to service. So investors rushed to sell assets, which in turn soured other leverage investments, leading to a snowball effect. The end result was the bank defaults and government bailouts of 2008. Blaming fancy financial products is easy. But the real culprit is even easier to sniff out: greed."[69] Or rather: people's greed for money.

It has to be added that people's personal behaviour has contributed to the crisis, although we should not forget that behind that lies the economicult understanding of interchanging the MEANS, money, for the end of every economic activity. Therefore it is really not enough to be disgusted about individual's so called 'immoral' or 'unethical' behaviour, as this is not merely a matter of individual choice but of structural conditions.

To transform debtors' mortgages into tradable stocks it is necessary to securitize them. As already pointed out, what is traded then is not a real asset, eg a house, but an imaginary representation of it, printed on paper, based on a mortgage on a house and agreed by a bank as collateral.

It was also necessary for (privately owned) rating agencies to value these securitizations, which can come in even more virtual forms. They agreed that there is real value in these virtual products, with high ratings a condition so that even pension funds can justify buying them. And so that's what happened.

The (privately owned) rating agencies which were paid for their ratings by their customers and can therefore, perhaps, be viewed as biased, are currently experiencing a high number of claims.

The US Ministry of justice, for example, is accusing them of fraud and hold the rating agency Standard & Poor responsible. The claim amounts to $5 bn.[70] On Wall Street it is expected that Moody's and Finch will also be prosecuted. In Australia it is reported that Standard & Poor had already been fined €24,3 million compensation. Consequently, one has to ask whether a public rating agency would not be better and would not do a more impartial job.

According to the Bank for International Settlement (BIS),[71] in June 2012 the total contracts value of over-the-counter OTC derivatives amounted to US $638.928 trn. No wonder Warren Buffet called them "instruments of mass destruction".[72]

What contributed to the size of the banking crisis was that the banks were able to enlarge their capital for these so-called 'investments'. After the second Glass-Steagal Act of 1933, which separated investment and commercial banks, was abolished in 1999 under the Clinton administration, the US banks were able to use their own capital *and* the money customers had deposited in their accounts for their own business. The reason for it was that it is understood that, when opening a bank account, the bank 'invests' the customer's money to make a profit, of which the account holder receives a share of the profit as interest[73] on his deposit.

---

69   Blogs.scientificamerican.com as published in: *Moneyweek* 15 February 2013, p. 34
70   As reported in *Frankfurter Allgemeine Sonntagszeitung* 24 February 2012, p. 30.
71   As reported November 2012
72   Larry Elliott, Dan Atkinson, *The Gods that Failed,* London, 2008, p. 264
73   The new draft law in Germany discussed in *Der Spiegel* 12 February 2013 demands that in future, the banks' business on their own account, such as speculative deals, high frequency trading or agreeing to credits for hedge funds, must be concentrated in a separate company.

Bankers' jobs changed from serving their customers by giving them sound advice on where to put their savings, to selling them products the banks were interested in trading for their own profit. For each such sale, the banks also charged a fee to the customers. The banks changed their service to their customers, who still believed that it was worth trusting them, into a self-serving deal.[74]

By transforming debtors' obligations into structured financial securities/vehicles of various types, the banks immediately got rid of their own risks. In the words of Will Hutton: "Looking at it from one angle, the whole history of financial institutions is that of trying to secure the rewards of a particular investment while passing the risk of that investment to someone else... For decades, the principle means of achieving this was the so-called 'greater fool' method, whereby institutions would routinely sell overpriced assets either directly to individual investors or to pooled investment funds such as pension schemes, unit trusts, savings plans and so forth."[75]

By offering their customers ready-made financial products, the service, based on the pattern of reciprocal interaction, banks gave to their customers was transformed into a one-sided interest on the sale of a commodity. The banking service was industrialized;[76] it was standardized when it should be personal, it was made one-sided when it should be reciprocal. The choice between different products replaced active participation of the customer.

The banks then started to set targets for these sales to their employees – how many sales they were to achieve every week. And they did not stop at that. They also invented incentives for their employees to fulfil their sales' targets. In addition to salaries, now additional payments as bonuses were offered to keep the employees on track. So the more each banker sells, the more their employer, the bank, would profit. The FSA found that firms were using a wide range of such sales, incentives schemes to encourage staff to part consumers from their cash. They included, according to a report in *The Guardian*:

- "• a 'first past the post' system where the first 21 sales staff to reach a target could earn a 'super bonus' of £10,000.
- At another firm, basic salaries for sales that could move up or down by more than £10,000 per year, depending on how much they sold.
- A scheme where sales staff could earn a bonus of 100 % of their basic salary for the sale of loans and PPI – but only if they sold PPI to at least half their customers.
- An incentive scheme where advisers were paid commission on products sold over the course of the year."

Such high risk deals are only to be financed with the banks' proprietary capital.
74 Will Hutton, ibid, p. 169, commented as follows: "Bankers did not try to be fair, proportional or to make profits that reflected due desert; they sought to manipulate, gamble and win without limit," and later on p. 211: "Paul Volcker suggests that deposit-taking banks should be prohibited from using that capital to support their proprietary trading operations thereby separating the two operations."
75 Larry Elliott, Dan Atkinson, ibid, p. 199
76 Alex Brummer, ibid, p. 299 mentioned, that Paul Tucker, former Bank of England's deputy governor, obviously is of the same opinion.

The bankers became the 'masters of the (money) universe' who by making more and more money could do no wrong, as they behaved according to the economicult understanding. Their business model was regarded as normal, as the right way to become richer. Everyone, especially politicians seemed to admire this. However, although the Bank of England had already been established by 1694 and private banks were certainly known to him, Adam Smith, as mentioned, had never claimed the finance industry was the source of the wealth of nations. He never confused money with real goods or took the financial industry for the real economy.

David Korten came to this conclusion: "The banks bundled the mortgages into securities they sold to investment banks that sliced and diced them, packaged them into complex securities, and then sold them to hedge funds, whose math wizards packaged them into even more complex securities that no one really understood. These securities were 'insured' against loss by other highly leveraged Wall Street institutions, such as AIG, which pocketed the premiums but kept only minimal reserves to cover potential losses, on the theory that housing prices could only go up. The investment banks and hedge funds that created the securities claimed that insurance eliminated the risk of holding such securities and hired ratings agencies to certify their claims,"[77] a view of the banking crisis that the German government shared, as stated in their "*Jahreswirtschaftsbericht*" of 2009.[78]

Michael Skapinder noted too the changed relationship of banks with their customers:[79] "Whenever my bank manager invites me in for 'a chat', I throw the letters into the recycling bin... 'The last time I responded to a similar invitation, it turned out the aim was to sell me home insurance'. Since then, I have been into my bank just once, to complain it had cut a savings rate to zero without telling me.[80] I was told 'it was my fault for not checking'.

It is no wonder that people have lost trust in the banking system, if 'trust' in it had ever been appropriate. When the Bundesverband der Verbraucherzentralen (vzbv) in Germany asked people about their experience with banking, 63 per cent expressed the fear that banks would betray them and said they wanted more market' controls by independent agencies.[81]

What prompted banks to stop offering customers a service and instead try to sell ready-made new products to them? The head of the Financial Services Authority, Martin Wheatley, thinks staff incentives were to blame. "The culture and practices of investment banking infiltrated retail banking," he says. After successive mis-selling scandals, banks have realized it's time to change; some have even begun rewarding good service. But it may be too late: an Ernst & Young report suggests that a third of customers now have dealings with three or more banks. There's no going back to the old days. "Banks may want to reinstate old-fashioned personal chats... but the customers have moved on."

---

77   David Korten, *Agenda for a New Economy – From Phantom Wealth to Real Wealth, A Declaration of Independence from Wall Street*, San Francisco, 2010, p. 33
78   P. 20
79   *The Week*, 17 November 2012
80   Although the banks were charging customers about 15 % interest on credit card debts.
81   *Speigel online* 3 June 2013

Over the last years a lot of books have been published in English about the banking crisis, and a list of them is given here.[82]

From the insight about the banks' transformed business model we can now conclude that Jean Fourastie and others were wrong with their prediction that highly developed industrial societies would become service societies, because they did not examine the intrinsic patterns of the three economic sectors, each typical and different from the others. Therefore, they could not see that the pattern typical for the second sector is transforming the tertiary sector. Reciprocal services have been replaced by the offer of ready-made products, made easy by the invention of new technologies which support the regression of tertiary services into secondary products. We can therefore presume that what we observe these days is industrialization on a hitherto unknown scale, being pushed through with the assistance of the new digitalized communication media.

This is even clearer when high frequency trading started to be used, whereby computers buy and sell securities from and to other computers according to special mathematical algorithms. People are no longer needed, either as sellers, or as buyers. People created these machines and now the machines can make autonomous decisions. So employees are no longer necessary for making money, as machines, being totally at the disposal of their owners, can achieve their aims more rapidly and reliably. Today, more than 70 per cent of deals in stock and derivatives are dealt with as high frequency trading.[83] So, money makes money. According to Larry Elliott and Dan Atkinson, "financialisation had created an inverted pyramid. Instead of having a broadly based productive economy supporting a financial sector which had speculation as one of its lucrative but less important activities, a diminished productive sector supported an ever-bigger financial sector which saw

---

82   Roger Bootle, *The Trouble with Markets, Saving Capitalism from itself*, London, 2009;
Alex Brummer, *Bad Banks, Greed, Incompetence and the Next Global Crisis*, London, 2014
Vince Cable, *The Storm, The World Economic Crisis and What it Means*, London, 2009;
Ha-Joon Chang, *23 Things They Don't Tell You about Capitalism*, New York, London, New Delhi, Sydney, 2010 – Chang is also the author of *Bad Samaritans*;
Larry Elliott, Dan Atkinson, *The Gods that Failed*, London, 2008;
Mitch Feierstein, *Planet Ponzi, How politicians and bankers stole your future, What happens next, How you can survive*, London, 2012;
Alan Greenspan, *The Age of Turbulence*, London, 2007;
Will Hutton, *Them and Us, Changing Britain = Why we need a fair society*, London, 2011
David C. Korten, *Agenda For a New Economy – From Phantom Wealth to Real Wealth – A Declaration of Independence from Wall Street*, San Francisco, 2010;
Michael Lewis, *The Big Short, Inside the Doomsday Machine*, London, 2011;
Paul Mason, *Meltdown – The End of the Age of Greed*, Edinburgh, 2009;
Dylan Ratigan, G. F. Lichtenberg, Jeffrey Spees, *Greedy Bastards! How We Can Stop Corporate Communists, Banksters and Other Vampires from Sucking America Dry*, New York, 2012;
Detlev S. Schlichter, *Paper Money Collapse, The Folly of Elastic Money and the Coming Monetary Breakdown*, Hoboken, 2011;
Gilian Tett, *Fool's Gold, How Unrestrained Greed Corrupted a Dream, Shattered Global Markets and Unleashed a Catastrophe*, New York, 2009

83   reported in: *Frankfurter Allgemeine Sonntagszeitung* 17 November 2013, p. 45, in an article with the headline "*Der superschnelle Computer macht die Boerse fair*", translated: The super-fast computer is making the stock exchange fair, a conclusion reached by Reto Francioni, CEO of Deutsche Boerse AG in Eschborn/Frankfurt.

speculation as the very reason for its existence."[84] The finance industry changed the complex interaction processes: from the investment of money in production, where products are manufactured and sold to make money, to the simple and direct activity of making money from money. The detour via production of real goods is no longer required. David Korten also referred to this when he pointed out: "While doing the research in 1997 for *The Post-Corporate World: Life after Capitalism*, I came across an article in *Foreign Policy* by John Edmunds, then a finance professor at Babson College and the Arthur D. Little School of Management, titled 'Securities: The New World Wealth Machine'... Foreign Policy is a highly respected professional journal with a strict review process. Yet here in its pages was an article recommending that the production of real goods and services should be regarded as passé because national economies can and should be organized around the inflation of financial-asset bubbles."[85] Korten comes to the result that: "Securization – the issuance of high-quality bonds and stocks – has become the most powerful engine of wealth creation in today's world economy. Financial securities have grown to the point that they are now worth more than a year's worldwide output of goods and services, and soon they will be worth more than two years' output. While politicians concentrate on trade balances and intellectual property rights, these financial instruments are the leading component of wealth today as well as its fastest-growing generator. Historically, manufacturing, exporting, and direct investment produced prosperity through income creation. Wealth was created when a portion of income was diverted from consumption into investment in buildings, machinery and technological change. Societies accumulated wealth slowly over generations. Now many societies, and indeed the entire world, have learned how to create wealth directly. The new approach requires that a state find ways to increase the *market value* of its stock of productive assets. Wealth is also created when money, foreign or domestic, flows into the capital market of a country and raises the value of its quoted securities... Nowadays, wealth is created when the managers of a business enterprise give high priority to rewarding the shareholders and bondholders. The greater the rewards, the more the shares and bonds are likely to be worth in the financial markets... An economic policy that aims to achieve growth by wealth creation therefore does not attempt to increase the production of goods and services, except as a secondary objective."[86]

Here, Korten explained an assumption that is widely held in the finance industry, in politics and by economicult theorists, that financial, mediated wealth is the same as real products and wealth produced by labour and nature, which Adam Smith was so aware of. We therefore need to remember: *Economicult has a twofold effect, exchange for money goes hand in hand with an interchange, substituting the MEANS of exchange for the end.*

The Skidelskys explained the change taking place as well in the private lives of bankers as follows: "In former times a banker bought an estate as soon as he could

---

84   Larry Elliott, Dan Atkinson, *The Gods that Failed*, ibid, p. 18
85   David C. Korten, *Agenda for a New Economy*, ibid, p. 29
86   David Korten, ibid., p. 30

and retired from the business; now he may buy an estate but makes sure he stays in constant touch with the stock market so he can accumulate further. It would be preposterous today, as it would not have been eight years ago, to explain why one did not work by saying 'I have enough to live as a gentleman.' Finally, capitalism enlarges insatiability by increasingly 'monetizing' the economy. This has two aspects. First, because of its tendency to marketize more and more goods and services – that is, make them exchangeable for money – capitalism constantly enlarges the sphere of monetary measurement and thus the case of direct comparison... More insidiously, by increasing the sphere of money measurement, capitalism inflames the love of money for its own sake... Traders in futures, derivatives and other rarefied financial products need know nothing at all of the actual goods that lie at the end of their transactions. Living in a world of pure money, they lose feeling for the value of things."[87] Of events, I would say.

The finance industry seems to have become totally self-serving, as well as claiming to be self-regulated, trading on their own account and not on their customers' behalf with borrowed capital. Economic understanding no longer seems to be embedded in society following the social rules of different societies, but is thought to have become independent of it, to the extent that it now instructs society on how it should work in its interest. Money appears to rule everything. And people appear to believe in it. So, is the economicult theory and practice really neutral to society?

We are now in a position to point out that we are not yet living in a post-industrial or post-modern society, but in a society where every interaction is still performed according to the pattern typical for the secondary sector – industry – while without having introduced qualitative criteria to differentiate the secondary from the tertiary sector, we would not even be able to have come to such a discovery.

As a last addition I would like include some remarkable statements, Mark Carney, the new governor of the Bank of England made in a speech at the Conference on "Inclusive Capitalism" in London 27 May 2014 as these give us a kind of summary about the banking industry, as seen by the BoE. Carney began with a statement about growing inequality in today's societies, saying for example that "equality of opportunity has fallen" and that "social mobility has declined in the US undercutting the sense of fairness at the heart of American society," when before everybody hoped, especially in America, that the "basic social contract comprised of relative equality of outcomes; equality of opportunity; and fairness across generations" (which he called the "trinity of distributive justice, social equity and intergenerational equity"). He pointed out the importance of beliefs as "part of inherited social capital which provides the social framework for the free market". "For markets to sustain their legitimacy," he went on, "they need to be not only effective but also fair. Nowhere is that need more acute than in financial markets; finance has to be *trusted*[88] and to value others demands *engaged citizens* who recognize their obligations to each other. In short, there needs to be a sense of society." He went on: "My core point is that, just as any revolution eats its chil-

---

87   Robert and Edward Skidelsky, *How Much is Enough*, ibid., p. 41
88   Highligthed by Mark Carney

dren, unchecked market fundamentalism" ("in the form of light-touch regulation, the belief that bubbles cannot be identified and that markets always clear") can devour the social capital essential for the long-term dynamism of capitalism itself. To counteract this tendency, individuals and their firms must have a sense of their responsibilities of the broader system. All ideologies are prone to extremes. Capitalism loses its sense of moderation when the belief in the power of the market enters the realm of faith. In the decades prior to the crisis, such radicalism came to dominate economic ideas and became a pattern of social behaviour. As Michael Sandel argued, we moved from a market economy to a market society." How remarkable is this insight to be heard from the governor of the Bank of England truthfully explaining the situation we these days are all in together. And with respect to the financial crisis Carney makes the following statements: "Ensuing events have further strained trust in the financial system. Many supposedly rugged markets were revealed to be cosseted:

- major banks were too-big-to-fail: operating in a privileged heads-I-win-tails-you-lose bubble;
- there was widespread rigging of benchmarks for personal gain; and
- equity markets demonstrated a perverse sense of fairness, blatantly favouring the technologically empowered over the retail investor."

As a governor of the BoE he points out to the necessity of restoring "monetary and financial stability" which "are cornerstones of strong, sustainable and balanced growth and therefore directly affect distributive justice," as for example "inflation hurts the poor the most and the real costs of financial instability – unemployment (reciting Janet Yellen about the risk that high unemployment could eventually lead to more-persistent structural problems) and the seizure of credit – are likely to be felt most acutely by the poor." Therefore the BoE with its central bank responsibility needed to act, "while to not have acted would have been catastrophic for all," and "in doing so, we need to recognize the tension between pure free market capitalism, which reinforces the primacy of the individual at the expense of the system, and social capital which requires from individuals a broader sense of responsibility for the system. A sense of self must be accompanied by a sense of the systemic."

Listing four financial reforms which "are helping to create this sense of the systemic and thereby rebuild trust in the system" he mentioned:

- ending Too-Big-To-Fail meaning that the public pick up the tab for the failure of bankers, a tasks which he says will be completed in 2014,
- creating fair and effective markets with the help of "market participants" and authorities, for example regarding LIBOR or the daily foreign exchange fixes, "increasing pre- and post-trade transparency in a host of fixed income markets and accelerating the G20 pledge to move the trading of all standardized derivatives onto electronic exchanges and platforms"

- reforming compensation schemes "that delivered large bonuses for short-term returns". "To align better incentives with the long-term interests of the firm – and, more broadly society – major changes are underway," for example "a new code for banks prescribing deferred variable performance payments" and" paying bonuses in stock rather than cash"
- building a sense of vocation and responsibility, where "business ultimately needs to be seen as a vocation, an activity with high ethical standards which in turn conveys certain responsibilities."

"The answer", Mark Carney said, starts "from recognizing that financial capitalism is not an end-in-itself, but a means to promote investment, innovation, growth and prosperity." How remarkable to hear this! He even describes the detachment of bankers from end-users... as a "reductionist view of the human condition," "the division of our lives into different realms, each with its own set of rules. Home is distinct from work, ethics from law; the individual from the system."

How liberating his comments are for a scientist, while at the same time it is so difficult to implement such rules when economicult thinking has become second-to-nature. To to be honest, it is hard not to feel grateful when hearing from an official British public servant that he seems to support a very similar insight as the one we are presenting in this study. However, analysis is not enough, we must act accordingly, if we are to have hope for the future.

9.5.3.3. From banking crisis to government crisis

When it becomes clear that a bank has made big losses and its own capital is not sufficient to cover these, this leads to:

- a fall in the value of the bank, as shareholders will try to sell their stock
- losses for the banks' owners[89]
- liability claims against the directors as well as against the boards of non-executive directors for their support of high-risk business models or even because of criminal behaviour which was not sufficiently controlled
- a stop on lending
- a run on the bank as account holders try to get their deposited money out[90]
- a possible public uproar, when a lot of banks make losses and their assets are not enough to cover their liabilities, which could lead to political instability
- problems for governments in financing their annual budget deficit
- governments being blamed for not seeing a financial crisis coming
- criticism of governments for little or no regulation of the banks.

---

89 It is very hard to understand why in the banking sector, bank owners are not held responsible for mismanagement, as they should be when the company fails, but are allowed to hand over their responsibility to taxpayers. And it is also hard to understand why banks do not have to pay VAT on the sales of their products.

90 Governments these days guarantee a certain amount of money, £80,000 in the UK, €100,000 in the EU zone, which will be paid to saving and giro account holders if a bank goes bankrupt.

- job losses for highly paid bankers – this problem should not to be marginalized[91]
- and in the long term perhaps: a general scepticism and distrust of people in the monetary system

Any government will try to avoid such outcomes at nearly any cost.

A government has an especially hard task on its hands if it is not just one bank with one business model, but the whole financial industry which has gone sour. Such a government would obviously think it preferable to bail out failing banks with taxpayers' money rather than to let them collapse. And when the government uses taxpayers money to help the banks – companies with limited liability – to survive,[92] losses for the bank owners as well as for their customers are avoided and public disturbances are prevented.

Governments do this in the hope that taxpayers' money to save the banks will be paid back in the future, when the banks again start making profits, and can continue to finance governments' debts. According to Mitch Feierstein:[93] "The credit crisis arose because of weak lending, excessive debt, inflated expectations, and overgenerous monetary policy. Worldwide, governments have chosen to respond by running huge deficits, bailing-out failed investors and lousy investments, adding to the pile of debt, and printing money."[94] The bailing-out amounted in France to 20 per cent of national welfare, in Germany to 25 per cent, in the USA to 35 per cent, and in the UK to nearly 90 per cent of national welfare. The crisis therefore was heavier in the UK than in any other nation, and while the UK government thinks that the banking sector is the reason for the wealth of that nation, others think it is 'debt generator'.[95]

German chancellor candidate and former finance minister Peer Steinbrueck, SPD, commented in his 30-page proposal to tame the financial markets, reported in *Der Spiegel,* 23 November 2012, that governments are addicted to credit – and the banks offer credit by buying up government bonds. As a return they expect a guarantee of survival: the state is expected to step in with taxpayers' money when banks are threatened with collapse.[96] Can this be seen as reciprocal interaction?

---

91 *Frankfurter Allgemeine Sonntagszeitung,* 9 December 2012, p. 33, reported that worldwide around 300,000 jobs for investment bankers were lost from 2011 onwards. Another 25,000 jobs were said to be cut by 2014. According to a report by the Centre for Economic and Business Research (CEBR) more than 100,000 bankers and finance managers have found themselves unemployed in the City of London.

92 *Der Spiegel* reported on 6 March 2013 that the banks which caused the banking crisis also profited from it, at least in Germany. Between October 2008 and December 2012, the national rescue fund SOFFIN, established in 2008 to save the banks, had to pay around €100 m to external advisors, eg the US bank Goldman Sachs or the investment group Rothschild, accountants and management consultants and lawyers. €90 Million or 90 % were accountants' fees.

93 Let us not forget that governments need to keep interest rates low so that they are still able to pay the interests on the public debt. And as long as the government's debts can be serviced, everything is perceived to be OK.

94 Mitch Feierstein, *Planet Ponzi,* ibid, p. 183

95 'Today' on BBC Radio 4, 6.15 h, 2 January 2014

96 "Die Regierungen sind suechtig nach Kredit und die Banken gewaehren ihnen diesen Kredit, indem sie ihnen ihre Staatsanleihen abkaufen. Als unausgesprochene Gegenleistung erwarten sie

The President of the German Bundesbank, Jens Weidmann, demanded a better control of the banks and claimed it was about time that the governments gilts in the banks' balance sheets should be backed up with capital, which is still not even the case five years after the crisis.

From the beginning of the crisis, the idea of fully legal tender is discussed, wrote Christian Siedenbiedel, in: *Brauchen wir ein neues Geldsystem?*[97] in: *Frankfurter Allgemeine Sonntagszeitung*, 18 August 2013, p. 30. The crux of the idea is this, to make the financial system secure and stable, the state should forbid banks from bringing new money into circulation when granting credit. The state could force the banks to hold a minimum reserve of 100 per cent for all short-time investments – or only permit the central bank to create money and distribute it. In Switzerland the organisation "Monetaere Modernisierung" wants to push through a plebiscite on the introduction of such a model and in Germany an initiative called "Monetative" is calling for the same. [98]

And while the problem was originally the banks liability, it now seems to have shifted from the banking industry to governments. However, such a view is only partly justified as governments have allowed the banks to become such an important part of the economy despite having insufficient proprietary capital. Otherwise they are necessary as it has been for them financing a growing part of the state's budget. And this explains perhaps why they have simply listened to the banks' interest. 'Self-regulation' and 'light touch' regulation instead of tough controls have become the order of the day, based on the belief that the markets' would take care of failing business models, and that countries cannot go bankrupt as long as their citizens pay taxes. No wonder the view is so common these days that a state is governed by the city's interest and not by the citizens'.

However, what if the market' is only an idea that is not working? Or if too many banks go under? Business Minster Vince Cable of the Liberal Democrats seemed to have been aware of the risks when he pointed out: "The sheer scale of the balance sheets of 'British' banks such as Royal Bank of Scotland/NatWest and Barclays – both of which have assets and liabilities bigger than the whole of the British GDP – is a reminder of how their business decisions impact so powerfully on the UK economy, and how their errors have inflicted widespread damage."[99]

That markets' can become unstable was perhaps a warning nobody wanted to hear. It is certainly not a possibility included in the economicult theory of so-called 'free markets'.

---

dabei nicht weniger als eine Ueberlebensgarantie: Der Staat soll mit Steuergeldern helfen, wenn den Banken der Absturz droht."

97 *Frankfurter Allgemeine Sonntagszeitung* 18 August 2013, p. 30

98 Ibid. "Seit der Krise erlebt... die Idee des sogenannten Vollgeldes eine Renaissance. Der Kern der Idee: Um das Finanzsystem stabil und sicher zu machen, soll der Staat den Banken verbieten, im Zuge ihrer Kreditvergabe neues Geld in Umlauf zu bringen. Dazu koennte der Staat die Banken zwingen, fuer alle kurzfristigen Einlagen eine Mindestreserve von 10 Prozent zu halten – oder ueberhaupt nur der Zentralbank erlauben, Geld zu schoepfen und weiterzugeben. In der Schweiz will der Verein "Monetaere Modernisierung"... eine Volksabstimmung ueber die Einfuehrung eines solchen Modells durchsetzen. Und in Deutschland fordert eine Initiative namens "Monetative" dasselbe. term – organization"

99 Vince Cable, *The Storm,* ibid, p. 144

Larry Elliott and Dan Atkinson pointed out that the US and other countries indeed "had experienced a 'Minsky moment'. In a paper for the Levy Institute based on the ideas of the late Hyman Minsky, Randall Wray Economics Professor at the University of Missouri," (1919–1996 and therefore not able to see his prognosis coming true), they write that "the long period of growth and long inflation had created an environment where markets were blind to the risks they were taking. Minsky came up with a theory of financial instability based on two propositions. The first, not especially original, was that there are two types of regimes for financial markets – one that is consistent with stability and one which is not. The second proposition, however, was more striking because Minsky argued that stability was destabilizing and carried the seeds of its own destruction because those operating in a stable world would take actions that would push the system towards instability."[100]

Vince Cable seems to have recognized that "... financial markets are subject to repeated bubbles, panics and crashes", and considered that these "should not be confused with markets in goods and services within and between countries"[101] when he wrote: "Banks are also on a massive scale losing the paradox of thrift. Having been taken to the brink of, or over the edge as a result of indulging in excessive leverage, and having inadequate capital to support the risks involved, banks are now furiously piling up capital reserves against bad debts, and restricting lending. As the Governor of the Bank of England observed recently of British banks: their behaviour is individually understandable but collectively suicidal – suicidal because they are dragging down the British economy, precipitating more bankruptcies and more bad debts for the banks themselves."[102]

So for a government: "The immediate priority is to protect the system from meltdown. But there has to be some line between short-term fixes and long-term structures. There is a real risk that governments will put taxpayers' money into the banking systems without banks, or the public, having any clear sense of where long-term policy is heading and, in particular, what kind of banking industry should and will emerge. Clarity over the reform agenda is therefore urgently needed."[103]

It seemed that one minister and the Governor of the Bank of England at least had some insight into the risks the financial industry had taken on these days. But how many others do? Where are their strategies to offer customers a service orientated banking system again? How could banking be made more secure for the future? Were Cable's words enough to thoroughly question the understanding of today's banking business? It does not look like it, especially when Cable warns at the same time that: "The worry some of us have is that legitimate arguments for re-regulating financial markets will become confused with a generalized movement towards dirigism and state control of economic activity." After all the insights, the market' model still has to be kept whatever the consequences. This may be called an ideological approach. It most certainly is not a scientific one.

---

100 Larry Elliott, Dan Atkinson, *The Gods that Failed*, ibid, p. 235
101 Vince Cable, ibid, p. 119
102 Ibid, p. 137
103 Ibid, p. 145

Gabor Steingart[104] suggested that in this bastard economy the government is no longer the neutral arbitrator it pretends to be. The government of today is a 'double being' that treads the red carpet by day in order to replenish its money supply by night in the shadowy realm of the global financial markets... Out of the former hierarchy grew a partnership for life and survival, in which the primacy of politics was suspended and the state viewed as secondary. The Left have since called it a failure of the market, the Conservatives a failure of the state. The truth is that we are now lamenting the failure of both market and state. Governments and bankers have together produced the conditions under which the West is suffering. The one was the accomplice of the other. The state opened the door through which the banking industry pushed into the public realm... Politicians committed to the common good and banks geared to maximizing profits are today building a community of goods with added reinsurance. Therefore the state rescues the banks, and the banks rescue the state. And if both lose their way, they order new supplies from the money-issuing bank in Frankfurt.

Steingart demanded a law disentangling banks and governments, and three-yearly reports from governments on its progress.

Germany's Conservative Chancellor, Angela Merkel also declared that countries need to become more independent from financial markets'.[105] And the best way to do that is to stop countries piling up new debts. In Germany it has been made illegal to refinance the budget by putting new debts on top of old ones by 2020 onwards, while existing debts are to be paid back instead.

However, a lot of people did not see the banking crisis as a failure of regulating the financial industry, but claimed that the crisis arose because banks had *not* been *free enough* to regulate themselves. To quote Hutton: "But once again, when the economists offered their explanations for the catastrophe, they reached the wrong conclusion: rather than realising that deregulation had been a disaster the consensus was that it had not gone far enough."[106]

So when the (US Republican) administration "exempted certain derivatives from regulatory oversight ... watered down requirements that banks balance their risk with safe assets; ... overruled state-level predatory lending laws ... exempted

104 *Der Spiegel* 16/2013, p. 81. Steingart is CEO of the Duesseldorf-based *Handelsblatt*: . "*In dieser Bastardoekonomie ist die Regierung nicht mehr der neutrale Schiedsrichter, als der sie sich ausgibt. Sie ist heute ein Doppelwesen, das tagsueber auf dem roten Teppich wandelt, um sich des Nachts im Schattenreich der globalen Finanzmaerkte seinen Geldnachschub zu besorgen... Aus dem einstigen Unterstellungsverhaeltnis wurde eine Lebens- und Ueberlebenspartnerschaft. Der Primat der Politik galt damit als suspendiert. Der Staat war sekundaer geworden. Marktversagen, rufen seither die Linken. Staatsversagen, behaupten die Konservativen. In Wahrheit muessen Markt- und Staatsversagen heute zusammen gedacht werden. Regierungen und Bankiers haben die Zustaende, unter denen der Westen leidet, gemeinsam herbeigefuehrt. Der eine war der Komplize des anderen. Der Staat oeffnete die Tuer, durch die das Geldgewerbe in den oeffentlichen Raum draengte... Die dem Gemeinwohl verpflichteten Politiker und die auf Gewinnmaximierung ausgerichteten Banken bilden heute eine Zugewinngemeinschaft mit angeschlossener Rueckversicherung. Deshalb rettet der Staat die Banken, und die Banken retten den Staat. Und wenn beide nicht mehr weiterwissen, bestellen sie Nachschub bei der Notenbank in Frankfurt.*"

105 According to *Handelsblatt*, 23 April 2013

106 Will Hutton, ibid, p. 164

credit default swaps from regulation as insurance products and... dialled back the Federal Reserve's regulatory powers"[107] – is this not an example of deregulation?

Instead, many people insisted that exactly the opposite of deregulation has taken place in the USA: "The true believers had never actually been in charge, the market had never truly been freed, and therefore the disastrous events of recent years cast no discredit on conservative ideas themselves. The solution wasn't to reconsider deregulation; it was to double down, to work even more energetically for the laissez-faire utopia." Again, it seems people simply cannot give up their long held beliefs in markets'. Even when confronted with the ugly consequences, they deliberately choose to separate themselves from reality, thinking they can still hold on to their belief – clearly a dangerous delusion. Who can defend an idea that instead of re-thinking misguided assumptions, we should follow the same path?

Isn't this totally different to real life? When we make a mistake, we learn from it, think about the reason we made this mistake and consequently change our habits and behaviour. But not in economicult society. Economicult has to be maintained at all costs. Why? Because these days our whole life seems to be defined by it?

It is obviously easier to burden millions of taxpayers than the banks and their owners with the consequences of their failing business model. Any other business would have to deal with its failure, but not the financial industry. How indeed do other industries react to this? And why were the banks' shareholders not forced to shoulder the losses from the beginning? Didn't they as the owners of the banks have more obligations than simply participating from the profits when there were profits?

The government could not let go of a whole branch of the economy, especially one which does not just manufacture any odd commodity but the very means of it. When the governments took this decision, to support the banks, they also tried to keep everyone's trust in this monetary system. Otherwise everybody would have lost out when the economicult model revealed its flaws – very publicly. So, there was not really an alternative to hand.

Now, the natural consequence might be that in future "every money-market saver and every bank will be rescued by the taxpayer... The giants of the financial system could gamble, lose everything, and yet walk away solvent,"[108] as Paul Mason rightly feared.

Some consequences of the various strategies governments have employed in response to the banking crisis will now be listed:

When banks today, especially system-relevant globally operating private banks, finance themselves with slightly more than 2 per cent, but rarely over 3 per cent of proprietary capital, while 98 per cent is borrowed, then the financial industry itself is founded on borrowing. Or the other way round: the big global banks were able to remove their own liability further and replace it with the liability of others. Nice work, indeed.

---

107 Thomas Frank, *We don't need no regulation*, in *The Guardian*, 7 January 2012, p. 28
108 Paul Mason, *Meltdown*, ibid, p. 21

Consequently governments have discussed making them hold a much higher leverage ratio, a higher share of proprietary capital (in the US 5 per cent) so they are better prepared for losses.

JP-Morgan-boss Dimon, however, has dismissed this type of attempt made by governments to gain more proprietary capital as "unamerican".[109]

Other banks have argued that increasing proprietary capital, by issuing new shares or retaining annual profits would only increase their costs. To this Rainer Hank and Winand von Petersdorff have made the remark that refusing a reform is neatly turned into a threat to society: we will reduce your wealth if you ill-treat us with high regulatory capital requirements. Those who argue in this way indecently ignore the costs with which they burdened the public in the financial crisis due to the paltry provision of proprietary capital.[110]

The Bank of England's Monetary Policy Committee agreed on quantitative easing – a programme of buying longer-term treasury securities and mortgage-backed securities to extend maturities (MEP) with the aim of increasing money supply and putting downward pressure on longer-term interest rates – to the tune of £375 bn in the UK. The Federal Open Market Committee agreed to an amount of $3.75 trn in the US[111] or US $85 bn a month, reduced to US $75 from December 2013.[112]

The Bank of England started a Funding for Lending scheme (FLS) in August 2012 amounting to £80 bn, enabling banks to access cheap funds in return for growing lending. 39 participating banks drew out a total of £13.8 bn, but, according to Ben Bernanke, Chairman of the Fed, USA's central bank, "net lending to households and businesses – new loans minus repayments – has slipped £1.5 bn since the scheme began and by £2.42 bn in the final quarter of 2012". For example "Lloyds shrank lending by £5.6 bn despite claiming £3 bn in FLS cash."[113]

---

109 *Spiegel* online, 9 July 2013

110 In: , *Frankfurter Allgemeine Sonntagszeitung,* 22 December 2013, p. 19, *Wie wir lernten, die Banken zu hassen:* "Geschickt wird aus der Verweigerung der Reform eine Drohung an die Gesellschaft: Wir schrumpfen euren Wohlstand, wenn ihr uns mit hohen Eigenkapitalvorschriften maltraetiert. Wer so argumentiert, der unterschlaegt auf ziemlich unanstaendige Weise die Kosten, die er der Allgemeinheit aufgebuerden hatte in der Finanzkrise infolge der miesen Kapitalausstattung."

111 On 31 August 2012 "Monetary policy since the onset of the crisis" at the Federal Reserve Bank of Kansas in Jackson Hole, Wyoming

112 How much the US quantitative easing strategy altogether amounts too, seems not possible to find out.

113 Reported *the i* 5 March 2013, p. 38. Ben Chu in *The Independent,* 25 April 2013, listed all similar schemes which the government "has been attempting to cajole and tempt our banks into increasing lending to the small business sector for two years now. First, in 2011, we had Project Merlin, in which the banks agreed gross lending targets with the Treasury for SME lending in return for a free hand to pay large bonuses to their heroic traders. Gross lending to the sector did indeed rise. But net lending fell. This was followed a year later by the National Loan Guarantee Scheme, in which the Treasury offered to guarantee banks' wholesale funding in return for an agreement from managements to boost SME lending. Net lending continued to fall. Then, last summer, the Bank of England took charge of the effort with the FLS, offering the banks cheap loans from Threadneedle Street in return for more SME loans. Over the first five months of the scheme net lending to businesses has continued to decline, even though the banks availed themselves of £14 bn of cheap loans. We were told by the Bank's Governor, Sir Mervyn

The UK government announced in February 2013 that it would once more separate commercial from investment banks. The same discussion took place in Germany.

In the UK, the government decided on a first draft of a new banking law on 6 February 2013, as demanded by a group of EU experts around the Finnish Central Bank boss Erkki Liikanen. EU Markets Commissioner Michael Barnier praised the proposals of Likanen's group of experts for demonstrating a way in which banks could act in the interest of their customers. In the past, financial institutions had taken excessive risks – at the expense of taxpayers.[114] Such risks, it should be added, were not taken for the tax payers to shoulder. And the banks did not do this to make profits to share with their customers, but only for their private interest, for their owners.

From November 2014, a European central control for the 130 biggest banks with a turnover of more than €30 billion will be established in the shape of EBA the European Banking Authority in the City of London[115] – following the discussion of the 28 EU finance ministers on 15 October 2013 in Luxemburg, while the 5,800 smaller banks in Europe will stay under the control of national regulators. A so-called 'cascade of liability' will be established, meaning that in case of losses, the shareholders and creditors of the bank will lose their money first, then account holders with more than £80,000 or €100,000. This is called 'bail-in'. If this is not enough, a European fund will take over, and only then will the taxpayer become involved.[116] However, when *Spiegel* online reported on 20 March 2014 that the European institutions, Parliament and Commission, had reached a compromise on how the banking union is to be developed, it turned out that 'the unholy alliance', between national states and banks is more to continue than to be transformed.

When eleven EU countries[117] voted for a financial transaction tax, the UK went to court against it claiming that it would not be the right solution for the British banking industry. With this new tax financial deals would be made slightly more expensive, deals of stocks by 0.1 per cent, deals of derivatives by 0.01 per cent. This measure seems fair as financial deals have hitherto been exempt from value added

King, last October that the scheme provided 'powerful incentives' for the banks to lend. Well, they clearly weren't powerful enough, because yesterday the FLS was relaunched with even bigger incentives for lending to SMEs."

114 Reported by the *Kieler Nachrichten* 4 October 2012: "*EU Marktkomissar Michael Barnier lobte die Vorschlaege von Kiikanen's Expertengruppe. Sie wiesen einen Weg auf, wie 'Banken im Interesse ihrer Kunden handeln' koennten. In der Vergangenheit seien Geldinstitute 'uebermaessige Risiken' eingegangen zu Lasten der Steuerzahler.*"

115 The EBA was established on 1 January 2011 and its website states that its "overall objectives are to maintain financial stability in the EU and to safeguard the integrity, efficiency and orderly functioning of the banking sector". It consists of the European Securities and Markets Authorities (ESMA), the European Banking Authority (EBA) and the European Insurance and Occupational Pensions Authority (EIOPA), the European Systemic Risk Board (ESRB) and the Joint Committee of the European Supervisory Authorities as well as the national supervisory authorities.

116 *Frankfurter Allgemeine Sonntagszeitung,* 15 December 2013, p. 26;
and on 15 April 2014 the EU Parliament agreed to this new bank regulation which its president, Martin Schulz, called "historic".

117 France, Belgium, Austria, Slovenia, Portugal, Greece, Slovakia, Italy, Spain, Estonia and Germany.

tax (VAT). Favouring the financial industry over every other industry was never understandable, and it is high time it was treated equally. Then perhaps high-risk deals will become more expensive making them less attractive.

The Deputy Governor of the Bank of England, Paul Tucker, came up with another idea. On 26 February 2013, as reported by the *i*, he suggested to MPs on the Treasury Select Committee that "rather than paying them interest", "the setting of negative interest rates... should be explored as a way of easing the flow of credit to the stagnant economy". Analysts warned that this would mean that the banks would cut interest rates on savings even more.

Another tactic intended to make banks realize their losses and not leave it to the future is, according to *The Daily Telegraph*, an "international agreement on accounting standards, but the IASB and its US counterpart, the Financial Standards Accounting Board, said last year that they have been unable to reach a deal."[118] At the moment, for example, German banks have to value all their assets according to the lowest value principle, while UK and US banks can value them at buying prices. "... the new code would force lenders to recognize upfront all the losses they could have to take against a loan over its life as soon as there is evidence of any deterioration in its value... Tony Clifford, an international accounting specialist at Ernst & Young, said the rules would be likely to force banks to increase their provisions against losses. He described the proposed rule change as the single biggest change in accounting the banks have ever had to deal with... The new 'expected loss' rule comes after several years of calls from senior regulators, including Sir Mervyn King, the Governor of the Bank of England, for banks to admit to the full scale of the losses on their balance sheets."

The other thing that "... quietly, modern governments have been trying to do: Britain's authorities silently rejoiced at sterling's 25 per cent depreciation, hoping – vainly, it turned out – that it would boost the export economy. The US authorities spent half their waking hours during 2009 trying to devalue the dollar against the Chinese RMB."[119] On March 2013, £1 was valued €1.14 and $1 at €0.77.

Furthermore, there are calls for bankers' incentives[120], bonuses and salaries to be limited. Adity Chakrabortty pointed out on 24 January 2012[121] that the boss of the Royal Bank of Scotland, of which 82 per cent is owned by the British tax payer through UK Financial Investments Limited, earns 97 times more than the average employee. "That can't be a good deal for the tax payer." And why did Barclays increase the bonuses of its employees by 13 per cent, when pre-tax profits fell 37 per cent in 2013 and return on equity plunged from 12.7 per cent to 8.2 per cent, asked *The Guardian*, 12 February 2014, p. 19?

On 3 March 2013, Switzerland held a referendum on salaries, coming to the decision that the owners of a company should decide about the salaries of their

---

118 8 March 2013, business pages.
119 Paul Mason in 2010 in: *Meltdown*, ibid., p. 212
120 *The Guardian* reported on 12 December 2013, p. 4, that Lloyds Banking Group was penalized with a record £28 m fine for a bonus-induced selling frenzy to customers who did not need these products.
121 In *The Guardian*, p. 5

employees – who else, you might ask?[122] Definitely not they themselves. But it should also be noted that in the USA attempts to let the owners of companies decide the salaries of directors – not just bankers – seem to have failed. *Der Spiegel* 28/2013 reported that the income of the top 200 CEOs of shareholding companies with at least US $1 bn turnover have risen in the last year by 16 per cent.

Perhaps another imbalance in today's system can be discussed alongside the size of salaries: the fact that employees in low paid jobs ("20 per cent of UK workers earn less than the living wage."[123]) are not able to make ends meet so their salaries need to be topped up by the government, ie the tax payer. In other words, companies reduce labour costs, seen as the cost for the production factor 'labour', by shifting it to the peoples' purse: another way to increase private profits by making the public pay for it. This cannot be a rational and fair way forward either.

The boss of Lloyds Banking Group, 40 per cent of which is now owned by the British taxpayer, is said to have received a bonus of £1.5 m for the year 2012 on top of his monthly salary.[124]

HSBC paid its chief executive, Stuart Gulliver, a pay and benefits package of £7.4 m in spite of the fact that HSBC was "fined a record £1.2 bn last year by United States regulators, who charged it with acting as a conduit for Mexican drug money and assisting with sanctions busting on behalf of the murderous regime in Iraq."[125] Simon Walker, the boss of the influential Institute of Directors called it "rewards for failure".[126]

Bankers' bonuses are really today under public scrutiny, although there was a real change to it. The *i* reported on the same day that: "Controversial plans to introduce a cap on bankers' bonuses across the European Union[127] appeared to hit the buffers last night as politicians failed to reach an agreement... News of the deadlock came as experts warned that capping bonuses could 'damage stability and growth'... Katja Hall, chief policy director at the CBI said: ... Such a move would fly in the face of financial stability, by removing companies' ability to quickly respond to a downturn by adjusting pay.' MEPs have been pushing hard for a cap on bonuses and the Irish presidency of the EU has made the reforms a

---

122 *Frankfurter Allgemeine Sonntagszeitung,*24 February 2013, p. 5; *The Guardian* reported that at the shareholder meeting in London of Burberry, "52.7% of investor votes opposed the company's pay report" about the salary of Christopher Bailey. "Investors are furious about the nearly £20 m of free shares handed to Bailey over the last four years, which they don't think have been adequately explained. Almost as irksome has been a £440,000 cash allowance – separate from Bailey's £1m salary and potential £2.2 m bonus – plus an additional one-off performance-related award of £7.6 m worth of shares when he took over as chief executive in May. These came on top of the £3.8 m worth of Burberry stock he already owns, according to the company's share register." However, "despite the scale of opposition the firm is not required to act as the vote is only advisory." You wonder, who had set up the constitution of the company when the owners have no rights to decide.

123 *The Week,* 9 November 2013, p. 6

124 Reported in *The i* , 20 February 2013 p. 41

125 Ibid, p. 29

126 *The Guardian*, 14 March 2013, p. 27

127 *Die Welt* 27 September 2013, p. 15, reported that the UK government had started proceedings against a limitation of bonuses at the European Court of Justice when payments were required to be limited to two annual salaries.

priority for the next six months..." One wonders how Hall, as chief policy director of the Confederation of British Industries, could make such a remark. Had the banks not almost brought down the whole financial system? Trying to deal with the consequences of the banking crisis is threatening 'financial stability' – when it was the banks threatening it? It is really hard to understand how cause and effect can be interchanged without a serious public outcry about it. When a company makes big losses, it would certainly be right that the responsible employee is sacked and taken to court or can expect his income to be reduced.

Like the one before, 2013 will be another rather lean year for bankers. Many will see a pay freeze for the second time running, as a survey of 30 German, Swiss and Austrian banks by pay consultancy Towers Watson showed, reported the *Frankfurter Allgemeine Sonntagszeitung*, 6 January 2013. The banks plan to raise basic salaries by just 1 or 2 per cent, and it's a similar picture for performance-related bonuses, according to the survey, 80 per cent of banks will leave them unchanged in 2013 or even plant to reduce them. Only 15 per cent of the surveyed banks are planning higher bonuses.[128]

"In a survey by Klein's consultancy (Hostettler, Kramarsch & Partner) the banks complained about the tide of regulations they have to implement. Nearly all new laws were developed internationally. They are partly based on resolutions by the 2009 G-20-summit in Pittsburgh, and partly on recommendations of the European Banking Authority EBA which have been translated into EU directives. There is not yet a legal limit for bonuses and salaries. An exception in Germany is banks which were bailed out by the government and of which more than 75 % are owned by the tax payer. Their top staff are only allowed to earn up to 500,000 Euros. A penalty for poor performance is also compulsory. The salary structure is audited by the German Banking Authority *BaFin*.[129] *Der Spiegel* reported on 28 February 2013, EU Parliament and EU member states have agreed to limit bonuses starting from 2014. According to a declaration by Parliament Vice-President Othmar Karas, bankers' bonuses will be regulated for the first time in the history of EU bank regulation.

But despite of all these announcements, the EU bank regulator (EBA) reported

---

128 by *Frankfurter Allgemeine Sonntagszeitung*
"*Das Jahr 2013 wird wie das vergangene ein eher mageres Jahr fuer Banker. Viele werden das zweite Mal in Folge eine Nullrunde erleben, zeigt eine Umfrage der Verguetungsberatung Towers Watson bei 30 Banken in Deutschland, der Schweiz und Oesterreich. Die Grundgehaelter wollen die Banken nur um ein bis zwei Prozent erhoehen, bei leistungsabhaengigen Boni sieht es aehnlich aus: 80 % der Banken lassen sie 2013 unveraendert oder wollen sie gar kuerzen, ergab die Umfrage. Hohere Boni planen nur 15 Prozent der Befragten...*"

129 "*In einer Umfrage von Klein's Beratung (Hostettler, Kramarsch & Partner) klagten die Banken ueber die Flut von Regeln, die es umzusetzen gelte. 'Fast alle neuen Vorgaben wurden auf internationaler Ebene entwickelt,' sagt Klein. Teils beruhen sie auf Beschluessen des G-20-Gipfels in Pittsburgh von 2009, teils auf Empfehlungen der Europaeischen Bankenaufsicht EBA, die in EU-Richtlinien umgesetzt wurden. Eine gesetzliche Obergrenze fuer Boni oder Gehaelter gibt es noch nicht. Eine Ausnahme sind in Deutschland Banken, die vom Staat gerettet und zu mehr als 7 Prozent in Steuerzahlerhand sind. Ihr Spitzenpersonal darf hoechstens 500.000 Euro verdienen... Auch ein Malus fuer schlechte Ergebnisse ist Pflicht...' Die Bankenaufsicht BaFin ueberprueft die Gehaltsstruktur.*"

in November 2013 that the number of bankers earning more than €1 m had risen by a quarter in 2012. 212 employees in Germany were paid more than €1 million,[130] while 2,714 bankers in the UK earned more than €1 million. America's biggest bank, JP Morgan Chase & Co. "paid more than 100 of its top staff in London an average of nearly £2.1 m each in 2012, according to new figures", while "the bank's London office racked up losses of about £3.9 bn during the early part of 2012" and "US and UK regulators held JP Morgan responsible for failures from portfolio level up to senior management, deciding it had made fundamental errors in both its risk management and financial reporting systems," for which in September 2013 "the bank was fined a combined total of $920 m (about £56 m) in the UK and US."[131] Why is this happening, one has to ask? It seems that the top bankers claim the same if not more power than the bank owners have.

Further, what happened about taking liable bankers to court, penalizing them individually for their deals with virtual assets which have caused financial instability worldwide?[132] The process has started here and there, but this is obviously not the only way to change behaviour, as the fine will be paid by the banks' customers. "The global banking industry has paid more than £ 166bn in settlement fees and fines between 2009 and 2013, the CCP Research Foundation has found," reported *The Guardian*, 13 November 2014, p. 30, six years after the so called banking crisis started."[133]

When *The Observer* reported on 24 February 2013, p. 44 - 45, on the pre-tax profit/loss of RBS and Lloyds it showed the following picture:

RBS	2008 in £	2013 in £
balance sheet size	2.4 trn	1.6 trn
pre-tax profit/loss	- 24.0 bn	- 4.4 bn
bonus pool	1.3 bn	650 m
Lloyds		
balance sheet size	1.0 trn	932 bn
pre-tax profit/loss	1.0 bn	- 1.4 bn
bonus pool	200 m	400 m,

where a correlation between bonuses/penalties and profits/losses was not always visible.

The BBC announced on 28 February 2013, that RBS had made a pre-tax loss in 2012 of £5.17 bn. The year before it lost £766 m. "Much of the pre-tax loss came from a £4.6 bn accounting charge for changes in the value of its own credit, which is a measure of how much it would cost to buy back its own liabilities." "RBS set aside £215 m to pay bonuses to its investment bankers, which Mr. Hester stressed was considerably lower than other comparable banks."

130 *Kieler Nachrichten* 30 November 2013, p. 5

131 *The Independent,* 2 January 2014, p. 15

132 We learned from *Die Welt,* 27 September 2013, p. 12, that JP Morgan is reported to have been fined with $11 billion, which will add to its expenditure on lawsuits of US $5 bn respectively in the last two years. On 19 October 2013 *Spiegel* online reported that JP Morgan was able to reduce the fine to US$ four billion. Two days later *Spiegel* online reported that the Bank of America had been fined with US $6 billion.

133 In his book, *The Demonization of the Working Class*, London, New York, 2012, p. XXI, Owen Jones commented as a resume of the London riots after the police shot dead twenty-nine-year old Mark Duggan on 6 August 2011: "Steal bottled water and end up in prison for six months. But help push the world into the most catastrophic economic crisis since the 1930s and expect to face no legal sanctions whatsoever. Even as much of the West's bankrupt financial system remains propped up by trillions of taxpayers' pounds, dollars and euros, not a single banker has

The discussion seems to be going in the wrong direction when not only the banks, but even the government is starting to talk about 'mis-selling' rather than criminal actions – an euphemism for a whole business branch which has caused thousands of people to lose their jobs, assets, especially pensions, and triggered worldwide financial instability.[134] Normally we use the word 'fraud' for an activity where someone tries to sell imaginary products with only exchange value to another. When the reality is played down like this even by governments, it is no wonder that the public demand for change is stifled. That might suit the government, but it will not do in the long term as governments will need to push through changes too. The US government, having already sentenced the banks with US $125 bn for their failure, announced 'Payback Time'[135] for the bailing-out costs. The Bank of America agreed to pay a fine of with $16.7 bn, the largest settlement ever.[136]

After the banking crisis, which began in the US mortgage market', a few more deals came to light where the banks had engaged in further 'mis-sellings', such as fixing the LIBOR rate, mis-selling complex interest-rate swap products, mis-selling payment protection insurance (PPI), rigging the UK gilt market, supporting tax avoidance, laundering drug money from Mexico, mis-selling cross-border-leasing products to communities – and perhaps more of which we are not yet even aware:[137]

Fixing the Libor rate

There has traditionally been no adequate regulation for the LIBOR rate, which is agreed everyday at noon. The big banks tell the British Banking Association the interest they could refinance themselves with on the day in question. From this information an average interest rate is then calculated which can be higher or lower depending on the accuracy of the information supplied by the banks. This average interest rate influences banks in terms of the amount they have to pay to

---

ended up in the dock. What is more, many of the British politicians baying for justice post-riots had, in the very recent past, helped themselves to millions of pounds of taxpayers' money. Two years before the riots MPs had been found systematically milking the expenses system. Only three ended up behind bars. Some had embezzled funds to pay for the same sorts of widescreen televisions that were later carted out of shops by rioters, admittedly in a more disorderly fashion. When Labour MP Gerald Kaufmann was found to have claimed £ 8,750 of public money for a Bank & Olufsen television set, he was simply asked to pay it back Post-riot Britain trashed the myth that Britain's justice system is blind to wealth and power."

134 In 2010, the German government introduced stricter legal regulations governing banks' advice to customers on which stocks to buy. Every stage of such advice now has to be documented. According to the *Frankfurter Allgemeine Sonntagszeitung*, 29 September 2013, p. 29, this has resulted in advice being given less often.

135 *Kieler Nachrichten*, 22 August 2014

136 *The Week*, 30 August 2014, p. 43

137 *The Observer* 24 February 2013 published an article by Lisa Bachelor stating that: "Some of Britain's biggest high-street banks, in this case NatWest and HSBC, are failing to make it clear to consumers who take out fixed-rate bonds, that they could lose some of their original savings as well as interest earned if they close their accounts early... The Financial Ombudsman Service says: 'We would urge any consumers who have been hit by these penalties and feel they were not made clear to come to us.'"

refinance themselves. It seemed that no one so far had regulated how the LIBOR rate can be found. This will change in due course as the banking authorities are now examining the information given by the banks. *The Guardian*, 7 February 2013, p. 26, published a summary of the Libor scandal:

"2005 Between 2005 and 2009 Barclays traders made 257 requests to fix Libor and Euribor rates. Initially traders sought to inflate the bank lending rate to boost profits – and their bonuses.

2007 After Northern Rock collapses, Barclays submits artificially low rates to give a healthier picture of its ability to raise funds. A Barclays employee tells New York Fed that Libor rate was being fixed at unrealistically low level.

2008 Wall Street Journal questions the integrity of Libor. Barclays is contacted by British Bankers' Association over concerns about Libor submissions. Fed begins inquiry and gives Bank of England proposals to tackle problems.

2009 BBA issues guidelines for Libor.

2010 Barclays makes effort to clamp down on Libor manipulation in email setting out standards of behaviour.

2011 Royal Bank of Scotland sacks four people for alleged roles in scandal.

2012 June Barclays chief executive Bob Diamond, ..., learns of emails sent by dodgy traders, says reading them made him feel 'ill'. Barclays admits misconduct. Regulators fine it £360 m.

July Barclays chairman Marcus Agius and Diamond resign, followed by chief operating officer Jerry del Missier. David Cameron announces review of sector, sets up Banking Commission. Serious Fraud Office (SFO) launches a criminal inquiry. Deutsche Bank says a 'limited number' of staff are involved. It clears senior management. SFO arrests three men. Swiss bank UBS is fined £940 m by regulators.

2013 January Barclays's new boss, Antony Jenkins, tells staff to sign up to new conduct code or leave.

February RBS is fined £390 m by UK and US regulators. RBS reduces bonus pot by £300 m.

Five other institutions still under investigation."

The *i* reported on 21 February 2013, p. 47, that "Britain's financial regulator is expected to publish its report into the Libor-fixing scandal early next month... The Financial Services Authority (FSA) will unveil the findings of an internal audit into manipulation of the inter-bank lending rate, which has already resulted in heavy fines for Barclays, Royal Bank of Scotland and UBS[138]...

Andrew Tyrie MP, who is the head of the Treasury Select Committee, yesterday warned that its findings needed to be comprehensive... Serious regulatory shortcomings also came to light..."

As reported in *Money Week* 12 July 2013 "Control of the Libor (London interbank offered rate) interest rate has been given to NYSE Euronext, owner of the New York Stock Exchange, for $1. Libor plays a key role in the trading of trillions of dollars of securities and loans. Control of the rate was removed from previous operators, the British Banking association (BBA), after several banks

---

138 According to an article in *Der Spiegel* 6/2013, UBS had to pay a US $1.5 bn fine.

were found to have rigged the rate to profit from derivative deals. *The Wall Street Journal* reports that Libor yields £2 m a year in revenues. The low sales price was partly to ensure the BBA did not profit from the scandal. However, it will cost NYSE abut £1 m a year to run, and £1.6 m to set up, says the FT."

Deutsche Bank was fined €725 m by the EU commission for LIBOR fixing. It had to pay 1/3 less than the original fine as the bank contributed significantly to clearing up the consequences.[139]

Mis-selling complex interest-rate swap products to small businesses
"Even before 'the dust had time to settle on the Libor-fixing controversy' British banks were already 'thrust into a new scandal', said Catherine Wheatley in *The Sunday Times*. After reaching a settlement with the Financial Services Authority (FSA), the big four – Barclays, HSBC, Lloyds and RBS – face a compensation bill of up to £6 bn for mis-selling complex interest-rate swap products to thousands of small businesses, many of which had no idea what they were getting into. The products (the most notorious of which is known as a 'structured collar') were sold as insurance against interest-rates hikes. The banks particularly targeted small and medium-sized firms seeking to refinance loans at the height of the 2007–08 credit crunch. Many 'failed to grasp' the 'casino' aspect of the hedging contracts; they weren't told that if interest rates fell, they'd have to pay banks the difference. Within months, rates duly collapsed to historical lows, and the giant bills began rolling in. Stories of hardship abound, said Harry Wilson in *The Daily Telegraph*. Some firms went bust. Others, faced with ruinous penalty fees for breaking the contract, were forced to find quarterly payments running to tens of thousands. Some 28,000 companies are affected."

In total, the compensation for these mis-sold papers may amount to £1.5 bn. When 173 cases were examined, more than 90 per cent were found to have violated the regulations.[140]

Mis-selling payment protection insurance (PPI)
'There are echoes here of the mis-selling of payment protection insurance (PPI) to retail customers, for which banks have also stumped up billions in compensation,' said Schumpeter on Economist.com. On 5 June 2014 a report on BBC News published that "banks alleged to have underpaid PPI compensation by £1 bn"[141]. 'The already-tattered idea of banks having their customers' best interest at heart has been shredded.' Calculating the compensation due to each customer 'is likely to be complex', stated Jill Treanor in *The Guardian*. Meanwhile fearful of another feeding-frenzy from claims-management firms, the FSA has urged affected companies to contact their banks directly."[142]

These cases of PPI mis-selling took place between January 2010 and March 2012 – "long after the financial crisis had begun, long after Lloyds had effectively

139 *Die Welt*, 5 December 2013, p. 9
140 *Die Welt*, 1 February 2013 p. 19
141 *The Guardian*'s headline on 5 June 2014
142 *The Week*, 7 July 2012

been taken over by the government, and long after Lloyds itself had previously been fined for dodgy sales incentives," as Patrick Collinson pointed out.[143] On 28 February 2013 p. 42 The *i* reported that "Lloyds Banking Group received almost 1.4 million complaints about mis-sold payment protection insurance (PPI) in 2012, it admitted yesterday." A week before The *i* reported that the boss of Lloyds had come under more pressure regarding a £4.3 bn fine for failing to pay compensation quickly enough to customers. "The group was by far the biggest mis-seller of PPI, with hundreds of thousands of customers affected. It has already set aside £5.3 bn for claims, with reports that this could rise by another £1 bn when it reports its 2012 results next week... Yesterday the FSA said more than 140,000 customers who were told they were due compensation by the bank between May 2011 and March 2012 were not paid within the 28 days Lloyds had promised... Tracey McDermott, the FSA's director of enforcement and financial crime, said: 'The industry let customers down badly in reaction to the sale of PPI. The volume of complaints is a product of (Lloyd's) own failing.'"[144]

On 23 July 2014, Jill Treanor reported for *The Guardian*, p. 25, that "Banking's biggest scandal has not yet run its course... As many as 5,000 people a week are still complaining to the Financial Ombudsman Service about the way they were sold PPI and the way their claims have been handled by their banks... The banking industry is in the shameful position of already having set aside more than £20 bn (according to *Which?)* to cover the cost of what has become Britain's biggest mis-selling scandal... But it is always worth remembering that this is a business that the City regulator has estimated brought in £44 bn of premiums for the banks on 46 m policies."

Rigging the UK gilt market

"Forget Libor fix,' says Damian Reece, there's a far more pernicious one in play that has now been running for years – the systematic rigging of the UK gilt market. The Bank of England's £325 bn quantitative easing programme[145] has proved so effective in manipulating Britain's borrowing costs downwards that yields on ten-year Government bonds (gilts) are now at a historical low of 1.63 per cent. That's quite something for a nation 'running a level of indebtedness as high, if not higher, than almost any other G20 country'. Rigging the gilt market serves a dual purpose: 'it keeps repayments on Gordon Brown's years of profligacy vaguely manageable', buying the coalition time (so far not used) to implement badly needed reforms to public finances. It also helps Britain's army of debtors. Yet this 'massaging down' of national borrowing costs is far from 'a victimless piece of market manipulation'. The chief impact has been to cost millions of ordinary savers billions of pounds.

---

143 *The Guardian*, 12 December 2013, p. 29

144 P. 41, which continues: "Lloyds was fined £1.9 m in 2003 for sales of high income bonds; £3.5 m in 2011 for mishandling complaints; and £4.2 m last year over mortgages.

145 From which "Britain's richest 5 per cent gained most", as the Bank of England reported in August 2012 to MPs using wealth distribution data from the Office for National Statistics. The fact that the gap between super-rich and normal people is widening, has been noted by the OECD and the International Monetary Fund, as highlighted by *Der Spiegel* 17/2012, p. 72

If you're wondering why the income from your pension of savings remains so abysmally low, 'don't look at the Libor fix, look at the gilt fix.'"[146]

Supporting tax avoidance

"End of the line for Barclays' tax avoidance factory 'run on fear and macho excess'". Under this headline *The Guardian* reported on 12 February 2013, p. 23: "As much as £1 bn a year of Barclays' annual profits in the years leading up to the banking crisis is believed to have come not from clever investments or banking services but from the prolific and secretive tax avoidance factory at the heart of Barclays' investment banking arm – much of which is expected to be lined up for closure today." This refers to Barclays' Structured Capital Markets division. "Former chancellor Lord Lawson last week described the business as 'industrial scale' tax avoidance." Barclays' new chief Antony Jenkins "told MPs last week that he was 'shredding' the legacy of his predecessor, Bob Diamond, as he seeks to clean up Barclays' image in the wake of a succession of huge fines and compensation pay-outs for Libor rigging and insurance mis-selling." On 4 December 2013, it was reported that the head offices and branches of the German Commerzbank had been searched by 270 tax officers following the tax authorities' suspicion that the bank helped 200 rich German customers to avoid paying taxes. The damage is thought to run into hundreds of million Euros.[147] On 25 July 2014, *The Guardian*, p. 32, reported that: "French judges have ordered Swiss bank UBS to pay a €1.1 bn (£873 m) guarantee while it investigates charges that it helped rich clients hide money from the taxman... In 2009 UBS reached a deal with US authorities to hand over the tax details of around 10,000 Americans whom it had allegedly been helping to avoid tax."

A new scandal about HSBC's activities, the largest bank in Europe, got global publicity in February 2015. In 2008 their employee Herve Falciani had stolen about 130,000 data of their customers from Zurich, Geneva and Lugano branches in Switzerland. First he tried to sell these data, then he handed them over to the French authorities, living now under police protection. When the data were decoded by an international recherche team (ICIJ) to which journalists working for the German *Sueddeutsche Zeitung* and the German broadcasting services NDR and WDR belong, it turned out that their international customers, among them financiers of terrorism, criminals, family members of dictators, dealers of arms, blood diamonds and drugs, had deposited € 75 bn in the bank in Geneva alone. Obviously HSBC helped them to hide this money by assisting tax evasion and money laundering. "Banks such as HSBC have created a system for making themselves rich at the expense of society..." explained Falciani in an interview with *Spiegel* online, 16 Juli 2013. And "HSBC was forced to pay a $ 1.9 billion settlement with the United States after a Senate committee found that failures in HSBC's money-laundering controls had enabled terrorists and drug cartels to gain access to the US financial system." This so called *Swissleak* is seen to be the biggest data leak in banking history.

---

146 Damian Reece in *The Daily Telegraph* reprinted in *The Week*, 7 July 2012
147 *Sueddeutsche Zeitung*, p. 1

Another HSBC deal was reported in the *i* 12 February 2015, p. 40, about the 11 February hearing of the House of Commons Public Accounts Committee. "Around 170 people with Jersey-based HSBC accounts are set to be told to pay up to £ 20 m by the UK tax authorities," causing Margarete Hodge, Chair of the Committee, to call tax evasion *endemic*. "The existence of the Jersey leak came to light back in 2012 and immediately sparked an HMRC investigation. HSBC at the time had three separate units on the island. They were a retail bank dealing with the day-to-day banking needs of Jersey's citizens; HSBC International which looking after ex-pat Britons and HSBC Private Bank Jersey." Rumors in Germany had it that the employees of the London branch of a state-owned German Landesbanken got their salaries paid into Jersey accounts.

Fixing the prices of gold and silver
It turned out that "London's financial sector was last night", 13 March 2013, "bracing itself for another official investigation into alleged price-fixing following reports that a US regulator is considering launching an inquiry into the City's gold and silver markets," reported *The Guardian* 14 March 2013, p. 27. "The Commodity Futures Trading Commission is discussing whether the daily setting of gold and silver prices in London is open to manipulation, according to *The Wall Street Journal*, which stated that the CFTC is examining whether prices are derived sufficiently transparently. The system of setting gold prices in London is unusual and involves a twice-daily teleconference involving five banks – Barclays, Deutsche Bank, HSBC, Bank of Nova Scotia and Societe Generale – while silver is set by the latter three. The fixings are used to determine prices worldwide."

And then these manipulations are sold to the public as the results of the free market'. One really wonders why the Banking Authority goes along with it. Has it totally closed its eyes to criminal activities?[148]

In November 2013 it was reported that the bank regulators in Germany and Great Britain had started an investigation into the gold price which "has fallen" dramatically by a quarter from its height of about $1,800 an ounce in October 2013. It turned out that it did not 'fall' – as if acting on its own –, but its value was reduced by banker's deals who first put it up arguing that gold is a safe haven for one's assets, when paper money loses its value and money in bank accounts pays low interest. This shows that it is high time to change the method used by the "London Bullion Market Association" to fix gold prices.

---

148 The explanation given by Mitch Feierstein in: *Planet Ponzi*, ibid, p. 193, is not convincing, even when he stated that: "Regulators are unpaid and often come from an academic background. Because economic theory tends (idiotically) to suggest that the financial world offers the most perfect possible example of markets in action, those theorist-regulators are woefully unsuited to tackle the grim realities of the financial sector. The situation will only change when regulators are better paid, have more real-world experience, and show real willingness to press for huge fines and, where possible, jail terms. At the moment, there's not the slightest hint of such a change." An explanation again purely following the 'money logic'.

Mis-selling cross-border-leasing products to communities

It turned out further that banks have offered special financial deals to European communities convincing them that they could make money by selling former publicly owned water, electricity, transport services, waste disposal facilities and hospitals and then leasing them back. The communities received one lump sum payment enabling them to be relieved of the costs of maintaining and moderniz-ing their utilities. The communities then used the one-off-payment to balance that year's budget and sometimes even to recruit more civil servants, the costs of which would have to be found every year, as they forgot to make sufficient provisions for financing these costs in the future, thus overstretching their budgets even more.

So, as predicted by *Der Spiegel*, when the US Security and Exchange Commission (SEC) finalizes its report on the banks' creative deals, the conduct of Germany municipal authorities before and during the financial crisis will have to be re-evaluated.[149]

Hitherto, local politicians and managers of municipal services were often held to be at fault – because, out of a mixture of naivety and greed, they purchased financial products with names that meant noting to them and they were not aware about the risks they entailed. It is now becoming clear how international bankers developed aggressive strategies for disposing toxic credit instruments via German municipalities.[150]

Take for example the German city of Leipzig. Just before the banking crisis broke out, the major Swiss bank UBS appears to have deliberately saddled the city with almost incalculable risks in order to earn itself a fat profit. By the time the responsible officials realized that the city, whose managers thought they were insuring their sewage plants, had in return bought collateralized debt obligations (CDOs) of American banks, it was too late.[151] Leipzig made a profit of about € 22m, but is now facing a loss of approximately € 300 m. If SEC can prove fraud, more banks could be held responsible. In Berlin, for example, J. P. Morgan is requesting € 155 m from a similar deal of transport services. We should add that these kinds of deals have come to an end as the US administration closed the tax-avoidance loophole in 2004, which the banks had used so far.

---

149 25/2013, p. 42: "... wird das Gebaren deutscher Staedte vor und waehrend der Finanzkrise neu zu bewerten sein."

150 *"Nach bisheriger Lesart waren die Lokalpolitiker und die Manager von Kommunalunternehmen oft selbst schuld – weil sie in einer Mischung aus Naivitaet und Gier Finanzprodukte kauften, deren Namen sie genauso wenig verstanden wie die Risiken, die sie damit eingingen. Jetzt zeigt sich, wie internationale Banker aggressive Strategien entwickelten, um toxische Kreditpapiere bei deutschen Kommunen zu entsorgen."*

151 *"Kurz vor dem Ausbruch der Finanzkrise hat die"* Schweizer Grossbank *"UBS der Stadt Leipzig offenbar bewusst kaum kalkulierbare Risiken zugeschoben, um selbst kraeftig zu verdienen... Dass die Stadt, deren Manager glaubten, ihre Klaeranlagen zu versichern, im Gegenzug fuer Immobilienpapiere amerikanischer Banken haften sollte, wurde den Verantwortlichen zu spaet klar."*

Mis-selling securities

Under the headline "Interner Verschiebebahnhof"[152] *Der Spiegel*, 37/2013, reported on a study carried out by scientists of the Frankfurt School of Finance & Management and the Frankfurt Goethe University. These scientists have done a fantastic job analysing data from the Bundesbank containing every asset of every German banking institutes, ie from private banks such as the Deutsche Bank as well as co-operative banks and the municipally owned Sparkassen. It turned out that in the investigation period from 2005 to 2009 an astonishing large amount of lousy securities, originating from the banks' deals, had been found their way into the customers' deposits.

It is therefore no wonder that the customers got significantly worse returns on their capital, while the banks cleared themselves of possible negative consequences of their deals. And while a lot of banks claim that they have given up making risky security deals, their balance sheets clearly show that they still hold huge amounts of risks from these deals.

The study established proof that banks are no longer dealing in the interest of their customers whose money they are supposed to manage for the better, and that they can no longer be trusted by customers, as they got rid of their own bad papers by transferring them to their customers, even charging them fees for it. The customers of these banks, it proves, can no longer count on the fact that they work for them, these banks only act in their self-interest.

Exploiting ailing companies

"Royal Bank of Scotland, the government-backed UK bank, has been referred to British financial regulators over allegations that it deliberately 'forced vibrant businesses into financial trouble' so that it could charge them high fees and ultimately seize their assets. The claims have been made by Lawrence Tomlinson, an adviser to British Business Secretary Vince Cable, in a report passed to the Financial Conduct Authority (FCA) by the Department for Business, Innovation and Skills today," reported iNVEZZ.com. on 25 November 2013. "Cable yesterday confirmed that he had referred the report to the City regulators and described the allegations as 'very serious', adding that he was waiting for an 'urgent response as to what actions have been taken'. Tomlinson's allegations focus on RBS's Global Restructuring Group (GRG) lending division, which handles loans classed as being risky. He believes that the bank has exploited the problems facing its customers, by transferring them from the main bank into GRG. This has enabled RBS to profit through higher fees and margins and the purchase of devalued assets by its property division, West Register... RBS has denied Tomlinson's claim." The report has been confirmed by the Bank of England.[153]

So just as we begin to hope that the banking crisis is finally over, all cases of mis-selling made public and the consequences made public, another scandal emerges. It is coming to light that the banks were also:

---

152 In English: Internal shunting yard.
153 *The Week*, 30 November 2013, p. 49

Fixing currency prices

The market' for currencies is huge, with currency dealers turning over about $5.3 tn every day. *Sueddeutsche Zeitung*[154] reported that the five biggest banks dealing in this market' have the following shares:

Deutsche Bank	15.2 %
Citi Group	14.9 %
Barclays Investment Bank	10.2 %
UBS	10.1 %

While all the other banks involved, such as HSBC, JP Morgan, Royal Bank of Scotland, Credit Suisse, Morgan Stanley, Bank of America and Merrill Lynch have a share of under 10 per cent.

National regulators in Germany, Great Britain, the USA, Switzerland and Asia have started investigations into the currency market', because they suspect that currency traders have manipulated prices. The suspicion follows the same line as the fixing of the LIBOR rate and the prices for gold and silver, as the prices for currencies are not determined as a result of trading, but set on a daily basis. It is known as 'over the counter' setting. The authorities have already found extensive faults with this kind of procedure for which regulation is necessary.

On 5 December 2013 it was reported[155] that EU competition Commissioner Joaquin Almunia imposed the following fines on some of the banks involved: Deutsche Bank €725.4 m, Citigroup €80 m and JP Morgan Chase €70 m. UBS and Barclays were exempt from punishment as they reported the scandal to the authorities."[156]

About months later Simon Goodley reported in *The Guardian* that: "The Serious Fraud Office has launched a criminal investigation into alleged rigging of the £3 tn-a-day foreign exchange markets. The move comes after about 15 authorities around the world said they were investigating allegations of collusion and price manipulation in the largely unregulated Forex currency market – which the Bank of England governor, Mark Carney, has suggested could prove to be a bigger scandal than Libor manipulation which has cost investment banks billions of pounds in fines imposed by regulators.[157]" However, the article concludes: "Marshall Bailey, president of the financial markets trade organisation ACI International, suggested that if any crimes are discovered, they should be blamed on rogue individuals rather than on the internal culture at any City institution...' The goal of any probe should be to root out wrongdoers on an individual basis, rather than vilify banks.'"

Betraying customers in "dark pool" trading operations

The Telegraph informed the public on 4 July, 2014, that the UK bank "Barclays falsified marketing material to mislead investors in its 'dark pool' trading opera-

---

154 4 December 2013, p. 20-21
155 *Kieler Nachrichten*, 5 December 2013, p. 5
156 *The Guardian*, 12 March 2014, p. 21
157 22 July 2014, p. 23

tions" which sent their shares to lose their value by 6.5 per cent, "knocking around £2 bn off the company's value at one point the day after it emerged that US authorities are suing the bank. New York attorney-general Eric Schneiderman claims the British lender duped investors by telling them they were putting their money into a safe place, when in fact they were exposed to high-frequency trading 'predators'. Barclays runs one of the world's largest dark pools, anonymous trading venues that do not make any trading information available until after the trades have been complete. 'The facts alleged in our complaint show that Barclays demonstrated a disturbing disregard for its investors in a systematic pattern of fraud and deceit,' Mr Schneidermann said."

A few banks have stopped trading with Barclays, for example Deutsche Bank, Credit Suisse and the Royal Bank of Scotland as well as the US banks JPMorgan, Goldman Sachs and Morgan Stanley, according to *Die Welt* , 28 June 2014, p. 19, a heavy set-back for Barclays which is said to be reducing its number of employees by 19,000 until 2019.

On 25 July 2014 *The Guardian* reported that, "Barclays fights back against US claims of 'dark pool' fraud", arguing that "many of the allegations have been taken out of context. Schneiderman's case, said Barclays, contains 'clear and substantial factual errors'," and the bank denied the attorney general to "have the authority to accuse the bank of fraud in this instance." However, "Barclays dark pool had fallen to 12th place – from second – in the league table of such trading platforms. According to the most recent data, volume in Barclays' dark pool slumped by 79 per cent in the 10 days after the allegations were made."

Breaching sanctions

The *i* reported 2 July 2014, p. 45, that "the US Justice Department said BNP had broken US sanctions between 2012 and 2014 by processing more than $500 m of dollar transactions involving a company controlled by an Iranian energy group. The US attorney general also accused BNP of processing more than $1.7 bn of transactions with Cuban businesses and, 'despite knowing the Sudan supported terrorism... and in the words of one compliance manager 'has hosted Osama bin Laden'', engaged in billions of dollars of illegal transactions to help the Sudanese government." "BNP pleaded guilty in a New York court on Monday night to falsifying records..." The bank will have to pay a record $8.9 bn (£5.19 bn) fine to settle sanction-busting charges in the US, its shareholders will not get a planned dividend rise this year, "but most bankers will get their bonuses."

However, the French bank BNP Paribas was not the only bank breaching sanctions. As *Spiegel* online published 8 July 2014 the German Deutsche Bank and Commerzbank as well as Standard Chartered, Lloyds Banking Group and Credit Suisse seem to have done the same. Commerzbank, a partly nationalized bank, will have to pay $500 million for the breach of US sanctions. The bank is reported to have sacked employees in Hamburg, responsible for these dealings.

Are all these dealings only random mistakes made by a few individuals getting it wrong? Or are we witnessing systematic structural failure committed by the banks?

The remarkable thing is that, given all this fraud by the banks and their responsibility for an almost worldwide financial collapse, this exact business model is still generally seen as normal, as the right form of doing business.

The opposition leader in the UK Parliament, Ed Miliband, Labour, proposed on 14 March 2013 in a speech to the British Chambers of Commerce that the country would need to adopt a "German-style regional banking system"[158], as in Germany 50 per cent of banks are municipally owned, the Sparkassen, 25 per cent are cooperatives, the Volksbanken, and only 25 per cent are private banks. Sparkassen and Landesbanken have a clause in their statutes to the effect that they have to support regional development, so they are not so easily developed into merely self-interested companies. Miliband's proposal followed a recommendation from Labour's Small Business Taskforce and also a series of visits by shadow cabinet members who had informed themselves about Germany's different banking sector.

It showed a different understanding of politics, exchanging more information between countries. For example, why not start regional 'Spark' banks by restructuring Lloyds (41 per cent owned by the taxpayer) and RBS (82 per cent owned by the tax payer) with responsibility for regional development and local people on the board?

When the British government claimed that it will install "the world's first green investment bank"[159] "capitalized with £3 billion to accelerate private sector investment in *high-risk* green projects[160] that are otherwise likely to proceed slowly or not at all, however, one cannot help but wonder why 'green' environmental projects are classified as high-risk, while the deals which have led into the present worldwide financial crisis are seen as 'normal'. Isn't it exactly this thinking that has to change?

An article in *The New York Times Business* entitled 'Green Lenders Reject Environmental Risk'[161] reported growing reservations of banks about financing projects which might have turned out environmentally unhealthy. "Over the last two years, Credit Suisse, Morgan Stanley, J P Morgan Chase, Bank of America, Citibank and Wells Fargo have moved to increase scrutiny of lending to companies involved in mountain top removal – blasting off the tops of mountains and dumping the debris in valleys ad streams below" "or churning out millions of tons of carbon dioxide to extract oil from sand in Alberta". "Still, the rise of issues like global warming, along with increasing scrutiny by environmental groups of banks' investments in many other industries – like oil and gas development, nuclear

---

158 *The Guardian*, 14 March 2013, p. 13

159 Which is not exactly right as the KfW Kreditanstalt fuer Wiederaufbau in Frankfurt, Germany, was founded in 1948, invested in 2010 €70.4 bn into Germany's Energiewende, the "energy transition programme, i.e renewable energy development, energy efficiency, town development with respect to energy use, energy saving, communal energy supplies, energy efficient street lighting, environmental protection, offshore wind energy or modernization of private houses. The KfW is a public bank, while there are at least three privately owned green investment banks in Germany, the UmweltBank AG, and the GLS Bank, which also finances social projects, and Triodos, a Dutch organization.

160 Author's emphasis

161 By Tom Zeller Jr. republished by *The Observer* 26 September 2010 p. 5

power, coal-fired electricity generation, oil sands, fuel pipeline construction, dam building, forestry and even certain types of agriculture – are nudging lenders into new territory… Rebecca Tarbotton, the executive director of the Rainforest Action Network, said that 'these companies have a high risk profile and that other banks should be beware. Bottom line,'she added, 'as access to capital becomes more constrained it will be harder for mining companies to finance the blowing up of America's mountains.'"

However, the fact that one of the stated targets of the new UK Green Investment Bank, is to finance waste disposal units, leads us to fear that this might have something to do with the issue of safe nuclear radioactive waste disposal, a hitherto globally unsolved problem. Such radioactive material, which will remain dangerous for about 24,000 years, comes mainly from the nuclear energy plants, and the British Government, elected in 2010, has promised that the safe disposal of such waste is to be financed by the private owners of these plants and not by taxpayers. It would be advisable, therefore, for the Green Investment Bank to make it clear which types of projects it will *not* finance (exclusion criteria). Nuclear electricity generation should be one such example, as it not only requires private finances for disposal of its waste, but also for the safe decommissioning of the power stations, as these are the liabilities of their owners, and not of the public. Equally financing huge coal fired power stations, weapons or military equipment, environmentally damaging goods and socially problematic production using child labour, genetically modified products and unfair business practices such as corruption, human rights breaches and so on, should be excluded from financing by the Green Investment Bank. The bank should make it clear that renewable electricity generation, district heating and zero-energy buildings will be financed (inclusion criteria), and that Integrated Accounting will be used so that the results achieved annually by the Green Investment Bank can be made public.

Boris Johnson, the Mayor of London, demanded an end of 'banker bashing'. Allow me – and others – to vehemently disagree. It is not about 'banker bashing', but making the failures of banks and bankers public to ensure that these are not repeated in the future.

Instead "more than four years since the banker-induced global financial crisis, and the evidence is mounting," wrote *Private Eye*,[162] that the banks are still doing business as usual, whilst successfully lobbying politicians and regulators to delay and dilute reforms that the public views as essential. Memories easily fade when money is to be made.

According to the Bank of England[163] a large part of the recurring problem is the toxic culture inside banks, which of course amounts to more than just individual behaviour. But the recent Conservative -Liberal UK government seems to favour a *no-change* policy, even giving the "highest-paid bankers" "a £100 m tax cut",[164] published The *i* noting that the top tax rate was cut by the government from 50p to 45p for those earning more than £150,000 in April 2013. This is a

162 No. 1332 p. 32
163 26 March 2012
164 The *i*, 24 December 2013, p. 6

present from the government to the bankers of £36,303 for each of the 2,714 bankers in the UK according to the latest European Banking Authority (EBA) figures for 2012,[165] amounting to more than double the size of an average annual family income in the UK. Can an additional £100 m hole in the budget due to tax cuts be really in the interest of the majority, whom a government should be working for?

Andrew Smithers of the *Financial Times*[166] was convinced that "the conditions for the next crisis are firmly in place. Financial crises occur when debt levels are excessive and asset prices fall. The severity of the recession that ensues can then be mitigated by large increases in government deficits and large cuts in interest rates. Today the conditions for the next financial crisis are already in place. Debt remains at pre-crisis levels and US equities and UK property are seriously overpriced. But the ability to reduce the impact of the next recession with large increases in government deficits and sharp falls in interest rates has vanished. Levels of private sector debt are also of concern, as demonstrated by the financial crisis in Ireland... In the US, private sector debt today is 2.6 times gross domestic product, and nearly twice the level reached after the 1929 crash, having fallen to only 31 per cent by 1945. Much of this debt is secured against real assets and, when asset prices fall, lenders worry about being repaid. But borrowers are not off the hook. They still have to repay their debts. The apparent value of net debt, which is always zero at book, then becomes negative. The impact of falling asset prices is thus amplified, and the greater the level of gross debt the greater the degree of amplification. Worryingly, these high levels of private sector debt coincide with an overvalued US stock market..." And the Bank of England's chief economist Andy Haldane warned in a speech at Birmingham University, published by *The Guardian*, 30 October 2014, p. 28, that the global monetary system poses a "threat to stability".

However, "the US Federal Reserve has called time on its $ 4.5 trillion bond-buying programme", introduced in 2008 to soften the international financial crisis, ascertained *The Guardian* in the same issue, p. 26. The "loose monetary police in the US has helped to foster growing confidence in global financial markets in the aftermath on the crisis." The European Central Bank is trying to follow this example from March 2015, even when her constitution does not allow to finance states, and there is a continuous quarrel among the ECB and especially the German government, not only because this proposed break of constitution, but also because the German Bundesbank holds 25 per cent in the ECB, meaning that German citizens will have to bear most of the risk, and also that no longer Parliaments decide about the policy in their countries, but it is decided without any Parliamentarien control.[167]   According to a 10-page report entitled 'The Destructive Power of the Financial Markets',[168] the conclusions reached by Heiner

---

165 Ibid, p. 2

166 19 July 2011

167 *Spiegel Chronik 2014*, p. 215. It is also to be remembered that when "according to the National Audit Office the scale of state backing for the banks peaked at an astonishing £ 1.162 trillion," ... "these banks were not made accountable to the people who had bailed them out: taxpayers did not have representatives sitting on their boards...", remarked Owen Jones in The Establishment, ibid, p. 259.

168 In: *Der Spiegel*, 22 August 2011

Flassbeck, Chief Economist at the United Nations Conference on Trade and Development are that "The time doesn't seem ripe, and the crisis wasn't severe enough, to grant – in defiance of the neoliberal zeitgeist – economic policy clear primacy over speculation-prone markets and to systematically restrict the financial industry to its function as a service provider to the real economy."

Indeed, what is needed is a new understanding, a new interpretation of reality, not a continuance of the situation which has delivered the crisis. This has been proposed by David Korten as well as Larry Elliott and Dan Atkinson, and this study takes the same line. An understanding is necessary which throws light on the economicult assumptions: money-as-MEANS to money-as-an-end, elected parliament as primary power to government, company owners to employed directors securing their own interests, civil servants behaving like elected politicians, public organizations which, when they offend the constitution which guarantees peoples' privacy, should be stopped and sanctioned instead of punishing those who blow the whistle on the wrong–doers… Why aren't we making more of an effort to illuminate the fundamental errors of the topsy-turvy world we are living in today? Why do we let these things happen and why do we simply accept that this is the nature of things, and the way things are will inevitably continue into the future?

9.5.3.4. Shadow banking

When the financial crisis is discussed, the so-called 'shadow[169] banking' system, a term attributed to Paul McCulley of PIMCO is often neglected. Therefore most people are not aware that there is a part of the finance industry that can entail even higher risks than the regulated banking system.

And because this is such an important issue, it is interesting to cite an article in the *Financial Times*, p. 1, 21 January 2015, by Miles Johnson, Harriet Agnew and Caroline Binham which read:

"Several years ago, a consultant was speaking to an offshore foreign exchange brokerage that was eager to start marketing its trading platform to retail investors in the UK.

Having looked over the business model, which involved setting up shop using off-the-shelf online trading software and a slender amount of starting capital, the consultant quizzed the entrepreneurs about risk management.

In an interview with the Financial Times, the consultant, a former senior executive at a retail Forex brokerage, recalled an entrepreneur replying: 'What is our risk management? Well, we all have foreign passports.'

The implosion of several retail foreign exchange brokers following the wild swings of the Swiss franc last week has brought into focus a lightly regulated industry long regarded in the City as an unsophisticated sideshow to the grander workings of high finance.

---

169 Not to be confused with the black market' where illegal products, such as drugs, are dealt and no taxes paid on the trading. It is estimated that this market' amounts to $2 trillion in the USA alone.

Yesterday, in the latest chapter in the fallout, IG Group, the UK spread-betting company, which is one of the most established operators in the industry, sought to reassure investors that it would stick with its new dividend policy despite the currency turmoil.

But it is the large number of operators based in Cyprus and offshore that has thrown open a debate over one of the ore shadowy areas of the City, which allows private individuals to use internet trading platform to speculate on currency markets for slender stakes.

'The retail brokers are a huge part of what makes the markets go round in London but the can't be let loose indiscriminately,' said Javier Paz, a senior analyst at financial research provider Aite Group. 'The UK regulator will have to err on the side of caution. The reputation of the City is at stake.'

The growth of retail currency trading over the past five years has been rapid. The average daily volume of individuals betting on these platforms had risen to about 20 per cent of the market by 2012, compared with just under 10 per cent in 2008, according to a recent report by Citigroup. Yet the majority of platform operators in the UK are not based in the country, instead operating in offshore locations, away from the scrutiny of the UK's market regulator, the Financial Conduct Authority.

Of about 90 firms that have permission to operate in the UK, 54 are based in Cyprus, according to the FCA."

The latest report of IWF global financial stability[170] showed that the importance of shadow banks is rising, from $ 26 bn in 2002 to more than $ 71 bn ten years later, the biggest shadow bank being Blackrock in New York with more than 10,000 employees and $ 3.6 bn assets from clients.

According to one definition, 'shadow' banks are 'non-bank financial intermediaries' such as "hedge funds, money markets and structured investment vehicles (SIV)"[171] collecting money from different clients for investment. Shadow banks do not need banking licences. The shadow banking system can take high risks, while offering high profits. So obviously this is not a banking service for the many, but only for those who would not mind losing a few millions if a deal turns out wrong.

Also, shadow banks do not have to cushion their investments with a certain percentage of capital, and are generally not subjected to the regulatory authorities. And "unlike their more regulated competitors, they lack access to central bank funding or safety nets such as deposit insurance and debt guarantees"[172] from governments.

A (staff) report by the Federal Reserve Bank of New York dated July 2010 divided the shadow banking system into three sectors.[173] Firstly, the government-sponsored shadow banking sub-system which "refers to credit intermediation activities funded through the sale of Agency debt and MBS, which mainly includes conforming residential and commercial mortgages"; secondly, an "internal" banking sub-system which "refers to the credit intermediation process of a global network of banks,

---

170 Cf *Frankfurter Allgemeine Sonntagszeitung*, 26 October 2014, p. 31
171 Ibid
172 Ibid
173 P. 26

finance companies, broker-dealers and asset managers and their on- and off-balance sheet activities – all under the umbrella of financial holding companies"; and thirdly an "external" shadow banking sub-system which "refers to the credit intermediation process of diversified broker-dealers (DBDs), and a global network of independent, non-bank financial specialists that include captive and standalone finance companies, limited purpose finance companies and asset managers."

Will Hutton had the following to say about the shadow banking system:[174] "The shadow banking system can claim to be the greatest machine created for personal enrichment in the history of the world. The fortunes in *The Sunday Times* 'Rich List' are overwhelmingly made in finance, private equity, hedge funds, investment banking and property, courtesy of leverage and one-way bets made with other people's money. They dwarf in both numbers and scale of wealth the United States' robber barons, English imperial adventurers, French tax-farmers, Spanish conquistadors and even corrupt Roman senators. And at least those earlier plutocrats left behind empires, monuments, cultures and great industries. Today's bankers have left nothing but trillions of pounds of permanently lost output throughout the world, while having had their jobs and businesses saved by the tax payer they deride. Professor Wilhelm Buiter (now chief economist at Citigroup) describes the situation today as nothing less than communism for the rich."[175]

The Financial Stability Board (FSB), a regulatory task force for the world's group of top 20 economies (G20), stated in its 2012 report[176] that a "credit intermediation involving entities and activities outside the regular banking system. Although intermediating credit through non-bank channels can have advantages, such channels can also become a source of system risk, especially when they are structured to perform bank-like functions (eg maturity transformation and leverage) and when their interconnectedness with the regular banking system is strong. Therefore, appropriate monitoring and regulatory frameworks for the shadow banking system need to be in place to mitigate the build-up of risks."

The shadow banking system had increased rapidly before the financial crisis from "$2 trillion in 2002 to $62 trillion in 2007. The size of the total system declined slightly in 2008 but increased subsequently to reach $67 trillion in 2011 (equivalent to 111 per cent of the aggregated GDP of all jurisdictions)." The FSB estimates its share of the total financial intermediation at around 25 per cent in 2009–2011, while "in broad terms, the aggregate size of the shadow banking system is around half the size of banking system assets."

In terms of financial risk, the shadow banking system is very important for a society. "The core activities of investment banks are subject to regulation and monitoring by central banks and other government institutions – but it has been common practice for investment banks to conduct many of their transactions in ways that don't show up on their conventional balance sheet accounting and so

---

174 *Them and Us, Changing Britain – Why we need a fair society*, London 2011, p. 174

175 Hutton also remarked on p. 181 that "Financial lobbyists do not buy votes in the British legislature in quite the way they do in the US Congress, but they do fund individual politicians' election campaigns. For example, 77 % of Boris Johnson's mayoral campaign in 2008 was funded by hedge funds, private-equity firms and their managers."

176 *Global Shadow Banking Monitoring Report 2012*, 18 November 2012, p. 3

are not visible to regulators or unsophisticated investors," Wikipedia made clear. And Simson Johnson, in *The Financial Times*, 18 June, 2014, p. 9, pointed out: "Financial shadows are dangerous. Even more dangerous are interactions between poorly understood shadows and essential financial intermediation activities... Who will step in to fill any liquidity gap, or even to provide support in the face of potential insolvency?.. We have again created the perception of risk mitigation, while allowing ambiguity to develop about who will bear what kind of risk."

Therefore a few more details from the FSB's report[177] might be useful to show the size of the shadow banking system and its systemic risk for societies:

- The largest shadow banking system is that of the USA with assets of $23 trillion in 2011, followed by the EURO area ($22 trillion) and the UK ($9 trillion).
- The Netherlands (45 per cent)[178] and the US (35 per cent) are the two jurisdictions where these non-bank financial intermediaries represent the largest sector relative to other financial institutions in their system.
- The share of non-bank financial intermediaries is also relatively large in Hong Kong (around 35 per cent), Switzerland, Singapore and Korea (all around 25 per cent).
- Jurisdictions where non-bank financial intermediaries are the largest relative to GDP are Hong Kong (520 per cent), the Netherlands (490 per cent), the UK (370 per cent), Singapore (260 per cent) and Switzerland (210 per cent), this concentration is explained by the fact that these are significant international financial centres.
- National authorities have performed more detailed analyses of their non-bank financial intermediaries to gain information about the risk factor involved (eg maturity/liquidity transformation, leverage, regulatory arbitrage).
- These analyses show that interconnectedness is a higher risk for the shadow banking system than for core banks.

The FSB report on the systemic risks in the shadow banking system calls for the following: improved and flexible monitoring, even for innovative products and mutations, especially for countries that lack fully developed Flow of Fund statistics, such as China, Russia or Saudi Arabia, or have low granularity resulting in a relatively large share of unidentified non-bank financial intermediaries, the use of additional analytical methods and the attempt to obtain more data on assets/liabilities, such as repo markets, securities lending and securitization.

According to a definition by the German Bundestag's research and documentation service, however, discussions on the regulation of shadow banking system have only just started. The core problem of the shadow banking system is that the regulated banks can transfer their deals to the ever-changing shadow banking system, so that the regulating authority has little insight into the risk. For example,

---

177 Ibid, p. 4+5
178 The reports hint in a footnote that the Dutch shadow banking sector shows that most non-bank entities are so-called special financial institutions (SFIs) rather than shadow banks, mainly driven by tax-avoidance.

if a crisis occurred in the shadow banking system, then that crisis would not be limited to this system, as links exist to the regular banking system via lending. Comparable deals have contributed substantially to the emergence of the financial crisis of 2007/2008 via a chain reaction. Obviously, the risks have not disappeared. They have only been moved into the shadow. For this reason, on 23 January 2013 the president of the German banking regulator, the Bundesanstalt fuer Finanzdienstleistungen, Elke Koenig, called for extensive international regulations and continuous supervision of the shadow banks. It seems time to shed more light into the shadow.

According to a report in *Die Welt*, 4 September 2013 p.15, stating that a proposal by the EU Commission is on hand, EU commissioner Michael Barnier called for a regulatory system for shadow banks. The German Chancellor Angela Merkel emphasized in a debate in the Bundestag that with the G20 holding a summit the weekend before, they would look silly if they did not come to an agreement on reasonable results. So, there will hopefully be regulations agreed on the shadow banking system before it is too late.

10. Understanding the environmental crisis and the quest for ecology

Having defined the basic economic pattern as a direct and immediate 'process of reciprocal interaction' meaning that it is decoupled from the exchange of money at the same time and having compared it to analyzed the 'oeconomia natura', we found it in the private and public household as well as in the tertiary sector of the economy. Now it is time to use this new understanding for analyzing the other crisis which threatens us today, the environmental crisis. We will see that using this newly defined economic pattern will allow us a better understanding of the environmental crisis, how it has developed and what can be done to develop an economic system without such problems.

First let us remember that, according to the pattern of direct reciprocal interaction, humans are in a constant natural, but culturally determined relationship with nature as the BASE of all life. In other words, humans extract everything they need from nature, transform it for their purposes and eventually return to nature the material they no longer have a use for. So nothing ever really leaves Earth eg if certain waste is removed from sight into waste disposal areas, it still exists. So, as humans and nature are in a constant process of reciprocal interaction, what we today treat as waste of our consumption still has an influence on nature. Radioactive nuclear waste from military weapons and power generating stations has to be securely stored for more than 24,000 years, in such a way that the resulting radiation cannot affect or destroy the health of living nature, of plants, animals or people, but no-one has yet come up with a solution to this storage problem. Hormones used as contraceptives are released from human bodies on a daily basis and flushed into water treatment plants. Now, remains of hormone contraceptives are found in natural surface water. Drugs that are used to treat humans' anxiety problems are now found in rivers "where they may be changing the behaviour of fish." "All sorts of synthetic chemicals used and excreted by humans end up accumulating in fish." Tomas Brodin of Umea University in Sweden had discovered a change in the behavioural pattern of perch when their water contains oxazepam, an anti-anxiety drug.[1]

In the winter of 2013/14 about 400 million people in the north and east of China were affected by extreme smog caused by fine dust, 17 to 20 times higher than the World Health Organization's (WHO) recommendation. A smog alarm was proclaimed for six provinces. 20 million people in Peking were advized not to leave their homes without wearing a face mask. According to estimates by the former Chinese Minister for Health, Chen Zhy, between 350,000 and 500,000 people die prematurely each year as a result of smog.[2] Jonathan Kaiman wrote from Beijing in *The Guardian*, 26 February 2014, p. 19, that the "Chinese smog" was being "likened to a nuclear winter", slowing photosynthesis in plants, due to a 50 per cent reduction in light and potentially wreaking havoc on the country's food supply – although it made producers to offer a new good, bottled Tianmu Mountain fresh air.[3]

Man's reciprocal interaction with nature means that waste and pollution rebound on humans. *The Week*[4] reported that "Beijing has admitted the existence of so called 'cancer villages', close to factories and polluted waterways, which first came to public attention in 2009, when a journalist plotted 40 on a Google map. China's rapid industrialization has been accompanied by a surge in cancer rates between 1970 and 2004, death from cancer rose by 80 per cent."

In its 2012 report, WHO pointed out that air pollution kills 7 million people yearly, according *Spiegel* online, 25 March 2014. And the UK television channel Channel 4 reported in its evening news on 3 April 2014 that the fog which had covered the UK for a few days was smog from air pollution, the worst since 1952. The head of air pollution at Public Health acknowledged that annually 29,000 people die from bad air quality in the UK, and the country will be fined £300 m, because it has not put the EU air pollution directive into national law.

The World Meteorological Organization's (WMO) annual Greenhouse Gas Bulletin, press release no. 1002, published 9 September 2014, reported that "the amount of greenhouse gases in the atmosphere reached a new record high in 2013, propelled by a surge in levels of carbon dioxide," which will inject "even greater urgency into the need for concerted international action against accelerating and potentially devastating climate change". And the UN weather agency found "broadly in the line with those of the US National Oceanic and Atmospheric Administration and other scientific agencies – average land and sea temperature soaring and 2014 on course of being the hottest year ever, published *The Guardian*, 4 December 2014, p. 3.

The World Wildlife Fund International reported in its 'LivingPlanet Report 2014', 30 September 2014, that the "population of mammals, birds, reptiles, amphibians and fish has declined by 52 per cent since 1970. Put another way," WWF International Director General Marco Lambertini wrote, "in less than two human generations, population sizes of vertebrate species have dropped by half. These are the living forms that constitute the fabric of the ecosystems which

---

1   *The Week*, 2 March 2012, p. 19, after an article in the *Daily Mail*
2   *Spiegel* online, 25 February, 2014
3   *The Week*, 29 March 2014, p. 15
4   2 March 2013, p. 7

sustain life on Earth – and the barometer of what we are doing to our own planet, our only home. We ignore their decline at our peril." We are "using nature's gifts as if we had more than just one Earth at our disposal. By taking more from our ecosystems and natural processes than can be replenished, we are jeopardizing our future... What kind of future are we heading toward? ... And we are all in this together. We all need food, fresh water and clean air – wherever in the world we live... Things look so worrying that it may seem difficult to feel positive about the future. Difficult, certainly, but not impossible – because it is ourselves, who have caused the problem, that we can find the solution. And it is by acknowledging the problem and understanding the drivers of decline that we can find the insights and, more importantly, the determination to put things right..."[5] The WWF found that Germany, for example, uses resources equalling 2.6 times that of planet Earth, and there is no evidence yet to suggest that this amount is decreasing.[6]

Furthermore, all the long-term consequences of human's interaction with the natural environment – in terms of the effect on 'external' nature as well as to their own nature – are not yet known. But there are obviously reasons to be much more careful about what we do, what we produce and consume and how we live, because this can no longer be neglected. Naturally, a few unwanted and unintended consequences can be dealt with, but trying to clean up and repair our interaction at the end of the production and consumption processes is far from easy.

Even before we analyze economicult theorists' understanding of the environmental crisis and their proposed solutions, could we therefore suggest that it would make economic sense to develop a kind of culteconomy which does not create these problems in the first place? Would it not be more economical to rethink the production and consumption process – in terms of the 'life helical' from cradle to grave – with the aim of avoiding such unwanted and unintended consequences? Even when whole industries make a living out of it? Should those who caused these problems not be held responsible for their actions, and should the consequences not cease to be seen as merely 'external' costs to society?

When approaching the environmental crisis from the viewing perspective of reciprocal interaction, one cannot help wondering, for example whether it makes sense to build new incinerators under PFI-contracts. Why, when the Conservative/Liberal coalition promised to be the greenest government ever, would they pursue such a policy, given that the requirement to supply these incinerators with enough waste – or 'fuel' – to burn for more than 25 years would contractually strangle any drive to reduce waste and increase recycling? Councils would even have to pay penalties to the incinerator companies if not enough waste – or 'fuel' – is produced.[7]

Instead, why not follow a coherent waste avoidance strategy? Why does everything seem to be decided without taking the long-term consequences for every aspect of life into consideration? Consideration of these consequences might

---

5   *WWF Living Planet Report 2014*, p. 4 and 5
6   Cf. the expression of an 'ecological footprint', coined by the Canadian human ecologist William Rees and Mathis, meaning that the human impact on Earth needs to be reduced.
7   *Private Eye*, No. 1334, p. 9

lead to a different solution for waste disposal, namely a systematic strategy of waste reduction. So, why are the supermarkets not required by law to take back plastic packaging and glass bottles, as is the case in other countries?

And – does our experience of the financial crisis not seem to mirror that of the environmental crisis? Private companies take risks and avoid liability for the consequences of their activities, leaving it to the public to pick up the bill, whether it be for the banks' bankruptcy, or for waste clearing with the consequence of a rising demand for health services?

And when companies are forced by EU laws to clear up their act, eg to comply with EU emission standards, they argue that this has cost the car manufacturing industry £7.4 billion, and say that firms have already incurred costs of £3 billion to reduce their greenhouse gas emissions.[8] These numbers may be right or wrong, they only prove that laws, EU laws, are obviously necessary to make these companies act, as perhaps they would not have done so otherwise?

So, if they are this good, why do these companies not inform the public about the amount of pollution that has been avoided? Would this not be interesting too, given the effect pollution has on people's health and on the environment? Altogether, would it not be preferable to develop a new economic model with no such consequences, a new nateconomic understanding which shows that acknowledging man's reciprocal interaction with nature is the way forward?

But let us first discuss in more detail what we mean when we talk about the environmental crisis and then analyze how economicult scientists respond to it, that is, if they see this as an issue which needs to be addressed – as most economicult theorists are not really concerned about it.

10.1. What is the 'environmental' crisis?

When we talk about the environmental crisis we generally mean the following events:

- **Pollution of air, land and water** with fine dust, waste and greenhouse gases (such as carbon dioxide,[9] methane, nitrous oxide and/or ozone), materials and chemicals, heat, radiation and noise etc. in a concentration not found naturally. An example is pollution by sewage sludge, no longer allowed to be spread on fields as a kind of fertilizer. Another example is acid rain, which leads to forest dieback or huge concentrations of plastic waste floating in the seas and killing wildlife.[10] CO_2 emissions lead not only to higher temperatures, but also to poisoning the soil and the over-acidify the sea today 26 per cent

---

8   *The Daily Telegraph*, 24 February 2014, p. 8

9   According to the *The Independent* ,25 April 2013, p. 57, the Committee on Climate Change (CCC) reported "that Britain's carbon footprint has grown by 10 per cent in the past two decades…"

10   A sperm whale was washed up on Spain's south coast having swallowed 17 kg of plastic waste dumped into the sea by farmers tending greenhouses that produce not only tomatoes and other vegetables for British supermarkets, but 2.4 tons of plastic waste per hectare each year, more than 45,000 tons altogether, reported in *The Guardian*, 9 March 2013 p. 34.

more acidic than at the beginning of industrialization,[11] (as included in the World Meteorological Organization [12] Bulletin of September 2014 for the first time), causing widespread damage and destruction;

- leading to a **greenhouse climate** with rising temperatures[13] and rising sea levels,[14] as glaciers and Earth's polar caps melt, causing changes to the paths of the jetstream and possibly the gulfstream, on which Europe's climate depends. The latter could bring Europe much cooler winter weather, whilst it is predicted that southern regions would suffer more droughts, causing more famine worldwide, as well as stronger rainfalls when it rains, hotter summer conditions,[15] as well as more storms and floods.[16]

A welcoming consequence of it is, on the other hand, that the north-west-passage of the Arctic is now open in summer and can be used for shipping goods more quickly from Europe to Asia. Connected with climate change also is a reduction of fertile zones of Earth.

The World Meteorological Organization (WMO) in Geneva reported on 6 November 2013, in 2012, CO_2 emissions in the atmosphere rose to a new record: since the beginning of industrialization the concentration of carbon dioxide, by 41 per cent to 393 ppm.

The organization Germanwatch noted in its 2014 Global Climate Risk Index that "Honduras, Myanmar and Haiti were the countries affected most by extreme weather events between 1993 and 2012... Altogether more than 530,000 people died as a direct result of approx. 15,000 extreme weather events, and losses between 1993 and 2012 amounted to more than 2.5 trillion USD," while the highly industrialized nations are overwhelmingly causing the catastrophe. Scientists working with Damon Matthews from Concordia Uni-

11 *Kieler Nachrichten*, 3 November 2014, p. 4
12 It was done in collaboration with the International Ocean Carbon Coordination Project (IOCCP) of the Intergovernmental Oceanographic Commission of UNESCO (IOC-UNESCO), the Scientific Committee on Oceanic Research (SCOR), and the Ocean Acidification International Coordination Centre (OA-ICC) of the International Atomic Energy Agency (IAEA).
13 The year 2012 was one of the warmest, according to the US space agency NASA as reported in *Der Spiegel*, 16 January 2013. Each decade is warmer than last: indeed according to *The Daily Telegraph*, 8 March 2013, p. 9, Dr. Shaun Marcott of Oregon State University in the US discovered that "the Earth is warmer than it has been at almost any time since the last Ice Age," ie 11,300 years ago at the beginning of civilization.
14 In an article with the headline "Melting ice may trigger faster rise in sea levels", Steven Connor reported that not only the south and northwest, but also the north-east of Greenland ice is melting faster than scientists expected. Were it to melt completely, this would raise global sea levels by more than seven metres,' said Professor Jeremy Bamber of Bristol University, one of the authors of the study published in the journal *Nature Climate Change*."
15 A recent UN climate change study reported, according to *Kieler Nachrichten*, 4 July 2013, p. 11, that the decade between 2001 and 2010 was not only the warmest since records began, but saw more than 370,000 people lose their lives through extreme weather events.
16 As warmer air can hold more water, more rain is to be expected. This is what the UK experienced with the devastating floods in summer 2007, followed by the wettest summer ever, when 420,000 people were without fresh water, and again in the winter 2013/14 where "electricity needed to be restored to 572,291 properties across the UK" according to *The Observer*, 16 February 2014, p. 6–7 .

versity in Canada looked into which states are most responsible for climate change publishing their study in 'Environmental Research Letters'.[17] It turned out that seven states are responsible for nearly three quarters of global warming:

- USA at 20 per cent, being responsible for a rise in ground temperature of 0.15 degrees Celsius;
- China and Russia accounting for 0.06 degrees each;
- Brazil and India about 0.05 degrees each;
- Germany and Great Britain about 0.03 degrees each.

If the rise is measured with respect to population, however, China and India, which together constitute nearly half of Earth's inhabitants, slide back to position 19 and 20 in the global warming stakes. Examining responsibility for climate change from this point, Great Britain comes first, followed by the USA, Canada, Russia, Germany, the Netherlands and Australia.

The Warsaw Summit on Climate Change in November 2013 was intended to provide the "opportunity to further detail the adaptation implementation by determining the role of adaptation in the 2015 agreement" to be reached in Paris in place of the 1997 Kyoto agreement "and by renewing the international adaptation knowledge management." The industrialized countries would have to "provide adequate financial and institutional support to further advance disaster preparedness and resilience of the poor countries." The result of that summit was, however, that industrialized countries and so-called developing countries are now obliged to report on their CO_2 emissions.

Considering the foreseeable problems and the inactivity of governments, eg with regard to the Warsaw conference in November 2013, one can agree with *The European Voice*, that short-time economicult interests still dominate long-term environment and energy policies. The (non-)result is that everything goes on as it is and nothing changes – a strategy which risks increasing global warming beyond the originally targeted maximum of 2 degrees Celsius, causing even more problems worldwide. Germany, the former role model, under the Conservative-Liberal government fell from being in eighth place to nineteenth place in the Germanwatch's climate index.

- H<u>ole</u>s in the **protective ozone layer**, causing more damaging space radiation to reach Earth.

- The loss of **soil fertility** through over-salting and over-cementing, and over-fertilizing, as well as overloading the soil with insecticides, fungicides and herbicides as part of monoculture farming as well as a decrease of invertebrates in the soil which play a vital role in decomposition and "ensuring soil remains packed with nutrients".[18]

17   *Spiegel* online, 17 January 2014
18   *The Week*, 9 August 2014, p. 19, reported that the "world's stock of spineless creatures – insects,

- **Soil erosion** due to the felling of rainforests and the forests of the Alps. And this despite the fact that a single tree absorbs about three tons of CO_2 just by growing, an amount equivalent to that produced by driving 15,000 km in a small car.[19]

- The consequent loss of the natural habitat's **ability to regenerate,** on which plants and animals depend.

- The **extinction** of plant and animal species,[20] such as bees which are necessary for pollination, as recently observed in Europe, the US, China, Japan and Egypt,[21], leading to reductions in harvests. The International Union for Conservation of Nature (IUCN) in Geneva, the biggest network of government and non-government environmental organizations worldwide, has published a *Red List* of all species on Earth which are in danger of extinction, once they are gone, they cannot be brought back to life, no matter how much money is spent. Society must recognize the significance of these species, which are sometimes alleged to be useless, but have their own right to existence, as pointed out by Ellen Butcher from the Zoological Society of London (ZSL).[22] The list of the 100 most endangered plants, animals and fungi is produced by more than 8,000 scientists of the IUCN and contains species from 48 countries. The reasons for extinction are overwhelmingly economic, according to Simon Stuart, chief of the IUCN Survival Commission.

- Extinction leads to **genetic erosion** and a reduction of **biodiversity.**

- The focus on extracting **finite, non-regenerative resources,** especially fossil fuels, leads to their depletion so that future generations will not be able to use them.

- Industrial plants also have a **high risk potential,** as in the catastrophes caused by the explosions at the **nuclear power plants** in Chernobyl/USSR in 1986, and Fukushima/Japan in 2011, or the **gas leak** at the chemical plant in Bhopal in 1984.

- A significant burden is placed on the environment by the **dumping of green-house gases** such as carbon dioxide into the atmosphere to an extent not found in nature itself.

---

worms, slugs, snails, spiders and the like – has slumped by 45 per cent over the past 35 years" according to a study of the University College London by the International Union for the Conservation of Nature.

19 In view of which the German UmweltBank AG has decided to donate €5 in support of an afforestation programme in Uganda for every new customer.

20 Niles Eldredge www.actionbioscience.org calles this the "sixth extinction", a man made event, following the first (ca. 440 m years ago), the second (ca. 270 m years go), the third (ca. 245 m years ago), the forth (ca. 210 m years ago) and the fifth (ca. 65 m years ago when "the remaining terrestrial dinosaurs and marine ammonites as well as many other species across the phylogenetic spectrum" were wiped out).

21 According to a report in *The Week*, 26 March 2011, p. 17: "The way we manage nature-based assets, including pollinators, will define our future, said Achim Steiner of the UN Environment Programme. 'The fact is that of the 100 crop species that provide 90 per cent of the world's food, over 70 per cent are pollinated by bees."

    It is no longer any wonder that so much is written about the nutritional values of insects these days. The aim is to change people's perception of insects so that they view them as food.

22 *Der Spiegel*, 11 September 2012

- Also significant is **the depth and speed** of our interaction with nature, as in the case of fossil oil, built-up over millions of years and consumed by man in a mere 150 years.
- Increasing **deforestation, as in the Amazon rainforest,** promotes climate change, where the trees which used to act as a 'green lung' of Earth are being replaced by farm land.
- And the latest warning comes, unusually, from Germany's Bundesnachrichtendienst (BND) which has pointed out that climate change can lead increasingly to strategic conflicts.[23] It foresees that the 450 ppm carbon dioxide line will be crossed even before 2040. This is the critical level which must not be exceeded if we are to prevent global temperatures from rising above two degrees Celsius. If, on the other hand, we continue to burn every fossil fuel known today, 1,700 bn tons of carbon dioxide will be emitted with the result that sea levels will rise even higher, more extreme weather conditions will occur, burdening national economies with huge costs, while people will start leaving their locality to find safer places to live.

Generally, when the environmental crisis is understood as a consequence of man's interaction with nature, we also have to consider that it also leads to problems for men themselves. In case of exhaust gases, for example, polluted air is not only damaging for nature, but also for humans who need to breathe it, especially children and the elderly. Similarly, surface water polluted with chemicals is also a problem for the people who need to drink it, and fertile soil polluted with poisonous chemicals used as herbicides or fungicides is a problem for the people who need to eat the vegetables and fruit grown in the polluted soil. So is the noise of heavy motorway and air traffic a problem, causing rising stress levels and health problems to the people living nearby. From the point of reciprocal interactions, we humans are not only the culprits, but also the victims of the environmental crisis.

In recent years, public concern about these problems has focused on global warming due to climate change.[24] "Tyndall and Fourier," wrote Gabrielle Walter and Sir David King,[25] "had discovered what we now call the greenhouse effect." "Greenhouse gases don't block the air itself, they act more like a one-way mirror," keeping the heat inside Earth's atmosphere, beginning with the Industrial Revolution around 1850. The carbon dioxide "that we animals breathe out," they explain "is taken up by plants, which use it to make their bodies, providing us with the food that completes the cycle"[26] in time – in the past 650,000 years levels have never been as high as today. As a consequence, "the IPCC[27] report predicts that between a fifth and a third of all species on Earth could be at risk of extinction by

---

23 *Spiegel* online, 1 November 2013, based on a report by Reuters

24 "Ice cores from Greenland and the Antarctic prove that the CO_2 concentration in the atmosphere in the last 800,000 years has fluctuated between 180 and 280 parts per million. But current readings at Zeppeling Mountain show 400 ppm." *Der Spiegel*, 'Norway Wants to Become Europe's Battery', 24 May 2012

25 In: *The Hot Topic*, London, 2008. p. 16

26 Ibid, p. 20, a "cycle" in time is open, and has therefore to be called a helix, as explained in ch. 7.

27 IPCC is the Intergovernmental Panel on Climate Change

the end of this century."[28]

Another consequence is that by the end of this century, as Walter and King predicted, or earlier as the US National Snow and Ice Data Centre (NSIDC) in Boulder/Colorado believes, the Arctic, "an ocean surrounded by land," while "Antarctica is a continent surrounded by water,"[29] could be completely ice-free. "The consequences of losing the Arctic's ice coverage for the summer months are expected to be immense. If the white sea ice no longer reflects sunlight back into space, the region can be expected to heat up even more than at present. This could lead to an increase in ocean temperatures with unknown effects on weather systems in northern latitudes." This prediction met with welcoming noises in some quarters, as said, in 2012, we heard that "at least 20 vessels are expected to travel north of Russia between northern Europe and the Bering straits. Last week a Chinese icebreaker made the first voyage in the opposite direction."

So, have governments been regularly dredging rivers, strengthening flood banks and preventing building on flood plains? The answer is that the present government has cut nearly £100 m a year from the Environment Agency's budget along with 15,000 jobs. Such a policy only makes sense if you believe climate change is not happening, or will have no consequences for our lives.

The most northern German Bundesland, Schleswig-Holstein, which has 1,125 km dykes to the North Sea on its west and the Baltic Sea on its east side, has recently updated its general plan for coastal flood defences for the next ten to fifteen years. The first protection plan against flooding was set in motion in 1962, after a disastrous flood killed more than 300 people in the north of Germany. The protective dykes are now to be built higher, wider and stronger, so that they can be raised with relative ease later on, if the situation demands. 354,000 people live in the endangered coastal area. €200 million is necessary to strengthen 93 km of dykes, the cost of which will be shared between the Federal Government, Schleswig-Holstein and the EU.[30] The reinforcements will be carried out even though the dykes were strong enough to hold back the floods of June 2013.

The German government has announced an action plan on climate, reported by *Kieler Nachrichten*, 4 December 2014. Until 2020 CO_2 emissions should be reduced by 40 per cent - compared to 1990, especially the energy efficiency of new buildings should be improved. That equals a greenhouse gase reduction of 78 million tons, especially in traffic, by supporting car sharing, saving petrol, supporting public traffic infrastructure, building cycling roads, supporting the transport of goods, were possible, on water instead of roads, in farming by regulating the use of fertilisers and increase organic farming, in energetic renovation of existing buildings and improving craftsmen's knowledge. However, it forgot to improve as well the ecological knowledge of architects and engineers, educated at universities, as well as setting a role model itself by ecological renovation public buildings, as ministries, schools, council houses, railway stations, police stations, care homes and others.

---

28 Ibid, p. 41
29 *The Guardian*, 24 August 2012, p. 22
30 *Kieler Nachrichten*, 12 December 2012, p. 12

News on climate change came from Mauna Loa observatory in Hawaii which measures greenhouse gases for the US National Oceanic and Atmospheric Administration (NOAA).[31] "The chances of the world holding temperature rises to 2 C – the level considered 'safe' by scientists – appear to be fading, with US monitors reporting the second greatest annual rise in carbon dioxide emissions in 2012... 'It's just a testament to human influence being dominant,'" remarked Peter Tans of NOAA. "The Mauna Loa measurements coincide with a new peer-reviewed study of the pledges made by countries to reduce CO_2 emissions. The Dutch government's scientific advizers show rich countries will have to reduce emissions by 50 per cent below 1990 levels by 2020 if there is to be even a medium chance of limiting warming to 2 C, thus preventing some of the worst impacts of climate change... 'So the climate has in one sense actually changed and we are now entering a new series of climatic conditions that we just haven't seen before,'" said Tim Flannery, head of the Australian government's climate change commission.

One consequence of climate change the scientists hold for certain that "the people least responsible for the problem will also be the ones to suffer first and most."[32] No fairness there.

Energy minister Ed Davey fears that "the world is losing the race to keep global warming in check."[33] "The Liberal Democrat minister said attempts to prevent global temperatures from rising more than two degrees Celsius above the pre-industrial level, generally regarded as global warming's danger threshold, were not on course to succeed... A World Bank report published the same week showed some of the dangers of a world warmed by four degrees... Average global temperatures have already risen about 0.8 degrees Celsius above pre-industrial levels. Attempting to keep the rise to below two degrees is the official aim of the UN's Climate Convention, and the official policy of Britain and the rest of the EU... But many observers are increasingly concerned about the so-called 'emissions gap' – the divergence between the CO_2 emissions limits that are necessary to keep below two degrees, and what is actually being emitted. The so-called 'emission gap' is widening every year, according to the UN Environment Programme referenced by Mr Davey."

It seems that governments are not doing enough to keep climate change at bay. They do not seem to inform the public about the dangers, leaving it to scientists who sometimes agree with each other and sometimes not, and instead of acting governments wait until everybody feels the consequences so that the inhabitants of a country can be convinced that more measures are necessary – mostly according to the logic of the traditional pattern: leave everything as it is but spend a bit of additional money on it. Die Welt reported that climate protection is marginalized in Europe'[34] because different interests of the 27 European governments prohibit activities against it. For example Great Britain and France want to retain nuclear power, while Germany's government has decided (again, but now with a

---

31   The Guardian, 9 March 2013 p. 10

32   Ibid, p. 57

33   The Independent,3 December 2012, p. 26

34   "Klimaschutz wird in Europa zur Nebensache", 19 April 2012 p. 10

Conservative and Liberal majority) to phase it out because of its radiation hazards and costs, focussing instead on renewable primary resources for electricity generation, which does not emit carbon dioxide.

The Climate Change Performance Index 2013,[35] published by Germanwatch e.V. and Climate Action Network Europe, compared 58 countries together responsible for more than 90 per cent of global energy related CO_2 emissions. Germany (€), United Kingdom (£) and USA ($) were valuated in terms of their emission levels, use of renewable energy, efficiency and climate policies:

Germany	67,54 points – 8th in the league table,
United Kingdom	67,33 points – 10th in the league table,
USA	53,51 points – 43rd in the league table.

The Climate Change Performance Index aims to: "encourage political and social pressure on those countries which have, up to now, failed to take ambitious actions on climate protection as well as to highlight countries with best-practice climate policies." However, the richest country, the US, made the least effort to cope with climate change.[36]

The Independent[37] pointed out that public concern seems to have gone cold, that "the 'perceived seriousness' of climate change has also fallen sharply since the unsuccessful UN Climate Change Summit in Copenhagen in December 2009. The summit ended in what was described as 'confusion, disagreement and disarray' as political leaders failed to agree a legally binding deal to curb greenhouse gas emissions... Doug Miller, chairman of GlobeScan said: 'Evidence of environmental damage is stronger than ever, but our data shows that economic crisis and a lack of political leadership mean that the public are starting to tune out.'"

It seems that politicians believe in the same economicult path as they have done before, mostly advized by economicult theorists, although the banking crisis as well as the environmental crisis could and should have lead to a re-think and perhaps even a new understanding.

The UN-climate report[38], presented on 27 September 2013 in Stockholm, the fifth of its kind, came to the following conclusions:

Since the beginning of the 20th century the sea level has already risen by 20 cm and the air has warmed up by 0.9 degrees, while snow and ice have melted considerably. This process will go on. Scientists are 95 per cent sure that climate change is caused by carbon dioxide which we release into the environment. CO_2 emissions from manufacture or electricity generation have increased in recent years by 50 per cent. More natural resources are used generating more emissions – and we view this development still as increasing rather than reducing prosperity, while the IPCC has warned that the consequences of our trades-as-before will

35   This can be downloaded from: www.germanwatch.org/en/ccpi
36   The global economic slowdown caused by the banking crisis might have been expected to play a role in reducing greenhouse gases, especially in the USA.
37   8 February 2013, p. 19
38   *Spiegel* online, 27 September 2013

change the world rapidly when this process would otherwise have happened over hundreds or thousands of years.

It is, however, a wonder that the EU summit of October 2014 had decided that CO_2 emissions should be reduced until 2030 by 40 per cent, while at that time it was 14.1 per cent in the EU, and that a bigger share of renewables should be used. China and the USA, countries which are with nearly 40 per cent responsibility the biggest emitters of greenhouse gases, seemed to have changed their position a little, "the coalition of former unwilling is now becoming a coalition of the willing," resumed *The Guardian*, 13 November 2014, p. 23.

In the next chapter we will list instruments and measures that can be taken, following the tertiary pattern, the process of reciprocal interaction. Before this we will discuss how environmental damage is viewed by economicult theorists – at least by these who are concerned about it, and have examined the consequences of our current interactions with nature.

If we study the published works of those who care about the environmental crisis, we can differentiate at least three different approaches in the search for an explanation of why such a crisis has developed:

- environmental economics,
- dual economics
- and ecological economics.

The three approaches are generally conflated in the public debate, however, so it is necessary to make their differences transparent:

10.2. The environmental crisis as seen by environmental economists

Environmental economists, eg Lutz Wicke, in: *Umweltoekonomie*,[39] argue that environmental damage is a daily by-product of human life, because humans always need to interfere with their environment. In this way, environmental damage, pollution and the loss of biodiversity are considered as a natural phenomenon. They are part of the law of nature. The problem is viewed as a natural one, not a cultural.

Arthur Koestler summarized this position with his famous saying that humans are an "error of evolution"[40] and consequently, it would serve them right if they were to die out.

---

39 Muenchen, 1982. Lutz Wicke was a former scientific director of Germany's Federal Environment Agency in Berlin.

40 Arthur Koestler, *Der Mensch Irrlaeufer der Evolution, Die Kluft zwischen Denken und Handeln, Eine Anatomie menschlicher Vernunft und Unvernunft*, Frankfurt, 1989

Reasons for the environmental crisis put forward by the environmental economists are:

- population growth,
- consumer greed which leads to unhealthy economic growth,
- overloading of the environment with damaging materials, which nature would not be able to absorb in the normal way,
- unknown future technical changes which could threaten the environment in unforeseen ways.

A commonly cited example of man-made environmental damage is the deforestation of the Mediterranean region, 2,000 years ago. However, those who use this example generally fail to recognize that, in ancient times, the region could easily have been reforested as the trees would have grown again. Today we are in a totally different position, plants and animals die out because their living conditions have been destroyed. We have to deal with a damage of a very different nature. This is not really seen by environmental economists.

Environmental economists further argue that economic theory has forgotten nature. They claim this because they see nature as a free commodity. This means that damaging material can be released into the natural environment at no cost at all for whoever wants to get rid of his waste. In this way instigators save costs which they would have to pay if the natural environment were not free to use. The costs are externalized from their individual balance sheet and will be paid – if at all – by the public.

Nature is seen as a free commodity, because, eg air and water, referred to as 'environmental media', are hard to demarcate and consequently impossible to trade. Although there is a need for a 'clean' environment – whatever this means, nobody produces it, as there is no market' price for it.

To internalize the problem and burden the instigators with the costs they have saved, environmental economists suggest that unspoilt nature – or 'clean' environment – should be defined as a fourth factor of production besides land, labour and money. It should be called a public factor. In this way politicians could set limits for pollution and create tools to secure the production of clean nature, for which then a market' price would result.

But, how can they do this? A market' price is a purely culturally invented expression which has no meaning in the natural world. And how can the depletion of resources, for example, be expressed in a price? Would it not mean that the price has to rise into infinity? And who would then be able to pay it?

This approach shows that the understanding and advice of environmental economists remains within the framework of classical economicult thinking. Nature is still seen as a factor, a commodity external to man, 'land', when nature's interaction with man is expressed. The natural "services" without which no life on Earth would be possible, are viewed as if they are capital, nature's capital. And a forth factor, clean environment, would not change this view. Environmental economists try to extend the present market' system understanding on to spheres which are not yet included, instead of asking whether exactly this thinking is the very reason for the problem.

We can conclude that such an approach is purely quantitative while not having modernized classical economicult assumptions. Therefore it cannot be the solution. However, this approach is shared by UNEP and the World Bank, calling it "green economy".

One method they recommended was to set up a market' for carbon dioxide. Under this system, governments grant private companies a certain amount of CO_2 emissions. If the companies do not use up their full CO_2 allowance, they can sell it to others. A market' for CO_2 emissions would be created with a price for CO_2 emissions. The hope was, that it would be cheaper to invest in CO_2 saving technologies and so reduce pollution, than buying CO_2 allowances from others.

Michael J. Sandel[41] discussed whether a government should limit emissions and punish companies which exceed that limit, or implement tradable rights for pollution. The latter, however, he pointed out, leads to emissions being treated as a cost, to be avoided, rather than waste, a damaging bi-product, and this would be important, but not essential.

Australia chose a different route: it introduced a carbon tax which 'forces about 300 of the worst-polluting businesses to pay a levy of about US$24 per tonne of greenhouse gases emitted. Protesters marched through Sydney against the 'toxic tax', and Tony Abbott of the Liberal (conservative) opposition vowed to repeal it if elected,' *The Week* reported 7 July 2012, writing on 26 July, p. 9, that Abbot, now prime minister, has scrapped the carbon tax.

In April 2013 Carbon Market Watch in Brussels concluded that the CO_2 emission market' was not working, the organization's director, Eva Filzmoser called it[42] a big flop." Too many pollution rights were on the market', and companies were inventing too many ineffective and therefore questionable Clean Development Mechanism projects to offset their CO_2 emissions. Hans-Josef Fell, Member of the Bundestag, Germany's federal parliament and architect of the Feed-In-Tariff law (a government guarantee[43] for the electricity produced locally and sold to the big power companies) remarked: "It is important to note that the number of tonnes of CO_2 traded under the emissions trading scheme, therefore causing costs, is much higher than the number of tonnes of CO_2 actually reduced as the desired result of the trading... Thus the cost for avoiding the emission of one tonne of CO_2 through emissions trading was 1325 euros in 2007. In comparison: with the help of the Renewable Energy Sources Act (EEG) the CO_2 emissions were reduced by about 57 million tonnes with additional costs of 5.56 billion euros in 2007, which is around 98 euros per tonne. In addition, 100-thousand jobs were created and a tremendous innovation was developed and the penetration of zero emission technologies was further promoted. After all, Europe has learned from this experi

---

41 Michael J. Sandel, *Was man fuer Geld nicht kaufen kann, Die moralischen Grenzen des Marktes*, New York, 2012, p. 94

42 *Der Spiegel* 14/2013, p. 64, "die grosse Luftnummer".

43 Copied meanwhile by more than 60 different nations, a 'feed-in-tariff' is not a government subsidy as no money is handed out by a government.

ence. From 2013 onwards, the emissions certificates should now be auctioned. However, it remains to be seen whether this actually will improve the effectiveness of emissions trading significantly."[44]

The reality, however, was that no market' developed to help saving CO_2 emissions, but a huge fraud started about German value-added tax, which seems to have cost the taxpayer €800 m, reported *Der Spiegel*, 24/2014, p. 78, and the Deutsche Bank seems to have played an important role supporting that swindle. The Frankfurt public prosecution office hold 160 employees in 150 companies responsible, 50 of it in Germany, with €127 m confiscated. The fraud seem to have started in 2009 in London. It was managed from Dubai through First Bancorp Ltd. and offshore centres in Cyprus and Hong Kong.

Furthermore, based on this sort of thinking of a market' for CO_2 emissions, it can never become the aim to avoid more than the permitted amount of environmental damages. It does not support the aim to try and live sustainably, because the assumption is that environmental damage always will take place, as the relationship between humans and nature is always damaging to nature.

To compensate for this idea that damaging the environment is a kind of natural law, subscribers to this view demand the protection of certain areas of 'natural beauty'[45]. These conservation areas should be kept free from all human activity, so that nature can flourish there – as if such a thing were possible, as if not everything on Earth is always engaged in a process of interaction in space-time.

The problem with such a view is that the question of why an environmental crisis is taking place has not been sufficiently thought through. If we try to answer this question, it becomes obvious that the cultural understanding of how we define and how we deal with nature, must have caused the problem, ie the economicult understanding of nature as production factor 'land'. It is not, that nature is forgotten in economicult theory. The question, as already discussed, is whether the opinion about nature/land being merely a production factor is right or wrong.

The amount of CO_2 in Earth's atmosphere is higher than it has ever been in the last 600,000 years. It must be related to human activity. And the explanation for the environmental crisis needs to be based on what we think of as normal in terms of our cultural relationship with nature over time. It cannot be right to merely extend today's economic theory without analyzing our understanding of nature. To leave our existing understanding unquestioned and even extend it to include unspoilt nature – as a fourth factor of production – will not solve the problem. We have to recognize that it is not just a quantitative procedure that is necessary, but also a qualitative one which analyzes our understanding of nature.

---

44   Hans-Josef Fell, *Global Cooling - Strategies for Climate Protection*, London, 2012, p. 125

45   Hundreds of so called "compensation banks" have been established in the USA, a documentation by the French journalists Sandrine Feydel and Denis Delestrac, broadcasted in Germany by arte tv on 3 February 2015, showed. These, for example, the Malua BioBank in Sabal, offer certificates of ownership of natural areas, as the ranforests on Borneo. Companies which want to realise a certain bulding project can set-off the damage caused on nature by buying a part of such areas without a change in their plans, without having to build in a sustainable, not damaging way. And the more these natural areas decrease, the value of the certificates will rise – nature as the object of even more speculation – which the protagonists call "green economy."

This is the problem: leaving our understanding as it is, treats the environmental crisis as an additional one, on top of all the other daily problems governments have to deal with, such as the provision of more well paid jobs for people instead of a subject which needs to be integrated. In this way the environmental crisis does not lead to a real qualitative change including all of governments' and citizens' activities, for example avoiding the production of waste from the beginning of every interaction with nature, or using renewable energy instead of fossil fuels. Instead it is only seen as a new opportunity for businesses, creating jobs at the end-of-pipe-industries.

Even investing into recycling would not be sufficient. According to Steve Bogan in *The Week*, "the UK generates 290 million tonnes of waste per year, of which 22.9 million comes from our homes. In 1995 we recycled just 7.5 per cent of our household waste; today that figure stands at 43 per cent and is well on course to meet an EU target of 50 per cent by 2020."[46] "Waste has become a commodity," said Pal Spillum, head of waste recovery at the Climate and Pollution Agency in Norway[47]... More than a third of the paper and plastic collected by British local authorities, supermarkets and businesses for recycling is sent to China... Norway is importing as much rubbish as it can get its hands on, in an effort to generate more energy by burning waste in vast incinerators." Waste is necessary for the end-off-the-pipe industry, as it is their resource, and it has become big business.

This raises the question of who owns the waste which businesses and households would like to get rid of? In Germany, remarkably enough, the Bundesverband der Entsorgungswirtschaft and the Bundesverband Sekundaerrohstoffe und Entsorgung published a study on the ownership of packing waste[48] on 9 July, 2013, pleading that the organization that collects waste, should own it and be allowed to do what it wants with it eg recycle it.

This interest in a growing amount of waste is naturally hindering any long-term strategy to avoid it or at least reduce it eg by changing production in such a way that goods last longer and are easier to repair, so that they do not need to be replaced with new purchases, a 'need' which is artificially built-in to them in the interest of the producers, as we have seen. The newly established recycling industry can then claim that reducing waste may lead to a loss of jobs and a reduction in the gross domestic product, something no government would want, an absolutely absurd consequence and the reverse of what is necessary.

Another industry is geo-engineering. Here we find the same principle: real change from the beginning is not happening, instead the economicult pattern is extended into hitherto unaffected areas, here: to remodel the whole planet.

The same goes for Carbon Capture and Storage technology (CCS). Carbon dioxide is produced by using fossil fuels, and a new industry is then created to store it[49] – with taxpayer's money of course. While the real thing to do would be

46   15 June 2013, p. 52
47   According to Helen Russell "Norwegians turn Europe's trash into cash but fuel concern over future of recycling" in: *The Guardian*, 15 June 2013, p. 37
48   According to *Kieler Nachrichten*, 10 July, 2013, p. 7
49   A proposition which none of the parties agreed to in the regional Parliament of Schleswig-Holstein Parliament, for example.

switching to renewable fuels which can be used without CO_2 emissions. According to the same logic, a similar 'new industry' was proposed to treat the oceans, so that they would be able to absorb more CO_2 emissions. Thankfully, scientists from the Alfred-Wegener-Institute (AWI) for Polar and Ocean Research in Bremerhaven rejected this plan. They assessed the energy required (including emissions) to mine the minerals and found that 'fertilizing' the oceans in this way would not make any sense.[50] People only invent such ideas to extend the traditional 'logic' and avoid the real problems instead of embracing change. Innovation, it seems, is something rarely welcomed.

Environmental economists still see the problem from an outdated viewpoint, according to which nature is a factor external to and separate from humans , and they believe that such an understanding of and relationship with nature is natural, when it is cultural.

They hardly recognise that our knowledge and our understanding of nature has evolved over the years. It is therefore out of the question for economicult theorists to accept the environmental crisis as a crisis initiated by man. They might register some of the problems, perhaps, for example that fossil fuels will come to an end as no new hydro-carbons will be created by nature in the near future, but they do not see this as a catastrophe, as they believe that new ways of finding fossil energy resources will emerge. They view the environmental crisis as an additional problem, for which, they hope, additional public funds will be provided.

It does not occur to them that their (cultural) model of the world needs to be re-thought. And they never seem aware of one other important factor, that renewable resources can be used by everyone, directly and free of charge, and 'Free is Cheaper'.[51] Perhaps this is even looked at as a disadvantage for businesses – who knows.

Therefore let's report about the effects one human being had on nature. Thomas Midgley Jr. (1889–1942) can be legitimately identified as the single organism in the world's history with the most damaging influence on the environment. As Bill Bryson[52] and others have pointed out, Midgley discovered in 1921, while working for the General Motors Research Corporation in Dayton/Ohio that a compound called tetraethyl lead "significantly reduced the juddering condition known as engine knock". Midgley mixed lead into petrol to stop such 'knocking'. It was called ethyl gasoline.

However, tetraethyl lead is a neurotoxin, which caused the death of nearly a hundred people and ill health in the untold numbers of others who produced it. Even Midgley himself got ill. Tetraethyl lead was historically mixed into plates and beakers and into paint, and is still found in venison. When it was put into petrol and used in car engines it was spread all over the world, causing irreversible damage. In 2000, the EU forbade its use. Today petrol is lead-free. And one wonders sometimes, why it has taken some countries so long to implement this EU directive.

---

50 *Der Spiegel* reported this on 22 January 2013 in *'Forscher erteilen Ozeanduengung eine Absage'*
51 Ken R. Smith, *Free is Cheaper*, Gloucester, 1988
52 Bill Bryson, *A Short History of Nearly Everything*, London, 2004 p. 193–194

Incidentally, recent studies in the UK and USA have shown that there is strong evidence of another consequence of using neurotoxin, a correlation between tetraethyl lead and criminality. The investigation found that the level of criminality was highest in inner cities, where was also the highest amount of lead in the environment. George Monbiot could not at first believe, that lead in petrol could have such an influence on criminality. "The hypothesis was so exotic that I laughed," he wrote,[53] then: "It seems crazy but the evidence about lead is stacking up. Behind crimes that have destroyed so many lives, is there a much greater crime?" Indeed there is. Scientific evidence showed that after all other variables like social, economic and legal factors have been taken out of the equation, "violent crime peaks around 20 years after lead pollution peaks. The crime rates in big and small cities in the US, once wildly different, have now converged, also some 20 years after the phase-out."

One would now expect such a neurotoxin will be banned not only from use, but also from production. Unfortunately this is not the case.[54] Monbiot reports: "There is only one remaining manufacturer of tetraethyl lead on earth. It's based in Ellesmere Port in Britain, and it's called Innospec." "... tetraethyl lead is being exported to Afghanistan, Algeria, Burma, Iraq, North Korea, Sierra Leone and Yemen, countries afflicted either by chaos or by governments who don't give a damn about their people... The UK government tells me that because tetraethyl lead is not on the European list of controlled exports, there is nothing to prevent Innospec from selling to whoever it wants... there lies, behind the crimes that have destroyed so many lives and filled so many prisons, a much greater crime." So bearing in mind its consequences, why is 'the greenest government ever' unable or unwilling to forbid the production of tetraethyl lead?

Bryson also described how Midgley then turned his attention to another technological problem: "Refrigerators in the 1920s were often appallingly risky because they used insidious and dangerous gases that sometimes seeped out. One leak from a refrigerator at a hospital in Cleveland, Ohio, in 1929 killed more than a hundred people. Midgley set out to create a gas that was stable, non-flammable, non-corrosive and safe to breathe. With an instinct for the regrettable that was almost uncanny, he invented chlorofluorocarbons, or CFCs."[55]

Let Bryson explain why it was not such a splendidly good idea to produce CFCs after all: "CFCs went into production in the early 1930s and found a thousand applications in everything from car air-conditioners to deodorant sprays before it was noticed, half a century later, that they were devouring the ozone in the stratosphere... A single kilogram of CFCs can capture and annihilate 70,000 kilograms of atmospheric ozone. CFCs also hang around for a long time – about a century on average – wreaking havoc all the while. And they are great heat sponges. A single CFC molecule is about 10,000 times more efficient than a

---

53 George Monbiot, "Yes, lead poisoning could really be a cause of violent crime," in *The Guardian*, 7 January 2013
54 *The Week* published 16 August 2014 an article from *The Independent on Sunday* reporting that three employees of Innospec went to jail because it was found that they had been "bribing officials in Iraq and Indonesia into buying chemicals from their firm, Innospec."
55 Ibid, p. 195

molecule of carbon dioxide – and carbon dioxide is of course no slouch itself as greenhouse gas. In short, chlorofluorocarbons may ultimately prove to be just about the most damaging invention of the 20th century."[56] Consequently in 1987 The Montreal Protocol on Substances that Deplete the Ozone Layer phased out these chemicals. The United Nations Environment Programme Ozone Secretariat could report that "atmospheric levels of key ozone depleting substances are declining… and will return to pre-1980 levels by around the middle of this century and the Antarctic Ozone around 15 years later."[57]

So – can the environmental economists really explain the environmental crisis and deny man's responsibility for it, if just one single organism can cause such far-reaching damage to nature? Obviously, they are not able nor they are not willing to.

10.3. ... as seen by dual economists

Dual economists – such as: Hans-Christoph Binswanger, H. Frisch, H. G. Nutzinger et al, in: *Arbeit ohne Umweltzerstoerung, Strategien einer neuen Wirtschaftspolitik*[58] – heavily criticize the environmental economists' understanding of the environmental crisis. They believe that environmental damage is not a constant of nature, but a consequence of the historic form of human dealings with nature in industrialized societies. Dual economists understand man as the author of environmental damage claiming that: economists have to give up their mechanistic view of the world,[59] a view which it is easy to agree with.

Dual economists think that environmental damage has cultural causes, arguing that environmental economists reduce the whole relationship between humans and nature to market' and money. In their view it is not only the production side, but also the consumption side of economics, plus the disposal of household waste that should be looked at. This part of economic activity, we know, remains in the shadow of economicult theory. They refer to themselves as "dual economists", because they want to include the consumption as well as the production aspect of the economy. And most certainly, they are right to do so.

Dual economists argue that environmental economists only want to market the environment further, while doing this would both legitimize present structures of allocation and neglect changing consumer habits. Therefore they propose a change in the way mankind deals with nature. They favour a change in the style of consumption and production with the aim of rendering both sides – from the outset – more sustainable. Economic growth could then continue in a qualitative sense.

---

56 Ibid, p. 196
57 http://ozone.unep.org; reported in a lot of newspapers, ie *Frankfurter Allgemeine Sonntagszeitung,*, 14 September 2014, p. 58
58 Frankfurt, 1983
59 Ibid, p. 90

Their concept can be summarized into three statements:

1. The merely quantitative term used by environmental economists with respect to money and the market' should be extended by considering qualitative criteria as well.
2. A new qualitative and consequently different kind of interaction with nature should be instigated. For example, instead of concentrating on making labour more efficient, the use of natural resources should be made more efficient, decoupling it from economic growth, and a more sustainable use of resources should be aimed at, in this way also reducing the dependence on finite resources.[60]
3. Unpaid and therefore informal labour should be valued higher than labour which is paid.

Dual economists claim that, at the moment, the welfare of a country is measured by the Gross Domestic Product (GDP), which, although not invented as a measure of welfare, only contains turnovers on the market. They propose that the human need for justice, self-determination and self-actualization should be also valued, and rather more than just the financial balance sheet. They want to decouple the increase of the GDP from the increase in consumption regarding energy and other finite natural resources. Products should be made more efficient by reducing the use of energy as well as natural material, on both sides, production and consumption. Products should last longer and be easier to repair, they propose.

From their point of view derives the call for an efficiency revolution, first proposed by Amory Lovins of the Rocky Mountain Institute in Snowmass, Colorado, USA. Lovins claimed that customers of energy companies do not want to buy electricity in kilowatt hours, but would prefer different sustainable energy services. He proposed a 'soft' path for the future energy strategy.

Generally, dual economists claim that the focus of economics should switch from the production of material goods to immaterial services ie from the secondary to the tertiary sector. They believe that increasing tertiary services will be more environmentally friendly, as less material resources are used – an argument which has already been discussed.

Since dual economists advocate increasing the productivity of resources rather than the productivity of labour, a new strategy for work is also proposed, suggesting that non-paid as well as paid labour should be valued. Non-paid labour includes, as we know, work which one does for oneself as well as for the members of a household. This proposal is based on their conviction that today's labour is wrongly separated into paid and unpaid labour, while the majority of working hours are done in the informal, unpaid sphere. Dual economists call this form of labour self-work[61] or in German: 'Eigenarbeit'.

---

60 As advocated by: Andrew Simms of the New Economics Foundation (NEF), in: *Cancel the Apocalypse: The New Path to Prosperity*, London, 2013
61 Christine and Ernst Ulrich von Weizsaecker, '*Eigenarbeit in einer dualen Wirtschaft*', in: *Anders arbeiten, anders wirtschaften*, published by Joseph Huber, Frankfurt, 1979, cf. ch. 7.

Their best-known political advice is – without doubt – to implement so called 'green taxes'. A few years ago, these taxes were introduced in Germany, however, their concept was not really understood by politicians. Therefore it is necessary to make a few remarks about the importance of 'green taxes':

Dual economists claim that today's political system is being moved in the wrong direction, as instead of rationalizing human labour, environmental damage should be rationalized. To achieve this aim, they propose to make it more expensive to use natural resources by taxing them. This would give businesses and consumers the incentive to save resources. This is the one side of the concept.

The other side is aimed at reducing the cost of labour. To do this, a government should spend what it collected from higher taxes on natural resources on decreasing tax on paid labour.

It shows, the concept of 'green taxes' has two components, it is dual: savings of resources by making them dearer, and spending the receipts to disburden labour. The aim is certainly not to allow the government to collect higher taxes, but to achieve a better balance between the use of natural resources and labour, thus creating more jobs as labour will be made cheaper. One side of their concept means to be burdened more with the aim of relieving the other side. Therefore, green taxes are neutral to the public budget, a zero-sum. So much for the theory.

In reality, people were not informed about the double-sided nature of green taxes, so, of course they opposed them, and the government was only interested in collecting a higher amount of tax while not reducing labour costs. It really is a pity that the dual economists' theory was so wrongly understood and applied, but who is to blame?

Consequently we can point out, that the dual economics concept is a relatively better explanation of the environmental crisis, because it also refers to the aspect of human activity, which is neglected in the classically-based theory. Also, it is a better explanation because it tries to include both quantitative and qualitative elements.

Nevertheless, the questions dual economists raise are not really answered. For example, how can the importance of paid labour be reduced and the importance of non-marketed labour increase if only paid labour enables people to finance their living in an economicult society? And: can dual economists' solutions justify cuts of paid jobs? Otherwise, what does their concept mean for women – because for women exactly the opposite is necessary: more qualified and highly paid labour, and certainly not more unpaid services, wherever? And what do they mean when they say that the industrialized labouring man is the cause for destroying the natural environment? Are human beings not also part of nature – natural living beings?

In raising these questions we come to the third attempt to understand the problem. This is the concept of ecological economics.

10.4. ... as seen by ecological economists

An ecological economist[62] agrees with dual economists that we are experiencing a crisis of culture, not of nature, a crisis in the relationship between man and nature.

To understand it, it is useful to return to the meaning of the word 'ecology', as mentioned in chapter 7, coined in 1866 by Ernst Haeckel, German biologist and friend of Charles Darwin, in his book: *Generelle Morphologie der Organismen*,[63] where he defined 'ecology' as relationships between organisms and their external environment. Therefore, the word 'ecology' has a very different meaning compared to its contemporary usage, hence the necessity of examining its roots. We can consequently assert that 'ecology' is no substitute for 'nature' or 'environment' or 'green', instead 'ecology' describes related processes rather than things or objects.

The relationship between humans and nature is constituted by reciprocal interaction, by work. Georg Picht[64] (1913–1982) was therefore right to state that with 'ecology' a new quality of rationality had arrived in the world. With it, the traditional classically scientific Human Exemptionalism Paradigm (HEP) has been extended and transformed into a New Ecological Paradigm (NEP) where humans are included as part of nature and different historic forms of culture, thus participating in both the preservation as well as the development of their society in time.

Edward O. Wilson[65] has formulated the difference between the approach of an economist and an ecologist to their subjects as follows: "The economist is focused on production and consumption. These are what the world wants and needs, he says. He is right, of course. Every species lives on production and consumption... The tree finds and consumes nutrients and sunlight; the leopard finds and consumes the deer. And the farmer clears both away to find space and raise corn – for consumption. The economists' thinking is based on precise models of rational choice and near-horizon time lines. His parameters are the gross domestic product, trade balance, and competitive index. He sits on corporate boards, travels to Washington, and occasionally appears on television talk shows. The planet, he insists, is perpetually fruitful and still under-utilized. The ecologist has a different worldview. He is focused on unsustainable crop yields, overdrawn aquifers, and ecosystems that are under threat. His voice is also heard, albeit faintly, in high government and corporate circles. He sits on non-profit foundation boards, writes for *Scientific American*, and is sometimes called to Washington. The planet, he insists, is exhausted and in trouble."

This allows us a first conclusion: ecological economics must be based on activities, on the tertiary pattern of reciprocal interactions between humans and between humans and nature in time. With this approach, people are included into economic theory as real, active and decision-making subjects who are involved in their own historic form of society. Their historic form of society can either be

---

62   A position, defined for example by the author in: *Oekologisches Arbeiten*, Wiesbaden, 1986
63   Berlin, 1866, p. 286
64   Georg Picht, '*Ist Humanoekologie moeglich?*' In: *C. Eisenbart, Humanoekologie und Frieden*, Stuttgart, 1979
65   Edward O. Wilson, *The Future of Life*, London, 2002, p. 24

preserved or changed into another form, for example where nature is understood as the BASE of all life with its own laws and its own purposes.

Such a conclusion allows us to formulate a genuine modern economic theory. Let us remember that when analyzing traditional economic thinking, we did not find a consistent definition of labour. Instead, the concept of labour was found to contain various divisions, for example between the labouring man and his own inalienable ability, between a given task and the result of that task, between dependent paid and independent unpaid labour, and so on. However, these divisions can now be removed. Instead, one exact definition of work can be introduced, based on physics, describing the labour of man as well as the labour of nature.

Environmental and dual economists viewed nature as a factor, seeing nature as man's external environment. They defined a human being as separate from nature, and in this thinking they continued to reproduce 17th-century ideas about the split between the material body and the immaterial soul. For Descartes, eg only human beings were alive and gifted with consciousness, whereas nature was lifeless, limitless, unchanging from the time it was created, *natura naturata*. As mentioned earlier, this view, implying that human activities have no effect on nature, helps in a way to understand the current disavowal of the environmental crisis.

With ecological economics all of these divisions can be overcome. Human beings can now be understood as natural, living, material beings, capable of self-awareness and consciousness. One of the most important insights of ecological economics, therefore, relates not only to the nature allegedly 'outside of' humans, but also to our understanding of ourselves. The natural philosopher Klaus-Michael Meyer-Abich has proposed that we should no longer talk about the environment as if it is external to us, but as our co-world, "*unsere Mit-Welt*".[66]

This leads to a <u>second conclusion</u>: in ecological economics, humans are seen as a part of nature, as living, natural beings, involved in the continuously ongoing process of reciprocal interaction through which they evolved from the animal realm. It follows that if human beings are viewed as part of nature and nature is considered their living BASE of existence, than air and water can't be labelled 'environmental media', but must be referred to as primary for life. Seeing air and water in this way is beyond environmental economists' understanding.

Additionally, if humans can be seen as part of nature and nature as their BASE of existence, the idea that human labour is something man does to nature must change, as now we can also view nature as working according to its own terms, remembering Adam Smith's insight. It means that human relationships with nature are two-fold, it is a process of give and take. Their relationship is reciprocal.

The easiest example which can be given for an reciprocal interaction, is of course the process of respiration: with every breath we take air from nature into ourselves, and we breathe out gases no longer needed back into nature. And when talking about the impact of labour on nature, we have to notice that nature itself is a continuously ongoing process, nature is not the same as it was million of years ago, it is *natura naturans*.

---

66 Klaus-Michael Meyer-Abich, *Wege zum Frieden mit der Natur,* Munich, Wien, 1984

Then the <u>third conclusion</u> is the following: the relationship between humans and nature is a process of reciprocal interactions. Consequently, if man destroys nature, he is not only the culprit, but also the victim.

The modern understanding of nature is a dynamic, open and self-organized process of evolution. This process moves from inorganic matter to organic matter, and from living plants and animals to human beings, with their gained capacity for self-awareness. Edward O. Wilson famously expressed this as follows: "... the biosphere as a whole began to think when humanity was born. If the rest of life is the body, we are the mind,"[67] a mind which is capable of consciousness, empathy, musicality and laughter, with the ability to learn and look into possible consequences of habits and behaviour, as well with the ability to find new ways of solving problems and developing new ideas about the world. Otherwise science would not be possible.

It follows that a reciprocal relationship between humans and nature can never be merely viewed as destructive, as environmental economists believe, as it can also become productive. However, this also means that, if we human beings destroy our co-world, living nature is reduced to an inorganic, lifeless state, and with this we reverse – mostly unconsciously and unintentionally – the process of evolution. Why do people think that this is a rational course when we know that nature is our BASE?

It seems to me that, even if we are rarely aware of it, we still have a sense of being part of nature. As Wilson puts it: "People prefer to be in natural environments, and especially in savanna or park-like habitats. They like a long depth of view across a relatively smooth, grassy ground surface dotted with trees and copses. The want to be near a body of water, whether ocean, lake, river or stream. They try to place their habitations on a prominence, from which they can safely scan the savanna and watery environment. With nearly absolute consistency these landscapes are preferred over urban settings that are either bare or clothed in scant vegetation...",[68] even if the natural environment these days mostly consists of cultivated land.

It is now possible to draw a <u>fourth conclusion</u> about what we mean when we talk about damaging or destroying nature, the 'world-with-us', so that it loses its ability to regenerate: destroying nature's ability to evolve, finally means eliminating life. If man interacts with nature in such a damaging way that the life conditions for plants and animals are destroyed, they die out. The result is that nature will eventually only exist in the form of dead matter. This is the real significance of the ecological crisis.

The outdated logic of environmental economists can also be set in a wider context: it is still seen as rational to replace human labour with machines in order to reduce labour costs – a kind of natural law to which we aspire. However, people are still needed as consumers, as someone who has to buy all the manufactured products, as someone who still has to hand over money in exchange for the goods, as money is only made by selling. From the consumer side of the economy this

67   Edward O. Wilson, ibid, p. 132
68   Ibid, p. 134

rationale looks different, as pointed out, because consumers do not aim at making money, rather they spend money for the goods and services they want. It follows that for production, the economic exchange is *for* money, in which the MEANS is made into the end, while for consumption the exchange is *with* money, meaning that money stays a MEANS.

These days, corporations claim that they cannot avoid damaging the environment and that they want to go on doing whatever they want without being publicly obliged to avoid or even reduce pollution, as this would cost them too much. For example, Exxon Mobil is that said that: "... it does not envisage a low-carbon scenario of the kind many climate researchers advocate. The company believes that the costs this would entail, and 'the reliable and affordable energy resulting from the policy changes ... are beyond those that societies, especially the world's poorest and most vulnerable, would be willing to bear.' Instead the company envisages only that the flow of emissions will stop increasing not give projections of concentrations of greenhouse gases in the atmosphere. It also does not address temperature effects of those concentrations."[69] Their position can now be formulated: we do not want to adapt to the consequences of man's interaction with nature. How strange and incomprehensible such arguments are! In traditional economicult thinking, based on classical assumptions, neither the presumptions, nor the consequences of how we deal with nature are considered or dealt with. Instead this theory assumes that nature is a static, limitless and lifeless phenomenon external to humans.

But from an ecological point of view, it is possible to acknowledge that the forms of human interaction with nature have varied throughout history and will differ in the future according to our ever-evolving experiences and insights. This allows us to anticipate that in future it will be possible to practise a very different and less-damaging form of interaction with nature – a very comforting thought, I find.

It is now easy to see that once we move beyond the classical point of view, different and much more realistic explanations of the ecological crisis emerge as well as strategies to overcome it.

Another point to be made is that once we view nature as an ongoing reciprocal process of interaction in four-dimensional space-time, recognizing that the many species found on land and in the sea have varied throughout history, just as the landscape has evolved throughout the thousand-years history of human cultivation which still goes on, we can re-address the question conservation, as posed by environmental economists. Does their demand for the conservation of nature mean that the natural world outside us should stay the same as it is today? When it is already the result of a million-year- long process? And how can the conservation of nature be achieved, if man and nature are constantly influencing each other?

Environmental economists do not understand such questions, as they do not realise that it's impossible for humans and nature to avoid interacting, in the same way as non-communication between humans is simply impossible.[70] Has environmental damage not already reached the North and the South Poles and the deep

---

69   Martin Wolf, in: *The Financial Times*, 18 June, 2014, p. 9
70   Paul Watzlawick (1921 - 2007) pointed out that, "we cannot not communicate".

sea? Why don't we recognize that the ability of Earth to absorb growing amounts of waste is finite? Because we do not want to look into it?

We cannot live without interacting with nature, and we cannot live without nature interacting with us, in one way or another. However, that interaction does not need to be damaging, it does not need to be negative. It is quite possible to sustain a constructive relationship, after all, man evolved from the animal kingdom. And who knows where this view of a productive relationship with nature will lead us in the future?

Now, a fifth conclusion can be drawn. When the question of the conservation of nature arises we can be more precise, stating that, what needs to be protected is the ability of nature to evolve, to build more complex living matter, creating more and perhaps different kinds of consciousness – rather than reverting to lifeless matter. This is an aim that needs to be included into every country's constitution.

Viewing the relationship between nature and humans as a direct, open, dynamic and reciprocal process of interaction *with* the use of money, but not *for* money, brings further advantages. One is that the contradiction between what is rational in microeconomics (producing more to make more money, even if it destroys the environment) and what is rational in macroeconomic terms (trying to 'repair' environmental damages by spending money) can be overcome.

Based on such an understanding, modern theory can now focus on: the consequences of every activity from the beginning of production to consumption and waste disposal with the aim of minimizing or avoiding damage, when everybody will be aware that environmental damage ultimately means self-damage. It is remarkable to see that even in ecological thinking we cannot avoid a bit of self-interest![71] However, we shouldn't change our relationship with nature merely because we can put a monetary value on nature's services to humans, eg when we strive to save hitherto wild, rarely disturbed forests because of the possibility that valuable remedies for human illnesses might be found there. Nature has its own self-value, beyond the human perception of it, and this must be respected.

When dealing with nature we need to aspire to a very economical, even frugal level of interaction. The flow of natural material into the sphere of human consumption and then back to nature needs to be slowed down and limited. Natural boundaries and limited resources need to be respected instead of us trying to widen the exploitation we may practise. Before production of any goods starts, all possible consequences, of consumption and future waste disposal must be considered.[72]

Primarily regenerative resources need to be used. Expressed in monetary terms that means: living off the interest, not the capital. Transport and traffic need to be reduced. Direct local and regional relationships need to be encouraged. Food needs to be grown locally, in season, and according to organic standards.

---

71 However, given our dependency on and our involvement with nature, trying to put a price on nature's services to humans becomes questionable, as attempted by Frederik Vester in: *Der Wert eines Vogels*, Muenchen, 1987. For it would follow that we reduce our damaging influence on nature only because of the fear that nature's services to man –expressed in monetary terms – will suffer.

72 This proposal for a helical life analyzis was first introduced in the group Ecological Economy of the Institute of Applied Ecology, Freiburg, in the 1980s, initiated by the author.

New ways of using products need to be made available: it is not always necessary to own the products one uses. The aim, that more people need to live on their own, because then more products can be sold, should be consigned to the scrapheap of history. In future instead of selling goods, their services should be sold[73]. The long-term use of products can then replace short-term sale. Continuous maintenance to protect the value of goods can be implemented. And with this shift the principle of responsibility can gain new importance, as when a product remains in the ownership of a manufacturer for its whole lifetime, the producer's interest in durability increases.

Let us remember what Milton Friedman, one of the free-marketeers, used to say: "Only a crisis – actual or perceived – produces real change. When the crisis occurs, the actions that are taken depend on the ideas lying around, the politically impossible becomes politically inevitable."[74]

At the moment two crises, the banking crisis and the environmental crisis, have occurred. It is up to us to analyze them thoroughly to find the reasons behind them and look for ways forward. And it is up to us to give up outdated beliefs, and change them into modern knowledge based on evidence and facts. We need to visualize a path and make a conscious decision as to why we are taking it.

However, real change will not come without modernizing traditional economicult thinking. Therefore, let us modernize our theories and democratize economics. Let's change the role of money so that it is no longer considered the end of all our activity rather used as than the MEANS.

I would like to finish this chapter with a reminder of what Klaus Michael Meyer-Abich, with whom I discussed my work, wrote in *Wissenschaft fuer die Zukunft, Holistischs Denken in oekologischer und gesellschaftlicher Verantwortung*, Muenchen, 1988, p. 115-117. Economists, he said, are glad that K. W. Kapp (1910–1976) who concentrated on the social costs of the economic process and whom they gave quite a hard time during his lifetime, was one of them. There are – albeit marginal – moves towards factoring environmental damage and the gradual exhaustion of natural resources into economics. However, that in no way means that the neglect of nature characteristic of recent economic thinking has been overcome, but rather that we need to think about economic assessments in much more fundamental terms, placing the focus of economic theory on the fact that our economy is the ecology of the human species in relation to nature, and can therefore only know, being *human ecology* what an industrial society needs to know. It would be good if this thinking took place less peripherally, for example in such courageous institutions as the Institute for Ecological Economy Research in Berlin or the Institute for Applied Ecology in Freiburg, and more in the core areas of the discipline. ... Does human interaction with our natural co-world not merit the same universal attention as the relationships between people and their relationship with themselves?[75]

---

73 Cf. Walter R. Stahel, *The Performance Economy*, New York, 2006

74 Cited from: Owen Jones '*Why let the right set the agenda? In the battle of think-tanks, the left is permanently on the defence,*' in The *i* 11 March 2013, p. 13

75 "*Die Wirtschaftswissenschaftler z. B. sind nun zwar froh darueber, dass K. W. Kapp (1910–1976), der sich mit den gesellschaftlichen Kosten des Wirtschaftsprozesses beschaeftigt hat*

10.5. Conclusions

The findings of this chapter can be summarized as follows:

- Environmental economics remains within the classical and neoclassical tradition of man's role in the world. Environmental economists see nature as external to man, and environmental damage as a natural consequence. They represent a one-sided, merely quantitative, static point of view when they propose to add a fourth factor of production, 'clean' environment. They propose that new markets' are needed to produce a 'clean' environment. They do not consider that their view of nature had lead us into the environmental crisis.

- Dual economists criticize environmental economists for their traditional view and propose to widen it. They argue that the hitherto forgotten side of economics, about everything which is not defined in monetary terms, for example 'self-work', now has to count. They complain that qualitative aspects have hitherto remained in the shadow of traditional economics. Sadly, besides their proposal for a green tax or better: a labour bonus, which has been thoroughly misunderstood by the public, the new quality they promised was not delivered, either in the analysis, nor by their proposals for solutions.

- This new quality is only obtained when an ecological point of view is taken. From a change of perspective about nature, outdated assumptions can be overcome and hitherto unquestioned ones discussed. The way nature and labour have been viewed in the past, can now be modernized, drawing on knowledge of modern physics. Human nature and nature external to man can now be seen as they really are, related in the process of reciprocal interaction. On this basis, a better understanding of the crisis is possible. A new, fair culteconomy can be created taking into consideration the whole helical life analysis of goods at the beginning of production. Such a modern understanding has advantages: it is more economical, as damages can be avoided before they occur rather than trying to repair them spending money. And new measures can be taken.

At the end of this chapter, and before going on in the next chapter to make proposals on how to modernise an economicult step-by-step, it is useful to look back at what has been achieved so far:

und dem sie es zeit seines Lebens nicht leicht gemacht haben, einer der ihren war. Es gibt auch - wiederum randstaendige - Ansaetze, Umweltschaeden und die allmaehliche Erschoepfung von Ressourcen wirtschaftswissenschaftlich zu beruecksichtigen. Die Naturvergessenheit der neueren Oekonomie (H. Chr. Binswanger 1979, E. K. Seifert, 1986) aber ist damit noch lange nicht ueberwunden, sondern dazu muesste viel grundsaetzlicher ueber oekonomische Bewertungen nachgedacht und im Zentrum wirtschaftswissenschaftlichen Denkens beruecksichtigt werden, dass unsere Oekonomie die Oekologie der Species Mensch im Naturzusammenhang ist, also nur als Humanoekologie wissen kann, was die Industriegesellschaft wissen sollte. Es waere gut, wenn dieses Denken weniger peripher, z. B. in so couragierten Unternehmungen wie dem Berliner Institut fuer oekologische Wirtschaftsforschung oder dem Oeko-Institut, und mehr in den Kernbereichen des Fachs geuebt wuerde... Verdient nicht der menschliche Umgang mit der natuerlichen Mitwelt hier ueberall eine etwa gleichrangige Aufmerksamkeit wie die Verhaeltnisse der Menschen untereinander und zu sich selbst?"

We started this study with the questions: are Adam Smith's insights into the wealth of nations still valuable, and are they today adequate in explaining and understanding our problems? These questions are worth asking, because politicians, businessmen, economists and journalists still claim that an 18ᵗʰ-century theory can offer solutions to the problems in the 21ˢᵗ century.

On closely studying the three publications containing Adam Smith's ideas, we found out that he came to interesting results, some based on classical sources, while others were really new, and hardly discussed by the people who follow him even today:

- that the real wealth of nations is produced by the labour of nature and of men, so we should strive to avoid damaging nature;
- that money is an economic MEANS, invented by humans, a medium which only has use value when changed into real things or services;
- that everyone is obliged to contribute to society in proportion to their ability, meaning for example that the richer people should pay relatively more taxes than the poorer;
- that wage labour should be paid liberally, sufficient for a decent life;
- that wage labour should not be taxed, as people are otherwise forced to pay taxes twice or more
- that education, the construction of roads and harbours, border control, policing, law courts, prisons, defence, inland revenue, and all the other tasks of the executive administration are public services for the many. They should not be performed for money;
- that human activities should be freed from rules dictated by an absolute monarch;
- that people's habits are always aligned to the rules of societies typical for a specific historical period;
- that people's interest in self-preservation is not reduced to money;
- that banking needs regulation, even when personal freedom might be limited;
- that all production is for the purpose of consumption;
- that Earth should be seen as divided into equal portions among all its inhabitants, enabling everyone to share its resources equally.

Additionally, we had to remind ourselves that Adam Smith's ideas were based on the thinking typical of his time – and how could it be otherwise, following the assumption that the world is a machine, that the world has been created by one external god and has remained unchanged, that the male gender is the norm, that agriculture is the basis of the economy and that 'labour' can be seen as a merchandise like any other commodity.

We saw that these views, widely held as norms in the 18ᵗʰ century, have changed in the last 250 years. Today we have a totally different understanding of the world including quite different laws of physics which could not have been foreseen by Adam Smith or by anybody else from his time.

Therefore, we found it remarkable that our modern insights have not yet been implemented in economic theory and practice. It is now high time to modernize economic thinking and to take it forward beyond classical and neoclassical assumptions, ancient traditions or abstractions, basing it on the evidence of what nature and human beings are – according to our knowledge in the 21st century.

What we also had to acknowledge is that today's sovereign is no longer an absolute monarch with an inherited kingdom, but that people are sovereign. We citizens make the rules. Our 'state' is not something apart from us, but is there for our participation. We live today in democratically constituted societies in which nobody is above the law. Every person is born into society with the same inalienable rights, regardless of gender, race, origin, hereditary status or belief – a list, to which should be added: regardless of their disposal power about monetary assets. We share the world through our activities and not through the ability of spending money.

Adam Smith based his economic theory on the principle of exchange, which he held as natural. What he did not pointed out, however, was, that his natural principle of exchange is transformed as soon as a MEANS of exchange is invented and implemented, and then exchange takes place <u>with</u> the use of money, being human invention that is 7,000 years old. And that the exchange with the use of culturally invented money is transformed another time, when the exchange takes place <u>for</u> money, a practice which became the cultural norm about 250 years ago. The former MEANS of exchange is then transformed so that it becomes the end of all cultural activities.

Today we no longer live in a natural form of economy, but in a culturally invented one, where the roles of MEANS and end are reversed. We therefore need to differentiate the three forms of economy as *nat*economy, *cult*economy and economicult.

While Adam Smith thought of 'land' and 'labour' as factors, we can today look beyond this understanding. What Adam Smith called 'land' means nature in reality, the BASE of all life, and what he termed 'labour' is in reality a natural inalienable ability of beings, the uno-actu process of perception and action.

Consequently, as long as people are not free *in* their work but have to sell their abilities – which are assumed to be seen as a separable object – from themselves to others, society can only be regarded as half-modern.

By widening our view and changing our perspective, we can now understand that what was formerly assumed to be a one-dimensional power of humans to dispose of external lifeless matter, is in fact a direct open and dynamic reciprocal process of interaction with our co-world. From this, the MEANS of economic activity, money, we have been discussing – is removed form its former understanding role as an end-in-itself, and repositioned while nature and man are the subjects. This modern understanding could be located in the tertiary sector of the economy as well as in the household economy. Such understanding is based on real facts, not on assumptions.

However, even in today's economicult society where everything seems to be exchanged *for* money, the traditional principle of one-dimensional disposal is still very much alive. In an economicult people are not free to follow their own desires;

instead they have to obey the intrinsic rules of money and markets'. The primary sector of the economy, agriculture, and the tertiary sector, services, are still operating according to that outdated one-dimensional pattern of disposal. We have therefore concluded that our society has not yet been developed into a post-industrial society.

So let us use the shoulders of giants such as Aristotle and Adam Smith to help us stand upright and come to a better understanding of what there is to do. And let's do that with our eyes and our minds wide open so that we can look deeper into the consequences of our activities and further into the future to develop a really modern and sustainable society. Change is not only possible. It is happening all the time. The only question is whether it happens with our conscious participation or without.

"Zeit, an den Ausweg zu denken."
Frank Schirrmacher, EGO, Das Spiel des
Lebens, Muenchen, 2013[1]

11. Short-term improvements

Our analysis has revealed that the mainstream economists' theory in which money is transferred from a MEANS to the kind of natural aim of all exchanges, is based on outdated 18th century assumptions about 'nature', man and the laws of nature. We can state this with absolute assurance because nature has never invented a MEANS for its exchanges and therefore, the MEANS can never become the natural end of all exchanges.

Quite the reverse: nature's exchanges are direct, open, self-organized[2] and unmediated.[3] Consequently, a form of economy based on natural exchanges can be referred to as a natural economy or *nat*economy. The pattern, typical for nateconomy is found in the 'household' of nature and of people.

A MEANS of exchange is a historic invention of people. Therefore, it derived from the cultural, not the natural sphere. Every economy using a MEANS of exchange – in whatever form – is a cultural construction. When humans invented a MEANS of exchange a few thousand years ago, it was to replace sacrifices to the gods, at first of people, then of animals. In contrast to a *nat*economy, an economy using a MEANS can only be referred to as a cultural economy or *cult*economy.

In the 18th century, the role of the MEANS of exchange had been transformed. From then on, exchanges were not only taking place *with* money, but *for* money. We needed to make this great cultural transformation transparent by changing the annex 'cult' from the beginning of the word *cult*economy to its end, which is economicult, to make it totally clear what is being done. This form of exchange, economicult, is today the norm for everything we do, not only in the formal, but also in the private sphere of our life. However, we were not always aware of the consequences of this transformation, neither for every person, nor for society as a whole.

We found in this study that due to this transformation, both nature and (the majority of) people were perceived as factors or commodities for the aim of making money. A person's labouring ability could be viewed as something separable from an individual and tradable on a market', so that the buyer of that ability could use it as he pleases, because he had paid for it. Society is thus split into buyers

---

1   translated by the author: Time to think of a way out.
2   Cf. Erich Jantsch, *Die Selbstorganisation des Universums, Vom Urknall zum menschlichen Geist*, Muenchen, 1979
3   Incidentally, science is also a direct unmediated reciprocal interaction of a scientist and his chosen object.

of labour with the freedom to decide about the labour of others, and the sellers of labour forced into wage slavery.

It seems that the criteria determining whether an individual is able to buy labour or needs to sell it, is the ownership of money. That means, a person's financial situation decides whether or not they can be an equal and free citizen or not. That money determines the status of people as either free subjects or dependent objects is typical for an economicult society. And such a society can only be called semi-modern. In a fully modern and fair economy, however, we would no longer allow money to determine a person's status. This is the goal we have to strive to.

The way forward is to establish a truly modern *cult*economy where everybody is truly equal, as all human beings are born with and live according to the same inalienable rights. In a truly modern *cult*economy, money is no longer allowed to divide people into economic subjects and objects. And a truly modern *cult*economy is no longer interested in the division of labour, as this idea is based on the monetary principle. We have discovered that the typical pattern for a truly modern *cult*economy is called 'reciprocal interaction', an unmediated and direct, open and dynamic, self-organized process. With the paradigm of reciprocal interaction we have moved on from the traditional view where a subject has one-dimensional disposal power over an acquired object. The new paradigm helps us to understand how multi-dimensional this interaction processes is. We have further found that in interaction both participants simultaneously take the status of subject and object as long as the process is ongoing, the subject-status being not only for humans, but also for nature. We have to remind ourselves that Adam Smith understood this well and that Gregory Bateson agreed.[4] Hartmut Rosa formulated that the good life means cultivating reciprocal interaction with oneself and the world in time.[5]

In interaction, we know, lies the answer why people have not only evolved as humans, but that both, nature and people, are still in the ongoing process of evolution.

When traditional economicult scientists insist on treating nature and the human labouring ability as objects, we now can refuse this traditional and restricted view, which is neither legitimized nor being found in any modern constitution. People – with their innate natural ability to work – and nature are unlike other goods and they are not 'produced' for the market'. All humans are equal natural beings who have the natural and legitimate right to follow the logic of their own life.

Such a truly modern understanding of nature and people is fundamental for a genuinely modern society. It has, remarkably enough, derived from our efforts to understand the environmental crisis and its roots. The analysis of nature as external to us has helped to enlighten us about our nature as humans.

---

4   Gregory Bateson saw men as part of his social and natural environment, in: *Oekologie des Geistes*, Frankfurt, 1981.

5   Hartmut Rosa, *Beschleunigung und Entfremdung*, Frankfurt, 2013, in: *Frankfurter Allgemeine Sonntagszeitung*, 27 October 2013, p. 8: "Das gute Leben ist, wenn ein wechselseitiges Antwortverhaeltnis besteht, das ich zu mir und zur Welt pflege. Und das braucht Zeit." However, how anyone can have an interaction with oneself, is a question he would need to answer.

However, instead of being aware of our nature, it seems that these days we are moving even further away from an acknowledgement of mans' involvement and dependency on nature as his BASE. In fact, the idea that we humans can be independent from nature seems to have grown even stronger,[6] a kind of self-illusion.

The problem that anybody faces when proposing change – in this case from a society based on abstract self-moving markets' to a modern fair society – is that people want to go on believing in these ideas, sometimes even against their self-interest, ideas that were imposed on them hundreds of years ago. So still today we all consider it as 'normal' that the majority of our exchanges are mediated, standardized and commercialized.

And we should also mention that separating ourselves from nature and dividing our ability to work from ourselves, can only be done in the abstract. Yet, it has been possible to convince us that this abstract idea is right and the way to proceed. This thinking seems to have become our 'second nature'. It is accepted nearly without question that people have to adapt to the market', rather than the market' has to adapt to peoples. Democracy has to be market'-conform, instead of the other way around, a democracy-conform market. And we observe people trying to transform themselves into market' products,[7] 'Money rules the world', we say. That is the way of the world. And we shrug our shoulders. Trying to change this view seems impossible. Because: who would have the power to do it? Who prefers interacting directly with others instead of doing so via money or the screen of a computer or a mobile phone?

Well, we all have the power to change. We can ask the question: in whose interest is it that we devalue our own ability for such small change? This is our society. We are the movers and shakers. We are the electors and doers.[8] We know that it is possible to act according to a different and more realistic logic.

So much effort is needed to modernise society, while showing how limited and outdated the traditional economicult logic is, is the first – and perhaps the easiest – step on this way.

I am convinced that an awareness of the opportunities offered by the modern paradigm of direct, unmediated and self-organized reciprocal interaction cannot and will not fall out of the heavens, but we all have to seize the initiative. And we can do it.

When we examined the effects of the traditional economicult assumptions, we found that another of their ideas ie that money is a quasi autonomous self-moving entity, is also wrong. It was the few who obviously were able to convince the majority of people to believe such an idea. But there is no 'law of nature' (and never can be) which gives a by people invented MEANS a higher status than a real

---

6   Irene Schoene, '*Vom Eigenwert der Natur, Ein Beitrag zur Oekologisierung der Oekonomie*', in: K. Grenzdoerffer et al, *Neue Bewertungen' in der Oekonomie*, Pfaffenweiler, 1995, p. 73 ff

7   To cite one example: a Hawaiian woman was asked by the authorities to shorten her name as it was seen as too long to be printed on her documents. The problem has since been resolved, by a change of the documents. Passports and driving licences are now issued with more spaces for the name.

8   Cf. the very enlightening article '*Auf Doktor Merkels Couch'* in: *Frankfurter Allgemeine Sonntagszeitung*, 15 September 2013, p. 49

human being has. This idea only has power over us as long as we follow its assumption. However, belief is not a modern attitude. Believe would revert us back into a state of immaturity before enlightenment. True qualities of modernity are: knowledge and direct participation as the basic principles of a democratic, self-ruling society.

It was in the 18th century that people began to develop enlightened views of the world. Nature had a history, it was discovered, and that nature is an interacting process, the process of evolution. Philosophers, such as Immanuel Kant (1724–1804), insisted that no person is an object, a MEANS for the purpose of others, but that everyone is an end-in-themselves. Nature and people have their own intrinsic value, and this has to be accepted and respected, a demand which economicult theory has not answered, yet.

In a truly modern society, therefore, we have to implement a modern view of nature as an ongoing evolutionary process of reciprocal interactions. This also means to acknowledge that with the creation of this universe, evolution had not come to an end, that it is still ongoing, although so slowly that we hardly register it in the short span of our lives. The process led from inorganic to organic matter, from immobile plants metabolizing[9] sunlight, water and chemicals from the soil, to animals with roaming ability. These animals then have evolved – as a result of their interaction with nature and each other, as at first Georg Wilhelm Friedrich Hegel (1770–1831) noticed – into humans with the capacity of consciousness and thought. Max Horkheimer (1895–1973), in his reference to Hegel, famously described humans therefore as *self-made*.[10] Mans' spirit and soul are natural functions, not something external to nature. And we can – in a way – anticipate some consequences of what we do, for example aiming to make money by selling goods for more than their production cost.

Secondly: we are aware that the natural world existed for billions of years without humans, while humans are unable to exist without nature. Nature is the BASE of all life, including human life. The consequence of this insight is twofold: nature's ability to evolve has to be safeguarded, and possible damage has to be prevented, as otherwise we risk our own life.

From such an understanding we can conclude that it is not very sensible to build a recycling industry, as we know that it would have to rely on the continuous production of waste, the material no longer useful to us which we give back to nature. Instead we should aim at a strategy of least waste from the very beginning. Earth's finite resources have to be used as economically as possible, as they cannot be replaced when once downgraded. Instead we should base our interactions with nature on resources which renew themselves.

Therefore thirdly: in a truly modern society people are no longer defined as being contrary to nature, but as a natural beings who build different kinds of cultures in spacetime. We are aware that every person has to incorporate fresh

---

9   This metabolism or interaction process is also going on, even when a plant is cut from its life base, eg apples lose water and shrink, wood continues to expand or shrink through interaction with its environment.

10 Cf. Max Horkheimer, *Zur Kritik der instrumentellen Vernunft*, Frankfurt, 1985

local air, fresh local water and fresh local food to release life energy, and that every person returns the digested residues back to nature. Through interaction with nature a person is able to do both, preserve and develop their life. This is our basic human self-interest. Being aware about the differences of the historic cultural context, in a modern economy the relationship between people and nature is fully understood and respected. Basic human needs have to be met and thus are not dependent on a medium (of exchange). Following this insight, building global markets' for the BASE of life, for example by speculation on global harvests, can no longer make any sense.

Every person born into a truly modern society has the equal right to direct interaction with nature and other humans and self-preservation. These human rights cannot be given up, neither can they be mediated by money. Let's remind ourselves that Adam Smith was the first writing that every man has the same share in the world, "had the earth been divided into equal portions among all its inhabitants". (TMS p. 215) This vision of everybody being entitled to an equal portion of air, water and food, is even after 250 years, a truly modern one.

And while every person has an equal right to self-preservation she also has the obligation to work to support herself directly. Splitting that direct process by inserting a division between the participants and their labour is neither advizable nor justifiable. We have experienced that such an imagined split only leads to inequality between those who own the MEANS and those who do not. In a truly modern *cult*economy, it follows, nobody is forced to sell her or his ability to work in order to get the MEANS for buying the necessities of life. And a market' for people's working ability can never be created.

In a truly modern *cult*economy, also the call to liberate markets' no longer makes sense, as there can be no markets' for the BASE of life, but direct reciprocal interactions. Modern *cult*economics is, we can conclude, fair both to nature and to people in their direct reciprocal interaction which differed in the past and will be different in the future.

Fourthly: we have discovered that the paradigm of direct and unmediated open dynamic and self-organized reciprocal interactions is based in the private and public household sector as well as in the service sector of the economy, as well as inside companies. In the service sector, producers and consumers are both active participants. Human services, we have seen, are produced and received simultaneously while the use of a MEANS is decoupled from that direct *uno-actu* interaction process. Instead of a 'division of labour' we discovered a 'division from money' – in other words, money is kept in the very role it was invented for, as a MEANS of exchange, and is not changed into an end-in-itself. The interaction paradigm shows an enlightened way for a totally modern society where nature and people matter. This is our vision. This is the way forward.

On the following pages important short-term improvements are presented, which could easily be implemented by everyone, outlining the way to develop society into a genuinely modern one.

Naturally, only a limited number of such improvements can be included in this study, while others have to be left out, as for example: how to prevent illness, how to learn for life,[11] how to be mobile, how to self-build warm and healthy accommodation,[12] how to clothe oneself and others, how to safeguard the role of print and electronic media as critical reporters of today's reality, how to support freedom of and access to information, how to encourage participation – and so on, bearing in mind that even language has a mediating role.

There are a lot of changes which can be made to improve knowledge and awareness of the form of society we live in, and how to develop it further, as history is an open process.

Some of these changes can be made in the short-term and are relatively easy. However, we are aware that while such small, short-time improvements will not be radical enough for some people, for others they will be too much.. And there is, of course, the danger that even the tiniest improvements are kicked into the long grass by politicians and administrators who may getting very creative presenting innumerable reasons why everything has to stay as it is. Often, in fact, far more energy is expended in arguing why nothing can be done, than is spent on actually doing something.

On the other hand, politicians can hardly refuse to support (at least in public) the idea of active participation by citizens in decision-making. Who says that only entrepreneurs have visions and can put them into practice? Why not by ordinary citizens keen to change things?

In this respect it is very helpful to compare practices in other countries so that nations can learn from each other, and avoid misinformation or repeat of mistakes. Politics can be understood as a direct, transparent and controllable activity aiming to serve the many, and not for money. Politics can give people a clear choice of goals to vote for – traditional ones, where the market' rules over people, or progressive ones, where people rule themselves and control the MEANS. We can expect more from our political representatives than the passive practise of waiting for data about what the majority of voters think before declaring their opinions on a given issue. A lot more. The process of interaction between political representatives and their constituents can be improved gradually. Just as the industry offers new products to citizens as if they were unaware of what people want, people can demand from politicians to act on certain strategies. Politicians might even support citizen's initiatives, even when they have never done so before.

A new understanding of nature and humanity really is overdue, one that does not depend only on spending taxpayers' money mediated by markets'.

Some promising initiatives have already taken place, though they have not yet been regarded as a move towards true modernity. Examples might include urban

---

11   Education, knowledge and culture as well cannot be seen as commodities, which can be bought and which remain, so to speak, "outside" the individual. Instead they need to be incorporated in a person, otherwise they do not make sense.

12   There are differences in the understanding of accommodation, for example between the UK and Germany. In the UK nearly 70 per cent of people own theirs, in Germany only 46 per cent. In the UK a property can be sold on after a year without paying taxes on the profit gained, in Germany you have to wait for 10 years. Therefore the house"market'" in Germany is a lot slower than in the UK. And also, German people do not view their place of residence in the same way, as a commodity.

gardening, distribution of locally produced organic farmed products, farmers markets, community-run shops, communication centres, local currencies, play groups, public internet cafes in local libraries, renewable electricity generation co-operatives and so on. All such self-organized groups and activities are established with the use of money but not *for* money. They offer local solutions in line with their local area and varying local cultures.

These are the real avant-garde, people living the principle of direct unmediated reciprocal interaction, the real role models, in direct contact with each other and nature, who are fair to other people and fair to nature. We can learn from them. These individuals experience more freedom in their work and are less dependent on the market'. Their lives are more fulfilled as they interact directly within their communities, and their understanding of themselves with learning and enhancing their skills all the time, and their compassion for nature is thus enhanced, in an ongoing process.

> "Anyone who believes in indefinite physical growth on a physically finite planet is either mad or an economist."
> **Kenneth E. Boulding (1910–1993), adviser to US American president John F. Kennedy, quoted in The The Canberra Times**

11.1. Nature has self-value

Nature is not only external to us – the air we breathe, the land we dwell on and the sea we fish and sail – but *also inside* us. We are nature. We human animals as Adam Smith called us, absorb nature with every breath and every sip of water enabling us to live. Nature is not merely a factor of production, as assumed by economi*cult* theory – nature has its own purpose, its own logic and follows its own evolutionary path.[13]

Life on this planet, we call Earth,[14] began about three billion years ago. At that time, Earth was in a very different state from its current one, eg the composition of the atmosphere contained no oxygen. And while the universe's heavy atoms were 'baked' in supernovae, perhaps the first complex organic molecules were brought to Earth from asteroids and comets, which bombarded Earth from deep space. That naturally means that nature must already have created organic life somewhere else.

Life is only possible in very particular conditions of oxygen, water, temperature, light, pressure and radiation, and it depends on the proximity of a star to a planet, for there is an optimum distance for the necessary delivery of light and heat. Today the thin Van-Allen-Belt combined with Earth's iron core and magnetic field[15] keeps cosmic debris away from the planet and limits radiation to safe levels for life.

---

13 Irene Schoene, ibid, p. 66–80

14 An 'earth' or 'Erde' also means the connection of an electrical charge for protection.

15 According to recent reports, new research into Earth's magnetic field organized by the European Space Agency (ESA) was launched on 22 November 2013 following scientists' discovery that it appears to have decreased in the last 150 years by 12 per cent.

Oxygen, essential for the process of life, is held within Earth's atmosphere and provides the first and most important 'food' for life.

Earth is self-sustaining, engaged in a continuous process of reciprocal interaction in curved four-dimensional spacetime, whilst it's own interior and surface is also moving. The land and the sea, where the conditions are favourable to organic life, floats on a hot nucleus of melted iron: volcanoes erupt, earthquakes occur, continents shift, and sometimes even former sea beds are turned into mountains. And plant life from millions of years ago is transformed into carbon energy resources.

From a subjective point of view from Earth, as we have discussed, Sun seems to be rising and setting. From an objective point of view, however, we know that it is the other way around. Earth is moving around Sun, and the so-called retrograde movements of planets were explained when Copernicus discovered that Sun is in the centre and that the planets move around it.

Earth spins on its own axis at a speed of 1.670 km/h, while revolving around Sun at a speed of 107.208 km/h. One rotation of Earth forms the rhythmical pattern which we name a year, and in time, a new year replaces the old one. Time moves forward.

The moon rotates around Earth at a speed of 3.659 km/h, always presenting the same side to Earth. "Moon" is the name we give to satellites orbiting a planet. Because of Moon's lack of an ozone layer, Earth's satellite is more prone to being bombarded with asteroids and comets from the universe. Even with our naked eyes we are able to see the impacts. Moon interacts with the waters on Earth, so that tides rise, moving the waters in and out every six hours. Isaac Newton (1642–1724) was the first to explain this phenomenon of interaction between Moon and Earth.

From the time organic molecules found a foothold on this planet and became able to reproduce, the conditions of Earth changed. The first blue algae in the waters exhaled oxygen, enhancing the atmosphere with oxygen. And life could progress from water to land.

Traditional economical theory regards 'land' as a factor of production, which can be cut into pieces and bought and sold. 'Land' was what the kings tried to conquer, its inhabitants were then being forced to work and produce soldiers for his their further conquests. 'Land' was what the Pilgrim Fathers hoped for, when they started dwelling on the apparently empty planes of the Americas, without respecting indigenous people and their self-chosen way of life. The new arrivals then claimed land for their own interest. Ownership of 'land' defined a free man who had the right to have his voice heard.

Today, our views have changed, as we have learned to respect the independence of other people, their self-chosen way of life and their countries. Former colonies became their own masters, which experienced some difficulties in forming national states in the way that the West has already done. At least in the 21st century, Europe has given up conquests of other lands replacing it with a co-operation contract between its member states.

However it can be stated that this 'external conquering' of land has been replaced by a kind of 'internal conquering': atoms can be split and made bond to form new elements, genes can be isolated, the human genome can be broken into its component parts, and we can know where our ancestors came from – leading to the view that we can and should construct the world according to our own interests.

In this study we do no longer regard 'land' as an object which can be 'produced' for a market' or cannot be moved from its cultural context or locality. To see 'land' as if it is one, relied on a certain cultural understanding in the 18th century[16], because it can be fenced off from others, so that these can be excluded from it and its use. Then it can be treated as if it is a tradable commodity. However, this idea has never been used with water or the sea, as they cannot be fenced off. The economicult perception of nature as land is based on a kind of limited view of what nature really consists of, as it excludes the insight that humans depend on nature for our life. And nature has more life experience, power and creativity than our human understanding has hitherto allowed us to recognise. Nature moves on according to its own laws, logic and rhythm. When we destroy and spoil it, it affects our own lives. Even when we try to establish new areas for wildlife to flourish,[17] this kind of wilderness is influenced by the culturally built-up land arond it and our own influence, eg by our use of air or water and other human activities. Everything we do to nature ultimately rebounds on ourselves. Nature is both within us and outside of us, and we are in a continuous process of interaction with it. So, when referring to nature, why not replace the term 'it' and 'which' with 'she' and 'who'?

Obviously, the economicult solution to implement a further, a fourth factor of production which they call "unspoilt nature" into the existing economicult model therefore cannot be a solution at all for the environmental crisis.

Furthermore, we have to learn that nature-conservation cannot mean the protection of what has evolved during the thousands of years of human cultivation in a state in which it is now as then we would forget to acknowledge that the evolution process is ongoing. Instead we have to protect nature's self-evolutionary ability. This is a much more complex process. It means that we need to prevent pollution at source rather than trying to repair damages, even if the latter could be achieved. Otherwise, how could an extinct species, for example, ever be revived? Spending billions would not help. Also, we must stop arguing that it is natural to pollute and damage nature. Once we realize that there is no other planet to seek refuge to when we have destroyed our BASE on Earth, how can we not seek to protect life on our planet? And how can it be seen as legitimate, in the 21st century, to burn off the existing fossil fuels and thus deny this resource to future generations? Is it fair to deny them the same possibilities we had? What right do we have

---

16 By the way: An important change in people's understanding of nature obviously had taken place in the 18th century, as documented in the so called 'Gottorf Codex', a huge collection of flower paintings commissioned by duke Frederick III. While before, nature and flowers were seen as symbols which come with layers of meanings (in myths, emblems, astrology as well etc.), like a nutshell was the symbol for the whole cosmos, now we recognize that they are presented in a kind of abstract knowledge. Flowers for example are no longer reproduced as symbolic blooms, but shown whole, from top to their roots, the roots however we normally cannot see, but only know that they are there, and separated from the soil without they cannot exist.

17 As planned in the mouth of the river Oder, Germany/Poland, or existing already near the Portuguese/Spanish border

to act that recklessly? And is it not arrogant of us to call the extracting of resources from nature as 'production'? Humans have not 'produced' any of them, we are only appropriating[18] them from the earth and are transforming them. That is all.

Nature shows us a far better model of interaction than economi*cult* human action. Nature, has the ability to create more and more complex structures, evolving from inorganic to organic matter, and from life to consciousness. Nature produces life which is more complex than inorganic matter, and the only force we know which can work against the law of entropy. If love of nature for itself does not come naturally to us, at least we should acknowledge that the evolution process has worked for billions of years.

11.1.1. The BASE

Life relies on reciprocal interaction to survive, propagate and evolve. Nature is the BASE[19] for every life, and has created awareness and cognitive powers.

To keep reciprocal interaction ongoing, humans need fresh air and clean water, food and energy. These basic needs are, depending on historic and local differences, the same for everyone. They are the BASE for human life.

We can only survive for a few minutes in the absence of air, and a few days without water – therefore clean air and fresh water are our most basic needs, the 'direct food'.

Besides these, we need to eat other food from nature, in the form of fruit, vegetables, milk, eggs and meat. These natural things release, taking into our bodies, the energy for human life.

Here again we see the process of direct reciprocal interaction in action: while fruit and vegetables are directly obtainable from the land, milk and eggs are the products of animals we have cultivated over thousand of years. The animals themselves can only be consumed if we kill them, and then they can only be eaten once. So consumption of meat can be viewed as perhaps an unnecessary luxury. What we incorporate and how we incorporate it, depends on different localities and different climates, and on changing social habits.

The food is taken from our natural environment in a continuous direct process of reciprocal interaction. This includes not only what we ingest but also what we excrete in a changed digested form back into our environment.

Furthermore, if we want to survive in different seasons and climate zones of planet Earth we need to keep warm. We need clothes and also energy in form of heated accommodation as well as hot water and power to run machines. The use of this external energy can - again - be seen as a process of taking-in from nature and giving-back to nature.

---

18 As proposed by Elinor Ostrom in: *Governing the Commons, The Evolution of Institutions for Collective Action*, New York, first published 1990, this edition 2011, p. 30 ff

19 The term BASE is pronounced in the same way in English and German, although in German it comes with more meanings: it is an old-fashioned word for a female cousin, and a word for a chemical substance, differing from an acid, according to the definition of Johanes Nicolaus Bronsted and Thomas Lowry 1923: a chemical substance which can give-off protons is called an acid, and one which can receive protons is named a base.

Having learned that a fair economy is a process of direct and unmediated, open and dynamic, self-organized reciprocal interactions, we can now propose that the energy incorporated into us and the energy we use externally should be produced in a direct, unmediated and self-organized manner. Everyone should be involved in its generation and not only in its use. Likewise everyone should be involved in understanding how the BASE of life is maintained and is made equally productive for all.

It would be unfair to go on allowing the BASE to be mediated by money in the future, as we have found, because the unequal distribution ensures that those with money have access to more basic resources than other people. And it is astonishing to observe how people continue to strive towards an unlimited increase in money when the BASE on which they depend is not only limited, but actually shrinking because of today's form of human activity. This demonstrates that by following the economi*cult* model today's economic activities, seen as the natural order of things, are separated from their consequences on nature and other people.

If we would go on viewing the BASE as a factor of production, an object, an environmental medium or an external factor, then we would continue to exploit and degrade it, seeing it only as a vehicle for absorbing or carrying away human waste, with no personal consequences for us, whilst it may effect our neighbour.

Clearly, our understanding of the BASE is still incomplete and needs to be developed further, based on Enlightenment idea that all people are born equal and have inalienable rights for all their life. It can be explained as follows:

Firstly, the direct reciprocal process of human interaction with nature and other people cannot only be seen as a right, but also as an obligation to be active in living a life which cannot be replaced or exchanged for money.

Secondly, it involves one of Adam Smith's most important, but less-known ideas, ie that Earth can be viewed as being divided into equal portions among its inhabitants. Then it becomes clear that people can no longer be seen as only *born* with equal rights, but have an ongoing equal right to self-preservation. Adam Smith was right to point out that the most important interest every person has is the preservation of his own life. Sadly, Smith's view was wrongly shortened to the selfish and egoistic interest in money.

This idea also harks back to the thousand year old Right of the Commons, according to which nobody could be excluded from the use of the land on which everyone could let their cattles graze. Everyone had an equal right to claim the same amount and the same quality of air, water and food during his whole life, as nobody can voluntarily refrain from breathing, drinking and eating, while being obliged by nature to work and to participate to achieve it. From this point of view it would be self-destructive madness to damage the common BASE as everyone would be aware that we depend on it with our life. These Enlightenment ideas can pave the way for an avoidance of damage to the BASE. The prevention of damage is, as we know, healthier both for humans and nature, and it also comes cheaper to avoid pollution than to damage the BASE first and then set up an industry which is expected to clear pollution as a condition for its business model.

This wider understanding of the BASE allows to deal fairly with nature as well as with people, with those living as well as those to come into life in the future as it passes on cultivated nature – in the real sense of the word – to the next generation without having destroyed it or thrown it back into a state of lifelessness where nature is no longer able to support life and is deprived of its ability to evolve.

Furthermore, this wider view understands that neither air, nor sea as part of nature can be divided into pieces to become tradable commodities. And both will always be effected with our activities. At the same time, if we view air and water as BASE, every person alive has to have unlimited, free and direct use of both. This understanding allows us to understand and improve our interactions with the BASE, making it equally available for everyone, while stop transforming it into a kind of merchandise for the aim of making money. The idea that markets' can be constructed for the BASE of life, as today, is obsolete and outdated.

And the last but also important detail this enlarged understanding refers to is the necessity of direct interactions. 'Direct' means spatial as well as temporal, unmediated and immediate, local and seasonal interactions. If direct interactions have become the necessity, we need to reduce transport and external energy use regarding the BASE, reduce the use of additives and preservatives to our food. Our focus will have to be put on raw food, local and in season and no-longer focussing on industrially produced food using ingredients from all over the world which could be a big step forward in improving people's health as well as people's own various activities and forms of participation, and therefore comes with it a possible reduction of the costs for treating illnesses. This is the way forward, preventing illness instead of concentrating of treatment, building an expensive industry for it.

According to the interaction paradigm, we view the people who live on Earth with us at the same time as equal with the same rights, able to organize their own BASE of living in a direct unmediated way. This insight no longer gives the MEANS – and people with monetary interests – the freedom to define what and how much a person should buy for self-preservation, regardless of the social and environmental consequences, which must always be considered.

Elinor Ostrom from the US Indiana University, and co-winner of the 2009 Nobel Prize for Economics, studied these direct participatory processes and published her findings with those of her colleagues in: *Governing the Commons, The Evolution of Institutions for Collective Action*. Ostrom wrote: 'The issues of how best to govern natural resources used by many individuals in common are no more settled in academia than in the world of politics. Some scholarly articles about the 'tragedy of the commons' recommend that 'the state' control most natural resources to prevent their destruction; others recommend that privatizing those resources will resolve the problem. What one can observe in the world, however, is that neither the state nor the market is uniformly successful in enabling individuals to sustain long-term, productive use of natural resource systems. Further, communities of individuals have relied on institutions resembling neither the state nor the market to govern some resource systems with reasonable degrees of success over long periods of time.'[20] She pointed out that "referring to natural

---

20   Ibid, p. 1

settings as 'tragedy of the commons', 'collective-action problems', 'prisoner's dilemmas,' 'open-access resources,' or even 'common property resources', the observer frequently wishes to invoke an image of helpless individuals caught in an inexorable process of destroying their own resources,"[21] which seems to call for an external intervention from whom whatever, still continuing to rely on the same assumption: people cannot organize themselves or do something themselves, this has to come from a kind of outside actor. "When the enforcement mechanism is not an external government agency, some analysts presume that there is no enforcement," Ostrom observed critically: "Many policy prescriptions are themselves no more than metaphors. Both the centralizers and the privatizers frequently advocate oversimplified, idealized institutions – paradoxically, almost 'institution-free' institutions."[22]

But while it is obviously true that we are leaving a scorched Earth if we go on destroying our BASE according to the traditional economic*cult* paradigm, we can recognise that this is neither necessary, nor has it ever been so, otherwise human-kind would not be alive. Or the other way around: damaging the BASE and destroying life is not happening according to a kind of natural law. It is only based on a certain understanding of nature and the cultural form of man's exchanges with natural life. We know from history that people before us were able to organize themselves according to very different cultural structures than those we think rational these days. These people were clearly able to avoid using, exploiting and polluting nature to the excess, and instead managed to maintain the BASE for thousands of years.

11.1.1.1. Air

We breathe in air, utilize it in our lungs and release the no longer useable gases back into the atmosphere surrounding us. This interaction happens automatically, though we may sometimes become conscious of the process when we take a deep breath.

The fact that breathing is managed by our autonomic nervous system might be one reason for being largely unaware about the continuous process of interaction with the surrounding nature we are in, while the other might be that air is trans-parent to our senses, giving us the mistaken impression that there is 'nothing' around us. However, we are living in a substance, as fish live in the substance water.[23] Air is our medium of life, also called the 'heaven', contrasting with the earth, the soil or the ground on which we stand and walk.[24]

In classical times, people thought of air as an element. This assumption was kept for about 2,000 years right through to the 18th century, when in 1771, the Swedish chemist Carl Wilhelm Scheele (1742–1786) classified a part of air as a gas supporting life, which he called 'oxygen', and so did Joseph Priestley (1733–1804) three years later, independently from him. Whether or not their discovery had

---

21   Ibid, p. 8
22   Ibid, p. 22
23   Are fish aware that they live in water?
24   There is even a dish in German speaking countries which is called '*Himmel und Erde*', translated: heaven and earth, made from apples and potatoes.

already become public knowledge by Adam Smith's time, we are not able to say.

Today we know that the air we continuously need to breathe in and out, is a mixture of different gases. It contains about 21 per cent oxygen, 78 per cent nitrogen, and 1 per cent trace gases such as argon, carbon dioxide and water vapour. And while we take in oxygen from the air for our metabolism, plants take carbon dioxide from the air and breathe out oxygen. We are in a process of open, direct and ongoing reciprocal interaction with plant life on Earth, and without it not able to exist.

The German chemists Fritz Haber and Carl Bosch developed a procedure, patented in 1910, to manufacture fertilizer from air's nitrogen content. This was based on a discovery presented by the British chemist William Crookes in Bristol in 1898, as a response to the dwindling resources of the natural soil fertiliser Guano. Nitrogen can be processed into nitric acid, or, by reaction with carbon dioxide, into the fertilizer urea to increase global agricultural production and to feed Earth's growing populations.[25]

The air we breathe today is billions of years old, being virtually the same as the one inhaled by the dinosaurs, because: 'Nothing is lost, nothing is created, everything is transformed,' in the words of Antoine de Lavoisier. Locally, air may contain traces of smoke, of salt, ash or pollen, as well as the residue gases from coal firing, steel melting or other chemical processes, of human waste which we are able to smell, sometimes even 'tasting' a corresponding flavour of the gases in our mouths. The air we breathe locally may also carry other aromas more pleasing to our senses, such as the smell of spring, of wet autumn leaves or of snow, or in the summer, the smell of flowers, like sweet-peas or pansies; while the air's movements can bring a sudden breeze of warmth or coldness.

We have stated that generally we experience air as transparent, but as soon as one ray of sunlight falls into our room we become aware of how many tiny pieces of material float in it, which we inhale into our lungs and which settle as dust on window-sills and furniture.

From outer space, the air belt which we can now recognize around Earth, our atmosphere, appears as blue. This belt is about 11 km thick, we know today, and it thins out the more it becomes distant from Earth. For us this makes it a problem to breathe in altitudes over 4,000 m, especially when people are not accustomed to it as tourists. However, it benefits aircrafts which use less kerosene as they meet lower air resistance in these regions. Birds and insects take to the air to travel between continents, transporting germs and seeds over distances of thousands of miles. Scientists have given different names to the levels of the atmosphere around Earth we differentiate: the troposphere, the stratosphere, the mesosphere, the thermosphere and the exosphere.

---

25 The product of nitrogen and nitric acid, salpeter, however, can also be used for the production of explosives. Fritz Haber was also interested in the development of poison gas for which he was held responsible after World War I, this should not be forgotten. So, in a way, Haber and Bosch can be held "responsible for the deaths of an estimated 100 million people", wrote *The Week* 16 November 2013, p. 23. Perhaps both chemists did more damage than the chemist Thomas Midgley, cf. chapter 10.

Air also helps to retain an average surface temperature on Earth of about 14 degrees Celsius.

Air exerts a pressure which varies locally and seasonally, and allows energy from the sun to travel to Earth's surface, illuminating and warming it, whilst radiation is held back by the ozone layer. Earth emits radiation back into space at longer wavelengths that we are able to see, because our senses are not sufficiently developed. The fact that it is invisible to us possibly explains why we are often not aware of it also.

While energy from Sun is delivered to Earth, the light photons might scatter in the atmosphere, allowing to understand us that Sun's energy or light is also interacting in a continuous process with Earth's atmosphere. If scattering happens, light then reaches Earth without causing a shadow, different to bright sunlight.

Air allows clouds of water vapour to build up and travel, which release rain down to Earth, sometimes resulting in violent thunderstorms.

Air retains the temperature of Earth while being heated up from Sun, making it warmer on the ground and cooler higher up in the atmosphere. However, being a gas, this process doesn't work as well as with water, for example. The lower density of air makes it cool down faster as well as heating it up faster.

Certain so-called climate gases, especially carbon dioxide, contribute to the retention of heat in Earth's atmosphere, suppressing the interaction with space. The consequence is that Earth can heat itself up to higher than average temperatures, with the result that a rise of a few degrees Celsius in the average temperature has already triggered the melting of the Artic pole and global climate change.

Air also allows sound to travel, in fact sound travels evenly in all directions. In the supposed void out in space, there is no sound. Most roaming animals have developed a voice with which to communicate in case they cannot see each other.

We call the movement of air 'wind'. It is caused by Sun as well as by the constant rotation of Earth around Sun and the temperature differences on this planet, for example the temperature differences of water and land.

I have included so many details about what we mean by 'air' in order to show how limited and unrealistic the understanding of economicult theory is, when it views air as an environmental medium. And it demonstrates clearly how important it is to extend the economicult definition of air.

It shows, to point this out again, that we human animals living on Earth together with other forms of life, are in a constant open process of direct interaction with the air around us, and that the whole planet is in interaction with other heavenly bodies, with our star, Sun, and with the void.

Some people, particularly those in industry, claim that it is too costly to agree to a stringent air pollution control. One cannot help but feel somewhat helpless in the face of such a narrow-minded view, supported by an out-of-date understanding of air. Are they really not aware that polluting air with chemical emissions can never be considered a right, a tradeable commodity or justified with nature's laws, but is effecting all forms of life – even if the damaging effects cannot immediately be seen or if the polluters themselves might be able to escape these consequences by living in a different location?

Let's remind ourselves that the Clean Air Act, initiated by the UK Parliament, was responding to London's great smog of 1953 in which 4,000 people were said to have died. From that time on, household fires with their smoke and sulphur dioxide emissions were banned in the capital, and smokeless fuels became compulsory.

However, in a report with the headline: "UK faces fines for failing to cut pollution in big cities,"[26] on 21 February 2014, Ian Johnston pointed out that: "The UK is facing fines of up to 300 m a year over its failure to cut levels of a gas that is believed to cause premature death and affect the growth of children's lungs." And the European Commission was supposed to take "legal action against Britain because it had not come up with a plan to get the amount of nitrogen dioxide – produced mainly by diesel vehicles – below agreed limits. Campaigners said people had 'the right to breathe clean air' and that the UK had some of the highest levels of the gas in Europe... Some 29,000 people are known to die prematurely every year from particles in air pollution, which can cause cancer." The areas in question are: "Greater London, the West Midlands, Greater Manchester, West Yorkshire, Teesside, the Potteries, Hull, Southampton, Glasgow, the East, the South East, the East Midlands, Merseyside, Yorkshire & Humberside, the West Midlands and the North East." Why, for example, can't regular chimney inspections be introduced in the UK as in other countries, to help control the emissions of waste gases and the results made available to home owners, so that they can install, for example, chimney filters or even new boilers.

In Germany, the '*Blauer Himmel ueber der Ruhr*'[27] initiative for the coal and steel-producing region in Nordrhein-Westfalen was announced in 1961, when Willy Brandt (SPD) stood against the Conservative Chancellor Konrad Adenauer. He called for social justice through environmental protection because children in particular were suffering from allergies and asthma, particularly in the Ruhrgebiet, due to bad air quality. It is interesting to learn what *The Spiegel* from August 1961 included in its list of the reasons for bad air quality in the area at that time:

- 56 Thomas steel converters,
- 75 colliery power stations and 18 other coal-fired power stations,
- 82 blast furnaces together with more steel melting or 'soaking pits',
- 17 concrete producers and oil refineries,
- 1,976 steam locomotives of the Bundesbahn and others.

The initiative was successful. By law, filters were inserted in chimneys of power stations, and emission gases from steel converters were 'cleaned' before releasing pollution gases into the atmosphere. However, it seems not a lot of countries have copied this strategy, as for example India or China did not. However, when the consequences of using lead in petrol and ozone damaging chlorofluorocarbons

---

26   In the The *i*, p. 9
27   Translated: blue sky over the Ruhr.

became clear, a law was passed to prevent the use of these chemicals. Today, people are more conscious of air pollution. Campaigns against smoking have been successful, as it can lead to lung cancer, not only to the smokers themselves, but for passive smokers as well, and now smoking cigaretts, pipes and cigars has been virtually eradicated in public places, with advertising banned.

In Europe, pressure is currently building up to further reduce car exhaust emissions. The European Union wants to tighten the limits for car emissions per kilometre to a maximal of 95 grams of carbon dioxide from 2020 onwards. This seems a necessary response to a continuing trend towards driving bigger cars which on average produce more exhaust gases. And it is hard to understand why, at the beginning of October 2013, the coalition government in Germany formed by Conservatives and Liberals was trying to postpone actions against it, as it will mean that an additional 310 million tons of climate gases will be emitted into the atmosphere, as the environmental organization Deutsche Umwelthilfe complained, stating that the German car manufacturers, in contrast to the French and Italians, make most of their money from big cars, which produce relatively more CO_2. And they seem to have in the German chancellor Merkel a loyal ally.[28] At the same time, newspapers reported that the Conservatives, Chancellor Merkel's party, benefited from a donation of the Quandt family, who own 46.7 per cent of the car producer BMW, amounting to €690,000. A few days later the public was informed that their partners in government, the Liberals, received €210,000 from this family. Can we really have doubts if such liberal donations had influences on the decision to delay the implementation of pollution limits?

And why are car manufacturers, who normally position themselves as being highly innovative, not cooperating with rail companies to produce small standardized solar-powered electric cars, which would be useful in towns and could also easily hop on and off high-speed rail carriages for long distances?

That said, we have to point out that according to the outdated economicult paradigm it would even make sense that air becomes more polluted, as then it could be the condition for establishing a market' for clean air, i. e. more air cleaning appliances could be sold. People could perhaps even be convinced that it is cool to carry their own clean air supply, as a kind of rucksack, as they have been convinced to carry their own bottled water. There would be he obvious consequence, of course, that the more money an individual has at his disposal, the more cleaner air he can buy and breathe. But this is exactly what should not be allowed to happen.

Well, I propose that we follow the new strategy, avoiding air pollution by giving everyone an equal right to free use of fresh and clean air throughout his or her lifetime on Earth. Air should be seen as everyone's unmediated direct primary food.

And it is good to learn that the awareness of the importance of clean air is rising. For example, Luce Irigaray and Michael Marder asked in an article called

---

28   *Der Spiegel* 2013, p. 32: "Die deutschen Autohersteller verdienen im Gegensatz zu den Franzosen oder Italienern vor allem mit grossen Autos Geld, die vergleichsweise viel CO_2 produzieren. In Merkel haben sie eine treue Verbuendete."

'Clean air is life itself,'[29] which discussed air pollution in Shanghai, Salt Lake City and Paris: "Is clean air, along with drinkable water, becoming one of the most precious resources on the planet? Or should we reframe the question and challenge the thinking that converts everything, including the very air we breathe, into economically measurable reserves and commodities?" They concluded that: "Unfortunately, in our western tradition, neither materialist nor idealist theoreticians give enough consideration to this basic condition for life. As for politicians, despite proposing curbs on pollution, they have not yet called for it to be made a crime," a crime against life itself.

11.1.1.2. Water

On a clear day when we enjoy the sunshine on a beach, the boundary between the air and the sea becomes nearly undistinguishable. The atmosphere and the sea seem to be melting into each other.

Air and water interact as well, they are in a continuous direct and unmediated reciprocal process of interaction with each other: air absorbs vapour and builds clouds. Water is released when these clouds become too heavy and falls back to Earth. We call it rain. Water absorbs gases from the air. Seawater incorporates carbon dioxide gases, which is the reason why scientists explain that global warming is not happening faster. The process is known as the hydrologic cycle or, to be more accurate – as a 'cycle' does not recognize time – the hydrologic spiral.

The water of sea, lakes or rivers seems to have a colour. Although water is transparent, it can look blue reflecting a blue sky, greyish or green, or brown if transporting mud, and it can even change to red if certain algae proliferate. However, groundwater is clear.

In religious ceremonies, water is often used, for example to baptise people to cleanse their sins.[30]

In classical times people viewed water as an element in continuous change, as illustrated by the famous saying that nobody can bathe in the same river twice. In these classical times, people would drink the surface water, use it for washing, catch fish from it, swim in it and release their waste into it without having to think of the consequences. Today, one would hesitate to copy this kind of interaction, because a high population density together with an industrial lifestyle makes the purity of such water use at least doubtful.

In ancient times, people settled near rivers and the sea. The first so-called 'high cultures' in Iraq and Egypt were established on the banks of the rivers Euphrates and Nile, also using their mighty waters for transport, while the regular flooding irrigated the land.

When water was scarce, ancient civilizations learned to regulate it in a process of self-organization, making sure that everyone had access to the same amount of water while been obliged to maintain equal levels of work on it. The irrigation systems that were invented then can still be seen today.

---

29 *The Guardian*18 March 2014
30 and such a religious ceremony is copied on board of an oceanliner when a passenger crosses the Equator for the first time, to the amusement of others.

Fifty years ago, fresh water was viewed as if it were an infinite resource. Now we know that it is billions of years old and finite.

Today, already a fifth of the global population suffers from a scarcity of fresh water, and this figure could rise to a third by 2025, as reported at the 'Global Economic Symposium' in Kiel, Schleswig-Holstein, in September 2011.[31] There are seven billion people living on Earth today, a figure which is still growing, and "their consumption of water-thirsty meat and vegetables is rising, and there is increasing competition for water from industry, urbanization and biofuel crops. In future, even more water will be needed to produce food because the Earth's population is forecast to rise to 9 billion by 2050." With the use of more pollutants, fewer fish in the sea and the reality of climate change, huge parts of the world will become less fertile, wells will need to be dug deeper and deserts will extend.

Today, we are aware that water is a bond of two gases, hydrogen and oxygen. A water molecule has the chemical formula H_2O, meaning that two hydrogen atoms are bound to one oxygen atom, a process in which both chemicals lose their form as gas and build a liquid – at a certain temperature and pressure. By electrolysis water can be split again into hydrogen and oxygen, as done by fuel cells, driving for example submarines, manufactured by HDW in Kiel, Schleswig-Holstein. Hydrogen and oxygen are the most abundant elements in the universe, we have discovered.

There is a strong force binding the two hydrogen atoms to the one oxygen atom, which leads to a high surface tension of water, which can be easily observed in a drop or water. Besides water has a high capillary force, it can move up the trunks of trees thus supplying them with the necessary food. Besides water is a good solvent and can absorb gases, as mentioned. Altogether, water has most astonishing qualities. Its maximum density is at about 4 degrees Celsius. That means that lakes or rivers can freeze on top, allowing the water under the ice to stay liquid so that fish and plants can hibernate. The greater volume of ice also allows icebergs to float on the sea, exposing only the top while the rest is under water.

When the temperature rises above boiling point, 100 Celsius at sea level, but lower on high mountains, liquid water changes its aggregation state from a liquid into a gas as steam and extends its volume, and when the temperature decreases in a cloud, it falls to Earth as snow, eventually forming solid ice. When that happens, the former transparent raindrops change into white snowflakes, forming crystals in such an astonishing variety that nobody has yet found two which are the same. Solid ice, as in glaciers or the ice caps of the North and the South poles, can exhibit different colours, translucent, white, light blue or green.[32]

Water, scientists think, was brought to Earth by asteroids and comets, which mostly consist of frozen water – and with it came the seeds of life. 70 per cent of Earth is today covered by water, mostly the salt water of the oceans. Water is also used as an indicator for life, when scientists analyze the spectrum of other planets.

Clean water is tasteless and odourless and does not contain calories. When

31   According to *Kieler Nachrichten*, 29 September 2011, p. 8
32   It is very recommendable to read *The Left Hand of the Electron*, by the American biochemist Isaac Asimov for a better understanding of the qualities of water, Zuerich, 1972.

there are differences in the taste of fresh water this is caused by the different local minerals it contains.

Water is life.[33] No organism can live without water. It is fundamental, as far as we know, to the photosynthesis and respiration processes. 90 per cent of the human body is water. No one is able to give up voluntarily drinking it. And catastrophes such as the recent hurricane Haiyan in the Philippines or the devastating floods in the United Kingdom, make us realise just how important fresh water is.

On the other hand, we can drown in water.

Saline water is not suitable for humans, but can be consumed by other life forms. In countries where freshwater is scarce, people have built desalination plants using solar power, and this water has to be enriched with minerals once generated.

Water consumption in Germany fell from 147 l/inhabitant/day in 1990 to 122 l/inhabitants/day ten years later, *Der Spiegel* informed us.[34] One reason for this decrease is that the installation of new toilet flushing systems has reduced freshwater use by 17 per cent.

However, why has no country yet made it the law for toilets to use 'grey water', the residue water from washing hands or using a washing machine, or why is the majority of the world not using humus instead of fresh water to safely break down excrement, as invented by Danish entrepreneurs? If the United Kingdom, according to the report by the Committee on Climate Change (CCC), is to expect hotter and drier summers, the rainfall necessary for plant irrigation will be reduced. At the moment the British farming industry uses 240 billion litres a year, but the supply will go down. This could make it very difficult to cultivate water-intensive crops.

Most nuclear power stations are built near rivers or the sea as they need water for operating. From Fukushima we learn, two years after the atomic catastrophe there, radioactive water is still being discharged into the Pacific Ocean.

Water is also used for extinguishing fires, for example the regular bush fires in Australia.

In order to use fresh water more efficiently, waste water meters should be installed in every house,[35] as Janice Turner wrote in *The Times*:[36] "Let's be clear about who's to blame for the shocking state of our water supplies. Yes, of course, we should pick out the privatized companies who, having piled up profits, paid hefty dividends to their foreign owners while failing to fix the leaks in their pipes before the drought hit. That's why they love a hosepipe ban: putting the onus of ending the wastage on the consumer diverts attention from their own bad management. But we consumers are at fault too. In the age of global warming, water is precious, but it's the one resource we squander 'without care'. The British use average of 150 litres a day; the Germans use 125 and the French 110. For

---

33 When Peter Brabeck-Letmathe, current chairman and former CEO of Nestle S.A., Vevey, Switzerland, "the largest producer of food products in the world", said that "access to water is not a public right", as Kevin Samson reported in *Global Research*, 14 December 2013, we wonder what kind of understanding he has about its importance, as it would imply that he wants to deny us the basic human right of life-preservation making it dependent on the market'.

34 *Der Spiegel* No. 30/2013, p. 47

35 As it will be the law in Germany from 2020.

36 *The Week*, 12 May 2012

households paying a flat rate for their supply, why bother to turn off the taps if it doesn't 'save a bean'? But instead of making water metering compulsory, as in Europe, past UK governments have backed off the idea for fear it would penalize the poor. But the poor needn't bear the cost of all those new meters. Why not just dip into the deep 'cash aquifers' of the water companies?"

It is the water companies that "are draining us dry," as Nick Cohen pointed out in *The Observer*.[37] "When the Tories privatized the water industry in the 1980s, they promised it would lead to more efficient services that would no longer 'suck on the public teat'. How wrong they were. In the event, it has produced profeteering companies that still need taxpayer support for major building projects, thanks to their habit of racking up big debts to maximize their returns to investors while escaping tax. The political class assumes that the status of privatized utilities is unchangeable; that businesses, run by 'reckless and greedy men', could never be replaced with, say, non-profit-companies. 'I wonder how long that line can hold.'"

Nobody uses more freshwater than the citizens of Abu Dhabi, as Alozsius Widmann and Winand von Petersdorff have pointed out.[38] In Abu Dhabi there are lots of golf courses, public parks and luxurious villas with gardens. Their average daily water consumption per inhabitant amounts to more than 600 litres, exceeding even that of US Americans.

The goal of a political water strategy cannot be to prevent water wastage alone, however, it has to aim to stop the pollution of water in the first place. This is the healthier and cheaper move forward. Schleswig-Holstein's Minister for the Environment, Robert Harbeck of the Green party, for example, has taken on a fight against the use of the herbicide Glyphosat. He initiated a ban on selling it to home owners and small holders in order to protect consumers as it already is showing up in groundwater and human urine. The long-term risk of Glyphosat and the danger of interaction with other environmental poisons have not been examined. But this herbicide is still widely used. This is wrong, he said.[39]

The principle of direct and unmediated reciprocal interactions allows us to consider the whole range of water use including waste water treatment, as it currently is fragmented. Therefore, it can no longer be a political strategy to first let people pollute the BASE – and then to establish a repair industry which deals with the damage, and makes money out of it. Waste does not disappear, even if it disappears from sight currently and its disposal has become 'somebody else's job'. As far as the health of the BASE is concerned, this current strategy is too short-sighted.

What is not considered in such a narrowing strategy is that, by interfering with the whole interaction process and mediating it by making money, we continue to damage life. And once people's growing health problems cause health organisations to create a new market', the situation worsens, especially when you have to buy the relevant treatments and medicines from private companies, as one needs

---

37   *The Week*, 10 August 2013, p. 14

38   In: 'Erklaer mir die Welt: Was mit dem Trinkwasser passiert', *Frankfurter Allgemeine Sonntagszeitung* ,28 July 2013

39   *Kieler Nachrichten*, 14 November 2013, p. 23: "*Das Langzeitrisiko von Glyphosat und die Gefahr der Wechselwirkung mit anderen Umweltgiften sind nicht untersucht. Dennoch wird das Herbizid weiterhin weit verbreitet eingesetzt. Das ist falsch.*"

money and more money to be able to acquire them. Therefore, such end-of-the-pipe industries really cannot be the political strategy for the future.

Every industry, including the pharmaceutical one, wants to increase and sell more products at higher prices to make more profit for its shareholders, and the government seem to support such strategies as it leads to more taxes coming in for a government which can be spend. This is all understandable and rational but dangerous for life on this planet, if the whole spiral of preconditions and consequences are taken into consideration. It follows that we should be aiming to avoid spoiling the direct and unmediated reciprocal interaction with the BASE. It means a different strategy: everyone should have free and equal access to clean water, the water supply being locally self-organized with the responsibility for local people. I would like to refer here to a speech the Prince of Wales gave at the BBC Radio 4 'Food and Farming Awards' in London, on 25 November 2009, where he came to a similar conclusion. We should aim at agri-culture rather than agri-industry. He said: "We are told, of course, that agri-industry is the only way that we are going to be able to feed our burgeoning population and that there are no health benefits to natural, organic, farming systems. But perhaps we need to ask ourselves a few searching questions before accepting such a proposition... For instance, if organically, or sustainably produced food has no health benefits, then why are the water companies in this country spending something like 100 million pounds a year removing the pesticides and other chemicals from our water supply? If our approach to industrially produced food (of which incidentally, we waste some 10 billion worth in this country) is so sensible, then why are we seeing a dramatic increase in Type-2-diabetes across the developed world? If an industrialized approach to animal husbandry – which increasingly treats animals as machines in an ever more 'efficient' system – carries no risk, then why are we seeing e-coli outbreaks in the United States from cattle raised on feedlots, fed on corn (when their stomachs were designed to cope with grass and leaves) and processed in ever decreasing numbers of abattoirs as big as car factories?" – or when grass eating cattle are fattened with body parts of other animals making them ill from mad cow disease? – "If every technological innovation to increase the productive capacity of industrialized animals far beyond what nature intended is considered safe, then why did the European Union decide to ban antibiotics as growth promoters in animal feed after they had been in use for fifty years? And if, Ladies and Gentlemen, all the evidence shows that when children or, indeed, prisoners are fed proper, nutritious food, their behaviour and concentration both improve, why do we then ignore it or dismiss it as irrelevant?... The truth is that by treating food as an easy commodity, rather than a precious gift form nature, we have started playing games with our health and with the environment, from which humanity can only stand to lose."

Furthermore, do we know what consequences the release of hormone contraceptives into the ground water might have in the long run when children and men drink hormone-rich water?

Avoidance of pollution is necessary, and laws preventing the discharge of harmful materials from domestic or industrial premises into the water must be enforced. Furthermore, there must be equally available and free fresh water for everyone. And thirdly, such a strategy must be regulated locally, as it was historically already practised for thousands of years, as Elinor Ostrom pointed out, ibid, cf. chapter "*Analyzing long-enduring, self-organised and self-governed CRPs*".[40]

A particular problem is the pollution of water with nitrates, as they can form cancerous nitrosamines and cause malfunctions of the human thyroid gland. Nitrates are transferred to ground water by chemical fertilizers and by an overload of liquid manure spread on fields, which results from intensive livestock farming, whilst there has been some reduction in harmful chemicals from household cleaners. One third of Germany's groundwater contains too high an amount of nitrate, experts estimate, which can only be reduced by tighter regulation of drinking water and a greater protection of water in certain areas (where water may have to be entirely prevented from running off into the ground). In the northern German Bundesland of Schleswig-Holstein, nitrate pollution is very high, even though agriculture has such a small part of the economy. Here, 22 out of 55 groundwater stations are overloaded with it. The Schleswig-Holstein Minister for the Environment, Robert Habeck,[41] has therefore demanded that in future every farmer should be required to produce a "farmyard balance", detailing which materials come into the farm and which leave it. Otto Ullrich[42] presented another model for an integrated strategy on freshwater. In Germany there are already water companies in rural areas which no longer invest in more water treatment installations, but in farmers who change to organic farming, as this would guarantee qualitatively higher drinking water as well as healthier and sustainably produced food together with more pleasant working conditions for people.

The equal use of freshwater should be made a Human Right. Freshwater is a basic human necessity, and cannot be viewed as a commodity and commercialized. Consequently, it is unsurprising that a million Europeans have protested successfully against an EU initiative to privatize water supplies,[43] although in the UK water companies are already privatized, meaning that they are run for the profit of their owners and not in the interest of the public. Considering the UK experience with unfulfilled political expectations, the water utilities in Great Britain should also be re-communalised, on a local level. This would make sure that the consumption of piped fresh water comes free, as it is our primary food, just like air.

The industry, however, has tried hard to establish a market' for bottled water. Water – as shown in a film by Res Gehriger for arte-tv with the title *Bottled Life* – has been made into a proprietary good, selling at ridiculously high prices, eg over £3 for half a litre at UK airports. And the industry has successfully trained today's consumers to follow this trend and constantly carry their private, plastic bottle of water. The Swiss concern Nestle is the biggest extractor of groundwater

40   Elinor Ostrom, ibid, p. 58, on p. XIV. "CRP" she defined as "common-pool resources".
41   *Kieler Nachrichten*, 25 October 2013, p. 11
42   who died in January 2015, with whom and others I founded the IOEW in Berlin in 1985 , in: *Regionalisierung: Die raeumliche Grundlage fuer eine zukunftsfaehige Lebensweise*, Lutz Finkelday (ed.), *Tausch statt Kaufrausch*, Bochum, 1999
43   *Frankfurter Allgemeine Sonntagszeitung*, 17 February 2013, p. 24

worldwide, their best selling brand in the USA being 'Poland Springs'. Last year, Nestle achieved a turnover of €6 billion with its 70 brands of bottled water, and this is rising.[44] Their latest marketing campaign is selling bottled groundwater under the global brand 'Pure Life', which although extracted in 27 countries, tastes the same everywhere. The consequences of their strategy are multiple: first, the groundwater table sinks in the countries were water is extracted, leaving less groundwater available for people, animals and plants; secondly, bottled water has a reduced quality compared to freshwater from the tap; thirdly, bottled water is much more expensive than tap water, it is a commodity for the richer people in the world; and fourthly, the bottles used are made of plastic,[45] transparent, unbreakable, but also indecomposable. While one-way-plastic bottles are already forbidden in several countries and have been replaced by re-usables, the problem of the disposal of waste plastic bottles remains unsolved. Plastic waste floats in huge concentrations in the sea, damaging sealife. Furthermore, bottled water needs "millions of barrels of oil to package and transport", clogging "up our world with plastic", while it is just purified tap water.[46]

Bottled water might be appropriate for health reasons in countries with high water pollution, and for a limited time until the pollution is solved, but in Europe or North America bottles should be reused and filled up with fresher tap water, recommended by Dagmar Schmauks.[47] Here, it is not necessary to carry heavy crates of water up the stairs to our homes, while the water industry could even be forced to sell their products in biodegradable bottles.

Nobody knows today how much plastic waste ends in the sea, Mark Lenz from Geomar Helmholtz Centre for Ocean Research at Kiel University warned. The estimates range from 6.4 to 26 million tons per year[48] while the conservation organization Naturschutzbund Deutschland (NABU) puts the figure at 10 million tonnes per year.[49] No part of the oceans is these days free of plastic which is a serious problem. UNEP, the environmental programme of the United Nations, has made the plastic problem one of its concerns proposing worldwide separation of waste and plastic recycling, already more or less in operation in Europe, while EU Environmental Commissioner Janez Potocnik launched an initiative at the beginning of November 2013, aiming to reduce the use of plastic bags by 80 per cent. Because 100 billion plastic bags are yearly used in Europe, the 28 EU countries have agreed on a compromise to limit the number of plastic bags at the end of 2019 to 198 head/year and in 2020 to 40 head/year,[50] to which national parliaments have to consent.

---

44 Joern Genoux reported in *Kieler Nachrichten,* 22 October 2013, p. 7
45 The problem, incidentally, is not only plastic bottles, but everything made from plastic, eg the consequences of a growing proportion of use of synthetics. This has prompted Nicholas Coleridge, President of the British 'Campaign for Wool' to raise the question, given that there are six billion people living on Earth, what happens to their old synthetic clothing in 100 years? Should we fill-in every valley with synthetics?
46 Eric Holthaus, on Slate.com, published in *The Week,* 30 August 2014, p. 17
47 *Frankfurter Allgemeine Sonntagszeitung,* 28 July 2013
48 *Kieler Nachrichten,* 5 November 2013, p. 7
49 *Frankfurter Allgemeine Sonntagszeitung,* 10 November 2013, p. 69
50 *Kieler Nachrichten,* 19 November 2014, p. 5

And fishermen on the island of Fehmarn in Schleswig-Holstein execute a dual system called 'Fishing for Litter' initiated by NABU to clear waste from the sea wherever they can, having to learn that plastic waste, such as a canopy from a sailing boat, can block a ship's propeller. Scientists estimate that up to a million sea birds and 100,000 sea mammals die every year due to plastic being dumped in the sea.[51]

A new problem is the recent discovery of microscopically small plastic parts in the stomachs of petrels, 84 per cent from plastic bags, food wrappings, caps, plastic bottles, etc., plastic which disintegrates into tiny parts due to the effects of sunlight and sea and is then swallowed by birds and fish. Moreover, it's not just containers that are the problem. Beaches already consist of up to 30 per cent plastic parts from shower gels, skin peelings, shampoo and tooth paste. These microplastic parts are released into the groundwater polluting freshwater supply.[52] These days they are even found in honey. It was reported in May 2014 by the BBC that they are already forbidden in the US state of New York. Microscopic plastic parts are eaten by sea fish and snails thereby preventing propagation. They also attract poisonous insecticides such as dichlorphenyltrichloroethane (DDT) or polychlorianted biphenyls (PCB), both banned worldwide by the Stockholm Convention of 2001 as they are dangerous to both animals and people in the food chain.[53]

Like air, water is our primary food, and it is not only food, but can also help generate electricity. Today, small hydroelectric power stations are built, eg at the mouth of the river Schwentine in Kiel where the water height can vary by 1.76 m according to the tide. Though on a small scale, this power station will deliver a continuous supply of electricity for 200 households, day and night, from November 2013 onwards. It cost the investors about €600,000. – and will pay for itself within 20 years.

The right to use the water from the Schwentine river has been leased from Kiel's city authorities for 30 years. The Stadtwerke Kiel, the local supplier, runs also other water power stations at Rastorfer Muehle and at Rosensee with a respective capacity of 1.2 and 0.75 megawatts of electricity per year.

And what is especially interesting, is that engineers have successfully invented a turbine without a gear box, so that a full 100 per cent of water energy can now be transformed, whereas previously at least 15 per cent of primary energy was lost. What is needed now, is a law allowing such small-scale power stations to be installed delivering electricity to the grid, independently of the big electricity-generating companies.

Another innovative example is being found in the Orkney Islands of Scotland, where tidal power is being exploited to generate electricity. We need more of this type of small-scale innovation.

---

51 *Kieler Nachrichten*, 19 November 2013, p. 3
52 *Kieler Nachrichten*, 18 November 2013, p. 8
53 *Frankfurter Allgemeine Sonntagszeitung*, 2 February 2014, p. 59
    According to *Spiegel* online, 14 October 2014, scientists have found the pesticide DDT still in every soil level and washed into lakes.

11.1.1.3. External energy

In the 19th century, electric power stations, mostly using coal, were installed in towns. While electricity is not a human invention but one of nature's, and it seems that even the ancients knew how to use it,[54] power generation follows the law of electromagnetic induction discovered in 1831 by British scientist Michael Faraday (1791–1867). Power stations and also electricity grids were first established by private entrepreneurs as well as by communities, known in Germany as local '*Stadtwerke*' or municipal utilities, many of which are still in operation today.

After World War II, most electricity generating stations were transferred from town centres to the greenbelt to reduce air pollution in towns and allowed expansion of the companies. Then only it became clear how poisonous the legacy of the electricity industry was: communities had to spend huge amounts of money to clean the contaminated grounds of heavy metals, coal tar, chlorocarbons and other poisonous chemicals before they were able to offer the land to new companies building there and creating new jobs, or for the construction of new houses. But it was not only the land which suffered the effects of this dangerous industrial waste. People living close to electric power stations had obviously suffered too, as the rise in the number of children with allergies, and elderly people with asthma and respiratory tract cancer showed. However, what was forgotten then was that communities had the planning powers to achieve change, while they were only aiming to support of electricity generation to cater for the rising population.

Also, many communities had sold their electricity generating plants as well as the local grids to private companies. These succeeded in their aim of closing smaller power stations, for example industrial ones in companies to avoid competition and force consumers to buy electricity from them, until the majority of the power supply in a region was owned by them. No wonder that they then were also able to define public energy policies according to their interest. In Germany, for example, only the Big Four suppliers now remain[55] – E.ON, RWE, EnBW Energie Baden-Wuerttemberg and Vattenfall[56] – and each control different regional markets. It is therefore understandable that politicians and consumers are demanding more competition in the electricity market', a reduction in emissions and lower prices – not only for the industrial, but also for the private consumer.[57]

---

54 cf. the 2,000 year old so-called Baghdad battery.
55 In the UK there are the Big Six power companies.
56 A company owned by Sweden, while EDF in the UK is owned by France.
57 *Frankfurter Allgemeine Sonntagszeitung* reported 1 February 2015, that while the price for a barrel of oil has fallen compared to last year, the amount of oil appropriated or "produced" has not been reduced. This showed a report by analysts Rineesh Bansal and Stuart Kirk for DB Research and it is absolute rational for the oil countries as they came to the conclusion that oil is a so called 'stranded asset', for which there will be less demand in future as 80 per cent of coal, half of its gas and a third of its oil will need to stay in the ground if global warming is to stay within 2 C. The oil 'producers' are therefore trying to sell today as much as they can, even at lower prices. Also compare *The Independent* 4 March 2015, reporting about a warning from the Bank of England that 'Insurers face huge fossil fuel losses' to their investment portfolio as the world starts combating climate change by changing to renewables.
    Spiegel online reported 28 December 2014 that in 2014 sun, wind, water and biogas had in Germany the highest share of primary resources used to generate electricity with 25.8 per cent.

A change in perception has occurred. 60 years ago the emissions from chimneys of steam and flames burning poisonous gases symbolized economic progress. Today, however, we consider these images no longer appropriate as they show the pollution, inefficiency and outdated machinery. Today we are aware that combustion and digestion are the same process, both enabled by oxygen, discovered by Antoine Laurent de Lavoisier (1743–1794). What goes into the air will be incorporated into our bodies, thus making us ill.

However, any organization which claims that a sustainable, competitive energy strategy should be followed (eg the Oeko-Institut e. V. in Freiburg, Germany, proposed) must also recognize that any proposed change in the energy policy of a country – however healthier, more efficient and therefore more rational – will always have to compete against the vested interests of the electricity-generating companies relying on meanwhile outdated business models.

Remarkably enough, the same is not true when the legacies of these electricity giants are discussed. Then the Big Four find it acceptable for a government, ie the taxpayers, to pick up the bill for the damages they have inflicted over decades. Taxpayers' money is then used for cleaning-up operations, whether it is installing filters in chimneys, replacing polluted soil, decommissioning nuclear power stations and/or finding a solution to the safe disposal of radioactive nuclear waste, which remains dangerous to life for thousands of years. These costs are subsidies to the electricity generating companies, yet one never hears these companies arguing that the government should not interfere in these cases.

Quite the opposite, the nuclear power companies demand more public money, meaning the taxpayer should pay to clear-up the waste they caused. *The Wirtschaftswoche* reported on 19 May 2014 that the Big Four wanted the government to shoulder the costs for closing down out of order nuclear power stations and the government should pay for the safe disposal of radiating nuclear waste, demands which were met with public disgust in Germany. The nuclear power companies are legally bound to put aside reserves for cleaning-up their sites when these have gone out of production. From the 29 nuclear power stations there, 8 have already been shut down, however, the decommissioning process hasn't actually begun at any of these. These companies seem trying to avoid their legal obligations – because environmental laws rely on the responsibility of the initiator of damages – and are especially keen to avoid financing a solution for safe final nuclear waste disposal not only because 70 years after the start of using nuclear power, there is no solution, but also because nobody knows how a solution will look and how much money it will cost. Besides, it should be remembered that the companies have the reserves and have paid their shareholders from the United States, Canada, Great Britain and France already from 2000 to 2013 more than €60 billion in dividends.

The question we must ask is this: do our elected politicians really have the courage to change the basic infrastructure of electricity generation from radioactive resources and limited fossil fuels to unlimited renewable resources, ie from a centralized to a decentralized local structure, from inefficient transformation of primary energy resources into electricity to much more efficient processes, from costly primary resources to free ones for the universal use by everyone, from dependency on coal and oil producing countries to national independence, from costly long transport chains to local use and participative production, from an emphasis on private company profits to low utility prices for citizens? And, of course, not forgetting the change from costly long-term disposal of radiating waste to a technology which does not generate such waste. The above should be the guideline for modern 21st century electricity policy. With respect to this, Tom Bower[58] recalls the words of Nigel Lawson, a former Chancellor of the Exchequer who was "convinced that Britain could rely on market forces. "We don't need an energy policy," he had said.

Let's beg to differ. Instead let us look into how a modern energy policy could be formulated.

In recent decades the economic interest concentrated on increasing labour productivity. Instead of using labour, energy was employed – one of the reasons for the increase in energy demand in industrialized countries. In the 21st century, we need to concentrate on increasing energy efficiency and reducing pollution, which can come new employment chances for people.

In 1971, Barry Commoner pointed out that the solution to energy shortage is not to find more resources, but to use energy more efficiently.[59] In 1976, in the light of the 1973 oil crisis, he pointed out that 85 per cent of global energy could be saved but the power companies are aiming to sell more.[60] Thus, the economic and political goal should be efficiency.[61] To follow his demand, we have to remind ourselves of the laws of physics: Energy can neither be produced nor destroyed, but can only be transformed from one form into another; as Julius Robert Mayer formulated in 1841. Hence, humans are only are able to transform one form of energy into another, ie fossil fuels into heat, movement or electricity. In these transformation processes, a part of the useable primary energy is irretrievably lost, and entropy increased, as Rudolf Clausius discovered in 1854, meaning that we use the wrong words when we talk about 'energy production'. We should use the words "energy transformation" instead, as humans, following the laws of physics, cannot "produce" energy. I wonder why even a big power company such as the German E.on makes the mistake to write about energy "production" instead of energy "transformation" or "electricity production", eg in an a back-page advertisement in *Der Spiegel,* 30/2013. Don't they employ physicists who would be able to correct such errors made by their marketing department? Instead of 'energy production' we need to write 'electricity generation' or 'power production'.

---

58 in: *The Squeeze, Oil, Money and Greed in the 21st Century,* London, 2009, p. 186

59 in: *The Closing Circle, New York,* 1971, presenting four laws of ecology: 1. Everything is connected to everything else. 2. Everything must go somewhere. 3. Nature knows best. 4. There is no such thing as a free lunch.

60 Barry Commoner, *Energieeinsatz und Wirtschaftskrise, Die Grundlagen fuer den radikalen Wandel,* Reinbek, 1976, p. 135

61 Commoner ascertained as far back as 1976 that every economic system depends on goods manufactured by the production system, while the production system itself depends on resources offered by nature, but the relationship between these systems is seen the other way around. The reason for this, Commoner argued, is deeply hid in the design of today's societies.

As pointed out, electricity is transformed from energy resources which therefore are called 'primary' resources. Consequently, electricity is not the same as primary resources, like coal, oil or wood. Electricity is of a different quality. It is secondary energy.

If people believe that electricity is 'clean' to use, then they forget that in the transformation process from primary into secondary energy greenhouse gases are emitted.[62] For example, a strategy of replacing petrol-driven with electricity-driven cars is not rational within today's energy structure, as electricity has first to be generated, mostly from finite carbon primary resources with all the well-known consequences of pollution. Therefore the replacement does not make sense if the power for driving electric cars comes from fossil fuel or nuclear power stations. Electric cars are only more environmentally-friendly if they are fuelled by renewables, such as solar power, wind, photovoltaics or water. To use them on a large scale would therefore need to built up first a different electricity generation and distribution.

Globally, predominantly finite fossil primary resources are used to produce secondary electricity. Steven Koonin, Scientific Director of British Petroleum BP and professor at the CalTech Institute, pointed out in a speech at John-Hopkins-University in Baltimore, USA, in November 2007 that the worldwide energy demand can be broken down as follows:

a) 40 % to generate electricity, predominantly from coal,
b) 40 % to heat water and buildings, predominantly from mineral oil or natural gas,
c) 20 % for transport, predominantly from oil.

These shares clearly correspond to the branches causing most air pollution:[63]

energy industry	38.6 %
transport	17.1 %
manufacturing industry	12.6 %
households	9.5 %
agriculture	7.5 %
chemical industry	2.3 %
waste disposal	1.3 %
others	11.1 %

out of a total of 916.7 million tons greenhouse gas emissions.

The fossil energy resources on which our welfare still seems to be based today were formed in the carbon era of Earth, hundreds of million years ago. Even if emissions of harmful substances from the use of fossil energy resources could be

---

62 A similarly narrow viewpoint is presented if people argue that hydrogen is the fuel of the future, as it is found in nature in abundance. As Helmuth Herterich correctly pointed out in *Frankfurter Allgemeine Sonntagszeitung*, 1 September 2013, p. 9, hydrogen exists on Earth only in the form of water. Firstly, the hydrogen has to be separated from oxygen. Even when fuel cells or photovoltaics are used to separate hydrogen and oxygen, the costs of these technologies and their degree of effectiveness also have to be considered. In the end, it seems that more energy is necessary to separate hydrogen than is gained from burning it.

63 According to figures provided by the German Umweltbundesamt

prohibited, the problem still remains that fossil energy resources on Earth are limited and will come to an end. BP reported in its 'Statistical Review of World Energy', published 2013, that on the basis of today's level of extraction, fossil fuel reserves will be exhausted as follows:

- crude oil in 2065,
- natural gas in 2068,
- coal in 109 years,

meaning that natural fossil primary resources, produced by nature million years ago, will be consumed by our societies in only hundreds of years. Koonin argued that because of the limited availability of fossil fuels we can assume that their prices will rise, not only because they would become more scarce, but also because it would be more costly to extract them from the ground. However, we experience today a very different situation, lower oil prices and a higher share of renewables for electricity generation, because Koonin did not see that global warming will demand a change to use a different kind of primary resources.

When finite fossil fuels are burned, harmful gases like carbon dioxide, stored in them, are released up to a level which would not occur naturally.

A new energy concept for energy policy therefore should aim at:

a) Reducing energy loss when transforming primary resources into electricity
So, when the electricity industry is the worst greenhouse gas emitter, energy efficiency should start in this industry to reduce pollution.

The transformation of primary energy resources into the secondary energy, electricity, cannot be performed on a 1:1 basis, as every time a transformation takes place, some energy is irretrievably lost, approximately one third, so that only about two thirds can be used.[64]

Therefore, electricity should never be used for heating, and this practice has already been forbidden in Denmark, as firstly electricity has to be generated from primary resources, and then it produces heat of a relatively low temperature. Politicians could implement laws forbidding the production of electric radiators. Electricity should only be used to power machines and for lighting, and these appliances should only be switched to the grid, when they are needed, as leaving them on 'stand-by' is an unnecessary extravagance and a waste of resources.

Consequently, engineers and scientists should be encouraged further to find new ways of improving energy efficiency.

Although coal-firing technology has improved in recent years and today coal-fired power stations are more efficient and use better filters, there are better ways to reduce emissions and increase energy efficiency, than by continuing the use of coal. Although the energy industry seems to be taking this route, 27 scientists at the Warsaw Climate Summit warned that the climate problem could not be solved only by changing to less emission coal-burning technologies, as even the most

---

64   The German Bundesministerium fuer Wirtschaft und Technologie in Berlin identifies this as a 55:45 ratio. The newest coal-fired power plant installed in Karlsruhe has a transformation rate of 46 per cent according to *Der Spiegel*, 37/2014, p. 68.

efficient new coal-powered station emits 15 times more carbon dioxide than renewable energy systems. These scientists called the continuing use of coal a danger which threatens to exceed all others, humanity has had to deal with.[65]

One method of improving efficiency is to use the wasted heat, which is normally just released into the atmosphere when electricity is generated. This technology is called 'district heating'. It was invented in Lockport, New York, by Birdsill Holly in 1877. District heating was for example used to heat the Crystal Palace in London.

Using district heat is not only useful for the environment, but also profitable for electricity-generating power stations as well as for electricity consumers because:

- power stations cannot only sell electricity, but also heat that is otherwise wasted, thus making more profit,
- consumers can buy a reliable source of heat for warm water and radiators as well as save money for maintaining individual boilers.

In this way, the efficiency can be doubled using otherwise wasted heat.

It is therefore hard to understand why governments still allow new coal-fired power stations to be built without installing district heating, even when it is used so successfully in so many other countries. In Kiel/Germany, the local power generating company had even built a tunnel under the fjord to be able to deliver district heat to the west side of the city. Parliaments should legislate ensuring that power stations are only given planning permission if they combine electricity generation with district heating. The necessary infrastructure, like pipes, to deliver such heat could be built by municipal authorities, and perhaps supported with subsidies from central governments.

b) Reducing transmission losses of secondary energy/electricity

Energy is not only lost when primary resources are transformed into electricity; it is also lost when electricity, the secondary energy, is transported over long distances, in average about 7 per cent. Transporting electricity should therefore be avoided and replaced by transporting primary energy.

A more efficient use of primary energy would therefore concentrate on the following:

- combined heat and power in urban areas (district heating),
- the use of micro generators combining heat and power for individual buildings, especially in rural areas.

Electricity-generating companies need to be convinced that finite primary energy resources are used more efficiently when the electricity is generated locally and not centrally.

---

65 *Kieler Nachrichten*, 19 November 2013, p. 5

c) Avoiding greenhouse gases by using local carbon-free infinite and low risk resources to generate electricity
It is not only necessary to follow a policy of installing combined heat and power locally so that finite primary energy resources could be used more efficiently, it is also necessary to replace finite fossil fuels with infinite renewables for generating electricity and heat. Renewables such as biomass, solar, water, wind or geothermics have the advantages of being:

- non-fossil and carbon-free,
- infinite and renewable,
- of low risk,
- cost-free for everybody, once the technology has been installed,
- available to be used locally by everyone,
- waste-free,
- supply-secure as there is no need to be bought from politically-insecure countries,[66]
- participative for citizens.

Wind power comes with regional advantages, especially for the North and coasts, thus also favouring hitherto structurally weaker areas.[67]

Spiegel online reported on 26 May, 2012, that solar power in Germany had produced 22,000 megawatts electricity, equivalent 20 nuclear power stations in 2011. In Abu Dhabi, one of the biggest solar thermal power stations went into generating in March 2013, supplying 20,000 households and saving 175,000 t of CO_2.[68]

Any energy policy concentrating only on cheap prices without aiming at energy efficiency and without informing the citizens about the renewables advantages, is 'elementarily wrong', as Hubert Weiger, President of the Bund fuer Umwelt-und Naturschutz in Germany, expressed it.[69]

While renewables have so many advantages, even in terms of people's interaction with nature and for their purses, it does not really make sense trying to extract more finite fossil resources by reopening former oil fields, for example in places such as Schleswig-Holstein, Germany's biggest oil extracting Bundesland, or by

---

66 Tom Bower, pointed out in: *The Squeeze, Oil, Money & Greed in the 21st Century*, London, 2010, p. 127, that in the 1990s "over half of America's daily consumption of 18 million barrels of oil was imported ...".

67 *Die Welt* stated on 20 June 2013, p. 17, that Schleswig-Holstein the most norther region of Germany, installed 237 wind power stations producing 35 megawatts of electricity in 1990, while in 2012 3,403 megawatts were produced, nearly 100 times more, and 6,500 people employed. By 2020, the Schleswig-Holstein government believes, three to four times more electricity from renewables will be generated than is consumed. The Statistische Amt in Kiel reported on 29 November 2013 that the share of electricity generation from photovoltaics had risen by 41 per cent in 2012 compared to the year before.
   Die Welt published 30 January 2015, p. 20, that 4,750 megawatt wind power has been newly installed in 2014, referring to the Bundesverband Windenergie, meaning that the German wind power stations have increased to 24,867.

68 *Spiegel* online, 17 March 2013

69 *Kieler Nachrichten*, 4 September 2013, p. 5

fracking gas from tar sands. Such a strategy would merely delay the exhaustion of finite resources, but would not really solve the long-term problem.

Besides, 700 German companies, water suppliers, breweries and the Mineral Water Well Associations have formed an alliance against gas fracking. They worry about the consequences for the groundwater and are demanding legal action against its use.[70] Fracking, or hydraulic fracturing, which involves pumping water and chemicals under high pressure into ground to release fossil fuels, has been forbidden by law in France since 2011,[71] as it has, according to Brian Vine[72] "the potential to contaminate underground water supplies, cause minor earthquakes and pollute the environment with vast quantities of toxic wastewater". US climate campaigner Al Gore has called the oil extracted from tar sands "'the dirtiest source of liquid fuel you can imagine', and labelled plans to build a major new pipeline from the tar sands of Alberta to refineries on the Texas Golf 'insane'." The Canadian province Alberta has the third-largest petroleum reserves.

One really wonders why the alternative route of using renewables with their many advantages is not generally followed? Why is it so hard to change to a better solution for our energy supplies?

The use of renewables for generating electricity is cheaper and more sustainable, especially since prices have fallen in recent years, mostly due to competition from China. Furthermore, fears that renewable resources cannot guarantee a steady supply of electricity can now be calmed. One solution for saving energy we are already aware of, is the use of pumped-storage power stations built on mountain lakes. These are being set up not only in Germany, but also in Scandinavia, with an undersea cable connection, as the Norwegian energy minister Ole Borten Mo announced on 20 June 2012. As reported by *Spiegel* online on 24 May 2012. He explained that the "Netherlands already have a connection to the Norwegian grid since 2008, the Danes are connected to their northern neighbours with several cables, England and recently even Iceland are thinking about cable projects".

Additionally, every government would have good reasons to support technical progress on small-scale-electric batteries. The biggest commercially-run battery park in Schwerin, Germany, went on the grid on 16 September 2014 with 25,000 lithium-ion-accumulators which was supported by the German government with €1.3 m of the €6m investment.

It is only rational to shift the emphasis of any country's energy policy from finite resources to infinite renewables,[73] although we should not forget that such

---

70 *Kieler Nachrichten*, 23 November 2013, p. 6

71 This was contested by the Texan oil company Schuepbach, but upheld by the French Constitutional Council, as reported by *Kieler Nachrichten*, 12 October 2013

72 'The Return of Black Gold', in: *The Week*, 9 March 2013

73 One example is the German North Sea island Pellworm, which currently is 100 per cent reliant on renewables. Wind and solar plants produce 21 gigawatt/hours electricity — three times more than the island itself needs, so electricity supply from the mainland is no longer necessary. And in Great Britain, Orkney "has become arguably the most self-sufficient community in the British Isles for its energy, and it is home to many of the world's most advanced wave and tidal power machines", according to *The Guardian*, 29 August 2012, p. 9.

a policy challenges the historical structure of the electricity industry in most countries. However it would give people everywhere the hope that progress in the right direction, less pollution and cheaper and secure participative use can be achieved. We should also not forget that the International Congress for the Use of Solar Energy had already stated in 1977 that Sun delivers 30,000 times more energy in a year than the whole world needs. So, let's use it more.

When we switch from central fossil-fuel electricity use to self-generated renewables, for example by installing photovoltaics on the roofs of buildings or by installing wind power parks owned by locals, and insulate houses so that they become independent from external energy sources, that means we reduce the demand, then we have more electricity than is needed for consumption. Such a surplus can then be sold for a certain price and fed into the power grid.

With the so-called *feed-in tariff*, implemented by a coalition of the Sozialdemokraten und Gruene/Buendnis 90 in 1990, following the US example of Idaho of 1980[74]. Politicians have made sure that local renewable users have the right to sell their electricity at a price guaranteed by the government. The advantage for every small local electricity producer is then, that he does not need to start negotiating with the big electricity companies if his electricity will be bought and at what price. However, with regard to the *feed-in tariff*, it cannot be called a subsidy, as no money is handed out by a government. Otherwise, it is a subsidy when the UK government supports the nuclear industry to the tune of £2.3 billion.

A further push for decentralised renewables would certainly occur, if all local self-production, in this case: renewable electricity, would be made exempt from business tax, as it is in the UK.

And additionally, in this way local electricity producers change their social status from passive consumers to active producers. To the end of 2014, 46 countries had already implemented a feed-in-tariff.

In 2012, the proportion of renewable generated electricity was increased in Germany from 16.4 per cent to 22.1 per cent.[75] That puts the use of renewable primary resources ahead of nuclear power, which accounted for 16.1 per cent of electricity production. The Umweltbundesamt in Berlin is convinced that it is possible to generating all electricity from renewables by 2050, thus stopping the country from being dependent on energy imports.

At the same time, the big power companies have warned that Germany's lights will go out. Instead of listening to the rational arguments which speak for locally used renewables, they have chosen to threaten politicians with a 'switch-off' of power stations.[76] However, threatening is never a good business policy, even if rational progress spoils the traditional business model of the big electricity companies, obviously having underestimated the success of the German

74   It is called in the USA *net-metering*, but contrary to the *feed-in-tariff*, locally produced renewable electricity is not paid a government guaranteed price, but is sold for lower prices.

75   *Kieler Nachrichten*, 3 Jul 2013

76   *Spiegel* online, 19 July 2013

'*Energiewende*' or energy transition.[77] Now they feel their only solution is to try to block the transition and frighten their customers with warnings that change is dangerous. They obviously want to keep their monopoly over the passive consumers. However, today energy's policy follows the law of nature and energy efficiency than keeping up a model invented 100 years ago. I think they should be well advised to change their propaganda and spear-head the change from centralized finite fossil fuels to decentralized infinite renewables, but there is reason for doubt if they will be flexible enough to do this.

While the points discussed above have focussed on the generation of electricity from primary resources, the next section will discuss further measures to improve energy efficiency.

d) Improving energy efficiency

Heat losses in buildings are the overwhelming cause for high energy demand. Tackling such losses is essential in order to improve energy efficiency – and to reduce energy bills for consumers. These days houses can be built which do not need energy for heating, warm water and running household appliances, but instead produce electricity and supply it to the grid. "Consultancy McKinsey reckons that, with a concerted effort, non-transportation energy consumption in America could be cut by around 25 per cent by 2020. In terms of cutting emissions, that would be like taking every car off the road... Bank of America Merrill Lynch suggests this will be a key investment 'megatrend' of the future... Any serious attempt to improve energy efficiency needs to involve the housing and construction industries. That's because energy consumption within buildings accounts for two-fifths of global energy use, according to the US Environmental Protection Agency (EPA), and a third of carbon emission... On a larger scale the European Union has set minimum energy performance requirements for new buildings. The aim is for all new buildings to achieve 'zero energy' status by 2020 – these are buildings that actually produce more energy than they consume via the installation of wind turbines or solar panels. To help achieve this, the European Investment Bank and the European Bank for Reconstruction and Development have helped facilitate nearly €15 billion-worth of investment since 2002."[78] And to quote *Scientific American* "New buildings aim to produce energy, not consume it."[79]

But it is not only necessary to built new houses which are better at energy efficiency, it is even more necessary to energetically modernize existing ones, as these make up the bulk of the buildings stock. Such a strategy would also create new jobs,[80] allowing more people to earn a monetary income. And these jobs would be in the service industry, working on solutions for different demands and needs of the houses. Unnecessary to point out, that they would adhere to the principle of reciprocal interaction.

77   *Frankfurter Allgemeine Sonntagszeitung*, 8 September 2013, p. 25

78   *Moneyweek*, 14 June 2013, p. 24–25

79   4 April 2011

80   A UN report of 2012 forecasted that up to 60 million new jobs could be created if the world would switch to renewables, *The Independent,* 6 August 2013.

Existing buildings can be modernized by insulating them to an optimum level (including outside walls, windows and especially window frames, entrance doors, ceilings and floors). Properly insulated buildings with optimal heat wraps can reduce heating cost by more than 80 per cent for the people living in them. In a way, insulation pays for itself. A German '*Passivhaus*', the first of which was built in 1990 in Darmstadt, uses only 10 per cent of the energy of standard buildings and 'net zero energy' houses use no external energy at all.

The support of the German publicly-owned bank Kreditanstalt fuer Wiederaufbau (KfW) founded in 1948 was essential in supporting energy efficient building. In 2012 the bank invested a total of €73.4 billion – in energy efficiency and modernization, also a big push for local craftsmen.

Politicians sometimes fear a growing sector of the population which is no longer able to afford rising energy prices,[81] meaning that low-income families will struggle with paying their energy bills. In response to this problem, governments could start a means-tested insulation programme for houses. This would be a far wider reaching rational government policy than providing billions of pounds of loans to fossil fuel projects in other countries, even to state-owned companies[82] for example; "Gazprom in Russia, Brazil's state owned oil company and petrochemical companies in Saudi Arabia are among those to have benefited from about £ 1.7 bn in government funding, Greenpeace has found. The UK Export Finance (UKEF) deals appear to fly in the face of the 2010 coalition agreement, in which the Conservatives and Lib Dems pledged to clamp down funding for fossil fuel operations abroad." Why financing other countries and not the UK taxpayers with the taxes they have paid? And why is the government which is normally so fond of privatisation not leaving it to other sovereign states to finance their own investments? Is it not much more necessary to get the local UK economy going, initiate jobs and knowledge to local people than shuffling money abroad?

In the very same edition of the paper on p. 37 Aditya Chakrabortty reports exactly about this, the lack of funding available for local initiatives, like Building Bloqs, "bringing jobs to jobless local economy, reinserting manufacturing into a deindustrialised husk of a place," especially when private banks do not support it, nor do Lloyds or the ethical bank Triodos.

The much bigger problem, however, is that all consumers are not offered equally fair tariffs by the power companies, because consumer tariffs are mostly structured in such a way that the industry pays less than the average small energy consumer. Here, consumers and taxpayers substitute the industry. A study by the GRUENEN party found that German households currently pay 27 cent per kilowatthour, 35 per cent more than in 2008, while the prices paid by the industry has remained at 10.1 cent.

In the UK there is for example the Stroud-based company Ecotricity offering 100 per cent green electricity at a lower price than the standard regional tariffs of the Big Six British energy generators. So it is possible to offer customers green power at fair prices.

---

81 *Der Spiegel* 38/2013, p. 16
82 *The Guardian*, 6 January, 2015, p. 7

Furthermore, many manufacturing companies which in the past were using their own waste heat have given up that activity, because the big suppliers have offered them energy at lower prices. Fair? Judge yourself.

In this way power suppliers also act wastefully. They make companies dependent on their cheap offers instead of letting them generating electricity themselves. This is another example of self-directed activities – as well as responsibilities – being replaced with the act of buying.

However, energy, in whichever form it is used, is a BASE of life and should not be made dependent on monetary terms, ie how much people are able to pay for it, as then people with MEANS can use more than others without it. And public services companies should not be allowed to strive for the highest possible monetary profits. They should remember that they have a social responsibility to their customers. Supplying the public with energy is a public service, which should be delivered locally following the most rational secure supply and the cheapest prices for everyone.

he question remains, as to why politicians have not yet started the systematic and energetic modernization of public buildings,[83] when on the other hand the government finances energy-saving programmes for their citizens. Here too it seems that politicians see their responsibility to influence the behaviour of other citizens while not changing their own,[84] developing themselves into much-needed role models.

Although the EU has proposed that every member state should commit itself to modernizing 3 per cent of public buildings a year, most regions do not make it their practise. One of the reasons is probably that they do not balance energy efficiency investments against future savings, perhaps a consequence of the outdated method of public budget accounting, another field that can profit from modernization. Furthermore, the knowledge of builders, architects and engineers needs to be improved, eg by forcing universities to modernize their teaching schedules and offer courses according to the demands of energy efficiency, i. e. reducing emissions.

For heating, relatively low temperatures are necessary. These can be achieved by renewables, such as solarthermic panels, geothermics, even wind turbines[85] and so on. However, when going solar, photovoltaics should be preferred, as these are more versatile. They produce electricity directly which then can be used for all

83 Thank goodness, it seems that the Church does not have the same fear of renewables than governments seem to have. *The Mail On Sunday*, 11 March 2012, reported that "One hundred vicarages, ten churches and seven church schools have had solar panels installed at a cost of more than £1.5 million in the past three months. This is in addition to the 300 churches, vicarages and Church of England schools in the region that use energy from Ecotricity, the Stroud-based renewable company that the Church has chosen as its green supplier. And there are plans to extend the solar scheme nationwide to 16,00 church buildings... Church of England procurement officer Russell Stables aid: 'This is far more than a cost-saving exercise - it is a means of demonstrating good stewardship and releasing money... Ecotricity founder Dale Vince said: 'The Church is setting a great example.'"

84 Although, to be fair to civil servants, in Germany an initiative called 'mission E' was introduced for saving energy in federal offices, although not on building them.

85 As installed on a four-storey townhouse made of wood in Steigereiland, Amsterdam, Netherlands.

domestic energy purposes, for household appliances, lighting, cooking, cooling and heating rooms or water.

Besides, it should not be overlooked, that the energy efficiency of consumer products needs to be improved. Governments have already made available more information on the energy consumption of household appliances so that consumers have a choice in saving energy. Still more needs to be done. Is it really necessary, for example, for home computers and radios to still use power when totally being switched off? And why should television sets be left on stand-by? Do we really need electric lemon presses?[86] And it would also be worthwhile if manufacturers would offer a range of household goods which provide certain basic mechanical operations which are easy to repair? This is a matter which has not been adequately discussed in public. Let us at least raise some more questions involving energy efficiency: Is it really necessary that most of today's communication technology to become "smart"? Is it really necessary for electric household appliances, such as radios, microwaves or ovens, to have built-in clocks which cannot be shut off, so that when you come into the kitchen at night, the whole room is lit up? Why do radios need to be totally reprogrammed if their power supply is removed ? Why do landline phones switch from one bright function to another, again to lit up a room in the night? Why do we have to actually unplug laptops to stop them using electricity? Why do electric toothbrushes show a flickering light when they only rest on their stand? It seems that the terms 'shut down' and 'remove' have become virtually meaningless in the world of electronic communication, as has the term 'deleted', when these emails turn up under the rubric 'deleted', meaning they are still existing. Is it really essential for pictures to be displayed in electric frames?

We have to be aware that the change of the medium, from paper to digitalized electronic information, also creates the possibility to edit pictures and so change the reality of the moment when they were taken, as this new facility allows us to 'improve' pictures – whatever that means – while in doing so, we change their history. And be aware, if every industrial product comes with these possibilities, the choice of consumers is more limited than extended.

When the city of Paris starts dimming the street lights at night, saving €200 million on its electricity bill and 250,000 tonnes of greenhouse gases, it is expected that more office lights will be switched off and shop window lights reduced. This could create the fear that "… urban centres will be plunged into a dismal and potentially dangerous gloom".[87] Instead of seeing this as an advantage, light pollution is seen as the natural order which has to be kept up.

However, we could follow the example of Sweden[88] making it the law that their self-governed communities switch to renewable energy by 2030.

When it became the economicult aim to replace human labour by the use of energy, as this is more productive for making money, this aim led to a rise in energy consumption. Then the energy industry came to believe that rise in pro-

---

86 A question posed by the journalist Winand von Petersdorf in the *Faz*, 2 September 2012, p. 39
87 *The Week*, 6 July 2013, p. 7
88 Nadine Oerhuber in: *Frankfurter Allgemeine Sonntagszeitung*, 18 May 2014, p. V7

duction and consumption will go on. Now it is made the basis of their expectation. It was expected that power companies would always be able to sell more electricity, thus making more profit. Are we therefore perhaps nudged into buying and using more and more electricity, because the industry invented more functions for machines and more machines, whilst there is no real choice left for consumers who would prefer appliances without them? There are so many areas where energy efficiency can be improved – and this without diminishing consumer services. However, can it be in interest of the industry to deal with consumers who want less electricity but more energy efficiency?

Last but not least, it has been reported that buildings can be cooled by using cold water from rivers and not only by electric air conditioning. On 24 July 2013, the German TV program 'Tagesschau' informed viewers that the French capital Paris has installed a 140 km long coldwater network, using water from the river Seine to cool houses. After use the warmed up water is returned to the river and then carried into the sea. This is an advantage, as electric air conditioning merely transports the heat out of a building, burdening the micro-climate of the town with even higher temperatures. But what about the consequences for life in the Seine? It has also been reported that the Chinese town of Dalian by the Yellow Sea has copied the example of Paris in its new International Conference Centre.

In 2005, the European Commission passed minimum energy efficiency standards to improve the environmental friendliness of products to which energy consumption is relevant, and added the following new product groups in 2013:

- heating systems,
- water heaters,
- vacuum cleaners,
- network standby and
- computers.

Furthermore, not only energy-using products (EUPs), but also energy related products (ERPs) are considered which can contribute to energy saving, such as windows, insulation material, shower heads, taps, etc. It is hoped that the annual electricity consumption in the 28 EU countries can be reduced by 20 per cent from 2020 on.[89] The European Commission aims to enhance product quality and ensure environmental protection, and also tries to make sure that goods of the same standard can move freely across the EU: "It prevents disparate national legislation of the environmental performance of these products from becoming obstacles to the intra-EU trade."[90] The EU Commission in Brussels thinks that 19 terrawatt hours of electricity can be saved, equalling the production of four nuclear power plants, if all household goods were manufactured according to the latest efficiency criteria,[91] saving as well money to consumers, if they do not chose to spend it on additional functions of products or have to adapt to rising energy prices.

---

89   www.dena.de, press release EU Ecodesign Directive
90   www.ec.europa.eu/energprise/policies/sustainable-business/ecodesign
91   *Kieler Nachrichten*, 27 August 2014, p. 7

e) Improving energy efficient transport

A public strategy for energy efficiency also has to consider transport. Mobility is one of the basic needs of people. Whilst the most energy efficient mode of transport is by ship, it is obviously only possible to use this in certain circumstances.

Methods of transport can be ranked according to their energy efficiency, and then this ranking can become a strategy to ensure mobility policy for everyone. A study of the environmental effects of different means of carriage in Austria was conducted by the IFEU-Institut in Heidelberg, Germany, in 2005 resulting in the following findings:

carrier	energy use in litres diesel/seat/100 km
bus	0.6 l
train	0.9 l
car with diesel engine	1.6 l
car with petrol engine	1.8 l
aeroplane	4.2 l

The ranking shows that buses and trains are the most energy-efficient carriers. Buses and trains offer public transport. It follows, of course, that public transport has to be prioritized over individual car use, and it should also be made a priority that buses and trains use electricity generated from renewable resources. There is no reason why buses and trains cannot be equipped with photovoltaic panels on their roofs to support electricity use. The additional argument for prioritizing public transport was that with future increases on finite fuels less people would be able to afford private transport by petrol driven cars.

In putting the focus on public transport by buses and trains as oppose to air travel, for example, it should also be emphasized that trains connect town centres directly while airports are normally outside towns. This means that if the time for travelling to an airport, checking-in, going through security and waiting are added, it transpires that over a range of 300 miles the use of trains can be more time efficient.

However, there is another problem that needs to be tackled: that is the fares paid by consumers of public transport. Today we find that air travel is sometimes cheaper than train travel, although less environmentally friendly and more time consuming. Because of relatively cheaper prices, people might prefer the plane. One of the reasons for relatively cheaper tickets is that airlines do not yet have to pay taxes on their fuel, while trains and buses have to which is an absurd situation and a form of subsidizing airlines by a government. But there is no reason for taxpayers to do so. A European initiative is necessary to tax kerosene in the same way as petrol and diesel. This measure would boost the public transport budget for investment helping to ensure that it remains a public obligation.

Furthermore, it is necessary to offer faster trains to the public with high-quality comfort for medium and long distances. Such high-speed trains are already in use in France, Germany, Japan, Spain, Turkey and Switzerland. Investment into a high-speed public train network should also separate passenger and freight trains. And the energy advantages for train travel need to be made transparent to people, eg by offering them perhaps free use of the high-speed network for one day, so can experience the benefits first hand themselves. Today, people are used to drive cars, but they do not know enough about the advantages of train travel. There is marketing to be done by the government.

In many countries there are continual complaints about the reliability of the public transport networks as well as their complicated pricing policies. Sometimes cheaper tickets can only be bought by booking a long time in advance or via the internet. This has to change. Public transport is a public service to citizens which should not aim solely at making the highest possible profit. There is no reason why railway staff shouldn't be able to sell tickets to passengers on the go on the trains.

Furthermore, as public mobility is part of our basic needs, it should come free, paid for by taxpayers, as the building and maintenance of roads is. It should be run as a public obligation to a country's inhabitants in the same way as facilitating direct mobility (walking, cycling). The Estonian capital Tallinn has set itself already to that task[92] copying Belgian, French and US American examples. And the magazine *Country Living* reported in its January 2015 issue, p. 37–38, that in the UK there are at least 2,000 schemes of not-for-profit mobility services with nearly 50,000 volunteers, helping people to get from A to B, at the same time promoting social inclusion and community bonds. "As cash-strapped local authorities withdraw the subsidies that used to shore up commercially unviable rural bus services, some of the most vulnerable people in our communities - the poor, elderly or disabled - are being left without any means of travel. As a result, they may be unable to access employment, medical treatment, leisure facilities or social events, perpetuating their isolation and disadvantage." The magazine then gave advice how to start an innovative community project for social transport and to get support, as for example from the Supporting Community Transport Fund, the Climate Challenge Fund or The Prince's Countryside Fund.

In the meantime, private train operators who leave people without seats because they profit if less carriages are used, should lose their contracts. It must be possible to improve existing contracts with private train companies by specifying the amount of seating, the quality of carriages, ticket price, punctuality, as well as improved marketing train services to the public.

Using public transport not only reduces greenhouse gas emissions, but it also relieves people of the stress driving long distances and finding a space to leave their car, perhaps even without paying for it, at the end of journeys. To convince more people to switch to public transport where possible , it is necessary to inform them how to use it, how to get from A to B as well as to whom to complain to if the service has let them down.

Running transport as an efficient and energy efficient service to the public, means learning from existing transport strategies in other countries. One such strategy is Switzerland's integrated transport policy, enabling citizens to use one ticket, one tariff and one timetable at moderate prices. A first start is made in the

---

92 *The Independent*, 29 November 2012

UK when First Great Western trains offer passenger aiming for London a ticket which includes the use of London transport. Switzerland's policy integrates the schedule of high-speed trains, local trains, buses, the underground and trams so that citizens can easily change from one carrier to the other. Integrated transport services should be the aim, and more bus and train companies should be forced to cooperate to ensure that it works.[93] The goal is to define transport from the point of the consumer as an efficient, environmentally friendly, integrated and easy-to-use service.

However, in the last 60 years the public policy was concentrated on destroying existing local train networks, closing railway lines and selling tracks, because politicians believed that the future would be to concentrate on individual car use. How short-sighted this was. And how many damages for people and the environment it has caused. When less and less public transport was on offer, people were even forced to use cars with the consequence that towns became polluted with exhaust fumes, motorways, roads and streets became congested, therefore car journeys took more and more time, and the possibility of finding a place to park a car without paying for it, shrank. Now towns have made their limited spaces more expensive to use, thus making car use and parking dependent on private financial MEANS, while the towns even financially profited from it. The transport problem still awaits a solution, and the solution is an integrated transport strategy.

Another aspect of an integrated transport strategy is the 'revival' of local train network, as it is currently followed in the German Bundeslaender Niedersachsen and Schleswig-Holstein. Neglected railway stations were renovated in an energy-efficient way and made a respected centre for the community with a personal service instead of ticket machines.

An integrated transport strategy does not only mean a better co-operation between different carriers, but also integrating it in town planning. When new houses are planned, they should, wherever possible, be built in easy reach of local railways stations.

However, as it is good that local train enthusiasts maintain and operate them in their free time, offering tourists a special experience, it would be a lot better if this would become the goal of official policy. The so-called 'Athens Charta' – a document of 1944 outlining a new understanding of how towns have to be planned, ie separated into quarters for living, working and leisure with these sections connected via roads using cars – is no longer appropriate in modern planning, and this model needs to be replaced by integrated planning strategies.

Furthermore, before new houses are build on green sites, research should be conducted into the amount of empty spaces in towns, eg brownfield sites left behind by industry or empty spaces above town centre shops, which could be transformed into accommodation, as these sites are already well connected to the necessary infrastructure, such as nurseries, schools, local authorities, hospitals, surgeries or homes for the elderly.

Empty rooms above shops in towns have mostly fallen into disuse as there are

---

93 If this can be done in Derbyshire in the holiday season, why can it not be extended everywhere at all times?

no separate entrances for potential residents. Councils could, for example, pay subsidies to house owners to help them build separate entrances and renovate such spaces for residential purposes, enlarge attics and even build roof gardens to so improve the micro-climate in towns. Inner-city living could thus be made highly attractive, and the existing infrastructure better utilised. A lot of traffic could be saved if people look for accommodation where they work, with the added benefit of making towns lively again. Of course, it has to be added that, if people living in inner-cities do own cars, the problem of how to offer them parking facilities needs to be solved, but there is also a solution to this. The council could offer to build multi-storey car parks exclusively for town-living. There is no reason to complain about urban desolation when there is so much potential to re-invigorate towns, mixing living and working quarters – with the support of participating citizens of course. There is no need to wait for big building companies to start on such plans, as we all can contribute to town regeneration.

In 2011, the share of gross renewable energy across Europe amounted to the following figures, according to the Statistische Bundesamt, Wiesbaden:

Austria	62.0 %
Sweden	55.5 %
Latvia	41.2 %
Finland	31.0 %
Slovenia	29.1 %
Denmark	28.7 %
Romania	28.4 %
Portugal	26.9 %
Spain	20.6 %
Italy	16.6 %
Slovakia	15.5 %
Germany	15.4 %

These countries have, more or less, already fulfilled the European targets, while France uses 14.4. per cent and Ireland 11.7 per cent, ie over 10 per cent. For every other European country the figure is under 10 per cent. In the UK, renewables currently account for only 5.6 per cent of gross electricity. In an article for *The Telegraph Magazine*,[94] Edward Platt complained that "so far, Britain has made slow progress towards the Renewables Obligation set by the European Union of generating 15 per cent of our energy needs from renewable sources by 2020, and towards the target mandated in the Climate Change Act of 2008 of cutting carbon emissions by 80 per cent by 2050.[95] Yet the government believes our reserves of wind, wave and tidal power will enable us to meet them. It estimates that offshore wind alone could meet Britain's current demand for electricity 10 times over, and

94 dated 28 July 2012
95 *Spiegel* online published on 6 March 2015 that the EU has now officially decided on new goals for a global climate agreement which all countries were demanded to present at the UN climate summit in Paris in December 2015. The EU aims at reducing greenhouse gas emissions about at least 40 per cent compared to 1990 by 2030.

environmental campaigners are urging the government to make the most of its potential. 'Forty years ago, we were discovering North Sea oil, now, as we find ourselves on the cusp of a technological revolution, we are sitting on the most fabulous resource once again,' Andrew Pendleton of Friends of the Earth told me. "It would be a tragedy if we didn't exploit it." Platt reported that the largest wind farm in the world, at Thanet, was set up in 2008, generating 300 megawatts, enough power for 240,000 homes in Britain, but an even larger wind farm is planned in the form of the London Array with 175 turbines and a 630-megawatt capacity, enough to provide electricity for 470,000 homes. The only problem, he sees, however, is that "the vast majority of Britain's offshore wind farms are built, owned and operated by foreign companies." It seems he concludes, "that we have lost faith in our engineers and innovators."

This complaint is also heard in Gloucestershire where people voted against a solar panel farm because it would be owned by foreigners, forgetting that it is not necessary to wait for 'the industry' to invest in renewables, but local landowners, farmers and other citizens can also cooperate to do it themselves as it is done in other countries.

In Germany, 40 per cent of renewable electricity is currently generated by the initiatives of citizens,[96] for example in the form of energy co-operatives. There are 656 energy co-operatives producing 580,000 megawatt hours of green electricity with which 160,000 households can be supplied.[97] So, why are other countries waiting? A government campaign to support such self-activity therefore would be most helpful. To make the technical revolution from finite fossil to infinite sustainable resources successful, it is necessary to not only to extend the grid, but also to secure the participation of every citizen. When it is only big private companies that are involved, this does not transform former passive consumers into active prosumers, and it does not empower people to partake actively in sustaining the BASE. Instead, the traditional economicult logic is allowed to operate: companies sell an anonymous ready-made product with the aim of making a monetary profit to consumers.

We learned after the federal election that the German association of Energy and Water, Bundesverband der Energie-und Wasserwirtschaft (BDEW), has published a new model to replace the Feed-In-Tariff[98] or the publicly guaranteed price for electricity. This new model would need to legislate producers offering locally generated power on an electricity stock exchange. The consequences, easy to see, would be that no small property owner would install renewables, as nobody could be sure that the self-generated electricity could be sold at a reliable price. Active prosumers would be forced again to revert to their traditional role as passive consumers. Any shift from a market' to reciprocal interaction of self-organised 'prosumers' would be reversed.[99] And the more rational and efficient solution would be given up, as a network of small local electricity prosumers, like

96 Bundesverband Erneuerbare Energie e.V., October 2012
97 *Kieler Nachrichten*, 25 July 2013
98 *Die Welt*, September 2013, p. 10
99 *Frankfurter Allgemeine Sonntagszeitung*, 17 November 2013, p. 28

that supported by the Hamburg company Lichtblick'. It is regrettable that the BDEW did not care to take this into his consideration.

f) Implementing energy security

On 30 June 2011 the German Federal Parliament decided again[100], this time following an initiative of the Conservatives and Liberals, that the use of nuclear power for generating electricity was to end in December 2022. The share of renewable primary resources should rise continuously to at least 25 per cent by 2020, 50 per cent by 2030, 65 per cent by 2040 and 80 per cent by 2050.[101] Such a political strategy was supported by 82 per cent of Germans.[102] It is called in Germany, as mentioned, the '*Energiewende*', another word which is now used by the international community alongside '*Waldsterben*', '*Zeitgeist*' or 'Kindergarten'. A survey by the Zentrum fuer Europaeische Wirtschaftsforschung (ZEW),[103] Mannheim, so-called '*Energiemarktbarometer*', asking 200 experts from science and industry about their thoughts about this *Energiewende* and how it is politically implemented, yielded – quite typically – a view only focussed on the price of energy; not on energy efficiency, on energy supply security, or even the participation of prosumers. Money is all that needs to be considered, it seems.

On 29 March 2014, EU Commissioner Oetinger called[104] for new and binding energy efficiency goals. The EU is the largest importer of primary energy, therefore energy efficiency is more important here than in other regions.

Experts talked of the disadvantages for conventional big global energy companies who might have problems adapting, whilst new companies, using renewables, will profit. This, however, is the way of the world: traditional habits are replaced by a new, more rational approach. And it is always up to the traditional companies to learn from new ideas, because if not, they will have problems to continue their business model.

The reason for the renewed decision of the German government to end the use of atomic power was the nuclear disaster of 2011 in Fukushima, Japan,[105] following an earthquake and a tsunami, which was the fourth global nuclear catastrophe since Windscale in Cumbria, UK in 1957, Three Mile Island in 1979 and Chernobyl, UdSSR in 1986.[106] These were catastrophes in which reactors exploded,

---

100 There had been a similar initiative a few years before under a Sozialdemokraten and Die Gruenen government.
101 Deutscher Bundestag: Die Beschluesse des Bundestages on 30 June.
    Conservatives and Liberals decided not to pursue an initiative for an action plan to improve energy efficiency and energy saving, while the Socialdemocrates voted for it.
102 Reported by the *Verband der Verbraucherzentralen*, 12 August 2013.
103 *ZEW* Supplement *ZEWnews*, July/August 2013, Special feature on the energy market.
104 In an interview with *Spiegel* online.
105 And while the Japanese government had given up nuclear power after the Fukushima catastrophe, the conservative government under Prime Minister Shinzo Abe decided in April 2014 to use it again.
106 It should not be forgotten that while more than 140,000 people were injured or died, such disasters also contribute to economic growth and the creation of new jobs as damage removal and repairs need doing. We have already pointed out the phenomenon that the economicult system profits from its self-generated damages.

releasing radioactive radiation into the environment.

But what about the incidents of more gradual radioactive poisoning, like the consequences of the Sellafield reprocessing facility in Cumbria dumping radioactive waste into the Irish Sea? Who is learning from it, stopping it and changes political strategy? And when catastrophic floods occur, like in the UK in the winter of 2013/14, what does the government do to prevent flooding of nuclear power sites, for example at Hinkley Point C, where the French company EDF is building a new power station?

Using nuclear power for peaceful purposes means generating electricity by using a nuclear chain reaction. Nuclear power was previously used only for military purposes,[107] for example the bombs which the USA dropped on Hiroshima and Nagasaki in 1945 to make Japan surrender.[108]

It was Albert Einstein who, out of fear that Nazi Germany might be the first to build atomic bombs, proposed in a letter to the American President Roosevelt that a fission weapon could be build, an initiative Einstein regretted throughout the rest of his life. The consequences were foreseen very clearly by John Foster Dulles, "Eisenhower's future hawkish secretary of state": "If we, a professedly Christian nation, feel morally free to use atomic energy in that way, men elsewhere will accept that verdict. Atomic weapons will be looked upon as a normal part of the arsenal of war and the stage will be set for the sudden and final destruction of mankind."[109]

While a lot more countries today own nuclear weapons, despite the international Non-Proliferation Treaty, the biggest arsenal is held by the United States of America. Hitherto, the world can only be thankful that nuclear bombs have not

---

In Chernobyl, for example, 3,500 people are currently employed to control the restricted area, make sure the cooling systems work and build a new sarcophagus around the exploded reactor, as reported by the *Frankfurter Allgemeine Sonntagszeitung*, 14 October 2012, p. 11.

107 The Campaign *Don't Bank on the Bomb* reported on 10 October 2013 that they had investigated 310 global banks and their involvement in the nuclear weapons industry. They found out that 12 banks – all European – do not finance this industry, while out of the remaining 298 banks, 8 German banks do, along with 2 from the UK and 166 from the US. Even in Japan, the first country which suffered nuclear bombing, 2 banks were found to be financing this industry, although there is a global Nuclear Non-Proliferation Treaty in place which should also include a law against financial investments into it.

The other question is that, out of the eight German banks financing the nuclear weapons industry, five, Bayern LB, Helaba, KfW, Sparkassen Finanzgruppe and the Cooperative DZ Bank, are public banks, while only three are private. One wonders if their public owners are informed about their deals and have supported it, because the end of nuclear power use in Germany also needs to include no public bank investment in this technology.

108 67 years later Oliver Stone and Peter Kuznick proved that the reason for the nuclear bombing of Hiroshima and Nagasaki was not so much to force the surrender of Japan which would have happened anyway, but much more to show the USSR how powerful the USA is and to "use the U.S. atomic monopoly to force Soviet compliance with U.S. demands," in: *The Untold History of the United States*, London, 2012, p. 184

109 Ibid, p. 177;

Arthur Koestler made in: *Der Mensch, Irrlaeufer der Evolution, Die Kluft zwischen Denken und Handeln, Eine Anatomie menschlicher Vernunft und Unvernunft*, Frankfurt, 1989, the same argument, seeing the 6 August 1945 as the most important date in our history because for the first time mankind is now able to destroy its own species, and perhaps life on Earth as well.

been used anywhere else besides Japan. And we can only hope that other nations are aware that a nuclear war cannot be 'won' in the old sense, as every country around the globe would be affected by the radioactive fall-out and a global winter, so nobody could be the 'winner'.

As well known, it was the American President Dwight D. Eisenhower who "began a campaign at home and abroad to promote what he called 'the peaceful atom', ... generated by his December 1953 UN address. The Atomic Energy Commission (AEC) marketed nuclear power not only as a protector against godless communism but as a magic elixir that would power transportation vehicles, feed the hungry, light the cities, heal the sick, and excavate the planet. The U.S. Postal Service issued a stamp celebrating 'Atoms for Peace: To Find the Way by Which the Inventiveness of Man Shall Be Consecrated to New Life.'"[110] But, testing nuclear bombs still went on. Oliver Stone and Peter Kuznick listed a few purposes for which nuclear bombs have been thought useful as 'peaceful' employment – before considering the consequences of course:

- bombs near the Arctic Circle which... would warm the polar area by approximately 10^{111} degrees Fahrenheit,
- planetary excavations (Project Plowshare),
- creating a 300-foot harbour in Alaska north of the Artic Circle (Project Chariot),
- freeing inaccessible oil deposits trapped in both tar sand and shale formation,
- creating huge underground reservoirs,
- producing steam,
- desalinising water,
- cracking copper and other impregnable ores,
- producing radioactive isotopes for use in medicine, biology, agriculture and industry,
- blasting a new, bigger and better Panama Canal,
- altering weather patterns "to accelerate melting of the polar icecaps by detonating ten 10-megaton bomb",

propositions which would be unthinkable today.

And then came the peaceful use of nuclear power for generating electricity. In July 1955, the first US nuclear power station began production. The peaceful use of nuclear power was agreed in 1955 at a conference attended by 1,200 scientists from 72 countries. This agreement was based on the hope that it would be possible to gain cheap electricity in abundance, and it caused many countries to spend billions on subventions for nuclear research, in 2011 the EU countries spent €35 billion on the nuclear industry.[112] "A recent environmental committee of MPs found that nuclear power gets an annual subsidy worth £2.3 billion a year..." Owen Jones pointed out in The i 14 November 2013, p. 15. So much for a free market'.

According to a Der Spiegel report summarizing the most important facts about the global nuclear industry, in 2009, 438 atomic reactors were in operation

110 Ibid, p. 282
111 Ibid, p. 283
112 *Kieler Nachrichten*, 2 November 2013, p. 4

worldwide, having already an average age of 25 years, generating 373 gigawatts of electricity, and 144 reactors in the EU countries, generating 131 gigawatts.

In recent weeks, it has become apparent that the EU now wants to allow even more subsidies for the use of nuclear energy. This was urged by EU Commissioner Alumnia, responsible for competition[113] (!) in the first drafts of a report on the future of energy and climate politics, with the aim of reducing the prices for nuclear energy being paid by citizens via taxes. That would mean, for example, that the UK government would contradict both current EU law and their own promise during the election campaign, that nuclear power stations and nuclear waste disposal units would never be financed by the taxpayer. Again, water under the bridge. And we read in *The Sunday Times* of 16 March 2013 that the government is now in "the final throes of tortuous negotiations" to agree a huge subsidy for EDF,[114] twice the level of today's wholesale price for the plant's output during its first 35 years in operation[115] for building the first new atomic reactor in Britain in 20 years. Should British taxpayers really be expected to finance state-owned companies of other nations? How liberal!

The Deutsche Institut fuer Wirtschaftsforschung (DIW) in Berlin has proved that the EU vision for using a mix of combined energy sources by 2050 cannot be relied upon as their assumption was based on four to five-year-old data, implying that third-generation nuclear power stations and carbon capture technology are working. The DIW reminded the EU Commission that nuclear power has never been competitive and never will be, and that carbon capture is not working. Apart from the United Kingdom, there is no country which trusts this technology anymore. "In its Green Paper, 'A 2030 Framework for Climate and Energy Policies', the European Commission calls for a framework for the future development of environment and energy policy beyond 2020. However, much like the 'Energy Roadmap 2050' adopted by the Commission in December 2011, the Green Paper is based on assumed scenarios that are, to a great extent, no longer relevant. The European Commission needs to provide updated model calculations immediately to enable energy policy decisions on the basis of transparent and comprehensible scenarios. A comparison of recent estimates conducted by DIW Berlin indicates that the Commission systematically underestimates the cost of nuclear power and carbon capture, transport and storage, while the cost of renewable energies tends to be overestimated. This applies in particular to photovoltaics where capital costs are, to a certain extent, already lower than the Commission's estimates for 2050.

---

113 Cf. *Der Spiegel* report in 30/2013, p. 63

114 Iain Dey, *Paying Through the Nose for Nuclear Power*: "The plan is to enable EDF to recoup its £14 billion construction cost via a minimum electricity price. Estimates as to this 'magic number' vary widely. But if, as expected, the agreed figure is around the £90/megawatt-hour-range, it will come in at 'roughly twice the current market for power'. Even then, EDF can't afford to do it alone. It has stepped up negotiations with another state-owned company, China Guangdong Nuclear Power, which could buy up to 50 per cent of the new plant — and cover half the bill — provided it likes the government's price guarantee. 'There's a good chance our energy bills are about to be pumped up to new record levels to suit the demands of governments in communist China and socialist France.' That isn't jingoism. It is a statement of fact. Wouldn't it have been easier just to build the plant ourselves?"

115 *The Week*, 26 October 2013, p. 6

In contrast to renewable energies, neither nuclear energy nor carbon capture, transport, and storage are cost efficient enough to play a central role in the future European electricity mix. It is therefore vital for Europe to continue to focus on the further development of renewable energies in future. This requires the setting of ambitious renewables targets for 2030 as well as clear emissions reduction and energy efficiency targets,"[116] DIW wrote.

The most annoying fact is that the proposals omit – again and again – any reference to the consequences, the total cost of using radioactive nuclear power, which include waste disposal, decommissioning as well as the cost of insurance against accidents. EU Commissioner for Energy and former Prime Minister of Baden-Wuerttemberg in Germany, Guenther Oettinger, announced on 1 November 2013, that he will propose the introduction of a European-wide liability insurance for nuclear power stations. The insured sum has to be as high as possible, but this has also to be signed by all 28 governments[117] in order to hold the companies responsible and not the taxpayer.[118] In Germany, the nuclear power companies are liable up to an amount of €2.5 billion, in France only up to €90 million. One wonders if his claim for a total insurance of the nuclear industry for damages and radiation could ever be paid by an insurance company without them becoming bankrupt - and then again it would be the obligation of the taxpayer.

The discussion was also taken up by the president of the German Umweltbundesamt (UBA). When Jochen Flasbarth gave an exclusive interview to *Die Welt*, 17 October 2013, p. 9, claiming that the Conservative-led German government is still handing out subsidies for purposes harmful to the environment, he listed subsidies to the agri-industry, building and transport, while he left out nuclear power subventions. Incidentally, the total subventions paid by the German taxpayer, without which none of these companies would make a profit, amounted to about €51 billion. Altogether it is a very unhealthy and illogical situation, especially considering that the costs for cleaning up (even if this is possible) Fukushima as calculated in November 2013 already ran to €187 billion.[119]

The public discussion about the consequences of the so-called peaceful use of nuclear power only started about 30 years later in Germany, when plans for a nuclear power station in Whyl, the wine-growing area of Baden-Wuerttemberg, came to light. Wine growers feared that emissions from the plant would spoil the micro-climate, damage their produce and force them out of business. Thousands of people protested against the plan, and a nuclear power station was never built.

---

116 DIW Wochenbericht Nr. 29 2013

117 *Kieler Nachrichten*, 2 November 2013, p. 4: "*Ich werde vorschlaen, eine europaweit einheitliche Haftpflichtversicherung fuer Atomkraftwerke einzufuehren. Die Versicherungssumme muss so hoch wie moeglich sein; aber sie muss auch von den 28 Regierungen unterschrieben werden.*"

118 E.on the biggest electricity supplier in Germany with 33 million customers and in high debt, informed the public at the beginning of December 2014 that it will split its business into two from 2016 on, one company will concentrate on delivering green electricity while the other will go on operating the old business using fossil fuels and nuclear, according to *Kieler Nachrichten*, 2 December 2014. Immediately alarm bells started ringing in the Energy Ministry in Kiel. Questions were asked what will happen to E.on's responsibility to abolish their nuclear power stations and safely waste storage, as well what will happen to the money E.on retained for these obligations.

119 Ibid

Because any individual does not have enough power to make his voice heard, people organized themselves in so-called '*Buergerinitiativen*' or citizens' action groups.

Discussions of the consequences of nuclear power use also demonstrated that the affected wine growers were unable to access scientific advice, proving their fears. Most scientists were employed by universities with the consequence that there was almost no institution with an interest to support the fears of ordinary citizens. As a result, the Oeko-Institut was founded in Freiburg in 1979. Individual citizens and environmental organizations joined and paid independent experts working in the interest of local people.[120]

Electricity is generated from radioactive material, for example uranium, by setting in motion a controlled chain of nuclear fission. Nuclear fission was discovered in 1938 by the German physicists Lisa Meitner and Otto Hahn. This process, once started, cannot be adapted immediately to people's changing need for electricity, which alters during day and night and from season to season. However, it is good for a steady basic delivery of electricity.

Generating electricity from primary nuclear resources does not produce the greenhouse gas carbon dioxides, it is claimed. However, when an exact study was made and recently published in *Scientific American*, it was found that: '"Nuclear power results in up to 25 times more carbon emissions than wind energy, when reactor construction and uranium-refining and transport are considered.' Atomic energy is no friend of climate."[121] Again, once all presumptions and consequences are considered and not just a part of the picture changes. Atomic energy is not so green as some claimed.

Moreover, the use of nuclear power comes with additionally far higher risks: Radioactive material is necessary for nuclear fission which, with good reason, is rarely found in nature, as it kills life as well as causes cancer and gene mutations in plants, animals and humans.[122]

---

120 This idea originated in the USA when independent scientists started working for citizens. The Oeko-Institute is an independent organisation, working outside a university and has today a brilliant reputation. Incidentally, no nuclear power station was built in Whyl.

121 As reported by Gideon Forman, Canadian Association of Physicians for the Environment, in: *The Week*, 2 April 2011

122 Fred Pearce, New Scientist Environment Consultant, wrote in *The Mail on Sunday* , 1 March 2012: Plutonium "is the most toxic pond in Europe. It will cost £10 billion to make safe. But (... and this is the good news) Harold Wilson won't have to pay for it": that "... the reluctance of our nuclear masters to clean up the billion-pound messes around Britain's coast is shameful... Why do we allow this? That's not giving the task to our children, but to our great-great-grandchildren... But once the nuclear fuel is removed the nuclear boffins don't plan to touch it again until at least 2096, when the difficult and expensive task of dismantling the reactor and disposing of the thousands of tonnes of radioactive rubble will begin... No other industry is allowed to do this. And no other nuclear nation is shirking responsibility for cleaning up its toxic nuclear legacy in this way. The Americans, French, Germans and Japanese all plan on dismantling most of their old reactors as soon as they can... The official line is that dismantling – decommissioning, as they like to call it – will be safer later, because some of the radioactivity will decay away... The real reason may be cost... Britain had never put money into a special fund for decommissioning. The idea was to pay the bill out of Government coffers... Hundreds of thousands of tons of radioactive waste will have to be stored safely and eventually buried deep underground – in a sealed vault we haven't started building yet... Many of the big-ticket decom-

The radioactive element plutonium was discovered in the 1940s in the USA, which is the most deadly material known to mankind. A millionth of a gram is enough to kill a person. Plutonium has a radioactive half-life of 14,000 years, meaning that its radioactive radiation halves after 14,000 years.

In closing-down nuclear power stations and military facilities and disposing of nuclear waste we have to make sure that radioactive material is stored safely for thousands and thousands of years away from living organisms. Building them has nowhere yet been started, if it ever will be done, nobody knows what it will cost and the costs are not included in the price of nuclear power. Nuclear power companies are obliged to do put money away for financing safe nuclear waste storage, but we could be sure that some of it will have to be shouldered by taxpayers, however no industry should be able to expect, perhaps with the banks already being bailed-out, that it is the public duty to take responsibility of their residues. So why should this be acceptable?

Additionally, electricity generation from nuclear power still uses finite primary resources. To get around this fact, physicists have developed reprocessing facilities – in Sellafield, UK, and in La Hague in France – where burnt-out fuel rods can be re-enriched. Nuclear scientists have also tried to invent a nuclear reactor that would 'breed' more radioactive material than it uses. In Germany alone, experimental work on a fast breeder nuclear reactor cost the taxpayer DM 20 billion before the unsuccessful experiment was finally abandoned.

There is no chemical process known to us by which radioactivity can be eliminated. Closing down nuclear reactors does not get rid of their radioactivity, so building long-term storage of nuclear waste underground is the only way it can

missioning items are at Sellafield on the Cumbrian coast... And Sellafield remains where we send the nastiest military and civil waste, such as plutonium-laced 'spent fuel' that has done its work in the power stations. Sellafield is a nuclear cesspit... They are almost proud to call it the most concentrated nuclear dustbin on Earth. Among much else, it contains three scary open-air ponds. Their constantly circulating waters keep cool hundreds of tons of highly radioactive reactor fuel and debris that were hastily dumped there half a century ago... Their minders say they are 'the most hazardous industrial buildings in western Europe'. Making them safe could cost a cool £10 billion... One of the piles caught fire in 1957, sending a radioactive cloud across the country — Britain's very own Chernobyl... So decommissioning the pile has been endlessly postponed. The current start date is 2019. Price tag unknown... Huhne" (former Energy Secretary) "said that decommissioning Britain's nuclear 'legacy' will cost £54 billion. I was told the real figure is likely to be double that. Just clearing Sellafield will cost £50 billion including removing enough radioactive soil to fill 77 lorry loads every day for 20 years."

On 7 November 2012 Sam Lister in the *i* pointed out that at Sellafield "... some of the older facilities have 'deteriorated so much that their contents pose significant risks to people and the environment... A long-term plan to clean up the Nuclear Decommissioning Authority-owned site, which is managed by Sellafield Limited, was agreed last year after an earlier one stalled because it was 'unrealistic'.

And Paul Brown on TruthDig.com (Los Angeles) commented according to *The Week* 7 September 2013: "Look at Chernobyl: work there to isolate the reactor damaged in 1986 won't be completed for another two years — three decades after the event. Even in Britain, 56 years after the fire at the Windscale nuclear reactor at Sellafield, there's still no workable plan to dismantle the damaged core. Tepco" the Tokyo Electric Power Company running the Fukushima nuclear plant "admits it will take at least 40 years to complete the clean-up, and even that will depend on technology yet to be invented."

be kept separate from living processes. Nuclear waste is far more dangerous and lasts longer than other forms of waste[123] – this should never be forgotten.

This is the reason why globally there is not *one* safe, long-term facility for the secure storage of nuclear waste available. And geological formations where radioactive waste could be safely stored over thousands of years are rarely available, but even if such formations would be discovered, they may not be welcomed by the peoples living there.

It seems that the UK government has come up with a clever idea about how to convince local communities that an underground long-term nuclear storage plant might be useful to them. *The Guardian* reported 25 July, 2014, p. 18, that: "local communities could be paid more than £40 m by the government simply for considering the building of an underground nuclear waste disposal facility in their area... However, the new approach would not allow any one level of local government to veto future site decisions." So, once a local community has agreed only to an investigation, it will not be able to say 'no' to it. Therefore, who will be convinced to do it?

"*Irish free to sue over nuclear contamination*" was the headline of an article by Mark Leftly in *The Independent on Sunday*.[124] Leftly pointed out that in 2014 "British nuclear operators face being sued for billions of pounds by the Irish government and Irish victims of any radioactive damage they cause under legal changes to be introduced this year. Politicians and campaigners in Dublin have long complained about the impact, both historical and potential, of the UK's civil nuclear programme close to its shores, with particular focus on the safety record of Sellafield. Greenpeace has warned that the dumping of the reprocessing plant's liquid waste has made the Irish Sea among the most contaminated waters in the world, even though Ireland itself produces no nuclear energy. Irish fishermen have been angered by catches of unsaleable mutated fish and by findings that they have been exposed to low-level radiation."

Additionally, the fall-out from nuclear tests and civil accidents which happened decades ago has been spread around the world and its radiating residue can still be found. Last year, 27 years after the explosion of the nuclear power generating plant in Chernobyl, USSR, "thousands of jars of Italian organic jam were found to be contaminated" with radiation. And still, the UK government is going ahead with the construction of new nuclear plants, starting with Hinkley Point C in Somerset, when the existing problems are not even brought closer to a solution. While Ireland was not able to go to court against it in the past, "legal experts say that Ireland's case will be radically strengthened when amendments to the Paris Convention on Third Party Liability in the Field of Nuclear Energy finally come into force this year, having been originally proposed in 2004." However, "the Nuclear Decommissioning Authority, which owns 19 sites in the UK, said that accident clean-up costs are covered by insurance." One wonders if

---

123 Eg the longest lasting organization on Earth, the Roman Catholic church, has operated for only 2,000 years, whereas nuclear waste has to be kept safely away from life for thousands of years. So how can anyone be sure that we are able to set-up organizations and run them, which make this happen?

124 5 January 2014, p. 17

this actually really is the case. Or is it only said to quieten public doubts?

Furthermore, in August 2014 we were made aware that currently 30 old nuclear power reactors are operating in the Ukraine, of which not one is secured against the dangers of war into which the country seems to have been forced now.

Spiegel online reported on 13 May, 2014, that the big German nuclear power plant owners, E.on, RWE and EnBW suggested setting up a Bad Bank in form of a public-law foundation which could be based on the about 30 billion accrued liabilities of the nuclear industries for decommissioning atomic power stations and safe storage of nuclear waste. It is now feared that this would mean that these nuclear power companies would try to shift their responsibilities for safe waste storage from a technology they have profited from for 50 years. It shows very clearly what this industry thinks about the consequences of their own dealings: obviously they are too dangerous to take the risk.

These consequences, nuclear power use came with, were never taken into account when the decision was made to use nuclear electricity generation 'peacefully'. Therefore we have to regard this former decision as totally irresponsible and unnecessary given that free to use, reliable, secure, infinite and waste-free alternatives exist in the form of renewables.

Why should we go on with such a technology? The only reason why it would make sense to do so might be the interest in military use of nuclear fission. Already in 1968, nuclear weapons had a total global overkill capacity of ten times. Do we really need more of it? And in more countries?

The USA not only manufactured and used the first atomic bombs, killing over half a million people in Japan, but also developed the first hydrogen bomb in 1952 and the first neutron bomb in 1977. This latter is somewhat different, as it leaves inorganic matter intact and only kills life. This is the reason why it is referred to as a 'perversion of thinking'.

In 1970, the Non-Proliferation Treaty was agreed by 43 states and an international Atomic Energy Commission installed to make sure such a treaty was maintained. However, one wonders if it is really doing what it is supposed to as more countries have started building nuclear weapons. The more countries will have radioactive fission weapons, the higher the danger they will be used. It is perhaps naive to expect that the world can only become more peaceful if there are less weapons and not more, especially nuclear bombs.

Finally, it needs to be added that a special security risk derives from nuclear research reactors, of which there exist around 130 worldwide. These reactors also contain highly enriched radioactive material which can be used to build bombs, yet they are not made sufficiently safe, according to the *New York Times*[125] which pointed out this danger. The installation of which goes back to Eisenhower's "atoms for peace" programme, as Oliver Stone and Peter Kuznick[126] reminded us, when 'the United States had sold dozens of research reactors to countries all over the world, including Iran, and had been supplying highly enriched uranium to fuel them. Some of the reactors used fuel enriched to 93 per cent.' A newly developed weapon was 'made out of depleted uranium, whose radioactivity and chemical

---

125 25 April 2010
126 Oliver Stone and Peter Kuznick, ibid, p. 410

toxicity would produce cancers and birth defects for years'[127] when used in Kuwait during the Operation Desert Storm in 1991.

There is no other solution to the nuclear problem than to cut the arsenal and shut down existing reactors. The world must aim at becoming totally nuclear free. Otherwise the nuclear threat to annihilate life on this planet remains – even if only by a mistake or misjudgment.

11.1.1.4. Food – the internal energy

Food as discussed here, is mostly harvested from the land in the form of the fruits and seeds of plants (eg potatoes), bushes (raspberries) or trees (apples) or whole plants, such as herbs, salads or cabbage. A more limited amount comes from the sea, in the form of fish, algae, crustaceans or mussels. We are considering here only food that sustains and prolongs people's lives, not drugs, the consumption of which makes people obese or shortens their life, even when governments profit from them through taxation, as with alcohol and cigarettes.[128]

Humans, being animals, are heterotrophic. We live on what is alive. Plants absorb light by chlorophyll and split it into hydrogen and oxygen. Oxygen is then released back into the air, and the hydrogen is used together with carbon acid from air to build carbohydrates, a process discovered in the 20th century by biochemist Otto Heinrich (1883–1970). Plants are autotrophic.

People and animals, domesticated in the continuous process of cultivation, have to rely on nature's produce. Millions of years ago human beings lived in the same way as most animals, hunting and gathering what nature provided locally, being forced to move to different areas once the resources of the locality were exhausted.

Then, about 30,000 years ago in the Neolithic Age, people learned by careful observation that it was possible to breed animals and cultivate the land for continuous harvests. This revolution enabled them to stay in one location. Now knowledge was gathered concerning how best to do this and solid shelters were built. People learned to ride horses, which enabled them to carry more and made them more mobile. They domesticated dogs for company. Settlement led to even closer observation of nature. Watching the sky and the stars and their momentum, helped them to prepare for winter. People learned to select and grow plants with more and bigger fruits. They experienced how nature operates; which plant or animal was best avoided and which was healthy to eat. They learned how to use natural remedies for illnesses, watching animals. By working with nature they changed their natural environment. We called this the process of reciprocal inter-action, which is self-organized, open and dynamic.

To show that a process is taking place it is necessary to compare events at different times, otherwise differences would not be noticeable. It is not helpful to

---

127 Ibid, p. 478

128 Marco Evers commented in 'Lizenz zum Toeten', *Der Spiegel* 7/2014, p. 128, that in the 20th century the global tobacco industry led to the death of about 100 million people and will kill up to one billion people in the 21st century, citing the estimation of the World Health Organisation. He pointed out that there is no other legal industrial product that threatens its user to such a degree when it is used in the way it is intended.

Besides, sugar and corn syrup should today be seen as drugs and heavily taxed to reduce consumption, according to scientists, reported by the newspaper The *i* 5 March 2014.

discuss only one event, as this could suggest that it always occurred in the same way. This would mean that things seem to be static, instead of being open, changing and evolving, as well as leading us to more experiences, better insight and deeper understanding.

Incidentally, a finished product allows less, rather than more insight and understanding because we are not involved in its production. The finished product is only decaying, not only in a natural, but also in a cultural way. As often experienced, when we attempt to take back a product straight away, a loss is usually incurred. We never get the same amount of money back for it than we have just spent on it.[129]

Settlement led to the most radical cultural transformation ever experienced in the historic evolution of mankind. By settling, watching, comparing events and learning, human animals transformed themselves into the *homo sapiens* and transformed their natural environment into cultivated, land.[130] This process is still going on, although we are not always aware of it as the human life span, compared with nature's processes, is extremely short. However, the more active we are in our open interaction with our fellow-men and our natural co-world, the more we look for examples of the damaging consequences of our activities and can change our actions for the better, even from the outset, and the more we will evolve. A fairer and more sustainable culteconomy is possible.

We can identify different types of interaction with nature's produce as our food: the first level can be subsumed into the category 'primary food'. Air and water belong to it, as described, as do fruit and seeds when taken from the plant, leaving it as it is. We can pick apples from the tree in our garden and the tree will go on producing new fruit in the next year. If we want more fruit, we can plant more apple trees by putting some ripe brown pips into the soil, and, if they are properly watered, a new shoot will result, eventually growing into a tree.

With much of today's food, however, this kind of interaction is impossible, ie when we consume not only the fruit or seeds of a plant, but the plant as a whole. Repeated harvesting in the following year therefore requires more care: a few of the harvested plants have to be saved, however hard the winter and scarce the food, stored and put in spring into the soil for a new harvest.

Actions, such as avoiding immediate consumption of available food and keeping some back to produce another year's harvest, are typical for human beings rather than for other animals. We are able to foresee – to a certain extent – the consequences of our actions and we can choose to behave accordingly. We are able

---

129 It seems today that products are even deliberately constructed with built-in obsolescence, making their use short-lived and making them harder to maintain/repair which means that they need be replaced more quickly with new products bringing new sales and generating new profits. This strategy was first introduced in 1920 by Alfred P. Sload, the President of General Motors, according to Wolfgang Heckel, *Die Kultur der Reparatur, Muenchen,* 2013, p. 45

130 One gramme of farmland contains up to ten billion bacteria the biggest genetic resource of the planet. Most people are not aware how important this reservoir of micro-organism in the soil is which we threaten with pesticides, monocultural farming and soil compression, *Der Spiegel* 44/2014, 132, pointed out.

to become aware[131] of the whole spiral of perception and action, and we know that our lives depend on our awareness.

Today, this process has been changed. Farmers can no longer rely on self-produced seeds. Instead seeds have to be bought. Agriculture has been changed into agroindustry. The big agroindustrial companies have grown new, more productive plant varieties, of which many lack the ability to propagate. Farmers are now obliged to buy seeds and seedlings from the industry. And the industry has patented their varieties – together with special fertilizer, special herbicides, insecticides and fungicides, without which these hybrid plants would not flourish.[132] Now farmers are dependent on the agroindustry with its monopoly on the production of seeds. The agroindustry has developed a new way of making money.

Alarmingly, 200,000 farmers are dying every year through pesticide poisoning. An UN report has shown that leukaemia and Parkinson's disease are seen as occupational diseases for farmers.

Even organic farmers and nurseries depend increasingly on buying-in such seeds, as there are not enough organic seeds offered on the market'. In this way the seed industry has ensured itself a steady trade. It also comes with the disadvantage that the purchasers of these seeds cannot be sure whether they are not buying genetically modified seeds. Currently, seed growers are not yet required to inform about the genetic modification of seeds. Only ecological associations, such as the global Demeter[133] association, are informing the buyers that their seeds are 'pure-line' or open-pollinated.

Monocultural production only works with the chemical assistance of special pesticides. The European Food Safety Authority (EFSA) discovered that bee populations, necessary for propagation, are suffering from pesticides, such as neo-nicotinoids, and also the developing brains of unborn babies are at risk. Therefore it proposed that, "the acceptable daily intake over a lifetime of acetamiprid and acceptable operator exposure level should be cut by two-thirds. For imidacloprid, the current acceptable daily intake was judged adequate, but the other limit plus the acute reference dose, the EFSA said, should be cut by a quarter."[134]

However, it is not only the quantity of herbicides being produced – with all the effects of their production – which is a problem. Just as with fossil fuels we must look at the bigger picture. When we view the whole process of industrial farming as an reciprocal interaction process, we will become aware that plant life can adapt to the use of pesticides in a similar way that microbes can become immune to antibiotics, ie when people are treated too often with antibiotics, these might no longer be effective to cure illnesses.

131 The question, if and to which degree plants have a rudimentary form of awareness is disputed.

132 There are special fruits grown in a seedless variety, such as grapes or oranges, as they are easier to be consumed.

133 Based on the anthroposophical theory of Rudolf Steiner, to which 4,500 farmers in 50 countries have subscribed, 1,400 of them in Germany.

134 *The Guardian* 18 December 2013, p. 9 "Imidacloprid and acetamiprid are produced by Bayer Corpscience. Imidacloprid was banned in the EU for many agricultural uses from 1 December, after the EFSA ruled it an unacceptable risk to bees. Bayer and the company Syngenta are taking legal action to try to overturn the EU moratorium."

So-called weeds, unusable plants that the farmer wants to eliminate on his fields, can grow immune to herbicides. In Germany, 18,000 tonnes of weed killers are spread onto the soil each year, reported *Der Spiegel*.[135] So-called 'superweeds' have appeared and there is no suitable product on the market' that can kill them. The only solution is human labour, ie people pulling-out every one of these 'super-weeds' by hand before they propagate, which is cost-intensive and reduces the farmers' profits, so is therefore not a realistic method in large-scale farming.

In the article, *Der Spiegel* reported that superweeds have become a threat for farmers growing cotton, maize, soya and wheat in the south of the United States. Already 28 million hectares farmland, a sixth of all arable soil, have been already made immune against herbicides, a fact to which the EU Parliamentarian Martin Haeusling reacted saying that the principle of agroindustrial farming was a way into a cul-de-sac, while only ecological agriculture offers a solution, as it works with and not against nature.

Today, farming the land is different from how it was even 50 years ago. Today, farmers are more dependent workers rather than independent entrepreneurs,[136] as their care and responsibility for the land migrated into the hands of the industry.[137] Global retailers control the food producers, their direct interactions more and more mediated by money and markets'.

Shortly before the start of the Internationale Gruene Woche in Berlin, the yearly international food fair, the Bundesverband der Verbraucherzentralen (VZBV) and the Umweltbundesamt (UBA) examined the ecological balance of food criticizing the German government, for failing to meet the government's environmental targets regarding the agricultural and food industries.[138]

---

135 39/2014, p. 76

136 Felicity Lawrence, *Eat your heart out*, London, 2008, p. 136.

   In: Not *on the label, What really goes into the Food on your Plate*, London, 2004, p. XIV, Lawrence wrote: "The damage to the landscape, the collapse of commodity prices, the exploita-tion of labour, the epidemics of disease and obesity, the concentrations of power we all worry about, are not the work of random or separate forces... I believe we are in the middle of one of the most significant revolutions since settled agriculture began 10,000 years ago... It is a revolution whose social and ecological consequences we have so far failed to address."

   I refer here only to Felicity Lawrence's statements instead of referring to the countless books about the food crisis, written in German and in English.

137 Fishing is not especially discussed here, but a similar process can be said to have taken place: "Small local fleets tend not to foul their own waters, since they know that to do so will kill their own future. But intensive international trawlers have had few such scruples", mentioned Felicity Lawrence, p. 188, remarking "that insanely 30–40 per cent of the world catch is still converted to fishmeal and oil, largely for the production of animal feed, fertilizer and food manufacture of products such as margarine," p. 192

138 *Spiegel* online, 15 January 2014: "*Der Ernaehrungssektor in Deutschland sei heute fuer ein Fuenftel der Treibhausemissionen verantwortlich. Vor allem die Belastung von Luft, Boeden und Grundwasser durch uebermaessigen Einsatz von Stickstoffen als Duenger muesse dringend reduziert werden... Schon jetzt weisen einer UBA-Studie zufolge mehr als ein Viertel aller Grund-wasservorkommen in Deutschland zu hohe Nitratwerte auf... Der Ausbau der Oekolandwirtschaft, die mit deutlich weniger Stickstoff, Pestiziden, Energie und CO2 auskommt, liegt ebenfalls weit hinter dem Plan. Die Nachhaltigkeitsstrategie der Bundesregierung sieht einen Anteil von 20 Prozent vor - bisher werden aber nur wenig mehr als sechs Prozent der land-wirtschaftlichen Nutzflaeche oekologisch bewirtschaftet... Die Nachfrage nach Bioprodukten ist gleichzeitig so hoch wie nie... Auch der immense Fleischverzehr in Deutschland belastet*

Therefore, UBA and VZBV have put forward for action the following proposals:

- The Federal Government should reform the regulation of fertilizers with the aim of reducing nitrates as well as promoting regulation at EU-level.
- The discussion about reducing waste concentrates too much on consumers, when it is retailers in particular who need to re-think their demands regarding the spotlessness, size and shape of fruit and vegetables.
- Meat production should be better controlled: the relationship of animals with the land needs to be made more direct with animal and environmental health better supported, and it should be obligatory to inform consumers about these matters.

With respect to the energy use of the agroindustry, Felicity Lawrence[139] wrote that, "Twenty-one per cent of the UK's total energy use is accounted for by its food supply. Synthetic fertilizers, hydrocarbon-fuelled farm machinery that has replaced manual labour, plastics made from oil, and pesticides made from its toxic by-products, have all helped improve global yields dramatically, but they have also meant that today's industrialized farming uses 50 times as much energy as traditional agriculture. And that's just on the farm. The plastics needed for packing food are now transported long distances... out-of-town stores that require us to drive our cars to do our shopping, all burn large quantities of fuel. Each British household consumes 130 kg of packaging from oil-derived plastics a year... Without a steady, cheap supply of fossil fuels, in other words, our food would look very different."

Similar changes to those having occurred in farming in the last decades, have been noted in consumption: fewer people produce food themselves. This is not merely a result of the trend towards urban living, leading to smaller gardens and a decrease in home grown produce. Even smallholdings have turned away from food production in favour of growing grass and flowers.

The consequence is that people not only need to buy every bit of their food, with produce being flown in from all over the globe, but are also no longer directly connected to the BASE, to the earth, the ground, the soil, the land, the plants, the animals and the process of growing. They have lost any knowledge they had about the growing conditions of plants, bushes and trees, and about how to prepare their fruits into a meal. Flats are even built these days without kitchens, as this is cheaper for the building industry. Some people now rely totally on eating-out or buying-in ready-meals which only need to be warmed up.

---

die Umwelt: In der Massentierhaltung entstehen Treibhausgase, die Regionen mit intensiver Tierhaltung produzieren einen enormen Stickstoffueberschuss durch die anfallende Guelle. Fast die Haelfte der Ackerflaechen wird fuer den Futtermittelanbau genutzt, zusaetzlich importiert die Branche grosse Mengen Futtermittel... Ungeloest ist auch das Problem der Verschwendug: Rund elf Millionen Tonnen Lebensmittel werden in Deutschland jaehrlich weggeworfen – nicht nur von Verbrauchern, sondern auch von Verarbeitern, der Industrie, im Handel und bei Grossverbrauchern wie Kantinen und Restaurants."

VZBV is the Federation of German Consumer Organizations and UBA is the German Federal Environment Agency

139 Felicity Lawrence, *Eat your heart out*, ibid, p. 40

And just when you think that this kind of impoverishment of an individual's activities can go no further, it is astonishing to find that people even buy a cup of coffee now, instead of making it themselves, as if they no longer know how to.

This cultural transformation creates paid work – possibly not well-paid – as well as large amounts of disposal wrappings while diminishing their experience with making something themselves. Interactions like consuming a cup of coffee are first separated into parts and then re-connected in a way that's based on monetary terms. Even our own ability to learn is changed into a market' demand. It transforms open participative processes into finished products. But – and herein lies its logic – it makes money. We haven't yet considered all the consequences of this change, perhaps because we are all locked into this pattern, leading to more market' dependency and fewer independent direct activities.

The next changes to discuss relate to the breeding of animals for human consumption. This process of interaction has changed in a similar way: we raise animals to consume them, but – and this is the difference – obviously it is not possible to propagate them as we do with most plants. Here too, the farmer needs to hold back a few animals of both sexes for propagation and feed them through the winter, even when the animals might be competitors for food during the cold months. Animals which we eat are here referred to as secondary food. The average person in Germany annually consumes 39 kg pork and 22 kg beef, chicken, turkeys and other meats. 75.1 per cent of people are unconcerned meat eaters, 11.6 per cent are 'part-time' vegetarians, who sometimes eat meat, 9.5 per cent are meat eaters trying to consume less meat, and only 3.7 per cent are real vegetarians, according to a report on meat-eating habits, reported in: *Frankfurter Allgemeine Sonntagszeitung*, 27 October 2013. Although if everyone in the world ate as much meat as people in this country do, 20 per cent more fodder for animals would be need to be produced than the entire global corn harvest, and still we would not have enough corn for our daily bread (as Felix Prinz zu Loewenstein, an organic farmer, has pointed out).[140]

Animals need primary food to grow and propagate, ie air and light, water, and plant fodder. Cattle, for example, generally need 10 kg of green fodder – all the while exhaling methane – so that a human being can consume 1 kg of meat. It seems wasteful to feed people in this way, as it also results in additional greenhouse gas emissions via animals' stomachs.[141]

And the former form of raising animals is also outdated. Specialist companies are happy to sell young animals to the farmer, who merely fattens them up and then sells them on to be slaughtered for consumption. The whole process of rearing animals has also become fragmented, and it also accelerates selling.[142]

---

140 in: *Frankfurter Allgemeine Sonntagszeitung*, 16 September 2012, Loewenstein stated that, on leaving Weihenstephan university in Germany students had incorporated an image of nature as a hostile force that could only be controlled by BASF, Syngeta and other global agrochemical giants.

141 Yet when the German party DIE GRUENEN proposed one meat-free-day a week in canteens in 2013, the press reported a public uproar.

142 This side of the division of labour comes with more opportunities for market' sales, resulting in more profit for the company as well as more tax income for the government. It also increases the Gross Domestic Product price-wise.

If the farmer believes in raising animals himself by feeding them through the winter, it is only necessary to keep a few females which can then be artificially inseminated. The artificial insemination of animals, as well as the cultivation of plants which are no longer able to propagate, has another consequence: both processes can be patented like any other product. According to *Die Welt*, 17 October 2013, p. 12, the German Bundeslandwirtschaftsministerium announced that in the first half of 2013 the number of so-called 'bio-patents' had increased to 176, a fact that is perhaps not yet sufficiently recognized. However, a patent on a living organism is totally different to a patent on an industrial product, German Bundeslandwirtschaftsministerin Ilse Aigner, CSU, pointed out when she presented these data. While patents on products can be owned and sold by a company, *creation belongs to all men[143]*, she said. And the initiative "No Patents on Seeds" criticized the European Patent Office that it had allowed already 2,400 patents on plants and animals.[144] In 2012 the German Bundestag voted against it. However, if breeding procedures come with technological innovations, whatever this means, it might be possible to get them patented. It is mostly the big global companies which seek to own patents, the so-called 'intellectual property', while farmers and - in the end - the consumers have to pay for it.

Mediating natural processes by money,[145] changing long-term into short-term interaction and transforming living animals into market' commodities[146] has even more implications: whereas in former decades a variety of animals was bred on a farm, today a huge number of animals of the same species are kept. Agro-firms with 10,000 chickens and thousands of cattle are common today; the biggest German firm, in Sachsen-Anhalt, has 62,000 pigs. Animals are raised in windowless sheds on concrete floors or in small metal cages. The land has been 'freed' from them.

Even their fodder is no longer grown locally coming from the farm, but is transported from other continents, eg maize or soya from South America. The reason is that transporting the cattle feed from far away is still cheaper. It has been pointed out repeatedly that rain forest destruction, mostly by big global food companies, has consequences not only for the people there, who have lost land needed to grow their own food, but also for people worldwide. The rainforest is the planet's biggest green lung, filtering carbon dioxide and dust out of the

---

143 accentuation by the author, "Die *Schoepfung gehoert* allen Menschen."

144 *Der Spiegel* 44/2014, p. 127

145 And when fish stocks are depleted by overfishing, industrial fish farming takes over, and fish farms with their high pollution of the water by chemicals, are 'destroying wild Scottish salmon', according to the headline of an *Observer* article on 16 February 2014, p. 18

146 *Der Spiegel* 6/2014 did an interview with Hilal Sezgin, author and philosopher, who has just published her book "*Artgerecht ist nur die Freiheit. Eine Ethik fuer Tiere oder Warum wir umdenken muessen*", arguing that breeding animals for our use puts man into an exceptional position which he does not have in nature, nor should he demand it as no animal is born for the sole purpose of being eaten by us. If humans are not allowed to treat each other as an object for a private purpose, then the same should be true for an animal.

atmosphere and producing oxygen.[147] When it is destroyed by the agroindustry, its function disappears.

A consequence of this kind of transformation is that animals are no longer raised in their natural habitat, roaming and looking for their own food, but are reared in totally artificial conditions. This often leads to their giving away or eating each others' feathers and tails, and being unable to suckle their young. Living organisms are treated as if they are things. It is a rational view about a product that once was an animal. The purpose is to produce a commodity for which there is worldwide demand, concluded Der Spiegel[148] also using the word 'product' for an animal.

A study for DIE GRUENEN's Parliament group, published in August 2013, found that industrial farming methods often makes animals ill. This prompted the Niedersaechsische Landwirtschaftsminister Christian Meyer from the same party to demand a political strategy whereby animals are kept according to the needs of their species, adapting stables to animals, not animals to stables.[149] Laws need to be introduced to realize this aim to improve animal well-being. We, as consumers, normally avoid being confronted with the living conditions of the animals we eat and mainly ignore such findings, which, as the latest scandal in pig breeding made public by Animal Rights Watch (ARIWA) in November 2013 showed, broke EU[150] laws and was only possible because the government failed to control the industry.

Another consequence of intensive livestock farming is that masses of animals generate masses of manure, materials which in former times the farmer would spread on the fields. But there is a limit to how much manure can be spread, as it soaks into the ground soil and overloads the groundwater with nitrates, when people rely on groundwater as primary food. It is costly to filter nitrates out, and, as Egon Harms of the Oldenburgisch-Ostfriesische Wasserverband, one of the biggest freshwater suppliers in Germany,[151] pointed out, even if filtered, such water is not really clean and has to be diluted with freshwater.

Naturally, keeping huge numbers of one species of animals together under these artificial conditions comes with the danger that illness will spread from one animal to others. Therefore the animals are given medication like antibiotics, in the hope of preventing infections. These antibiotics pass then through the chain of animal manure into the soil, into crops and groundwater and finally into peoples' food with the consequence that antibiotics will no longer be effective on humans when needed because the germs have become resistant.

Today, epidemiologists fear[152] a new 'post-antibiotic' age dawning where anti-

---

147 Decisions to cut down the rainforest are made by local landowners. When in an economicult society direct interactions are transformed and mediated by money, is it really any wonder that South American politicians offer to keep the rain forest intact if they are paid by others to do so, while seeming not to realize that they too depend on its oxygen production?

148 43/2013, p. 69: "Es ist eine rationale Sicht auf ein Produkt, das mal ein Tier war. Es geht darum, eine Ware zu produzieren, fuer die es weltweit Abnehmer gibt."

149 In an interview with NDR Info radio station 14 August 2013

150 Spiegel online, 28 November 2013

151 Ibid

152 Der Spiegel, 46/2013

biotics will no longer help. And "'no new class of antibacterial has been developed since 1987... partly because companies can no longer make enough money out of antimicrobials to justify investing in the research needed,' says Prof. Dame Sally Davies, Chief Medical Officer for England."[153] So when people consume mass market' meat every day with the aim of staying healthy, it might in fact have the opposite effect.

On 30 July 2013, the German Bundesamt fuer Verbraucherschutz und Lebensmittelsicherheit published figures about the amount of antibiotics sold directly to farmers by veterinarians, a right which *Der Spiegel* called it "*das suesse Privileg des Dispensierrechts*",[154] an exception to the pharmacy monopoly – leading to a situation where 80 per cent of the turnover of some large veterinary clinics is derived from selling pharmaceutical products. This double function of prescribing and selling is already forbidden in Denmark and in Sweden.

Antibiotics use by German farmers totalled 1,706 tonnes in 2011, with human consumption of antibiotics amounting to 800 tonnes. The biggest quantities were tetracyclines (564 tonnes) and aminophyllinie (501 tonnes), followed by makrolides (173 tonnes), sulfonamides (185 tonnes) and polypetid-antibiotics (127 tonnes), overwhelmingly used in the south of the Bundesland Niedersachsen, where these days intensive livestock farming is concentrated. The reason for collecting this data on the use of antibiotics in livestock farming is that there is an interest in finding out about antibiotics and resistance. In 2011, Germany used 211 mg per kg of treated biomass, while the UK used 51 mg and Denmark 43 mg, demonstrating Denmark's 60 per cent reduction in antibiotic use for animals over the last 20 years. This reduction of the use of antibiotics should therefore become the aim of other countries too. It is possible.

On 1 April 2014, the 16th amendment to the drug law came into practice. From then on, a databank will record every detail of antibiotic use for every farmer. With 20 per cent of farmers using around 80 per cent of the antibiotics, it will then be possible to give accurate advice to these farmers regarding ways of reducing the amount of drugs used, hopes epidemiologist Professor Thomas Blaha from the Tieraerztliche Hochschule Hannover.[155]

Der Spiegel published the following data on intensive pig farming in Germany with the headline:

---

153 Gillian Tett, *Can we avoid an anbitiotic apocalypse?* in *The Financial Times*, according to *The Week*, 14 December 2013, p. 51
154 *Der Spiegel*, 16/2012, translated: the sweet privilege of the dispensing licence
155 *Der Spiegel*, 43/2013

"Die grosse Sauerei":[156]

Freshwater consumption:	50 billion litres
Number of slaughtered pigs:	58.7 million pigs in 2012
Breeding conditions:	0.75 sqm space for a pig weighing between 50 and 110 kg
Genetic impoverishment:	more than 95 % of all pigs come from only 3 different breeds
Farming land:	40 % of harvested wheat, rye, oats and maize is animal fodder
Freshwater needed to produce	1 kg pork: 5.988 litres
Freshwater needed to produce	1 kg potatoes: 287 litres
Antibiotic use:	40 times more than in German hospitals
Concentration:	32.7 % of fattening firms keep more than 1,000 pigs, compared with 3.4 % in 1999, the 500 biggest firms together raise more than 4.6 million pigs

As the full costs of industrial farming are not integrated into the price the consumer pays for meat, meat seems to be cheap. The real costs are paid, but by others. At first, there is the taxpayer who hands out money to the European Agricultural Fund, and then the European Agricultural Fund hands it on to farming firms. "There is little of the free market here," Felicity Lawrence found.

Then, when groundwater needs to be cleared of too much nitrate, the consumer pays the water supply companies to prepare the water fit for human consumption. These costs are not included in the price of the meat. And when consumers become ill by eating polluted food or drinking polluted water, their health insurance has to pay for the treatment.

Lots of new businesses take chances with new profit-making opportunities – but why? Does this economicult model really make sense? Is this rational? Could we not live with less expenditure if we were to invent a model of food production without such consequences, avoiding them from the beginning? Would it not be fairer and cheaper if the industrialized model of farming is replaced by a model which pays greater respect to nature and to people?

Traditionally this process is referred to as the 'division of labour'. And the most frequently heard phrase in the real economy is: 'We do not have any liability for this product, you have to contact... about it?'[157] The fragmentation breaks up the unity of interaction as well as responsibility.[158]

---

156 43/2013, p. 71, The *'grosse Sauerei'* means a right mess, referring to a *'Sau'*, the German word for a sow.

157 Rebecca Smithers, in 'Which? finds shoppers misled on faulty goods', *The Guardian*, 19 December 2013, p. 30, reported on the findings of a study by consumer group Which? revealing that retailers such as Amazon, Apple, Argos, Currys, Euronics and John Lewis did not inform their staff about their responsibility as retailers, instead were referring claimants to the manufacturing company in breach of consumer protection regulations.

158 Indeed the historic process of fragmentation can be viewed as decreasing responsibility on the

If it was the job of the farmer to look after all the consequences of his business, eg dealing with the pollution of ground water by manure, it would not be possible to shift the problem onto someone else. Perhaps the farmer would then come to the conclusion that he should not raise so many animals of one species in limited spaces if he considered its effects? And if he had experienced epidemics once or twice among livestock, would he not then aim to broaden the range of species that he rears?

If the farmer cared about avoiding the consequences we've been discussing, perhaps he would also extend his balance sheet with information on everything coming into and going out of his farm.

And if consumers were made even more aware of the conditions of industrial farming, would they not try to buy different products using their power to achieve change? Most people have empathy with living beasts when they see them treated so badly.

The farming industry in Germany produces food for nearly 100 million people and turns over €163 billion a year. It is the country's fourth biggest industry. This sector, with its SME-type businesses ought to be rooted in society, but in reality it has an disastrous image. Normally it brings 160,000 different goods quietly onto the shelves of even the most isolated village store. At the same time, attracting only public attention when it adulterates, tricks or deceives. How can it be, that successful products of this industry receive high-profile undesirable awards such as the 'Golden Cream Puff' from consumer protection organisations? That every individual misdemeanour seems to confirm the misconduct of the whole industry? People's basic trust in the sector has been 'eroded', the advertising paper *Horizont* recently wrote, also as a result of the 'culture of silence' it has maintained for years. Indeed, year after year producers have done everything they could to hide from consumers. In an age of fully automatic production processes, their advertisements still feature manicured female hands slicing individual strawberries and dropping them into yoghurts rather than revealing to their customers that the 18 kg of yoghurt consumed per year by the average German aren't stirred by hand. Companies have long relied on global flows of goods and retain chains, but don't want it to become public knowledge. When critisised, they react by employing public relation agencies instead of disclosing all their ingredients as well as their suppliers.[159]

---

production side: home and work are divided, work is done outside the home in a company, a company is set up by law employing the owner as well as workers, then the legal status of the company is transformed into one with limited responsibility, the ownership is split into shares, more people can buy a share of the ownership, making their money 'work', not themselves.

159 *Der Spiegel*, 31/2013, p. 35: "*Die Branche muesste mit ihren mittelstaendisch gepraegten Unternehmen eigentlich in der Bevoelkerung verwurzelt sein, tatsaechlich aber hat sie ein verheerendes Image. Sie bringt 160.000 unterschiedliche Waren in aller Regel geraeuschlos und ohne groessere Sicherheitsrisiken in die Regale jedes noch so abgelegenen Dorfladens. Gleichzeitig faellt sie nur dan auf, wenn gepanscht, getrickst oder getaeuscht wird. Wie kann es sein, dass erfolgreiche Produkte dieser Industrie von Verbraucherschuetzern oeffentlichkeitswirksam Negativ-Preise wie den "Goldenen Windbeutel" erhalten? Dass jede Verfehlung von Einzelnen das Fehlverhalten einer ganzen Indusrie zu bestaetigen scheint? Das Grundvertrauen in die Branche sei "erodiert", meldete vor kurzem das Werbeblatt "Horizont" - auch weil diese "viele Jahre eine Kultur des Schweigens" gepflegt haben. Tatsaechlich taten die Hersteller jahrelang alles*

In a survey of consumers' concerns, published by the German Bundesverband der Verbrauchezentralen (VZBV), led by Infas-Institute it was discovered that ⅔ of those questioned feared that they had been betrayed by the food industry as much as by the banks.[160] Only 43 per cent trusted the industry to deal with faulty products and 92 per cent wished to see more market control by independent organizations. Brussels is raising an alarm: the food industry is increasingly betraying and deceiving us. The risk of discovery is small and the penalties are too low, wrote the EU Parliament's Enviroment Committee in a draft report, reported *Spiegel* online on 15 November 2013.[161] Some of the fraudulent activities listed by the committee included: ordinary flour being sold as organic flour, eggs from caged poultry being sold as organic eggs, and salt for de-icing roads being sold as cooking salt. The authorities found methanol in spirits and horse meat in products which should have contained beef. There are clearly recurring patterns:

- Key ingredients are replaced by cheaper alternatives.
- Meat products do not correspond to the animal species on the label.
- The wrong weights are given.
- Conventional food is sold as 'organic'.
- Farmed fish is marketed as 'wild'.
- Food past its sell-by date is put for sale again.[162]

The industry was found to have deceived the public over sales of the following groceries primarily: olive oil, fish, organic food, milk, cereals, honey, maple syrup, coffee, tea, spices, wine and fruit juice – nearly everything we take into our bodies. The committee complained about gaps in control because nobody in the EU even knows how many companies are involved in the food trade. Retailers do not need to register. This should be made the law now.

The deception of consumers, who are expecting fresh and safe food, also happens when the food industry fails to employ enough food safety inspectors and to comply with hygienic standards. Dave Prentis, General secretary of Unison complained in a letter to *The Guardian* 25 July 2014, p. 37, that: "It is no surprise

---

dafuer, sich vor dem Konsumenten zu verstecken.In Zeiten vollautomatisierter Produktionsab-laeufe werben sie imer noch lieber damit, dass manikuerte Frauenhaende einzelne Erdbeeren sch-neiden und in den Joghurt fallen lassen, als dem Kunden klarzumachen, dass die 18 Kilogramm Joghurt, die jeder Deutsche im Schnitt pro Jahr verzehrt, nicht von Hand geruehrt werden. Die Unternehmer greifen zwar laengst auf weltweite Warenstroeme und Handelsketten zurueck, wollen das aber moeglichst nicht publik machen. Auf Kritik reagieren sie mit dem Engagement von PR-Agenturen, statt all ihre Zutaten und Lieferanten offenzulegen."

160 According to a report by *Spiegel* online, 3 June 2013

161 "*Bruessel schlaegt Alarm: In der Lebensmittelbranche wird offenbar zunehmend getaeuscht und betrogen. Die Entdeckungsrisiken seien gering und die Strafen zu niedrig, schreibt der Umweltausschuss im EU-Parlament in einem Briefentwurf.*"

162 "*Wichtige Inhaltsstoffe werden durch billigere Alternativen ausgetauscht. Die Tierarten auf Fleis-chprodukten werden fehlerhaft gekennzeichnet. Das Gewicht wird falsch angegeben. Konven-tionelle Lebensmittel werden als "Bio" verkauft. Zuchtfisch wird als Wildfang gekennzeichnet. Lebensmittel werden wieder in den Verkehr gebracht, nachdem deren Haltarkeitsdatum ueber-schritten wurde.*"

to Unison that two-thirds of fresh chicken in the UK is contaminated with campylobacter (*Poultry industry's dirty secret*, 24 July). Back in 1994, privatization allowed poultry meat producers to do away with independent, government-employed, poultry meat inspectors. Instead the industry was allowed to employ its own poultry inspection assistants (PIAs). In the smaller plants, the PIA is often the plant owner. Talk about giving the fox the key to the hen house. Meat inspection is a highly skilled job that has been hopelessly undervalued by the Food Standards Agency (FSA) for too long. There is no national standard or qualification for PIA so many staff are poorly trained – through no fault of their own. Companies are under market pressure to produce a cheaper product for ever more demanding supermarkets. This in turn puts pressure on slaughterhouse staff not to reject unfit birds. Added to this, there is a high staff turnover and high rates of sickness absence. Major plants are consistently understaffed and use agencies to fill the gaps. Only when a qualified and independent meat hygiene inspector is present is the job done properly. Sadly this is getting much harder. Recently, under the instruction of the government, the FSA lobbied to overturn a decision by the European parliament's environment, public health and food safety committee to reject visual-only inspection of pigs, for example.

Protection of the human food chain must be the first and most important duty of the FSA. These roles should not be privatized or weakened. The people who carry out these vital roles feel that both the FSA and the government have abandoned them and put the public at risk, simply to increase the profits in the meat industry..."

We can try to find explanations for consumer scepticism over the food industry's offers, perhaps not just in the bad experiences they may have made, but also in their in general awareness that it would be better if their meals should come directly from nature; from real fruit, vegetables, cereals, milk, butter, eggs, cheese, meat and so on. People are aware that they should prepare and consume fresh, raw, seasonal and locally grown food. However, at the same time they are easily tempted to consume processed food which has the opposite characteristics, especially when it is cheap and well-marketed as appetizing, when those around them are also consuming it, and when it is offered as a quick solution when they are hungry. Paying money for a ready-meal may also allow us to feel that someone has worked on something for us, that we don't have to be active but can remain relaxed and passive while paying for the efforts of somebody else. It is a bit like the situation in childhood where you only have to express hunger and mother will immediately respond to your needs. Indeed, when food such as soft white bread is so easy to swallow, isn't this reminiscent of the eating habits of a child who is not yet able to chew properly?

It is no wonder that the food industry tries to market its processed products particularly to children. Cute pictures of small animals nudge children to convince a grown-up that this is the product to buy, as if these images, for example small dogs on breakfast cereal packaging, had something to do with its contents. "Food companies are accused today by the World Health Organisation, the public arm of the UN, of finding ways to bypass the rules on advertising products to children and fuelling the obesity epidemic. Attempts by the authorities in Britain to clamp down on marketing to children through television advertising are not enough to protect them, a major report by the WHO concludes.[163] Britain has done more than some other European countries to guard children against advertising of unhealthy food, snacks and sweets, the report notes, but it is not one of the five countries – Denmark, France, Norway, Slovenia, Spain and Sweden – that have fully implemented the EU code on restricting marketing to children. There are, says the report, gaps and weaknesses in the UK regulations." Furthermore, it is not only the marketing of food *to* children, any advertising campaign *with* children should also be forbidden, even if appealing pictures of babies make the proud parents money.

Countless numbers of articles and books have been written about the detriments of processed food compared with fresh, raw, seasonal and locally grown food, and the food chain growing longer and longer, increasing the time between production and consumption, for example because of transport. These publications publish the chemical ingredients necessary to extend the shelf-life of processed foods, and highlight the lack of information consumers are given about artificial ingredients. Indeed, they inform us about what is done to make the food cheaper and easier to produce as well as increasing its longevity so that the producer does not lose money. Such ingredients are never used in fresh food because fresh food comes in its natural form. They include: antioxidants, colourings, emulgators, leavening and pickling agents, enzymes, processing aids, filler substances, thickening agents, aromas, taste intensifiers, raising agents, preservatives, artificial sweeteners, glutamate, vitamins[164] and more. In Hamburg, a special museum for additives has even been established, the Deutsche Zusatzstoffmuseum. Some of these artificial substances in processed food are listed in the International Numbering System (INS), the Codex Alumentarius, and given E-numbers. Consumers need much more information about additives, and governments need to protect consumers more and further regulate the food industry.

However, governments always try to find compromises between the interests of industries – cheap costs with higher profits – and those of the consumers, who want to know what is in their food and stay healthy. E-numbers, for example, do not really help consumers make decisions, as nobody is able to remember the meaning of these numbers, and what consequences they might have.

Although more government control and regulation is necessary, quite the opposite has also happened in Germany. According to *Der Spiegel*[165] the food control service is at least 1,600 inspectors short. The outcome is that consumers

---

163 *The Guardian*, 18 June 2013

164 Additionally people like to consume special vitamins and minerals to supplement their food. This market is worth US $28 bn a year. However, scientists from John Hopkins University in Baltimore, reviewed studies on additional vitamin in-take and found that people do not stay healthier or prevent themselves from developing chronic diseases or avoid death that way as *USA Today* reported on 16 December 2013. In fact, it was the other way round: high doses of vitamin E and A as well as beta-carotene can cause health risks. So 'more' does not always mean 'better'.

165 31/2013

are informed about food scandals *after* they have taken place, when the aim should be to prevent problems in advance. A few of the latest food scandals are listed here to remind us:

- Ham sprayed with chemicals, a process which is quicker than drying in fresh air, is transported from all over the world to the Italian town of Parma, where it is re-wrapped and then marketed as original 'Parma ham', as if the pigs were raised in Italy.
- Horse meat from Romania was put into lasagne instead of beef indicated on the package. However, the call to mark food with a 'country of origin label' was opposed by Spain and Great Britain.[166]
- Meat, especially pork and chicken, is injected with water to increase its weight so it can be sold a higher price. And when the water disappears during cooking it leaves small shrunken pieces.
- Baby milk is described as better than mother's milk, yet often diluted with water and white colouring as was done in China when thousands of children became ill.
- Fruit yoghurt contained no natural fruit but only chemical substitutes for flavour and colour, with synthesized vitamins such as vitamin 'D' added to make it 'healthier', the German organisation Foodwatch[167] reported, complaining that the EU-wide Health-Claim Directive that was made law in 2012 did not live up to its promise.
- Lager is produced with chemicals, instead of water, barley and hops, as the 500-year-old German 'Reinheitsgebot' or 'purity law for beer brewing' commands.
- Bread baked using ready-made mixtures is purported to be individually-handcrafted by artisan bakers, whilst coming from a factory.
- Chocolate was found to contain the chemical additive piperonal for improved flavouring when this should have been achieved with better quality ingredients.

Jenny Russell in *The Times* identified a few more incidents: "Vodka laced with antifreeze. Fake ham made from dyed chicken. Mozzarella comprising less than half real cheese. These and other horrors were recently exposed by trading standards officers in West Yorkshire... Indeed, of the 900 foods they tested, more than a third proved to be dodgy in some way. An official report commissioned after last year's horsemeat scandal found that food fraud is becoming a major international problem, with criminal gangs seeing it as an easy alternative to drug or people smuggling... Part of the attraction to criminals is that, with cash-strapped local authorities cutting back on food testing, there's very little risk of detection. Some authorities no longer test at all. It's a dangerous situation. Even in straitened times, the state needs 'to spend enough to ensure that those who are swindling or poisoning us have a real fear of being found out'."[168]

---

166 *Frankfurter Allgemeine Zeitung*, 5 December 2013, p. 10
167 *Spiegel* online, 9 December 2013
168 *The Week*, 22 February 2014, p. 15

"Professor Chris Ellott told the Commons Environment, Food and Rural Affairs Committee that food fraud needed to become an item in the company risk register," reported *The i* 9 January 2014. "He said: 'Any particular incidents of suspected food fraud that are happening in large companies should be reported to the board.' ... food authenticity had been taken 'very seriously' in the UK, with the Food Standards Agency regarded as a global leader, but that had been 'eroded over a number of years, to the point that governmental testing was at an all-time low.' He said a unit should be set up as an independent force able to deal with 'complex food crime perpetrated by highly organized and dangerous, potentially violent, organized crime groups'," and added that there is "the potential for 'huge profits and low risks' in food fraud and there remained, in Britain, a worrying lack of knowledge' regarding the extent of their operations." On its website, Lebensmittelwarnung.de, the German Bundesamt fuer Verbraucherschutz und Lebensmittelsicherheit (BVL) publishes the latest food warnings, according to paragraph 40 of the Food Safety Act. As welcome as these intentions are, the problem remains that food safety control is, as pointed out, mostly a reaction to something that has already gone wrong, when it would be much better to monitor all food before bringing it to the market' to avoid risks to health. This is a process which the industry does not want to happen and is therefore resisting.

As Felicity Lawrence concluded in *Dinner is served, courtesy of the mafia*:[169] "What we are witnessing is not so much the breakdown of the rule of law as the systematic removal of law. We may not have the political instability of a fragile state, but we have weakened the public institutions that keep the market in check... So government inspection and testing in the food industry has been cut in favour of allowing the private sector to police itself. The regulator, in this case the Food Standards Agency, has been eviscerated, cut and stripped of powers, and left inadequate for the task of investigating. Individual local councils and trading standards officers – responsible as the home authorities for imposing the law on any giant company headquartered in their patch – have lost most of what little money they had to rise to the unequal challenge. Crime, not surprisingly, has rushed into the vacuum, and the industry's own policemen turned out to be of the sleeping kind. It's not just the food sector... The rule of law does not much trouble the criminal networks that have run illegal labour rings in the UK either. For years they have supplied casual workers to our food and packing factories, the catering trade, building sites and care homes. Their connections with people-trafficking and money-laundering have been established. But, even if detected, few are likely to be prosecuted..." It is no wonder that people are disappointed with the governmental obligation as they should "be able to depend on the state to police crime and enforce the law". This reflects the pattern already pointed out: avoiding risks in advance is not made the aim of governments, instead risks are dealt with afterwards, when the consequences have already become obvious for everyone, the damage already done and suffering already experienced.

In general, it can be said that the food industry is trying to replace natural living processes (on which human beings depend) with artificial substances (these

169 *The Guardian*, 19 December 2013, p. 36

days even genetically modified) , the consequences of which are not known. And this development is fuelled by financial considerations, with the aim of making products cheaper to produce and cheaper to buy, without the participation of consumers. It is a process of industrialization. The problems it causes for animal or human health, for example, rising allergies and food intolerances, are then made into a growing business for the health industry, where additional doctors, nurses and hospitals are needed, along with additional allergy specialists, and more drugs to help people recover from these illnesses. And while economists and politicians welcome increasing turnovers, Martin Jaenicke[170] accurately character-ized this situation as the industrial system profiting from its own consequences. Why is there rarely anyone asking whether this is the kind of economic develop-ment we really want and we really need?

Another factor that is rarely recognized is that the process of industrialization means transforming open immediate and unmediated reciprocal interactions into finished commodities.

Wouldn't it be cheaper, fairer, healthier, more participative and much more effective, if such consequences – for nature and people – were avoided from the very beginning, following the pattern of reciprocal interaction rather than the one of fragmentation?

Instead, we can watch a continuation of the industrial pattern of fragmentation going further. For example, on 25 November 2013, the German television pro-gramme *Report Muenchen* broadcasted details of a new Free Trade Agreement with the USA, which, scientists fear, will lead even to a wider deterioration in food standards and to more erosion of people's participation and their governments rights. The Agreement states that US food concerns would be able to sue national administrations of every country which refuses them the right to trade in it, on the grounds of non-adherence to the national quality standard, eg selling US chicken treated with chlorine to increase its keeping potential. These global food compa-nies can raid nations, fears Friends of the Earth, and they can claim costs that the taxpayer has to bear, and countries would no longer have the sovereignty to decide on their own standards.

This is the process of further transformation from local agriculture into global agroindustry, and farms into firms, leading to an even wider break of the unity of production and consumption. Individuals locally no longer produce food themselves, producers do not consume their own products. Both buy from a globalized food industry which manufactures processed food with little regard for its connection with source or destination.

To resume the arguments:

The transformation on the consumer side

The 21st century consumer no longer produces food or exchanges the harvest surplus at a real market; instead he takes his choices from ready-made products manufactured in anonymous industrial processing plants (which he doesn't know and usually cannot access, and which often try to escape liability for their

---

170 *Wie das Industriesystem von seinen Missstaenden profitiert*, Opladen, 1979

products),while not being involved in production decisions.

Ready-made food might sometimes be convenient, but it lacks detailed information about the production process as well as the exact contents and their origin, and it is this information that the consumer needs in order to even make a properly informed choice.

The advantage for the 21st century consumer is that the food is immediately ready to eat while raw food needs time for preparation and cooking as well as someone with the knowledge of how to cook it. Raw food cannot be tampered with in the same way as processed food. These days food comes from all over the world, not necessarily from the country where the consumer lives, resulting in additional distribution costs and increased traffic which causes additional greenhouse gas emissions.[171] And everyone can enjoy international(ized) food: American burgers and ice-cream, Italian pizza and lasagne, French baguettes and fries, Chinese egg-noodles and stir-fries, Indian curries, Turkish doner kebabs, South American chili con carne or British baked beans.

The variety of provenance also means that the food is grown in different seasonal climates enabling the consumer to consume fresh fruit in the European winter. Our dependency on the natural fertility helix in our own country is broken or enlarged, depending on the view from which it is regarded. As Jane Merrick commented in *The Independent*, 2 January 2014, p. 29, this shows"... how producers and supermarkets are furthering our disassociation from the seasons and eroding our ability to enjoy food that grows naturally in different months of the year. By pandering to an ever-tasteless (in more ways than one) palate, the food industry is not celebrating British produce but helping to kill it off. Giving consumers British strawberries at all times weakens our link with the changing year, turning us even further away from seasonal, less popular fruits like damsons, quinces and plums that are naturally ripe and juicy in winter.[172]"

The transformation on the producer side
Small scale farms offering a variety of products and animals are replaced by big firms with a huge amount of land growing one product, eg maize,[173] to be

---

171 Bonn based agricultural scientist Michael Blanke has compared the energy balance of apples with the following result: he found that one kilo New Zealand apples consumed in Germany generates 400 gram of CO2 emissions, while apples from the Alte Land near Hamburg generate one third less emissions. The consumer's own transport emissions have to be considered too, however, if the consumer uses his car to drive two kilometres to the supermarket, the round trip generates half a kilo of greenhouse gases, said Joerg Albrecht in *Frankfurter Allgemeine Sonntagszeitung*, 21 September 2012.

The ecological balance sheet for every product needs to be established. In 2011, the Darmstadt Institute for Applied Ecology conducted a meta-study for the Nordrhein-Westaelische Landesamt fuer Natur, Umwelt und Verbraucherschutz, based on 200 studies examining 600 products. The biggest emitter of CO$_2$ was found to be pork (224 kg CO$_2$ per inhabitant/year), followed by cheese and butter (170 kg and 164 kg), beef, fish and beer generated 90 kg, 69 kg and 96 kg respectively, followed by coffee, mineral water and eggs (43 kg, 55 kg, 36 kg). The lowest emissions are generated by apples (17 kg), potatoes (13 kg), tomatoes (6 kg) and pasta (6 kg).

172 It would perhaps be better to have mentioned autumn instead of winter.

173 In Germany, maize monoculture is referred to as 'maizification'/'*Vermaischung*'.

transformed into biogas instead of food,[174] and fields on which bigger and bigger machines sow, fertilize and harvest. Industrial farming reduces the number of labourers and their costs. However, it also limits human cooperation. A big farm can afford its own machines working on bigger fields, whereas smaller farmers needed to cooperate for the use of harvesters.

Firm-farmers are contracted to grow produce for the global food processing industry. The firm-farmer no longer works direct to supply local food for local people. They no longer live directly off their own produce, but indirectly by sales to retailers as well as on European Union subsidies handed down to them via national governments, administered by civil servants.

The whole process of interaction with nature is split into smaller parts, each concentrating exclusively on one task, eg fattening pigs or raising chickens in their thousands, treating the animals as objects, in totally un-natural and inappropriate circumstances, as they are not in contact with a range of different animals or with soil or daylight, but dependent on medication, such as antibiotics to stop one illness destroying a whole herd of the same kind. Grass-eating animals like cows have even been fed the residues of other animals, consequently developing the mad-cow-disease. Firm-farmers no longer have direct contact with the real consumers of their goods.

The way forward, however, should be different: convincing consumers and the agroindustry to seek direct interaction with nature as well as with the buyers of their produce, for example in farm shops, to enrich the relationship between producers and consumers in all their facets.

Another consequence of industrializing agriculture is the large amount of food which is thrown away as the food is cheap, relatively.[175] Wasting food is of no concern to the food industry, as long as it has sold its products and therefore its aim to make money is fulfilled.

The amount of waste is nowhere bigger than in industrialized nations. *Spiegel* online, 11 September 2013, contained a report from the United Nations noting that, globally more than a quarter of farmland is used for the production of food which goes directly into the wastebin. The report estimated that the financial losses (excluding fish and seafood) amount to €565 billion a year. At the same time 870 million people worldwide are starving. The European Union aims to reduce the amount of wasted food by half by 2020.

As *Der Spiegel* pointed out, it is not only the food that is wasted, but also energy and water, necessary for production. The amount of water wasted in Germany is equivalent to five times the volume of Lake Constance. Besides the wasted food,

---

174 which takes land away from food producing. If the European Union were to cease mixing biofuels into petrol, more than 120 million people could be fed, the democracy network Campact argued (see *Der Spiegel*, 9 December 2013) at a time when EU energy ministers were aiming to extend the production of biofuels from 5 to 7 per cent.

175 It was reported in *The Week* 26 October 2013, p. 25, citing *The Independent* that "68 per cent of bagged salad bought and sold by Tesco never makes it onto the plate. 33 per cent is thrown away before it gets sold, but 35 per cent is binned by the consumer. The average British family throws away £680-worth of food each year." In Germany a government study found that food waste there amounted to 82 kilos.

greenhouse gases amounting to 3.3 billion tonnes of carbon dioxide are emitted.

The US report stated further that in general 54 per cent of wasted food is already lost in production, or due to late harvesting or in storage especially in developing nations, while food waste arising from processing, distribution and consumption is a particular problem for industrialized countries. So, to feed more people it would be recommendable to implement strategies for avoiding such waste.

Another problem is that in recent years the food industry has offered food in ever-larger quantities. There are many oversized sandwiches, such as a 'foot-long' sandwich from Subway costing $5 in the US.[176] There are also bigger servings of soft-drinks,[177] which New York's city town council tried to a limit to 16 ounces (470 millilitres), a measure which failed to gain court approval. Both are examples of the industry's strategies to sell even more. The consumer is now forced to buy much more than he wants, with the consequence that he either keeps the food for too long for it to be fresh or that he eats more than he needs, leading to weight and health problems, eg due to too much sugar and fat.

And it is not only the quantities of food for sale that have been made bigger, this has been followed by bigger glasses and plates, bigger chairs and sofas, as well as lamps and beds. Because people have put on more weight by eating more, the dimensions of household goods have had to increase proportionately with the things around them.

This trend comes with especially problematic consequences, when a consumer with a headache is forced to buy 20 pills instead of the five they may need to get rid of the pain. The consumer often neither needs nor wants these quantities, as more and more people live in single households, but the industry increasingly restricts consumer's choice when it comes to the quantities offered.

Today food is more and more often wrapped in plastic, not only for hygienic reasons. The plastic wrapping denies consumers the chance to recognise whether the food is really fresh because they are no longer able to smell it. Their perception is limited to sight.

And another consequence as already noted is, that children grow up less and less aware of what their food looks like when it is fresh. Their knowledge of the essential connectedness of man with nature and our necessary dependence on nature is reduced.

A further consequence is that the plastic wrapping needs to be thrown away by the consumer, contributing to the mountains of plastic (along with electronic waste from computers, mobile phones, Kindles, CDs, TV sets and so on). Plastic does not biodegrade naturally but needs to be stored safely. A lot of it is now exported to less industrialized countries as this is sometimes the cheapest way to get rid of it.

In her film *Crops of the Future*[178] Marie Monique Robin informed us that plastic carries another risk, the release of so-called endocrine disruptors which act like artificial hormones, disturbing cell growth and possibly leading to the development of cancerous tumours.

176 *The Week*, 6 July 2013
177 *Kieler Nachrichten*, 1 August 2013
178 Shown 16 July 2013 on the German/French TV channel *arte*

The solution to all these problems should be to widen the freedom for consumers allowing him more choice as well as involvement respecting his wish for:

- smaller quantities of food,
- less pre-washed or pre-peeled vegetables, fruit and salads,
- more loose food,
- paper bags or biodegradable plastic bags for transport,
- retailers to remind consumers to bring their own bags,
- direct sales from local farmer to local consumer,
- transparent growing and production processes,
- local consumer involvement, as practised for example on George and Giles Eustice's farm in Cornwall,[179]
- and more control on food production and retail.

The food industry needs to be re-engineered from BASE, and this seems to already be happening: consumers have become far more conscious of what they eat and what the consequences can be. To support this development, food additives and pesticides should be heavily taxed, so that the food industry would no longer find it so profitable to use these chemical substances but prefer natural ingredients instead.

At the same time the food regulator should force the industry to print precise contents and quantities on labels, avoiding general descriptions, such as 'preservatives', but indicating instead exactly what kind, and how many grammes of it, is in the product, what kind of artificial colour and how much. Information by e-numbers is not sufficient.

Consumers have a choice. Nowadays even the big supermarkets offer organic food which is sometimes – if you compares prices for butter for example – cheaper than industrially produced global products. This puzzled economicult scientists; however we know that organic farming involves less chemicals and lower mechanical input, so it might be cheaper, though more working people are necessary to look after land and animals (which we view as an advantage, and not only a cost factor) and less transport.

In Germany, a number of organic farming associations have been established, such as Demeter, Allnatura or Naturata, which label their products with special trademarks assuring the customer that the food is grown ecologically in direct and unmediated relationship with nature. This means no artificial additives, no use of fertilizers or pesticides and especially no incorporation of genetically modified material (GM).[180] And instead of killing living organisms with chemicals in order

179 Featured in the program '*On our farm*' by Sarah Swadling, broadcasted on BBC Radio 4, on 5 January 2014, from 6.35 h. The Eustice's family farmed for more than 400 years in Cornwall, George swapped strawberry farming for Westminster while Giles gave up working in computer sales to run the business. Covering 28 acres and employing 70 people, it includes a farm restaurant, deli, farm market, bakery, pick-your-own, and a centre for teaching children farming and showing consumers that everything which is offered is grown on the farm, from food for the rare pigs to 100 different varieties of food for consumers.

180 *The Week*, 6 October 2012, p. 15, reported that "in 2003 51 per cent" of people "said they were

to grow only one species, thriving soil life is encouraged as the benefits of this are well understood.

Let me present only one of the examples of how to work better with nature: in August 2013 *Wired* magazine published an article by David Baker about the experience of Leontino Balbo Junior, who started organically farming sugar cane[181] in the Brazilian state of Sao Paulo in 1986 to "increase a crop's productivity, boost its resistance to pests, reduce the resources needed to cultivate it, and broaden the biodiversity of the land on which it was grown. Balbo called his approach 'ecosystem revitalising agriculture' (ERA) and claimed that it could revive not only ailing crops... but also ailing land that had been 'starved of vitality' by decades of modern farming. If it was successful, the impact would be felt far beyond agriculture." Balbo, who produces 34 per cent of the world's organic sugar today, which is "used in about 120 high-profile products from Green & Black's chocolate to Yeo Valley yoghurt, sees his aims of agricultural self-sufficiency, as a way "to preserve the natural resources we need now – water, soil fertility, biodiversity and the atmosphere. Otherwise, we won't be able to maintain a civilized society. If we have a water crisis, for example, we will end up having a global war because of natural resources. And human beings as a civilization will be gone." This was the fear of Balbo..." "ERA is organic in its approach but, Balbo says, it goes much further than simply not using artificial pesticides or fertilizer. At its core is a respect for soil. Farming has tended to treat soil more as a receptacle for water and nutrients than as something that makes an active contribution to plant growth. 'Soil is not just a container,' he says, 'it's also the content of the ecosystem. It holds the biodiversity, both living and mineral, that's essential for life. If the soil loses this function, all other things are compromised.' According to Balbo, modern agriculture damages soil in three ways.

Farm machinery compresses it, making it less able to hold water; fertilizers upset its natural chemical balance; and monocrops reduce its biodiversity, which he sees as essential for healthy plants. 'So much soil used for agriculture is dead,' he says. 'We need to revitalize it, to restore the energy of its ecosystem.'"

Before it was seen as normal to burn fields before harvesting. "Crop burning eliminates pests and snakes, and burns the 'trash' – the living and dead leaves – from the canes... So the harvesters have to cut and collect not only the cane, but the melt, which is full of soil" and needs to be washed. "We were using three million litres of water every hour just to do that." "Balbo spent five years, from

---

'concerned' or 'very concerned' about GM crops. A decade on, attitudes have softened only slightly: in a new survey by the British Science Association, 46 per cent felt the same."

Spiegel online 11 February 2014 reported that the British government will now say 'yes' to GM 'corn 1507'.

Frankfurter Allgemeine Sonntagszeitung commented on 15 December 2013, p. 65, that genetically modified potatoes 'Amflora' and 'Fortuna', produced by BASF and Monsanto, will not become the big business the chemical giants hoped as neither farmers nor consumers buy them.

On 11 February 2014 we also learned, *Spiegel* online, although 88 per cent of Germans have reservations about genetically modified US corn – German Chancellor Merkel has cleared the way for GM corn as she wishes the German government to abstain from voting against it.

181 Sugar production was once one leg of the Triangular Trade of slaves between Europe, Africa and the 'colonies' in West India and South America.

1988 to 1993, developing a mechanical harvester that would cut the cane 'green', that is with its leaves still on... Harvesting this way, Balbo says, returns 20 tonnes of trash per hectare to the soil each year, restoring nutrients, especially nitrogen, and forming a mulch that helps keeps weeds down." Additionally, he started to use ultrasoft tyres on the machines to prevent the soil becoming compressed. Then "he turned his attention to the byproducts of the sugar production process itself." At one of the estate's mills in Sao Francisco which had been turned over to organic production, "the liquid residue left over after the cane pulp is fermented, is collected and sprayed back on to the fields, and dry matter is fed directly into a furnace which produces 200 tonnes of steam per hour. Some of this is used to extract sugar from the cane. The rest of the electricity powers the mill and its associated buildings, with excess sold to the grid."

At first his efforts were disappointing. But Balbo who "is passionately opposed to GM crops" remained convinced that "everything in nature has a function. Everything is doing something. You can't just go into an ecosystem and apply insecticide and eliminate 30 or 40 species of insect, because they have a role there." After a while bugs came back. "'The bugs, combined with using softer tyres, changed the geometry and the composition of the soil. We soon started to see a fourfold increase in water retention, a fivefold increase in resistance to erosion and a threefold increase in organic content,' he says... By leaving all the insects in place,' says Balbo, 'we enabled nature to keep them under control.' ERA had finally arrived. It has taken him 27 years, but Balbo has not only improved cane production on his land. He has also increased its biodiversity far beyond fungi and wasps. The Balbo fields are now home to hundreds of forest animals including foxes, deer, capybara and armadillos, four types of big cat and countless bird and insect species. But he sees sustainability as something more than this, a philosophy that encompasses not only environmental concerns, but economic and social ones too." "All Balbo employees now have access to welfare, medical and sports facilities, and low-cost housing." "'What he practises is phenomenology,' says Evaristo de Miranda, a senior researcher at Embrapa, Brazil's state-owned agricultural-research centre in Brasilia, who has been following Balbo's project for more than 20 years. 'It's what farmers have done for over 10,000 years. He observes, experiences, analyses, innovates and transforms. He knows, as a good agronomist, to ask the right questions. He interrogates nature all the time and nature responds. His advances are empirical, in the full sense of the term.'" Balbo is now taking his ideas "out of his testbed in Sao Paulo state, into the wider world. To market his ideas... he will be launching Agros Fortis (based on the Latin for 'strong fields'), a technology-transfer company that will help others adopt ERA."

We need to help natural processes to remain healthy and active, this should be the aim, learning from Balbo's example. This is also the aim when politicians decided that organic farming and direct marketing of its produce are supported. Even the Bauernverband[182] believes that there is a high potential for organic farming.[183] Schleswig-Holstein will put €130 m more into subsidies for organic farming, amounting to a total of €430 m until 2020. According to its Minister for

---

182 Germany's Farmers' Association including all kinds of farmers
183 *Kieler Nachrichten*, 10 February 2014, p. 6

Agriculture and Environment, Robert Habeck, food policy will be reset with increased protection of nature, better sustainability of food production, animal health and species-appropriate husbandry. The Minister for Agriculture in Niedersachsen, Christian Meyer, whose region offers the largest amount of arable land in Germany with the highest density of livestock per square metre, is even of the opinion[184] that the era of unregulated intensive factory farming is over.

Let's look at another example of what can be done[185]: agronomist Knut Ellenberg of the Demeter farm yard 'Klostersee' near Cismar, Schleswig-Holstein, found that the traditional feeding of calves does not make sense. First the other cow is milked, then later a part of the milk is warmed up to the cow's body temperature and given to the calf in a bucket.[186] He started developing a more "mother-bound" feeding method on his farm – a transferable, practical and economical procedure. Now, after the first few days, the calves go into a separate compartment, if the mother decides to stay in instead of grazing on the pasture. After milking, the cows go together with their calves into a big cowshed. There the calves can drink, let themselves be licked and run about, and then move back into their separated place. A new cowshed was built in which every cow was given nearly 20 sqm space, allowing the animals double the amount of space traditional farming offers to them. The shed was cheap to build. It was financed by citizens by so-called 'cow bonds', with fixed interest being paid in the form of cash or organic products, whilst the reformed process needs more manpower to look after the animals. It created more jobs.

The adoption of chickens by egg consumers is another form of direct interaction between producers and consumers. In fact, this direct relationship can be extended even more, if the consumers lend a hand here and there to the organic farmer with weeding or harvesting, also bringing pleasure to children as they too benefit from extended contact with animals. This is a good example, and more farmers should be encouraged to follow it. In the UK it is practised by the Community Supported Agriculture (CSA) scheme. "People come from our village... to share the work, responsibilities and decision-making, complete with the risks and rewards – produce from our plot," said Ben Tregenna who runs such a scheme in Cambridgeshire.[187]

Furthermore, politicians should make sure that locally produced, organically grown food is bought for meals in public canteens, eg in the army and navy, in ministerial offices, hospitals, homes for the elderly, schools,[188] nurseries, police stations, fire service, parliaments and so on, as already the case in Denmark. Cooking with fresh local products, additive-free, with a short cooking time and fresh herbs instead of processed ingredients should become the norm. And the public administration should be the role model for this. This practice can reduce aller-

---

184 *Spiegel* online, 1 March, 2014

185 *"Zurueck zu den Zitzen, mehr Mutterbindung beim Milchvieh"*, *Kieler Nachrichten*, 22 October 2013

186 "Da melkt man die Mutterkuh, erwaermt einen Teil der Milch spaeter auf Kuhkoerpertemperatur und gibt sie dem Kalb in einem Eimer."

187 www.countryliving.co.uk, April 2013, p. 51

188 Jamie Oliver has already tried to promote this initiative.

gies, food intolerances and illnesses as well as keeping people more active, which in due course would save money as they would no longer need time off to recover from illnesses. Such an initiative needs to be well-marketed so that workers become aware of its benefits. Canteens should inform their customers exactly where the ingredients of meals originated from, how many food miles were necessary and the name of the producer. This would also be in favour of local food producer. Why should politicians not follow examples from other countries such as Denmark, or France, where for example a new law asked that only the places where meals are freshly cooked with fresh ingredients[189] are allowed to call themselves 'restaurants'.

The justification of an increasingly industrialized lifestyle is that a world with a growing population needs more and more food to feed its inhabitants, while the prices of food should stay stable or should even decrease, enabling everybody to consume more, especially sugar,[190] salt, fat and meat in their everyday diet, while today's waste is not taken into the equation, as said.

Such a view still seems to be advocated as the only normal and the right way forward. As the *Kieler Nachrichten* reported on 6 August 2013, scientists of the Dutch university of Maastricht are attempting to produce artificial meat from stem cells, as they believe that meat from a laboratory could help to stop global hunger and satisfy the growing hunger for meat. Global consumption of meat, they think, will increase by about 3 per cent by 2050. At the same time, livestock farming could be limited, even in helping to combat climate change, as meat production swallows up more agricultural land, water and grain than the production of any other human foodstuff.[191] Although viewing meat as the only type of food that counts is unreasonably restrictive, the issue of population growth – again, seen as a natural and uncontrollable law – is neglected as other ideas than technical quantitative ones. This is, of course, clearly in line with the industrial approach which offers more indirect products for sale by money, less direct recip-

189 *Spiegel* online reported on 8 June 2013 that 31 per cent of French eating establishments today use pre-packaged green salad, industrially produced fries, and potato flakes as well as deep frozen *creme brulée*. They replace their 'self-work' with buying-in. The new law aims to guarantee that a restaurant meal is freshly prepared with fresh natural ingredients.

190 "The growing obesity epidemic could be 'halted or reversed' in less than five years if the food industry makes cuts in the amount of 'hidden sugar' in our food, leading doctors have said. Sugar is a major cause of obesity and also increases the risk of type-2 diabetes. Leading experts today launched a new campaign group, Action on Sugar, to alert the public to the high levels of sugar in their food and lobby government and the food industry to reduce its use of 'unnecessary' sugar. ... Experts said that if major manufacturers reduced the amount of sugar in their products, adding up to a 20 to 30 per cent decrease in sugar content in three to five years, the obesity epidemic could be stopped in its tracks. Graham McGregor, professor of cardiovascular medicine at the Wolfson Institute of Preventative Medicine and chairman of the new group, said that the Government's 'Responsibility Deals' with the food industry had failed and a new approach was needed... 'to reduce the completely unnecessary and very large amounts of sugar the food and soft drink industry is currently adding to our foods.' The obesity epidemic is costing the UK over £5 billion a year, he said, estimating that costs could rise to £50 billion by 2050," The *i* reported on 9 January 2014, p. 6.

191 Here, even climate change is used trying to legitimate even a deeper level of industrialization, ie the production of synthetic meat.

rocal interaction and an even higher fragmentation of the relationships between producers and consumers as well as people and nature.

Consequently, it is helpful to remind ourselves of some interesting data. "Currently, 36 per cent of the calories produced by the world's crops are being used for animal feed, and only 12 per cent of those feed calories ultimately contribute to the human 'direct' diet (as meat and other animal products). Additionally, human-edible calories used for biofuel production increased fourfold between the years 2000 and 2010, from 1 per cent to 4 per cent, representing a net reduction of available food globally... We find that, given the current mix of crop uses, growing food exclusively for direct human consumption could in principle, increase available food calories by as much as 70 per cent which could feed an additional 4 billion people (more than the projected 2 - 3 billion people arriving through population growth)," commented Emily S. Cassidy, Paul C. West, James S. Gerber and Jonathan A. Foley of the Institute on Environment, of the University of Minesota, Saint Paul, USA, on 1 August 2013, adding: "... to increase food availability, we may also consider how the world's crops are allocated to different uses and whether it is possible to feed more people with current levels of crop production." Efficiency of use should come before production of more.

Another voice, the one of Tara Garnett of the University of Oxford, has pointed out that instead of technical solutions the global distribution of food needs to be improved, as at the moment 1.4 billion people in the world are overweight and obese, while at the same time 1 billion people go to bed hungry. Not only must we re-think farming and distribution methods; we also need better quality, locally produced food allowing people more contact with nature and the sale of smaller quantities.

It is also necessary to support people growing their own food instead of making them labour to buy products from the global market'. Such an approach obviously would have many consequences which do not yet fit into the traditionally fragmented pattern of economicult production and consumption. Consider again how the fragmented pattern is understood:

Land is for the exclusive use of its owner. Landowners decide what to produce with respect to the most profit they gain on the global food market'. What is produced is less dependent on the natural local conditions of soil and climate, than on expected sale prices. Natural competitors in the form of insects or plants are killed off. Soil exploited by monocultural production is artificially enriched by fertilizers manufactured by using fossil fuels.

The landowner pays people to labour on his land for his profit. Receiving wages minus taxes, the labourers buy food and the other necessities for life preservation. They might even be able to buy the globally marketed food which they helped to produce.

Sales of food, now commodities, as well as the profits gained from its sales, are taxed by the government. Food imports are taxed by government.

The process of reciprocal interaction between man and nature has been transformed and made indirect. Countries are no longer able to produce and supply staple food for everybody, but import it from other countries. Global investors speculate on future harvests.

David Hachfeld from Oxfam argues that food is not an object of speculation to be gambled on, and it should not be treated as such.[192] Oxfam has published a study stating that German banks and insurance companies are heavily involved in food market' speculation leading to higher prices for consumers and therefore to more hunger. According to them, global speculation amounts today to €70 billion, in which the German insurance group Allianz and Deutsche Bank are major players. In 2011 Allianz invested more than €6.2 billion and Deutsche Bank nearly €4.6 billion.[193] The investment bank Goldman Sachs is said to be involved in 25 to 30 different global 'raw' material markets', for coffee, soya, wheat and cattle, which is about 20 per cent of their business. Fact is, a huge market' for financial products has been established in recent years allowing people to gamble on the development of food prices. And so the markets' on which contracts for agricultural raw materials are dealt, have developed a kind of *life on their own*. The volume of financial deals is now 20 to 30 times bigger than the deals in the real economy.[194] Germany's Finance Minister Wolfgang Schaeuble raised the ante in the fight against food speculation. He had supported a proposal by the Council of Finance Ministers in June to reform the European Financial Market Directive. But this was condemned by non-governmental organizations, such as Foodwatch and Oxfam, as virtually useless trying to limit it. In a paper sent to all member states, the German Ministry of Finance advocated, that uncontrolled trade outside stock exchanges should be regulated. Additionally, some kind of limit on speculation should apply to large concerns, to prevent small subsidiary companies from taking speculation deals to their limits. Schaeuble also wanted to put right the biggest weakness of the Council's proposal pointed out by the Non-Governmental Organizations: in his view the European Securities and Markets Authority (ESMA) should set uniform European-wide limits so that speculators cannot side-step into countries with lower standards[195] according to *Der Spiegel* 37/2013, p. 68.

192 *Spiegel* online, 23 October 2013
193 *Spiegel* online, 9 May 2012, Deutsche Bank said that it is examining this critic. Allianz refused to comment.
194 *Der Spiegel* 5/2013, p. 74-75: "*Fakt ist: In den vergangenen Jahren ist ein riesiger Markt fuer Finanzprodukte entstanden, mit denen auf die Entwicklung der Nahrungsmittelpreise gewettet wird... Und so haben die Maerkte, auf denen Kontrakte fuer Agrarrohstoffe gehandelt werden, ein Eigenleben entwickelt. Das Volumen der Finanzgeschaefte ist inzwischen 20- bis 30mal groesser als das der realen Geschaefte.*"
195 Deutschlands Finanzminister Wolfgang Schaeuble "*legte im Kampf gegen Nahrungsmittelspeku-lanten nach. Zwar hatte er im Juni den Vorschlag des Rates der Finanzminister zur Reform der Europaeischen Finanzmarktrichtlinie mitgetragen. Dieser war von Nichtregierungsorganisationen wie Foodwatch und Oxfam als nahezu wirkungslos verurteilt worden in Bezug auf die Beschraen-kung von Agrarspekulationen... In einer Stellungnahme, die an alle Mitgliedslaender verschickt wurde, fordert das BMF unter anderem, den abseits der Boerse stattfindenen unkontrollierten Handel einzuschliessen. Zugleich soll eine Art Spekulations-Limit fuer Gesamt-konzerne gelten, damit nicht jede kleine Tochterfirma das Geschaeft ausreizen kann. Auch die aus Sicht der Nichtregierungsorganisationen groesste Schwaeche des Ratsvorschlages will Schaeuble korrigieren: Die Europaeische Wertpapier- und Marktaufsichtsbehoerde ESMA soll seiner Meinung nach europaweit einheitliche Grenzen festlegen, so dass Spekulanten nicht auf Laender mit niedrig-eren Standards ausweichen koennen.*"

Spiegel online reported on 13 March 2013 that Deutsche Bank CEO Juergen Fitschen had to face a lot of criticism regarding the bank's speculation on food in a hearing of the Bundestag's Committee on Development. He tried to defend himself arguing that Deutsche Bank does not speculate on agricultural raw materials/soft commodities itself but only offers index funds, for which the buyer of such a financial product is responsible. German MPs called this "a cynical argumentation and an antiquated moral understanding." The German Minister for Agriculture, Ilse Aigner, praised the decision by the DZ Bank, an 'umbrella' group off more than 900 German cooperative banks, to withdraw from speculation on food.

The way forward now is to end fragmentation and encourage direct reciprocal interaction between man and nature. Instead of working against nature leading to the loss of soil fertility and biodiversity, as well as damage human health, we need to develop life-affirming interactions and treat our co-nature with fairness, respect and responsibility, since we, as human beings, depend on it. The BASE for human life is more than just a business.

When discussing the primary and secondary BASE for life, something else comes to mind: the Ancient Greeks, 2,000 years ago viewed air, water, soil (producing food or internal energy) and (external) energy as the elements which could not be split any further. According to today's understanding of physics, they obviously can, and are better understood as well. Yet if we extend the ancient theory a little more and call them the basic elements *of life*, then we have to recognize that our ancestors were not completely wrong.

These insights also enable us to extend the enlightened view that people are born equal and have the same inalienable rights, now being able to formulate this more precisely: people are not only born equal, but they also share the same right to interact with the BASE as well as having a shared interest in self-preservation as long as they live. It follows that the human relationship with the BASE of life – in the ongoing natural uno-actu-process of perception and action – should be constructed in such a way that it stays always direct and unmediated, that it is the same[196] for everybody and of equal advantage to people and to nature.

11.2. Humans have self-value

Every organism and every human being is different from another. No person is totally identical to another with respect to sex, age, height, weight, health, eye colour, hair colour and quality, skin colour or fingerprints. All these characteristics define a certain person, as well as their abilities, experiences, interests, preferences, heritage, willingness to show compassion or assume responsibility, views and even beliefs. Every person is unique. Every individual has value for himself, to be respected by others.

Every human being has only one life; there is no second chance to live one's life again. Every individual lives in their own time and interacts with others at

---

196 ...as if Earth were divided into equal parts for everybody's use, as Adam Smith noted.

their own pace according to their own rationale. Individuals make their own decisions on how to live, where and under what circumstances. And this right to self-determination cannot be taken away from a person. Every person is the subject of their own destiny, and therefore no life is the same as others.

This does not mean, however, that people are not influenced by natural disasters such as storms and floods, volcanic eruptions or cultural disasters such as wars, or by social habits. Every individual has the basic human potential for self-development, whilst the form in which self-development can take place will differ from person to person, from culture to culture as well as from past to present. ·

The individuality of a person allows a government to issue non-forgeable identity cards and passports which confirm a person's identity, containing their unique name, image, date of birth, eye colour and current place of residence.

Furthermore, by nature humans are a kind of super-organism because different ranges of bacteria live inside them for the purpose, for example, to break down food, digest it and release it. Without those micro-organism human life would not be possible.

The natural law of biological diversity means that *one* specific look should never be made the norm, as the consequence of this would be that one characteristic is seen as 'better' compared to the norm than another one, when in reality they are of equal value, but just different. Natural differences need to be accepted. They can be ascertained but really not judged, and encountering them can make a person more self-conscious. In cultural terms, however, people create certain norms for 'appropriate' behaviour and habits, perhaps even a norm for looks. Children learn the cultural norms understanding what is judged as good and acceptable in their culture and what not. A specific culture, however, can reduce the level of differences and emphasize what people have in common as humans.

Today global human culture – in spite of our natural differences – allows the view that every person is born into the world equal and with the same inborn and undeniable rights. This is the true inheritance of the Age of Enlightenment. It is the basis of people's struggle for democracy.

Besides, every socially constructed group such as a family, an association, company or organization as well as every public body develops its own rationale. This kind of self-rationale is also embodied into every material product, and it is even found in every human interaction, as previously discussed. Every cultural institution, every agency of exchange comes with its own intrinsic logic and acts according to its own rules.

The question is why, even in the 21st century, are these natural conditions not yet accepted, respected or considered fertile ground for economic insight and understanding?

11.2.1. People and their work are one

Economicult theory has hitherto been based, as we have found out, on the idea that the working abilities of people can be split from them and sold, as if their ability is a commodity. This is another inappropriate and abstract view like the one economicult has of nature when it is merely seen as an object that is external to us. In reality, separating the ability from the person is obviously not possible. This can only be done in abstract thinking, as a person's ability to labour is still incorporated even when sold. 'Labour' cannot be isolated from the person who labours.

This is not only true in the formal economy, but also in a household or 'nateconomy' where everyone participates while the tasks needing to be done are self-determined. During our free time, the private part of life, we are what we think, say and do. In the nateconomy, no one would claim that it is possible or even necessary to differentiate between a person and their ability, in contrast to today's economicult era, where people are thought to be able to sell their ability, thus transforming themselves in to a commodity easily exchangeable and replaceable by money and the market'.

Why? Because without such an abstract construct economicult theory would not work.

The justification for the economicult misconception of 'labour' is based on the belief that today people are the owners of their 'labour' and free to do with it what they want, while in former times they were serfs or slaves owned by a master. Today we are able to talk about markets' for 'labour', although this is only an abstract, it is still seen as social progress.

We have found that, in reality, it is a matter of semantics, because today the free people who sell their labour in exchange for money as compensation, have also to give up their own free will and submit to that of others. People, however, inflict this so called 'Arbeitsleid'[197] on themselves as free individuals, and it is suggested that individuals sell their labour freely for a financial reward which is determined by collective industrial bargaining. This is one side of the argument.

The view, less frequently advanced, is that people living in an economicult society, need money to live, because they need to buy the basic necessities of life, as they do not produce these themselves. The means for life have become indirect and mediated in an economicult society. Therefore most people, being without means, are forced to sell their labouring ability – or, more accurately, themselves – to the minority who have money to buy their labour. This necessity to sell oneself is forced on the majority, even when it is argued that people do it of their own free will and at their own decision. Trading a person's working ability is based on the idea that people are in total control of it – a nice idea if the unity of human nature were such as to allow it. Selling one's own ability means to 'verdingen'[198] oneself, to hire oneself out. And again the question needs to be asked: who is the 'I', from whose perspective it would be possible to sell one's own inalienable ability, separately from oneself?

It is only if people have disposal power through money, that they are free subjects, because they are not forced to sell themselves. For most, with the sale of their 'labour' the social status of people changes to that of an object. Consequently we have to state, that it is done by financial rather than constitutional terms that

---

197 Usually translated as 'disutility of labour'.

198 This German verb 'verdingen' is seen as old-fashioned but hits the mark, as it contains the idea of turning oneself into a thing, from a human being into 'labour'.

people are defined – and define themselves – to be 'free subjects' or 'depending objects'. As the whole logic of economicult theory is based on monetary gains via selling, it becomes clear, that money is the aim, and is the criteria that turns both people and nature into objects, and that they are the instruments which are used to make money. Regardless of the type of organization to which the working ability of a person is sold, people can now be expressed in terms of jobs, time and costs, into 'labour' only.

The human invention of money, though a socially useful medium, should, however, never be used to impose one's will on somebody else, as this changes the social status of equal people and creates inequality. To modernize the outdated thinking about people and nature, therefore is the challenge.

The economicult model aiming to raise profits and reduce expenditure makes every organization rationalize costs, for example by giving labouring people so-called zero hours contracts, of which there are 1.4 million in Britain,[199] or by replacing 'labour' with machines, setting 'labour free', just as it was before the sale of 'labour' took place. When that happens, a labourer has to find another organization which is willing to pay him, as otherwise he is not able to preserve his life. New additional jobs are necessary because people need to earn an income. The economicult spiral increases. New products need to be invented and new sales brokered, not only because of the so-called consumers' infinite demand, but also because of people's need for a paid job or money.

From a scientific point of view there is no reason why, even in the economic sphere of life, labouring people should lose their status as free subjects, and therefore there is no reason for them to be reduced to the status of objects. Instead of transforming free subjects according to the market' mechanism into fettered objects we could also view them as free within the culteconomic sphere. This would mean that the underlying traditional economicult understanding, according to which we buy an object and do with it what we want, needs replacing with the modern understanding of free people co-operating with each other as respected individual subjects. No form of economic theory should deny people their equal right to be free in their work. To implement this view into a modern culteconomic practice, a few steps are required:

First, let's view people's labour as an incorporated ability, as a service. Human working services are more than just costs included in the manufactured products. They can be reported on their own separately in the annual Gross Domestic Product (GDP) of a country.

A service is, as discussed, the uno-actu process of reciprocal perception and action from which money is decoupled, during the time production and immediate consumption take place. This could mean for example, that everybody applying their labouring ability who is interacting within an organization would receive a monthly part-payment. Everybody working in this organization is paid the same amount of money, regardless of his position. At the end of the year, when

---

199 *The Daily Telegraph*, 1 May 2014, p. B 8, reported referring to the Office for National Statistics. Zero-hours contracts mean that they do not guarantee people work and pay, while the hired people are forbidden to earn money from other jobs, a perversion of a 'free' labour market'.

the organization's profits are calculated, the surplus – minus investment and dividends to the organization's owners – is divided into equal parts bearing in mind that it implies equal responsibility. A company which already uses a very similar model, is the British John Lewis Partnership.

The next step would be to make all employees the owners of the company by handing out to them a certain number of shares as part of their income. That way, ownership is based on direct interaction, on the people working there. And every worker in the organization will have an equal vote, as the organization is the result of the efforts of all the people working there, according to their ability, as Adam Smith famously wrote, in the same way as every citizen has one vote when electing a representative for Parliament.

Furthermore, people's ability to work should never be taxed, ie their salary from their work as well as recompense when they are over the age of 60 years. At the moment, people in the UK do not pay tax on the first £10,500[200] or €12,600 income, while in Germany only €8,130 is tax free.

It is also necessary to consider the fact that when every good or service, such as the service of a builder, is taxed, with Valued Added Tax – strangely enough with the exception of the sale of financial products – we should be sure that people should only pay tax once.

Freeing labour from income tax was Adam Smith's proposal, made 250 years ago, and it is one of his ideas which has not yet been realized.

Once the economy is no longer based on the abstract idea of separation of a person from their labouring ability, the 'division of labour', people become free in the economic sphere. They are not freed from their work, but in their work.

Then it follows that, each person born into a culteconomy needs to be provided with a basic and unconditional income in order to fulfil their basic needs. This step forward would free people further, to seek possibilities of interaction with others according to their genuine interests, as they no longer have to sell themselves and take a job offered. People would of course be able to top up their income by taking on additional work, but of their own choice. If their preference was to work only for themselves, then they will be able to do this entirely on their own terms as far as the number of hours or type of work and co-operation with others are concerned. This would liberate people's imaginations as well as their creative powers to a great effect.

The final chapter, No. 12, will discuss such concepts for long-term improvements. The only obstacle to make people free in their work, and not from it, is the traditional economicult thinking or 'thinging'. However, by making this transparent, we have become aware of it, so that this barrier can be overcome.

---

200 The i, 17 March 2014, p. 3

11.2.2. People are active, self-involving and participating

We have already referred to another misconception of economicult theory – the view that only producers are active whilst consumers are passive. This thinking is outdated because:

- Everyone, even a producer, is a consumer – in his private life, where he is free to do what he wants. Economic theory needed to include the consumption side too.
- Also, everything is ultimately produced for consumption, as Adam Smith has pointed out. Machines can replace human labour, but they cannot replace consumers.
- According to the pattern of reciprocal interaction a service is produced at the demand of the consumer. Therefore, the view that the manufacturing process produces anonymous goods without the initiating demand of the consumer no longer makes sense. Also, people as consumers are diverse and have different needs.
- The pattern of reciprocal interaction showed that (the human ability to) work is an uno-actu process, combining perception and action, activity and passivity. Wolfgang Heckel expressed a somewhat similar idea when he pointed out that economic(ult) culture has fragmented the unity of production, use, maintenance and repair in favour of production only.[201]
- Human beings have evolved from an animal state through a self-organized reciprocal interaction process with others as well as with their natural local environment, shaping their outside nature and their internal nature at the same time. This insight is limited when only the producer is seen as active.

The idea that the majority of people are passive and therefore need to be organized, that people need to be allocated to jobs and have their futures shaped by external factors rather than being self-determining, should be viewed as an anachronism in the 21st century. Anyway, such a view may have been invented, only to legitimize the actions of a minority in forcing the majority to follow its rationale. Self-organization it is, so let's illustrate this with a few examples:

- The break-up of the former Deutsche Demokratische Republik in East Germany was achieved by the people, when citizens demanded that the promise of democracy be made real, peacefully demonstrating against a life of being spied on and suppressed by a so-called 'socialist' dictatorship.
- In Germany, people have self-organized so-called 'Wissenschaftslaeden', associations offering scientific research to citizens, when the knowledge necessary to decide, for example whether to continue with plans for the so called 'peaceful' use of nuclear power, was unavailable to the people. The Oeko-Institut in Freiburg, and the IOEW Institute for Ecological Economy Research in Berlin have provided such knowledge.

---

201 Wolfgang Heckel, *Die Kultur der Reparatur*, Muenchen, 2013, p. 174

FAIR ECONOMICS

- Tenants have put their money and responsibilities together to self-organize the renovation of derelict factories in towns, turning them into accommodation according to their abilities and needs, as in Hamburg-Ottensen, when previously, they, as tenants, were only able to rent ready-built mass-market' flats.
- Students have self-organized so-called summer universities, ie the 'Sommer-Hochschule' at Hamburg University, discussing fresh ideas from outside of the 'ivory towers', once they found out that the only economic theory offered to them by their professors, was only the economicult model.
- Parents have self-organized so-called 'Kinderlaeden', caring-facilities for their youngsters, with both parents obliged to be involved directly and employing only part-time employees.
- Citizens have called for more direct 'Buergerbeteiligung'/citizen involvement in town planning since they are the ones who have to live in the resulting built-environments and use the public transport. It is now the law in Germany to involve citizens in planning wherever building is to take place.
- People have self-organized so-called 'community shops', ie in Horsley and Uley, Gloucestershire, when the local shop-cum-post-office threatened to close. More than 100 people donated money to retain their local shop, which is now so well frequented that it returns a kind of dividend to its founders, in the form of a voucher which can be exchanged against purchases, or if not used, is given to the local Food Bank.
- People have established supervised Adventure Playgrounds, such as the Elbe-Aktivspielplatz in Hamburg. An Adventure Playground differs from a normal one, as here children can learn how to build. They are not restricted to using just the toys that are offered. This encourages them to learn that they can change their environment, and shows them how to do it. I feel this practice is extremely important as it demonstrates to children that they do not have to follow the intrinsic rules of ready-made toys, games or machines, but that they can invent new rules, as children always did in the past. And they also learn that self-activity comes with obligations and responsibilities.
- People have started generating and consuming heat and electricity from renewable resources, leading to a 40 per cent share of renewables generated by former 'passive' electricity consumers in Germany.

And they can discuss their experience with the public in order to inspire others, as occurred in the meeting 'Energiewende – dezentral und genossenschaftlich'[202], held in Berlin on 19 November 2012.

Rail enthusiasts saved UK railway lines from closure, for example between Settle and Carlisle, restored stations and promoted railway use for everyone.

Self-organized activities do not only take place when services are unavailable or inadequate. People have always organized themselves, ie developed ways to use scarce freshwater, share fishing grounds or ensure fair access to common land, so that natural resources should not be overused or exploited only by a minority, as Elinor Ostrom showed. However, self-organized processes have not received

202 Energy transition – decentralized and cooperative

enough attention. Ostrom also pointed out: "The issues of how best to govern natural resources used by many individuals in common are no more settled in academia than in the world of politics. Some scholarly articles about the 'tragedy of the commons recommend that 'the state' control most natural resources to prevent their destruction; others recommend that privatizing those resources will resolve the problem. What one can observe in the world, however, is that neither the state nor the market is uniformly successful in enabling individuals to sustain long-term, productive use of natural resource systems."[203] Together with her colleagues, she studied the rules of self-organization and found that equal commitment from participants is needed together with respect for nature, but without free-riding. Ostrom's work proved that self-organized activities are neither chaotic nor do they come without rules. The basic rules for self-organization, likely to have been experienced by anyone who has been involved in a self-organized project, are as follows:

- People come together of their own free will, and as equal subjects.
- People are aware that some tasks can be better tackled by co-operation than individually.
- People begin a self-organized project for different reasons, but they can make effective joint decisions on tasks, learning that decision-making is an open process which can be adjusted to changing circumstances.
- People need to set up an agreement on how a project is self-organized, and how much work everybody has to put in – according to their personal abilities and experiences.
- People have to agree on how and when every participant will profit from the project.
- People need to agree to a procedure to solve conflicts. These will always arise, due to jealousy, for example. The procedure has to be cheap and easy to access.
- People have to monitor their initially agreed rules to check that they remain appropriate and equally applicable to everyone.
- People have to make sure that everybody sticks to the agreed rules. And these rules need ongoing discussion as to whether they need to be developed further.
- And last but not least, governments should look out for ways how to encourage and support self-organization. Self-organized work or its products should always be free from tax

The habits and rules which our varying cultures invent, are then treated as if they are norms one has to obey. In a very similar way, people tend to follow the rules of certain organizations without questioning them or developing them further. However, people should never forget that all norms have been invented and implemented by people in the past, and that they are therefore adaptable.

What is necessary today is to formulate a political strategy to support the learning of active self-participation in order to stimulate the role of citizens as

---

203 Elinor Ostrom, *Governing the Commons, The Evolution of Institutions for Collective Action*, New York, 2011, p. 1

activists[204] for more fairness and democracy in a society. Politicians need to understand that participation needs to be learned and encouraged, involving children as early as possible in activities as well as responsibilities appropriate for their age. Teaching them only how to buy and consume is nowhere a sufficient instruction for anyone who wants to be truly involved in a democratic society. Direct engagement and citizens' initiatives will always determine how a country's democratic constitution is practised in real daily life.

Participation and self-determination are the BASE in a democracy. As the philosopher Rainer Forst from the Goethe University, Frankfurt, argues, it is a question of recognising not just the right of people to a materially good life, but also the autonomy of a being who is not only subject to norms but sets them as well. It is insufficient to think only about the distribution of wealth. Otherwise we would not need to make a distinction between the victim of a natural catastrophe who has lost everything in the earthquake or flood, and the victims of exploitation and social exclusion whose poverty has a structural cause.[205]

When questioned further as to whether a society in which people own more goods and with their use lead better lives is not already a fairer one, Forst replied[206] that this idea seems to him to be wrong and only half-understood. Clearly, such a society is in many respects better than a society of scarcity, he argued, but being better doesn't make it fairer. Because fairness is about the extent to which the social conditions are justified by the members of that society themselves.

Therefore let us point to another insight: *the only need which a market' society cannot supply is fulfilling the need to be self-active*; this cannot be bought. Instead it has to be fulfilled by doing. And having already discussed how a meal can be self-prepared using raw and fresh ingredients from local, seasonal and organic production, we can now add that this is an activity which everyone can enjoy. It is more satisfying than microwaving a ready-made meal. It requires greater self-involvement, both physically and psychologically.

In terms of a political strategy we repeat Elinor Ostrom's advice: "What is missing from the policy analysts' tool kit – and from the set of accepted, well-developed theories of human organization – is an adequately specified theory

---

204 Will Hutton wrote in: *Them and Us, Changing Britain - Why We Need a Fair Society*, London, 2011, p. 88: "Fair process confirms that I have the opportunity to determine my fate. Self-determination of this type, as psychologists have long recognised, is a crucial stimulant and confirmation of self. This incorporated three different but related needs: I need to be able to act autonomously and organize my own actions; I need to have some capacity to view myself as capable and effective by acting in the external environment; and I need to be respected as a member of a group, connected to others in a web of reciprocal relationships. Get these things right and people flourish; remove them and they wilt."

205 *Der Spiegel* 34/2013, p. 106: "*... sondern der Autonomie als eines nicht nur Normen unterworfenen, sondern auch eines Normen setzenden Wesens. Das reine, reduzierte Verteilungsdenken greift zu kurz. Sonst brauchten wir keinen Unterschied zu machen zwischen dem Opfer einer Naturkatastrophe, das in einem Erdbeben oder einer Ueberschwemmung alles verloren hat und den Opfern von Ausbeutung und sozialer Exklusion, deren Armut strukturell bedingt ist.*"

206 "*Da scheint mir ein falsches, halbiertes Gerechtigkeitsverstaendnis am Werk zu sein. Klar: Ene solche Gesellschaft ist in verschiedener Hinsicht eine bessere als die Mangelgesellschaft. Aber dass sie besser ist, bedeutet nicht, dass sie gerechter ist. Denn die Gerechtigkeitsfrage ist die Frage nach der Rechtfertigkeit sozialer Verhaeltnisse durch die Mitglieder dieser Gesellschaft selbst.*"

of collective action whereby a group of principals can organize themselves volun-tarily to retain the residuals of their efforts." She cites here law firms as well as cooperatives as examples, because "until a theoretical explanation... for self-organized and self-governed enterprises is fully developed and accepted, major policy decisions will continue to be undertaken with a presumption that individu-als cannot organize themselves and always need to be organized by external authorities."[207]

Examples of what such a political strategy would look like, should include experiences from co-operatives, but also from the 'repair cafes'[208] initiated in Amsterdam in 2009 or Muenchen's '*Haus der Eigenarbeit*'/self-work-shop or in Kiel or London. These initiatives support people's natural interest, curiosity and pleasure in finding things out, and generate satisfaction from solving a problem by cooperating with others.

While it no longer makes sense to buy a new product when the old one only needs repairing, producers can also offer lifelong repairing services, eg as Henkel Stahlrohrmoebel in Forchtenberg-Emsbach, Germany, practise.[209]

Another welcome development is the shared use of products. We have shown that there are already a lot of organizations which offer car-sharing in German cities, for example Stattauto.[210] It does not make sense to own a car in a city when it is only used for an hour a day, as there is not enough public space in towns for parking, and the public transport offers good connections. The Bundesverband Carsharing reported 16 September 2014 one million people as registered car-sharers in Germany.

The Week published on 14 June 2014, p. 15, a list of more sharing operations, such as Airbnb, "... 'Lyft' and 'Ueber' for ride-sharing, operating in dozens of cities; 'EatWith' for sharing suppers with chefs in their homes; 'Spillister' to rent bicycles; 'ParkingPanda' to borrow a parking space; 'TaskRabbit' to assign choes; 'BorrowMyDoggy.com' ..." Sharing has been extended to other products too, such as streaming of music from the internet instead of buying recorded music.

However, we have to differentiate the various forms of sharing if we want to be able to make a judgement as to whether this development is following the paradigm of reciprocal interactions or not:

- If producers would stop focusing on selling goods and only rent them out, we would notice that the relationship between producer and consumer, as well as the relationship of the producer with nature, changing for the better, because then he would make goods longer-lasting, easier to repair and to recycle with-out damaging effects, as these effects would become the producer's and not the consumer's responsibility. Turnover with natural material would slow down. And the consumer would save money on maintaining costs, and because the use price of a good would be relatively lower than the sale price is.

---

207 Elior Ostrom, ibid, p. 25
208 see e.g. http://repaircafe.org
209 According to an interview on *Spiegel* online 14 May 2012
210 A play on the German words '*Stadt*' = town and '*statt*' = instead.

- If mediating agencies, like Stattauto, purchase goods and then lease them to consumers, this too is a business model that enables people as consumers to save money, as well as achieving as positive effects for their environment and nature, for example towns would not be clogged up with privately owned cars in the same way as they are now, because the fewer cars would be used more often rather than remaining parked and stationary.

- However, if consumers buy a good and rent it out to others because they own the good and can do with it whatever they fancy, then they follow the traditional economicult logic. Consumers are now in their own free time transforming themselves into entrepreneurs, for example when they rent their own private place with the aim to make money out of it. This behaviour of these people therefore is not a new model and it does not follow a new paradigm. Instead, it is deliberately extending the all too familiar logic of the monetary sphere into their free time. Although it would be progress, if consumers would let strangers stay in their home overnight for free, because they are hospitable people. Another consequence of this might be that such hosts take business away from the tourist industry and contribute to the risk that insured, regulated and trained professionals lose their jobs. It is therefore no wonder that Evgeny Morozov criticizes the "'share-economy' as strengthening the worst excesses of the ruling economic model: It is neoliberalism on steroids."[211]

- Philip Oltermann reported from Berlin in the same edition of *The Guardian* that the city has a growing number of borrowing shops, eg for items such as electric drills which you might only use twice a year and therefore do not need to own. Borrowing helps to save finite natural resources as well as being easier on the own purse. "'So far, most of these developments have taken place without the support of the city itself,' said Dorothee Landgrebe, of the Heinrich Boell Foundation. 'The state could do a lot more to support genuinely ecological projects such as borrowing shops and help identify those who exploit sharing schemes for their own profit.'"

On 1 June 2014 the Regionalwert AG Hamburg, a citizen-owned shareholder company will start where farmers, retailers and customers are brought together. Citizen's money is invested in regional, independently working businesses from farming to processing, retailing and restaurants. The companies are obliged to keep high ecological and social standards as well as mutually use as much of their products as possible, [212] reported *Kieler Nachrichten* 15 April 2014, p. 7. Citizens will profit from excellent quality food and small ecologically working businesses are given a new perspective when engaging in such an organization. By the way: the first of such citizen shareholding company in Germany was established 2006

---

211 *Der Spiegel*, 34/2014, p. 63

212 "*Das Buergergeld wird in regionale, selbstaendig wirtschaftende Unternehmen von der Landwirtschaft ueber Weiterverarbeiter bis hin zu Handel und Gastronomie investiert Die Betriebe verpflichten sich, hohe oekologische und soziale Standards einzuhalten und sich untereinander moeglichst viele Erzeugnisse abzunehmen.*"

in Freiburg, while another of these initiatives is working in the south German Isar-Inn region.

For a democracy, it is necessary that everybody makes use of their inborn ability to create and design – in participation with others. Acknowledging as well as supporting people's self-organized activities are real steps forward for society.[213]

Another measure would be to convince – or even to force – producers of mass-market' products as well as banking services to implement boards of consumer representatives in shareholder companies. Consumers need a bigger involvement in the production process than their current role of merely being questioned by market' researchers, as has been the case up to now. It is only manufacturers and the engineers they employ who decide which products to manufacture and offer to consumers, what purpose these goods have, how they look, how much energy they need and how they can be disposed of when they are no longer wanted. However, manufacturing processes can be made far more transparent for society, especially in food processing, waste disposal, the banking industry and the health sector. A consumer board should have the responsibility of deciding on such issues as how to produce goods using less electricity, how to prolong their lifetime by making them more reliable, how to make products easier to repair, how to reduce the consequences of their use and how to ensure recycling. These are all questions which receive insufficient attention from producers because they have no interest in what happens to their goods once they are sold.

It is obvious that at first such consumer participation is unlikely to be seen to benefit producers' interests in autonomous decision making. However, as everybody will become aware that natural resources are finite, new procedures might be accepted.

These proposals do not directly suggest how to involve more people in politics, but they might be steps into that direction. To support direct political participation, we should also aim to teach children how local government is organized and funded and about the real people doing the jobs, and how councils make decisions regarding budgeting and spending. Children should be encouraged to attend council meetings, allowed to ask questions, and encouraged to learn about the obligations and responsibilities of councils, even if they are properly representing the genders. They should travel to London to observe both Houses of Parliament in session. Children should also learn how they can make themselves heard and how they can influence politics by playing games imitating the political process. This should become part of the curriculum in every school.

11.2.3. People and their data are one

On 3 June 2013 the world changed – from the point of view of the public. This was the day Edward Snowden informed journalist Glenn Greenwald in a hotel in Hong Kong that US and UK security agencies collect information, mediated by digitalized communication technology, about everyone and everything, not only in their home countries, but also in the independent countries of other people,

213 This thinking and experiencing oneself could also be supported by the universities.

including members of democratically elected governments.[214] Consequently there was a public outcry as people using all forms of electronic communication – from telephones to social networking sites – discovered that their privacy had been compromised. From the summer of 2013 onwards, every few weeks, new information about governments spying on their people was made public.

Ten months later, the UK newspaper *The Guardian* and the US newspaper *Washington Post* were honoured with the famous Pulitzer price for making the surveillance public, mostly executed by UK and US government agencies.

Greenwald wrote: "Ultimately, beyond diplomatic manipulation and economic gain, a system of ubiquitous spying allows the United States to maintain its grip on the world. When the United States is able to know everything that everyone is doing, saying, thinking and planning – its own citizens, foreign populations, international corporations, other government leaders – its power over those factions is maximized. That's doubly true if the government operates at ever-greater levels of secrecy. The secrecy creates a one-way mirror: the US government sees what everyone else in the world does, including its own population, while no one sees its own actions. It is the ultimate imbalance, permitting the most dangerous of all human conditions: the exercise of limitless power with no transparency or accountability,"[215] when "... those Internet tycoons who are apparently so willing to devalue our privacy" handing over information to government agencies, "are vehemently protective of their own."[216] Greenwald reminded us that: "Privacy is essential to human freedom and happiness for reasons that are rarely discussed but instinctively understood by most people, as evidenced by the lengths to which they go to protect their own. To begin with, people radically change their behaviour when they know they are being watched. They will strive to do that which is expected of them. They want to avoid shame and condemnation. They do so by adhering tightly to accepted social practices, by staying within imposed boundaries, avoiding action that might be seen as deviant or abnormal."[217] They kind of give up their human right of evolution to create new thoughts, new habits and in the end more modern views on how their societies can move forward.

After the terrorist attacks on 11 September 2001, when thousands of New Yorkers died, such surveillance operations became rational, as it was assumed by governments that anyone could be a threat to a country. US President George W. Bush launched the so-called 'war on terror' on everybody to pursue possible terrorists. The Patriot Act was rushed "through Congress... and Bush signed it into law on October 26, 2001. The Patriot Act expanded government surveillance and investigative powers. In 2002, Bush empowered the National Security Agency to conduct warrantless wiretaps in violation of the legal reviews required by the Foreign Intelligence Surveillance Act (FISA) courts and to monitor U.S. citizens' e-mail... To convince the American people to accept such blatant infringement of their privacy and civil liberties, the administration barraged the public with con-

---

214 Glenn Greenwald, *No Place to Hide*, London, 2014, p. 34
215 Ibid, p. 169
216 Ibid, p. 171
217 Ibid, p. 173

stant alerts, heightened security, and a five-tier system of colour-coded warning that fluctuated based on each day's danger of terrorist attack."[218] The assumption was that spying on everyone would make a country safer..[219] As Oliver Stone and Peter Kuznick conclude: "Bush made it clear that this was a new kind of war – a war fought not against a nation or even an ideology but against a tactic: terrorism. As retired Ambassador Ronald Spiers pointed out, framing it that way was deliberate and pernicious... 'A *war on terrorism* is a war without an end in sight, without an exit strategy, with enemies specified not by their aims but by their tactics... The President has found this *war* useful as an all-purpose justification for almost anything he wants or doesn't want to do... It brings to mind Big Brother's vague and never-ending war in Orwell's 1984.' It was also a new kind of war in that it would require no sacrifice from the overwhelming majority of Americans."

Laws were relaxed for national security organizations, which was previously only legal subject to court decree, when the authorities had convinced the courts that there was a well-proved reason for surveillance.

Now, the basic human right to privacy was restricted, with the consequence that the relationship between citizens and their governments changed. Any ordinary citizen in any country could now on be viewed as a suspect, whereas before such an understanding was more typical of autocratic governments, such as the Nazi-regime between 1933–1945 or the so-called Deutsche Demokratische Republik between 1945–1989 in the east of Germany. Government – elected to protect the constitutional rights of people – was now seen as exempt from following the law.

This kind of reaction to the 911 attacks was possible, because for the first time in history, the technology for mass observation was available. Digitalized communication technology created the potential for external parties to extract huge amounts of data from the various technical devices people use in private, process this data and connect it with other data from other sources. Huge plants were built to store these huge amounts of data, and no one really know what the consequences would be if someone were to raid such data storage plants.

People woke up to the fact that they no longer talked to each other directly when they used the internet and realised that there is always a *third* party involved, one which can easily store information and find out who is talking to whom, for how long, from which numbers and from what location.

And profiles of individuals can now be made connecting data, showing their typical patterns of behaviour, not only in the formal working place, but also in the time that is spent in their own free sphere where they are independent subjects, in their households. Governments can find out what people do, what they read, with whom they are friends. And governments believe in the validity of this procedure, as their assumption is that once we know how people acted in the past, their future activities can be predicted, producing a linear understanding of the world.

This allows us to answer the question, why, apart from the need to find terror-

---

218 Oliver Stone and Peter Kuznick, *The Untold History of the United States*, London, 2012, p. 505
219 Matthias Rueb, '*Postamerikanisch*', in: *Frankfurter Allgemeine Sonntagszeitung*, 27 October 2013, p. 10

ists, it is so important for democratically elected governments to have as much information about their citizens when the same citizens – according to their countries' constitution – have the right to their own independent decisions and self-fulfilment, to think and act as they wish as long as they follow the democratic constitutional laws; and when the same citizens also have the right to elect different people in government and can change laws which they decide are not appropriate or useful any more.

The assumption that the knowledge of the past enables us to predict the future should be abandoned in the 21st century, as we are aware that everybody has the ability and the capacity to change, to do something new and to behave differently from what was typical before, according to learning and insight, and additionally, that everyone is free to do so every time. This assumption does, however, allow us insight into the only half-modern and static vision that most people still have of their fellowmen as well as of their society. This needs to change. The future is open.

Such industrial-scale spying technology, although forbidden, had already been used by businesses to spy on other companies. Examples show that people working for the private media have hacked into other people's phones for the purpose of making money from publishing stories which otherwise would have been kept private. Such journalists, and the newspapers and magazines they worked for, broke the privacy laws, yet when this came to light, their offence was rarely appropriately prosecuted. This became clear years afterwards, when the public heard that police officers were paid for selling information to the press. There was public outrage about the consequences of the violation of the right to privacy, and newspapers closed.

Consequently we need to point out: when a company spies on its competitors, when criminals try to make money from stolen identities via the internet,[220] they break the privacy law, but when civil servants spy on everyone and every country, can it be seen as lawful? Should we really think that is the norm that one democratically elected government is spying on another democratically elected government[221] with whom they enjoy friendly relations, even perhaps belonging to the same defence organization such as NATO? Should any government be allowed to do everything which is technically possible, and when found out, attempt to justify it – but still try to prosecute the informer? Should a government not be a role model, obeying constitutional rules, rather than behaving as if these do not apply to them? Are administrations above the law? Can Edward Snowden really be called a traitor, when he made the public aware of the amount of surveillance which was occurring, which is now seen as if it is normal? Don't we need to see him as a hero upholding the constitution, and not as someone who has to fear for his life, as he told the journalist Hubert Seipel, in a broadcast by Norddeutsche Rundfunk on 26 January 2014? Why is it always the one who exposes the law-

---

220 *Der Spiegel* 5/2014, p. 40

221 As far as we know they also spied on the heads of states of Brazil and Mexico; a report called 'Markets for Cybercrime Tools and Stolen Data' released by RAND (Research And Development) Corporation and sponsored by Juniper Networks, published by RT TV station on 29 March 2014, "says that one's twitter account credentials can actually become a gold mine – especially if a person is too lazy to invent new passwords for all their accounts in different networks" while "the value of credit card credentials has recently seen its decline..."

breakers who is hounded, when the real misdeed is done by people who break the law but are not sufficiently controlled by the legislative?

The Week 1 February 2014, p. 13, commented that America appeared to be spying on Germans more than on the inhabitants of any other European country:[222]

- "Germans are far too relaxed about US spying". The majority of people seem to believe that there is no problem with others processing your data, if you have done nothing wrong.
- After it was discovered that American authorities spied on German Chancellors Merkel (CDU) and Schroeder (SPD), the Germans government started to work "on a 'no-spy' agreement to repair relations – now at an all-time low – but even that has fallen apart" as "the Americans insist on their right to spy".
- US President "Obama's speech… detailing so-called reforms of the spy programme, was a farce" as he made it "abundantly clear 'how little interest he has in the privacy concerns of allies. It may console Americans to be told that a US court will henceforth get to judge whether their emails should be read or not, but 'for the rest of the world, that's not reassuring'.
- "Yet for the German attorney general, there is apparently not enough evidence to warrant a criminal investigation. Translation: airing the truth about exactly how our leader's privacy was compromised isn't worth the cost of embarrassing our ally."
- "Was there all along 'an agreement under which Germany collected the data and made it available' to the US?"
- "The truth is that, in information technology Germany, indeed all of Europe, is merely 'a kind of colony of the US', dependent on the overlord for know-how… Our data sits on US servers and is easily harvested by US spies. If we want to protect it, we must develop our own IT capabilities. 'Rather than whining about the power' of the Americans, we colonists must declare independence."
- And possibly the worst of all: isn't spying on others using the internet happening everywhere, if not in the same detail and with the same degree of professionalism as that demonstrated by the American National Security Agency (NSA) and the British General Communication Headquarter (GCHQ) in Cheltenham, Gloucestershire? And if other countries are doing it, are we not permitted to do the same?

Who has ever been asked if they really want to live in a world where detailed information about everything an individual says or does is observed, stored, processed and used for profiling, while no meaningful regulation has yet taken place regarding the development and use of communication technology, which – to repeat it – is manufactured by producers as is every other consumer good without any genuine democratic involvement of the consumers who are expected to buy and use it?

And as the observation of people is made easier by digitalized communication

technology, shouldn't we be concerned that all areas of life for all people will become transparent and therefore controllable?
To what extent will this interfere with people's freedom, their self-determination, their ability to learn from insights-gained and their development?

Furthermore, control of other citizens by spying may also be exerted by organizations which are run by unelected and therefore entirely non-legitimate individuals. This is especially significant when we note that nearly one-in-three such 'observers' in the USA are employed by a private security company.. So are we justified in worrying that the communication industry will perhaps even encourage a fear of authoritarian governments that already exists?
The new possibilities connected with digitalized communication technology make the huge global communication companies less democratically controllable and even more influential than nations, as everybody uses their free 'services', which leaves a trail of information about themselves – though they may be unaware of this and even unwilling at the same time.

The open letter, Mathias Doepfner, CEO of Axel Springer SE, wrote to Eric Schmidt of Google,[223] the biggest of these giant service companies, added to chapter 6, speaks for itself. Although the problem is treated by Doepfner as if it is the software giant Google, but not the digitalized communication technology itself which is the problem. Once again a significant fact is ignored: that every product and its user are in a process of reciprocal interaction. We could have expected that this awareness would increase with the information about governments' adminis-trations spying on users of digitalized communication software. Instead, we uphold the delusion that every user has autonomous power over a technical prod-uct and the freedom to dispose of it.

And more, people using free digitalized communication technology are paying for this by giving away their own data, their identity. In this way, they become factors for making money. Doepfner named it the 'behavioural currency' with which the users pay. So using so-called 'free' communication technology as search engines on the internet, is not really 'free', but you have to pay a price for its use.

As justified as Doepfner's fears are, however, we can never be sure that his company, given the prerequisite, would not act in the same way as the computer giant he was complaining about. Our experience has proved that: whatever a new form of technology makes possible, is done, because companies aiming to make money would never sacrifice their opportunities.

The only alternative to this dismal perspective on digital communication,[224] is that the internet is transformed into a public domain which comes truly free as an infrastructure which is set up by peoples' taxes. When Doepfner names the former public post and telephone companies as 'state monopolies', then we have to answer: they were set up as organizations of public infrastructure, produced for the many to use, and not to provide money for private companies.

The late journalist Frank Schirrmacher pointed out in the *Frankfurter*

---

223 It might even be more suitable to rename Google 'Goggle'.
224 And never trust a government or a scientist who claims that there is no alternative.

Allgemeine Sonntagszeitung[225] that we live in a time of retrogression in terms of our social order in the Western democracies, which might also lead to loss of national sovereignty – and the independence and freedom of the people too, one has to add. Instead of increasing the freedom of the individual, Big Data has instigated a cultural re-evolution which cannot really be compared to anything that previously existed. New technologies have produced new capabilities in the market' space that allow us to do things with information we've never been able to do before,[226] said Gus Hunt 2011 at the Amazon Web Service Summit,[227] chief technician of the CIA and a highly valued source of information about events which the NSA prefers not to make public.

Schirrmacher feared, furthermore, that a 'fluid digital I' will in the future replace the real empirical I, for example, on the internet we can use different imagined personalities and play different roles. A man can be a woman, an old person can pretend to be a teenager, a banker or a politician, in short: every role is possible. Internet criminals approach people pretending to represent respectable and reliable companies; for example, you may receive an email that purports to come from British Midland Airways thanking you for booking a flight of which you have no knowledge, or one from Barclays asking you to respond immediately otherwise your account will be closed, when you do not bank with them. You know that if you open such emails out of curiosity, your computer will be infected with a virus.

The real 'I' has a body, or rather: is a body with the uno-actu capacity of perception and action, capable of compassion and feeling. However, as Jakob Augstein concludes,[228] in the digital age we are forced to contemplate the disappearance of the physical body, with the consequence that our emotions and senses connecting us to the real world may also become obsolete, because we are also lead to further fragmentation of the individual. We all use this technology, but who has consciously agreed that this is the way he wants to go forward? When he is deliberately fragmenting his experiences and abilities man has developed in the long process of evolution?

Retrogression has another effect, and we have already pointed it out: what has been observed and recorded in the past will be seen as the norm for the future, which means that nothing new can be thought or done. Everything has to answer to the rationale already in place. For example, efforts towards more democratic self-development will halt when seen to be threatening traditional structures. Society will become linear and static, instead of open and dynamic.

When, previously, citizens were striving to defend freedom and privacy, much of their personal information has now become available. And while the government's activities should be transparent, easily observable by the people, the governments' actions can stay now private, another situation which seems to have

---

225 25 August 2013, p. 3
226 Die "*Maerkte erlauben uns, Dinge mit Informationen zu tun, die wir niemals haben tun koennen.*"
227 Perhaps this should be listed as an addition the intrinsic market' rules - compare chapter 7.
228 *Sabotage, Warum wir uns zwischen Demokratie und Kapitalismus entscheiden muessen,*
    Muenchen, 2013, p. 256: "*Im digitalen Zeitalter muessen wir mit dem Verschwinden des*
    Koerpers rechnen."

reversed – or should we call it a 're-evolution', this event of time turning around our beliefs of privacy and transparency, as Greenwald has pointed out.[229]

It will even be possible to change history, to reverse people's memories as well as their experiences by adapting the electronic records. It is the totalitarianism of the status quo, it is the prison of the present which has shut out both past and future from discourse, as if already reflecting the changing mentality of an ageing society: our political parties can only imagine the future as a prolongation of the present.[230]

And the latest chance of mis-information came from the US-online medium 'The Intercept'[231] informing the public that the British GCHQ developed programs to smear people on the web, though it is not yet clear if such 'cybermobbing' has already taken place or was merely planned. In this way, fears the journalist Glenn Greenwald, the civil service would have even more opportunity to manipulate and control people.

However, big data can be totally wrong. A study conducted by the Information Commissioner's Office, a non-departmental public body of the UK Ministry of Justice, brought to light the fact that a quarter of the data collected by Experian, a credit reporting agency, was incorrect.[232] We should ask how, if ever, this inaccuracy could be corrected when people do not even know of its existence. It would indeed be interesting to see what would happen if large numbers of people clamoured for information on the data stored about them in order to correct any errors.

Furthermore, it is possible that once such information is collected, even when wrong, will never be totally destroyed but instead stored in a special file marked 'Deleted', as though someone believes that the information, even if incorrect, would still be useful in the future.

And it is worrying that the data of people who claim to know what information is stored about them, executing their right to have wrong information deleted,[233] might be filed in a special, easily monitored category marked 'the usual suspects'.

Media and the public should defend the democratic right to privacy. The development of facial recognition software by the American state or the declaration by Google that Google mail users cannot count on privacy would have raised a storm of anger in the past or at least prompted inquiries.[234] Today this rarely happens, even when, according to the EuGH-ruling 16,500 people (see *Der Spiegel*,

---

229 Glenn Greenwalt, ibid., p. 209
230 Wrote Claudius Seidl, *Frankfurter Allgemeine Zeitung*, 4 August 2013, p. 41: "*Es ist der Totalitarismus der gegebenen Verhaeltnisse, es ist das Gefaengnis einer Gegenwart, die das Vergangene genauso wie das Kuenftige ausgesperrt hat aus dem Diskurs, es ist, als ob sich hier schon der Mentalitaetswandel der alternden Gesellschaft zeigte: Die Zukunft koennen sich unsere Parteien nur als Fortschreibung der Gegenwart vorstellen.*"
231 *Spiegel* online, 25 February 2014
232 '*Secrets of Your Credit Rating*', Channel 4, 24 February, 2014
233 According to the EuGH-ruling, the European Court, that Google has to delete information if a person asks for it.
234 "*... zur demokratischen Substanz gehoert, dass Medien und Oeffentlichkeit Gegenwehr entwickeln... Dass der amerikanische Staat eine Software zur Gesichtserkennung von Menschenmengen sehr weit entwickelt hat oder dass Google erklaert, dass Googlemail Nutzer nicht mit Privatsphaere rechnen koennen, haette in der Vergangenheit einen Sturm der Entruestung, zumindest Nachfragen ausgeloest.*"

28 July 2014, p. 121) approached Google asking for the deletion of their data with the effect that Google complained about having to employ more than a hundred new people to deal with these requests and compared to the million people who use this search engine daily, this really is a small number.

These are all more reasons to make the economicult-driven, fragmenting paradigm transparent. It is necessary to discuss who is following it and who is driving it, and – as always – in what interest. And it is necessary to ask ourselves whether we really want it, given that we, the people, decide on the way society moves forward. Or do we?

Before proposing a few improvements to counteract this fragmented objectification of people, let us list a few more examples of the separation of the individual and their data, as we have already experience. These examples clearly demonstrate how far the economicult thinking has infiltrated our daily lives:

- A bank asks you what you would like to do with your money when you withdraw it from your account which the bank administers in your name.
- The doctor you consult fixes his eyes on the computer screen displaying your data rather than listening to your description of the symptoms, not even giving you a physical examination.
- City councils in Germany sell inhabitants' data to private companies to make money.
- A letter to *The Daily Telegraph,* entitled 'Sharing my medical data,' printed in *The Week* 1 February 2014, p. 23, read: "Last year I was told my medical data would be shared throughout the NHS unless I opted out. Concerned about the data accuracy, I asked to see a copy, even digitally. The reply was that I should make an official request on a WMG form (whatever that is). If my request was accepted, and if I paid £10, I could call into the surgery to inspect the data. Any copies would be charged at 50p a page, up to a maximum of £50. I decided it was easier to opt out."

However, if you do opt out, you are informed by the surgery that if you go directly to a hospital they may not have necessary information for your treatment. Data about an individual seems to have become more important than the individuals themselves.

Furthermore it seems that the NHS will not only collect and share people's medical data, but hand it on to private companies, as The *i* reported on 7 August 2013. Regarding the "NHS database fears", we read in *The Week*, 25 January 2014, p. 6, that: "Privacy campaigners have criticized a plan to sell information about NHS patients in England to drug firms. The NHS would like to collect anonymous patient data and store them on one nationwide database." Everyone's records – including NHS numbers, date of birth and postcode – will also be made available to pharmaceutical companies and medical researchers. Researchers argued that such records are crucial for investigating the causes of disease, but privacy experts have warned that the public will have no way of knowing who has knowledge of their medical records, or what they are being used for.

The i reported on 17 March 2014, p. 11, only eight weeks later, that already: "A database containing details of every NHS patient to enter the hospital system has been sold to a marketing consultancy firm," the healthcare intelligence company Harvey Walsh – without the knowledge or consent of patients.

Citizens were informed of the NHS's wish to share patients' health records with other organizations through an insert in a newspaper, posted through letterboxes. A personal NHS letter to each of the patients with such information would have been preferable. Although the most important issue for a patient was omitted in this information, ie what do my NHS records contain? Are they correct? Why does the NHS charge a fee when I want to see my own data? Will I be informed when the NHS sells this data? Why is the patient not the owner of his data, but the NHS? Why does the patient not profit from selling his data, but the NHS – when the NHS has not bought the data from a patient?

It seems the people working for the UK National Health Service are not able to treat their fellow citizens as equals: instead they are treated as passive objects, and their data as free. How come?

The Daily Telegraph, 24 February 2014, p. 1, wrote that "the medical records of every NHS hospital patient in the country have been sold to insurers," so the NHS is already doing what it merely promised to do in the future, once people had given their consent. "... A report by a major UK insurance society discloses that it was able to obtain 13 years of hospital data – covering 47 million patients – in order to help companies 'refine' their premiums." Is there one patient of the NHS in the UK who has been given his consent to this?

When the Parliamentary Health Select Committee asked Max Jones, director of Information and Data Services at the HSCIC, about details of the sale of patients' data, he replied that "it would not be possible to produce any information before the centre was set up in April 2013 as its predecessor 'no longer existed.'"[235] One wonders whether there is a law in the UK about the storage of data, especially for public services? It is no surprise when Phil Booth from privacy campaign group medConfidential points out in the same article that "'the language in the document is extraordinary; this isn't about patients, this is about exploiting a market.'" Well, it should not be for a market', but offer a service.

And not only that. The report by the Staple Inn Actuarial Society – a major organization of UK insurers – "... boasts that 'uniquely' they were able to combine these details with information from credit ratings agencies, such as Experian, which record the lifestyle habits of millions of consumers."

235 The Guardian, 26 February 2014, p. 7

- An electricity supplier not only asks for your address and telephone number to send you their bill, but also wants to know your date of birth.
- You receive an unsolicited offer from a baby outfitting company after registering the birth of your daughter, as the registration office sells your information to commercial companies. Who has permitted the government office to do so?
- Google takes photos of your house without asking your permission, so that everybody can view it from their remote computer, and perhaps decide whether it might be worth burgling.
- American Express sends you a letter offering their Preferred Rewards Gold Card, and when you want to know where the company got your address from and your financial status, they tell you that they have purchased it from Experian, a company which bought it in turn from Transactis. And when you question Experian[236] they assure you "... that Experian uses the information entirely in accordance with the Data Protection Act and other best practice guidelines such as the Direct Marketing Association (DMA UK) Code of Practice and British Code of Advertising and Sales Promotion at all times."
- Retailers nudge their customers into handing over their data to them, in return for which they obtain a price reduction via a 'club' card or bonus points. Now the retailer can dispose of your data.
- Buying a kindle and then electronically mediating your reading enables the producer to control your reading habits, as all the data about what you have read, how you have used the kindle, your highlighting, chapters left out or time of reading can be known to the book's producers, perhaps even to such an extent that books are re-written, as Frank Schirrmacher pointed out in: *EGO, Das Spiel des Lebens*, ibid, p. 192.
- When you want to view internet offers you have to 'register' so that the companies concerned will know who you are. Why? Because this information is valuable as it can be sold.
- An airline debits your credit card with £19.90 on 26 June 2014 for a deal dated 20 May 2014, as their knowledge about your credit card details allows it, without any explanation to the card company or to you as the owner, why they have done so.
- The organization SCHUFA AG *Schutzgemeinschaft fuer allgemeine Kreditsicherung* in Wiesbaden, an information office collecting the data of 66.2 million Germans, their bank accounts and financial status, offers information about people with poor credit ratings, thus allowing others to approach only the so-called 'better off' prospective customers, and data protecting officers in Germany have already raised doubts about such a practice.
- Smart LG TV sets are programmed to send information about people's viewing habits back to the manufacturer, enabling them to show targeted advertising to people, which means, that the money a consumer pays in exchange for a product no longer guarantees the buyer total control of what they have purchased.

---

236 Dated 5 January 2012

- In the USA so-called 'talking cars' are developed, as *Kieler Nachrichten*, 2 August 2014, p. 3, reported.
- In the EU, car owners could be forced to install an 'e-call' system, giving information about the location of a car, if this information can't already be gained via the mobile phone of the car users - even when it is not activated. Insurance companies could use the system to control the habits of drivers.

On 17 January 2014 US president Obama announced in a long awaited speech "a series of surveillance reforms in the wake of six months of revelations from whistle-blower Edward Snowden, announcing that the government would no longer hold databases of every call record made in the United States."[237]

But what about listening to calls? And what about listening to and recording international calls between people in the USA and people in other countries?

What about stopping the practice of paying the US networks Google, Amazon, Facebook and others for developing technical devices to allow the government to access the data they have stored on their customers?

"Obama said the US government had to be held to a higher standard than private corporations that store user data or foreign governments that undertake their own surveillance. 'We have to make some important decisions about how to protect ourselves and sustain our leadership in the world, while upholding the civil liberties and privacy protections that our ideals and our constitution require,'" the US President pointed out, "in other words, the goal isn't to truly reform the agency; it is to deceive people into believing it has been so that they no longer fear it or are angry about it," wrote Glenn Greenwald in the same issue, adding that Obama is "not an agent of change but the soothing branding, packaging for it."

However, "the same could not be said for the UK," Nick Hopkins pointed out in the same article. "Untroubled by the kind of political brouhaha Obama has faced, Downing Street and the chiefs of the intelligence agencies have refused to acknowledge there is a need for any debate at all, let alone consider reforms to the bodies and laws that govern the conduct of British spies."

Tim Berners-Lee, the inventor of the world wide web demanded[238] a so-called Magna Carta "to protect and enshrine the independence of the medium he created and the rights of its users worldwide," in which "principles of privacy, free speech and responsible anonymity" should be included. "Berners-Lee also spoke out strongly in favour of changing a key and controversial element of internet governance that would remove a small but symbolic piece of US control. The US has clung on to the Iana contract, which controls the dominant database of all domain names, but has faced increased pressure post-Snowden. He said: 'The removal of the explicit link to the US department of commerce is long overdue. The US can't have a global place in the running of something which is so non-national. There is huge momentum towards that uncoupling but it is right we keep a multi-stakeholder approach, and one where governments and companies are both kept at arm's length.'"

---

237   Headline of the *The Guardian Weekend Edition*, 18 January 2014
238   *The Guardian*, 12 March, 2014

Here the economicult pattern is obvious: the dispossession of an individual of their own data, treated as if it is not connected to or belonging to the person's identity, but as if it is an autonomous product which can be processed and traded, at the one-sided decision of the buyer. A person is now divided from their data – another fragmentation, another abstract following the same pattern which had led to the division of 'labour' from a labouring person. Data is now a commercial good which can be sold and bought – but: is this really possible without the involvement of the specific individual? How can anybody view this as 'neutral' and 'impartial'??

The only difference in comparison with 'labour' is that the working person is seen as able to sell their working ability themselves, as if they do 'own' this ability and, in the historical process, having become a subject, while a person's data can be seen as an object, totally separated from the individual, with the consequence for example not allowing people the power to sell their own data.

Data is seen as a commodity. Have people fought for centuries to change their status, becoming equal subjects with equal rights, only to become aware that they are still the objects of economicult interests by following outdated assumptions? What is happening to the respect which everyone should show others in a democratic society?

Unfortunately, a very similar approach is taken by scientists, although they should know better. These days, scientists are also able to collect data about people with the help of digitalized communication technology, such as mobile phones. A person's smartphone can be viewed as a measurement device. In this way, scientists no longer need to question people directly. They are now able to access the communications technology that people use. Alex Pentland called it "reality mining".[239]

Data is perceived to have become independent from the person it characterizes, and it can be connected with other data without the knowledge or consent of the individual. Contacts, friends, banking details, habits, shopping or reading preferences, every form of behaviour can be compared and typical patterns can be diagnosed. At this point it might also become easy to classify and digitalize people, for example by giving them a number. The process will reach a point where humans can be 'read' by machines. Wasn't it originally supposed to be the other way around?[240]

Whenever human rights are neglected in this way, one must question what has happened to the right to informational self-determination which was demanded by the German Bundesverfassungsgericht in 1983?[241] How has the above become an accepted practise? And who is considering the long-term consequences for society, when it is supposed to be progressing towards a more free democracy with more direct participation of the people?

Although technology has the ability to signpost ways in which society can advance, this cannot be forced on us. However, we can alter the way things have 'naturally' developed.

239 Frank Schirrmacher, ibid., p. 177

240 Ansbert Kneip, DE70200000000020001585, *Der Spiegel* 48/2013, p. 67, "*Der Mensch muss maschinenlesbar werden. Gedacht war das mal umgekehrt.*"

241 The German Court of Constitution

I remember that this significant change from data identifying a person to seeing data as a tradeable object, was documented as far back as 1979 in the proposal for a data protection law by the Hamburg government (document no. 9/1112). It allowed the government to collect, store and process their citizen's data, and even sell them to private authorised (of course carefully selected) companies. Should it not be the other way around, I wondered, if somebody whoever this is, should at first inform the person about collecting, storing and processing of his or her data, to make sure that he or she is aware about it and secondly then ask the permission of the person? And who would then be able to sell, the person whose data represents him, or the government? Do we not "own" or data? Or better: are we not our data?

Such laws need to be abolished. This was my opinion then, and it is now.

In future, personal data should only be collected, stored and processed if people have been asked and signed a contract permitting this to happen. People need to be informed if someone wants to process their data. People need to be informed if a private company wants to store their data. Every person has the inalienable right of owning their own data. The human right for informational self-determination needs to be included in the EU-Charter of the basic human rights. And it is good that in April 2014 the European Court of Justice in Luxembourg declared the EU data storage directive unlawful.

The most obvious thing for everybody to remember now is: do not give your data to anybody. Do not allow anybody to start a business using your personal information. Always click 'no' when a company offers you a newsletter or wants to pass on your data to other 'carefully selected' organizations.

Be aware that every company's interest in you is a commercial one. Businesses are not offering you a favour and they are not acting fair. They are only taking, not giving. In this way, you can avoid unconsciously transforming yourself into merchandise.

11.3 Qualifying and extending Data

We have found that it is both possible and necessary to develop culteconomics beyond classical and neoclassical assumptions, by broadening our view and taking into account previously unconsidered criteria.

These criteria sometimes go beyond that which can only be expressed in quantitative data or monetary terms, as will now be discussed.

11.3.1. Respecting the differentiations between products typical for the three economic sectors

When the products of the tertiary sector were analyzed in terms of their own logic instead of that of the secondary sector, we found that the typical tertiary pattern differs from the one typical for the secondary sector: the typical tertiary pattern is a direct, ongoing uno-actu process of perception and action, initiated by the consumer, while the exchange of money is happening indirectly, and the typical pattern for the secondary sector is the production of an anonymous ready-made commodity, according to the exclusive disposal power of the producer.

Official statistics, therefore, need to reflect the typical patterns of sectors, extending the obviously inadequate practice of merely listing every product according to the area of business which produces it.

One of the services we have been looking at is the work a person can deliver. Therefore, 'work' should no longer just be subsumed under the costs of the product manufactured – instead, it should be separately listed as the category 'expended working hours', which should be divided into self-work, independent commercial work and dependent paid work. Such an improvement in information would have two advantages:

- Counting working hours is fairer than listing the costs of work in terms of prices, as the term 'hours' allows equal measurements, when the price of work differs regionally according to the wage paid.
- Listing 'working hours' in its own category makes it easier to monitor whether 'work' is increasing or decreasing. If the statistics show that 'working hours' are in decline, this could prompt new political measures to activate more people.

With respect to the primary sector, it is also necessary to extend the categories of measurement with the aim of differentiating between the following:

- natural resources which renew themselves (for example infinite primary resources from sun, wind and water for electricity generation),
- natural resources which are finite, such as fossil carbon fuels,
- primary food from natural plants such as fruits and seeds,
- secondary food where the animal has consumed the primary food.

Such a differentiation would show whether every society is really moving towards increased sustainability.

Furthermore, as has already been pointed out,[242] in reality humans interact directly with nature. It follows that the use of nature or human turnover of natural resources should be expressed in physical measurements, such as metres, tonnes, minutes, watt hours/joule and degrees Celsius/Fahrenheit, litres, pascals and so on, but not in financial terms, as money has no meaning for nature. Listing our interaction with nature by pricing it makes our direct interaction indirect, which is inappropriate and should therefore be avoided. Additionally, market' prices are always changing, even when the rate of inflation is taken into consideration, while physical measurements are standardized.

When we strive to reduce the quantity of greenhouse gases, this needs to be monitored in tonnes and not prices, as this would give us imprecise information if market' prices fall. It is therefore not logical to put a price on greenhouse gases and allow a market' to be built. This kind of 'solution' pretends that something is being done, as it follows the economicult paradigm. Science must develop an awareness of the restrictions of this paradigm in order to develop it further.

---

242   In chapter 9: The shift in the use of natural resources

11.3.2. Implementing differentiations in the Gross Domestic Product (GDP)

The concept of the Gross Domestic Product (GDP) of a nation was invented as an indicator in 1934 in the USA by Simon Kuznets, as the government wanted to find out whether the consequences of the international inflation crisis had finally been overcome. This indicator was designed to show whether the economy had picked up again, ie whether market' transactions in terms of prices had risen.

A Gross Domestic Product is the sum of all annual sales of goods and services, expressed in market' prices. The GDP, we need to remember, is an historical and social construct. Its currently applicable definitions, concepts and classifications are "compulsorily laid down in the European system of accounts of 1995 (ESA 1995)", as the German Statistische Bundesamt stated.[243]

If market' turnovers had risen in a specific period, then this would give society confidence for the future; people would re-invest and borrow more to finance investments because the demand would be expected. Increasing monetary figures would mean that more people were in employment as more jobs had been created. Rising turnovers lead to rising profits for producers, and would also mean that trade unions could claim pay increases for their members.

Any government would welcome a rise in GDP as this would appear to show that it has followed the right policies to kick-start the economy, and politicians could hope to being re-elected.

It would also mean that tax revenue is rising. The government could then plan to increase spending on the infrastructure or reduce the new debt necessary to finance the annual budget, or even pay back previous debts. The GDP prognosis is the basis for the annual government budget.

Also, the central bank could issue more money – up to the amount of the GDP increase. So, when the GDP figures are rising, this would be a good sign for everyone, and would suggest that a country is performing well, for example in comparison with other nations.

These arguments have led to the internationally upheld presumption that an increase in the GDP for one year compared to the year before, improves the welfare of a nation. Christian Leipert resumed that even after the intensive debate about the insufficiencies of the BSP[244] as a welfare measure and the presentation of social indicators as alternative instruments for measuring quality of life in the 70s, the BSP has maintained its position as a central performance indicator for economic development. How can this contradiction between a clearly theoretically proven unsuitability of BSP as measure of welfare and society's actual practice of treating BSP growth as the key criteria for success be explained? Only perhaps by cnsidering the behaviour-shaping interest of the institutions defining economic and social life - private companies, the state and trade unions.[245]

---

243   Subject-matter series 18, p. 22

244 BSP stands for the German term 'Brutto Sozialprodukt' as it was called until 1999, corresponding to the UK Gross National Product (GNP), however, an exact definition of GNP or GDP (Gross Domestic Product) is not required here.

245 Christian Leipert, *Erfolgsmessung im Spanungsfeld zwischen etablierter und alternativer Oekono-*

When we discuss the internationally held trust in GDP figures, we have to make it clear that the GDP figure for one year can never be expressed only as the historic, current or nominal price. To compare the market' turnover for one year with the previous years' figures, we need to adapt these nominal figures into constant or real value figures, ie by considering the inflation or deflation rate, as Adam Smith recognized. And it is only in real prices that the figures can be compared for different years and with different countries.

However, this is not as simple as it seems. For example "'the UK government does not publish formally how they take into account inflation for GDP', but... the recent discrepancy (between the government's figures and the other inflation measures) appears to be down to how the government takes inflation into account on its own expenditure," as Merryn Somerset Webb, editor of moneyweek.com pointed out.

Additionally, we need to be aware that prices do not only rise or fall through inflation or deflation. They can also rise because monopolies have been established and price-rigging has taken place, as Adam Smith also knew.

Instead of all this, today 'growth' in the sales of marketed goods and services in real prices is generally regarded as the basis for people's wellbeing. 'Growth'[246] means higher income, more choice and access to more goods and services, and this is always viewed positively. However, the inventor of GDP never intended that a rise in turnovers expressed in prices should signify that the welfare or wealth of a nation had improved.

Today the whole economy is seen to be about the push for 'growth'; there seems to be no other way forward than to increase turnovers, and it would be rather silly to questions this, Henning Klodt, Director of the Zentrum Wirtschaftspolitik at the IfW Institut fuer Weltwirtschaft in Kiel, Germany, pointed out.[247] In the opinions of most economists and politicians, the problems of the world cannot be solved without an increase in sales. Their focus thus only allows for discussions of the future distribution of a surplus – however this surplus is defined. It does not permit discussions relating to a fairer distribution of existing wealth. Materialistic behaviour – very much in the ordinary sense of the word - seems natural and right, and socially accepted as 'normal'. This materialistic mentality assumes that social problems can

---

mie, in: *Alternative Oekonomie und oekonomische Theorie*, published by Jens Harms, Christian Leipert und Philipp Sonntag, Frankfurt, 1980, p. 52-58: "*Auch nach der intensiven Debatte ueber die Unzulaenglichkeiten des BSP als Wohlfahrtsmass und der Praesentation von sozialen Indikatoren als alternative Messinstrumente von Dimensionen der Lebensqualitaet in den 70er Jahren hat das BSP seine Position als zentrale Erfolgsgroesse der wirtschaftlichen Entwicklung weitgehend behauptet. Wie ist dieser Widerspruch zwischen der theoretisch klar nachgewiesenen mangelnden Eignung des BSP als Wohlfahrtsmass zu fungieren und der tatsaechlichen gesellschaftlichen Praxis, die Wachstumsrate des BSP als wichtigstes Erfolgskriterium zu betrachten, zu erklaeren? Erklaerbar ist er wohl nur dann, wenn die verhaltensleitenden*
Interessen der das oekonomische und gesellschaftliche Leben bestimmenden Institutionen – der privaten Unternehmen, des Staates und der Gewerkschaften - ins Spiel gebracht werden... (die) diese zu einem Wachstumskartell zusammenschweisst."

246 Please note again that the word 'growth' should not be used, as it derives from the biological sphere and, thus supports the assumption that a monetary increase in prices is natural, when we know that it is a cultural phenomenon. The word which should be instead used is 'increase'.

247 *Kieler Nachrichten*, 29 January 2013, p. 3

be solved by merely throwing money at them. Economic 'growth' is sold to people as progress, an acknowledgement shared by the vast majority. The central problems of humanity are reduced to their material and economic aspects. Conflicts of distribution, environmental damage, the North-South divide etc. appear to be solvable only through further economic 'growth', concluded Karl Georg Zinn.[248] Tasks like the reform of existing structures, the analysis of what is done and how it is done and the assessment of the consequences must be avoided as they are seen as impossible.[249]

Before discussing the efforts which have been made to develop the Gross Domestic Product further, let me cite one argument why the idea of infinite 'growth' on a finite planet, is really absurd and is only possible using financial terms. Money can be increased infinitely, while natural material can not. The investment banker Jeremy Grantham had calculated, as George Monbiot informed us,[250] what a steady growth of 4.5 per cent over 3,000 years would mean: "Let us imagine that in 3030 BC the total possessions of the people of Egypt filled one cubic metre... How big would that stash have been by the Battle of Actium in 30 BC?.. It's 2.5 billion billion solar systems." It is easy to understand that infinite 'growth' exploiting natural resources is not possible. "It does not take you long, pondering this outcome, to reach the paradoxical position that salvation lies in collapse," Monbiot points out. "To succeed is to destroy ourselves. To fail is to destroy ourselves. That is the bind we have created. Ignore if you must climate change, biodiversity collapse, the depletion of water, soil, oil; even if all these issues miraculously vanished, the mathematics of compound growth make continuity impossible... As the philosopher Michael Rowan points out, the inevitabilities of compound growth mean that if the predicted global growth rate for 2014 (3.1 per cent) is sustained, even if we miraculously reduced the consumption of raw materials by 90 per cent, we delay the inevitable by just 75 years. Efficiency solves nothing while growth continues." You wonder, why economicult theorists and politicians still try to convince us that 'growth' is necessary and possible.

In recent years, many studies have tried to include more indicators of the quality of life, trying to improve on the Gross Domestic Product as a measurement of the well-being of nations. In spring 1997, *The Independent*[251] reported on a study

---

248 In: *Die Selbstzerstoerung der Wachstumsgesellschaft, Politisches Handeln im oekonomischen System*, Reinbek 1980, p. 58: *"Das materialistische Verhalten - ganz im Sinne der Alltagssprache gemeint - erscheint als das natuerliche, richtige und ist ja auch als 'normales' Verhalten gesellschaftlich gebilligt. Dieser materialistischen Mentalitaet entspricht ein Verstaendnis fuer gesellschaftliche Probleme, das die Problemloesung auf das Vorhandensein oekonomischer Quanti-taeten reduziert. Das als Fortschritt suggerierte und von einer grossen Mehrheit der Menschen auch als Fortschritt wahrgenommene Wirtschaftswachstum bzw. die dieses Wachstum verursachenden Faktoren bestimmen das Problemdenken, d. h. die zentralen 'Menschheitspro-gleme' werden auf ihre materiell-oekonomische Seite reduziert. Die Verteilungskonflikte, die Umweltzerstoerung, das Nord-Sued-Gefaelle etc. erscheinen (nur) loesbar durch weiteres Wirtschaftswachstum."*

249 This also reminds us of how government administration operates: existing structures are seen as natural, they cannot be changed, and everything additional would cost additional money, instead of changing the existing structures.

250 *The Guardian*, 28 May 2014, p. 32

251 '*How our quality of life has become the poor relation of economic growth*', by the Economics Editor Diane Coyle

by the New Economics Foundation and Friends of the Earth[252] regarding a new index to "overcome some of the disadvantages of Gross Domestic Product, the conventional indicator of an economy's growth... calling on political parties to switch the focus of their economic policies from growth *per se* to the quality of life...". It criticized the fact that "GDP adds together all forms of economic activity whether these enhance well-being or not, and takes no account of the depletion of resources or any kind of loss of assets. So, for example, a hurricane which destroys several houses will boost GDP because of all the reconstruction work that follows it. Much of what it adds in fact serves to reduce the quality of life. It is as if economists have not yet learned to subtract."

Ten years ago the OECD (Organisation for Economic Co-operation and Development) rejected GDP as the only measurement of quality of life in a country,[253] stating instead that 22 new indicators were needed. These included more social inclusion, better education, investment into research, longer life expectancy, clean air, a reduction in the inequality of income and wealth, and greater freedom, together with lower climate-changing gas emissions, less nitrogen and more diversity of bird species.

It is worth noting, that the kingdom of Bhutan has already invented a 'Gross National Happiness' indicator. The northern most German Bundesland, Schleswig-Holstein, created a special department at its regional statistical office, following a conference in January 1990, to explore the potential for a more reality-orientated wealth and welfare reporting system.[254] This department takes account of elements previously un-valued and un-measured, including self-work and charity work, as well as monetarized market' figures. The cost of health services, which should decrease if people become healthier, is also factored into the equation. The result shows that well-being in Schleswig-Holstein's has risen faster than in other German Bundeslaender, by 9.4 per cent in comparison to an average figure of 3.2 per cent.[255]

In September 2009, Joseph Stiglitz and Amartya Sen presented a report with proposals to the French President,[256] to which "a first reaction ... came from the Franco-German Council of Ministers in February 2010, which requested the two countries' councils of economic experts to prepare an expert report on how the Commission's recommendations could be implemented."[257] "What is now required," the Statistische Bundesamt concluded, "is to set up a consistent and internationally coordinated statistical reporting system which covers not only a country's economic performance but also the people's quality of life, social progress and sustainability aspects of that development."

And the United Nations held a conference on 19 May 2014, as The *i* reported, p. 11, discussing "calls for the way in which governments measure economic progress...". However, we find that what required is not a continuation of the discussion for another 40 years, but to address the contradictions of the GDP as it is

252 Called: '*More Isn't Always Better*'
253 *Kieler Nachrichten*, ibid
254 Cf. Irene Schoene, documentation of the conference: *Moeglichkeiten einer realitaetsgerechteren Wohlstandsberechnung*, Kiel, 1990.
255 '*Schleswig-Holstein rechnet sich schoen*', *Spiegel* online, 19 May 2011
256 Will Hutton, *Them and Us, Changing Britain – Why we Need a Fair Society*, London, 2011, p. 53
257 The German Statistisches Bundesamt reports on its website 'How to measure well-being'

currently defined and used. Now.

Changes to the GDP should also include decisions about the role of government in a country's budget. Today, increased government spending on such things as helping people into employment, social security, putting more policemen on the streets, defence, building, maintaining and modernizing the infrastructure is welcomed as a good thing. This increase in spending contributes to a rise in GDP, but must be financed by the taxpayer. Government spending and taxation ultimately results in a zero sum: what comes in goes out. Therefore it is legitimate to question the wisdom of including government spending in the GDP figure.

And it is also necessary to mention that governments have found a way to spend more than they collect, ie by borrowing on financial markets'. Gabor Steingart[258] argued the same case when he said that a rise in GDP no longer represents a real rise in well-being – as if, indeed, rising GDP and well-being would be the same – but is a consequence of governments taking on more debt.

Let's discuss what contradictions and inconsistencies the GDP figure contains, without GDP reforms, and propose that these inconsistencies are corrected:

- The first point to be made is that only market turnovers expressed in money are included in the GDP. A lot of human activity however is not, as we know, mediated by market' and money, nor should it be, for example all self-work and household activities which take place in people's free time, including raising children and looking after the elderly.

   Even when these unpaid activities are excluded, nobody can deny that they are not adding to the well-being of a nation. As Leipert reminds us that behind the historic increase of the BSP lies not only an actual rise in production, but also a significant shift of productive activities from the non-marketed sector to the commercialized sector. [259]

---

258 Gabor Steingart reminded us on the fact that in former times the rise in GDP used to mean a rise in welfare. Today, it mostly means an increase in debt. If the German GDP for the years 2000 to 2012 is reduced by the amount of government borrowing, we get the true figure: as soon as the credit injections are taken away, the average growth rate for this period falls from 1.3 to just 0.1 per cent. Only a fool would take on a credit of $10,000 and then argue that he is now $10,000 richer, said the former economic adviser to Vaclac Havel, Tomas Sedlacek. But government exhibit this foolishness every day. They buy additional welfare on the capital market, with the result that the reality, in which we live is in fact artificial. Fiction triumphs over reality.

   "Frueher war der Anstieg des Bruttoinlandprodukts gleichbedeutend mit einem Zuwachs an Wohlstand. Heute bedeutet er vor allem einen Zuwachs an Schulden. Wer vom deutschen Bruttoinlandsprodukt der Jahre 2000 bis 2012 die staatliche Kreditfinanzierung abzieht, erhaelt die ungeschminkte Wachstumszahl: Kaum rechnet man die Kreditinjektionen heraus, sinkt die durchschnittliche Wachstumsrate dieses Zeitraums von 1,3 Prozent auf nur noch 0,1 Prozent. Nur ein Narr wuerde ein Darlehen von 10.000 Dollar aufnehmen und anschliessend behaupten, er waere um 10.000 Dollar reicher, sagt der ehemalige Wirtschaftsberater von Vaclav Havel, Tomas Sedlacek. Aber genau diese Naretei begehen die Regierungen mittlerweise jeden Tag. Sie kaufen Wohlstand am Kapitalmarkt dazu, mit dem Ergebnis, dass die Wirklichkeit, die uns umgibt, synthetisch erzeugt wird. Der Schein triumphiert ueber das Sein." in: 'Entflechtet euch!' Der Spiegel 16/2013,

259 *"Bekanntlich steht hinter dem historischen Wachstum des BSP nicht nur eine tatsaechlich realisierte Produktionssteigerung, sondern zu einem nicht unbetraechtlichen Teil auch die Verlagerung von produktiven Taetigkeiten im aussermarktlichen Sektor in den erwerbswirtschaftlichen Bereich hinein."*

- The second point is that every activity exchanged on the so-called 'black market'", meaning illegal and criminal activities like selling drugs or weapons, racketeering, usury, gambling, forgery of banknotes or fashion brands, human trafficking, burglary or money laundering, cannot be included in the GDP total sum, even though such activities are performed for financial benefit and involve monetary transactions. Organised international crime, said the United Nations "is worth up to $870 billion (£560 billion) a year,"[260] and it is not taxed, while the The *i* reported on 27 March 2014, p. 30, that: "The combined turnover of Italy's Mafia clans has overtaken that of the European Union's budget as the mob spreads its tendrils overseas... Giovanni Brauzzi, a security policy director at the foreign ministry, claimed the mob's annual income had passed €200 billion (£166 billion), compared with a total EU spend of €140bn."

- Thirdly, it is assumed that a certain rise in GDP, let's say of 2 per cent, should take place each year – this was the "growth in Britain actually averaged..." "between the economic troughs of 1991 and 2009".[261] If the same percentage is achieved each year, it is considered as a stable level of 'growth'.

  The remark we have to make here is that a rise of the same percentage each year means that the GDP is not showing stable growth, but rising growth, as the same percentage is counted from a basic figure which is rising all the time. To analyse this in detail, let's take the GDP figures from Germany as an example.

  In 2012, the Gross Domestic Product in Germany amounted to €2 643.9 bn[262]. A 2 per cent increase on €2 643.9 billion would amount to €52.878 billion, so the GDP for 2013 would rise to €2 696.778 billion. A further 2 per cent increase on this 2013 figure would amount to €53.93556 billion, so the GDP for 2014 would be €2 760.7735 billion. A further 2 per cent increase on the 2014 figure would amount to €55.21547 billion, so the GDP for 2015 would rise to €2 815,9889 billion. And a 2 per cent increase on the 2015 figure would amount to €56.319778 billion, taking the GDP for 2016 to €2 872.2086 billion.

  It is easy to see that the 2 per cent from an annually rising basis, though obviously the same 2 per cent, does not equate to the same amount in absolute figures, but shows a rising amount from €52.88 to €53.94 to €55.22 to €56.32 billion.

  On the other hand if the original 2 per cent equalling €52.878 billion were to be added every year, the percentage would fall because of the rising basis:
  €52.878 billion of the basic €2 643.9 billion equals 2.00 %,
  €52.878 billion of the basic €2 696.778 billion equals 1.96 %,
  €52.878 billion of the basic €2 749.656 billion equals 1.92 %,
  €52.878 billion of the basic €2 802.534 billion equals 1.89 % and
  €52.878 billion of the basic €2 855.412 billion equals 1.85 %.

---

260 Emma Graham-Harrison, in: *The Guardian*, 17 July 2012
261 Will Hutton stated this in: *Them and Us*, ibid, p. 221
262 According to the Statistisches Bundesamt, Wiesbaden

The figures show that a yearly addition of the same – apparently stable – amount of money to the GDP figure leads to a continuously lower percentage of 'growth'. These mathematical relationships have to be considered when complaints about a lower percentage rise are expressed in public. Only if the absolute figures in terms of prices are also published, can it be judged whether there is cause for complaint. So, let's always publish the absolute figures *and* the percentage of the annually changing real GDP data, because we have learnt that percentages on their own are not sufficient for a well-founded judgement as to whether an economy is expanding or contracting.

- The fourth point which needs to be discussed relates to the fact that, hitherto, the GDP figure has been expressed as a total. This total should in future be presented as a balance. At the moment the GDP is the sum of all products and services traded on the market' at a price, including increases of prices.

  However, by totalling up sales figures, the GDP does not give any indication of the reason why the sale occurred; for example did sales increase because there was demand to compensate for damages? When, for example, thousands of houses are flooded, as was the case in the winter of 2013/14, the carpet, furniture and decorating industry can obviously expect more sales because the houses need to be restored for their occupants.

  Let us consider a few more examples which increase the GDP and decide whether they can really be viewed as an increase in welfare:

- Is an increase in sales of unhealthy junk food good or bad for people's welfare? Is an increase in spending on the National Health Service good or bad, when the reason behind this is that more people need treatment because of obesity due to eating too much junk food, which has lead to more diabetes and heart problems? Or when more people need treatment because of a rise in car accidents?

- In 1989, Exxon had to pay billions of US dollars in compensation for environmental damage caused by the oil spillage from the wrecked Exxon Valdez ship, which destroyed around 400,000 birds and the Alaskan fishing industry. It was estimated that it would take 70 years for the environment to recover from the disaster.[263]

  Now, in terms of GDP, could the economic activity resulting from the clean-up operation really be seen as increasing public welfare? Surely Exxon's contribution to GDP can only be viewed as neutral, as it was merely spending a compensation for the damage caused by its own negligence.

  Are the costs for decommissioning nuclear power stations and safely storing radioactive waste for thousands of years a sign of more welfare?

  And can the increasing appropriation of limited natural resources – what we used to refer to as 'production' – really be seen as a welcome development

---

263 Tom Bower, *The Squeeze, Oil, Money & Greed in the 21st Century*, London, 2009, pp. 161 and 178

because it increases the GDP?

Lewis Mumford pointed out back in 1977[264] that these cause for an increase in GDP may look good on paper but are being far from positive in reality. To merely add up sales figures is to disregard all the negative effects: the exhaustion of the soil and Earth's resources, the pollution of air and water, the creation of cemeteries of rusting cars and mountains of paper and other waste, the poisoning of living beings and the injuries sustained by millions of people on motorways. These are viewed as unavoidable consequences for today's life, but Mumford understood them to be the toxic outcomes of our affluent society.

Is the rise in the sales of carbon dioxide, based on the EU logic of establishing a market' for carbon trading, a good thing when our aim should be to reduce carbon dioxide emissions?[265]

Is a rise in the sale of waste products good, when our aim should be to reduce waste?

Is it really a desirable development for a family who find they need to buy a car and spend hours commuting, because they are unable to pay the rising house prices in London?

It is quite easy to see that establishing a market' and relying on it to solve our problems, does not work.

However, in terms of GDP as it is currently calculated, the answer to all these questions is 'yes'. Every sale on the market', for whatever reason, even if it is only to restore things damaged by accidents or natural catastrophes or war, means an increase in GDP. What we have to conclude is, that it is necessary to qualify the data used. The GDP should be changed from a sum to a balance, distinguishing positive increases from merely compensatory costs, subtracting the later from the first.

Let's remind ourselves of two more examples, known to every student of economicult theory which demonstrate the absurdity of 'growth' in GDP as currently measured:

- If a female professor of economics employs a male cleaner, his wages, including expenditures on social security and health insurance, increase the Gross Domestic Product. If, however, the female professor marries the male cleaner, the GDP figure is reduced as the cleaner would then be expected to do the cleaning for free and not for a wage.

- If one father pays a salary to another father for looking after his children, and the other father pays the same level of salary back to the first father, the GDP figure rises twice, as both their salaries are counted, while in reality the double salary increase of the GDP turns out to be a zero-sum.

---

264 Lewis Mumford, *Mythos der Maschine, Kultur, Technik und Macht*, Frankfurt, 1978, p. 706
265 Cf. Christian Leipert, *Die heimlichen Kosten des Fortschritts. Wie Umweltzerstoerung das Wirtschaftswachstum foerdert*, Frankfurt, 1989

Why are we continuing to find a figure which is not meaningful so important? Why don't we change our reasoning? Why do we prefer not to acknowledge the weaknesses of GDP, avoiding the discussion about reforming it – still? It would be hard to imagine how natural sciences such as physics would have progressed, had they relied on constructs as inconsistent and contradictory as the GDP. But every politician and every journalist still uses it.

What we need to do is to reform the GDP figure. Instead of being calculated as a total, it should be expressed as a balance between real, productive increases and merely compensatory expenses (currently estimated at 20 per cent of GDP and rising). The resulting figure would give us perhaps real information about what is increasing and why.

11.3.3. Make Integrated Balancing the law

Hitherto, companies have drawn up their annual balance sheets in monetary figures, because a financial profit is the reason for their existence and their goal. Today, the law requires companies to report annually on their financial balances and according to performance.

The financial balance sheet has two sides. It records the '*activa*' (assets) on one side and the '*passiva*' (liabilities) on the other side, ie what the company owns and what it owes – resulting in a balance showing whether it has made a profit or a loss in the past year. Double-entry accounting was invented in Italy in 1494 by Luca Pacioli. This type of financial statement is obviously very useful and should remain. It shows the socio-economic side of accounting.

When in a culteconomy, the basic paradigm is expanded from object disposal to reciprocal interaction, however, recognizing nature as the BASE of human existence, the annual balance sheet has to be extended to include reporting about the ecological, physical side of interaction too, namely with nature. This side cannot be expressed in prices, but needs to be stated in physical measures like tonnes of carbon dioxide emissions. If we go on neglecting the physical side of the economy, we reduce the ability of nature – the BASE's ability – to evolve further, because the ongoing greater, deeper and faster human intervention with nature has already led to reduced biodiversity and genetic erosion, resulting in a less resourceful, less vibrant planet.

Expanding the documentation of our interaction with the ecological base requires political will, but this alone is not sufficient, making it into a goal must become the daily practice of all individuals and businesses. Therefore we need an integrated accounting system, which allows a company the chance to find out where it stands.

As already stated, documenting a company's interaction with nature requires enlarging the form of reporting from financial prices to natural physical quantities because we are aware that expressing the reciprocal interaction between the BASE and people in monetary terms is not sufficient. This is an approach which is more useful than trying to include so-called externalized costs into the monetary balance sheet, as proposed by the German economist Karl William Kapp[266]

---

266 *Soziale Kosten der Marktwirtschaft*, Frankfurt, 1979

(1910–1976), and it is encouraging that the German Bundesamt fuer Statistik and the German Umweltbundesamt are already using physical measurements when reporting about the use of natural resources.

Then it is no longer enough for any company to document financial profit or loss alone; it must also report on how its interaction with nature has developed and how much ecological profit for nature was gained, for example through its efforts to reduce the company's carbon dioxide emissions.

Once this integrated double-entry accounting has been carried out for a few years, comparisons of the profits accrued for nature can be made, as is already done for financial profit, and progress can be stated. Such comparisons can then also be made between companies. We have called this new expanded accounting 'Integrated Accounting' or 'Integrated Balancing'.

Though some might think that Integrated Balancing merely involves the amalgamation of financial, social and environmental reporting,[267] it is actually much more than this: it allows the company to work towards two equally important goals for its business, economic profit *together with* profit for nature. It would be a welcoming step forwards if all companies, especially shareholder companies, inserted the aim of reducing their interaction with the BASE into their constitution or statutes, making it a binding goal for their activities. This has not yet occurred. The only shareholder company which already practises Integrated Balancing is the UmweltBank AG in Nuernberg, Germany, a specifically green private investment bank financing sustainable projects such as electricity generation from renewable resources, the building of zero-energy houses or projects involving organic agriculture.

Nowhere in the world does the law require the financial balance sheet to be extended into a system of Integrated Balancing. But it would be welcomed, naturally, if more innovative enterprises started to use such reporting so that standards for it can be established. In particular, environmental organizations and green parties or local and federal governments could provide important role models.

It is surely unlikely that there would be resistance to such an extended Integrated Balancing system since, for example, German efforts to reform reporting (Bilanzrechtsreformgesetz of 18 October 2005) so as to include non-financial indicators have been particularly well received.

While the economic side of Integrated Balancing can remain as it is, according to today's law, the ecological side of Integrated Balancing needs to follow new criteria. It should culminate in a balance between expenditures and emission savings, not expressed in money but in physical terms. It would then show at the end of a term, whether the strain on the BASE could be reduced or increased, and therefore whether more or different measures are required.

The ecological side of the company's balance sheet is differentiated into three categories:

---

267 Georg Giersberg, '*Der Geschaeftsbericht der Zukunft*', in: *Frankfurter Allgemeine Zeitung*, 1 October 2012, p. 12

- **Operational ecology.** This contains information about self-generation and use of energy, differentiated into finite fossil and renewable resources, release of waste heat, use of fresh and grey water. It also includes the use of material resources, such as paper and covers recycling, waste disposal, noise pollution, use of land and space, environmental protection and, of course, the mobility policy of a company, including for example company cars or subsidies paid to employees for the use of public transport;
- **Product ecology.** This contains information about the company's production processes, differentiated into raw material use, material savings relating to production and consumption, the   durability of products, and the extent to which they can be maintained, repaired, recycled or disposed of.
- **Human ecology.** This is a category about which companies might feel uncertain.[268] Human ecology can be defined as an interdisciplinary study of all relationships between humans and their natural environment in its special historic form. This means using instead of the classical human exemptionalism paradigm (HEP) the new ecological paradigm (NEP) in which human are no longer viewed as an exceptional but understood as one of many species that interact with their external natural environment.

However, if man is viewed as part of nature, nature can no longer be perceived as merely external to mankind – any discussion of the natural BASE of existence must be extended to include human beings, as had been explained. Furthermore, people's working hours, their interaction, have to be listed in every balance sheet, as work is seen as their reciprocal interaction with their natural and social environment, and not just a cost factor in relation to the price of a product.

All this information is important for internal as well as external stakeholders.

For internal stakeholders, information is required about job development, working hours, qualifications, apprenticeships, employment of people with disabilities, single parents, job fluctuation, further education and ongoing training, payment structure, registered patents, industrial safety or levels of sickness and occupational diseases. What should also be included is information about the local connections a company has built, eg it may use locally grown organic food in its canteens.

For external stakeholders, the social responsibilities of the company to its owners, suppliers and a wider public, for example consumers, have to be listed.

Finally, the annual reduction in carbon dioxide emissions resulting from all three categories should be reported. Where it is not yet possible to calculate the exact figure, qualified data, together with aims for further reduction in CO_2 emissions, should be given. A company which is serious about decreasing emissions can contribute by using low-emission rather than high-emission materials, reduc-

---

268 While this term is widely used in the USA, it is less known in the UK and Germany;
   here are studies in which it is used: Joseph Huber, *Humanoekologie als Grundlage einer praeventiven Umweltpolitik?* published by: *Internationales Institut fuer Umwelt und Gesellschaft at Wissenschaftszentrum* Berlin, IIUG-dp 83–8;
   P. Ehrlich, A. Ehrlich, J. Holdren, *Humanoekologie, Der Mensch im Zentrum einer neuen Wissenschaft*, Berlin, Heidelberg, New York, 1975;
   Georg Picht, 'Ist Humanoekologie moeglich', in: C. Eisenbart, *Humanoekologie und Frieden*, Stuttgart, 1979

ing its use of packaging or changing from plastic to biodegradable wrappings. This would clearly benefit the natural BASE. The UmweltBank AG, for example, reported for the year 2013 that they were able to reduce paper use by 7.8 per cent[269] compared to the year 2012. This company also runs a campaign known as 'bankers on bikes', meaning the bank encourages employees to use bikes instead of cars for commuting, and they award a prize to those who travel the most miles. The prize means that money for the miles bankers cycled will be invested in special environmental projects all over the world. Furthermore, the bank's own building in Emilienstrasse 3 has been sustainably renovated. Environmentally friendly furniture and other building materials have been chosen, and electricity is generated both by its own solar power station and by windparks the bank has invested in.

The UmweltBank AG has published the ecological side of its annual Integrated Balancing report for the period 2009–13 as shown on page 446.

The UmweltBank AG reports on its annual savings of carbon dioxide emissions regarding all three ecological categories. In 2013, the total savings of CO_2 amounted to 2,619,952.6 tonnes, which amounted to a 473.1 kg CO_2 reduction per share. This is known as the 'ecological dividend' and along with the economic dividend, it has steadily risen in recent years. It shows Integrated Balancing can be a very useful instrument for calculating the actual relief for the environment resulting from the bank's activities.

Moreover – and this too is exemplary – the UmweltBank AG implemented an Environmental Board. This board parallels the board of non-executive directors according to the laws which inspect the financial side of the business. The members of the Environmental Board should do the same for the ecological side of the bank's business, guaranteeing to its owners as well as to its customers that the company practises what it preaches by only financing environmental projects. The Environmental Board of the UmweltBank AG consists of around 20 scientists, politicians and representatives of environmental organizations and manufacturing companies, and is run by an executive committee of three people, currently one woman and two men.

The UmweltBank AG has received considerable acclaim for its innovative work, achieving the following:

- in 2002, the highest sustainability rating (AAA) of the Zuerich Kantonalbank,
- in 2005, listed as one of the top 20 sustainable global companies,
- in 2009, the 'Golden Bull Award for Sustainability' recommended by the *Euro Greentec Journal*
- in 2013, the German Corporate Social Responsibility (CSR) prize for its authentic business model.
- while in 2007, the UmweltBank was entered in the Global Challenges Index, initiated by the Hannover stock exchange. The index follows the following goals: fighting climate change, securing people's right to sufficient fresh water, foresting[270] sustainably, securing bio diversity, fighting poverty and supporting responsible managing structures in companies.

---

269 *Integrierte Berichterstattung* der UmweltBank AG fuer 2013, p. 54
270 From which the word 'sustainability' originally came.

Ecological side of the UmweltBank AG's Integrated Balancing from 2009–13
CO_2 emissions, CO_2 savings and Ecological Dividend in CO_2 per share[271]

CO_2-Emission Einheit t CO_2	2010	2011	2012	2013	Veränderung zu 2012
					%
Geschäftsverkehr					
- Bahn	5,9	4,4	6,7	4,1	- 38,8
- Pkw	2,4	2,5	3,6	2,4	- 33,3
- Flug	2,1	1,9	3,8	8,9	+ 134,2
Zwischensumme Geschäftsverkehr	10,4	8,9	14,1	15,4	+ 9,2
Gebäudenutzung					
- Heizung	34,1	29,3	31,3	33,7	+ 7,7
- Ökostrom	0,0	0,0	0,0	0,0	0,0
Zwischensumme Gebäudenutzung	34,1	29,3	31,3	33,7	+ 7,7
Papierverbrauch (bis 2012)	29,4	42,3	37,0		
Papierverbrauch (aktueller Umrechnungsfaktor)	6,3	9,1	7,9	7,3	- 7,8
Summe CO_2-Emissionen	73,9	80,5	82,4	56,4	- 31,6
CO_2-Emissionen pro Mitarbeiter/-in kg/MA	714,4	740,5	781,8	541,8	- 30,7

CO_2-Einsparung Einheit t CO_2	2010	2011	2012	2013	Veränderung zu 2012
					%
Bestands-Kreditprojekte	1.679.000,1	1.797.044,5	2.029.835,4	2.321.618,3	+ 14,4
Neu finanzierte Kreditprojekte und Beteiligungen					
- Projektfinanzierung	105.694,6	191.909,6	148.726,3	209.641,9	+ 41,0
- Private Solaranlagen	20.639,7	25.994,9	33.768,2	50.189,3	+ 48,6
- Privater Hausbau und Altbausanierung	1.865,8	1.552,4	1.127,0	787,9	- 30,1
- eigene Stromerzeugung aus Beteiligungen	18.571,5	27.858,9	39.641,4	37.771,5	- 4,7
Zwischensumme Kreditprojekte	146.771,5	247.315,8	223.262,9	298.390,7	+ 33,6
Summe CO_2-Einsparung	1.825.771,7	2.044.360,3	2.253.098,3	2.620.009,0	+ 16,3

Ökologische Dividende pro Aktie Einheit kg CO_2	2010	2011	2012	2013	Veränderung zu 2012
CO_2-Ersparnis pro Aktie	329,7	369,1	406,8	473,1	+ 16,3

The London International Integrated Reporting Council (IIRC), "a global coalition of regulators, investors, companies, standard setters, the accounting profession and NGOs... shares the view that communication about businesses' value creation should be the next step in the evolution of corporate reporting". On its website, it describes an "integrated report" as "a concise communication about how an organization's strategy, governance, performance and prospects lead to the creation of value over the short, medium and long term".

However, the IIRC reporting system still has shortcomings. It lacks the facility for indicating the extent of cuts in annual carbon emissions and therefore can

271 *Integrierte Berichterstattung, Jahresbericht UmweltBank AG*, Nuernberg 2013, p. 56/57

not list how much 'profit' has been made for nature; it lacks as well a modern understanding of *cult*economics, and it has failed to develop its understanding beyond the outdated thinking derived from Adam Smith in the 18th century. These deficiencies have to be resolved before its proposals can be followed.

11.4. On the MEANS of human activity

Money is no object, UK Prime Minister David Cameron from the Conservative Party told the flood victims on the Somerset Levels in February 2014. He was assuring them that the government would provide the necessary funding[272] to dredge rivers and strengthen river banks so that a repeat of the catastrophic flooding in Somerset and Gloucestershire, which caused around one billion pounds' worth of damage. Since we warm the planet up, there is warmer air in the atmosphere which can hold more water, and therefore more storms and increased rainfall have to be expected.

With this statement, the Prime Minister may have revealed more of his political understanding than he perhaps intended. He appears to have fallen into the economicult trap of viewing money as the economic subject, and not as a man-made object, while nature and man are seen as economicult objects which only have value when used to make more money. Such a view has previously been discussed in detail.

Money was invented by man as a MEANS of exchange. To view it as if it can have the status of a subject is to confuse its true meaning. Money is not a subject and never can be. It cannot move on its own. The economy can be run with money, as shown in the tertiary pattern, but it should not be run merely for money. There is no such thing as a 'GDP rise', but increased prices and increased sales according to people's activities, there is no 'growth momentum',[273] there is no rising pound (as stated in *The Week* 22 February, p. 46), just people trading in currency in the hope that it might give them a profit when they sell it again. There is no 'share price increase', merely people speculating, resulting in lower or higher prices depending on the future value of a company. And saved money cannot work, contrary to the headline "How are your savings supposed to work if they just lie about?"[274] of an ad of the DWS Deutsche Asset & Wealth Management in the *Frankfurter Allgemeine Sonntagszeitung*, 28 September 2014, p. 10. Well, money is not working and it cannot. Instead it is people and nature who do the work. And there are more misused expressions, for example: "If demand does increase," wrote Gerard Lyons, chief economic adviser to Boris Johnson, Mayor of London,

272 *Private Eye* No. 1360, p. 8, pointed to the fact that money never was an object, as for example last year £600,000 "was made available by Somerset county council and the European Union to recruit and pay for 'locally based farm liaison officers' to help farmers cope with the consequences of increased flooding". This was a consequence of a changed policy concentrating on less intensive farming to "encourage habitats like permanent grassland raised water levels areas' which are more conducive to a wide variety of flora and fauna." "£3 m a year of taxpayer's money is currently given to farmers on the Levels to fund 528 'agri-environment' agreements. Such agreements cover more than 50,000 acres of the Levels and Moors and pay the farmers involved as much as £180 per acre a year..."
273 OECD according to *The Guardian*, 12 March 2014, p. 26
274 *"Wie soll Ihr Erspartes arbeiten, wenn es nur rumliegt?"*

in: *The Daily Telegraph*, 24 February 2014, p. 82. We know that Mr. Lyons got it wrong: "demand does not increase", it is people who buy more.

The use of language obscures the reality. People are the actors. We cause changes. We expect a rise or fall in prices. We buy and sell to make money. A kind of belief system has evolved, expressed in the words we use whereby money is an active agent, a social subject, which would be able to move autonomously. This is an illusion. Money cannot act on its own. We, the people, we can. And we do when we invest money. It is our decision to make more, not 'money's'.

Those who profit from the transformation of money from an economic object to a subject have argued that their habit shows the natural order of things. This cannot be the case, because nature has never invented a MEANS of exchange and is therefore incapable of substituting MEANS with the end, as we do with money.

Therefore, in future let us call money what it really is: a MEANS or a "wheel" as Adam Smith called it for our social interactions. It is now incumbent upon us to start the long process of making sure that money remains a MEANS.

As a MEANS, money needs to be carefully observed and regulated by the elected representatives who have been granted this power by the people. This task cannot be left to private interests. To achieve this, no central bank should ever be privatized, instead it should always be in local and mutual ownership as a legal public body, because supplying people with the MEANS is a public obligation. Therefore, why are the banks which are today in public ownership (having been bailed out with taxpayers' money) not turned into locally controlled services offering reliable, customer-orientated and cheap basic banking, as this is what people mostly need?

Recently, many initiatives have been launched to create local MEANS, such as the so-called 'Chiemgauer'[275] or the 'Stroud pound'[276] or the 'Kaereti' on the Greek island of Kreta[277] The word 'Kaereti' means 'offering a little astistance', as the Greek director Alex Macheras explains. Nearly 500 people exchange goods, services and knowledge in this way. The Kaereti is a regional addition, like the regional currency Chiemgauer in Germany. It has been extended from the village of Ierapetra into the surrounding area. There are other similar networks in Crete. You can't become a Kaereti millionaire. The Kaereti doesn't pay interest. It is meant to facilitate the experience of solidarity and belonging, as well as communication between people. In the old days olive oil was a kind of currency, and this oil standard is being revived, as it is also the case with honey.[278]

---

275 Created in 2003 and established within the Chiemgauer-listed organization which numbers 3,000 members, including 600 companies and 250 charity organizations. In 2010, over 400,000 Chiemgauer MEANS were in circulation.

276 Created in 2009 by local the Transition Towns group, and the third local currency scheme in England after the Totnes Pound and the Lewes Pound. 30 businesses in Gloucestershire are enrolled in the programme and in 2011 £4,000 worth of Stroud pounds were issued.

277 *Der Spiegel*, 25/2012

278 "Der 'Kaereti' bedeutet '*Nutzen durch eine kleine Hilfe*', berichtet der griechische Regisseur Alex Macheras. '*Knapp 500 Leute tauschen so Waren, Dienstleistungen und Know-how. Der Kaereti ist eine regionale Ergaenzung wie bei euch die Regiowaehrung Chiemgauer. Er hat sich von unserem Ort Ierapetra auf die Umgebung ausgedehnt. Es gibt auch andere, aehnliche Netzwerke auf Kreta. Kaereti-Millionaer kann man nicht werden. Der Kaereti verzinst sich nicht. Er soll 'Erfahrung von Solidaritaet und Zugehoerigkeit sowie in der Kommunikation zwischen den Menschen' vermitteln.*

It is not only in the UK, Germany and Greece that people have created local currencies, in France for example, local means of exchange are booming, reported *Der Spiegel,* 4 August 2013. Dozens of small currencies with colourful notes will support the local economy and social cohesion - while making a stand against the financial crisis and stock market speculation.[279] There are said to be 17 local currencies in France with the same value as the €.

All the different local currencies have one thing in common: all working hours are of equal value, and no interest is paid, so it makes no sense to hoard the MEANS. Indeed, the more of the currency is spent locally, the more it is exchanged into real goods and services produced locally, the more everybody profits. Incidentally, the mayor of the German village of Joergel in Bayern also use the local currency of 'Chiemgauer' to pay unemployed people. In summary, the more local MEANS is used, the wealthier the whole community becomes.

11.4.1. A transparent concept for public service payment

The last point about short-term improvements to be made here is that every country needs one public transparent structure informing everyone what is paid to elected politicians. And we need one transparent wage structure for all civil servants, from parish councils, through town and county councils up to the central government, as well as for anybody working in a public organization, such as the National Health Service, school or universities or theatres. Then and only then, can such excesses as paying bonuses to high-ranking civil servants, who are merely carrying out their function of executing Parliament's decisions, be stopped once and for all.

A transparent public wage structure is based on the conviction that every civil servant's job needs firstly to have a specific job description. All tasks should be executed by employing well-trained people with the necessary qualifications, regardless of age, gender, religion and ethnic or social background.

A transparent fee structure for elected politicians and a transparent wage structure for civil servants has the advantage that everyone in a country knows what anyone in a specific public position is earning. Secret wage negotiations would thus become a thing of the past. Journalists would no longer be able to complain that a local council leader, as in Cheltenham, or the vice-chancellor of a university like Birmingham,[280] or a Network Rail executive, earn more than the Prime Minister of a country, for example (in the case of the university twice more and in the case of the Network Rail executive nearly four times more).[281] A public debate and decision about the whole pay structure for civil servants is long overdue.

Frueher war das Olivenoel eine Art Waehrung, dieser 'Oelstandard kommt heute wieder in Gebrauch, uebrigens auch mit Honig.'"

279 *"Dutzende von Kleinwaehrungen sollen mit bunten Scheinen die oertliche Wirtschaft und den sozialen Zusammenhalt foerdern - und ein Zeichen gegen Finanzkrise und Boersenspekulationen setzen."*

280 Cf. *The Week*, 22 March 2014, p. 15

281 *Private Eye* No. 1362, p. 11

"Beyond all this we would hope for a cultural shift, towards decency, fairness and social stability, away from the demented pursuit of 'shareholder value' and 'yield'."

Larry Elliott, Dan Atkinson,
The Gods that failed, How Blind Faith in Markets Has Cost Us Our Future[1]

"We can shape our future."
Will Hutton, Them and Us, Changing Britain –
Why We Need a Fair Society.[2]

"We humans are awakening to the reality that we are living beings who inhabit a finite living Earth to whose ways we must now adapt by creating economies that mimic the biosphere's fractal structure and capacity for self-reliant local adaptation through cooperative self-organization."

David Korten, *Agenda for a New Economy*[3]

12. The long view

The results of this study show that our understanding of the world can be improved which can then, in due course, lead to social *cult*economic progress. In order to implement these new insights and follow them in daily life, they should also be made the basis of every country's constitution.

First, let's summarize our findings:

- We realized that in modern *cult*economics no person[4] can be viewed and treated as a mere 'MEANS of production'. No longer can a person's – abilities be objectified as a 'thing' which can be at the disposal of its 'owner'. Such a historically outdated assumption, we discovered, only existed because traditional economicult theory viewed 'labour' as separable from an individual. In reality, however, experience shows us that this separation is impossible to execute as labour cannot be split from the labouring person. Economicult

---

1   London, 2008
2   London, p. 406
3   San Francisco, 2010, p. 150
4   Instead of 'man', as distinct from an animal (with the connotation of maleness), John Stuart Mill, MP, proposed in the 1867 parliamentary debate on the Reform Bill that the expression 'person' should be used to indicate a conscious individual with rights and obligations in relation to judicial and public order, as cited in: *Duden 5, Fremdwoerterbuch,* published by the Bibliographisches Institut Mannheim, Wien, Zuerich, p. 583.

theory contains a false understanding of the human condition. One consequence of our insight is that it is no longer possible to construct a so-called
'market" for labour.

In the constitutions of many democratic countries, a person is regarded as the
free subject of their own life, yet this appropriate modern view is not yet applied
to everyone. Whilst an entrepreneur can work as an independent subject according to economicult theory, the people he employs (or their 'labour') are viewed as
if they were dependent objects. Economicult theory has until today a divided
misguided understanding of labour, and it has always puzzled me that no-one has
pointed out the errors of this divided conception of man, when no other science
would tolerate a dual meaning for one of its basic categories. There is clearly a
contradiction between the view of man in modern democratic constitutions and
the view of man in economicult theory, yet no-one has claimed that the objectified
status of an employed person is unconstitutional.

Today, we understand each person to be a unique individual with the ability to
develop new insights and arrive at new solutions for which there is yet no historical archtetype,[5] similar to the way in which nature's ongoing evolutionary process
leads to totally new forms of life.

- We also found that traditional economicult theory splits people in a further
  way, into producers and consumers, where producers have the exclusive right
  to decide what is produced and offered to the consumers, who are excluded
  from these decisions. However, in a more advanced *cult*economic theory it
  is important to include the consideration that in the end all goods are
  manufactured for consumption, and that every individual is a consumer.
- Additionally, we found that every person is to be understood as a natural
  being. We know that human beings have developed from animals over millions of years in the evolutionary process, gaining consciousness and foresight
  while continuously learning from, as well as influencing nature in its historic
  cultivated form, the 'world-with-us' (rather than external to us).
- The modern understanding of people as natural beings and equal subjects has
  consequences for our modern understanding of nature. In the 21st century,
  we acknowledge nature as the BASE of all life. Nature is a dynamic and open,
  self-organized process which has its own rationale and self-value. The anthro-
  pocentric view that nature is a kind of 'capital' for us to dispose of must be
  overcome in the 21st century. Therefore, nature can also no longer be treated
  merely as an object at our disposal.
- Whereas the traditional economicult theory identified three production
  factors, land, labour and capital, modern fair economic theory offers a new
  perspective, because people and and nature are subjects with life
  purposes of their own.

---

5   As expressed by Gregory Bateson, *Oekologie des Geistes, Anthropologische, psychologische,
     biologische und epistemologische Perspektiven*, Frankfurt, 1981, p. 410 ff. Bateson saw the mind
     as a systemic phenomenon of life.

It follows that 'capital=money' is the only production factor. It should be recognized for what it truly is: a man-made culturally-developed MEANS, that is sometimes useful for mediating human reciprocal interaction, but should not be used to replace it or seen as the only one. So, when the role of the MEANS is thus understood, the MEANS can no longer be treated as if it were an independent and autonomous, self-moving entity that is able to somehow set the rules which people have to follow.

Instead, now it is clear that those wishing to convince others that the MEANS is the end of all human activity but the 'wheel' as Adam Smith wrote, are arguing from a position of self-interest, as they are the ones who would profit from such a view. It most certainly follows that the MEANS needs to follow the rules agreed by the people, not the other way round. This new understanding of the vital differences between natural human beings and their self-invented instruments, markets', technologies and money, is part of the necessary process of modernization and democratization which economic theory is to undergo.[6]

We achieved these conclusions by analyzing the typical pattern for the household economy with its direct and unmediated interactions, the natural economy, as well the typical pattern for the third economic sector which is intangible services.

Whilst the third economic sector accounts for the majority of all today's production, it has not yet attracted sufficient attention. This is perhaps because it contains a different logic, one which can be described as an open, direct, uno-actu reciprocal interaction process between consumer and producer, initiated by the active consumer, while being decoupled from the exchange of a MEANS.

However, we found also that the direct uno-actu pattern of reciprocal interactions has been reversed according to the typical pattern for the secondary sector, ie standardized ready-made products in total control of the producer and in immediate exchange for the MEANS.

The results of this study must now be taken further and used to develop traditional economicult thinking. They must be incorporated into every country's constitution as the modern basic understanding of man and nature and their interactions, to be implemented into society. That way, the traditional thinking of economicult theory and practice is modernized and democratized – which is definitely the way forward.

12. 1. The written Constitution for a democracy

Many people do not yet live in democratically constituted countries. Though reforms are continually introduced which aim to achieve what we value today as the best form of government, there is a lot to do in order to enshrine equality,

---

6   *The Atlantic* online reported in *The Week*, 5 September 2009, p. 42: Richard Posner "... economists ignored messy realities 'that don't lend themselves to expression in mathematical models or are intractable to formal analysis'. That's not a failure of economists, it's a failure of economics itself. In its search for scientific certainty, economics has arrived at a point where no two economists agree on what they see in front of them, much less on what the future may hold... The discipline needs 'to acknowledge its inadequacies and re-orient its training and research', or face a future of growing irrelevance."

fairness and freedom-for-everyone as the leading principles to be respected and followed by all. This is sometimes even the case in countries which believe themselves to be democratically governed already.

The International Declaration of Human Rights, as adopted by the United Nations General Assembly in Paris on 10 December 1948, includes a few principles which should be supplemented and clarified with the following statements:

- Everyone born into a society is equal, regardless of gender, age, nationality, belief or different MEANS.
- Individuals are their own subjects living in peace, free from slavery and torture. Every individual has the right to a fair trial and to justice, which is unmediated by MEANS.
- Only natural individuals have the right to vote, one person has one vote. This right cannot be bought or sold.
- Every person has the right to freedom and anonymity of communication. Every person has the right for individual conscience, language and belief without surveillance from others. Every person's data belongs to this person. Data cannot be bought or sold, it cannot be stored and processed without the person's written approval.
- Human beings need to learn more rather than to use the technologies we invent. People have the right to free life-long learning in schools, colleges and universities, unmediated by MEANS, as well as free access to libraries, museums, theatres and the internet[7]. Women in particular should be encouraged go to school because it has been found that educated women will not only have smaller families, but they will also teach their children how to write, read and calculate.
- Every individual has the right to mobility, unmediated by MEANS.
- Every individual born into a community has the right to satisfy their basic natural needs, for example with respect to clean air and water, food and housing, to be active and stay healthy, unmediated by MEANS.
- Every person has the lifelong right as well as the duty to active participation in the local community, a right that cannot be bought or sold, while communities have the right to self-government.
- As well as the diversity of peoples, the biodiversity of nature's evolutionary process, the BASE of all life, must be protected. Human beings can only take so much out of nature as nature annually produces, and they can only hand back to nature materials that they are not using anymore if this is in amounts which nature can annually take.

These basic understandings need to be generally accepted. In some cases, people have fought for thousands of years to achieve the above, and there has been opposition to certain ideas here, especially those seen to restrict the so-called divine power of self-proclaimed absolute rulers. However, changes can be won.

---

7   An expertise for the German Federal Education Ministry presented in November 2014 found that students want less and less to make self-reliant decisions creating their own ideas or find new ways to explain reality, according to *Frankfurter Allgemeine Zeitung*, 7 November 2014, p. 44.

For example, in 1215 the English King John was forced to seal the Magna Carta granting everybody the right to a fair trial; in 1789, the French King Louis XVI was forced to concede the rights of liberty, equality and communality to everyone, and when in 1776 the North American colonies declared independence from the English kingdom under George III, they did this because they were being forced to pay taxes, but denied representation in the London Parliament.

Therefore, it seems unthinkable that a democratic constitution can be retained without amendment, when Will Hutton characterized the (unwritten) constitution of Great Britain as follows: "Britain developed its democratic constitution seamlessly out of its pre-democratic feudal constitution, without ever setting out how it wanted to be governed. As a result, the existing democratic arrangements are built within a framework of monarchical government: the king or queen opens Parliament, laws require the monarch's assent, and the capacity for discretionary monarchical power exists everywhere. There is no formal system to coordinate departments because the constitution supposes that the monarch and Privy Council will do it – as they would if the monarch were still head of the executive branch."[8]

We would add further, that the Members of the second chamber of the British Parliament also ought to be elected[9]. And instead of having a monarch as the head of state, the highest representative of a country should likewise be elected by the people. State and church should be kept separate as belief is a private conviction.

No government should ever be permitted to collect taxes directly from peoples' private bank accounts, as it is the individual who is the owner of such an account and therefore the only one who has the right to dispose of it. Privatization of tax collection is not allowed. Also, no government is permitted to collect taxes for the church, even when another government decades ago has signed a concordat with a church on this, and the church now wants to make people believe that it has a claim for compensation if this concordat is given up.

The people of a nation own the land they live in, not a monarch.[10] The meaning of 'land' is to be transformed from an object we can speculate on to the BASE for life preservation.

In the modern formulation of basic individual human rights, it says that all people are *born*[11] free and equal in dignity and rights. They are endowed with reason and conscience and should act towards one another in a spirit of brotherhood.

Today, we have to add that the meaning of the word 'born' needs to be clarified or an amendment added. It only refers to the time of birth, which is not sufficient, as the declaration should include the whole lifetime of every individual, because the next but one article states: "Everyone has the right to life, liberty and security of person." This is later extended in Article no. 25, which reads: "Everyone has the right to a standard of living adequate for the health and well-being of himself" –

---

8   In: *Them and Us, Changing Britain – Why We need a Fair Society*, London, 2011, p. 342
9   Perhaps as representatives of different regional parliaments
10   Cf. Kevin Cahill, *Who Owns the World, The Hidden Facts behind Landownership*, Edinburgh, 2006, p. 43
11   Author's italics

and herself – "and of his family, including food, clothing, housing and medical care and necessary social services..."

Nowhere in the Declaration of Human Rights is it written that these basic inalienable rights of every person can or should be mediated by MEANS. As we know, the disposability of the MEANS is unequal. We therefore have to make sure that in future the MEANS will not compromise this commitment to life-long equality.[12] Perhaps the rights should be formulated as follows: Everybody is free and equal in dignity and rights, and the BASE of life should be equally and freely available to the same degree for everyone, not mediated by MEANS.

Democracy also requires that people participate directly in their own affairs, in accordance with the idea of equality, as enshrined in The Declaration of Human Rights Article 21, which states that everyone has the right to participate in the government of a country, directly or through freely elected representatives, and that the will of the people is the basis of the authority of any government.

Therefore, we would add here that while the representatives of the people are chosen in free elections, this does not yet apply to the administration of government which is charged with executing the representatives decisions. Likewise, these should be elected.[13] Otherwise the administration's employees who shape politics, would have no legitimation to do what they are doing.

People make the laws and decide how to live freely and they will also have to take care not to pollute or degrade the BASE for future generations.

In a democracy nobody is above the law. Nobody has more rights than anyone else. And nobody can claim to have more influence than any other because of their disposable power of MEANS.

No one country has the right to invade another country or base their own military troops or weapons there,[14] as otherwise the freedom and independence of other nations would be challenged.

In a democracy every person has one vote, as said, whereas hitherto, in the economicult sphere, voting rights depend on MEANS, ie how many shares a person owns in a joint-stock company dictates how many votes shareholders have at their disposal – another example of the fact that different levels of disposability of MEANS cause inequality.

Democracy is built from the bottom up. It is an ongoing process in which people elect their representatives as well as standing for election themselves, from the smallest parish up to a central legislative body. And democracy should not only be a feature of the public sphere – it should also be learned and practised in the private sphere. Gender difference, for example, should never again translate into gender inequality.

---

12 On 20 May 2014, 9.00 am, BBC 4 Radio broadcasted a debate entitled 'Why Vote?' at the London School of Economics and Political Science, hosted by Michael Sandel. The audience of LSE students was asked to consider whether they would sell their vote for money.

13 As called for by the former Liberal leader Nick Clegg for example in an interview with Nicholas Watt, in: *The Guardian*, 29 August 2012, p. 11.

14 We could argue that such an understanding would also make it necessary to insert a paragraph into a written constitution stating that the people in a democracy will never attack another country or even consider it. They will only defend themselves when parliament decides by a majority of 75 per cent to do so.

In a democratically constituted country, people relate to each other as equally free natural beings in charge of their own life and in direct reciprocal interaction both with each other and with nature, the BASE of life, while nature follows her own evolutionary process and her own logic with its own intrinsic value. The traditional economicult assumption that nature is given to humans to be controlled by us, is outdated in the 21st century.

Every democratically constituted country needs a written constitution, agreed by the people, identifying their rights as well as their duties, and incorporating a modern understanding of people and nature. That way, everybody knows their constitution and can rely on it to ensure that their defined rights and duties are realized. The practise of turning people and nature into instruments for private profit such that they are seen, in economicult terms, as a *thing*[15], is now a thing of the past. And a Constitutional Court can enable every individual to claim their constitutional rights, without being mediated by MEANS, and reinstate them if necessary.

People are the rulers in a democratic state, there should be full public involvement in any debate about formulating or reforming a constitution. The modern views of man and nature must be fully discussed prior to being written into the constitution. This process could take several years. It is appropriate for the debate to begin in schools, as it is the young who inherit the future. Children who are old enough to attend formal education are also old enough to reflect on ways of living well with each other as well as with nature. They are old enough to make judgements about what is good in today's society and what can be improved. This gives teachers as well as politicians the responsibility of showing children how people are currently represented at all levels and how their right to self-government is secured. Children can analyze how such decisions are made through role-play exercises discovering how the interests of all are balanced against the interests of a few – the real task of politics – and how compromises can be achieved.

Children should then discuss with adults at home what they have learned at school and what they found important about this process. Starting this debate in schools would hopefully mean that children would grow up with a better ability to organize themselves as adults, actively participating in their local community.

This need for direct public involvement means that it is of course not possible to set down a complete written proposal for a constitution here. All that can be done for the moment is to list a few basic modern insights:

The first is, naturally, that differences in age, beliefs, language, ethnicity or gender should not exclude anyone from the debate. A written constitution is the foundation which binds people in a country together on the basis of their shared values.

It is heartening to note that in countries which do not yet have a written constitution, many groups are campaigning for such a reform. Details of these initiatives, such as the 'Unlock Democracy' movement can easily be found on the internet – and joined.

---

15 We have to keep in mind, that using the term '*thing*' is only a figure of speech. This so-called *thing* is not necessarily a material object. It can also mean: an idea, a living being, a process or a social construction as a constitution.

I would like to make an additional suggestion to these initiatives: it is not enough to put up a website or send people papers here and there. Instead what is necessary is to set up face-to-face discussion groups in every community. People need to meet directly to discuss how democratic aims can be achieved together and which categories are more important than others. People need to see for themselves who is representing an initiative and who they are working with. They have to be convinced by first-hand experience that such an initiative can be trusted, that the people involved will take their obligations seriously and act responsibly. Only then can people join in and contribute support, only then is the process direct and fair.

The other sphere of duties which need to be written into any constitution of a democratic country is that of making sure that Parliament has the power to formulate political decisions and legislate accordingly, whilst ensuring that a fully elected government exists to execute the decisions of Parliament. Some of these duties are listed below:

Parliament sets the date for an election, not government. Only individuals have the right to vote, not organizations of any kind.

Parliament votes for its president, the most important function in a country. Parliament also elects people into government and administration.

It is also necessary to clarify the roles of the executive and legislative powers. These need to be carefully separated. If a person has been voted into government, then that person can no longer be a Member of Parliament.

Parliament is the body who puts the annual budget together, and decides on every item in it.

Parliament is also the body entrusted with putting through land reform.

Parliament decides on the structure of salaries for every civil servant in a country, setting up a transparent income structure depending on the importance of the tasks with which civil servants are entrusted. In this way, nobody in public service is allowed more remuneration for their work than the President of the Parliament and the Members of Parliament. This principle extends to local administration as well as to public organizations, such as, in the UK, the British Broadcasting Corporation (BBC) or the National Health Service (NHS) or the Bank of England (BoE), as well as to university or defence staff, for example. Parliament also makes sure that no bonuses are paid for public services and no public servant should be able to determine their own remuneration package.

Parliament should likewise make sure that the public infrastructure is modernized and maintained to a high standard with an emphasis on regional and long-distance high-speed railway networks, that the utilities, like fresh water and sewage treatment, electricity and health care, are run in the interests of all and not for the financial profit of a few.

It is also Parliament's obligation to ensure that no public infrastructure is privatized or outsourced, as tax-paying citizens in a democractic country are not expected to guarantee private profits, either to the fracking or the nuclear or the armaments industry. Tasks which are currently outsourced, such as the administration of prisons, schools, social services, defence, control of the MEANS and so on, must be taken back into public administration.

Furthermore, Parliament should decentralize legislation as well as administration. It is therefore essential that Parliament makes sure that local people in administration are well trained.

Parliament should make sure that the military forces only exist to defend a country against an attack from outside, and are never deployed within the country itself. This is the task of the police. Parliament must be careful to ensure that the industrial-military complex, as US President Eisenhower called it, is restricted to the level for defence. Importantly, both the military and the police need to be sworn in on the written Constitution and controlled by Parliament like every other civil service.

No part of the civil service is there to develop its own rules and structure, but has to make sure that the rules established by Parliament on behalf of the people of a country are followed.

12.2. The modern understanding of nature

Every constitution needs to be based on a modern understanding of nature, as nature is the BASE of life. A democratic constitution must obviously be rooted in a modern view of nature and the world, together with a modern understanding of the individual person.

It had been shown that, even now in the 21ˢᵗ century, all our vitally important interactions with nature have still not been given enough attention, because of the erroneous view that humans are put on this planet to dominate the natural world, solely for their own purpose. A modern understanding switches the focus to the relationship between people and nature, based on dynamic, open and direct reciprocal interactions. Consequently, reciprocal interactions need to become the centre of our attention, especially as the consequences of today's human activities seem to be jeopardizing the existence of life on Earth as we know it, for the first time in history. Life is now threatened to such an extent that the evolutionary process itself is in danger. Continuing such a procedure based on outdated assumptions about men and nature is not an option any more as it only leads to a dead end.

It is, therefore, not sufficient to include the 'preservation of nature' in a country's constitution, as Schleswig-Holstein did in 2008,[16] as it is nature's ability to evolve that has to be protected. Whereas hitherto people argued, following economicult theory, that environmental damage has always happened and is external to human beings, today we recognize that environmental damage is the result of a certain and outdated form of reciprocal interaction between man and nature.

Protecting nature's evolutionary ability has consequences, as we can no longer go on viewing nature as an infinite resource, for example. Natural resources, such as fossil fuels, have developed over millions of years, but will become so depleted over a few generations, that our successors will be excluded from using them to the same degree as we have done. This is, of course, not fair. The idea that people get

---

16 Jonathan Watts reported in *The Guardian*, 3 September 2012, that "Ecuador is the only country in the world to have recognised the rights of nature in its constitution".

richer by exploiting nature and can go on doing so infinitely, seems short-sighted and slightly naive, because these days we know that the more we exploit this planet, the BASE of life, the more barren it becomes. Once this is done, there is no second planet we can move to, continuing the same form of exploitation.

Consequently, we now realize that the way forward is to concentrate on two strategies: reducing the use of finite resources, while monitoring it carefully, and switching to activities using renewable resources, eg generating green electricity and growing food locally. This not only saves CO_2 emissios because less transport, but also allows people to experience real relationships with nature and extends their own understanding, knowledge and skills.[17]

The new modern understanding of nature also calls for a re-think of the traditional idea of land ownership, as many still believe that privately owned land can be dealt with by its owner in whatever way they please. We need to develop a more realistic approach, as equal use of the BASE must mean equal access to land for everyone, a fact which even Adam Smith noted 250 years ago. Land should be seen as the common BASE on which all inhabitants of a nation can live, work and grow food, and this has to be secured not only for today's generation – but also for future generations. The concept of the commons, old as the hills, should be reintroduced and run in a modern participative form. It should be our understanding that every person has the right to use the common land to an extent that has been agreed upon, with the obligation to keep it in fertile condition. This concept also suggests self-government by the people, who set their own rules for its use.

The model for such an understanding of interaction with nature is our ongoing interaction with the sea. No individual would presume to demand a certain part of the sea for their exclusive use, for the particular amount of years that they live. Everyone understands that they have the same right to use the sea. Fishing techniques can be regulated, not only in order to make sure they are equitable, but also to protect the rights of animals to their own life and their own evolutionary process. The same goes for the water itself.[18]

The rights and obligations of land use should be organized locally and contracts entered into a public land registry, open for inspection by everyone, which can only be altered with involving a lawyer.[19]

Anyone wanting to use a section of land should receive a contract of use from the local council to ensure careful maintenance of the land for locally organic farming, eg by preserving soil fertility and not damaging it with life-endangering

---

17 Dr. Peter Hooda of Kingston University, London, who co-authored a study published in the journal Environmental Science and Policy, said, according to the *Independent on Sunday*, 18 January, 2015, that: "The climate change impact of flying food into the UK is considerable... the UK's most popular greens produces more than ten times its own weight in greenhouse gas emissions if it is flown in from outside Europe".

18 For readers interested in the consequences of this action for freshwater rivers, we would highly recommend Roger Deakin's book: *Waterlog*, London, 1999, particularly from page 30 onwards where the author discusses swimming in rivers and the sea.

19 Recent proposals by the Conservative/Liberal coalition government to privatize the land registry whose use is not even fully obligatory, seems to be motivated more by the aim of keeping information about landownership private, than giving people transparency about who owns what.

chemicals, so that waters from brooks and rivers can be safely used by animals and people without installing costly cleaning processes. It is well known that organic farming has the least damaging impact on the land. Organically grown food should be grown locally in accordance with people's needs and under their direct control, rather than being imported from far away regions with high transport costs, where crops are often only grown for cash whilst locals are denied the right to grow their traditional staple foods.[20]

And this, despite evidence that local people's digestive systems have adapted over thousands of years to their local food.

The idea that everyone in the world should consume the same food all year round without regard for the seasons belongs on the scrap-heap of history, because behind it lies an assumption that the world is monotonous and monolithic; instead biodiversity and cultural diversity should be made the goals of every modern country. "Earth's biosphere is segmented into countless self-organizing ecosystems, each exquisitely adapted to its particular place on Earth to optimize the sustainable use of locally available resources in service to life," stated David C. Korten.[21]

Consumption of locally grown organic food is also preferable as it can be offered more quickly for consumption. It can be harvested at the point of ripeness. Therefore the quality of the food is better, it is more nutritious, and it smells and tastes better. People growing their own staple foods locally are in direct contact with their natural BASE, even in the city gardens of New York and La Habana, Cuba, and have an interest in protecting nature's ongoing evolutionary process. People can feel responsible because every day they see that their own lives depend on the BASE. Their local food should be offered directly at genuine market places, self-organized by local people.

The modern understanding of nature as the BASE of all life, including human's, also needs to consider that buildings are erected which generate more electricity than they use.

12.3. The modern understanding of a person

The 18th century French Revolution and the Enlightenment process were based on the principle that everyone is born free and equal. Let us come back to this expression again. Why does it state that people are 'born' free? Why should they be only free at the time of their birth? Should they not be free and equal subjects for the whole of their life, equipped with rights as well as duties in their process of direct interaction with each other as well as with external nature? We have already mentioned that such a wider interpretation of the human condition has to find a way into the written constitutions of democratic countries.

Understanding freedom in this way, has consequences: it means that the BASE of every individual's life should also be made freely and equally available throughout that individuals' life.

---

20 If it is right that in the UK only10 per cent of fruit and 55 per cent of vegetables are grown, as the *i* reported 24 February 2015, then the goverment could initiate a programme to support market gardens by local people.
21 David C. Korten, ibid, p. 145

Everyone needs to work for a certain number of hours daily for their own livelihood in direct interaction with the local community. The obligatory working hours that have been agreed need to be recorded. And everybody born into this society will need the same unconditional basic income. We will use a MEANS, but we will no longer view the MEANS as a subject equal to a living being and able to act as a lawgiver to us. Because when the basic interaction process is made dependent on MEANS and mediated by it, as it is today, the principle of participative rights and duties is only half-realized.

The most important change associated with a fair cultural economy as compared to the traditional economicult thinking is likely to be that of challenging the assumption that there can be a market' for labour, which is, as we have found, an outdated social construction based on the assumed separation between a person and their ability to work, and applied to individuals who are employed. Or to put it another way, in future nobody will have to 'sell' his labouring ability to another person as the only way to gain the necessary MEANS for self-protection, and people will no longer be split into self-employed subjects and employed objects. The basic resources, we all need, will be produced and supplied in a reciprocal process of interaction with nature and other people locally. As a general principle, human interaction will no longer be mediated by money and executed for money. In future, no-one will be an object serving the interests of another person, neither in their private nor in their public life, and no branch of science or organization will view an individual as an object.

The direct process of interaction is called cooperation. Everybody participates in local self-government. The aim is to involve everybody in local affairs, giving people personal responsibility rather than paying an administration to make decisions on their behalf, using taxes.

In a direct self-governed democracy people will have less interest in the surveillance of other people without their consent. People will have greater autonomy and therefore more individual freedom than today. Let us remember that the freedom of the individual is a kind of basic principle in all Western democracies, even if only partially practised, yet today that individual freedom seems threatened, more by the interests of global corporations than by national governments. "Living democracy manifests the ultimate ideal of popular sovereignty – government of the people, by the people, for the people," said David C. Korten.[22] "We humans are awakening to the reality that we are living beings who inhibit a finite living Earth to whose ways we must now adapt by creating economies that mimic the biosphere's fractal structure and capacity for self-reliant local adaptation through cooperative self-organization."[23] This indeed is the aim, the way forward. As Peter Wilby noted in *The Guardian*, 6 September 2012, p. 31, summarizing the actual situation in the UK and the USA: "The big idea of the post-1970s right in Britain and the US was that everyone would acquire a stake in capitalism, through home ownership (and treatment of houses as speculative investments); money-purchases pension, where what you got depended on the stock market; modest

---

22 David C. Korten, ibid, p. 155
23 Ibid, p. 150

ownership of shares or bank 'products' linked to share indices; and opportunities, created by deregulation, to shop around for 'deals' on services such as power supply, phones, savings rates and insurance. We would all, at least in our private lives, become members of the bourgeoisie, naturally sympathetic to 'wealth creators' and their political allies... For a time the strategy worked. Voters hesitated to support any part which threatened economic change that might cause house prices or shares to fall... Now the neoliberal revolution has gone into reverse... A report last year from the Smith Institute suggested owner occupation could be lower than 60 per cent by 2025, and private renting well over 20 per cent. If so, nearly two million fewer people will be living in their own homes. In the US, home ownership and the predictions for its future follow a similar curve... Neoliberalism, then, has failed to deliver on its promises. Houses have provided stores of wealth for the majority of Britons born before 1970... But younger generations struggle to access both pension schemes and houses... More and more voters, therefore, will be worrying about jobs, benefits, rents and debt interest rates, not about the value of houses, pensions or shares. The neoliberal attempt to create mass capitalism has hit the buffers..."

The economicult concept, upheld by so many politicians has obviously not delivered what it had promised. Acknowledging that fact is one thing we need to do.

The other, without doubt, is to recognize that the neoclassical economicult concept of nature and the individual being was inappropriate to both. It was based on mere assumptions about nature and the nature of a person, invented nearly 300 years ago. In the 21st century it is outdated and in need of modernization. We have to acknowledge that, in the long run, this concept hasn't worked, neither for nature, nor for people. This is hard to accept, and it is problematic for us to overcome this heritage. But historic assumptions need to be updated and replaced by a modern understanding based on real facts, in the same way that physicists are to continuously updating and modernizinge our understanding of nature.

In this study, we have presented a new theory of how to modernize and democratize economic thinking, whilst correcting misconceptions, in order to show a way forward for societies so that they can act fairly to nature as well as to people.

This new culteconomic concept of a fair economy could now be made into a model for the way we make decisions about how to lead our private lives, where we are free from objectifying according to the interests of others.

We do not have to wait for politicians to adopt the new understanding. We are free to do it ourselves. Directly and immediately, face to face. We can discuss it with each other. We can interact with each other, directly. We can involve ourselves and participate locally. We can care for the world we will one day leave to our descendents. Let us start now. This is how every cultural change occurs: when people make it happen.

13. Bibliography

13.1. Books

Arendt, Hannah, *Vita activa oder vom taetigen Leben,* Muenchen, 1981

Aristotle, *The Politics* (P), translated by T. A. Sinclair, third reprint, 1993

Asimov, Isaac, *The Left Hand of the Electron,* Zuerich, 1972

Augstein, Jacob, *Sabotage, Warum wir uns zwischen Demokratie und Kapitalismus entscheiden muessen,* Muenchen, 2013

Bachofen, Johann Jakob, *Das Mutterrecht,* first published 1861, Frankfurt, 1975

Bataille, George, *Die Aufhebung der Oekonomie, Muenchen,* 1985

Bateson, Gregory, *Oekologie des Geistes, Anthropologische, psychologische, biologische und epistemologische Perspektiven,* Frankfurt, 1981

Bateson, Gregory, *Geist und Natur, Eine notwendige Einheit*, Frankfurt, 1984

Bell, David, *Die nachindustrielle Gesellschaft*, Reinbek, 1979

Berekoven, Ludwig, *Der Dienstleitungs-markt in der Bundesrepublik,* Goettingen, 1983

Binswanger, Hans Christoph, et al, *Arbeit ohne Umweltzerstoerung, Strategien einer neuen Wirtschaftspolitik*, Frankfurt, 1983

Binswanger, Hans Christoph, *Geld und Magie, Eine oekonomische Deutung von Goethe's Faust*, Stuttgart, 2010

Bloch, *Ernst, Die Lehren von der Materie,* Frankfurt, 1978

Boehme, Gernot, *Die Natur vor uns, Kusterdingen,* 2002

Bootle, Roger, *The Trouble with Markets, Saving Capitalism from Itself,* London/Boston, 2009

Bornemann, Ernst, *Das Patriarchat, Ursprung und Zukunft unseres Gesellschaftssystems,* Frankfurt, 1975

Bornemann, Ernst, *Psychoanalyse des Geldes,* Frankfurt, 1977

Bower, Tom, *The Squeeze, Oil, Money and Greed in the 21st Century*, London, 2009

Braun, Christina von, *Der Preis des Geldes, Eine Kulturgeschichte,* Berlin, 2012

Brooks, David, *The social animal*, New York, 2011

Alex Brummer, *Bad Banks, Greed, Incompetence and the Next Global Crisis,* London, 2014

Bryson, Bill, *A Short History of Nearly Everything,* London, 2004

Cable, Vince, *The Storm, The World Economic Crisis and What it Means,* London, 2009

Cahill, *Who owns the World - The Hidden Facts behind Landownership,* Edinburgh, 2006

Carus, Lucretius T., *Von der Natur der Dinge,* Leipzig, 1831

Chang, Ha-Joon, *Bad Samaritans*, London, 2007

Chang, Ha-Joon, *23 Things They Don't Tell You About Capitalism*, New York, 2011

Commoner, Barry, *The Closing Circle, Nature, Man and Technology*, New York, 1971

Commoner, Barry, *Energieeinsatz und Wirtschaftskrise, Die Grundlagen fuer den radikalen Wandel,* Reinbeck, 1976

Curtius, Ernst, *Der religoese Charakter der griechischen Muenzen*, Berlin, 1870

Damaschke, Adolf, *Geschichte der Nationaloekonomie,* Jena, 1922

Davies, Glyn, *History of Money - From Ancient Times to Present Day,* Cardiff, 2005

Davies, Nigel, *Opfertod und Menschenopfer, Frankfurt,* Berlin, Wien, 1981

Descola, Philippe, *Die Oekologie der Anderen*, Berlin, 2014

Ehrlich, P. und A, J. Holdren, *Humanoekologie, Der Mensch im Zentrum einer neuen Wissenschaft*, Berlin, Heidelberg, New York, 1975

Ekins, Paul, *The Living Economy*, London, 1986

Eliade, Mircea, *Die Religionen und das Heilige*, Frankfurt, 1986

Elias, Norbert, *The Civilizing Process*, London, 1939

Elliott, Larry, and Dan Atkinson, *The Gods that Failed*, London, 2008

Feierstein, Mitch, *Planet Ponzi, How politicians and Bankers Stole your Future, What happens next, How you can survive,* · London, 2012

Fell, Hans-Josef, *Global Cooling, Strategies for Climate Protection*, London, 2012

Ferguson, Niall, *The Ascent of Money, A Financial History of the World*, London, 2009

Finkelstein, Israel, and Silberman, Neil Asher, *The Bible Unearthed, Archeology's New Vision of Ancient Israel and the Origin of its Sacred Texts*, New York, 2001

Fourastie, Jean, *The Great Hope of the Twentieth Century*, 1950

Forsyth, Mark, *The Etymologican, A Circular Stroll Through the Hidden Connection of the English Language*, London, 2011

Frazer, James George, *The Golden Bough, A Study in Magic and Religion, first published 1890, A New Abridgement from the Second and Third Editions*, Oxford, 1994

Freeman, Charles, *The Closing of the Western Mind, The Rise andFall of Reason*, New York, 2009

Freud, Sigmund, *Moses and Monotheism*, first published 1939, New York, 1967

Freudenthal, Margarete, *Gestaltwandel der staedtischen, buergerlichen und proletarischen Hauswirtschaft zwischen 1760 und 1910* , Frankfurt/M, Berlin, 1986

Gartner, Alan, and Frank Riessmann, *The Service Industry and the Consumer Vanguard*, New York, 1974

Gazzaniga, Michael, *Who's is in Charge*, New York, 2011

Gershuny, Jonathan, *Die Oekonomie der nachindustriellen Gesellschaft*, Frankfurt, 1981

Goettner-Abendroth, Heide, *Die Goettin und ihr Heros, Muenchen*, 1983

Gorz, Andre, *Kritik der oekonomischen Vernunft*, Berlin, 1989

Gould Davis, Elizabeth, *Am Anfang war die Frau, Die neue Zivilisationsgeschichte aus weiblicher Sicht*, Muenchen, 1977

Greenspan, Alan, *The Age of Turbulence*, 2007

Greenwald, Glen, *No Place to Hide*, London, 2014

Grober, Ulrich, *Die Entdeckung der Nachhaltigkeit, Kulturgeschichte eines Begriffs*, Muenchen, 2013

Habermas, Juergen, *Theorie kommunikativen Handelns*, Frankfurt, 1981

Haeckel, Ernst, *Generelle Morphologie der Organismen*, Berlin, 1866

Hammond, J. L. and B., *The Village Laborer 1760-1832, A Study of the Government of England before the Reform Bill*, first published 1911, London, 1967

Hampshire, Stuart, *Spinoza and Spinozism*, Oxford, 2005

Hawking, Stephen *The Universe in a Nutshell*, London, 2001

Heckel, Wolfgang, *Die Kultur der Reparatur*, Munich, 2013

Hegel, Georg Wilhelm Friedrich, *System der Sittlichkeit, first published 1802/03, in: Fruehe politische Systeme, by Gerhard Goehler (ed.)*, Frankfurt, Berlin, Wien, 1974

Heinsohn, Gunnar, *Privateigentum, Patriarchat, Geldwirtschaft, Eine sozialtheoretische Rekonstruktion der Antike*, Frankfurt, 1974

Herder-Dorneich, Philip, *Honorarreform und Krankenhaussanierung*, Berlin, 1970

Herder-Dorneich, Philip, *Wirtschaftssysteme, Opladen*, 1972

Hobbs, Thomas, *Leviathan, first published 1651, nineth edition*, Cambridge, 2006

Hobsbawn, Eric, *The Age of Revolution 1789–1848*, London, 1975

Horkheimer, Max, *Zur Kritik der instrumentellen Vernunft*, Frankfurt, 1985

Huber, Joseph, *Humanoekologie als Grundlage einer praeventiven Umweltpolitik?* published by the Internationales Institut fuer Umwelt und Gesellschaft am Wissenschaftszentrum Berlin, IIUG-dp 83–8

Hutton,Will, *Them and Us, Changing Britain – Why We Need A Fair Society*, London, 2011

Ingersoll, Robert Green, *What's God Got to Do with It? God in the Constitution – 1890*, Hanover, 2005

Jaenicke, Martin, *Wie das Industriesystem von seinen Missstaenden protifiert*, Opladen, 1979

Jantsch, Erich, *Die Selbstorganisation des Universums, Vom Urknall zum menschlichen Geist*, Muenchen, 1979

Joehr, W. A. *Organische Wirtschaftsgestaltung? in: Die Ganzheit in Philosphie und Wissenschaft, Wien*, by Walter Heinrich (ed.), 1950

Jones, Owen, *The Establishment, And How They Get Away With It*, London, 2014

Kaku, Michio, *Physics of the Future: How Science Will Shape Human Destiny and Our Daily Lives by the Year 2100*, London, 2011

Kant, Immanuel, *Kritik der reinen Vernunft,* 1781

Kant, Immanuel, *Was ist Aufklaerung? Berlinische Monatsschrift*, Dezember 1784

Kapp, Karl William, *Soziale Kosten der Marktwirtschaft*, Frankfurt, 1979

King, David, and Walter, Gabriele, *The Hot Topic*, London, 2008

Klein, Naomi, *This Changes Everything, Capitalism vs. The Climate*, New York, 2014

Koestler, Arthur, *Der Mensch Irrlaeufer der Evolution, Die Kluft zwischen Denken und Handeln, Eine Anatomie menschlicher Vernunft und Unvernunft*, Frankfurt, 1989

Korten,David, *Agenda for a New Economy – From Phantom Wealth to Real Wealth – A Declaration of Independence from Wall Street, 2nd edition*, San Francisco, 2010

Kuhn, Thomas, *Die Struktur wissenschaftlicher Revolutionen*, Frankfurt, 1976

Kumar, Manjit, *Quantum, Einstein, Bohr and the Great Debate about the Nature of Reality*, London, 2009

Kurnitzky, Horst, *Triebstruktur des Geldes, Ein Beitrag zur Theorie der Weiblichkeit*, Berlin, 1974

Kurnitzky, Horst, *Der heilige Markt*, Frankfurt, 1994

Lange, Ernst Michael, *Das Prinzip Arbeit, Frankfurt, Berlin, Wien*, 1980

Laum, Bernhard, *Heiliges Geld, Eine historische Untersuchung ueber den sakralen Ursprung des Geldes*, Berlin, 2006

Lawrence, Felicity, *Eat your heart out*, London, 2008

Leipert, Christian, *Erfolgsmessung im Spannungsfeld zwischen etablierter und alternativer Oekokonomie, in: Alternative Oekonomie und oekonomische Theorie*, Jens Harms et al (ed.), Frankfurt, 1980

Leipert, Christian, *Die heimlichen Kosten des Fortschritts, Wie Umweltzerstoerung das Wirtschaftswachstum foerdert*, Frankfurt, 1989

Lewis, Michael, *The Big Short, Inside the Doomsday Machine*, London, 2011

Lippe, Rudolf zur, *Am eigenen Leibe, Zur Oekonomie des Lebens*, Frankfurt, 1979

Lippe, Rudolf zur, *Naturbeherrschung am Menschen*, Frankfurt, 1981

Locke, John, *Second Treatise of Government, first published 1690*, Indianapolis, 1980

Manstetten, Reiner, *Das Menschenbild der Oekonomie, Der homo oeconomicus und die Anthropologie von Adam Smith*, Freiburg/Muenchen, 2000

Marchant, Jo, *Decoding the Heavens, A 2,000-Year-Old Computer – And the Century-Long Search to Discover its Secrets*, Cambridge, 2009

Marcuse, Herbert, *The One-Dimensional Man*, 1964

Marshall, Alfred and Mary, *The Economics of Industry*, London, 1879

Mason, Paul, *Meltdown – The End of the Age of Greed*, Edinburgh, 2009

Mathias, Peter, *The First Industrial Nation, The Economic History of Britain 1700–1914*, London, 1969

Maus, Marcel, *The Gift*, London, 1966

McKenzie, G. Tullock, *Homo oeconomicus*, Frankfurt/New York, 1984

McRobie, George, *Small is Possible*, London, 1985

Merchant, Carolyn, *The Death of Nature. Women, Ecology and the Scientific Revolution*, San Francisco, 1980

Meyer-Abich, Klaus-Michael, *Wege zum Frieden mit der Natur, Muenchen*, Wien, 1984

Meyer-Abich, Klaus-Michael, *Wissenschaft fuer die Zukunft, Holistisches Denken in oekologischer und gesellschaftlicher Verantwortung*, Muenchen, 1988

Meyer-Dohm, P., *Wirtschaftswissenschaft als Wissenschaft vom Menschen, in: THEMEN*, published by Universitaet Witten/Herdecke, April 1984

Morris, Ian, *Why the West rules – for now*, London, 2010

Mueller, Rudolf Wolfgang, *Geld und Geist, Zur Entstehungsgeschichte von Identitaetsbewusstsein und Rationalitaet seit der Antike*, Frankfurt, 1977

Mullin, Chris, *A View from the Foothills*, London, 2010

Mullin, Chris, *Decline and Fall*, London, 2011

Mumford, Lewis, *Mythos der Maschine, Kultur, Technik, Macht*, Frankfurt, 1978

Muttitt, Greg, *Fuel on the Fire, Oil and Politics in Occupied Iraq*, London, 2011

Nasar, Sylvia, *Grand Pursuit, The Story of Economic Genius*, London, 2011

Negt, Oskar, *Lebendige Arbeit, enteignete Zeit, Politische und kulturelle Dimensionen des Kampfes um die Arbeitszeit*, Frankfurt, New York, 1984

Neumann, Erich, *Die grosse Mutter, Eine Phaenomenologie der weiblichen Gestaltungen des Unbewussten*, Zuerich, 1985

Ostrom, Elinor, *Governing the Commons, The Evoltion of Institutions for Collective Action*, New York, 1999

Pagel, Mark, *Wired for Culture, The Natural History of Human Cooperation*, London, 2012

Paine, Thomas, *Rights of Man, first published 1791*, London, 1985

Petty, William, *A Treatise of Taxes and Contribution*, 1662

Picht, Georg, *Ist Humanoekologie moeglich? in:* C. Eisenbart (ed.), *Humanoekologie und Frieden*, Stuttgart, 1979

Polanyi, Karl, *The Great Transformation*, Boston, 1944

Porter, Roy, *Enlightenment, Britain and the Creation of the Modern World*, London, 2000

Postel, Verena, *Arbeit im Mittelalter*, Berlin, 2006

Postman, Neil, *Amusing Ourselves to Death*, New York, 1985

Priddat, Birger, *Geist der Ornamentik, Ideogrammatik des Geldes, in: Kapitalismus als Religion,* by Dirk Baecker (ed.), Berlin, 2003

Ranke-Graves, Robert von, *Die weisse Goettin, Sprache des Mythos*, Reinbek, 1988

Ratigan, Dylan, together with G. Lichtenberg and Dr. Jeffrey Spees, Greedy Bastards, *How We Can Stop Corporate Communists, Banksters and Other Vampires from Sucking America Dry*, New York, 2012

Reichelt, Helmut, Adam Smith, *in: Pipers Handbuch der Politischen Ideen*, by Iring Fetscher and Herfried Muenkler (ed.), Muenchen, 1985

Reichwald, Ralf, *Arbeit als Produktionsfaktor*, Muenchen/Basel, 1977

Russell, Bertrand, *History of Western Philosophy*, first published 1946, London/New York, 1996

Sacks, Oliver, *Musicophilia*, New York, 2008

Sandel, Michael J., *Was man fuer Geld nicht kaufen kann, Die moralischen Grenzen des Marktes*, New York, 2012

Schirrmacher, Frank, *EGO Das Spiel des Lebens*, Muenchen, 2013

Schlichter, Detlev S., *Paper Money Collapse, The Folly of Elastic Money and the Coming Monetary Breakdown*, Hoboken, 2011

Schoene, Irene, *Oekologisches Arbeiten*, Wiesbaden, 1988

Schoene, Irene, *Moeglichkeiten einer realitaetsgerechteren Wohlstandsberechnung*, Kiel, 1990

Schoene, Irene, *Schleswig-Holstein - eine Dienstleistungsgesellschaft*, published by Landeszentrale fuer Politische Bildung Schleswig-Holstein, 1992

Schoene, Irene, *Vom Eigenwert der Natur, Ein Beitrag zur Oekologisierung der Oekonomie*, i: K. Grenzdoerffer et al, *Neue Bewertungen in der Oekonomie*, Pfaffenweiler, 1995

Schumacher, E. F., *Small is Beautiful, A Study of Economics as if People Mattered*, London, 1973

Sennett, Richard, *The Craftsman*, London, 2008

Sennett, Richard, *Together: The Rituals, Pleasures and Politics of Cooperation*, London, 2012

Sheldrake, Rupert, *The Science Delusion*, London, 2012

Shell, Marc, *The Economy of Literature*, Baltimore and London, 1978

Siculus, Diodorus, *Historical Library, in:* Selina O'Grady, *And Man created God, Kings, Cults and Conquests at the Time of Jesus*, London, 2012

Simms, Andrew, *Cancel the Apocalypse: The New Path to Prosperity*, London, 2013

Skidelsky, Robert and Edward, *How Much is Enough, The Love of Money and the Case for the Good Life*, London, 2012

Smith, Adam, *An Inquiry into the Nature and Causes of the Wealth of Nations (WN)*, first published 1776, Petersfield, 2007

Smith, Adam, *Theory of Moral Sentiments (TMS)*, sixth edition, published 1790 (first published Edinburgh, 1759), this edition published London 2009, foreword by Amartya Sen

Smith, Adam, *Early Writings (EW)*, edited by J. Ralph Lindgren, publisher Auguustus M. Kelley, New York, 1967

Smith, Ken R., *Free is Cheaper*, Gloucester, 1988

Snyder, Laura J., *The Philosophical Breakfast Club, Four Remarkable Friends Who Transformed Science And Changed the World*, New York, 2011

Sohn-Rethel, Alfred, *Geistige und koerperliche Arbeit*, Frankfurt, 1973

Solnit, Rebecca, *A Rape a Minute, a Thousand Corpses a Year, Hate Crimes in America (and Elsewhere)*, on: TomDispatch.com, 2013

Stahel, Walter, *The Performance Economy*, New York, 2006

Stavenhagen, Gerard, *Geschichte der Wirtschaftstheorie*, Goettingen, 1969

Steiner, Uwe, *Die Grenzen des Kapitalismus, in: Kapitalismus als Religion*, by Dirk Baecker (ed.), Berlin, 2003

Stone, Oliver, and Kuznick, Peter, *The Untold History of the United States*, London, 2012

Tett, Gilian, *Fool's Gold, How Unrestrained Greed Corrupted a Dream, Shattered Global Markets and Unleashed a Catastrophe*, New York, 2009

The News Chronicle, *Everything within – a Library of Information for the Home*, London/Edinburgh, presumably printed 1930

Thomas, Hugh, *The Slave Trade, The History of the Atlantic Slave Trade 1440–1870*, New York, 1997

Toffler, Alvin, *The Third Wave*, New York, Toronto, London, Sydney, Auckland, 1980

Treiber, H., and Steinert, H., *Die Fabrikation des zuverlaessigen Menschen, Ueber die,Wahlverwandschaft' von Kloster- und Fabrikdisziplin*, Muenchen, 1980

Tusser, Thomas, *Five Hundred Points of Good Husbandry*, Oxford, 1984

Ullrich, Otto, *Regionalisierung: Die raeumliche Grundlage fuer eine zukunftsfaehige Lebensweise*, in: Lutz Finkelday (ed.), *Tausch statt Kaufrausch*, Bochum, 1999

Vester, Frederic, *Unsere Welt – ein vernetztes System*, Stuttgart, 1978

Vester, Frederic, *Der Wert eines Vogels*, Muenchen, 1987

Watson, Robert N., *Back to Nature, The Green and the Real in the Late Renaissance*, Philadelphia, 2006

Weber, Max, *Die protestantische Ethik und der Geist des Kapitalsmus, in: Gesammelte Aufsaetze zur Religionssoziologie*, Tuebingen, 1920

Weinberger, Katharina, *Kopfzahl-Paranoia, Von der Selbstzerstoerung der Konzerne*, Muenchen, 2009

Weizsaecker, Carl Friedrich von, *Die Geschichte der Natur*, Goettingen, 1979

Weizsaecker, Ernst Ulrich und Christine von, *Eigenarbeit, in: Anders arbeiten, anders wirtschaften*, by Joseph Hueber (ed.), Frankfurt, 1979

Weizsaecker, Viktor von, *Der Gestaltkreis, Theorie der Einheit von Wahrnehmen und Bewegen*, Frankfurt, 1973

Werlhof, Claudia von, *Comments on "Shadow-Work" by Ivan Illich*, read at the ECOROPA Conference "*Towards an Ecological Economy*", Kassel, 1980

White, Gilbert, *The Natural History of Selbourne*, 1788

Wicke, Lutz, *Umweltoekonomie*, Muenchen, 1982

Wilson, Edward O., *The Future of Life*, London, 2002

Woehe, Guenther, *Einfuehrung in die allgemeine Betriebswirtschaftslehre*, Muenchen, 1973

Wolf, H. *Der homo oeconomicus, Eine nationaloekonomische Fiktion*, Berlin/Leipzig, 1926

Wood, Gordon S., *The American Revolution, A History*, London, 2005

Woodward, John, *Essay Towards a Natural History of the Earth*, first published 1695, in: *Enlightenment, Discovering the World in the 18th Century*, by Kim Sloan with Andrew Burnet (ed.), London 2003

Xenophon, *Oeconomicus*, translated by E. C. Marchant, O. J. Todd, *Loeb Classical Library*, first published 1923, Cambridge/London, 2010

Zinn, Karl Georg, *Die Selbstzerstoerung der Wachstumsgesellschaft, Politisches Handeln im oekonomischen System*, Reinbek, 1980

13. 2. Magazines/Newspapers

Bank & Umwelt
Canberra Times
Computerwoche
Country Living
Der Spiegel
Die Welt
Financial Times
Frankfurter Allgemeine Sonntagszeitung
Kieler Nachrichten
Money Week
New York Times
Private Eye
Radio Times
Scientific American
Spiegel Online
Sueddeutsche Zeitung
The Daily Mail

The Mail on Sunday
The Daily Telegraph
The Guardian
The i
The Independent
The Independent on Sunday
The Observer
The Sunday Telegraph
The Sunday Times
The Times
The Week
USA Today
Wired
Wirtschaftswoche

13.3. Radio & Television stations

BBC Radio 4
NDR Info Radio
TV BBC 1
TV BBC 2
Tagesschau, the daily German TV information programme
TV channel "Arte"
TV programme "Report Muenchen"

13.4. Others

The Holy Bible, Containing the Old and New Testaments, translated out of the Original Tongues and with the former Translations diligently compared and revised by His Majesty's special command,

A. D. 1611, Appointed to be read in Churches, printed in London and published by the British and Foreign Bible Society

Duden, Fremdwoerterbuch, published by Bibliographisches Institut Mannheim, Wien, Zuerich

Handwoerterbuch der Sozialwissenschaften, Band 3, Stuttgart, Tuebingen, Goettingen, 1961

Oxford Concise Dictionary of World Religions, published by John Bowker, New York, 2000

Bundesamt fuer Verbraucherschutz und Lebensmittelsicherheit

Bundesverband Erneuerbare Energie- und Wasserwirschaft (BDEW)

BP Statistical Review of World Energy, 2013

Deutscher Bundestag, Berlin

Deutsches Institut fuer Wirtschaftsforschung (DIW), Wochenbericht

Statistisches Bundesamt, Wiesbaden/ Germany (www.destatis.de)

UmweltBank AG, Geschaeftsbericht 2012

Umweltbundesamt (UBA), Dessau/ Germany (www.umweltbundesamt.de)

U.S. Census Bureau

Verband der Verbraucherzentralen

ZEW news

www. Huffingtonpost.com

INDEX